The Right to Fight

Three American soldiers in France during World War I. Shown are Lieutenant Colonel Otis B. Duncan, 370th Infantry in the center. Major J. R. White, left, and Lieutenant W. J. Warfield. (National Archives)

THE RIGHT TO FIGHT

A History of African Americans in the Military

Gerald Astor

PRESIDIO

Published by Presidio Press
505 B San Marin Drive, Suite 300
Novato, CA 94945-1340

Library of Congress Cataloging-in-Publication Data

Astor, Gerald, 1920–
    The right to fight ; a history of African Americans in the military / Gerald Astor.
        p.   cm.
    Includes bibliographical references and index.
    ISBN: 0-89141-632-3
    1. United States—Armed Forces—Afro-Americans—History. 2. Race discrimination—United States—History. 3. United States—Race relations—a history. I. Title.
    UB418.A47A84   1998
    355'.0089'96073—dc21   98-17063
                                            CIP

Printed in the United States of America

Contents

Preface

In the course of writing six books on World War II, I contacted many hundreds of survivors for their eyewitness or oral histories. Occasionally, I was turned down on the grounds of weak memories or an unwillingness to invest the time I required. For the most part, however, veterans were quite willing to share their experiences.

For this book, dealing with race relations in the military, I encountered considerable reluctance. A retired white general who had commanded African Americans in World War II and Korea wrote me, "My decision [not to cooperate] reflects no disrespect for your competence as a writer. I observed the commotion that publication of the history of the 24th Infantry Regiment [an all-black outfit] caused and I do not care to be involved in a similar controversy." He was only one of many Caucasians unwilling to respond.

Many black veterans also rejected me. Their refusals ranged from "I've talked to white writers before and they never get it right."; "Why should I give my time to someone for free?"; "It's all ancient history and nothing is going to change."

Nevertheless, about eighty people added their stories to the official documents, the oral histories captured by the armed services, the newspaper and secondary accounts. There is a mix of black and white voices and different generations because the only way to grasp what happened over the years requires listening to people with varying viewpoints and backgrounds. I was never able to find someone willing to defend the notion of segregation; it is a mark of progress, that except for the radical fringe, it is no longer politic to publicly express white supremacy.

Personal accounts of those engaged in the business of war, and for that matter, any endeavor, strike me as at least as significant as the official reports, investigations, studies, and theories. All histories, no matter who their authors, are skewed. No source is incontrovertible. The biases of the anecdote, the individual experience shaped by perception and memory, are no more a distorted history than those of the nonhuman statistical analysis, the second-hand reports by those not on the scene, the often self-serving, prejudged investigations. One had to be there to experience racism, to know how traumatic and wounding it is to the individual and to the greater society. The histories of minorities in the military too often focus only on them; neglecting the actions and thoughts of the majority. That whites for so many years could ignore the conditions for blacks in the military is as much a part of the story as the effects upon the victims of discrimination. Furthermore, race relations involve both parties; the insights and experiences of both are highly germane. We still have great gaps between racial and ethnic groups but we are still one nation. That is the essence of *The Right to Fight.*

Acknowledgments

This book could not have been written without the generous expenditure of time and energy by the members of the armed forces listed under Roll Call. I am indebted to every one of them.

I received invaluable help from Dr. Richard J. Sommers and Dr. David Keough at the Archives Branch of the U.S. Military History Institute, Carlisle, Pennsylvania. Equal aid came from Alan Aimone at the U.S. Military Academy Library at West Point; Amy Cantin, curator of the Personal Papers Archives of the Marine Corps Historical Center in Washington, D.C.; Gina Akers of the Navy Historical Center in Washington, D.C.

Brigadier General John Mountcastle, Col. George MacGarrigle, and William Hammond at the U.S. Army Center of Military History in Washington, D.C., were kind enough to allow me to review interviews used in *Black Soldier, White Army*. Colonel Julian Olejniczak at the U.S. Military Academy suggested several good sources. Walton Moody and Yvonne Kinkaid at the U.S. Air Force Center for History at Bolling Field, Washington, directed me to relevant materials. Joseph D. Caver of the U.S. Air Force Historical Research Center, Maxwell Air Force Base, Alabama, provided material from the oral histories of that service. Colonel Alan L. Gropman, historian and renowned authority on the Tuskegee airmen and the Air Force, assisted me in making contact with the African American pilots of World War II. J. Robert Moskin, an old magazine colleague, suggested fruitful avenues. Paul Stillwell at the Naval Institute in Annapolis, as in previous books, helped with names, research, and the oral histories produced at the institute.

Commander Mike Brady of the Navy, Bill Schwartz of the Army, Capt. Pat Johnson of the Marines, and Capt. Ronald Watrous, Judith Grojean, and Maj. Stevie Shapiro of the Air Force, all responded with answers to my queries.

Copy editor Carmen Capalbo, as in my past books, worked heroically on matters of fact, spelling, style, and clarity.

While I have endeavored to quote sources verbatim I have corrected spelling errors and grammar for the sake of clarity.

Quotations from *Benjamin O. Davis, Jr.* by Benjamin O. Davis, Jr. (Washington, D.C.: Smithsonian Institution Press, 1991) by permission.

Quotations from *The Golden Thirteen* by Paul Stillwell (Annapolis, MD: Naval Institute Press, 1993) by permission.

Quotations from *Proudly We Served* by Mary Pat Kelly (Annapolis, MD: Naval Institute Press, 1995) by permission.

Quotation from *Firefight at Yechon* by Charles Bussey (McLean, VA: Brassey's [US] 1991) by permission.

1
The Long Voyage

Ordinarily, the right to kill or be killed as a member of the military has been an almost inalienable right, or more likely a duty for citizens, particularly for those without the economic clout or the class status that enables them to avoid the dangerous or onerous. The obligation has even been extended to cover resident aliens. It is one more measure of the depth of antiblack sentiment in the United States that even at the cost of a significant reduction in available manpower, military leaders and civilian officials, backed by whites in and out of uniform, traditionally limited African American service in the armed forces, denying blacks the dubious right to be exposed to enemy fire.

While other ethnic groups—Jews, Italians, Irish, Chinese and Japanese, Mexicans and Native Americans—were victims of discrimination by individuals, the systematized exclusions from and within military service never applied to them with a single exception. During the early days of World War II the authorities restricted deployment of those of Japanese extraction but eventually they were issued weapons and granted the privilege of combat.

The reluctance to put deadly force in the hands of African Americans, accompanied by rigid segregation of servicemen and -women, lasted for some 175 years after the "shot heard round the world" signaled the labor pains of a new nation that claimed "all men are created equal." Blacks in the armed forces traditionally lived separately from whites, and when allowed to fight, bled and died separately. For the most part, the barriers that created Jim Crow education, housing, economic opportunity, and justice, and during this period usually denied men of color the right to shoot and be shot at, consigned them to haul, lift, dig, drive, and clerk.

During the battle for the South Pacific island of Peleliu in October 1944, a band of leathernecks from the U.S. 1st Marine Division, huddled in a steep ravine while above them Japanese troops occupied entrenched positions. Private First Class Ed Andrusko, who had been wounded and then healed sufficiently to rejoin Item Company, says, "It was high noon, 110 degrees, no shade, and a merciless tropical sun. The hostile defenders were now firing down on us from all sides. The cross fire was deadly and we were trapped.

"Our radioman used the last working radio to get artillery or heavy mortar support. He pleaded for immediate help and soon we heard the booming of our distant cannons. Our incoming shells whistled and exploded on the ridge above us for several minutes. Then the shells rained down on our beleaguered company. We were now being heavily shelled—by our own artillery. I had no concept of time but it was eternity until our radio contact finally stopped the bombardment.

"As the message runner, I returned to the command post and reported our new losses and serious situation to the Top Sergeant. He radioed for reinforcements, for medical corpsmen, water, and as many stretcher bearers as he could get. The word came back negative. No reinforcements. No stretcher bearers. All reserve units were committed in an all-out battle throughout the island with heavy casualties. There was no help available."

Desperate for aid, the sergeant ordered Andrusko and one other marine, nicknamed "Ski," to accompany him on a dash to the beach area and recruit anyone available. Under covering fire they sprinted to the rear and vainly sought succor from other unit commands. "Exhausted from the heat, we rested near the beach in the shade of a damaged supply truck. A young black sergeant who had overheard our plight, walked up and said, 'I heard you all were looking for some troop replacements.'

"Our Top Sergeant looked a little stunned and speechless at the black, uniformed sergeant. The Top cleared his throat and asked, 'Who are you? What unit or company are you with? Are you Army, Navy, Seabees, or what?'

"'I am a U.S. Marine platoon sergeant. My men and I are all U.S. Marines.' I remembered seeing and talking to the black troops on the beach when I first returned to battle weeks before. He continued, 'My men have all finished their work on the beach. We are cleared with the division headquarters to volunteer where needed. We are Marines from an ammunition depot and have had some infantry training.'

"Our top sergeant appeared very puzzled. How could he bring in an all-black unit to rescue members of a line company that was part of the famous, all-white 1st Marine Division? It was heavily complemented with Southern officers and men, home-based at New River, North Carolina and 'the pride of the South.' This was our Division's third major campaign and the situation had never occurred before. He tried to discourage the volunteers stating they were not trained nor qualified for the terror of battle. But by now the black marines had armed themselves heavily and lined up behind their platoon sergeant who insisted we lead the way to the front lines.

"Our top sergeant said, 'Well, don't say I didn't warn you people.'

"Ski and I snickered, 'Wait till those red-neck rebels and segregating Yankees see who is coming to their rescue!'

"As we got closer to our lines, several enemy snipers fired at our rescue party. Our new volunteers withstood their baptism of fire and skillfully returned fire when needed. I felt good about what we were doing, like the cavalry coming to the rescue. Or maybe it was stupidity because of the heat. I said to our grim, pouting top sergeant, 'Hey, Top, do you think we will get a medal for this rescue mission?'

"After a short silence, he said, 'You're lucky if those rebels in our company don't shoot our butts off for this! You're from New Jersey and a damn Yankee who doesn't understand what we're doing here. Now keep moving those troops up the ravine. Keep your head down, and your stupid mouth shut!' which I did.

"When we reached our mauled company area, it looked like General Custer's last stand. The top sergeant came upon our new replacement officer in command of the company and said, 'Sir, I have a platoon of black— I mean a platoon of Marine volunteers who came to help.'

"The young, new Commanding Officer said, 'Thank God. Thank you, men. Sergeant take over. Get our wounded and dead out.'

"We gave covering fire and watched in awe as our new, gallant volunteers did their job. Some of these new men held a casualty stretcher gently in one hand as true angels of mercy. Then when necessary, they would fire an automatic weapon with the other hand, while breaking through the surrounding enemy. The grateful wounded thanked the volunteers as each survivor was brought to the rear aid station and safety. One badly wounded Southerner said, 'I felt like I was saved by Black Angels sent by God. Thank you. Thank you all!'

"The platoon of black Marines made many courageous trips to our company area for the wounded. With each return from the rear they brought back badly needed ammunition, food and water. It was nightfall when the evacuation of all the wounded was completed. The volunteers moved into our empty foxholes and helped fight off a small, night-time enemy counterattack.

"The next morning, our company commander ordered us to take the hill. After several bloody hours of fighting, Item Company survivors and our black volunteers did just that. We were relieved from the gruesome mountain by a U.S. Army infantry company. As the soldiers passed, they asked sarcastically, 'Who are the black guys in your outfit?'

"Our top sergeant bellowed, 'Why some of our company's best damn Marines, that's who!'"

Ten thousand miles away in Europe, a few months later, desperate for combat infantrymen, Gen. Dwight D. Eisenhower, commander for the Allied Expeditionary Force in Europe, authorized recruitment of volunteers from rear-echelon troops, including African Americans. Unwilling to fully integrate the black men into infantry line companies, the newcomers formed extra platoons assigned to infantry and armored divisions fighting the Germans across the Rhône. Brigadier General H. T. Mayberry, the assistant division commander of the 99th Division, which incorporated three "Negro rifle platoons" said, "The Negroes participated in some intense fighting. They were subjected on occasion to some artillery and mortar fire. All in all the fighting in which they took part was of such character as to give them a pretty good test.

"They would go anywhere their leaders would take them. Their performance was consistently good. I watched their casualty list. They had a strength of about forty-three when they came to us and when hostilities ceased they were down to about thirty-two. We thought they fought very well. One of the platoon leaders [the black infantrymen served under white officers] said to me. 'I'll take these people anytime. They'll go anywhere I want to take them.'"

Despite the praises heaped on them by white observers, when Ed Andrusko's Marine unit pulled back, the "Black Angels" reverted to their previous status of segregated, noncombatant service troops. After the shooting stopped in Europe, the volunteer black riflemen left the white infantry divisions to rejoin segregated outfits headed either for demobilization or nonbattle assignments.

The proscriptions of the military, which covered freemen as well as slaves through the Civil War, instead of relaxing after that conflict hardened following the Spanish-American War. Grudgingly and with disparagement toward almost all, the authorities in and out of uniform, granted only a small percentage of blacks the right to fight for their country during the two world wars and well into the Korean conflict, while maintaining them in a separate but unequal military.

Dismal as the history of the U.S. military experience in race relations was for so long, in the 1950s the armed forces finally banished segregation and offered full opportunity, making minorities not only eligible to suffer the ordeal of combat but also to command whites, years before African Americans achieved full statutory rights in civilian society through the Civil Rights movement.

If there is such a phenomenon as a defining moment, one occurred during the Vietnam War. In 1966, a French TV crew accompanied a thirty-three-man army platoon from the 1st Cavalry Division over a period of several weeks. The TV producer titled the documentary, *The Anderson Platoon*, because the soldiers, about an equal number of black and white men, were led by Lt. Joseph B. Anderson, an African American graduate of West Point. At one point, the outfit came under heavy fire from Vietcong soldiers. As the embattled Americans awaited a helicopter to evacuate the casualties, a seriously wounded black sergeant in severe pain lay on the ground. The camera focused on a white trooper patting the distressed sergeant's hand to comfort him. When the chopper finally put down, an integrated quartet of soldiers bore the injured man off. Bleeding together, succoring one another, without regard to race, white men acting under the orders of a black, integration in the line of fire had fully arrived. But it had been a long, arduous, painful, often agonizing voyage. And the journey was actually not over.

2
The Struggle Begins

The first blood shed by an American flowed from the body of a husky, knock-kneed, middle-aged man, the celebrated Crispus Attucks, in the square around the Boston custom house as a rowdy crowd according to one observer, "[some] armed with musquets, but most with clubs, bludgeons and such like weapons," confronted ten British redcoats. Although one scholar insists Attucks was a full-blooded Natick Indian, he has usually been described as a former black slave from Framingham and as such the recipient of the dubious credit as the first fatality of the Boston Massacre in which the musket balls fired by the soldiers struck eleven civilians, killing four besides Attucks.

At the trial of the British soldiers, a slave named Andrew testified that a stout man with a "long cordwood stick" bashed the officer, "struck the grenadier's gun at the captain's right hand . . . knocked his gun away and struck him over the head . . . This stout man held the bayonet with his left hand, and twitched it and cried, 'kill the dogs, knock them over.'" Andrew identified the assailant as "the mulatto who was shot."

John Adams, who would become one of the leaders in the American Revolution, acted as defense counsel for the accused British soldiers. He focused on Attucks, conjuring up the traditional American image of the rampaging African American, "whose very look was enough to terrify any person," [who] "had hardiness enough to fall in upon them and with one hand took hold of a bayonet, and with the other knocked the man down." He concluded his oration: "an Attucks from Framingham, happening to be here, shall sally out upon their thoughtless enterprises, as the head of such a rabble of negroes . . . as they can collect together . . ."

No one can fully ascertain the motives of Attucks or for that matter those of the white men who died in the incident. Attucks could have been simply a boisterous member of a mob, fresh from what was called a "victualling house" or perhaps been a genuine martyr imbued with resentment against the oppression of his former status as a slave and spurred by the local attitudes of hostility toward the provocative acts against the colonists by the home country. Whatever the source of his behavior, Crispus Attucks might well have passed into near anonymity were it not for the continuing need and desire of African Americans to demonstrate to themselves and to the rest of the country, their involvement in the birth and growth of the nation.

Although credited as the first casualty in the preliminaries to an actual war, Attucks bore only a thick piece of wood in his brief moment of combat and he was not a member of any army. In fact, a number of nonwhites actually served in militias prior to the American Revolution as the settlers fighting the French and Indian War enlisted blacks, mostly slaves consigned by their masters. The general policy, particularly in the South, frowned on the practice, largely because it gave vassals potential access to guns. For the most part, the units restricted them to the roles of batmen and menials. After the end of the French and Indian War the reduction in militias also sharply reduced the recruitment of blacks.

As the opposition to British rule gathered steam following the Boston Massacre, the Continental Congress recommended that able-bodied men in each colony form militia companies, the celebrated minutemen of the early days of the war for independence. Initially, nonwhites were enrolled; in some cases like that of Peter Salem, his owners granted him the freedom that enabled him to enlist. Black men thus fought and bled at Lexington and at Bunker Hill where the bravery of one Salem Poore earned him a petition, signed by fourteen Massachusetts officers, stating "a negro called Salem Poore . . . behaved like an experienced officer, as well as an excellent soldier." Without specifying any particular action, the signatories continued, "We only beg leave to say in the person of this said negro centers a brave and gallant soldier. The reward due to so great and distinguished a character, we submit to Congress." Poore later fought at Valley Forge and the Battle of White Plains.

Within a year after the clash of the minutemen and Redcoats at Concord and Lexington, the authorities in those areas of a heavy concentration of blacks had second thoughts about putting guns into the hands of slaves or freemen who might make common cause with their brothers in bondage. The 1775 Continental Congress created an army, and its adjutant general Horatio Gates promptly ordered recruiters not to enlist "any stroller, negro or vagabond." The Congress itself rejected a resolution from a South Carolina delegate that required all blacks, freemen, and slaves be discharged from the ranks of the army but the generals charged with the siege of Boston while canvassing for soldiers agreed to exclude all nonwhites. Communities forming fighting units purged them of blacks and Native Americans as well. By the summer of 1776, local, state, and Continental policy restricted military service to whites. The desire to exclude African Americans from the fighting pervaded not only the Southern plantation society but also the North where as late as 1790 some 35,000 African Americans remained slaves, even as a number of state legislatures began to outlaw the condition during the last decades of the century.

The resistance to the use of freemen and slaves to fight the English stiffened with an attempt by John Murray, as Earl of Dunmore, and the royal governor of Virginia, to enlist them under his banner with the promise that anyone who did so would receive his freedom. Dunmore's ploy threatened to inspire a full-scale insurrection of the slaves and the destruction of the economy of the South. The Virginians passed a series of statutes with punishments as severe as death or work in lead mines for any slaves caught in their attempt to join the Dunmore legions. The royal governor enrolled about three hundred former slaves, garbing them in uniforms inscribed LIBERTY TO SLAVES and they were officially designated, Lord Dunmore's Ethiopian Regiment.

Dunmore threw a force of six hundred troops, nearly half of them black, into a decisive battle at Great Bridge where the rebel Virginians decisively whipped the Redcoats. Defeated in battle, the Dunmore legion fell victim to an epidemic of smallpox and retreated into oblivion with their leader.

Were it not for the pitiable effect upon human lives, the entire Dunmore affair could be a scene from a comedy of the absurd. The Committee of Five, which included Thomas Jefferson, in its first draft of what would become the Declaration of Independence condemned George III for having "waged cruel war against human nature itself, violating its most sacred rights of life and liberty in the persons of a distant people who never offended him, captivating and carrying them into slavery in another hemisphere . . ." On the other hand, many of the rebellious, including the patron saint of freedom Patrick Henry, painted the British as outside agitators who roused the blacks "to destroy us." And, when writing the final version of the Declaration, Jefferson, aware that bondage remained a feature of the American scene, removed the charges of slave trading as one of the king's crimes rather than remind the world who profited most from George III's sponsorship.

The barriers to black participation in the American Revolution crumbled when the leaders contemplated the real possibility of defeat. In a protracted struggle, the Continental army could ill afford to ignore a segment that added up to nearly 20 percent of the total population. (The proportion of blacks to whites for what would become the United States actually reached its zenith at 19 plus percent in 1790.)

In an effort to field troops for the Continental army, some states actively began to enlist blacks, particularly as recruiting officers received as much as ten dollars a head for every volunteer brought into camp. When the Congress in 1777 fixed quotas of soldiers for states, resistance to using blacks crumbled, even in the face of state statutes that forbade use of nonwhites. For their part, many of these free newcomers, hard-pressed to earn subsistence wages, eagerly accepted the bounty offered and the promise of food, clothing, and shelter. Adding to the manpower pool, Northern states provided for enlistment of slaves if their master agreed. The latter not only received a sum of money—in some cases the usual bounty paid a recruit—but also became exempt from support for a former slave who fell upon hard times when freed. Under the system that granted able-bodied men exemption from the draft if they produced a substitute, blacks, free or in servitude, often stood in for whites. Southerners would misrepresent their slave substitutes as freemen in order not to run afoul of the rules that banned slaves from bearing arms. For their part slaves were highly motivated to serve in the military because that might mean liberation when the fighting ended.

Salem Poore, commended for his courage at Bunker Hill was one of a number of nonwhites who drew praise from commanders. The *Pennsylvania Evening Post* of 7 August 1777 reports the daring raid, led by a Lieutenant Colonel Barton, that captured the British general Prescott at Newport, Rhode Island. "They landed about five miles from Newport, and three-quarters of a mile from the house, which they approached cautiously, avoiding the main guard, which was at some distance. The Colonel went foremost with a stout active negro [named Prince] close behind him, and another at a small distance; the rest followed so as to be near but not seen."

Barton diverted a sentry with talk about recovering some wounded rebel prisoners and gossip, then grabbed him before he could cry out. The party reached the bedroom of Prescott. The *Post* said Prince butted the door open with his head. According to a surgeon attached to the American army, "A Negro man, named Prince, instantly thrust his beetle head through the panel door and seized his victim while in bed."

Letters from various commanders of the colonist companies often note the presence of "Negroes" as well as "Indians" and frequently add comments on how well they performed. The very fact that the white officers felt compelled to make these remarks only heightens the sense of low esteem in which nonwhites were held. But about all the men of color could expect in reward were words of praise. At the Battle of Mobile, an American counterattack was repulsed with the Continentals retiring in disorder. Jeffrey, a slave taking the place of his master, according to a contemporary account, "seeing the disastrous results about to befall [his comrades] rushed forward, mounted a horse, took command of the troops, and, by an heroic effort rallied them to the charge—completely routing the enemy, who left the Americans masters of the field. He at once received from the General [Andrew Jackson] the title of 'Major,' though he could not, according to the American policy, so commission him."

His valor notwithstanding, Jeffrey reverted to the status of slave after the peace. At the age of more than seventy he struck a white man in self-defense and incurred a punishment of thirty-nine lashes which caused his death.

Obviously, service with the Continentals did not guarantee liberty. An adolescent slave named Samuel Charlton received a silver dollar from his New Jersey master when he enlisted as a teamster as a substitute for his owner. Charlton engaged in the Battle of Monmouth and while attached to George Washington's baggage train earned a commendation from Washington for his courage and devotion. Upon expiration of his time in service, Charlton returned to slave status, gaining his freedom only after his master, in his will, freed all in bondage to him and provided a pension for his surrogate soldier.

To get around the distaste for adding blacks to the Continental military and loss of a valuable piece of property through manumission in return for service, the whites resorted to hiring blacks as laborers for the armed forces. Some states like Virginia, Georgia, and South Carolina bought or rented slaves from planters for purposes that included work as armorers, wagoners, or at building fortifications. Additionally, state governments in possession of slaves—blacks captured from British units—or expecting to obtain them in the future from booty or in the bondage trade, used them as bounty to induce whites to enlist. South Carolina, for example, offered "one sound negro between the age of ten years and forty . . . for each and every year's service" to men who enlisted for three years.

There were leaders who recognized the inconsistency of the Declaration of Independence with schemes that perpetuated slavery in order to gain the right to freedom the document proclaimed. James Madison, a Virginian, referring to the use of the "negro bounty" by his state legislature said, "Without deciding on the expediency of the mode under their consideration, would it not be as well to liberate and make soldiers at once of the blacks themselves, as to make them instruments for enlisting white soldiers? It would certainly be more consonant to the principles of liberty, which ought never to be lost sight of in a contest for liberty . . ."

Madison claimed that the policy he offered would not endanger the property rights of the plantation owners, arguing "experience having shown that a freedman immediately loses all attachment and sympathy with his former fellow slaves." That dubious assertion failed to convince the powers of the Old Dominion and they refused to recruit the local blacks.

The enemy, the British armies and navies, likewise hungered for able bodies. They too overcame a reluctance to depend upon men of color and overturn an economy based on slavery. Actively campaigning in the South, the royalist troops numbered thousands of nonwhites among their spoils and many willingly took the king's shilling which brought with it freedom. Proclamations that offered liberty to slaves who deserted the rebels attracted thousands of fugitives to the British lines and these n under the Union Jack. The major distinction from Continentals was that few blacks in the loyalists' cau the red coat of a combat soldier.

The English exploited the knowledge of the forn for espionage. Since they were particularly susceptible pox, the Britons even used sick ones as a primitive f .... warfare, distributing the ill and dying in areas where they might infect rebels. But with some exceptions, nonwhites were almost exclusively limited to provisioning, building pathways or breastworks, acting as servants and grooms for horses. Explicit orders from top echelons directed that blacks, along with Native Americans and enemy prisoners be removed from the muster rolls of the regular troops. Instead, they were formed into militia companies, segregated units. In this guise, particularly as the enemy threatened British installations the blacks were equipped with weapons and fought alongside the English. The Hessians, themselves mercenaries, had less compunction about filling up their ranks with any bodies they could find.

However employed, blacks entering into the service of George III entertained no particular affection for the English or the king's cause. The prospect of freedom governed their decisions.

As the struggle dragged on, the need for manpower deepened. The Continental navy and states sponsored ships. Particularly short of sailors, the service eagerly recruited blacks, many of whom had considerable seafaring experience. Some were knowledgeable enough to serve as pilots in the tricky inland waterways. The separate state navies that enlisted men for shorter periods of time and granted crews larger shares of prize money from seizure of enemy vessels naturally attracted blacks who, as in the case of land forces, swapped freedom from slavery for waterborne service. The Royal Navy liberally employed black seamen and those with knowledge of the local waters also served as pilots in coastal and inland voyages. Because of the dismal life ashore for all of color, these men, unlike many whites, were not inclined to jump ship.

Conditions for army units were particularly critical in the South where the British had successfully sought aid from a significant number of loyalists while also offering freedom to the blacks who deserted their masters and fled to the mother-country's lines. A committee on behalf of the Continental Congress proposed to strengthen the troops available for South Carolina and Georgia by raising a 3,000-strong army of blacks under white officers and noncoms. Masters would receive one thousand dollars for each slave furnished. The soldiers themselves would not be paid but supplied food and clothing and at the end of the war were rewarded with a fifty-dollar bonus and their freedom. A leading proponent of the idea, Continental Congress ident Henry Laurens, himself a former slave trader and subsequently a beneficent landowner and slaveholder who now sought to end his own participation in the practice, wrote to George Washington for support. The commander in chief temporized, unwilling to commit himself publicly on such a sensitive subject. However, through Alexander Hamilton, Washington presented a proposal for slave soldiers enlisted in South Carolina and Georgia to the Continental Congress.

When Laurens's son brought the notion to the South Carolina authorities, they were quick to react. Governor John Rutledge told the younger Laurens the measure "was received with horror by the planters, who figured to themselves terrible consequences." Rather than arm their chattels and relinquish the labor upon which their fortunes depended, in return for a better chance at independence, South Carolinians resoundingly voted against such a radical notion. Upon word of a proposed British expedition against South Carolina, the legislators would not even entertain a request for non-arms-bearing black wagoneers, pioneers, artificers, and servants. Washington expressed no surprise and reportedly advised Laurens that private interests outweigh public weal among most humans.

With the Southern states firmly set against the mobilization of blacks, particularly as full units, for the most part, the Continental armies integrated nonwhites in their forces. Muster rolls for the 1st Rhode Island Regiment indicated as many as 225 nonwhites served in menial as well as combat positions. During the Battle of Rhode Island in 1778, essentially a retreat to preserve forces that might otherwise be cut off, black soldiers ably defended against intense attacks by combined British and Hessian troops. Their performance was on a par with that of whites, and the praise from commanders and observers noted their gallantry. The party with George Washington that crossed the Delaware on Christmas night 1777, to capture more than 900 Hessians included Prince Whipple, a black ordinarily assigned as a bodyguard to one of Washington's aides. In the painting of the feat, Prince Whipple pulls one of the oars.

The French, upon entering into an alliance against the British, added 545 residents of Haiti to their forces and employed them in an unsuccessful siege against Savannah. The men from Santo Domingo prevented a defeat from turning into a disaster by repelling a British counterattack.

Documents from the period refer to the accomplishments of many individual freemen and slaves in the fight for independence. Usually assigned the unpleasant tasks of manual labor, waiter, and valet for officers, foraging for supplies when not called upon to bear arms, the African Americans enjoyed more creature comforts than ordinarily available to men of color. In both the navy and the army, blacks were not considered for positions above the lowest ranks.

In spite of the achievements of many of the minority men enrolled, the traditional hostility against them persisted. One observer commented about his regiment, ". . . there were a number of negroes, which to persons unaccustomed to such associations, had a disagreeable, degrading effect." A captain in the 4th Pennsylvania Battalion wrote his wife that the mixture of "Negroes, Indians, and whites, with old men and mere children . . . make a most shocking spectacle . . . sufficient to make one sick of the service." General Philip Schuyler complained that "Negroes disgrace our arms." He continued, "Is it consistent with the Sons of Freedom to trust their all to be defended by slaves?" General William Heath wrote to Samuel Adams of his discomfort at seeing "negroes" mixed with whites.

With the surrender of Cornwallis at Yorktown, Virginia, in 1781, the Revolutionary War was over, although because of poor communications and the involvement of distant parties official peace lay a year and a half off. The status of slaves involved in military operations by both sides presented a thorny problem. The provisional treaty signed in Paris in 1782, contained language covering the evacuation of the British and disposition of property belonging to Americans. The colonists wanted runaways who signed up with the enemy to be returned to their owners. The British, however, felt some obligation to those who had volunteered and in good faith served the home country. They had been promised their freedom. In the South, attempts to negotiate a solution that allowed those pledged liberty from those who were simply runaways or booty broke down. When the British sailed from Charleston, South Carolina, they took with them more than 5,300 former slaves, depositing most of them either in Jamaica or East Florida. Others wound up in the Bahamas, Canada, Nova Scotia, or even England itself. George Washington, as a Virginia plantation owner, sympathized with his regional neighbors demanding the surrender of valuable assets. He tried vainly to convince the British commander in chief, Sir Guy Carleton, to turn over the former slaves. Carleton, reluctant to accommodate the desires of the slaveholders from the start, eventually allowed thousands of refugees from bondage to sail from New York, much to the annoyance of Washington. Adding to the unhappiness of the slave owners, France, the ally in the war, carried off several thousand blacks under its custody. Altogether, as many as 20,000 African Americans may have departed from the country as a result of the war. Not all who left went free. Loyalists carried away their human chattel and some British officers and soldiers had been given slaves as bounties for their efforts.

The one consistent theme of African Americans during the American Revolution is they were regarded as property by the colonists and the British. They were used as payment or surrogates for military service, given as rewards for services rendered, and even their induction into the military with the promise of freedom was a commercial transaction, in effect renting their bodies in return for liberty.

The use of blacks in the Revolutionary War followed a pattern that continued for about 175 years in the American military. At first, the authorities declined to enlist them. As the shortages of manpower became apparent, they were grudgingly enrolled, largely for menial work rather than combat duty and denied positions that might give them authority over white servicemen. With the passage of time the consumption of cannon fodder would grant some the right to bleed for the country. And when the shooting was over and the number of men under arms sharply reduced, they were the first to be dismissed.

In the years immediately after the American Revolution, men like George Washington, Thomas Jefferson, and James Madison apparently recognized the incompatibility of the Declaration of Independence with its nonrestrictive insistence upon the freedom and equality of all men. But while they provided for manumission of bondage for their slaves upon their own deaths, they did not personally champion a movement to end the conditions of servitude inflicted upon African Americans. Nevertheless, the Constitution adopted by the thirteen original colonies contained a clause that set a cutoff date of 1808 for those states that wished to import slaves. The abolitionist movement, slowly building up in the Northeast, was able to banish slavery altogether in New England and the North Atlantic states. The infant federal government went so far as to prohibit the practice in the Northwest territories, guaranteeing freedom throughout the northern tier of the new country. While that offered some relief to the oppressed, the military basically remained closed to nonwhites. For even free blacks in states where slavery did not exist, discrimination in the armed forces was only one of many injustices inflicted upon them. Aside from all of the social indignities heaped upon them, they were unable to vote, their testimony was unacceptable in a court of law, and they were taxed for educational facilities they could not use. Denied equal opportunities in employment, housing, and wages, it is difficult to understand why they should even want to serve in the defense of the country, but they did.

The United States felt little need for a sizable military in the years immediately after the Revolution, but within a few decades, serious issues with both the French and the English brought the nation to the brink of war. As Napoleon rampaged throughout Europe and fought with nearly every neighboring country the British headed the opposition. Both warring parties trampled the rights of neutral America. Most egregiously, they raided American shipping when the vessels entered into commerce with the enemy. In addition, the Royal Navy not only seized U.S. vessels but also impressed their seamen in the service of the king. Adding to the grievances of the

Americans, the British Orders in Council also imposed trade restrictions which were particularly onerous for the agricultural South.

Europeans regarded the new democracy as a weakling peopled by an undisciplined rabble hardly worthy of consideration. In 1811, the Royal Navy's corvette *Little Belt* drubbed a U.S. frigate *President* in an impromptu sea battle that confirmed the British belief in the inferiority of their American cousins. Although George III technically still occupied the throne, he was certifiably insane and a bellicose politico-military establishment, still smarting from its defeat twenty-five years earlier, savored the taste of revenge.

At the same time, the prospect of another war with England tempted some Americans. They saw opportunities to gain land in Canada and the Far West. Settlers also believed the British, intent upon expanding their empire, instigated trouble with Native Americans. Action on the diplomatic front and protest induced the representatives of Bonaparte to act conciliatory. Meanwhile, the British offenses exceeded the toleration of the administration under President James Madison. He asked for a declaration of war from a Congress sharply divided on the issue. The measure passed by only nineteen to thirteen with the Federalists, particularly those representing the banking and shipping circles of New England and New York, staunchly opposed. In fact, the British Parliament had already repealed the notorious Orders in Council, the chief complaint of the Americans, but word reached the States only after the vote decreed war.

When the War of 1812 erupted, the American army authorities again were disinclined to include nonwhites, although the population now included almost 1,400,000 blacks, of whom 1,181,362 were slaves with the remainder freemen. However, the conflict never aroused the enthusiasm that marked the war for independence, which produced state-sponsored militias and enlisted massive numbers of volunteers. The armed forces refused to enroll slaves but welcomed freemen, particularly in the navy where one-sixth of the sailors were blacks.

Some commanders, like Oliver Hazard Perry expressed unhappiness with such seamen. Assigned by his superior, Commodore Isaac Chauncey to head the Great Lakes fleet, Perry wrote Chauncey, "The men . . . were a motley set, blacks, soldiers, and boys. I cannot think that you saw them after they were selected." Actually between 10 and 12 percent of the sailors were blacks.

From his flagship, Chauncey dismissed the complaint. "I regret you were not pleased with the men sent you . . . for to my knowledge a part of them are not surpassed by any seamen we have in the fleet and I have yet to learn that the color of skin or the cut and trimmings of the coat can affect a man's qualifications or usefulness. I have nearly fifty blacks on this boat and many of them are among the best of my men."

Subsequently, Perry, having distinguished himself with a great victory against the enemy, said of his black crewmen, "They seem to be absolutely insensible to danger." The famous painting of Perry abandoning the stricken *Laurence* for the *Niagara* shows a black sailor, Cyrus Joshua Tiffany, accompanying Perry in the longboat.

African Americans also sailed aboard privateers. After an exchange of gunfire with a British frigate that killed two blacks and wounded six other Americans, Nathaniel Shaler, commander of the privately armed schooner *Governor Tompkins,* notified his New York agent "The name of one of my poor fellows who was killed ought to be registered in the book of fame, and remembered with reverence as long as bravery is considered a virtue. He was a black man by the name of John Johnson. A twenty-four-pound shot struck him in the hip and took away all the lower part of his body. In this state, the poor brave fellow lay on the deck and several times exclaimed to his shipmates, 'Fire away, my boy: no haul a color down.' The other was a black man by the name of John Davis and was struck in much the same way. He fell near me, and several times requested to be thrown overboard, saying he was only in the way of others. When America has such tars, she has little to fear from the tyrants of the ocean."

Usher Parsons a navy doctor at the time of the War of 1812 wrote to the Massachusetts Historical Society some years later, "In 1816, I was surgeon of the 'Java,' under Commodore Perry. The white and colored seamen messed together. About one in six or eight were colored.

"In 1819, I was surgeon of the 'Gorier,' under Commodore Macdonough; and the proportion of blacks was about the same in her crew. There seemed to be an absence of prejudice against the blacks as messmates among the crew. What I have said applies to the crews of other ships that sailed in squadrons." Unlike the situation during the Revolution, the mother country could no longer be tarred as friendly to slavery. Parliament had ordered an end to the profitable trade although as a colonial power the country continued to exploit the residents of its possessions in every way except that of bondage. Mindful that once generated insurrection could spread and infect areas like the West Indies and Bahamas, the British secretary for war and the colonies, Earl Bathurst, cautioned his military commanders, "You will not encourage any disposition which may be manifested by the Negroes to rise upon their masters." His directions were ambivalent, however, with a proviso that individual African Americans could enlist in a black corps—a segregated unit—or flee to freedom in a British colony.

Short of troops because of the need for the army to deal with the waning but still puissant power of occupied France, the British saw the blacks, rejected by the American forces, as a key to their victory. Those charged with carrying out the war expressly appealed to slaves to quit their masters and support the English cause. Admiral Sir Alexander Cochrane, based in Bermuda, plotting a thrust at Chesapeake Bay, explained to his superiors that he would invade there and the preliminary conquests would provide an area where thousands of unhappy slaves would rally to his side. "The great point to be attained is the cordial support of the Black population. With them properly armed and backed with 20,000 troops, Mr. Maddison [sic] will be hurled from his throne."

While American whites claimed nonwhites made inferior soldiers, Cochrane insisted, "The Blacks are all good horsemen. Thousands will join upon their masters' horses, and they will only be required to be clothed and accoutered to be as good Cossacks in the European army [an army made on the cheap always gladdens the hearts of government ministers] and I believe more terrific to the Americans than any troops that could be brought forward."

Cochrane's prediction of widespread defection proved far off the mark as three months of recruiting registered only 120 men. One reason lay in the option for slaves to become freemen in British colonies. Given that alternative from combat against their former masters, the African Americans saw no reason to expose themselves to hardship and peril. Many undoubtedly realized their prospective liberators only wished to exploit them and could muster little enthusiasm to be tools of either side. Although the British persisted in the attempt, they were never able to induce any substantial number of black residents to take up arms against the enemy. Upon abandoning the Chesapeake campaign, the British carried with them about 2,000 runaways, most of whom settled in the maritime provinces. A few Virginians, however, were actually sold back into slavery in the Bahamas.

As His Majesty's armies massed to attack New Orleans, Andrew Jackson issued a proclamation to the Negroes.

> To the Free Colored Inhabitants of Louisiana:
> Through a mistaken policy, you have heretofore been deprived of a participation in the glorious struggle for national rights in which our country is engaged. This no longer shall exist.
> As sons of freedom, you are now called upon to defend our most inestimable blessing. As Americans, your country looks with confidence to her adopted children for a valorous support, as a faithful return for the advantages enjoyed under her mild and equitable government. As fathers, husbands, and brothers, you are summoned to rally around the standard of the Eagle, to defend all which is dear in existence . . .
> To every noble-hearted, generous freeman of color volunteering to serve during the present contest with Great Britain, and no longer,

there will be paid the same bounty in money and lands, now received by the white soldiers of the United States, viz: one hundred and twenty-four dollars in money, and one hundred and sixty acres of land. . . .

On enrolling yourselves in companies, the Major-General Commanding will select officers for your government from your white fellow-citizens. Your non-commissioned officers will be appointed from among yourselves.

Due regard will be paid to the feelings of freemen and soldiers. You will not, by being associated with white men in the same corps, be exposed to improper comparisons or unjust sarcasm. As a distinct, independent battalion or regiment, pursuing the path of glory, you will, undivided, receive the applause and gratitude of your countrymen.

Jackson's offers must have been bittersweet to those who were eligible. The boilerplate about the "sons of freedom," "glorious struggle for national rights," and "a faithful return for the advantages enjoyed" ignores the conditions under which the freemen or their ancestors as well as their fellow blacks still in bondage came to America. To enjoy the privileges of putting up their lives, the freemen would have to accept the subservience to a wholly white officer leadership, although the ranks of noncommissioned were open. And they would be segregated from their fellow soldiers whose sole distinction lay in color of skin.

However dubious the terms of the proclamation to the African Americans, much of the country endorsed the idea, for reasons of exigency rather than justice. The Redcoats had made substantial inroads, burning the national capitol, capturing huge areas of territory such as Maine, and threatening the dwindling remnants of the ground troops. The New York state legislature passed a bill that sought to enroll "free men of color" into several regiments with white officers in command. In addition, the legislation carried a provision for slaves, with permission of their owners, to enlist, with the master or mistress receiving the bounty and pay of the soldier. Upon the discharge, manumission would be granted.

Before the War of 1812 broke out, Gov. William C. C. Claiborne of Louisiana with its slaveholders and extensive plantations tried to organize black militia companies composed of freemen for future contingencies. White residents of New Orleans denounced the black militia, tarring them as the bloodthirsty "wretches" who had overthrown the French in Haiti and created an independent republic. But as the fighting spread over America, officials reactivated black militias, with the proviso of "white only" for officers. Claiborne, however, signed a commission for one black lieutenant, and subsequently several more men of color entered the officer ranks.

As the British army neared New Orleans, Jackson spouted more bombast designed to inspire his 6,000 troops, which included the black militia units and other freemen, recruited for a total of two battalions numbering 500. He specifically addressed them: "To The Men Of Color—Soldiers! From the shores of Mobile I collected you to arms—I invited you to share in the perils and to divide the glory of your white countrymen. I expected much from you; for I was not uninformed of those qualities which must render you so formidable to an invading foe. I knew that you could endure hunger and thirst, and all the hardships of war. I knew that you loved the land of your nativity, and that, like ourselves, you had to defend all that is most dear to man. But you surpass my hopes. I have found in you, united to these qualities, that noble enthusiasm which impels to great deeds . . ."

When battle erupted on the outskirts of the city, both contending armies fielded blacks. Both of the American battalions participated and the British had imported a regiment from the West Indies. Although the fighting actually occurred some two weeks after the peace treaty had been signed at Ghent, the forces under Jackson decisively defeated their enemies on 8 January 1815 and subsequent accounts commended the performance of the American nonwhites.

Isaac Chauncey later proved less of a champion for equality in the service. As acting secretary of the navy in 1839 he issued a restrictive circular. "Frequent complaints having been made of the number of blacks and other colored persons entered at some of the recruiting stations, and the consequent underproportion of white persons transferred to seagoing vessels, it is deemed proper to call your attention to the subject, and to request that you will direct the recruiting officer at the station under your command, in future, not to enter a greater proportion of colored persons than 5 percent of the whole number of white persons entered by him weekly or monthly; and under no circumstances whatever to enter a slave." For that matter the marines, army, and even state militias, with the odd exception of Louisiana, refused to accept any blacks.

During the Mexican War, which lasted less than eighteen months, 1,000 blacks participated as members of the navy but the campaigns of American forces invading Mexico required no large-scale infusion of men, thereby forestalling any call upon nonwhites for military service.

The issue of black presence in the military would remain dormant until the outbreak of the Civil War in 1861 and the subsequent demands of both the Union and the Confederacy for huge numbers of men.

3
The Civil War

As in the past, the outbreak of the Civil War brought no concerted rush to enlist African Americans as soldiers either in the North or the South, although individual areas and commanders recruited some. While the navy had continued to enroll black seamen, there was a quota system and those who came aboard did so mostly as menials. The marines were firmly lily-white. The army carried a handful of blacks and Native Americans on its rosters but the use of nonwhites as ground troops was discouraged.

The Confederate assault on Fort Sumpter, South Carolina, galvanized Northern determination to crush the secessionists. When President Abraham Lincoln issued a call for the defense of the Union, tens of thousands of volunteers eagerly signed up with the state militias to bolster the strength of the Regular Army. The federals, confident of their strength, figured they would crush the South within a matter of months. Enlistments were for ninety days or even less.

For the brethren of the oppressed the conflict loomed as a crusade. In Massachusetts they sounded their tocsin:

> The following Resolutions were adopted at a recent meeting of the colored citizens of Boston—
>
> Whereas, the traitors of the South have assailed the United States Government, with the intention of overthrowing it for the purpose of perpetuating slavery and,
>
> Whereas, in such a contest between the North and South—believing, as we do, that it is a contest between liberty and despotism—it is as important for each class of citizen to declare, as it is for the rulers of the Government to know, their sentiments and position; therefore,
>
> Resolved, That our feelings urge us to say to our countrymen that we are ready to stand by and defend the Government as the equals of its white defenders—to do so with "our lives, our fortunes, and our sacred honor," for the sake of freedom and as good citizens; and we ask you to modify your laws, that we may enlist—that full scope may be given to the patriotic feelings burning in the colored man's breast—and we pledge ourselves to raise an army in the country of fifty thousand men.

Resolved, That more than half of the army which we could raise, being natives of the South, knowing its geography, and being acquainted with the character of the enemy, would be of incalculable service to the Government.

Resolved, That the colored women would go as nurses, seamstresses, and warriors, if need be, to crush rebellion and uphold the Government.

Resolved, That the colored people, almost without exception, "have their souls in arms, and all eager for the fray," and are ready to go at a moment's warning, if they are allowed to go as soldiers.

Resolved, That we do immediately organize ourselves into drilling companies, to the end of becoming better skilled in the use of firearms; so that when we shall be called upon by the country, we shall be better prepared to make a ready and fitting response.

The *Philadelphia Press* two days later carried a story in which it reported "A number of prominent colored men are now raising two regiments . . . and hundreds of brawny ebony men are ready to fill up the ranks if the State will accept their services. Peril and war blot out all distinction of race and rank. These colored soldiers should be attached to the Home Guard. They will make Herculean defenders. Colored men, it will be remembered, fought the glorious battle of Red Bank, when the city was in peril in 1771."

The account then printed portions of a speech by Alfred M. Green in which he orated, "The time has arrived in the history of the great Republic when we may again give evidence to the world of the bravery and patriotism of a race, in whose hearts burns the love of country, of freedom and of civil and religious toleration. It is these grand principles that enable men, however proscribed, when possessed of true patriotism, to say, 'My country, right or wrong, I love thee still.'"

Green went on to note that in spite of "the brave deeds of our fathers," as attested by Washington, Jackson, and others, he and others of his race had not been granted the rights of citizens and their injuries included fugitive slave laws, the Dred Scott decision, indictments for treason, and other grievances. Nevertheless he said, ". . . let us endeavor to hope for the future, and improve the present auspicious moment for creating anew our claims upon the justice and honor of the Republic . . ."

The themes contained in Alfred M. Green's speech—patriotism in spite of discrimination, willingness to put lives on the line in the face of grievous acts, and most significantly, the belief that if they could serve and show their mettle, blacks would be accepted as equals with all the rights of Americans— would echo for nearly 100 years.

The offer of men, even women to bear arms, the assertion of fealty to the Union failed to impress either the authorities or much of the white population who scorned blacks as inferior in intelligence and ineffective as warriors. The Providence, Rhode Island, police broke up drills organized by the local freemen as "disorderly gatherings." When a black man attempted to attach himself to a Pennsylvania force headed for the defense of Washington, Baltimore citizens stoned him. Felix Brannigan, a nineteen-year-old corporal in the New York 74th Volunteers, declared, "We don't want to fight side and side with the nigger. We think we are too superior a race for that."

Except for its ardent abolitionists, the North initially rejected antislavery as the mission. Recruiters refused applicants with the wrong skin color. Major General Thomas W. Sherman, who commanded the Union forces landing on the South Carolina coast pledged not to overthrow the "peculiar institution." Brigadier Ben Butler offered federal troops under his command to aid the governor of Maryland to put down a rumored slave rebellion.

Major General John C. Frémont who had run for president on an antislavery platform in 1856, was an exception. As commander of the Department of the West he proposed to free slaves of secessionists in the territory he governed. Lincoln, mindful that the border states while adherents of a federal union and the supremacy of the central government did not oppose slavery, countermanded the orders issued by Frémont.

In fact, in August 1862, Lincoln advised a delegation from Indiana that "to arm the Negroes would turn 50,000 bayonets from the loyal Border States against us." Six weeks later, he reasserted this position to visitors from Chicago. Certainly, many who rejected the South's right to secede held no brief against slavery. Almost an entire regiment from southern Illinois deserted with the statement that they would "lie in the woods until moss grew on their backs rather than help free the slaves."

The president had set out his priorities in a letter to newspaper editor Horace Greeley. "I would save the Union. I would save it the shortest way under the Constitution. The sooner the national authority can be restored; the nearer the Union will be 'the Union as it was.' If there be those who would not save the Union, unless they could at the same time *save* slavery, I do not agree with them. If there be those who would not save the Union unless they could at the same time *destroy* slavery, I do not agree with them. My paramount object in this struggle *is* to save the Union, and it is *not* either to save or destroy slavery. If I could save the Union without freeing *any* slave I would do it, and if I could save it by freeing *all* the slaves I would do it; and if I could save it by freeing some and leaving others alone I would also do that. What I do about slavery, and the colored race, I do because I believe it helps save the Union; and what I forbear, I forbear because I do *not* believe it would help save the Union . . ."

The policy enunciated by the Great Emancipator in 1862 foreclosed any widespread effort to make the African Americans an integral part of the Union effort. By the same token, while Lincoln was too much of a moral human being to have condoned slavery, when he did move to free all slaves and enlist the full support of black Americans in the federal cause he still acted on the basis of preserving the Union. Until that moment in 1863, however, he continued to resist liberation of slaves for nearly two years.

The issue enveloped the White House as well as the Congress with the efforts of Maj. Gen. David Hunter during the spring of 1862. Lincoln negated another mini-emancipation decreed by David Hunter to cover the population he controlled in the Department of the South. Charles G. Halpine, a New Yorker born in Ireland, a journalist and Union officer serving with Hunter in South Carolina, produced accounts under the *nom de plume* of Private Miles O'Reilly. One sketch reported that General Hunter, finding himself with fewer than eleven thousand men under his command and charged with the duty of holding the whole tortuous and broken seacoast of Georgia, South Carolina, and Florida, had applied often and in vain to the authorities at Washington for reinforcements.

"No reinforcements to be had from the North; vast fatigue duties in throwing up earthworks imposed on our insufficient garrison; the enemy continually increasing both in insolence and numbers . . . when General Hunter one fine morning with twirling glasses, puckered lips, and dilated nostrils (he had just received another 'don't-bother-us-for-reinforcements' dispatch from Washington) announced his intention of 'forming a negro regiment, and compelling every able-bodied black man in the department to fight for the freedom which could not be the issue of our war.'"

Because of the strictures against enlistment of the indigenous nonwhites, Hunter sought to issue arms, clothing, equipment, and rations for this regiment by listing the men as laborers hired by his chief quartermaster. He anticipated gaining the approval of higher authorities who would then authorize payment through the War Department. However, said Halpine, if the government balked, Hunter, who possessed considerable property, planned to pay his irregulars out of his own pocket.

Even before the financial details could be worked out, Hunter confronted the problem of who would command his newly recruited troops. Wrote Halpine, ". . . it was not a trivial difficulty. Where would experienced officers be found for such an organization? 'What! command niggers?' was the reply—if possible more amazed than scornful of nearly every competent young lieutenant or captain of volunteers to whom the suggestion of commanding this class of troops was made. 'Never mind,' said Hunter, when this . . . was brought to his notice; 'the fools or bigots who refuse are enough punished by their refusal. Before two years they will be competing eagerly for the commission they now reject.'"

Hunter then announced that any noncommissioned man, who volunteered for the duty and passed an examination in military proficiency, would become an officer. Noted Halpine, "Ten had the hardihood or moral courage to face the screaming, riotous ridicule of their late associates in the white regiments." Halpine reported that one applicant was immediately offered a first lieutenancy, with the promise of being made captain when his company filled up to the required standard—probably within ten days.

"The inchoate first-lieutenant was in ecstasies; a gentleman by birth and education, he longed for the shoulder-straps [insignia of an officer]. He appeared joyously grateful; and only wanted leave to run up to Fort Pulaski for the purpose of collecting his traps, taking leave of his former comrades, and procuring his discharge papers from Col. Barton. Two days after that came a note to the department headquarters respectfully declining the commission! He had been laughed and jeered out of accepting a captaincy by his comrades; and this . . . was but one of many scores of precisely similar cases."

In spite of this obstacle, the 1st South Carolina formed into a creditable unit. Halpine boasted, "At once, despite all hostile influence, the negro regiment became one of the lions of the South." However, word of Hunter's unauthorized actions struck unsympathetic ears in Washington. The War Department, aroused by a Kentucky congressman, refused to approve and the House of Representatives introduced a series of questions about Hunter's operations.

The general riposted with an argument that rather than employing fugitive slaves as charged, he had enrolled a fine regiment of loyal persons, "whose late masters are fugitive rebels—men who everywhere fly before the appearance of the national flag, leaving their loyal and unhappy servants behind them. . . . In the absence of any 'fugitive master law,' the deserted slaves would be wholly without remedy had not the crime of treason given them the right to pursue, capture and bring those persons of whose benignant protection they have been thus suddenly and cruelly bereft."

Having wittily dismissed the charges against him—when his letter to Secretary of War Stanton was read aloud in Congress, most of the representatives burst into laughter—Hunter added, "The experiment of arming blacks, so far as I have made it, has been a complete and even marvelous success. They are sober, docile, attentive and enthusiastic; displaying great natural capacities in acquiring the duties of the soldier. They are now eager beyond all things to take the field and be led into action; it is the unanimous opinion of the officers who have had charge of them that in the peculiarities of this climate and country, they will prove invaluable auxiliaries, fully equal to the similar regiments so long and successfully used by the British authorities in the West India Islands."

For all of his guile, Hunter could not overcome the resistance of official Washington. Hunter abandoned the project for lack of money to equip and pay the troops. He managed, however, to create one company of blacks to police the island of St. Simon. Later, the 1st South Carolina Regiment, composed of black enlisted men would be reestablished and participate in the fighting.

One noticeable effort by the Confederacy to use its resident blacks to defend secession and the right to slavery enrolled a regiment of "1,400 colored men" according to the *New Orleans Picayune* and the newspaper commented after a review held in February 1862, "We must also pay a deserved compliment to the companies of free colored men, all very well drilled and comfortably equipped." But two months later when the siege by Union troops threatened to trap the Southern defenders, all of the Confederates were evacuated with the exception of the blacks. Their training would be put to good use by the invaders.

Another stillborn effort to bolster the defenders occurred in Memphis where a committee undertook "to organize a volunteer company composed of our patriotic freemen of color of the city of Memphis, for the service of our common defense." The attempt provided little aid.

The optimistic views of the North quickly crumbled after a series of resounding defeats during the first months of the conflict. The Southerners, who had attracted many of the military's professionals, demonstrated better strategy and tactics. The Confederate troops, believing their way of life was threatened, entered battle with far more zeal than their opponents. One of the first converts to the use of nonwhites in the Union forces had been Lincoln's secretary of war, Simon Cameron, who earlier dismissed use of this manpower. When he insisted the federal government had the right, even the duty to arm slaves against their masters, Lincoln promptly sacked him and Edwin M. Stanton assumed the post.

As usual, principle succumbed to need, and in the summer of 1862, only a few months after the abortive attempt by Hunter, although still relying on a volunteer system rather than a draft, Congress authorized the enlistment of black men, albeit offering them less money than paid to whites. Ben Butler, previously eager to stomp out a nonexistent slave uprising in Maryland, now refused to enroll freemen in the Louisiana territory that he governed. Washington, D.C., dispatched a general with word that Butler would have to forego his prejudices in favor of the cause. Butler, not averse to confiscating slaves in areas he controlled and using this "contraband" for labor and servants to officers, succumbed.

The Union promised the blacks of Louisiana a payment of $38 in advance and between $13 and $22 a month, weapons and equipment free, with their families eligible for army rations. Upon the triumph of the North, each man was to receive $100 or 160 acres of land. In two weeks the quota for the 1st Regiment, Louisiana Native Guards filled up. Called *Chasseurs d'Afrique*, the soldiers guarded bridges, military installations, fortifications, railroads, and strategic bayous.

For most of the Civil War the South recoiled from arming its black residents in pursuit of secession. Rebel armies enrolled blacks mostly as auxiliaries but there was a potential for combat. When the Confederate forces drove into Maryland after inflicting horrendous defeats of Union troops in the Second Battle of Bull Run in September 1862, Frederick Olmsted observed their march. "The most liberal calculations could not give them more than 64,000 men. Over 3,000 negroes must be included in this number. These were clad in all kinds of uniforms, not only in cast-off or captured United States uniforms, but in coats with Southern buttons, State buttons, etc. These were shabby, but not shabbier or seedier than those worn by white men in the rebel ranks. Most of the negroes had arms, rifles, muskets, sabres, bowie knives, dirks, etc. They were supplied in many instances with knapsacks, haversacks, canteens, etc., and were manifestly an integral portion of the Southern Confederacy Army. They were seen riding on horses and mules, driving wagons, riding on caissons, in ambulances, with the staff of Generals and promiscuously mixed up with all the rebel horde . . . rather interesting when considered in connection with the horror rebels express at the suggestion of black soldiers being employed for the National defense."

Always hungry for able-bodied hands the Union Navy had followed a more open policy than the land-based forces. From the beginning of hostilities, federal gunboats mounting a blockade of Southern ports encountered small numbers of fugitives fleeing bondage on anything that could float. Robert Smalls, a slave serving as a pilot in the waters around Charleston, South Carolina, waited for the night that the three white officers of the 300-ton sidewheel steamer *Planter* chose to spend the night ashore. Smalls guided a party of sixteen escapees, seven of them women and children, including his wife and three offspring, onto the *Planter* in the dark of early morning. At 3:00 A.M. Smalls fired up the boilers and within half an hour cast off from the dock. He hoisted the Confederate and palmetto flags and steered the ship past a series of harbor positions. At each one, Smalls saluted with a blast from the steam whistle.

As they approached the final barrier, Fort Sumpter itself, Smalls positioned himself in the pilothouse, folding his arms and covering his head with a big straw hat, the customary posture of the white captain. Challenged, Smalls responded with the proper countersign—three shrill bursts of the whistle and one hissing noise. Satisfied, the sentries issued permission for the *Planter* to head out to open sea and supposedly one shouted, "Blow the damned Yankees to hell, and bring one of them in." A voice on the *Planter* yelled back, "Aye, Aye."

Continuing to run a moderate pace rather than arouse suspicion by speed, Smalls skippered his vessel beyond the range of the Confederate guns. Only then did he strike the Southern colors and run up a bedsheet to signal truce. Just as he announced himself, crewmen on the *Onward,* a Union gunboat in the blockade armada, manned their guns, prepared to unleash their cannons on the enemy ship. *Onward*'s captain, spying the white flag, ordered his sailors to hold their fire.

A prize crew from *Onward* boarded *Planter* to be pleasantly surprised by the booty. Not only did the Union fleet gain a formidable new ship but it also seized a thirty-two-pound gun, a twenty-four-pound howitzer, four smaller pieces, and a seven-inch rifle destined to be installed at a Confederate fortification in the harbor. Smalls and his associates were recognized as having brought to the Union a prize, and a Congressional bill authorized them to share half the value of the ship and her cargo, a sum of $4,584. Flag-Officer S. F. Du Pont, commander of the South Atlantic Blockading Squadron commended Smalls to the secretary of the navy, Gideon Welles, and the former slave remained with the *Planter* as a pilot while it plied Southern waters on behalf of the Union Navy.

With heat and disease felling many sailors, Secretary Welles demonstrated an eagerness to absorb blacks into his service. He issued an order on 30 April 1862 that contained the statement, "The large number of persons known as 'contrabands' flocking to the protection of the United States flag affords an opportunity to provide in every department of a ship, especially for boats' crews, acclimated labor. The flag-officers are required to obtain the services of these persons for the country by enlisting them freely in the navy with their consent, rating them as boys, at eight, nine, or ten dollars per month and one ration . . ." Open as he may have seemed, to whites, Welles sugar-coated his endorsement of black seamen with the bottom rating as "boys" and at minimal cost.

On 1 January 1863, Lincoln, who had warned the Southern states that if they did not surrender by this date he would declare all slaves free people, issued his Emancipation Proclamation after the Confederates refused to lay down their arms. As part of the document, Lincoln stated "such persons [the now liberated blacks] of suitable condition will be received into the armed service of the United States to garrison forts, positions, stations, and other places and to man vessels of all sorts in said service."

By his language, the president fully sanctioned the use of African Americans in the military and where authorities had once disdained their enlistment they now fiercely competed for men of color in order to fill the quotas for troops levied by the federal government. Initially, the results disappointed the adherents of an open policy. In the six weeks after the establishment of the 54th Massachusetts Regiment, aimed at fielding a black contingent, the state could attract only 100 men of color. Boston civic leaders dispatched envoys to other portions of the country and even to Canada.

Agents of other northern governments roved the southern territory held by the Union with instructions to recruit the former slaves. But the national government also coveted these "persons of suitable condition" to fill their federal ranks. Secretary of War Edwin M. Stanton sent the adjutant general of the Union Army into the Mississippi Valley to create brigades of the blacks. A Bureau of Colored Troops was established to supervise the organizing of the units and to examine prospective candidates for commissions with them.

Prominent blacks reacted with enthusiasm to the new attitude of the Lincoln administration. They spoke out strongly, encouraging their fellow ethnics to join the Union forces. Frederick Douglass lent his considerable skills as an orator and writer to the cause. "A war undertaken and brazenly carried on for the perpetual enslavement of colored men [a provision of the Confederate Constitution specified the legitimacy of slavery] calls logically and loudly for colored men to help suppress it. Only a moderate share of sagacity was needed to see that the arm of the slave was the best defense against the arm of the slaveholder . . ."

Douglass assured his fellow blacks that "Massachusetts now welcomes you to arms as soldiers. She has but a small colored population from which to recruit. She has full leave of the general government to send one regiment to the war and she has undertaken to do it. Go quickly and help fill up the first colored regiment from the North. I am authorized to assure you that you will receive the same wages, the same rations, the same equipment, the same protection, the same treatment, and the same bounty, secured to the white soldiers. You will be led by able and skillful officers, men who will take special pride in your efficiency and success. They will be quick to accord to you all the honor you shall merit by your valor, and see that your rights and feelings are respected by other soldiers."

The African Americans rallied to the cause with enthusiasm, well aware what victory could mean. H. Ford Douglass, a freeman who had enlisted in white outfits before the formation of the black ones joined up to "be better prepared to play his part in the great drama of the Negro's redemption." Christian A. Fleetwood who would become sergeant major of the 4th U.S. Colored Troops believed he was fighting "To save the country from ruin."

Pomp, circumstances, and high expectations were lavished upon the 54th Massachusetts by the Brahmins and the hoi polloi. On 28 May, little more than four months after it had been established and trained, the regiment marched to a wharf to embark for the battlefields. To see the outfit off, flags hung throughout the city, a band played while 20,000 citizens cheered the troops. The 54th carried a national flag furnished by the "Colored Ladies' Relief Society" along with a banner depicting the Goddess of Liberty emblazoned LIBERTY, LOYALTY AND UNITY with the white silk regimental insignia bearing the Massachusetts coat of arms on one side while the other flashed a golden cross and the Latin IN HOC SIGNO VINCES, an exhortation signifying a holy crusade. None of the previous fifty-three regiments from the Bay State were accorded such a splendid send-off. In the ranks of the 54th marched two sons of Frederick Douglass.

As the potential of black volunteers became more apparent, Lincoln waxed increasingly enthusiastic. By March 1864, just a few months after the Emancipation Proclamation, he declared, "The colored population is the great *available* and yet *unavailed of,* force for restoring the Union. The bare sight of 50,000 armed and drilled black soldiers upon the banks of the Mississippi, would end the rebellion at once."

The issue of soldiers' pay provoked considerable controversy, even after it appeared that the government now sought full use of its nonwhite residents. The standard pay for all blacks in the army, even after Lincoln issued the Emancipation Proclamation and made service a right of all freemen, amounted to ten dollars a month of which three dollars could be in clothing, as stipulated in the Militia Act of 1862. White equivalents received a basic stipend of thirteen dollars a month. Adherents of equitable compensation pointed out that the Militia Act was intended to cover recently freed persons of African descent who worked as laborers and menials for the military but did not bear arms.

Governor John A. Andrew of Massachusetts vigorously fought the differential in soldiers' pay. In championing the 54th and 55th, all African American regiments, he had promised the recruits they would be treated the same as the men in the other state-sponsored units. Andrew made it his business to travel to Washington and appeal to Lincoln, Stanton, and other top officials, eventually winning a decision by the attorney general that the salary of ten dollars a month was only meant to apply to those who had been slaves.

It was, however, a victory without the spoils. The War Department kept a tight lid on its coffers rather than stir resentment among whites. Stanton dismissed protests uttering a preposterous statement: "The duty of the colored man is to defend his country, whenever, wherever and in whatever form, is the same with that of white men. It does not depend on, nor is it affected by, what the country pays. The true way to secure her rewards and win her confidence is not to stipulate for them, but to deserve them." He made no mention of the obligation of the country to defend its citizens nor did he suggest that while one segment of the population would have to fight for her rewards and confidence another received these as a birthright. With elections approaching, Lincoln also hesitated.

Resolved to secure justice, Andrew persuaded his state legislature to ante up the differences in the monthly pay of the federal government to the two black regiments. The 54th promptly declined to accept any money from its home state. Their leader, Colonel Hallowell, reported that the men, having enlisted on the same basis as others, would rather serve without pay than accept less than that given their white equals. In fact, on three previous occasions the soldiers of the regiment refused to accept their stipend unless it matched that of all soldiers.

Resentment over the inequity boiled over among the black troops. A group in a South Carolina regiment refused to carry out their duties unless paid on an equal basis. The regimental commander termed the action mutinous and a firing squad snuffed out the life of the sergeant who led the protest. A similar incident and result quashed the complaints of a Rhode Island artillery unit stationed in Texas. The aggrieved members of the 55th Massachusetts wrote to Washington that following "thirteen months spent cheerfully and willingly doing [their] Duty most faithfully," they would prefer to be discharged from the service rather than continue to be paid less than their white counterparts.

One soldier, James Henry Gooding, wrote to Lincoln: "Now the main question is, are we *soldiers* or *laborers?* We were fully armed and equipped; have done all the various duties pertaining to a soldier's life, have conducted ourselves to the complete satisfaction of general officers who were, if anything, prejudiced *against* us, but who now accord us all the encouragement and honor due us, have shared the perils and labor of reducing the first stronghold that flaunted a traitor flag, and more Mr. President, today, the Anglo-Saxon mother, wife, or sister are not alone in tears for departed son, husbands, and brothers. The patient, trusting descendants of Africa's clime have dyed the ground with blood in defense of the Union and democracy. . . . Now Your Excellency, we have done a soldier's duty. Why can't we have a soldier's pay?"

This issue would continue to plague the Union cause and burble through the halls of Congress until 1864 when the solons finally enacted a law that provided equality in money, uniforms, arms, rations, medical care, and other military necessities. The bill also covered retroactive benefits dating back to April 1861 for any black soldier who had not received the same wages as whites during this period.

The 1864 statute stands as the first meager step in the long hike to obtain equality in the military. Never again would the armed services, however much they demeaned the contributions of minorities, differentiate in terms of pay, with the exception of Filipino messboys and stewards taken into the navy following the Spanish-American War.

The same law had also mandated equality in other aspects of service but practice frequently fails to follow policy. White physicians resisted assignment to medical assignments with black regiments. To alleviate the shortage, the authorities simply declared hospital stewards to the posts. Outrage quickly followed. No one could defend the employment of such unqualified men to treat even minor conditions to say nothing of those that required surgical knowledge and skill. More than 38,000 black soldiers died in the Union uniform and the excessive casualties may owe something to the inadequacy of their medical care.

A highly trained and well experienced black physician, Dr. Alexander T. Augusta, a Virginia native who learned his craft in Canada and remained in Toronto to treat a largely white practice, accepted the offer of a commission as a major. But when he subsequently boarded a train at Baltimore, a railroad guard assisted by half a dozen thugs ripped off the oak leaf insignia from his uniform. Augusta got off the train, told his story to the provost marshal in the station and was escorted back to the train with a military squad plus police detectives. Nevertheless someone managed to punch him in the face and only when his bodyguards drew their pistols could he take a seat.

His troubles continued at Camp Stanton, Maryland. White assistant surgeons who reported there for duty wrote in dismay to Lincoln of their unhappiness at finding themselves subordinate to a black man. Their appeal reached some sympathetic ears and Augusta was removed from a position of command and placed on detached service. Furthermore, the local paymaster refused to give him more than seven dollars a month for his service. It took a letter from a senator to the secretary of war and then a direct order to the paymaster before Augusta could finally receive his due, some fifty-three weeks late.

Separate also meant unequal in equipment. One general advised his senator that his black troops went into battle with "arms almost entirely unserviceable." Another regiment of nonwhites carried flintlock muskets, which an inspector had condemned twice.

Worst of all, the Southerners refused to treat captured blacks in Union blue as soldiers. The Confederates referred to them as "slaves in arms" or "slaves in armed rebellion," ignoring even the fact that some had been freemen well before the Civil War. The government under Jefferson Davis, in 1863, decreed that blacks taken in battle against the Confederate States or who gave aid or comfort to the enemy should be dealt with in accordance with the laws of the state in which they were seized. Because every one of these mandated execution for insurrection, it was a death sentence. The North retaliated with the threat of an eye for an eye. Lincoln approved an order stating that for every Union prisoner killed in violation of the laws of war a Reb would die. Any Union soldier enslaved or sold into slavery would mean a Confederate would do hard labor on public works. Over time, the South settled for less drastic treatment. Some black soldiers taken by the likes of Nathan Bedford Forrest, who after the war founded the Ku Klux Klan, were murdered but most were either put in prison camps or set to work on Confederate installations.

Despite the unfairness and the general hardships of military life, the African Americans adapted well to army life. They were used to hard labor and to taking orders. Many of the former slaves enjoyed better food and clothing than in their state of bondage. And they were better motivated than most of the whites for freedom from fetters was a far more tangible goal than the abstraction of the Union.

The African American soldiers were well aware of the disdain for them. After they were grudgingly welcomed into federal service, some sang a swatch of doggerel:

> McClelland went to Richmond with two hundred thousand braves,
> He said, "Keep back the niggers and the Union he would save."
> Little Mac, he had his way, still the Union is in tears,
> And they call for the help of the colored volunteers.

Using his pseudonym of Private Miles O'Reilly, Halpine also wrote a popular song to explain the attitudes of some whites toward their black colleagues: Entitled "Sambo's Right to be Kilt," the lyrics said:

> Some tell us 'tis a burnin' shame
> To make the naygers fight;
> An' that the thrade of bein' kilt
> Belongs but to the white;
> But as for me, upon my sould!
> So liberal are we here,
> I'll let Sambo be murthered instead of myself
> On every day in the year.

Within approximately 186,000 men of color among the 2,100,000 enrolled members of the Union Army, another 30,000 blacks sailing under the federal colors in the navy, only a handful of nonwhites reached the commissioned ranks. Aside from chaplains and battalion surgeons, fewer than 100 from the minority became officers and none held higher grade than captain. The whites who commanded the bulk of the African Americans in the 166 segregated regiments, according to historian Benjamin Quarles, as a group, were "officers of above-average character and efficiency." There were, of course, exceptions, men who achieved their posts because of political connections and occasionally a brutal incompetent slipped through the screening board.

The creation of black regiments under white officers and noncoms converted some opponents, not to a sense of equality but because they now saw opportunity. An Illinois soldier wrote, "A year ago last January I didn't like to hear anything of emancipation. Last fall, accepted confiscation of rebels' Negroes quietly. In January took to emancipation readily, and now . . . am becoming [color] blind that I can't see why they will not make soldiers . . . I almost begin to think of applying for a position in a [black] regiment myself." The hopes of advancement in such units would attract military careerists even for a few years after the Civil War.

Opening up enlistment to blacks could not compensate for the lack of able-bodied men willing to soldier on beyond the initial terms of enlistment, from as little as nine months to two years. On 3 March 1863 the federal government instituted the Enrollment Act, making every fit male citizen between the ages of twenty and forty-five eligible for a draft. The Union thus followed the suit of the even more hard-pressed Confederacy, which had begun to require service a year earlier. The system set up quotas for each congressional district and an area could meet its numbers with volunteers but if it fell short, conscription would supply the required amount. The practice of bounties for recruits became a profitable business as brokers, for a price, offered to provide a community with its quota. The base price was $300 but by manipulating federal, state, and local emoluments, a total of $1,000 might accrue. Candidates from one district sometimes accepted the bounty, then deserted and signed up somewhere else a number of times. The possibility of hiring a substitute added to the commercial potential in the filling of quotas. As the poorest members of the American lower classes, blacks obviously provided candidates for the draft and as surrogates for whites unlucky enough to have been conscripted. The Civil War draft, which occasioned a fearfully bloody riot and antiblack reactions in New York City, actually directly put only 46,000 in arms although 118,000 who had been called avoided service by furnishing substitutes. The overwhelming number of men who fought for the Union cause were volunteers.

Although most white Northerners remained convinced of their superiority to their black Unionists, the bulk of the literature from the Civil War, the letters, accounts, journals, and official reports commended the African American fighting men for their efforts. Charles Stinson, serving with both the 13th New Hampshire Volunteer Infantry and subsequently the 19th U.S. Colored Infantry wrote a letter to his sisters in 1864, "The colored troops have done some gallant fighting and are praiseworthy. Bully for the colored volunteers."

John Habberton, a New York City white, serving as a junior officer with the 20th Colored Infantry kept a diary. His outfit sailed to Louisiana and once ashore he wrote: "The first mate got out his banjo and the darkies, who can, dance with great energy and the others look on and criticize and [praise] the best performances after the manner in which their brethren do such things with the exception of those who have been slaves. Very few men of the South can dance. Neither are they professors of any other African accomplishments."

As the 20th reached the mouth of the Mississippi near Fort Jackson and Fort St. Philip, Habberton recorded his impressions of the reception given it. "The colored population along the shore turned out en masse and with yells, shrieks, howls, laughter and gestures, grimaces and contortions welcomed their brethren to the shores of Louisiana. The juvenile portion of our regiment, both black and white are highly affected by the sight of calico [women]." The youthful whites cited by Habberton were officers or even a scattering of noncoms since the high rate of illiteracy among blacks at the time forced the involvement of whites as sergeants able to read the manuals and orders of the day.

Habberton paid tribute to the quality of the troops. "They are fast becoming old soldiers. There isn't a man in the company who can't run a guard equal to a veteran of the Army of the Potomac. And as to foraging, though the officers' mess hasn't been able to get boards for flooring, most of the men's tents are neatly floored.

"[They] don't carry their pieces like hoes," he noted after a fruitless search for the enemy. "I noticed two men in the company who showed signs of fear and they were loudly laughed at, lightly punched by their more manly comrades. A darky has this advantage: his face don't turn white with fear as some white faces do."

Habberton decided to test the night guards. "I went outside the works [fortifications] and then ran up towards them, holding my sword to prevent its rattling so they could have no clue who it was. They all challenged me. I crept up within ten feet of one and suddenly stood up before him. His back happened to be turned . . . he started liked a scared picket. In an instant came the stereotyped 'Halt! Who goes there?'

"I had instructed them not to fire until they had challenged twice. I stood motionless and silent. Again he challenged and the 'click' which accompanied it [cocking of the weapon] informed me that if I didn't want to become a vacancy in the regiment I might as well tell who I was. I made up my mind they could take care of the place. These men in common with their uniformed brethren all over the Union are gradually forcing their way to respect of honest men. They are quick to learn, remember well, have plenty of pluck and what's necessary to help a man endure the hardship of a soldier's life. They are civil and respectful, more clearly than white troops generally are, and as proud as possible of their occupation."

Habberton remarked that while he had been in a garrison in New York it was not uncommon to find whites assigned to guard missing when morning came, their muskets lying on the ground. He bitterly noted that while his "unbleached Americans" reenlisted, huge numbers of whites did not when their time elapsed.

Colonel Thomas Wentworth Higginson commanded the 1st South Carolina Volunteers, an aggregation largely of recently emancipated men. In his book, *Army Life in a Black Regiment*, he mused, ". . . the mass of men are naturally courageous up to a certain point. A man seldom runs away from danger which he ought to face, unless others run; and each is apt to keep with the mass, and colored soldiers have more than usual of this gregariousness. In almost every regiment, black or white, there are a score or two of men who are naturally daring, who really hunger after dangerous adventures, and are happiest when allowed to seek them. Every commander gradually finds out who these men are, and habitually uses them; certainly I had such, and I remember with delight their bearing, their coolness, and their dash. Some of them were negroes, some mulattoes. . . . The mass of the regiment rose to the same level under excitement, and were more exciteable, I think, than whites, but neither more nor less courageous."

Higginson observed that when deciding whether Northern free blacks or Southern slaves made the best soldiers, officers generally showed a fondness for men with backgrounds of bondage. "I preferred those who had been slaves, for their greater docility and affectionateness, for the powerful stimulus which their new freedom gave, and for the fact that they were fighting in a manner for their own homes and firesides. . . . They seemed like clansmen, and had a more confiding and filial relation to us than seemed to me to exist in the Northern colored regiments."

Higginson expressed a remarkable sensitivity to what would remain a key aspect in the relationships of a minority people in the American armies, then and at least through World War II. "As far as the mere habits of slavery went, they were a poor preparation for military duty. Inexperienced officers often assumed that because these men had been slaves before enlistment, they would bear to be treated as such afterwards. Experience proved the contrary. The more strongly we marked the difference between the slave and the soldier, the better for the regiment. One-half of military duty lies in obedience, the other half in self-respect. A soldier without self-respect is worthless. Consequently there were no regiments in which it was so important to observe the courtesies and proprieties of military life as in these. I had to caution officers to be more than usually particular in returning the salutations of the men; to be very careful in their dealings with those on picket or guard duty; and on no account omit the titles of the noncommissioned officers. So in dealing out punishments, we had carefully to avoid all that was brutal and arbitrary, all that savored of the overseer. Any such dealing found them as obstinate and contemptuous as was Topsy when Miss Ophelia undertook to chastise her. A system of light punishments, rigidly administered according to the prescribed military forms, had more weight with them than any amount of angry severity. To make them feel as remote as possible from the plantations, this was essential. By adhering to this, and constantly appealing to their pride as soldiers and their sense of duty, we were able to maintain a high standard of discipline."

Higginson noted that the "sense of inferiority" impressed upon them in plantation life caused some to balk at orders from black noncoms because they could not accept commands from any but whites. Over time, the troops learned to salute white officers not because of the color of their skin but because of their rank. "Then we taught them to take pride in having good material for noncommissioned officers among themselves, and in obeying them." That was achieved even at the cost of transferring first-rate white sergeants. ". . . it was a help to discipline to eliminate the Saxon, for it recognized a principle."

The ardor of the black recruits notwithstanding, the newly formed units operated with at least one major handicap. Lieutenant James Monroe Trotter serving with the famous Massachusetts 54th said, ". . . in our colored regiments a very large percentage of the men were illiterate, especially in those composed of men from the south and so lately escaped from under the iron heel of slavery. Indeed, in many of them there could scarcely be found at the commencement of the service a man who could either read or write. Many an officer can recall his rather novel experience in teaching his first sergeant enough of figures and script letters to enable the latter to make up and sign the company morning report."

Idealistic and practical white leaders including Col. James Beecher, a brother of the famous, and subsequently somewhat infamous because of an extramarital affair, Henry Ward Beecher, instituted classes that would give the rudiments of an education to make the minority soldiers literate, enabling them to be better soldiers as well as fit for their lives as private citizens after the war. The whites who plunged into this kind of extracurricular instruction taught alongside of the best educated of the blacks, the chaplains.

For the most part, one must depend upon the whites for a description of the black soldier in battle. African Americans, particularly the most recent fugitives from slavery who then enlisted in the military, ordinarily lacked education. It was believed by many slaveholders that literacy could lead only to difficulty in maintaining their supremacy. One exception was Christian A. Fleetwood. Born a freeman in Baltimore, he was awarded a Medal of Honor by the Congress for heroism while with the 4th U.S. Colored Troops. Fleetwood, as a young man visited Liberia, the African country which some hoped would become the new home of freed slaves, and graduated from Ashmun Institute in Oxford, Pennsylvania. The school later became Lincoln University.

Fleetwood, thirty years after the peace at Appomattox, wrote a brief history entitled *The Negro As A Soldier.* He devoted a few pages to the presence of blacks in the American ranks during the Revolutionary War and the War of 1812 but the bulk of his manuscript deals with the Civil War. Fleetwood quoted the letter from General Hunter's defense of his policy and the song written by Halpine as Miles O'Reilly.

According to Fleetwood, "The first fighting done by organized Negro troops appears to have been done by Company A, 1st South Carolina Negro Regiment at St. Helena Island, November 3–10, 1862, while participating in an expedition along the coast of Georgia and Florida under Lt. Col. O. T. Beard, of the 48th New York Infantry, who says in his report: 'The colored men fought with astonishing coolness and bravery. I found them all I could desire, more than I had hoped. They behaved gloriously, and deserve all praise.'"

Fleetwood, in prose tinged with purple, wrote of the assault upon Port Hudson, Louisiana, during the 1863 Vicksburg campaign, by a force that included the 1st and 2d Regiments, Louisiana Native Guards. He reported, "[Colonel Stafford of the 1st Regiment] made a brief and patriotic address, closing in the words: 'Color Guard: Protect, defend, die for, but do not surrender these colors.' The gallant Flag-sergeant Plancianos, taking them replied, 'Colonel: I will bring back these colors to you in honor, or report to God the reason why.'

"Six times with desperate valor they charged over ground where success was hopeless, a deep bayou between them and the works of the enemy at the point of attack rendered it impossible to reach them, yet strange to say, six times they were ordered forward and six times they went to useless death, until swept back by the blazing breath of shot and shell before which nothing living could stand. Here fell the gallant Captain Cailloux, black as the ace of spades, refusing to leave the field though his arm had been shattered by a bullet, he returned to the charge until killed by a shell.

"A soldier limping painfully to the front was halted and asked where he was going, he replied; 'I am shot bad in de leg, and dey want me to go to the hospital, but I guess I can given them a little more yet.' The colors came back but crimsoned with the blood of the gallant Plancianos, who reported to God from that bloody field."

A white officer confirmed the courage shown, "You have no idea how my prejudices with regard to Negro troops have been dispelled by the battle the other day." The *New York Times* editorialized that their conduct "settles the question that the negro race can fight." Further engagements in the Vicksburg area added more believers. An assistant secretary of war, tagging along with the army under Ulysses S. Grant, reported, "The bravery of the blacks in the battle at Milliken's Bend completely revolutionized the sentiment of the army with regard to the employment of negro troops. I heard prominent officers who formerly in private had sneered at the idea of the negroes fighting express themselves after that as heavily in favor of it."

The testimonials impressed Secretary of State William H. Seward who authored a pamphlet *Review of Recent Military Events:* "As the national armies advanced into the insurrectionary territories, slaves in considerable numbers accepted their freedom and came under the protection of the national flag. Amidst the great prejudices and many embarrassments which attend a measure so new and so divergent from the political habits of the country, freedmen with commendable alacrity enlisted in the Federal army. There was in some quarters a painful inquiry about their moral capacity for service. That uncertainty was brought to a sudden end in the siege of Port Hudson. The newly raised regiments exhibited all necessary valor and devotion in the military assaults which were made, with desperate courage, and not without fearful loss, by General Banks."

Nathaniel Banks, who had dithered over the use of them, himself praised his "negro troops." In the assault . . . the behavior of the officers and men was most gallant, and left nothing to be desired. . . . On the extreme right of our line, I posted the first and third regiments of negro troops. The 1st Regiment of Louisiana Engineers, composed exclusively of colored men, excepting the officers, was also engaged in the operations of the day. The position occupied by these troops was one of importance, and called for the utmost steadiness and bravery in those to whom it was confided.

"It gives me pleasure to report that they answered every expectation. Their conduct was heroic. No troops could be more determined or more daring. They made, during the day, three charges upon the batteries of the enemy, suffering very heavy losses, and holding their position at nightfall with the other troops. . . . Whatever doubt may have existed before as to the efficiency of organizations of this character, the history of this day proves conclusively to those who were in a condition to observe the conduct of these regiments, that the Government will find in this class of troops effective supporters and defenders . . . They require only good officers, commands of limited numbers and careful discipline, to make them excellent soldiers."

During the North's drive into Virginia in 1864, Robert E. Lee himself dispatched his vaunted cavalry at a site called Wilson's Landing. The *New York Times*'s correspondent reported the South's best "was badly worsted in the contest last Tuesday with Negro troops composing the garrison at Wilson's Landing." A few days later, Gen. Benjamin Butler crowed, "With one thousand seven hundred cavalry we have advanced up the Peninsula and forced the Chickahominy. . . . These were *colored cavalry,* and are now holding our advanced pickets toward Richmond."

The film *Glory,* focusing on the 54th Massachusetts Regiment, has helped make that unit the most famous of the Union blacks. The Union commander for the assault upon Fort Wagner, South Carolina, in July 1863, Gen. George C. Strong, announced to the 54th that it had the honor to lead the attack. An observer claimed "A cheer went up from six hundred throats." Christian Fleetwood wrote of this engagement where "[the 54th's] grand young commander, Col. Robert Gould Shaw, passed into the temple of immortality. After a march of all day, under a burning sun, and all night through a tempest of wind and rain, drenched, exhausted, hungry, they wheeled into line, without a murmur for that awful charge, that dance of death, the struggle against hopeless odds, and the shattered remnants were hurled back from the mouth of hell, leaving the dead bodies of their young commander and his noble followers to be buried in a common grave. Its total loss was about one-third of its strength.

"Here it was that the gallant Flag-sergeant Carney, though grievously wounded, bore back his flag to safety, and fell fainting and exhausted with loss of blood saying, 'Boys, the old flag never touched the ground.'"

The battles for Petersburg, a railroad hub some twenty miles south of Richmond, stands as one of the more dramatic engagements involving Union blacks. When a battery of Confederate artillery opened fire on the advancing army near Baylor's Farm, the African American brigade under Gen. W. F. "Baldy" Smith, composed of four regiments of infantry, two of cavalry and two artillery batteries counterattacked. The men slogged through a swampy patch, then charged up a slope against near point-blank fire. They drove off the Rebels at a cost of perhaps 100 soldiers.

With the enemy outpost captured, 3,000 of the black volunteers rushed toward the main line of defenses. The immediate objective lay some 800 yards off and the Blue Bellies, says a contemporary account, "were obliged to advance across an open field, exposed the whole distance to deadly fire, completely enfilading their two lines of battle to fire from two batteries directly in front, and to a cross-fire from an intermediate battery." Despite heavy losses they gained the position and then prepared for the final rush.

The setting sun flashed on their bayonets as they scrambled forward through a wall of enemy shot and shell. Despite fearful losses they scaled the breastworks and at close quarters vanquished the Southerners who withdrew. The black soldiers claimed capture of the majority of enemy artillery pieces and bagged two-thirds of the 300 prisoners. But Christian Fleetwood noted that the 4th U.S. Colored Troops alone lost about 250 of their complement of fewer than six hundred.

One might dismiss Fleetwood's superheated prose as fired by ethnic pride. But Fleetwood was not simply an observer; he participated in that brutal campaign before Petersburg, Virginia. It was here he won his Medal of Honor and the right to proclaim, "See them on the 15th day of June 1864, carrying the outpost at Baylor's Field in early morning, and all the long, hot summer day advancing a few yards at a time, then lying down to escape the fire from the works, but still gradually creeping nearer and nearer, until just as the sun went down, they swept like a tornado over the works and started upon a race for the city, close at the heels of the flying foe, until mistakenly ordered back. Of this day's experience General Badeau writes, 'No worse strain on the nerves of troops is possible, for it is harder to remain quiet under cannon fire, even though comparatively harmless, than to advance against a storm of musketry.' General W. F. 'Baldy' Smith, speaking of their conduct, says, 'No nobler effort has been put forth to-day, and no greater success achieved than that of the colored troops.'"

Fleetwood quotes Smith's order of the day, "To the colored troops I would call the attention of this command. With the veterans of the Eighteenth Corps, they have stormed the works of the enemy and carried them, taking guns and prisoners, and in the whole affair they have displayed all the qualities of good soldiers."

He poured on the praise to Assistant Secretary of War Charles A. Dana who had come to visit with General Grant. "Smith told us that the Negro troops fought magnificently, the hardest fighting being done by them."

Lincoln himself visited Grant in his encampment a few days later and expressed eagerness to inspect the heroic legions. "I want to take a look at those boys. I read with the greatest delight the account given in Mr. Dana's dispatch to the Secretary of War how gallantly they behaved."

Charles Stinson in a letter home from the Petersburg area, "ten miles from nowhere," says, "Our troops are not in possession of Petersburg yet and I don't know when that will be. We have charged them out of some very formidable works. The colored boys did it." Unfortunately, the Union commanders failed to exploit their advantage immediately and in the delay the South rushed up reinforcements. During the subsequent siege the Union attempted to tunnel under the fort that controlled entrance to Petersburg with an eye to blowing the place up with 8,000 pounds of gunpowder. But the explosion did not destroy the defenders who fell upon the lead attack division composed of eight black regiments inflicting an appalling number of casualties in what became known as the Crater. Northern commanders rather than admit botched strategy blamed the African American troops' lack of experience and failures of discipline.

A bare two months later, the battered unit from Petersburg, with Fleetwood in attendance, went to the slaughter at New Market Heights and Fort Harrison in Virginia. He wrote, ". . . out of a color guard of twelve men, but one came off the field on his own feet. The gallant Flag-sergeant Hilton, the last to fall, cried out as he went down, 'Boys, save the colors,' and they were saved."

Subsequently Ben Butler issued an order based on this action, "Of the colored soldiers of the third divisions of the 18th and 10th Corps and the officers who led them, the general commanding desires to make special mention. In the charge on the enemy's works by the colored division of the 18th Corps at New Market, better men were never better led, better officers never led better men. A few more such gallant charges and to command colored troops will be the post of honor in the American armies. The colored soldiers' coolness, steadiness, determined courage and dash, have silenced every cavil of the doubters of their soldierly capacity, and drawn tokens of admiration from their enemies, have brought their late masters even to the consideration of the question whether they will not employ as soldiers the hitherto despised race."

Before Congress, Butler later spoke of the carnage. "There, in a space not wider than the clerk's desk, and three hundred yards long, lay the dead bodies of 543 of my colored comrades, slain in the defense of their country, who had laid down their lives to uphold its flag and its honor, as a willing sacrifice. [Butler could be as florid as Fleetwood in the tradition of the day.] And as I rode along, guiding my horse this way and that, lest he should profane with his hoofs what seemed to me the sacred dead, and as I looked at their bronzed faces upturned in the shining sun, as if in mute appeal against the wrongs of the country for which they had given their lives, and whose flag had been to them a flag of stripes, in which no star of glory had ever shone for them—feeling I had wronged them in the past, and believing what was the future duty of my country to them—I swore to myself a solemn oath:'May my right hand forget its cunning, and my tongue cleave to the roof of my mouth, if ever I fail to defend the rights of the men who have given their blood for me and my country this day and for their race forever. And God helping me, I will keep that oath." In fact, this speech to Congress advocating full civil rights to the formerly benighted, occurred ten years after the battle, and fulfilled Butler's pledge.

Even as the Confederacy began to sink under the weight of the Union power, the Rebels rejected pleas that the only chance lay in mobilization of the local blacks. "Satisfy the Negro," said Tennessee general Pat Cleburne, "that if he faithfully adheres to our standard during the war he shall receive his freedom and that of his race." [Butler had alluded to such a proposal in his order after New Market.] Not even a plan for a gradual elimination of slavery could win the endorsement of the Confederate establishment who may have believed that without slavery their entire life would disappear anyway. Only in the final days of the Civil War, far too late for an opportunity to gain victory via use of a substantial amount of manpower, did Jefferson Davis seriously consider arming blacks and the eventual end of slavery.

Not the least evidence of the effectiveness of the minority men who fought for the Union lies in the Medals of Honor Congress awarded to them. Fleetwood, who earned one, lists seventeen blacks including Flag-sergeant

Alfred B. Hilton who fell at New Market as recipients, although other histories put the number at fourteen. Whatever the medal figures, there is little doubt that African Americans played a crucial role in the Union triumph.

The association with African American fighting men profoundly affected some of their white officers. Command of black troops devolved on some young white officers whose abilities and survival brought them promotions that made them eligible for senior positions. Samuel Chapman Armstrong was such a one. He was born on Maui where his missionary parents taught Polynesian people the Bible along with secular skills like carpentry and agriculture. A graduate of Williams College at Andover, Massachusetts, in 1862, Armstrong recruited a company of men to serve in the 125th Regiment near Troy, New York. They engaged the enemy first with the Union forces at Harpers Ferry and suffered the ignominy of a mass surrender of 11,000 men without having fired a shot. Under the circumstances of the day, the captured men, instead of going to a miserable encampment such as Andersonville, Georgia, received a parole that barred them from war for a year.

When the 125th reentered the war it fought valiantly at Gettysburg, fending off charges by a Mississipppi brigade and the ultimate strike of the Confederate onslaught, a coordinated assault by divisions under Generals Pickett and Pettigrew. Armstrong, on his own initiative, planted an ambush that halted Pettigrew's units well before they could achieve their objective.

Promoted to lieutenant colonel, Armstrong received command of a newly formed black regiment. For the final two years of the war, Armstrong directed African American soldiers against the rebels in major campaigns at Richmond and Petersburg. Although the experience was not unique, in Armstrong it led him to devote the remainder of his life to working with blacks to enhance their lives. In 1866 he joined the Freedmen's Bureau set up by the federal government to aid the former slaves. Responsible for inhabitants in a group of counties at the mouth of the James River in Virginia, Armstrong created an educational plant that provided both academic instruction and training in trades. Named for a nearby town, the place became known as Hampton Institute. Nearly 100 years later, descendants of Samuel Chapman Armstrong would become involved with the fate of African Americans in the armed forces.

4
The Buffalo Soldiers

The bloom of the African American soldier faded quickly in the eyes of most whites. Southerners opposing the reconstruction of their territory took dead aim, literally sometimes, on the local black militias. The whites, whether part of the nascent Ku Klux Klan started by Nathan Bedford Forrest or in their own separate organizations, shot at the militias while they drilled, murdered some of their leaders, and openly attacked a lawfully constituted unit in South Carolina, killing five men. The intimidation eroded the power to vote, restricted economic opportunity, and closed off social improvements. The all-black militias, formed to preserve the rights contained in the Thirteenth, Fourteenth, and Fifteenth Amendments, along with specific statutes passed by Congress, collapsed.

On the federal level, officials resisted the opportunities for blacks in the services. Ulysses S. Grant wrote to a Massachusetts senator that while he personally did not object to their use, he regarded them as best utilized for emergency reserves behind the standing army rather than as peacetime regulars. In the Congressional debates, antiblack legislators asserted that the African Americans were less able, less qualified, would fill slots needed by unemployed whites, and when armed under the auspices of the government would offend the bulk of the country. The arguments played well in the border states and of course among white Southerners, even though in the first years after the Civil War they held little political power.

In spite of the strong negatively inclined forces, in 1866 Congress decreed that the regular army would have four black infantry regiments and two black horseborne units, the 9th and 10th Cavalry Regiments. A consolidation of the established armed forces in 1869 reduced the contingents of foot soldiers to a pair, the 24th and 25th Infantry Regiments. Although the quartet of regiments all appeared designed to operate as battlefront troops, they remained, as did the bulk of the Civil War units, segregated and commanded by white officers.

In the aftermath of the Civil War, as the military entered into a period of peacetime downsizing, those intent upon making a career out of the army scrambled for berths. Charles Halpine in his Miles O'Reilly mode wrote, "Black troops are now an established success, and hereafter—while the race can furnish enough able-bodied males—the probability would seem that one-half the permanent naval and military forces of the United States will be drawn from this material, under the guidance and control of the white officers. To-day there is much competition among the field and staff officers of our white volunteers—especially in those regiments being disbanded—to obtain commission of like or even lower grades in the colored regiments of Uncle Sam . . . [the] board of examination cannot keep in session long enough, nor dismiss incompetent aspirants quick enough to keep down the vast throngs of veterans, with and without shoulder-strap [officers], who are now seeking various grades of command in the colored brigades of the Union . . . what a change in public opinion are we compelled to recognize! In sober verity, war is not only the sternest, but the quickest, of all teachers . . ."

What galvanized the whites to volunteer for service with black organizations was not respect for their effectiveness but ambition. Blacks may have established their ability to fight but they were deemed unfit to lead themselves or to be mixed in with their white counterparts. In spite of the limited possibilities, there was no shortage of volunteers among black men. A certain Sgt. Samuel Harris believed a hitch in the regular army would enable him to obtain a decent government job after his discharge. Private Charles Creek remarked, "I got tired of looking mules in the face from sunrise to sunset, thought there must be a better livin' in this world." Another man, the offspring of a black woman and a white man, enlisted to escape from his family. Some sought adventure, but for the most part, even at the height of Reconstruction, the lure of the army lay in its economic opportunity and status. Low as the esteem was of white society for the private soldier, the career ranked higher than that of the civilian African American, particularly among people of color.

Regardless of the sentiments of the public, government officials, and military leaders, there was a mission for the newly constituted 9th and 10th Cavalry Regiments. With the end of the Civil War, pioneers and settlers headed toward the West where they inevitably confronted Native Americans seeking to preserve their way of life. The migrants relied on the military arm of the U. S. government to reconcile their concept of private ownership of land and the Indian belief that the vast plains belonged to no one.

In 1867, the 10th Cavalry, commanded by Col. Benjamin Grierson attempted to prepare for campaigns on the frontier. As soon as Grierson's outfit arrived at Fort Leavenworth, Kansas, the establishment made it clear that they were not welcome. The post commander assigned the troopers a campsite in a swamp and then criticized the men for muddy tents and uniforms. He ordered that none of the 10th Cavalry men approach closer than fifteen yards of a white soldier. Poorly outfitted, issued horses whose best years lay behind them, the 10th Cavalry under Grierson hastily headed out to its assignment.

The regiment came under fire for the first time 2 August 1867 while on patrols designed to protect workers laying track for the Kansas-Pacific Railroad in northwestern Kansas. A troop of thirty-six men retreated in the face of an onslaught by as many as three hundred braves. For more than a decade, the 10th participated in a grueling series of campaigns that pitted the black soldiers against such foes as the Apaches, Kiowa, and the Cheyenne. The 10th Cavalry was responsible for the eventual defeat of Indian leaders Black Kettle, Victorio, and Black Horse.

Setting up headquarters in what would become Fort Sill, Oklahoma, the 10th not only battled the hostile Native Americans, but also controlled behavior on reservations, chased horse and cattle thieves, and tried to suppress the whiskey trade. Their superiors, recognizing the deficiencies in their education, set up schools to teach literacy during periods in which the troopers were not engaged in military duties. Black chaplains played a major role in instructing the men.

Most of the white troopers were also largely illiterate, but the black cavalrymen deserted far less frequently, either out of loyalty to the service that offered them a measure of self respect or perhaps because they could count on less in the way of living wages outside of the army. It was a brutal life, aside from the danger of battle. Away from the fort facilities, which they built themselves, they lived in tents or in the open, spent long hours in the saddle riding great distances, coped with stifling heat, subzero cold, and acute shortages of water and food. A number perished not from hostile action but exposure, disease, and deprivation.

Even in garrison it could hardly be described as comfortable. During the first decades after the Civil War, the forts of the day resembled ramshackle villages rather than the neatly stockaded citadels depicted in films. The enlisted men shared vermin-infested hovels and depended upon nearby creeks for bathing and washing clothes. Occasionally fruits or vegetables grown in gardens supplemented the steady diet of beef, bacon, and beans, but there was not enough fresh produce to prevent an epidemic of scurvy, ordinarily a disease visited upon seamen. Given the miserable housing and sanitation, outbreaks of dysentery, tuberculosis, and other respiratory ailments were common. Venereal infections, the bane of military organizations for centuries, flourished, particularly with the whiskey ranches that sprouted on the outskirts of encampments. There, along with the potables and gamblers coveting soldiers' pay, whores proliferated. Within the forts, the men paid for the services of laundresses who combined their legitimate trade with prostitution.

The efforts of the black soldiers on behalf of the frontier residents gained them neither respect nor fair treatment. In one incident, men from the 9th Cavalry, hunting rustlers, came under fire from a ranch house. As the troopers pulled back, an ambush shot two of them to death while one assailant died from return fire. Their commander, Col. Edward Hatch, led a detachment that captured nine men whom he believed were responsible. But a grand jury not only released eight—the other man was acquitted— but indicted three of the cavalrymen for killing one of their attackers. Colonel Hatch himself was charged with falsely imprisoning the suspects he rounded up. It took a change of venue to get Hatch off the hook.

Somewhat surprisingly, there is little record of friction between blacks and whites when quartered on the same post, albeit in segregated units. They even shared some guard and housekeeping duties. However, white soldiers constantly denigrated their black colleagues. A white captain remarked that a unit in the 10th Cavalry had an "Ethiopian lieutenant [Henry Flipper, first of his race to graduate from West Point] and sixty of the very best darkies that ever stole chickens."

They habitually received less than their due in rations and equipment. In the field, they were a motley lot. A white officer wrote of a cavalry column, "Most of the men ride in their blue flannel shirts . . . one big sergeant wears a bright red shirt . . . ; some of the men take off their shirts and ride in their gray knit undershirts. There are all sorts of hats worn, of American and Mexican make, the most common being the ugly army campaign hat of gray felt . . . There are few trousers not torn or badly worn, especially in the seat. [Some troopers even exchanged their army blues for civilian overalls.] Here is a man with a single spur; here one without any." Again, the Hollywood version of the cavalry approximates only what the men sported during dress parades.

They could expect no hospitality at other installations where local commanders would demand they camp outside the post. Ignoramuses in high places condemned them for inherent defects. One general announced that black men were suited only for duty in warmer southern climes and those dispatched to the northern Dakota territory could not survive. Nevertheless, the cavalry units served and performed as well as white outfits in the colder regions.

They had few champions but one was artist Frederic Remington who painted the exploits of frontier cavalrymen. He offered a rhetorical evaluation. "Will they fight? That is easily answered. They have fought many, many times. The old sergeant sitting near me, as calm of feature as a bronze statue, once deliberately walked over to a Cheyenne rifle pit and killed his man."

Sometime around 1870, the black cavalrymen became known as the "Buffalo Soldiers." One explanation says the Indians so dubbed them because they thought the color of their skin and their hair resembled the hide of the buffalo. Another derivation is based on the buffalo-hide overcoats worn by troopers in the colder climes. An officer's wife wrote "The Indians call them 'buffalo soldiers' because their woolly heads are so much like the matted cushion that is between the horns of the buffalo." When the 10th Cavalry got around to choosing a design for the regimental coat of arms, it incorporated the animal in the crest.

The two infantry regiments, the 24th and 25th, less mobile than the cavalry, occupied outposts stretching from the Southwest to the Alaskan territory. Northern areas of the United States provided no friendlier an atmosphere than the southern ones. With only a tiny number of blacks in the upper tier of states, particularly in the West, the perennial tension over black men [soldiers] associating with white women aroused animosity and in several instances led to murder and mob violence in the guise of vigilante justice.

For all of the success of the four segregated units, African American soldiers continued to be pariahs. General William Tecumseh Sherman, in his capacity as commanding general of the army, aware how the separate but equal strictures imposed terrible difficulties in locating units and assigning officers, in 1877 proposed an end to the distinction of "black" and "white" as was then the official policy of the navy. Although Sherman added that he believed whites were better suited for the task of combating "the enemies of civilization" he declared himself "willing to take black and white alike on equal terms, certainly a fairer rule than the present one of separating them into distinct organizations." However, opponents defeated a Congressional bill aimed at eliminating segregation in the military.

Neither the cavalry nor infantry regiments for African Americans contained any nonwhite officers. Pressure from some civilian leaders forced the U.S. Military Academy at West Point to accept blacks. Of the first twenty-five appointed during the 1870s and 1880s, a dozen passed the entrance examinations. But only three would manage to graduate. The atmosphere at the Point was violently hostile. Major General John M. Schofield, while commandant at the academy during this period, dismissed claims of excessive hazing of a black cadet as an example of racial prejudice. Instead, he insisted the true prejudice was "a just aversion to the qualities which the people of the United States have long accustomed to associate with a state of slavery and intercourse without legal marriage, and of which color and its various shades are only the external signs."

As so many of his ilk had in the past and would in the future, he discerned the baleful influence of agitators. Rather uniquely, he identified them as the radical Republicans who appointed blacks to slots at West Point. "To send to West Point for four years' competition a young man who was born in slavery is to assume that half a generation has been sufficient to raise a colored man to the social, moral, and intellectual level which the average white man has reached in several hundred years. As well might the common farm horse be entered in a four-mile race against the best blood inherited from a long line of English racers."

The bias at the Military Academy under Schofield led to an incredible piece of investigation and subsequently a court-martial by the officers in residence. After a black cadet was found bound to his bunk and bleeding, the inquiry and the trial concluded that the injured youth had written himself a threatening note, slashed his face, slit open an ear, and then tied himself so tightly to the bed that those who found him were forced to cut him free. Robert Todd Lincoln, son of the murdered president, secretary of war in the administration of Chester A. Arthur, and an adherent of a better shake for nonwhites in the army, reversed the court-martial but the cadet was dropped from the rolls for alleged academic deficiencies.

The fifth black candidate to enter the U. S. Military Academy and the first of his color to complete four years and earn a commission was Henry Ossian Flipper, born in 1856. His mother Isabella Buckhalter, described by a contemporary historian as "a mulatto" in the keep of the Reverend Reuben H. Lucky, married a shoemaker named Festus Flipper, who was owned by Ephraim G. Ponder, a businessman whose enterprises included slave trading. Both slaveholders gave permission for the couple to wed and the marriage produced five sons. All of them achieved prominence—one became a church bishop, another a wealthy farmer and landowner, a third a professor, and a fourth a physician.

Festus somehow managed to buy the freedom of his wife and the first two sons when Ponder shifted his operations from Thomasville, Georgia, to Atlanta. The end of the Civil War saw the Flipper family permanently established and Festus prospered in his trade. As a boy Henry Flipper had learned to read with the help of another slave. He then entered schools founded by the American Missionary Association, which like many other organizations as well as some individuals opened institutions of learning catering to the now free blacks. Flipper then attended Atlanta University, one of a number of colleges offering higher education for African Americans, and while enrolled there he received his nomination to the Military Academy from a Georgia congressman.

In *A Colored Cadet at West Point* (1878) Flipper recalled his arrival at West Point. "The impression made upon me by what I saw while going from the adjutant's office to the barracks was certainly not very encouraging. The rear windows were crowded with cadets watching . . . with apparently as much astonishment and interest as they would, perhaps, have watched Hannibal cross the Alps. Their words, jeers, etc., were most insulting."

That description may be accurate but Flipper was not a unique phenomenon on the campus. There was already one black, James Webster Smith, in his third year in residence and another, Michael Howard, who entered with Flipper. Howard disappeared almost immediately when the authorities discovered he lacked a basic background in all academic subjects. However, Smith, apparently a cantankerous sort, roomed with Flipper.

Newspapers of the day had editorially debated whether Flipper would achieve any success. Although some praised his initiative and intelligence others doubted his chances of success. The *Chicago Tribune* asserted "Flipper will never be allowed to graduate; the prejudice of the regular Army instructors against the colored race is insurmountable . . ." In his memoirs, Flipper wrote that most of his fellow cadets ignored him. He indicated that he had expected ostracism and he made no effort to insert himself into a social relationship with the whites. For that matter he sneered at the qualities of some of his colleagues. "There are some from the very lowest classes of our population. They are uncouth and rough in appearance, have only a rudimentary education, have little or no idea of courtesy, use the very worst language and, in most cases, are much inferior to the average Negro."

Claiming his chief desire lay in promoting the status of the black soldier, Flipper said, "One must endure these little tortures—the sneer, the shrug of the shoulder, the epithet, the effort to avoid, to disdain, to ignore—and thus to suffer." Flipper declined to report the more egregious hazing to the authorities, knowing he would only be labeled a troublemaker. He observed that many of those who shunned him on the academy grounds were polite off post. Flipper attributed their contrasting behavior to fear of the more rabid racists with whom they associated on campus.

Flipper's roommate, James W. Smith, either unwilling to accept the abuse, or because of alleged academic deficiencies, left the academy before graduation. But in 1877, as the first African American to complete the course, fiftieth in a class of seventy-six, Flipper received his diploma and second lieutenant's bars. As superintendent, General Schofield delivered a keynote address in which, despite his bias against blacks, he remarked, "Anyone who knows how quietly and bravely this young man—the first of his despised race to graduate at West Point—has borne the difficulties of his position [bearing the hopes of his race while ostracized by his fellow cadets] . . ." Flipper himself recalled applause as he was awarded his certificate. "Even the cadets and other persons connected with the academy congratulated me. Oh how happy I was. I prized the good words of the cadets above all others. They did not hesitate to speak to me or shake hands with me before each other or anyone else. All signs of ostracism were gone."

There was some talk of a post as commander in chief of the Liberian army but Flipper rejected that possibility in favor of the 10th Cavalry. Some thirty years later, Flipper wrote *A Negro Frontiersman* about these experiences. At Fort Sill he initially was a curiosity to the African Americans in residence and "there was a constant stream of colored women, officers' servants, soldiers' wives, etc., to see the colored officer." But to his surprise he was accepted by a number of whites, as evidenced by invitations to attend social affairs. On the occasion of the first such party he did not plan to attend. "I did not go because I thought it was only a courtesy invitation. I went to bed early, but Lieutenant and Mrs. Maney came to my quarters, roused me out and wanted to know why I had not gone to the party." Persuaded he was welcome, Flipper dressed and then at the insistence of Mrs. Maney participated in every dance.

There were also the expected unpleasantries. When he visited Fort Concho, the junior officers organized a dinner in his honor but the commanding officer, a major from Flipper's own 10th Cavalry, canceled the affair. The embarrassed younger officers apologized to Flipper.

Although the regiment at the time was occupied with pursuit of the Apache chief Victorio over a distance of 1,200 miles, the young lieutenant never engaged in any significant combat. He performed such worthy tasks as supervising the erection of poles for a telegraph line, assisted in maintaining law and order in the frontier territory, and on one occasion put the engineering skills he learned at West Point to good use enabling the troops to cross a flooded creek. "I had all the wagons unloaded, took the body from one and wrapped a tent fly around it, making a boat of it. I then had a man swim across with a rope, each end of which he tied securely to a tree. In that way I rigged up a ferry on which we ferried over all our effects, the women and children [the train of an army until World War II often included families, personal belongings, and many of the trappings of a more settled community] and then swam the horses and mules. We then put the wagons together and pursued our journey."

Perhaps his most dangerous assignment was a mission to carry messages through almost 100 miles of territory controlled by the enemy to Grierson at 10th Cavalry headquarters. It required twenty-two hours to cover the distance and Flipper said, "I felt no bad effects from the hard ride till I reached the General's tent. When I attempted to dismount, I found I was stiff and sore and fell from my horse to the ground, waking the General. He wanted to know what had happened and the sentinel who had admitted me, had to answer for me. One of the men unsaddled my horse, spread the saddle blanket on the ground, I rolled over on it and, with the saddle for a pillow, slept till the sun shining in my face woke me next morning."

The end of Flipper's career in the army began with a posting to Fort Davis, Texas, where he was given the unattractive jobs of handling quartermaster duties, commissary subsistence, and other bookkeeping duties. The atmosphere there also proved much less hospitable. Flipper complained that on New Year's Day 1881, only one officer paid the customary courtesy call upon him. "The rest of the officers on the post were hyenas." However, the black officer found some solace in the company of Miss Nell Dryer with whom he enjoyed horseback rides.

The interracial friendship or perhaps courtship generated resentment among some white officers, particularly a Lt. Charles Nordstrom, a former suitor of Dryer. In a successful effort to win back her favor, Nordstrom invested in a grand buggy and soon she abandoned her rides with Flipper for ones with Nordstrom. Because Flipper regarded Nordstrom as an ignorant fellow, and a brute lacking social graces, he may well have advised the young woman that her swain was unworthy of her gentility. In any event, the animosity toward Flipper heightened.

In a change of command, Maj. N. B. McLaughlin, described by Flipper as "a very fine officer and gentleman" who befriended him, was replaced by Col. William R. Shafter. An infantryman and an adversary of Grierson, the colonel was described as "coarse, profane and harsh with junior officers." Shafter had a long history of commanding blacks—both during the Civil War and subsequently. Shortly after he assumed command, Shafter relieved Flipper of some of the supply responsibilities but left him temporarily in charge of the commissary and its funds.

In July 1881, a discrepancy in Flipper's accounts for the commissary funds surfaced. Charged with embezzlement, Flipper claimed he kept some government money in his own quarters because "as I was responsible for their safety, I felt more secure to have them in my own personal custody." Clouding that arrangement was access to Flipper's belongings by a black servant, Lucy Smith whom some allege also acted as his mistress. Shafter said he became suspicious that Flipper planned to flee to Mexico with the loot and had him arrested.

During the subsequent court-martial the defendant argued that he had discovered an unexplained shortage in the accounts and while seeking an answer and a way to recover what was missing he had filed false reports that indicated the books balanced. He expected to cover the deficit with the royalties on his book *A Colored Cadet at West Point*. He and his counsel charged that a clique of officers, including Nordstrom, had conspired to bring about his downfall. Immediately after being seized, Flipper's personal belongings including a watch and jewelry were confiscated. He was remanded to the guardhouse, although customarily officers, unlike enlisted men, when facing a court-martial were merely confined to house arrest. Not until the general in command of the Department of Texas intervened was Flipper granted the privilege of his own digs. He noted, "I was confined in my quarters, which were barricaded, nailed up and made as secure as the guard house was . . . and was guarded night and day by an armed sentinel. These extreme measures were not warranted by the nature of the offense charged against me, and were in violation of the 65th Article of War and the customs of the service." The judge advocate general agreed, "[there was] no case . . . in Army history which an officer was treated with such personal harshness and indignity as was Lt. Flipper."

A group of local businessmen collected about $1,700 as restitution for the missing money, and in a bizarre gesture, Shafter himself offered $100 although later he held onto Flipper's watch as collateral for what he now called a loan. The colonel forced Lucy Smith to undergo a strip search and from her bosom the investigators recovered a batch of commissary checks, one from Flipper, along with a gold coin listed as part of the inventory of the funds. She explained that she feared another untrustworthy servant might be a thief and by keeping the items on herself, she was protecting her employer.

Although any missing money had now been restored and another prime suspect had emerged, Shafter pushed the criminal charges against Flipper. The testimony revealed a tangled bureaucratic web in the military accounts with everyone from Shafter down through several ranks of officers to Flipper, shifting money about and making little effort to properly manage it. Throughout his testimony, Shafter constantly used the word "nigger" and the defense counsel deftly demonstrated the colonel's slipshod style of administration. As a witness, Lucy Smith, perhaps concerned for her own future, pled a poor memory and maundered on to no effect for either side.

The court found Flipper not guilty of the charge of misappropriating funds for his own use but guilty of "conduct unbecoming an officer and a gentleman," referring to the false record created by him immediately after he learned of a discrepancy, sentencing him to be dismissed from the army. The head of the Texas Department of the Army added insult as he reversed the first verdicts, making Flipper also guilty of embezzlement.

While awaiting appeals or confirmation of these decisions by the authorities in Washington, D.C., Flipper's former superior Colonel Grierson arranged to transfer him to the cavalry jurisdiction "as quickly as possible from unsatisfactory and, I may add, dangerous surroundings and influences." The judge advocate general of the army reviewed the case and concluded Flipper had not defrauded the government. He recommended a lesser punishment. Secretary of War Robert Todd Lincoln endorsed this position, but inexplicably President Chester A. Arthur approved the sentence.

In *A Negro Frontiersman*, Flipper would write, ". . . he [Shafter] and his adjutant Lieutenant [Louis] Wilhelmi and Nordstrom began to persecute me and lay traps for me. I was warned by civilians and never did a man walk the path of uprightness straighter than I did, but the trap was cunningly laid and

I was sacrificed . . . All the men connected with that nefarious scheme are long since dead. Lieut. ———— came in one night from some detached duty and caught his wife sitting nude on another officer's lap. Lieut. ————'s wife went into a sporting house in Los Angeles and he died in disgrace. Lieut. ———— died at Santa Fe, leaving his wife and two daughters in dire poverty, and [another officer's] only daughter was ruined by a private soldier. There has surely been retributive justice in my case. Every man that participated in the case against me, including the members of the court-martial, are all dead."

John M. Carroll, a historian of the Buffalo soldiers, found a letter from an officer in the same command who flatly called the allegations against Flipper trumped up and that he was really only charged "because he had been 'too familiar' when speaking to the wife of another officer on the post. 'Too familiar' meant that Flipper spoke to her at all." There are, it must be said, also revisionist historians who insist Flipper was guilty of the charges and the verdict was not the result of racial prejudice.

Whatever the merits of his case, the cashiered Flipper at first could only find a position as a clerk for a steam laundry. But he then turned his talents to engineering and built a substantial career for himself in that profession. He acted as a surveyor and became an expert on land grants. Nearly 100 years after he graduated from the Military Academy, the Department of the Army, after a campaign led by a Georgia schoolteacher, awarded Flipper an honorable discharge.

A somewhat overage member of the 1886 class at West Point, John "Black Jack" Pershing at age twenty-six began his active duty career with the all-white 6th Cavalry, commanded a troop of Sioux scouts, did a stint as an instructor at the University of Nebraska where he also studied law and then in 1895 accepted a slot as a first lieutenant with the 10th Cavalry at Fort Assiniboine in Montana. His most arduous assignment with the 10th involved moving nearly 200 starving, wandering Cree Indians, with 500 ponies and baggage, who had crossed the border into Montana back to their home turf in Canada after diplomatic negotiations between Washington, D.C., and Ottawa.

The mission required close, intensive work with his cavalrymen. In his memoirs Pershing wrote, "Service with colored troops demands much greater effort on the part of officers than with white troops." Having said that, he dismissed the usual complaints of poor discipline or sloppiness and noted his men behaved bravely, efficiently, and cooperatively. Tempering his praise with paternalism, he insisted his "attitude towards the negro was that of one brought up among them [Pershing had been raised in Missouri]. I had always felt kindly and sympathetic toward them and knew that fairness and due consideration of their welfare would make the same appeal to them as to any other body of men. Most men, of whatever race, creed or color, want to do the proper thing and they respect the man above them whose motive is the same."

Pershing represents about the best attitude in a white commander that a black soldier could expect during the nineteenth century. There were almost no candidates from his own race. Not until 1887, ten years after Flipper graduated, did another African American follow in his footsteps. John Hanks Alexander passed through the United States Military Academy and served with the 9th Cavalry in the Dakota Territory. He remained a second lieutenant with the Ninth until he died of natural causes in 1894.

By the time of Alexander's demise, the so-called Indian Wars were over. The frontier soldiers, like the 10th Cavalry under Pershing, carried out more benign missions for the Great White Fathers. But in the years of conflict, sixteen individuals from the quartet of black regiments won the Medal of Honor for their efforts in these campaigns. A typical citation, the award to 1st Sgt. Moses Williams of the 9th Cavalry, noted, "Rallied a detachment, skillfully conducting a running fight of 3 or 4 hours, and by his coolness, bravery, and unflinching devotion to duty in standing by his commanding officer in an exposed position under a heavy fire from a large party of Indians saved the lives of at least three of his comrades."

No one from the period seems to have remarked on the irony that one minority had been employed to suppress another. With the Native Americans subdued, the black troops had a brief respite from wars against the alleged enemies of the United States but their status continued to be in jeopardy.

There was little progress for African Americans seeking a career with the seagoing service. The United States Naval Academy accepted sixteen-year-old James H. Conyers, a black from South Carolina, in 1872. Although Conyers escaped most of the vicious brutal beatings and humiliations practiced at the academy, he was, according to research by Lt. Comdr. R. L. Field, USN (Ret.), the source of "considerable uproar upon his arrival and remained the center of attention throughout his stay." The *New York Times* reported the plebe was totally ignored by classmates who agreed to avoid personal contact even at the risk of violating orders. One midshipman refused a command from a lieutenant to fence with Conyers. Reported for disobedience, and given an alternative of apologizing to the lieutenant or leaving the academy, the youth chose to be separated.

Accused of various infractions, Conyers was court-martialed several times and dismissed. However, on each occasion, the secretary of the navy restored his status. To the academy commander, Adm. Robley D. Evans, "the boy was really unbearable" and added that even if he had been a model of deportment, the insititution was not prepared to deal with a black midshipman.

Conyers quit the scene after only a few months because of deficiencies in his studies. He returned in 1873 but again dropped out due to academic failings.

The candidates who followed Conyers met the same fate, although the severity of the hazing appeared to have intensified. A newspaper story said that an officer had to draw his sword to protect one black plebe and on another occasion a gang of midshipmen joined in a general assault. Invariably, the African Americans were turned out for their weakness in the classrooms.

5
The War With Spain

As the nineteenth century petered out, the nonwhite elements of the armed forces struggled for recognition, at least in the eyes of white society and the dominant hierarchy. But they were bucking a strong tide. The Supreme Court with *Plessy v. Ferguson* set its imprimatur upon the principle of separate but equal, which was honored only in the first word. The Marine Corps clung to its exclusionary policy. In the age of sail and wooden hulls, with responsibilities largely confined to coastal waters, the navy had relied on people of all races who shifted back and forth between merchant ships and men-of-war. Prejudice barred men of color from commissions and African Americans aboard navy vessels worked as messmen or below decks in the sweaty work on the steam engines. Few held deck ratings but still the navy seemed friendlier than its fraternal services. No real effort was made to segregate men aboard ships or even at shore stations. However, the navy, in whose ranks during the Civil War African Americans accounted for perhaps a quarter of the personnel, already was undergoing a drastic sea change, the conversion to a large, permanent fleet. The viewpoint of *The Influence of Sea Power Upon History* by Adm. Alfred T. Mahan had convinced political figures and military authorities of the need for a powerful navy capable of ranging far beyond domestic waters. That led to recruitment of career sailors and better educated, more technologically experienced individuals. Black sailors were increasingly detailed to the most menial jobs with the bulk of them serving food to white officers or at best stoking the boilers with coal.

In the army, as the resistance of the Native Americans to "Manifest Destiny" declined to the level of isolated skirmishes, the four black regiments, increasingly stationed in proximity to white towns and cities, bumped against growing hostility. Brawls, shootings, and even murders indicated the high antagonism of residents against black soldiers quartered in their areas.

Vested interests, however, praised the 25th Infantry Regiment, summoned in 1894 to Missoula, Montana, to preserve order and property in a railroad strike. Commented the *Anaconda Standard,* a local newspaper, ". . . it is generally admitted that the conduct of the soldiers, during the time that they were on duty here, [was] exemplary, and demonstrated beyond a doubt the excellence of the Negro as a soldier . . . The railroad authorities are naturally loud in their praise of the troops, and the majority of the strikers admit that if the soldiers had to be called out there could have been none better than the companies of the 25th Infantry who were encamped here. [Actually, the union-oriented railroad employees and later miners in another conflict of capital and labor complained that the black soldiers cursed and abused them.]

"The prejudice against the colored soldiers seems to be without foundation, for if the 25th Infantry is an example of the colored regiments there is no exaggeration in the statement that there are no better troops in the service. During the strike, opportunity was afforded to compare them with the white soldiers and in no instance did the 25th suffer by the comparison." Black soldiers may have been chosen for this duty because their skin color made them less likely to find common cause with white strikers.

Policies that extinguished British, Spanish, Mexican, and Native American sovereignty over land that would become the forty-eight states, expanded to visions of a wider sphere of influence. The sole offender of the Monroe Doctrine was Spain, whose island of Cuba lay less than 100 miles from Florida. Refugees fleeing oppression escaped to New York to work in the cigar industry. Revolutionaries flitted between Cuba and the States. Money, weapons, and encouragement flowed to the rebels. Publishing entrepreneurs William Randolph Hearst and Joseph Pulitzer engaged in a circulation race that would be celebrated as the birth of "yellow journalism," featured atrocity stories describing the cruelty meted out to insurgents.

By late 1897, however, the Spanish government seemed to have curbed the worst excesses committed under its imprimatur and to be prepared to offer a measure of independence to the island. In a move supposedly to guarantee American interests, the United States dispatched its battleship the USS *Maine* to anchor in the Havana harbor. On the night of 15 February, a massive explosion shattered the *Maine*. It sank with the loss of 266 sailors, including 22 blacks, mostly serving as stewards for the officers. Jingoes shouted for a declaration of war and drew support when a board of inquiry concluded that a mine attached to the keel blew up the ship. [One investigation in 1911 confirmed this explanation but later research suggests the possibility of an accidental internal detonation.]

Spain, not eager for a fight, strove to conciliate the American authorities. But political forces in the United States and most particularly in the Congress relished the prospect of a conflict. President William McKinley, while unenthusiastic—his assistant secretary of the navy, one Theodore Roosevelt, sneered, "McKinley has no more backbone than a chocolate eclair"—gave in to the war-hungry. He failed to advise Congress of the opportunities to negotiate a settlement agreeable to the United States and the legislature indulged itself with a declaration against Spain.

There is nothing like a war to unite and energize a nation. "The splendid little war" as Secretary of State John Hay proclaimed, attracted a grand rush of young males anxious to demonstrate their patriotic ardor, and for the most part black Americans joined the stampede to the colors. They volunteered to serve their country, even as it enacted an increasing number of Jim Crow laws designed to separate and subjugate them. A few black leaders, like Henry M. Turner, senior bishop of the African Methodist Episcopal Church, questioned the enterprise, arguing that whatever the Spaniards inflicted upon the Cubans could not be any worse than the outrages perpetrated by American whites upon the black citizens.

The bishop uttered a minority voice in the minority community. As in the previous challenges, first for independence, then in 1812, and again in 1861, African Americans chose to enlist because of fealty to a nation they considered their homeland, for economic opportunities, for adventure, and most significantly because they believed performance under arms opened the road to equality. Trooper John E. Lewis of the 10th Cavalry wrote to the editor of the Illinois *Record,* "I hope that you dear sir, will appeal to the young colored men of this country in defense of a common cause. It is time every patriotic young colored man should come to the front and defend its honor and show that we are true American citizens; that we can protect our homes and government."

For the first time in American military history, the barriers to command dropped a notch. Charles Young, the third success story at West Point, an 1892 graduate, was at the outbreak of the war, the only man of his race qualified to lead combat troops. The son of slaves, Young had a father who volunteered for an artillery unit during the closing months of the Civil War. When the family moved to Ohio, Young attended public schools and matriculated at Wilberforce University, an institution created to provide higher education for blacks. Upon graduation he accepted a position teaching at Wilberforce. Hearing of opportunities to compete for the West Point program, Young promptly entered the competition, scoring second highest in his region and ultimately enrolled at the academy. Like Flipper and others before him he struggled not only with the academics but also the racial slurs, shrugging off his nickname "load of coal." He persevered and earned his second lieutenant's commission, orginally serving with the 25th Infantry before winning a transfer to the 9th Cavalry. His background led to appointments as a teacher first at the Fort Duchesne post school and then at Wilberforce.

Stashed in the military training program of that university, First Lieutenant Young received a temporary rank of major and command of the 9th Ohio Colored Infantry, which took up station at Camp Russell Alger, near Falls Church, Virginia. Reportedly, when a white regiment arrived from

South Carolina, the newcomers cursed at the proximity to "damn niggers." One of them refused to salute Major Young who said nothing about the incident, but the camp commandant heard of the insult. He summoned the soldier and Young, directed the major to remove his jacket and hang it on a chair. The white enlisted man was then ordered to salute the chair with the coat. Then Young put it back on and the soldier saluted him, supposedly learning that the courtesy was earned by rank, not the individual who happened to hold the commission.

Some black veterans, usually noncoms, were given commissions by the governors in their home states for service with the militias. A handful of African Americans who had some standing in civilian life—a member of the state legislature, a barber, and a musician in North Carolina for example, also qualified as officers. Whites, however, continued to dominate even among the segregated outfits, with the lower echelons of officers chosen from white noncoms who had experience with black units. A suggestion that the president restore Henry Flipper to duty as leader of an all-black regiment failed to pass muster.

Previously, because of regional opposition, except for an abortive attempt at Fort Myers, Virginia, none of the black units had ever been stationed in the South. Cheers from townfolk, mostly white, rang in the ears of 9th Cavalry troopers as they entrained from Lander, Wyoming, to travel southeast for the eventual voyage to Cuba. They, along with the newly formed militias, recoiled from a far more malevolent reception below the Mason-Dixon line. The civilians ferverently sought to enforce their Jim Crow laws with utter disregard for common courtesy to say nothing of disrespect for those who wore their country's uniform. Captain John Bigelow Jr., a white man who commanded a 10th Cavalry squadron, believed some of the unpleasant incidents might never have occurred were it not for the ugliness of the attitudes enforcing segregation.

Townspeople in Lakeland, Florida, Mobile, and Anniston, Alabama, abused the black soldiers, denying service at stores or enforcing separation on streetcars. At Tampa, a drunken band of white volunteers fired their rifles at a two-year-old black child. Fortunately their aim was poor enough so only the boy's clothing was ripped but when members of the nearby 24th and 25th Infantry heard about the incident they rampaged through the city destroying whites-only businesses and brothels. When neither military nor civilian cops could halt the riot, authorities summoned a white regiment from Georgia. The disorder ended but not before injury to some thirty blacks.

Having spent their entire military careers posted to territories with little or no Jim Crow laws, the regular army blacks experienced culture shock and reacted forcefully to attempts to restrict them. Sergeant Horace W. Bivins had joined the army more than a decade earlier, "having a very great desire for adventure, and to see the wild West." He wrote a brief autobiography during the Cuban campaign. "I entered Hampton School, June 13, 1885 [he was then twenty-three years old] at which place I received my first military training. I enlisted in the United States Army, November 7, 1887." Posted to Jefferson Barracks, Missouri, Bivins says he received a few lessons in mounted and dismounted drill before assignment to the 10th Cavalry. As a trooper, Bivins participated in various operations designed to curb or control Native Americans. Perhaps because of his time at the Hampton School, Bivins was detailed as a clerk in the regimental adjutant's office. However, he soon demonstrated a talent with a rifle. "My first target practice with the rifle was at San Carlos. I stood number two in the troop of sixty men although it was the first time that I had ever shot a rifle. I was made sharpshooter in that year, 1889, and have ever since led my troop in markmanship." In the years leading up to the fighting in Cuba, Bivins, for his prowess with his weapon, collected a batch of medals and badges, including the first gold award handed out when he represented the Department of the Dakotas at an army competition.

Assigned to the 10th Cavalry, he had participated in campaigns against "hostile Indians" for a few years before settling into more uneventful duties at Western outposts. His narrative notes, "We left Fort Assiniboine, Montana, April nineteenth . . . We received great ovations all along the line. Thousands of people were thronged at the places where we would stop and we were treated royally; at Madison, Wisconsin, we were presented with enough flags to decorate our train and were given cigars and many other pleasantries. Our band would play in response to the ovations that were given us from time to time.

"After reaching Illinois we received both flags and flowers from the ladies and schoolgirls. I planted one of the flags given me on the crest of San Juan Hill, July 1, 1898. As we neared the South the great demonstrations became less fervent. There were no places that we entered in which we were courteously treated.

"The signs over the waiting room doors at the southern depots were a revelation to us. Some read thus: 'White waiting room.' On the door of a lunch room we read, 'Niggers are not allowed inside.' We were traveling in palace cars, and the people were much surprised that we did not occupy the 'Jim Crow' cars, *the curse of the South* [his italics].

"At Nashville, Tennessee, we were met by thousands of people, both white and colored. Our band played in response to the cheers that went up from the great multitude."

Buffalo soldier John Lewis, in his letter to the *Record,* described the passage to the land of segregation, saying, "we knew no difference until the line of Kentucky was reached, at Hopkinsville, Ky. It seemed strange that on one side of the road stood the white and that on the other colored. The people of Nashville, Tenn., gave us a rousing reception and many of the boys longed to return to that city. At Chattanooga, our pleasure was entirely cut off. Several days before the 9th went in [black soldiers] broke up the Jim Crow car and took several shots at some whites who insulted them . . . The Jim Crow car that ran from Lytle, Ga. to Chattanooga was discontinued. The 25th Infantry broke that up.

"[Lakeland] with all its beauty is a hell for the colored people who live here, and they live in dread at all times. If one colored man commits any crime, it does not make any particular difference whether they get the right party or not; all they want is a black. The main man, Abe Collins, who was such a dread to the colored people was shot and killed on May 16, 1898 by some [black] soldiers. On that date, some of our boys, after striking camp, went to Lakeland, went into a drug store and asked for some soda water. The druggist refused to sell them, stating he didn't want their money, to go where they sold blacks drinks. That did not suit the boys and a few words were passed when Abe Collins (white barber) came into the drug store and said:'You d—— niggers better get out of here and that d—— quick or I will drive you B—— S—— B—— out,' and he went into his barbershop which was adjoining the drug store and got his pistols, returned to the drug store. Some of the boys saw him get the guns and when he came out of the shop they never gave him a chance to use them. There were five shots fired and each shot took effect. I suppose that he was of the opinion that all blacks looked alike to him; but that class of men soon found out that they had a different class of colored people to deal with."

The shipment of the four black, regular army units had begun even before Congress issued its declaration against Spain. The War Department marshaled them all at Chickamauga Park, Georgia. In some circles, the existing black troops were considered to be the most qualified to fight in the tropics. Not only were they touted as more able to cope with the heat but a popular misconception held that they carried some raceborne immunity to the deadly scourge of yellow fever. Initially, the governors of states in the South, Midwest, and Northeast refused to mobilize the black volunteers. Again, however, necessity plus the demands from African Americans and their white supporters wrought a change. Officials charged with providing militias manufactured out of civilians formed a number of black units as Congress approved the recruitment of ten regiments composed of what were delicately known as "immunes."

Some white soldiers supported their black counterparts when they refused to accept Jim Crow. John H. Helm, an African American, answered the call for enlistment in the 6th Virginia Volunteers. In a letter to historian Marvin Fletcher he wrote, "When a number of men on pass from the

6th Virginia [a black militia outfit] entered a saloon in Macon [Georgia] as soon as the bartender saw them he yelled, 'No niggers allowed in here.' Some soldiers of an Ohio Regiment took charge serving the negroes, breaking up the place."

Lewis reported that many white Southerners sought to inflame racial animosities. "One white Southerner talking to a white soldier was running down the colored soldier, and because the white soldier would not approve of what he said, he commenced to abuse him. It ended in the white Southerner being killed and not one thing was said about it. You would be surprised, although you live where very little prejudice exists, [at] the friendly feeling that exists between the colored and white soldiers and they have resented many an insult that was cast at the colored troops. Many a resort had to close on account of refusing them [Negro soldiers] certain privileges."

In his letter to Marvin Fletcher, John Helm said, "When the second call was made in 1898, there was talk of white officers for the sixth Virginia volunteers. The objection was so strong that the War Department allowed the Negro militia to have their own officers. Lt. R. C. Croxton [white] of the Regular Army was commissioned Lt. Colonel, commanding at Camp Corbin, Virginia with the 6th Virginia. All seemed to be working well. At Knoxville, Tennnessee, it was apparent that Lt. Col. Croxton had no use for his Negro officers. Many times I heard him reprimand captains or lieutenants in front of the men. After being in Knoxville a few days, we were told that the major of the 2d Battalion, five captains and three or four lieutenants had been ordered to take examinations. They promptly resigned. Just what the Lt. Colonel wanted.

"The officers said they passed the state board at Richmond. The white regiments were being discharged. Now the Lt. Colonel had what he wanted, white officers. When these officers came, the 1st Sergeant of Company G went around for signatures agreeing not to obey the newly appointed officers. Drill time came. Right shoulder arms. Not a man moved. Shortly afterwards a colonel from an Ohio Regiment took command. Same result. 'I have been in the service 20 years and have never had an order disobeyed [he said].'

"That night the 6th Virginia was surrounded by three regiments and ordered to stack arms. All drills were given without arms. After several days the rifles were returned. White officers were now in command. Flushed with success, the Lt. Colonel ordered the remaining Negro officers [to undergo] examinations. They all took them. We heard no more."

Major William H. Johnson of the 6th Virignia was among those who resigned their commissions. He explained, ". . . by act of Congress, the commanding officer of a regiment is allowed at any time he sees fit, to ask for a

Board to examine into the qualifications, efficiency, conduct and capability of the officers under him.

"This of course, gives a commanding officer an opportunity to get rid of any officers who may be objectionable to him, whether on account of color or anything else. A West Pointer can have room made for his fellow school mates to the detriment of the volunteer officers, and the colored officers can be gotten rid of for the volunteer officer of his choice."

Johnson claimed that "the intention to get rid of colored officers was evident. We did not fear a fair examination as some of us had been examined more than once, and one of us three times, being always successful, but we were satisfied that it was a case of trot them out and knock them down.

"We consider that the officers composing the military board of the State of Virginia, Colonel Jo Lane Sterp, General Charles J. Anderson and other prominent gentlemen who examined us, or some of us at least, and pronounced us qualified for our positions knew their business as well as the commanding officer of the 6th Virginia Regiment."

Woefully equipped and ill prepared for the conflict, the Army could not supply lightweight khaki uniforms for a tropical campaign, and the troops went into Cuba perspiring profusely in the blue wool designed for winter garrison duty. The regulars carried the standard Krag rifle but volunteers coped with Springfields that used black powder. Conditions just before embarkation required the soldiers to stand for hours while waiting to board the transports. John Bigelow's men reached the piers in railroad coaches equipped with ice in the water coolers but no food other than a 3:00 A.M. breakfast of hardtack and coffee. Bigelow reported, "I wanted to give my men some supper. I went to a restaurant on the pier to make arrangements to have the men eat there, and was told by the lady who kept it that to have colored men eat in her dining-room would ruin her business." Other than what they could buy from peddlers, the troopers bedded down for the night unfed. The next morning, they loaded their baggage, still with no food.

Adding to the disarray, the shortage of ships forced the first cavalry units landing on the beach to leave their mounts behind. Only those steeds belonging to officers accompanied the troops. When these along with mules were pushed into water to swim for the shore, some headed out to sea. However, they responded swiftly to a bugler's cavalry call and made their way to the beach.

The 9th and 10th Cavalry Regiments, together with the Rough Riders organized by Roosevelt and led by Col. Leonard Wood, formed one brigade of dismounted troopers in a division under Gen. Joseph Wheeler, an erstwhile Confederate commander. The American commander, the obese Gen. William R. Shafter, nemesis of Henry Flipper, vetoed a plan devised by the Navy for a landing at the entrance to the port of Santiago de Cuba on the southeastern coast of the island. Shafter feared the fortifications at that site. Instead, he chose a beach fifty miles west, at the village of Daiquiri. Cuban partisans promised to draw off the Spanish soldiers defending the area.

Following a naval bombardment, the honor of first ashore on 22 June at Daiquiri [a few days earlier Marines had landed to the west near Guantánamo] fell to these troopers on foot. They scrambled onto the sand without facing enemy fire. The Spaniards had withdrawn, either frightened by the threat of the guerrillas or because the general at Santiago wanted to bolster his forces. Left behind were stout emplacements stuffed with arms and ammunition sufficient to have devastated the floundering Americans. As it was, the only casualties were two members of the 10th who drowned when their longboat either capsized in the surf or as by one account, they slipped while climbing from a lighter to a pier.

Three days after the landing, squadrons from the 10th in conjunction with white regulars from the 1st Cavalry and the all-volunteer Rough Riders, having dried their rain-soaked clothes over bonfires, began an assault on a Spanish strong point, a pass through the mountains known as Las Guásimas. The three organizations struck out in separate columns through dense underbrush. Elements from the lead groups converged half a mile from a breastworks thrown up on a hill before Las Guásimas. It was still early morning as the Americans formed into a crude battle line. Uncertain whether the straw hats visible above the top of the emplacement belonged to the enemy or to rebels, General Wheeler ordered a small cannon to fire a few rounds. A retaliatory volley of shot and shell confirmed the identity of the Spanish defenders who outnumbered the attackers, 1,500 to 1,000.

Command and control were barely in evidence as the brigade's separate outfits closed with the enemy. Eager for the fight, the Rough Riders rushed across open ground to assault the defensive positions. Heavy fire stalled the volunteers, but fusillades from the Rough Riders backed by the black and white troopers drove off the foe who may also have been frightened by the sight of reinforcements, including troopers of the 9th Cavalry, advancing behind the attackers. Only ten Spanish dead and eight wounded were found at the site but the American volunteers lost eight killed and thirty-four wounded while the regulars, black and white, counted another eight dead and eighteen injured.

Black Jack Pershing missed this skirmish of his old unit. When the war with Spain first broke out, he was teaching tactics at West Point. He threatened to quit for a post with the Rough Riders unless allowed to rejoin the 10th Cavalry. Delayed enroute to Las Guásimas by his duties as regimental quartermaster for the 10th, Pershing, after speaking with men involved, complimented his troopers for "relieving the Rough Riders from the volleys that were being poured into them from that portion of the Spanish line."

The American veterans of Las Guásimas rested for six days awaiting the arrival of thousands more soldiers, stocks of ammunition, rations, and other military accoutrements. The troops faced a far more difficult series of battles for the village of El Caney and a pair of hills, San Juan and Kettle, which barred entry to a major objective, Santiago de Cuba. Unfortunately for the invaders, the nearly week-long hiatus allowed the defenders enough time to dig rifle pits, string barbed wire, plant cannons, and install themselves in blockhouses and in El Viso, a stone fort.

On 1 July, thousands of Americans struggled through mud along a narrow trail toward El Caney. Although the attackers far outnumbered the defenders as much as ten to one, the roughly 500-man force ensconced in the fortifications, discouraged advances with withering, well-aimed fire from their Mauser rifles. Once more, the Americans were ill equipped for their task. They could train only four pieces of light artillery on the ramparts protecting El Caney. Because the U.S. Army still used black powder, the positions of soldiers were revealed while poor aim of the cannoneers did little damage.

Foot troops then rushed the Spaniards. Men of the 25th Infantry attacked in the vanguard. Lieutenant James A. Moss, serving with the unit, described the battle for the strong point of El Viso. "The dead, dying and wounded are being taken past to the rear; the wounded and their attendants are telling the Twenty-Fifth: 'Give them hell, boys; they've been doing us dirt all morning.'

"A member of the Second Massachusetts, carrying several canteens, and going to the rear for water, says to our soldiers: 'The buggers are hidden behind rocks, in weeds and in underbrush, and we just simply can't locate them; they are shooting our men all to pieces.'

"The procession is, indeed, terrible. Men with arms in slings; men with bandaged legs and bloody faces; men stripped to the waist, with a crimson bandage around the chest or shoulder; men staggering along unaided; men in litters, some groaning, some silent, with hats or blood-stained handkerchiefs over their faces; some dead, some dying! . . .

"'Forward, guide left, march!' is given, and advancing two hundred yards through a grass field, hidden from the enemy's view by a double row of trees, they reach a barbed wire fence. Some soldiers are supplied with wire cutters—the command at once cuts its way through and crossing a lane, enters an open pineapple patch. Ye Gods! It is raining lead! The line recoils like a mighty serpent, and then, in confusion advances again! The Spaniards now see them and are pouring a most murderous fire into their ranks! Men are dropping everywhere! . . . The bullets are cutting the pineapples under our very feet—the slaughter is awful! . . .

"The bullets . . . are raining into our very faces. A soldier comes running up, and cries out, 'Lieutenant, we're shooting into our own men. Mid the cracking of rifles, the whizzing of bullets, the killing and wounding of men, and the orders of the officers, great is the confusion! How helpless, oh, how helpless we feel! Our men are being shot down under our very feet, and we their officers, can do nothing for them.' . . .

"Our officers . . . decide there is only one thing for United States Regulars to do—Advance! Advance until they find the enemy! . . . Our firing line is now no more than one hundred fifty yards from the fort, and our men are doing grand work. A general fusillading for a few minutes, and then orders are given for no one but marksmen and sharpshooters to fire. Thirty or forty of these dead-shots are pouring lead into every rifle-pit, door window, and porthole in sight . . . The Spaniards are shaken and demoralized; they are frantically running from their rifle-pits to the fort, and from the fort to the rifle-pits! Our men are shooting them down like dogs . . . The fort has been silenced!"

Moss's shot-by-shell account finished, "However, a galling flank fire is now coming from the village and a small block-house on our left . . . It is, therefore, decided to rush forward . . . The line is now being formed for the final rush—all is ready—they're off . . . Men are still dropping by the wayside, but on, on, up, up they go, those dusky boys in blue. The heavy firing has ceased, and after twenty-five or thirty minutes of desultory firing, El Caney itself surrenders!"

Sergeant M. W. Saddler wrote to *The Freeman,* a newspaper for blacks published in Indianapolis, "On the morning of July 1, our regiment, having slept part of the night with stones for pillows and heads resting on hands, arose at the dawn of day, without a morsel to eat, formed a line, and after a half day of hard marching, succeeded in reaching the bloody battleground of El Caney. We were in the last brigade of our division. As we were marching up we met regiments of our comrades in white retreating from the Spanish stronghold. As we pressed forward all the reply that came from the retiring soldiers was, 'There is no use to advance further. The Spaniards are intrenched in block houses. You are running to sudden death.' But without a falter did our brave men continue to press to the front.

"The first battalion of the 25th Infantry . . . was ordered to form the firing line, in preference to other regiments, though the commanders were seniors to ours. [Under the circumstances a questionable honor that may have been motivated by a willingness to sacrifice black instead of white lives.] . . . The enemy began showering down on us volleys from their strong fortifications and numberless sharpshooters hid away in palm trees and other places . . . Our men began to fall, many of them never to rise again, but so steady was the advance and so effective was our fire, that the Spaniards became unnerved and began over-shooting us. When they saw we were 'colored soldiers' they knew their doom was sealed."

Sergeant Saddler stated that "the advance was continued until we were within 150 yards of the intrenchments; then came the solemn command, 'Charge!' Every man was up and rushing forward at headlong speed over the barbed wire and into the intrenchments, and the 25th carried the much coveted position."

Although Saddler, in common with soldiers throughout the history of war, vastly exaggerated the enemy numbers—he said there were 5,000 defenders—the brief battle was a bloody one. At El Caney, 235 of the defenders were killed or wounded and 120 seized as prisoners. The Americans lost 81 dead, and 360 wounded. The splendid little war had a price.

While the 25th Infantry helped roust the enemy from El Caney, the "Negretos Soldados" or "Smoked Yankees," as the Spaniards called them, from the 24th Infantry and the 9th and 10th Cavalry Regiments participated in the celebrated assault upon the defenders holding San Juan Heights whose most dominant elevated mass, San Juan Hill, bore atop it a well-defended blockhouse. The plan envisioned by Shafter and his staff called for the cavalry division, which included the 9th and 10th and the Rough Riders, along with the 1st and 2d Infantry Divisions to make their way through the lowland jungle before climbing San Juan Hill. The atttack would wait upon the 2d Infantry Division's capture of El Caney, a maneuver expected to require only a few hours. When El Caney proved a much tougher nut to crack and the 2d remained tied up in that assault, revised strategy dictated a strike by the 1st Cavalry and the 1st Infantry Division under whose command the 24th Infantry Regiment marched.

Again, the black powder of American weaponry revealed to keen-eyed enemy gunners the whereabouts of the foe, and they laid down accurate artillery and rifle fire. The Spaniards, wearing green uniforms that enabled them to blend into the vegetation and packing smokeless powder remained near invisible. To add to the exposure of the Americans, a Signal Corps balloon, pulled first by wagon and then by men straining at guy wires, floated overhead. The balloon, sent aloft with the laudable purpose of spotting fordable spots to cross the San Juan River, pinpointed the location of the American forces. Pershing, now accompanying the troopers of his unit, noted, "When the Tenth Cavalry arrived at the crossing of the San Juan River, the balloon had become lodged in the treetops above and the enemy had just begun to make a target of it—no doubt correctly supposing that our troops were moving along this road and were near at hand. A converging fire from all the works within range opened upon us that was terrible in its effect; the 71st New York, which lay in a sunken road near the ford, became demoralized and well-nigh stampeded; our mounted officers dismounted, the men stripped off at the roadside everything possible, and prepared for business. We were posted for a time in the bed of the stream to the right, directly under the balloon, and stood in water to our waists awaiting orders to deploy. Remaining there under this galling fire of exploding shrapnel and deadly Mauser volleys the minutes seemed like hours."

What is most significant about Pershing's remarks are his matter-of-fact report of the breakdown of the 71st New York, a white volunteer regiment while his own Smoked Yankees performed with discipline and distinction under the same intensive fire.

Because some senior commanders had fallen ill, the nominal leader of the Rough Riders, Leonard Wood, breveted to brigadier general, moved up to boss a brigade while a delighted Teddy Roosevelt, armed with a full colonel's eagles took charge of his volunteer unit. Nevertheless he chafed at the disposition of the troops, which placed other outfits including the 9th Cavalry ahead while the Rough Riders were designated reserves.

The temperature climbed to a humid, stifling 100 degrees as the men plowed through waist-high grass. The Mauser bullets from the heights mowed down the humans toiling upward at a frustratingly deadly pace. To TR's joy, word came for a charge on a nearby height known as Kettle Hill. The Rough Riders, on foot, behind their leader on his horse Little Texas, surged forward and drove the enemy from the summit.

In a memoir of the event, Roosevelt wrote, "Being on horseback I was, of course, able to get ahead of the men on foot, excepting my orderly, Henry Bardshar, who had run ahead very fast in order to get better shots at the Spaniards, who were now running out of the ranch buildings . . . Some forty yards from the top I ran into a wire fence and jumped off Little Texas, turning him loose. He had been scraped by a couple of bullets, one of which nicked my elbow, and I never expected to see him again. As I ran up the hill, Bardshar stopped to shoot, and two Spaniards fell as he emptied his magazine. These were the only Spaniards I actually saw fall to aimed shots by any one of my men, with the exception of two guerillas in trees. Almost immediately afterward the hill was covered by the troops, both Rough Riders and the colored troops of the Ninth and some men of the 1st."

The Americans had little time to savor the triumph of Kettle Hill before turning their attention to San Juan Hill. At this site, the enemy mounted its fiercest defense. In a letter to his sister, Cpl. John Conn of the 24th Infantry details the horror; the confusion; the visions of glory, valor, and panic, the curious mixture of pomp and religion; and above all the madness that envelops the combat soldier. "After we had advanced about a mile, we began to meet the wounded coming to the rear, and thought seriously of the situation, and then in a short time the road was almost choked entirely with the wounded and stragglers. Our progress was very slow so when we got into the zone of the small arms firing it was about 11:30 o'clock. It was terrible. There were wounded and dead men lying all alongside and in the road, and the air seemed alive with bullets and shells of all descriptions and caliber. You could not tell from what direction they were coming; all that we could understand was that we were needed further in front, and we could not shoot, for we could not see anything to shoot at. We advanced until we were assured by our divisional commander that our mettle was about to be tested; that he was depending on his boys of the 24th to make history, and that the fate of his record and possibly of the nation depended on the quality of the mettle mentioned.

"We piled up all our extra baggage and our blanket rolls, nothing but our arms, ammunition and canteens being needed and, fully stripped for fighting, we advanced with our regimental chaplain's last words ringing in our ears: 'Acquit yourselves like men and fight.' We were right in it then, in good shape—lots of music and very few drums. From the appearance we passed two or three regiments lying in the road, so that we had to stumble over them and pick our way through them to advance . . . until we were in the desired position, and it was terrible—just one continual roar of small arms, cannon and bursting shells; but our position was comparatively secure on account of the river bank."

Corporal Conn said that "the orders from our colonel were: '24th Infantry move forward 150 yards.' With a last look at our arms and ammunition—and yes a little prayer—we started, and such a volley as they sent into us! It was then that Sgt. Brown was shot almost at the river bank. We had to cut and destroy a barbed wire fence . . . How or by what means it was destroyed no one scarcely knows; but destroyed it surely was, and in that angry mob, nearly all their officers having been disabled, there was no organization recognized. Men were crazy. Someone said: 'Let us charge,' and someone sounded 'Let us charge' on a bugle. When that pack of demons swept forward the Spaniards stood as long as mortals could stand, then quit their trenches and retreated . . . When we gained the hill they were in full retreat . . . It seems now almost impossible that civilized men could so recklessly destroy each other."

The Spaniards might have been able to dislodge the Americans from their newly acquired positions after the first day of the San Juan Hill battle but except for artillery the defenders made no concerted attempt to oust the invaders. Within a day, American reinforcements ensured the eventual defeat of the Spanish.

Conn mentioned the men from other regiments over and through which his 24th picked its way. Actually, the 71st New York Volunteers referred to by Pershing was one of these units and it was rallied by two officers, one from the 24th and the other a member of the 71st. The whites of the latter mixed with the blacks of the 24th in gaining the top of San Juan. In fact the Americans in front of Santiago fought almost as if an integrated army. Theodore

Roosevelt wrote, "There was very great confusion . . . the different regiments being completely intermingled—white regulars, colored regulars, and Rough Riders . . ." Although he omitted them, soldiers black and white from volunteer units also participated. The battlefield integration was symbolized by the action of a sergeant from the 10th Cavalry who snatched up the flag from the fallen bearer of the white 3d Cavalry and carried both units' banners forward. While the exigencies of combat wrought desegregation, the expedition to Cuba saw a greater equality and respect for blacks than would be evident over the next nearly fifty years of military history. There was no difference in the equipment issued to men of color and when the assignments were handed out it appears that the generals did not hesitate to use the black soldiers.

Among the individuals cited for their efforts was Sgt. Horace Bivins of the 10th Cavalry. He wrote to a friend even as the siege of Santiago continued. "We had a hard fight. It began at 6:30 a.m. July 2, and lasted until noon, July 3. We drove the enemy within one mile of the city. The city is at our mercy; we can destroy it at any time. Our loss is very heavy . . . We have the Spaniards bottled up; the only chance they have is to take wings and fly. Sampson [Admiral William T.] did good work. We were within three miles of the naval battle; the very earth trembled.

"I was sixty hours under heavy fire," said Bivins. "Four of our gunners were wounded. I got hit myself while sighting my Hotchkiss gun [a British-made machine gun]. I was recommended in the official report for bravery in action . . . Bravery was displayed by all of the colored regiments. The officers and reporters . . . said they had heard of the colored man's fighting qualities but did not think they could do such work as they had witnessed in the sixty hours' battle." Bivins earned the citation he mentioned for his action in bringing up a battery of Hotchkiss guns to pin down the defenders at Kettle Hill affording his fellow cavalrymen an opportunity to charge up the slope.

Sampson's Atlantic Squadron destroyed the ships of the Spanish Navy, which tried to flee the harbor. With their fleet demolished, the Spaniards occupying Santiago de Cuba faced a hopeless situation. American soldiers ringed the city and the defenders could neither expect reinforcements nor escape by sea. On 17 July, after days of negotiations punctured by artillery barrages raining upon the beleagured inhabitants of the town, the Spanish surrendered. Fighting in Cuba was over.

For their valor in Cuba, five troopers from the 10th Cavalry received the Medal of Honor. Fireman, First Class Robert Penn was the only black sailor to earn an equivalent honor from the navy. When a fire broke out aboard the USS *Iowa* in the sea off Cuba he risked exposure to scalding water while dousing the flames.

The victors now mounted an expedition to Puerto Rico where resistance hardly ever reached a level above a skirmish. A single black unit, a company from the mostly all-white 6th Massachusetts, was involved. In less than thirty days, some of the American soldiers reboarded their transports bound for home.

On the other side of the world, the abrupt defeat of the Spanish flotilla by Admiral Dewey, which inaugurated the war, convinced the Spanish they could not retain possession of the Philippines. Rebel forces there, led by Emilio Aguinaldo, anticipated independence but the United States had developed a thirst for empire, although politicos rationalized any overseas territorial acquisitions as designed for strategic purposes rather than economic exploitation. Whatever the reasons, Spain had officially ceded control of the archipelago to the United States and with independence denied, Aguinaldo and his fellow insurgents opened fire. To suppress the opposition, the War Department dispatched the 24th and 25th Infantry Regiments beginning an extended use of various black units in the Philippines in coming decades. In one more play of the race card, the United States employed African Americans against the Filipinos, an arrangement that generated protest from some black leaders.

At the end of the splendid little war black fighting men shared much of the glory and basked in a brief spate of white esteem. Rough Rider Frank Knox, who would become secretary of the navy during World War II and obstruct the progress of blacks in that branch of service, wrote home of his experiences on San Juan Hill after he was separated from his own unit, ". . . I joined a troop of the 10th Cavalry, colored, and for a time fought with them shoulder to shoulder, and in justice to the colored race I must say that I never saw braver men anywhere. Some of those who rushed up the hill will live in my memory forever."

Pershing, like many of the white officers assigned to the black regiments, expressed pride in what their men had accomplished. "Our regiment has done valiant service. No one can say that Colored troops will not fight; 18 percent of the regiment killed or wounded, 50 percent of the officers . . . killed or wounded and all fought gallantly." High marks for performance of course reflected well upon those who led the troops but as prejudice hardened in later years white officers denigrated the men under their command.

Pershing was one who believed the struggle brought a new unity among the races. "White regiments, black regiments, regulars and Rough Riders, representing the young manhood of the North and the South, fought shoulder to shoulder, unmindful of race or color, unmindful of whether commanded by an ex-Confederate or not, and mindful only of their common duty as Americans."

Correspondent Stephen Bonsal, who covered the fighting at San Juan Hill wrote, "I was not the only man who had come to recognize the justice of certain Constitutional amendments in the light of the gallant behavior of the colored troops throughout the battle, and indeed the campaign. The fortune of war had, of course, something to do with it in presenting to the colored troops the opportunities for distinguished service, of which they invariably availed themselves to the fullest extent; but the confidence of the general officers in their superb gallantry, which the event proved to be not displaced, added still more, and it is a fact that the services of no four white regiments can be compared with those rendered by the four colored regiments . . ."

But memories were short or subject to abrupt change. Immediately after the capture of San Juan Hill, which presaged the fall of Santiago and the continuing defeat of both the Spanish ground and sea forces, Theodore Roosevelt lavished compliments on his nonwhite associates in the campaign. He informed a reporter that black cavalrymen had fought alongside the Rough Riders and he could want "no better men beside me in battle than these colored troops showed themselves to be." He expressed only some surprise that the so-called immunes appeared to be just as suceptible to illness and insects as whites.

However, in 1899 Roosevelt authored an article for *Scribner's Monthly* in which he denigrated the black soldiers, asserting that whatever they achieved it was largely because of the leadership by white officers. He insisted he had come upon a group of them leaving the battlefield and he persuaded them to return by flourishing his pistol. Presley Holliday, a 10th Cavalry veteran of the Cuban campaign refuted the magazine thesis and facts. "I believe the Colonel thought he spoke the exact truth. But did he know, that of the four officers connected with two certain troops of the 10th Cavalry, one was killed and three were so seriously wounded as to cause them to be carried from the field, and the command of these two troops fell to the first sergeants [blacks] who led them triumphantly to the front? Does he know that both at Las Guásimas and San Juan Hill the greater part of Troop B of the 10th Cavalry was separated from its commanding officer by accidents of battle and was led to the front by its first sergeant?" Holliday's comments are confirmed by the official records which show a high rate of casualties among the white officers.

Roosevelt also erred in attributing cowardice to the blacks he saw heading to the rear. As an eyewitness, Holliday wrote, "There were frequent calls for men to carry the wounded to the rear, to go for ammunition, and as night came on, to go for rations and entrenching tools. A few colored soldiers volunteered, as did some from the Rough Riders. It then happened that two men of the 10th were ordered to the rear by Lieutenant Fleming, 10th Cavalry, who was then present with part of his troop, for the purpose of bringing either rations or entrenching tools, and Colonel Roosevelt seeing so many men going to the rear, shouted to them to come back, jumped up and drew his revolver, and told the men of the 10th he had orders to hold that line and he would do so if he had to shoot every man there to do it. His own men immediately informed him that 'you won't have to shoot those men, Colonel. We know those boys.' He was also assured by Lieutenant Fleming . . . that he would have no trouble keeping them there, and some of our men shouted, in which I joined, that 'we will stay with you, Colonel.'

"Everyone who saw the incident knew the Colonel was mistaken about our men trying to shirk duty, but well knew that he could not admit any heavy detail from his command, so no one thought ill of the matter. In as much as the Colonel came to the line of the 10th the next day and told the men of his threat to shoot some of their members, and, as he expressed it, he had seen his mistake and found them to be far different men from what he supposed, I thought he was sufficiently conscious of his error not to make a so ungrateful statement about us at a time when the Nation is about to forget our past service."

Roosevelt's disparaging remarks probably owed more to his inordinate hunger to glorify himself and the Rough Riders than to any conscious bigotry. But whatever his motivation, he provoked distrust among African Americans, and within a few years he would give them far more reason to oppose him.

Presley Holliday's comment about national lapse of memory was appropriate, for the cessation of hostilities and subsequent demobilization saw renewed ill treatment of African American members of the military. Units like the 6th Virginia Volunteers with men like John Helm who wrote of the sudden demand for black officers to pass examinations were deactivated. Helm said, "White officers were not better qualified than Negroes. We were all civilians. White officers seemed eager to command black troops but objected only when they saw Negroes with shoulder straps."

Like all citizen soldiers, the nonwhites longed for a quick release once their country was no longer challenged. Some directed their anger at the one living black West Pointer still on active duty, Maj. Charles Young. Winslow Hobson, a black soldier from Ohio expressed his dismay with the treatment given black volunteers stationed at Camp Meade, Maryland, "every man with a bit of pride and love for family is more than anxious to get out of this hell. The war is over now and Roosevelt, Miles [Gen. Nelson A. who took command of the U.S. forces] and others (white of course) have all there is to be gotten out of it. Now shame on our officers! They are willing to be called at the last moment to play the lackey and watch-dog for the remaining white men who want to remain in the service—not for glory but for the money in it. . . . We have worked hard since being in the service and we need a well-earned rest, but will never get it as long as there are any white people to see us drill. I say white people because the major [Young] does not try as hard to please his colored visitors as he does the whites."

A fellow member of the 9th Ohio Infantry, T. Miles Dewey, complained, "It is true that he [Young] takes pains to gratify the curiosity of white people to the neglect of our race. Whenever there is a large crowd of white people on the grounds, we can be expected to be 'drilled to death' as the boys say."

Dewey also voiced unhappiness with the medical treatment. "Whenever a sick man goes to the hospital our physician gives him a sarcastic smile and says 'Why you are all right,' or 'there is nothing the matter with you.' . . . It makes no difference what the complaint is. A man suffering with diarrhea, or indigestion gets a pill from the same bottle as the man with a sprained ankle or weak back."

As testified by Miles Dewey and others of the 9th Ohio, command by a black officer could be onerous. A number of soldiers from the 8th Illinois Infantry occupying Cuba, indicted their light-skinned colonel, John R. Marshall, as "the man with a white face and a black heart and hand." Marshall was accused of cruel modes of punishment, failure to obtain proper provisions or medical care for those serving in the 8th Illinois. The complaints about black officers are little different than those aimed at white rankers. But a commissioned African American faced a unique dilemma. His superiors usually were doubtful if not downright negative about his qualifications. Proving himself to them meant separation from his natural brethren, the oppressed minority.

As might be expected, Southern communities particularly resented the black soldiers encamped in their region while awaiting demobilization and those from the North became furious over the abuses. While the 7th Infantry, an Ohio organization was billeted in Georgia, C. W. Cordin advised a Cleveland newspaper, "The true condition of the southern Afro-American is indeed deplorable. They fear the white man about as much as the rat does a cat, and have very few privileges such as we enjoy in Ohio." Cordin spoke fondly of another Ohio unit made up of whites ". . . they have proven to be our friends and several times have taken our men from the police when they were about to be put under arrest for a trifle. In one case a white man called one of our soldiers a vile name and the soldier hit him in the mouth. A policeman placed the soldier under arrest. A corporal and two men (Second Ohio) put in an appearance and demanded the release of the soldier and the demand was granted. Had it not been for the white soldiers he would have had a long sentence to work out on the chain gang."

Having worn the uniform of the United States, the African Americans strongly resisted the treatment habitually meted out to members of their race. In Macon, Georgia, they balked at riding in Jim Crow trailers hitched to the rear of trolley cars. Conductors shot to death at least three black soldiers when a fight erupted over orders to evacuate the whites-only section.

Aside from a temporary gain in the respect accorded by white soldiers and reporters who observed African Americans fight in the war, black members of the military recognized the power they accrued while in service. Cordin noted, "The hatred of the Georgia cracker for the Negro cannot be explained by pen. In every contemptible way do they show it to all except our soldiers. They are too cowardly to bother them to any extent. I have not heard of one soldier being insulted. Most of the boys who have no gun or revolver borrow one whenever they get a pass to town. Therefore, the white people have learned the boys are prepared for unwanted insults."

Although Cordin's remarks seem at variance with his reports on black soldiers murdered by the likes of streetcar employees, the thrust of what he said demonstrates the truth of the worst fears of those who sought to deny African Americans the right to bear arms. If capable of forceful action, blacks might resort to other means than passive resistance.

6
New Beginnings and Brownsville, Texas

When war with Spain began one of the eager black volunteers was an eighteen-year-old youth from Washington, D.C., Benjamin O. Davis. He had attended an integrated school named for abolitionist Lucretia Mott and then graduated from the M Street High School. There he enrolled in a cadet program and a black battalion in the District of Columbia National Guard. His father, a messenger for the Department of the Interior, encouraged all three of his children to apply for government jobs but Benjamin set his sights on the army. Davis, who saw Sitting Bull in one of the Native American groups that visited the capital said "colored cavalrymen" inspired his choice.

With the establishment of the 8th U.S. Volunteer Infantry, Davis, by dint of his military training, obtained a lieutenant's commission in a company raised by one Robertson Palmer. The latter had no army experience and the task of training fell to Davis who acknowledged great help from an illiterate veteran of five years with the 9th Cavalry.

Of the commander of the regiment, Lt. Col. Archelaus M. Hughes, a soldier who had served under Nathan Bedford Forrest for the Confederacy, Davis said, "I do not remember any instance where he displayed any racial prejudice." He had his first real taste of discrimination when the unit moved to Fort Thomas, Kentucky. A drugstore in Cincinnati drew the color line, barring blacks, to the mild dismay of Davis. However, when the regiment reached its staging area at Chickamauga Park, Georgia, he was appalled. Distressed by the railroad depot signs for WHITE and COLORED he recalled, "I shall never forget my first visit to that city. It had a most depressive effect upon me. Much of my patriotism was dampened. As far as I was concerned and all persons classed as colored, this country, this land for which we were called upon to defend and if necessary make the supreme sacrifice was 'not a land of the free.' No phase of American life is so discouraging to the colored people as segregation."

With the cessation of hostilities, Davis's regiment was demobilized. He sought an appointment to the U.S. Military Academy. "My father, through a friend, was able to reach the President of the United States [McKinley], only to be informed that for political reasons, the President could not 'at this time' appoint a colored to West Point. My military record was excellent, my mental qualifications were good, but my color or race, a condition over which I had no control presented a problem to me. I had had contact with many white boys. My association with the white officers during my short active service did not impress me as making them superior merely because they were white. I stood above some of them in several subjects and general average."

Still resolved to have a career in uniform, Davis signed up as a private soldier. "At that time in the community where I was born and lived, an enlisted man was looked down upon as an undesirable person. Several boys who had gotten into difficulty with the police had escaped arrest by enlisting in the army or navy." The practice of dumping young men who ran afoul of the law on the military would continue until well into the Vietnam War.

Posted to the 9th Cavalry at Fort Duchesne, Utah, Davis said, "I was surprised at the large number of [men] that could not read and write. A majority of them Xed the payroll. They learned their general orders for sentinels on post from repeating them after the NCO in charge of their recruit training. They were real professional soldiers in Troop I. These men knew the 'know how' of soldiering." He took it upon himself to teach some how to at least write their names.

"I remember one old fellow coming down the steps with a big grin. They asked, 'What are you smiling about, Old Issue?' He said, 'I done signed the payroll. That recruit has taught me to write.'"

Davis, a business student in high school, said, "I could write well, take dictation and type. There was a need for clerks. I got along well with the officers in part because I helped them with their records." With his background, education, and dedication, Davis quickly moved up the ranks to the highest noncommissioned level, sergeant major. In 1900, upon Congressional authorization for expansion of the army and its officers, Davis, encouraged by his white superiors and Charles Young, now a first lieutenant with the unit, applied for a commission. Tutored in mathematics by Young, Davis underwent a series of examinations that covered his physical qualifications as well as written tests that covered army regulations, grammar, constitutional law, and even world history with questions about Hannibal, the campaigns of Caesar, and the Franco-Prussian War.

Davis scored well enough and backed by recommendations from superiors received his lieutenant's bars. Another black candidate, John E. Green, also earned a commission. With Charles Young that gave the army three African American officers. Actually, several weeks passed between the time of the final interviews and the announcement of Davis's success. In the interim, Troop I embarked for service in the Philippines. Only after they docked in Manila did he get word that he was now a lieutenant and assigned to the 10th Cavalry.

To wipe out the Filipino insurgency over the period of 1899–1902, the United States had shipped to the Philippines 70,000 soldiers including large elements from all four of the black army units, plus two regiments of black volunteers. Among those posted to the islands was Charles Young. Influential African Americans urged that men of color receive commissions in the volunteer organizations, the 48th and 49th Infantry Regiments. The War Department agreed to appoint company grade officers—captains and lieutenants—for this purpose.

Many of the black soldiers developed an immediate rapport with the indigenous people, a relationship fostered by the insults and discrimination heaped on them by white civilians and military forces who applied the word "nigger" with equal venom to the troops wearing army blue and the Filipinos. White residents and authorities established segregated facilities in restaurants, barbershops, and bordellos.

While African Americans frequently expressed sympathy for the people of the occupied country they continued to battle those identified as enemies of the United States. C. W. Cordin, who had been a member of the 7th Ohio Infantry during the Spanish-American War, had become a career soldier in the 25th Infantry. He described a firefight that resonates with accounts from Vietnam, "we noticed a file of queer-looking people coming out of the bamboo woods, and as about 200 Chinese coolies had been carrying bamboo from these woods to our lines, to build our supply road, we did not pay much attention to them as they were dressed just as the Chinese coolies are. All at once they threw out their skirmish line. As the body of men did this another body to their left marched out of the woods as skirmishers, and before we could send word to the company, the insurgents opened the battle . . . We lost ten men killed and one wounded. I don't know how many were killed on the other side as they carry away their dead and wounded. They have two men to one rifle."

Another soldier who faced the rebels, Cpl. S. T. Evans with the 24th Infantry noted that "we laid under one of the heaviest fires for three hours that any man was ever under, and we never had but five men wounded. They were in their entrenchments and let us get within 200 yards of them before they opened fire on us. We were marching in columns of four at the time when they raised right up out of their trenches and poured a volley into us. We had no more shelter than is on your parlor floor."

The American firepower and numbers crushed the organized opposition. Troops captured the insurrection leader Emilio Aguinaldo in 1901 and although isolated bands continued to bedevil American troops for years, the threat of a war for independence in the archipelago faded. Benjamin O. Davis recalled leading patrols into the countryside in search of the rebels, but they had vanished. At one location he was told they had not been sighted in the vicinity for more than a year. His Troop F, 10th Cavalry devoted its working hours to supporting a United States–controlled civil government, an early version of the hearts and minds programs in Vietnam.

Davis seized the opportunity to school himself in both Spanish and the indigenous language of Bisayan. His linguistic abilities served him well. After the regiment returned to the States in 1902, Davis said, "At the station in Las Vegas, New Mexico, I went into the dining room to get something to eat. A waiter told me that colored people could not be served. I responded to him in Spanish. He was profuse with his apologies and served me."

His troop settled in at Fort Washakie, Wyoming, an outpost far from any sizable town. "By regulation, we would send out parties to supplement the rations. It was part of our training. Cavalry was supposed to do a lot of patrolling, learning to locate yourself in the country." Using the Krag carbine rifle, the cavalrymen laid up meat which they preserved in icehouses.

His situation kept Davis isolated from racial problems. Elsewhere, the situation for black soldiers deteriorated. They were no longer needed to quell uprisings by Native Americans, the Spanish-American War was a hazy memory, and the Philippines appeared pacified. Thus, the soldiers entered into garrison life at a time when the advocates of segregation and domination pursued their aims more forcefully than ever. Mindful of the assertiveness of African American members of the armed forces and perhaps their access to weaponry, numerous Southern communities strongly objected to having them stationed in their vicinity.

Symptomatic of this problem, Secretary of War William H. Taft wrote to Texas senator C. A. Culberson on 4 June 1906, rejecting a demand for removal of black soldiers from Fort Brown, Brownsville, Texas. "The fact is that a certain amount of race prejudice between white and black seems to have become almost universal throughout the country, and no matter where colored troops are sent there are always some who make objections to their coming. It is a fact, however, as shown by our records, that colored troops are quite as well disciplined and behaved as the average of other troops, and it does not seem logical to anticipate any greater trouble from them than from the rest. Friction occasionally arises with intemperate soldiers wherever they are stationed, but the records of the Army also tend to show that white soldiers average a greater degree of intemperance than colored ones. It has sometimes happened that communities which objected to the coming of colored soldiers, have, on account of their good conduct, entirely changed their view and commended their good behavior to the War Department."

Some six weeks after Taft wrote his letter, however, the aggressive behavior of the racists inevitably provoked the proud regulars of the 1st Battalion from the 25th Infantry which replaced a garrison made up of whites from the 26th Infantry. The black troops had been shifted from Fort Bliss, Texas, to Fort Brown, which in fact lay within the city of Brownsville, separated from town residences only by walls. The men endured the typical slights and discrimination of a firmly segregated community. Many businesses rejected black customers. City parks denied entry to nonwhites. For the most part, saloons refused to serve the African Americans although some establishments opened a back room for nonwhites.

E. P. Thompson, a white lieutenant from the 26th Infantry, in an affidavit recalled the reaction of the local citizens when they heard the 25th was to be stationed at Fort Brown. "Many derogatory remarks were made . . . 'We don't want the damn niggers here'; 'Niggers will always cause trouble'; 'To hell with the colored soldiers, we want white men . . .' A saloon keeper related a row that had occurred in the White Elephant. "That one Bates, a Federal officer was at the bar drinking when a colored soldier entered and asked for a drink; that the said Bates then turned to the soldier and said no nigger could drink at the same bar with him and that upon the soldier remarking that he was as good as any white man, said Bates drew his revolver and hit the soldier over the head; said Bates then going to the police headquarters offering to pay his own fine."

The bars also operated gambling houses that banned black players. When quartered at Fort Brown, white soldiers spent much of their pay in these dens and a subsequent report on conditions in the town speculated that "the parties engaged in the gambling and saloon business were extremely anxious to have the colored troops withdrawn from Brownsville and replaced by white soldiers."

On 5 August, little more than a week after the men arrived at Fort Brown, on a Sunday evening, Privates James W. Newton and Frank Lipscomb from Company C strolled down a street that led from the gate of the garrison. On the sidewalk stood several white women. According to the testimony of Brownsville civilians, Newton and Lipscomb "rudely jostled" the "party of ladies" and an outraged employee of the customs service named Tate struck Newton with his revolver, knocking him to the ground. When the soldier picked himself up Tate had his pistol trained upon him. The pair from Fort Brown left the scene but Newton protested his treatment to Capt. E. A. Macklin, his company commander, who promised to seek redress.

A second incident, a week later, involved another Company C soldier, Clifford Adair, who visited Matamoros across the border where he bought a silver penholder. According to Adair, when he stepped back onto U.S. territory, an official from the customhouse accosted him and announced, "Here, I will not allow any nigger to bring anything over here. You are smuggling; I am going to report you to your company commander." After searching Adair, the customs man confiscated the penholder, which was a nondutiable article. When apprised of what happened, Captain Macklin promised to try and retrieve the penholder.

A third case that riled the troops concerned a Private Reed, admittedly returning from an alcoholic spree in Matamoros. As Reed came along a boardwalk between the American and Mexican towns, one of the employees of the customhouse shoved him off into the shallows of the muddy Rio Grande.

The temper of local whites turned even uglier. On the same day that the customs agent harassed Adair tales circulated of a black soldier who dragged a white woman by her hair over the ground. Although that was only the most recent unfounded story of sexual abuse of white women by black soldiers, in a town where almost every one of the citizens walked around with a pistol or other weapon, this rumor concerned officers at Fort Brown sufficiently enough for them to send patrols into town to usher soldiers back into the fort.

Shortly after midnight of the following day, it was alleged that shots were fired into the air from Fort Brown and then a number of men, estimated at from nine to twenty, climbed over the walls and began randomly firing rifles into houses. As these soldiers advanced through the streets, a mounted police lieutenant confronted them. Bullets killed his horse and smashed his arm, eventually requiring amputation. The men fired at other cops, putting a bullet through one's hat and one group headed for a saloon that refused to permit them to drink alongside whites. When the barkeep heard the commotion, he sought to close the door but he was fatally shot.

The ten-minute outburst within earshot aroused the sentinel at the fort, and the sergeant of the guard ordered the bugler to summon the garrison to arms. With some troops believing they were under siege by townfolk, sergeants and corporals, responsible for the security of weapons, opened the locked gun racks with their keys, except for one that had to be broken into because the key was unavailable, and prepared to defend themselves. But no attack followed. The firing in Brownsville died out and the officers restored order to their command.

When morning came, the police discovered in the streets cartridges and ammunition clips for the Springfield '03 rifles recently issued to the 25th Infantry. Based on that evidence and the testimony of citizens who swore they saw men in uniforms rampaging through the darkness, a military investigation into the incident began. The first such inquiry was conducted by Maj. Augustus P. Blocksom under instructions from the commanding general for the area. Meanwhile the civilian authorities convened a grand jury.

Blocksom took testimony from soldiers, which he supplemented with affidavits and oral examinations of witnesses conducted by a local committee.

At least fourteen residents swore they saw black soldiers shooting up the town. Not surprisingly, Blocksom concluded that the offenses were indeed perpetrated by soldiers from the 25th although no one could identify a single individual as responsible. The troops, it was claimed, declined to name any of their fellows as guilty, even when they were advised that if the individuals "who planned and committed these murders and attempted murders [could not be identified], it would be necessary to discharge all the men present at Fort Brown that night without honor and to bar them from reenlistment in the Army or service in the Navy or in the civil service."

The Brownsville grand jury, stymied because of an inability to accuse anyone by name could not return a true bill. Blocksom and his associates announced that the men had entered into a conspiracy of silence to protect their comrades. Claims that shots had been fired into the fort from outside were dismissed on the grounds that no bullet holes could be found in the post's buildings. Blocksom and company also concluded that in spite of what the sergeants and corporals supervising the gun racks swore, the firing in town had continued after the racks were unlocked and their testimony was in error or a lie. Furthermore, the investigators decided that when the companies were formed up in the fort by officers after the shooting began, those involved quickly returned to their places to respond to roll call or someone else answered for them. Although the white officers inspected all of the battalion rifles in the morning and detected no sign they had been fired, the investigators explained that between the shooting and the examination of the weapons, the culprits or their friends cleaned the rifles.

Based upon Blocksom's report, the southwestern Texas commanding general recommended dismissal of the entire battalion, excepting only those men not at the fort when the affair occurred. Recognizing the drastic nature of this punishment, the War Department sent Brig. Gen. Ernest A. Garlington, inspector general of the army, from Washington to Texas to conduct a second inquiry. He questioned the men, all now confined to the guardhouse at Fort Sam Houston. No one would admit to taking part. Garlington issued an ultimatum, which set a time limit for others to come forward and provide information that would "lead to the detection of the few men guilty of the crime . . ." In his report he noted, that although all of the men admitted they knew of the incidents involving Newton, Adair, and Reed, "As soon as the subject of the trouble at Brownsville was introduced, the countenance of the individual being interviewed assumed a wooden, stolid look, and each man positively denied any knowledge of the circumstances connected with or individuals concerned in the affair. . . . The secretive nature of the race, where crimes charged to members of their color are made, is well known." Apparently, the only man to volunteer for questioning was Sgt. Mingo Sanders who provided no information but only protested that with twenty-six years of service he did not deserve the proposed sentence.

Garlington then endorsed the recommendation, that all men in the three companies, except for those who had been on leave, on detached duty elsewhere, or in the hospital for illness, be dismissed. Secretary of War Taft concurred with the findings and the suggested punishment. As the nation's commander in chief, a title he may have relished even more than "president," Theodore Roosevelt, claiming the Constitution gave him the right to such administrative action, directed that all enlisted men and noncommissioned officers at Fort Brown on the night of the shooting be dismissed forthwith "without honor." The sentences were applied to 167 men, including half a dozen holders of the Medal of Honor.

The African American community and some whites, including those who divined in the case political leverage against TR, voiced unhappiness with the way the matter was handled and the draconian disposition which penalized the innocent along with the guilty. Booker T. Washington telegraphed Secretary of War Taft urging that a final disposition be delayed. "There is feeling of intense grief and disappointment throughout the country among colored people," but the decision had already been made and the sentence carried out.

Taft, in a report summarizing the affair, argued, "Under these circumstances the question arises, Is the Government helpless? Must it continue in its service a battalion many of the members of which show their willingess to condone a crime of a capital character committed by from ten to twenty of its members, and put on a front of silence and ignorance which enables the criminals to escape just punishment? . . . Can the Government properly therefore keep in its employ for the purpose of maintaining law and order any longer a body of men, from 5 to 10 percent of whom can plan and commit murder, and rely upon the silence of a number of their companions to escape detection?"

Not surprisingly, Taft answered his own questions with a resounding negative. He saw nothing excessive in the expulsion of the entire battalion and insisted the justice doled out was "an utterly inadequate punishment for those who are guilty whether of committing the murder or of withholding or suppressing evidence which would disclose the perpetrators of such a crime." Having called the verdict "inadequate punishment," Taft then contradicted himself, making precious distinctions that could hardly have appeased critics. "The use of the word penalty in the proceedings is a mere misnomer and unfortunate. The dismissal from the service of members of this battalion under the circumstances is not a punishment, however great the hardship. There is a dismisssal technically known as a dishonorable discharge, which is only imposed by sentence by a court. This is punishment.

But the members of this battalion were not dishonorably discharged . . . They were discharged for the good of the service, as the technical phrase is, 'without honor,' to distinguish the discharge from a discharge with honor, or an honorable discharge . . . The discharge 'without honor' is merely the ending of a contract and separation from service under a right reserved in the statute . . ." But in fact, by whatever label one pasted on it, the termination eliminated rights to pensions, civil service jobs, or even enlistment in any other military branch.

When the Senate questioned the actions taken, TR, on 19 December 1906, replied vigorously, defending the way his administration and the army officers dealt with the situation. He noted "there had been considerable feeling between the citizens and the colored troops of the garrison companies. Difficulties had occurred, there being a conflict of evidence as to whether the citizens or the colored troops were to blame. My impression is . . . in these difficulties there was blame attached to both sides . . ." Roosevelt provided no source for this conclusion and neither of the military investigations offered any information suggesting the soldiers had misbehaved.

The president recited the crimes committed and lashed out at the defense, scoffing at the implication that it was townspeople who opened fire on one another as part of a plot to discredit the soldiers. He described those who turned their rifles on the civilians as "assassins," denounced their comrades as "men [who] have banded in a conspiracy to protect the assassins," and announced "They have stolidly and as one man broken their oaths of enlistment . . ."

Maintaining that the soldiers served under contracts of enlistment, Roosevelt declared, "It was my clear duty to terminate those contracts when the public interest demanded it; and it would have been a betrayal of the public interest on my part not to terminate the contracts which were keeping in the service of the United States a body of mutineers and murderers."

Roosevelt, like his secretary of war, ruminated on the severity of his actions but far from apologetic he intensified the rhetoric. "People have spoken as if this discharge from the service was a punishment. I deny emphatically that such is the case, because as punishment it is utterly inadequate. The punishment meet for mutineers and murderers such as those guilty of the Brownsville assault is death; and a punishment only less severe ought to be meted out to those who have aided and abetted mutiny and murder and treason by refusing to help in their detection." It was a dazzling leap of jurisprudence to add mutiny and treason to the crimes of the soldiers, particularly since neither their immediate superiors nor those who investigated mentioned offenses ordinarily subsumed under those headings.

To justify the punishment of those who may have participated in the outburst along with men whose crime was to remain silent, Roosevelt offered a number of precedents. He reported that during the Civil War, several state militia regiments were disbanded as "disorganized," "mutinous," "demoralized," with "numerous desertions." These examples, based on behavior in wartime, hardly fitted the profile at Brownsville where the troops belonged to the regular army and none of the adjectives applied. It could hardly have helped Roosevelt's standing with African Americans when he cited two cases, researched by a former Confederate soldier, that involved Robert E. Lee who had led the armies aimed at preservation of slavery.

Roosevelt confronted the race issue. He said he had expressed "abhorrence which all decent citzens should feel for the deeds of the men (in almost all cases white men) who take part in lynchings, and at the same time I condemned . . . the action of those colored men who actively or passively shield the colored criminal from the law." He launched into a most peculiar twist on the separate but equal theme. "It is of the utmost importance to all our people that we shall deal with each man on his merits as a man, and not deal with him merely as a member of a given race; that we shall judge each man by his conduct and not his color. That is important for the white man, and it is far more important for the colored man. . . . If the colored men elect to stand by criminals of their own race because they are of their own race, they assuredly lay up for themselves the most dreadful day of reckoning. Every farsighted friend of the colored race in its efforts to strive onward and upward should teach first, . . . alike to the white man and the black, the duty of treating the individual man strictly on his worth as he shows it. Any conduct by colored people which tends to substitute for this rule, the rule of standing by and shielding an evil doer beause he is a member of their race, means the inevitable degredation of the colored race. It may and probably does mean damage to the white race, but it means ruin to the black race."

He concluded his brief dissertation on the needs of African Americans to behave better than their white counterparts with a ringing testimonial to himself as a champion of equality. "In the North as in the South I have appointed colored men of high character to office, utterly disregarding the protests of those who would have kept them out of office because they were colored men. So far as was in my power, I have sought to secure for the colored people all their rights under the law. I have done all I could to secure them equal school training when young, equal opportunity to earn their livelihood and achieve their happiness when old . . ." Roosevelt proclaimed "the same revolt at wrong done a colored man as I feel wrong done a white man" and reiterated his condemnation of lynching.

In an addendum issued about a month later, the president responded to questions from the Senate about the "sufficiency of the evidence." To convince the doubters he transmitted the testimony of witnesses taken under oath along with maps and photographs of the scene as well as such physical evidence as empty shells, a bandolier, ball cartridges, and clips for rifles. He ridiculed those who claimed the rioters were whites who somehow obtained army uniforms, blacked their faces, "disguised their voices so that at least six witnesses who heard them speak mistook their voices as being those of negroes." Because they were heard talking in English he declared they could not have been Mexicans (the American whites in Brownsville were far outnumbered by people from across the border). He pointed out that the ballistics evidence indicated Springfield rifles, not available to anyone except U.S. troops.

Roosevelt's fulminations failed to stifle those who perceived an injustice. The Senate Committee on Military Affairs spent the better part of a year reviewing the events at Brownsville and the banishment of the men from the 1st Battalion. While a majority of the solons endorsed the decisions of the army and the president, a minority, led by Sen. Joseph Foraker, issued a dissent after they grilled a number of witnesses, including some experts introduced for the purposes of defense.

Their objections noted that the three companies in the "exact language of Major Blocksom," had "an excellent reputation up to the 13th of August, the date of the shooting." Major Charles W. Penrose, an 1884 graduate of the Military Academy testified that from 30 to 40 percent of his men had been under fire in battles or skirmishes and were "well drilled, [among] the best I have ever seen. As a rule they behave themselves very well." He added that the records for courts-martial bore him out. It had already been developed by Blocksom, that Newton and Adair, the two men involved in incidents that were seen as motivation for the affray, were known as model soldiers and not the type to instigate untoward behavior. General Andrew S. Burt, commander of the 25th for ten years until his retirement in 1902, told the senators, "There is no better first sergeant in the United States Army than Sgt. Mingo Sanders. His veracity as he sees a thing is beyond question. . . . I can say in general terms that those men are all to be believed on their oath. I would believe them if I were sitting in a court-martial and they were even called in their own defense."

Other white officers in the 1st Battalion also spoke highly of the men. One observed, "I have commanded white soldiers a good deal, and I found that drinking among our men was much less." A second swore, "They were a most excellent lot of men, and an excellent lot of noncommissioned officers."

Foraker and his associates elicited statements on the attitudes of Brownsville whites, bringing in such witnesses as Lieutenant Thompson. The senators also reviewed the effects of an alleged assault upon a white woman by a black, which inflamed the local people. The mayor of Brownsville, fearing a riot by his citizens, had met with Major Penrose and asked that he restrict his men to quarters on the night of 13 August. "The people in town are very much incensed and excited . . . if you allow these men to go into town tonight, I will not be responsible for their lives."

The critical evidence offered involved the actual discharge of weapons and the testimony of those claiming to be eyewitnesses. Awake and in his quarters at the beginning of the incident, Penrose remembered, "The first two shots I heard were undoubtedly pistol shots, sir . . . The other shots I heard were from high-power guns . . . the Springfield rifle such as we use in the army . . . the Winchester and all the sporting rifles [Krag, Savage, Marlin, Mauser, and Mannlicher]. Another officer from the battalion agreed with Penrose as did the sentinel on duty and a civilian employed as a "scavenger" who happened to be in the fort. Even the mayor roused from his sleep by the noise believed the initial firing came from pistols. All of this directly contradicted the claims of townspeople and investigators Blocksom and Garlington who averred the opening fusillades poured from rifles aimed by soldiers inside the fort at nearby houses. The three rounds triggered by Pvt. Joseph Howard while on guard duty might have confused some witnesses.

Major Penrose, company commanders, and platoon leaders had immediately begun to muster their men when they heard the shooting. Roll call of the three units accounted for all of the men and a check of the weapons in the rifle racks indicated none missing. None of the officers saw among the men any signs of excitement or hard breathing, which would have suggested that they had rushed back to the reservation fresh from a riot a few blocks away. As a result, Penrose never considered his men had engaged in an attack on the town until the mayor called upon him that night, relating the statements given to a hastily organized committee by civilians. Penrose said the mayor also presented some items, allegedly collected at the scene of the shooting, such as shell casings, rifle clips, and a bandolier.

Confronted with the words of eyewitnesses and physical evidence Penrose and two of his officers agreed that some soldiers must have been involved. Over several weeks, however, they changed their minds. Between the time of the shooting and the disposition of the case, with the men transferred to Fort Reno, Oklahoma, the major and his associates interviewed the soldiers. None of them could or would say who was guilty but all protested their innocence. Nor did they put the blame on townspeople. They simply responded they did not know who was involved.

Penrose explained to the Senate committee that he had originally believed there was sufficient street illumination for the residents of Brownsville to identify the culprits as soldiers. But he had subsequently learned the riot occurred in almost total darkness. During the Senate inquiry, testimony revealed experiments that indicated the darkness all but precluded identification of clothing or other characterstics of individuals more than a few feet away. It was also learned that one of the principle witnesses in the one fatal shooting of the fateful night had changed his story. Even Secretary of War Taft advised the president not to give credence to that account.

Furthermore, subsequently conducted ballistics tests found that almost a dozen of the shells discovered by civilians and the Brownsville police could only be traced to a weapon that had been securely locked up on the night of the shooting. Penrose testified that the shells in question actually had been collected some days earlier and left on the back porch of B Company where they were accessible to any passerby, soldier, or civilian. He suggested that anyone might have taken them and placed them where they would indict the troops. Other spent cartridges recovered around the scene of the crime likewise appeared not traceable to the Springfields issued to the 25th Infantry. Adding to the mystery, much of the physical evidence was located in a small area, an impossibility due to the ejection mechanisms for the Springfield rifles. And Penrose reiterated that as soon as it was light enough, he had ordered a check of weapons and ammunition, which were reported in order, the guns clean, every cartridge accounted for.

The Senate minority opinion on the case pointed out that all of the testimony gathered by a citizens' committee, Major Blocksom, and an assistant U.S. attorney general, whether formally or under oath, was taken "ex parte, without any opportunity to the soldiers to be present or to be represented, to cross-examine, or put to the test in any way whatever the statements made by various witnesses." Foraker and his allies reasoned that the townsfolk, the army investigators, and the assistant U. S. attorney general, all operated on the basis that the troops were guilty and it was only a question of which individuals had participated. Blocksom, for example, declared, "that the raiders were soldiers of the 25th Infantry cannot be doubted." Foraker interrogating Blocksom brought out that the investigator would not believe any soldiers who denied their part in the shooting without corroboration— in his view they were obliged to prove themselve innocent.

Blocksom blamed the soldiers for ill feeling, proffering, "that there was no doubt Mrs. Evans was seized by the hair and thrown violently to the ground by a tall negro soldier." Yet, even more than a year later that charge was not supported by any sworn testimony.

The report of the dissenters denounced the military findings and sentences as unjust. As a remedy they introduced a bill in Congress to allow any of the discharged soldiers eligibility to reenlist, upon swearing an oath that he did not participate in the affray and did not know who did. The legislation never gathered enough votes, although a few years later, the War Department conducted hearings that enabled 14 of the 167 men discharged from the 1st Battalion to obtain reinstatement.

Murder, assault, and riot occured at Brownsville in 1906. Undoubtedly, the army's upper echelons and the politicos of the period, fearful of further disorder and antagonism between townspeople and those in uniform, felt a need to quickly level blame. Given the climate of the times and the location of the incident, it is not surprising that the stampede to judgment trampled upon the black soldiers. However, even in that era when the administration of military justice was harsh and peremptory, the abuse of rights for the troops, sanctioned by civilians like the president, the secretary of war, and the attorney general, and ratified by the Senate, bespeaks a callous disregard for the basic fair play in any court of law.

In 1972, responding to pressure, President Richard M. Nixon and Acting Attorney General Richard Kleindienst directed the army to redress the wrongs. Rather than consider the merits or lack of same in the evidence, the administration pushed the army to award honorable discharges to the soldiers of the 1st Battalion on the basis that Garlington approached his investigation with an unwillingness to accept as truth anything a black said, and by the absence of any legal or proven precedent for mass dismissals. Congress offered a token payment of $25,000 to the one surviving soldier, eighty-six-year-old Dorsie Willis, who had struggled since 1906 as a porter and bootblack. No provision was made for the survivors of the other men who undoubtedly had fallen on hard times as a result of their sentences.

7
Navy White, Pancho Villa, and Houston

Isolated in Wyoming, the 25th Infantry disgrace had no impact upon Benjamin O. Davis, intent on advancing to a captaincy. "We knew about the *Crisis* [the NAACP publication that publicized the case] but we regarded [W. E. B.]. Du Bois [editor of the magazine] and the NAACP with suspicion. We weren't concerned about Brownsville. It was the Army."

In the aftermath of Brownsville, as president, Theodore Roosevelt continued to signal mild support for blacks. In 1901 he extended an invitation to Booker T. Washington to dine at the White House. The furor that ensued caused Roosevelt to confess error due to a momentary lapse of control. Not for another twenty-eight years would an African American be invited to officially break bread with a president. Much more immediately, the military had begun to slam shut its doors even more tightly to African Americans pursuing equality and opportunity.

The perception of Brownsville encouraged those intent on restricting the roles of nonwhites in the military. When Emmett J. Scott, secretary to Booker T. Washington at Tuskegee Institute, asked Roosevelt to expand opportunities for blacks by opening up slots in field- and coast-artillery batteries, the War Department scotched the idea. Its experts declared blacks lacked the intelligence or the skill required for operating the sophisticated machinery of such weapons. An additional argument against the deployment of artillery-trained African Americans pointed to the problem of coordinating these batteries with local militias, now that the newly authorized National Guard (1903) allowed exclusion of blacks. The state units, almost exclusively white, were more concerned with the maintenance of segregation than mounting the best possible defense.

Booker T. Washington wrote to Secretary of War Taft questioning whether the army would recruit "additional colored soldiers to take the place of the three companies [because of Brownsville] that were dismissed." He added, "I very much hope . . . some plan will have been thought out by which to do something that may change the feeling the colored people now as a whole have regarding the dismissal of the three colored companies." Ever mindful of his self-chosen stance as a conciliator, Washington noted, "The race is not so much resentful or angry, perhaps, as it feels hurt and disappointed. I am not excusing or justifying this feeling, because I do not know the detailed facts upon which the action was based." He concluded with a reference to riots by whites against blacks in Atlanta.

For a time, the two of the three black officers of the army, Charles Young, a West Pointer, and Ben Davis, up from the ranks, marched through diplomatic sloughs or assignments that kept them out of line commands with the sensitive possibility of supervision over whites. Young had been appointed superintendent of two national parks in California, commanded a troop at the Presidio of San Francisco, and served as military attaché in Haiti. A clerk he hired stole his maps and the intelligence he had gathered and sold it to Haitians. An embarrassed Young returned to the States, then did tours in Wyoming and the Philippines before shipping out to Liberia as military attaché there. In that capacity, he succeeded Ben Davis who had previously been posted to teach military science at Wilberforce University in Ohio, the assignment once held by Young. Ambushed and wounded in the Liberian bush during one of his missions to organize the nation's military, Young received a commendation from Gen. Leonard Wood, the former army chief of staff. "His service in the Army has been highly creditable to his race from any standpoint."

The similarity of the Young and Davis careers was hardly an accident; the War Department could find few positions where it could hide its African American officers. Both men would return to stateside duties by 1913.

For the Marine Corps there was absolutely no change. It simply continued its exclusionary practices. Its parent organization, the navy, started to secure all possible ports of entry. At the Naval Academy, after several African Americans appointed to the school during the mid 1890s, for one reason or another did not enter, nearly forty years would pass before a black again presented himself.

Below the most-junior levels of command, blacks were frozen out of even the more menial assignments aboard ships. In place of the modest-size vessels crewed by no more than 100 men, the new battleships required a complement of more than 1,000. To fill these ranks, the service actively recruited across the land. But the talents needed involved less seagoing experience than skills with steam-driven engines and more sophisticated weapons, which in turn placed a premium on education or experience with farm machinery, factory production, or paperwork, all of which were largely closed to African Americans. In addition, the expansion of Jim Crow laws and attitudes influenced the all-white navy leaders to shun black volunteers. When Theodore Roosevelt decided to flaunt the flag before the Japanese in 1907, a flotilla of dreadnaughts known as the Great White

Fleet, appropriately painted and largely manned by white men, steamed across the Pacific. Even the lowly berths of messmen were less of an option for blacks, as Filipinos, who were deemed more docile, filled many of these positions.

Theodore Roosevelt and his successor in the White House, William Howard Taft at least talked of equality and fairness. But with the inauguration of Virginian Woodrow Wilson as president after the 1912 elections the status of African Americans fell several notches further. During this administration, Jim Crow took up residence in many federal agencies, as the nation's capital segregated government offices, functions, cafeterias, lavatories, and other facilities. The ambiance created by Wilson and his cohorts encouraged the more extreme racists. Lynchings increased.

Overall, the American military felt little urgency to change. The major active arenas involved sporadic uprisings in the Philippines and the border with Mexico where revolutionary convulsions dictated concern. In 1913, Ben Davis, while in command of Troop B of the 9th Cavalry along the line separating Arizona from Mexico awakened to the sound of heavy firing. Two bullets whizzed through his tent as he dressed. The troopers drove off the *federales* although several Americans were wounded.

Troubles continued to percolate along the border until in 1916 Pancho Villa and a band of marauders crossed the Rio Grande where they spilled American blood. Villa, a rebel against the government of Mexican president Venustiana Carranza and in some quarters considered a simple bandit, led a night attack that savaged Columbus, New Mexico, killing fifteen Americans, seven of whom were soldiers. Another thirteen people, including eight more men from the local garrison were wounded. The American troops on the scene rallied sufficiently and even pursued the raiders into Mexican territory inflicting some seventy casualties upon them.

President Wilson authorized a force of 5,000 men led by Brig. Gen. John J. Pershing to cross the Rio Grande with the aim of punishing the Villa army and eradicating it as a threat to Americans. In the vanguard rode the 10th Cavalry with Charles Young, now a major, in the saddle.

The retreating Villistas proved difficult to find, even though Pershing tried scouting with a new tool, the airplane. For some 300 miles his army tracked the enemy forces and the entire affair took on added complications when the Carranza government, while hostile to Villa, resented the presence of Yankee soldiers on their turf. The Mexican forces resisted the intruders from across the border.

Cavalrymen under the command of Major Young, backed by machine guns, charged on foot and ousted a batch of Villistas encamped at Aguascalientes. From there Young's regiment rushed to the relief of the white 13th Cavalry under siege from some 600 soldiers serving the Carranza government. When the black soldiers rescued the embattled Americans, their leader, Maj. Frank Tomkins, gushed, "By God, Young, I could kiss every black face out there."

Young supposedly replied, "If you want to, you may start with me."

Colonel William C. Brown, the regimental commander, praised Young as "excellent in all categories." Pershing himself presided over the examination that led to Young's promotion to lieutenant colonel.

A major clash between the Mexican army troops and the 10th Cavalry occurred at Carrizal. (Young was not with these units.) Pershing had instructed Capt. Charles T. Boyd to lead his C Troop and the men of K Troop who combined numbered only eighty-two soldiers, on a scouting expedition in the vicinity of Carrizal. Pershing would insist later that he had cautioned Boyd not to attempt to force his way through Carrizal, defended by a garrison of from 400 to 600 soldiers.

Corporal Henry Houston of Troop K at the request of one of his officers wrote a letter describing the experience. He reported a three-day journey in which the cavalrymen covered more than 100 miles, including a long stretch across a desert.They reached the outskirts of Carrizal where Boyd met with representatives of the Mexican forces. The American was informed that the general in command refused them permission to pass through the town. "Captain Boyd rode back to us with his head bowed and when he got back to where we were he raised his head and said, Quote, 'Boys, this looks fine, the General says the only direction we can travel is north, my orders are to travel East to Villa Ahumada which is eight miles on the other side of this town and I am going through this town and take all you men with me.'

"When Capt. Boyd made the last remark all of our boys cheered and began singing phrases of spirited songs to show their willingness to accompany Capt. Boyd in his charge through town and to show their contempt of the Mexicans as foemen."

The troopers began their advance with the main body formed to meet the enemy forces head-on while a pair of platoons guarded the flanks. "We started forward deployed in line of foragers, moved forward until we were within 500 yards of the enemy, then we dismounted and our horses moved to the rear and we moved forward, the Mexican cavalry started riding around both flanks and when we were about 200 yds. from the enemy we received a heavy volume of fire from rifle and machine guns and we knew that the ball was opened then.

"We received the order to lie down and commence firing, using the battle sight (which is the way we aim our rifles when we are fighting at close range). All of our men were taking careful aim, and Mexicans and horses were falling in all directions but the Mexican forces were too strong for us as they had between 400 and 500 and we only had 50 men on the firing line, so even though we were inflicting terrible execution they outnumbered us too greatly for us to stop their advance around our right flank.

"At this stage of the game the Mexicans were so close that it was almost impossible to miss them, they were even so close that it was possible to hit them with stones had we desired. After about 1 ½ hours hard fighting they were about thirty yards from our right flank. I tried to swing the left half of our platoon (of which I was in command) around so as to help out our platoon on the right but it was impossible, about that time our Capt. (Capt. Morey) yelled out to Sergt. Page, Quote, 'Sergt. Page! Good god man, there they are right upon you,' and Sergt. Page responded, 'I see them Capt. but we can't stop them and we can't stay here because it is getting too hot.' By that time bullets were falling like rain and the Capt. ordered all of us to look out for ourselves and our men moved off the field by our left flank. No one can truthfully say that our men ran off the field because they did not. In fact they walked off the field stopping and firing at intervals."

At the edge of an irrigation ditch, Houston came across Morey who had been wounded and was being helped by a pair of troopers. Houston lent a hand, giving the captain a drink of water out of his campaign hat. "By that time the men were rallying for a final stand but our Capt. said, 'I am done for boys, You had better make your getaway.' And then we scattered each for his own self."

Houston escaped in the company of Howard Queen, another corporal. Both barely survived a hike that took them into mountains where they nearly expired from thirst before discovering water. Altogether, Houston estimated that he traveled for twenty-four hours without water, covering a distance of as much as fifty miles.

The ill-fated decision to advance through Carrizal cost Boyd his life. Altogether a dozen Americans died, ten were wounded with twenty-four, including some of the injured, taken prisoners. The postmortem estimated enemy casualties at seventy-five. Initially, the army chief of staff blamed Pershing for a military debacle. Subsequently Black Jack explained that according to Morey, who, despite his wounds, managed to flee, Boyd had misinterpreted Pershing's orders as a mandate to reach Ahumada even if that meant a direct confrontation at Carrizal.

The Americans had been forced to retreat but now large numbers of U.S. soldiers gathered at the border. President Carranza ordered the prisoners released and entered into negotiations that would squelch further incursions from his side of the Rio Grande. Their honor intact, their captured men restored, the 10th Cavalry units returned to U.S. posts.

The administration of Woodrow Wilson faced up to a much more serious threat to American sovereignty. As World War I entered its third year, the Germans resorted to unrestricted U-boat war and sank neutral ships, including those flying the Stars and Stripes. Early in 1917, British intelligence advised Washington that it had discovered a German plot to engage Mexico as an ally in the event the United States entered the war on the side of Great Britain. The alleged scheme provoked considerable anti-German sentiment. In March, when torpedoes sank three merchant ships within twenty-four hours, Wilson called on Congress for a declaration of war which the legislators delivered on 6 April 1917. Although like much of the population, African Americans had been split on whether the United States should enter the conflict, they soon closed ranks to support the decision. Some like Du Bois, a Socialist as well as an integrationist, believed the war would cause vast changes in society, leading to both economic and social justice.

In the months preceding the entrance of the United States into the war, some Americans like Theodore Roosevelt and Leonard Wood vigorously pushed for an expansion of military training. Joel Spingarn, the white head of the National Association for the Advancement of Colored People, and who had attended a military training camp at Plattsburgh, New York, in 1915 and 1916, proposed that a training camp be established for African American officers. By the time he could persuade anyone of the value of such a facility, World War I had enveloped the United States.

To create black officers, the War Department chose Camp Des Moines, in Iowa, as a separate, segregated facility, which aroused some spirited opposition among blacks. A basic goal of the NAACP was integration yet here was its leader, Spingarn, arguing for one more Jim Crow institution. Newspapers like the *Chicago Defender* and the *Baltimore Afro-American* contended that such an operation was bound to be unequal to that provided for whites, guaranteeing that the officers produced would be less qualified. Racists would then claim their case proven, that military command was beyond the mental and psychological capacities of African Americans.

The debate caught up Charles Young, serving with the 10th Cavalry at Fort Huachuca, Arizona. In correspondence with Du Bois, the militant editor of the NAACP's *Crisis* who initially opposed a segregated arrangement, Young wrote, "Dr. Spingarn is right in practice, you see, as you are right in theory. We are going to need leaders for the Colored regiments." Eventually, Du Bois discerned a lesser between two evils, a segregated camp for black officers or no camp and no black officers. African Americans would then all serve under whites. He now agreed that the gain might justify temporary abandonment of the principle of integration. However, many influential blacks continued to resist establishment of Camp Des Moines.

Hopes for the opening up of the armed forces to nonwhite officers were jolted only a week before Congress acceded to Wilson's call for war. The army general staff, anxious to make some use of the nation's blacks, urged the secretary of war to create for this segment of the population a limited-sized, modestly equipped infantry division. Logic suggested that Charles Young receive the stars of a general and take command. However, powerful political and military figures sought to block advancement by Young. At Fort Huachuca, a pair of examiners wrote that he was "a very intelligent colored officer, hampered with the characteristic racial trait of losing his head in sudden emergencies." No evidence of such a flaw was offered but then there was no requirement for the detractors to make their case.

By the time the nation was officially at war, Camp Des Moines had been opened, but while his superiors wrangled over a proper assignment for him Young remained at Fort Huachuca. Jerome Howe, a white second lieutenant with the 10th Cavalry that chased Pancho Villa, recalled, "When the country became involved in war with Germany, and we were recruited to war strength, we were required to send our suitable noncoms to school, to Colonel Young of our regiment, a wonderful black soldier who had been one of our squadron commanders in Mexico to be trained to be officers of a Negro division. I sent [Corporal Henry] Houston."

Said Howe, "I admired Col. Young as did all officers with whom he served. Moreover I found him very likeable. I often visited him in his quarters and heard him play beautifully on the piano. He had a fine family but never had them with him on a military post. [Life for a black officer's wife at a military installation would have been the utmost in segregation, separated not only from the spouses of the white officers but because of rank denied easy association with the women attached to enlisted men.] He was a fine specimen of an athletic soldier and a perfect gentleman."

The urgings to give Young a command slot mounted until the army demanded he undergo medical tests. His records indicated hypertension and Gen. Tasker H. Bliss, chief of staff, ordered Young to Letterman General Hospital in San Francisco to determine whether he was fit for promotion and a continued career. With the exception of a bout of blackwater fever while in Liberia, Young had never been absent from duty. "No one in the regiment, either officer or man, believes me sick and no one save the doctors here at this hospital," Young wrote Du Bois. "Without ache or pain, I sit here twirling my thumbs . . . when I should be at Des Moines helping to beat those colored officers into shape."

Newspaper editorials, letters, and telegrams to the White House demanded Young be made at least a full colonel and assume the appropriate responsibilities. But even as the physicians and general staff pondered the case, Sen. John Sharp Williams of Mississippi advised President Wilson that one of his constituents had written of his unhappiness at having to serve under a black officer. Wilson sent a memorandum to his secretary of war, Newton Baker, about the lieutenant's distress. "Senator Williams of Mississippi called my attention to a case the other day which involves some serious possibilities, and I am venturing to write you a confidential letter about it.

"Albert B. Dockery, First Lieutenant in the Tenth U.S. Cavalry, now stationed at Fort Huachuca, Arizona is a Southerner and finds it not only distasteful but practially impossible to serve under a colored commander. The Tenth Cavalry is temporarily in command of Lieutenant Colonel Charles Young, who recently relieved Colonel D. C. Cabell, and I am afraid from what I have learned that there may be some serious and perhaps even tragical insubordination on Lieutenant Dockery's part if he is left under Colonel Young, who is a colored man. Is there or is there not some way of relieving this situation by transferring Lieutenant Dockery and sending some man in his place who would not have equally intense prejudices?" Evidently, a white commander such as the one who had instructed an enlisted man to salute Young's uniform was not at Fort Huachuca.

In a handwritten note to a subordinate, Baker complained about Dockery, "He should either do his duty or resign," but undoubtedly aware of the pressure upon and the predilections of his president, he asked if there was any graceful way out. Subsequently Baker responded to Wilson, "Several Senators, curiously enough one from North Dakota, have presented . . . to me [names] of your officers in the 10th Cavalry who are under the same embarrassment as Lieutenant Dockery with regard to service under Lieutenant Colonel Charles Young. The situation is, of course, very embarrassing, but I am endeavoring to meet it by using Colonel Young in connection with the training of colored officers for the new Army at Des Moines." Noting that Young, "apparently is again in perfectly good health" and would be studied at Letterman, Baker ended, "There does not seem to be any present likelihood of his early return to the 10th Cavalry so that the situation may not develop to which you refer."

The physicians, in spite of Young's record and the conclusions of an examination board that he was "entirely fit for promotion" diagnosed him as suffering from advanced nephritis and heart disease. Woodrow Wilson then assured Senator Williams that the situation would be resolved on the grounds that questions about Young's health would preclude his assuming command. Newton Baker, inclined to waive the doctors' report, succumbed to the anti-Young forces and the obvious desire of the president to satisfy the feelings of white Southerners. Not even a ride on horseback by Young from his home in Ohio to Washington, D.C., was sufficient to convince the decision makers that he was fully able to meet the demands of a military command. Young was forced to retire. As a sop he was appointed military adviser to the adjutant general of Ohio, a paper post for a paper unit.

Not even Young's separation from the 10th Cavalry satisfied Dockery, a graduate of the U.S. Military Academy and now elevated to captain. Wilson sent to Baker still another memorandum about Dockery's alleged plight. The president apologized for bothering his secretary of war but continued, "the trouble it would seem is not now the fear of Captain Dockery that he will be put under a negro officer but that it has got on his nerves that he himself remains an officer in a negro regiment, and I was wondering whether without violation of the best practices of the department some officer of Northern birth could be substituted for him." Subsequently, the unhappy white officer obtained a transfer. Meanwhile, the lone other black officer available for combat duty, Ben Davis Sr., posed no similar problem. By July 1917, he and the 9th Cavalry had settled down for duty in the Philippines.

Although their careers seemed to follow parallel trails leading to blind alleys, Davis believed he and Young were hardly similar. "Young and I were opposites. He was very sensitive of his color. I was an officer and I expected to be treated as such and was. I never had any trouble. I was not concerned whether people liked me. I wanted them to respect me and they did."

With Pancho Villa still on the loose, despite the Carranza government's promises to prevent raids upon American turf and the apparent plot by the Germans to enlist Mexico on its side, the U.S. Army maintained a large standing force in Texas. Among the units deployed there was the 3d Battalion of the all-black 24th Infantry. Lieutenant Colonel William Newman commanded eight officers and 654 enlisted men detailed to furnish guards while civilians constructed Camp Logan.

Race relations in the Lone Star State had, if anything, deteriorated in the ten years since Brownsville. The soldiers of the 24th Infantry set up a temporary home on the ragged edges of Houston. A quarter of the local population was black but the majority whites practiced a hard line on segregation, quite at odds with the conditions the soldiers of the 24th had met in the Philippines or the Far West.

High on the list of obnoxious Jim Crow rules was segregation aboard streetcars, a phenomenon absent from previous areas occupied by the 24th Infantrymen. An employee of the trolley line reported that the soldiers appeared angry about riding behind screens erected to shield whites from them. Within the first few weeks of their arrival, the troops, frequently shouting profanity, ripped down signs restricting sections of the omnibuses. In several nasty confrontations, operators and conductors summoned the cops. According to an investigation, "A motorman called a police officer and reported to him a 'nigger' who wouldn't comply with the law; the police officer said, 'Nigger, you are violating the law here,' and he says, 'I don't give a ——— about no law or anything else.' [He] had a big knife,' said the cop, 'and I knocked him in the head and took him to jail . . .' More than once, policemen beat up black soldiers.

The white workers erecting Camp Logan demonstrated their contempt for the men in uniform by setting up special water cans labeled "colored." They also constantly referred to the guards as "niggers," a word commonly used by the Houston whites and the city police. The lawmens' use of offensive language continued unabated even though after a protest from the regimental commander, the Houston chief promised his men would abstain from that insult. Almost every case that involved a black soldier and a charge of disorder involved use of the "n" word coupled with angry reactions from the soldiers. Anxious to avoid more trouble, Maj. Kneeland Snow, who replaced Colonel Newman, reached an agreement with Police Chief C. L. Brock wherein sixteen of the best enlisted men would act as military police and they would handle soldiers who offended Houston laws. Nevertheless, the grievances of the men from the 24th continued to create flammable conditions. The resentment simmered as the troops sought recreation in saloons, poolrooms, gambling houses, and other harbors of vice.

On the morning of 23 August, Lee Sparks, a policeman on duty in the black 4th Ward, broke up a dice game "played by some Negro boys," according to a statement by army investigators. Sparks then pursued the youths into a private house from which he emerged "with a colored woman who, it is reported he was striking. A Negro soldier of the 24th Infantry, reported to be somewhat under the influence of liquor, remonstrated with the officer for his treatment of the colored woman and in turn was beaten up by Officer Sparks and sent to the chief of police under the charge of interfering with an officer."

Word of the altercation reached Cpl. Charles W. Baltimore, one of the hand-picked MPs. Posted to that same 4th Ward, Baltimore approached Sparks and, said army investigators, "as part of the duty required of him, made inquiry of Officer Sparks as to the circumstances of the arrest of the soldier. There is a disagreement between Officer Sparks and Corporal Baltimore as to the latter's manner in asking for this information. Officer Sparks claims Corporal Baltimore used profanity; Officer Daniels, Sparks' partner, present during the arrest, says he heard no profanity. Officer Sparks struck Corporal Baltimore with his pistol; Corporal Baltimore turned and ran; Officer Sparks fired three times, he states, at the ground merely to frighten Corporal Baltimore, who ran into a house followed by Office Sparks, who there overtook Corporal Baltimore and struck him over the head one or more times and sent him to police headquarters in arrest. It was soon reported in the 24th Infantry camp that Corporal Baltimore had been shot by a policeman . . ." It would become apparent that the facts of the affair would depend upon which version of an eyewitness one believed with the outcome driven by rumor and confusion.

Battalion adjutant Capt. Haig Shekerjian, a native of Torrington, Connecticut, and a graduate of the Military Academy, was the first officer informed of the trouble in town. "At 2:30 P.M.," testified Shekerjian [His statement became the foundation of the entire investigation by military authorities], "a soldier and a civilian came up to the camp in an automobile. The soldier told me Corporal Baltimore had been shot through the head in the San Felipe District and was lying in the middle of the street with no one to care for him. I questioned both and they said they were sure Baltimore was shot in the head because they could see the blood. I took both men to Major Snow and then went to a telephone and called police headquarters and spoke to Superintendent Brock. He told me Baltimore had just been brought into the police station and Baltimore was not shot but beaten up. I went to Major Snow and told him what Brock had told me. He told me to go down and investigate.

"There were two police officers in camp looking for a Negro boy whom they claimed had stolen a bicycle. They took me to the police station and I went to Supt. Brock's office where I saw Baltimore. I asked him how he was. He said, 'All right, sir.' He had a bad cut over his right forehead. The blood had been washed away. Chief Brock, the officers McPhail and Fyfe and myself were in the room when I questioned Baltimore. Baltimore said he had seen two officers on San Felipe Street and he had gone over and asked one of the officers why he had arrested a soldier that day. The policeman gave no answer except to curse him and tell him to mind his own business. Cpl. Baltimore said he said, 'I am on duty on this beat and when I return to camp I must report it.' The policeman drew his pistol and hit Baltimore over the head. Baltimore dodged and ran. The policeman pulled out his pistol and fired three shots. Baltimore ran into a house and the policeman chased after him, pulled him out of the house and took him to the station. This was what Cpl. Baltimore told me and was also the substance of an affidavit sworn to by Cpl. Baltimore before McPhail and I got there.

"I asked Cpl. Baltimore who the man was. He pointed out Sparks. I questioned Sparks and he said that Baltimore had talked fresh to him. Sparks told him, 'I don't have to report to any nigger.' Baltimore, according to Sparks had said, 'What in the hell do you mean by arresting the soldier!' He, Sparks, fired three shots merely to scare Baltimore and not to hit him. Officer Daniels substantiated the statement made by Sparks with the exception that 'if Baltimore used profanity, [I] did not hear it.'"

Shekerjian's account continued, "An officer investigating on behalf of the police department felt that the entire fault was Sparks's. We discussed as to how he should be punished. One idea was to suspend him, which Mr. Brock had the power to do. Another was to file charges against him. And a third was to have him indicted. I was assured, however, that probably no jury would fine and punish him. Mr. Brock said he would suspend Sparks until the matter was talked over with Major Snow. As I left the office I heard Mr. Brock tell Sparks that he was suspended. I asked whether I could take Baltimore back to camp with me and he said I could.

"Just as I was leaving, another soldier, Pvt. Edwards of Company L was brought in. He was bloody. That was the one Baltimore was inquiring about. Sparks claimed that the soldier came up to him just as he was arresting a colored woman and tried to get her away from him. He eloquently stated that the soldier was drunk when he brought him into the police station. On my way back to the camp, I told Baltimore to do no talking at the camp about the matter, to belittle it so as not to cause any trouble. He told me he understood and that he would do no talking. I then took him to Major Snow . . .

"Major Snow called all the 1st Sergeants together. Cpl. Baltimore was present. Major Snow told them how the matter stood, that the soldiers should be assured of full justice. He told the sergeants to make a full explanation to the companies. This explanation was made at retreat at about six o'clock. Previous to my order, to my returning to camp, Major Snow gave orders for no man to leave camp until further notice. All passes were cancelled. A water-melon party which was to be held that night was postponed to a later date. The camp seemed quiet. I ate supper at 6:30 and then walked around the camp. There were no groups about and I asked several trustworthy men about the feeling in the camp. The answer was that the feeling had died down, that the explanation satisfied the men."

Shekerjian either badly misjudged the mood of the troops or else in little more than an hour something suddenly changed the climate. Just before eight o'clock, the captain started to make a telephone call when he said, "Acting Sgt. Vida Henry called Major Snow and I heard him tell Major Snow he was afraid there was going to be trouble. As I got to the head of the I Company street, I met Major Snow and he said he had just caught three men stealing ammunition from the K Company supply cabinet. Assembly was called at once. . . . Major Snow told me to direct a thorough search of all the companies and for no man to leave the ranks. I went to each company to make sure that the men who were checked were actually present. The companies checked their men off one by one.

"Major Snow explained to the men that the police were at fault and they would be punished. I Company seemed very restless. The men were shifting about on their feet. Several men asked Major Snow questions, they were dissatisfied evidently with the treatment they had received at the hands of the police. I issued orders that all rifles were to be taken to the supply tent and a guard placed over it. I returned to I Company, stopping at each of the companies to be certain that the rifles were turned in. Major Snow told Sgt. Henry to make a check of the company every half hour. He told me to have a guard placed around the tents. . . .

"All this was happening much faster than I am telling it. Men were rushing around wildly. A shot rang out in the I Company street which was followed by two shots near the supply tent. Immediately I Company burst into fire. The shooting was mostly . . . in town but a good many were in the camp. I rushed from one man to another calling on them to cease fire but no attention was paid to me. I was grabbing and shaking each man. Then it gradually came to a cease fire."

Walking about the camp, Shekerjian discovered a group of men lying on the ground, aiming their rifles over a tree stump. He shook each soldier, he said, ordering them to cease firing. "One man helped me," testified the battalion adjutant. "He said to me, 'Captain, for God's sakes, help me hold the ammunition and see if we can stop the firing. . . . Within a few seconds I realized the men had as much ammunition as they wanted. I could do more down in the streets, so I went there."

After a brief lull, recalled Shekerjian, gunfire again shattered the night. "The men were now hollering all over the company street, 'C'mon, let's go. Let's get to it. We've got work to do. Hell, we're going to France. Let's clean up the city.'"

The officer accosted Sergeant Henry and claims he pleaded with the noncom, "For God's sakes, help me make these men realize what they're doing." Shekerjian added that it never occurred to him that Henry might be involved in the disorder, even as the sergeant allegedly told him, "This check that Major Snow has now ordered, it's going to be awfully hard to make a check every half hour." Shekerjian said he responded by pulling out his watch to certify the time and advising Henry that all he had to do was obey his order. "He said, all right, sir."

As the officer reached his tent he said he heard yells. "I looked over and saw a mob going through the I Company supply tent. I grabbed a lantern and ran out. The first man I saw [was] Sgt. Fox. He had a rifle. I grabbed it and said, 'What are you doing with that rifle!' He said, 'Nothing. All the men are getting theirs.' I rushed to the mob and called 'Attention!' to them. No attention was paid to me. I asked them what was the matter. Someone said, 'The mob is coming.' I called out to the men. 'There is no mob coming.' Someone said, 'Yes it is.' I called out again, 'Men, no one will come to this camp to harm you.' They paid no attention to me. They said, 'We're tired of this. We'll take the law into our own hands.' There were cries, 'Give me some more ammunition. Be sure you get enough. Give me a rifle.' I tried to grab a man who had some boxes of ammunition. Everyone was trying to get as much as they could. Someone knocked me over. I got up and put my flashlight on and threw it on him. He said, 'Drop that light or I'll blow a hole through you.'"

Shekerjian identified his assailant as a soldier from Company I. He then named another man who ran by him and ignored a demand that he help the captain quell the disturbance. Shekerjian knew several other soldiers. "I saw them rise and surge forward. I heard them call, 'M Company's gone. Let's go.'"

According to Shekerjian, near-anarchy gripped the battalion as the men rushed about, some intent upon rampaging through Houston while others struggled to remain as ordered in spite of the entreaties of their comrades to follow the mob. "K Company was deserted except for the 1st sergeant. He was walking around dazed, almost in tears. Noncommissioned officers were trying to quiet the men. [Some rioters] told M Company to join them, 'We're staying by our captain. We have a good captain.' I heard Captain Jack's voice. He was going up and down the line keeping order. He said the whole company was all right. L Company . . . was in good shape. There were other men going off the post and yelling. I told them to shut up. Just then someone came up and reported that Pvt. Strong had been shot in the stomach."

What Shekerjian described as a "column" of men surged toward the gate. "I had the feeling it had to be stopped. Cpl. Brown was at the head of the column. He said, 'We'll stick by you, if you'll come with us.' Someone said, 'Put a bullet into him and stop that ——— dog!'" Fortunately for Shekerjian, the soldiers ignored the suggestion and while the armed troops headed into the city streets, he focused on what could be done inside the camp. "Captain James had now secured fair control over his men. There was considerable talking, grumbling, but the men were standing about. I went to Pvt. Strong and had someone carry him into the kitchen and I sent for the doctor (who could not be located)."

At the supply tent, Shekerjian instructed a sergeant to write down the names of those men who were still on post. The soldiers present understood the consequences if they were not listed and made sure that the sergeant inscribed their names. But when the captain told them to surrender their weapons, they refused. "They were much too frightened and said, 'No, we're going to keep our rifles.'"

Ordering everyone to remain in place, Shekerjian sought help. He found some officers from a black Illinois National Guard regiment, including Capt. Joseph Mattes, a white. "He asked if there was anything they could do. 'I told him to get your men into town. That's where help is needed.' Captain Tuggle came up and asked if he could be of any help. I told him help was needed in town and to form his men in a line along Washington Avenue to keep city police from entering the camp and to arrest all colored soldiers."

It was near midnight before Houston quieted down. Troops hastily summoned from Galveston now enforced martial law. Shekerjian spoke to Police Superintendent Brock who reported many of the rioters corralled at the ballpark. Several members of the 24th straggled back to camp during the early morning hours and were lodged in the guardhouse. Two civilians armed with shotguns brought in a soldier but Shekerjian told them to haul the man out of camp and to the county jail.

That afternoon, with the white 19th Infantry Regiment in control of the premises, the battalion formed up and a blanket arrest was made. From the roll calls taken periodically during the night, as many as 156 men appeared to have been involved. An inventory of ammunition supplies revealed 15,200 rounds missing from Company I alone, with lesser but substantial amounts from other units. Bullets had killed sixteen whites or Hispanic Americans and wounded eleven more.

Among the dead was Captain Mattes, gunned down while riding in an open touring car on San Felipe Street with E. S. Meineke, a Houston policeman. They had come upon soldiers shooting up the town, and when Mattes attempted to stop them, the rioters blasted him and the other occupants of the automobile, possibly assuming in the darkness that the vehicle carried city cops. The local police wore olive drab uniforms, impossible to distinguish in the dark from that of the military. In addition to Mattes, Meineke was killed and two of the three soldiers with them wounded. Also murdered was police officer Rufe Daniels who had demurred when his partner Sparks claimed that Corporal Baltimore swore at him. Daniels apparently confronted advancing rioters who approached within five feet of him before they fired the fatal shots.

Four of the men from the 24th died, three from gunfire, including possibly of bullets from their comrades, in violence. The fourth casualty, Sgt. Vida Henry, an eighteen-year veteran who had warned Major Snow of impending trouble and subsequently advised Shekerjian that he thought control impossible, had entered into the orgy of shooting. When he saw order on the brink of restoration and realized what lay ahead for him, he committed suicide.

The military authorities shipped the entire 3d Battalion, the assumed guilty and the clearly innocent, to New Mexico while an inquiry proceeded and arrangements were made for a court-martial. Unlike at Brownsville, an effort was made to develop genuine evidence and to punish only those who committed crimes. And in the Houston riot, there was no question that some black soldiers had indeed shot up the town and murdered a number of citizens, some police officers as well as a member of the army, Captain Mattes. The prosecutors on this occasion not only had eyewitness testimony from white officers like Shekerjian, but through their questioning, persuasive powers and offers of immunity convinced a number of soldiers to testify against their fellows.

Ultimately, in November 1917, sixty-four soldiers stood on the dock at Fort Sam Houston, charged with mutiny in time of war as well as premeditated murder, in the first of several trials. Both the prosecution and the defense counsel, Maj. Harry Grier, stipulated to certain "facts" entered into the court record. Referring to the frequent clashes between city police and civilian workers with the soldiers, the transcript says, "Most of the incidents consisted mainly in applying epithets of opprobrium . . . particular offense to being referred to as 'niggers' even when the term was used without intention of causing any slur on them . . . was invariably met by angry responses, outbursts of profanity and threats of vengeance . . . several cases resulted in soldiers being beaten up . . . colored soldiers actually did receive injuries at the hand of the city police. . . . Mutual mistrust and fear [existed] between the citizens of Houston and the soldiers . . . The military police were instructed to cooperate with the civil authorities but similar instruction to cooperate had not been promulgated to the civil police of Houston."

A total of 165 witnesses paraded before the three-judge court although none of them could provide the prosecution with a coherent account of what actually happened. Nevertheless, a number of townspeople as well as soldiers offered damning, if hearsay, evidence. A female friend of a soldier told the court that she heard Corporal Baltimore boast, "I didn't get the man who beat me but I got his partner." Most of the accused refused to testify and the ones who did denied participation.

The defense relied on raising doubts about the identities of some of the accused and the mitigating factors. Grier stressed statements, "The mob is coming" as indicating the men sought arms for self-preservation rather than to commit murder. The testimony suggested the soldiers believed army regulations specified that "superiors are forbidden to injure those under their authority by tyrannical or capricious conduct or abusive language [or treatment] to preserve their self respect. . . . The colored soldiers could not reconcile themslves to actions of the police authorities with [this] principle." Vida Henry, it was theorized, had been brooding over the recent vicious riot of whites, which killed as many as 125 African Americans in East St. Louis.

The officers who conducted the trial convicted fifty-nine men of various offenses, ranging from the most extreme to lesser ones. The trio of all-white officers sitting as judges sentenced twenty-nine to death, others to long terms of imprisonment and five were acquitted. Three days before Christmas in 1917, Charles Baltimore and a dozen more went to the gallows. Neither Secretary of War Baker nor President Wilson chose to review their sentences before the executions were carried out. Even though white newspapers, North and South approved the action, protests at the swiftness of this action and the absence of any appeal procedures convinced Baker to recommend that Wilson reexamine the cases of the sixteen still condemned. The president commuted six of these but another ten men were hung for the crimes at Houston.

African American leaders and newspapers were not mollified. W. E. B. Du Bois scorned what he viewed as a form of separate but unequal justice. For the murder of 125 citizens in East St. Louis the maximum sentences for convicted whites was five to fifteen years. Ten blacks arrested during those melees received fourteen years in prison. In contrast, with seventeen whites murdered in Houston, nineteen soldiers were hung, another fifty-one went to prison for life and forty more spent time behind bars.

The rancor from events in Houston poisoned prospects for African Americans in the military, even as efforts to employ more men of color continued. Well before the controversy over Charles Young, Secretary of War Baker, in a note to Gen. Hugh L. Scott, the army's chief of staff who successfully lobbied the Wilson administration and Congress to impose a draft, said, "The operation of the selective conscription system will undoubtedly bring into the forces to be trained a substantial number of colored men. It will not be possible to officer these men entirely with white officers nor would it be desirable." He went on to suggest a separate camp, reporting that Howard University might be ideal with its many college graduates.

Fort Des Moines was chosen over Howard, but more significantly, the principles of separation and of who would lead whom were enunciated. Brigadier Joseph Kuhn, speaking for the War College Division of the army wrote, "The War College Division has no hesitation in recommending that if camps for colored citizens are to be established that they be separate from the camps for white citizens." He added, "That colored officers should not be assigned to white organizations requires no argument . . . it is believed that there are many colored men of good character and education who with proper training, would make suitable company officers for the colored organizations forming part of the contemplated drafted force . . . but in general it is believed that our colored citizens make better soldiers if commanded by white officers than they do under officers of their own race."

As a twenty-one-year-old graduate of Howard University, Charles Houston [no kin to the cavalryman] eagerly reported to Camp Des Moines for the course that would make him a second lieutenant. "Morale was high when the camp opened June 15. The fact that we were the first Negroes being trained by the hundreds to become officers of men . . . made the training serious business. We took to training easily and liked it."

Those who had applied to other areas than the infantry inquired why the specialized training was delayed. They were told they could serve only as foot soldiers and if that did not suit them, they would resign. Houston complained, "Other arms of service were being withheld from us solely because we were Negroes. Still it was better to go to war as an infantry officer than to be drafted as privates into labor battalions."

The officer course at Camp Des Moines was in its second month when the riot at Houston occurred. Charles Houston noted that sentiment in the barracks criticized a decision that placed blacks "into a nest of prejudice," but there was general agreement that those who had broken military law should of necessity face the consequences. Trouble closer to home broke out at a local Chinese restaurant that refused service to some black soldiers, although state law specifically prohibited racial discrimination in public eating places. After the mild disturbance, Col. Charles C. Ballou, the white commandant, lectured the men on behaving properly and staying out of places where their presence might cause friction.

The African Americans intent on becoming officers at Fort Des Moines, however uncomfortable with discrimination, probably did not realize that the Brownsville and Houston disorders not only severely punished the soldiers but also would profoundly influence the treatment of all men of color in uniform.

8
World War I

Although some African Americans, including people of substance and influence held differently, many agreed with the view of W. E. B. Du Bois who editorialized in the NAACP's *Crisis,* ". . . *first* your Country, then your rights . . . Certain honest thinkers among us hesitate at that last sentence. They say . . . is it not true that while we have fought our country's battles for one hundred fifty years, we have *not* gained our rights? No, we have gained them rapidly and effectively by our loyalty in time of trial.

"Five thousand Negroes fought in the Revolution; the result was the emancipation of slaves in the North and abolition of the African slave trade. [Actually these results did not follow immediately upon the enlistment and participation of blacks in the cause.] At least three thousand Negro soldiers and sailors fought in the War of 1812; the result was the enfranchisement of the Negro in many Northern States and the beginning of a strong movement for general emancipation. Two hundred thousand Negroes enlisted in the Civil War, and the result was the emancipation of four million slaves, and the enfranchisement of the black man. [One could argue again on the connection of alleged cause and effect.] Some ten thousand Negroes fought in the Spanish-American War, and in the twenty years ensuing since that war, despite many set backs, we have doubled or quadrupled our accumulated wealth."

Having justified the position, Du Bois urged, " Let us not hesitate. Let us, while the war lasts, forget our special grievances, close our ranks shoulder to shoulder with our white fellow citizens in the Allied Nations that are fighting for democracy. We make no ordinary sacrifice but we make it gladly and willingly with our heads lifted high, our eyes lifted to the hills."

However, there was little inclination of whites to have blacks stand shoulder to shoulder with them. Early in the buildup of U.S. forces, a senator questioned the navy's limitations upon blacks. Secretary of the Navy Josephus Daniels, one of the prime movers in the Wilson administration's deprivation of equality for African Americans, tartly answered, "there is no legal discrimination shown against colored men in the Navy. As a matter of policy, however, and to avoid friction between the two races, it has been customary to enlist colored men in the various ratings of the messmen branch; that is cooks, stewards and mess attendants, and in the lower ratings of the fire-room, thus permitting colored men to sleep and eat by themselves." The statement implied that blacks wanted separation and it ran counter to the history of the navy, which until the time of the Spanish-American War did not segregate its sailors.

A memorandum to the army chief of staff in November 1917 reported, "The Commanding General of the 33d National Guard Division has repeatedly pointed out that it is impracticable to use the 8th Illinois Infantry (colored) [the unit to which the ill-fated Captain Mattes belonged] as part of his Division. . . . The Commanding General of the 37th National Guard Division has also repeatedly pointed out that it is impracticable to use the 9th Separate Battalion, (Ohio Infantry 9th Colored) as a part of his division. The Commanding General of the 26th Division took his outfit to France and left the Massachusetts Separate Company and the Connecticut Separate Company (both colored) in the United States."

On the other hand, draft boards in certain localities frequently regarded even physically unfit nonwhites as suitable for meeting the manpower quotas, thereby enabling able-bodied young white men to stay at home. Such practices forced Newton Baker to relieve three draft boards of their powers. Baker also appointed NAACP executive Emmett Scott as an advisor on race relations. The War Department when calling up nearly 700,000 men through selective service sought to maintain a ratio of one black for each seven whites. The draft statutes for World War I contained a specific provision, "White and colored enlisted or enrolled men shall not be organized in or assigned to the same company, battalion, or regiment." For the most part, the African American population was relegated to service, supply, and labor duties. White supremacists regarded putting weapons in the hands of blacks as a threat. Because of what happened at Brownsville and Houston, and how the news was played, even those less antiblack felt anxiety over arming nonwhites. Furthermore, although the army still contained the four regular black units of trained personnel, the 24th and 25th Infantry and the 9th and 10th Cavalry Regiments, it chose not to deploy these outfits for combat service abroad. Instead the professional soldiers and cavalrymen received assignments along the border with Mexico or at outposts in the Philippines and Hawaii.

Although there was a general willingness to make use of blacks as support troops, pressure for the right to fight brought the activation in November 1917 of the combat-intended, 92d Infantry Division, to consist of black draftees with graduates of Fort Des Moines as the junior officers while whites held the senior posts. (Among the noncoms who received commissions were Henry Houston and Howard Queen who as members of the 10th Cavalry engaged the Villistas.) A second infantry division, the 93d, surfaced a month later to absorb African Americans belonging to federalized National Guard units. Some veterans drawn from the regular army black units became cadre for these operations. During World War I, of the 404,308 African Americans in the army, somewhere around 42,000 could be listed as combat soldiers with 90 percent of them serving in the two infantry divisions. (Hewing to its exclusionary policy, the navy enrolled only 5,328 nonwhites, the lowest percentage of blacks ever to serve in that branch during any American war.)

Some of the men newly commissioned, having passed the Fort Des Moines course reported not to the 92d and 93d but for tasks with the service units. Until their arrival, white officers and noncoms directed tasks such as loading supplies in the States and then handling the cargo when it reached France. But when a black officer reported to one of these quartermaster operations, the white noncoms received transfers rather than have them serve under black superiors. A number of National Guard units composed of African Americans included field-grade-level officers—majors and colonels— but when the War Department put together the 93d Division, these individuals did not continue in command slots except for one regiment.

The exclusionary tendencies extended to the Army Nurses Corps, which steadfastly refused to enroll any nonwhites until December 1918, after the Armistice ended World War I. Nor did the American Red Cross admit African Americans. In a perverse display of logic it registered black nurses and then rejected them on the grounds that there were no women of color in the army's medical corps.

With the largest mobilization of Americans since the Civil War and the greatest number of nonwhites ever in uniform, racial incidents involving the military and civilians became frequent. Soldiers whose hometowns were in the North and Far West, less restrictive areas,were stationed in areas where segregation was not only the custom but the law. The white officers in command accepted and attempted to enforce the local discriminatory practices.

All across the South, where many military installations were hastily erected, communities strongly objected to the encampment of nonwhites, particularly those whose home areas lacked a strong Jim Crow tradition. Mayor J. F. Floyd of Spartanburg, South Carolina, spoke for many. "I am sorry to learn that the Fifteenth Regiment [a New York National Guard outfit of blacks which would evolve into the 369th Infantry, a part of the 93d Division] has been ordered here, for with their northern ideas about race equality, they will probably expect to be treated like white men. I can say right here they will not be treated as anything except negroes. We shall treat them exactly as we treat our resident negroes."

His chamber of commerce chimed in. "If any of those colored soldiers go into any of our soda stores and the like and ask to be served they'll be knocked down. Somebody will throw a bottle. We don't allow negroes to use the same glass that a white man may later have to drink out of. We have our customs down here, and we aren't going to alter them." To avoid further offense to the sensitivities of the Spartanburg citizens, the War Department ordered the New York–originated regiment to ship out for France, a bare two weeks after it arrived in South Carolina.

During the spring of 1918, at Camp Funston, Kansas, as the 92d Division passed through the final stages of preparation for combat, a black sergeant denied admittance to a local theater responded with a tirade. The dispute threatened to develop into a full-blown conflict and forced Charles C. Ballou, breveted to major general, who had served with the 24th Infantry, to take notice. He acknowledged that by law, the movie-house manager was not allowed to ban the sergeant but Ballou told his troops he blamed the sergeant, the victim of a discriminatory act, for the trouble. ". . . the row should never have occurred and would not have occurred had the sergeant placed the general good above his personal pleasure and convenience . . . [he was] guilty of the greater wrong in doing anything, no matter how legally correct, that will provoke race animosity." As he had at Camp Des Moines, Ballou urged his men to accommodate the practices of segregation and to avoid places where their presence was not accepted. In a subsequent speech to his troops, Ballou demolished any respect for himself with a naked sanction of white supremacy. "The facts are that white men established this camp and gave you this great opportunity, and if members of this camp make its presence obnoxious, white men will say they don't want it and will not have any colored camps."

The tension between whites and blacks also surged when the two races occupied the same area at a military installation. As a member of the 368th Infantry Regiment, the Fort Des Moines graduate Lt. Charles Houston recalled their dismal location at Camp Meade, Maryland, "the least desirable section of the camp. It was so low that much of it flooded with every rain." He noted one exception to the strict segregation of the races. Both white and black conscientious objectors were housed together in a barracks in the area of the 368th with an armed white guard over them. Houston observed, "The army considered COs as cowards and scum . . . The camp command considered them too low to associate with white soldiers."

Houston had hoped to serve with the field artillery but his request for a transfer was denied. He pondered the curious ways of the army's placement system, with the uneducated, even functionally illiterate black farm hands sent to the artillery, which needed more learned personnel able to understand modern technology, while the better-schooled individuals came to the infantry.

Off post, Houston ran afoul of a white officer who tried to create a lynch mob out of some enlisted men. Fortunately, a military police captain appeared and dispersed the crowd before any violence. Subsequently, there was an altercation involving a black enlisted man during a training exercise. Houston, designated as the prosecutor for a court-martial of the alleged offender, dutifully questioned witnesses, examined the evidence, and concluded the accused was not guilty of any wrongdoing. When the colonel of the regiment learned of Houston's plan to dismiss the charges he became furious. "He wanted to teach the regiment a lesson," said Houston. The colonel abolished the court-martial and had the soldier lodged in the stockade. The incident directed Houston to his later career. "I would study law and use my time fighting for men who couldn't strike back." He eventually became special legal counsel for the NAACP.

Serving their country through the grace of the majority race, attacked or denigrated by civilians and whites in uniform, the soldiers of the 92d and 93d Divisions underwent the typical preparation for combat at facilities in the United States. The men of the 93d as former National Guardsmen seemingly had more military experience than the draftees of the 92d, but most of their previous army training consisted of close-order drill and instruction in armories, hardly the stuff of trench warfare.

Although the two all-black outfits readied themselves for combat, Pershing placed an urgent request for "laborers for forestry, railroad construction and general work." The army chief of engineers proposed that much of this manpower be drawn from African Americans under white noncoms. He admitted, "The class of white men who would seek service . . . in these battalions could not be very desirable and more time would be required to train them than would be necessary with the intelligent colored man . . . There will be vacancies in the noncommissioned grades which must be filled from time to time and unless white men are taken from other ranks and transferred to these battalions there results a permanent vacancy or promotion of a colored man. The promotion of the colored man is then impossible as it gives a mixed class [race] of noncommissioned officers." He also noted a policy that mandated white superiors would be destructive of morale, curb incentive, fail to exploit the talent of well-educated, technically proficient black soldiers, and create serious administrative problems. Nevertheless, he proposed the straw bosses be white to avoid any possibility that the color line for command be breached.

The issue of whites serving under blacks continually vexed the War Department when the quartermaster general was assigned a batch of African Americans, declared unqualified for their original assignments as artillery officers, for stevedore and labor units. To accommodate them, white noncoms in certain of these service battalions were transferred out and replaced by the officers. Major General Frank McIntyre, assistant to the chief of staff, suggested to his boss, "to prevent a recurrence of this nature, it would seem advisable not to commission colored men in the Field Artillery as the number of men of that race who have the mental qualifications to come up to standards of efficiency of the Field Artillery officers is so small that the few isolated cases might be better handled in other branches."

McIntyre failed to mention that the black officers who were deemed incompetent for duty with field artillery because of inadequate "mental qualifications" never took any courses for field artillery. A memorandum to the chief of staff from the War Plans Division pointed out that although they went through infantry instruction "these colored officers did not receive artillery training. They are, therefore, the only officers who have been assigned to artillery regiments of the National Army without previous artillery training, and without undergoing elimination on the grounds of mental or other capacity for artillery work."

Colonel D. W. Ketcham, who wrote this report, followed up, "It is obvious that the colored lieutenants now on duty with the 349th and 350th Field Artillery have received their commissions under less exacting circumstances than any white officers . . . since they have not been required to undergo elimination in an artillery training camp. To this extent, favoritism has been shown them." The War Plans Division officer seems to have felt that the mistake was due to a desire to please African Americans, rather than the result of a segregated system that denied access to schooling in specialties and the inevitable inefficiency of operating separate armies.

Faithful as they were to the principle of segregation, the upper echelons of the War Department staff also wrestled with a shortage of manpower. In June 1918, the director of operations floated the possibility that "colored men might be used to advantage in the lower grades in the supply and ammunition trains of Infantry divisions, the officers, noncommissioned officers and higher grades of mechanics being white . . . arrangements could be made, such as are common in large construction works, whereby the white and colored men can be quartered and messed separately . . . that the use of colored men in this way would be economical and relieve a corresponding number of white men for combatant duty." [Being a white soldier in the U.S. Army in World War I and subsequently in World War II was a mixed blessing.]

The director of the War Plans Division, Brig. Gen. Lytle Brown, wrote a memorandum commenting on this option. "The fighting value of colored men has been much discussed and while there is considerable doubt as to their value for furnishing officer material, it seems to be pretty generally agreed that under white officers or largely officered by white men, their capacity and work as noncomissioned officers and privates, even on the firing line . . . has been considerable . . . It can hardly be said that the negro soldiers are either useless or very greatly inferior when they are properly led.

They should therefore be required, both out of proper appreciation of their own capacity, pride and patriotism and out of proper consideration for other classes of men, to do their full and proper share in winning the war."

The author recognized the political and social implications in how the army deployed African Americans. "It is, moreover, considered a very unsafe policy to utilize colored men in a way to accentuate race discrimination against them. This is not a time to stir up race-feeling which is, under the best conditions, a serious problem with us. If they are to be used in such a way that only subordinate positions are open to them and if they are made to feel that faithful and satisfactory service cannot bring them the reward of advancement to higher grades in the unit which they are serving, it can hardly be supposed that they will give their best efforts or that a proper pride and morale can exist in such units. The colored drafted men will include the best of that race, and it is to be expected that some excellent noncommissioned officer material will be found which should be recognized and utilized."

Having stated a case for a more open approach, Brown focused on the negatives. ". . . experience in this war has shown that the colored draft has furnished material much inferior to the rank and file of the colored regiments of the Regular Army, and in many ways inferior to the excellent material furnished by the white draft. A large proportion of these colored men are of the ignorant, illiterate, day labor classes. A great many of them are of inferior physical stamina and would not hold up under the conditions of strenuous field service and could not withstand the rigors of the damp, cold winter in France. The percentage of sickness among them has been very high, particularly of venereal disease. In colored units it has been extremely difficult to find sufficient noncomissioned officer material and it is almost impossible to find men for clerical and administrative work."

Brown went on to point out that "aside from the question of color, the combatant value of colored draft troops is considerably lower than that of the white draft troops, and that the proportion of reliable fighting men among the colored men must be smaller than among the white men." Brown asserted that while a limited number of nonwhites qualified for combat, the most effective use of these soldiers lay in "communication and service of the rear." He added concerns about troubles arising from both races encamped at the same sites. "In the field it may be extremely difficult to always provide for separate messing and quartering." He concluded that "white and colored men should not at this time be mixed in the same units."

Once on the Continent, the African Americans became the subject for a delicate discussion with the host nation. A secret directive from the French military authorities, apparently at the request of U.S. officers, cautioned against any closeness between their officers and black Americans. "We may be courteous and amiable with these last but we cannot deal with them on the same plane as with white officers without wounding the latter. We must not eat with them, must not shake hands or seek to talk or meet with them outside of the requirement of military service." Furthermore, the French high command warned against high praise for the performance of black Americans and the citizens should refrain from "spoiling the Negroes. [White] Americans become greatly incensed at any public expression of intimacy between white women and black men." (According to W. E. B. Du Bois, he was the first to publish the document, although after the war. When the French Ministry heard of the directive, it ordered all copies collected and burned.)

The first element of the two black infantry divisions to debark in France as part of General Pershing's American Expeditionary Force was the 369th Regiment, nominally part of the 93d. None of the regiments belonging to that organization, however, fought under its banner in World War I as they were parceled out to various French divisions. In the case of the 369th, with the French army ridden by mass defections and mutinies over the senseless slaughter of *poilus* earlier in the year, Pershing gladly sloughed off the black soldiers whom none of his commanders wanted, to the home forces. The French who were accustomed to black soldiers drawn from their colonial possessions in Africa, welcomed the reinforcements. The 369th would become known as the "Men of Bronze."

Colonel William Hayward, commander of the 369th Regiment, told a friend, "Our great American general simply put the black orphan in a basket, set it on the doorstep of the French, pulled the bell and went away." Hayward, a lawyer active in New York State's Republican party, had helped organize the National Guard unit. Historian Bernard C. Nalty describes Hayward as a man who "respected his black troops . . . did not spare himself in looking out for them."

In spite of their loss of American parentage, the orphans, at least in the eyes of the French, adapted extremely well. Shortly before Hayward's men and those of the other three regiments of the 93d went into battle, Col. T. A. Roberts toured the units and reported on all four to Pershing's chief of staff. "The appearance of officers and men is excellent. Discipline is reported to be excellent. The French officers on duty with the regiment [372d] as well as civilians express themselves as highly pleased with the conduct of the men, their discipline and their aptness under instruction. . . . It is a new regiment [371st] formed of men obtained from the draft and the majority of them with no former military experience or training. They are reported to be progressing very rapidly . . . I met the division commander [French] and a number of other officers of adjoining sectors and all were enthusiastic in their comments about the progress and bearing of the 369th." Roberts commented in similar fashion on the 370th.

Toward the end of the war, Hayward submitted a report on his outfit's activities to Pershing, and it reveals that although the troops appeared to have been smoothly absorbed by the French, multiple problems afflicted the organization. "This regiment came to France in 1917, with about 2,000 men and about 50 officers [a very low ratio of the latter to the former], permission to go to war strength [a shortage of perhaps one-third the enlisted men and officers normally dictated in the table of organization] having been denied in the United States. The regiment came to the French Army in March and was reorganized and equipped French at that time, taking over a sector April 8th."

Hayward's account skips over important details. "Equipped French" meant that nation's rifles, bayonets, gas masks, even mess kits, and packs. Following a short, totally inadequate briefing for battle, the men of the 369th still struggling to master the alien gear, marched into the maw of combat, where they depended upon supplies from often uncertain French sources. Language differences bedeviled communications, making coordination with adjacent units haphazard.

After three months of operations, the 369th had settled into its role said Hayward, when the three other regiments from the 93d arrived from the States. With these troops assigned also to the French, "a new scheme of organization was worked out . . . entirely different from the one . . . successfully used by us." Considerable confusion arose, requiring appointment of many "acting" noncoms until after months passed the high command granted permission for a table of organization.

The three restructurings of the 369th undoubtedly affected performance and morale but even worse was the handling of new men. "From time to time replacements have been received in detachments of several hundreds. They have always come without previous notice to the regiment, sometimes equipped, sometimes not equipped and never trained. No officers have accompanied them except for the purpose of delivering them to the regiment. For example, some three hundred recruits reached the regiment a day or two before the Battle of Champagne, July 15, 1918, when the regiment was waiting with its French Division for the attack of the Germans. The day before the Champagne offensive started, September 26th, 1918, in which this regiment participated as one of the assaulting units, six hundred untrained recruits arrived, equipped with gas masks and helmets but having never worn them."

Hayward complained, "The regiment has never had anywhere near its quota of officers. It has had as low as thirty-seven present during the Battle of Champagne and when a considerable gain in officers was apparently in sight, fifteen or twenty officers were always ordered away to school as instructors or students." He added that as a result of the most recent Allied thrust, he was down to fewer than twenty-five men with commissions.

In spite of a lack of manpower and the overseers to lead the troops, Hayward observed that the 369th bore heavier burdens than others. "It has continuously held sectors, with two battalions in line, for a much longer period of time, so I am informed, than any other American regiment, having two weeks rest in six months continual service." Shortages of materials plagued the 369th. "Beginning in March, the regiment theoretically equipped by the French had barely enough equipment to get along with, there being particularly a shortage at all times in horses and wagons."

Hayward griped that Pershing's headquarters even thwarted attempts to pin medals upon his men. "In many cases, during the six months the regiment has been continually under fire, conspicuous examples of bravery among the officers and men has been shown, oftentime in operations concurrent with the French. In these cases our Division General of Army Gouraud has desired to cite the men, and has written to GHQ, AEF for permission. This has been going on continuously since last May and no reply has ever been received nor apparent attention paid to the request, although in one case, the Commander-in-Chief, AEF [Pershing himself] saw fit to mention the gallantry of two of the members of this regiment in an American communiqué. The men of this regiment have accordingly seen their French comrades decorated for the same acts which they have performed at the same time in the same manner."

Efforts by Hayward to obtain leaves for his men, a feature common among other units, were blocked. While all other regiments rotated a certain number of enlisted men home, the opportunity was never afforded the 369th. Nor were any of its captains allowed to return to the States to serve as instructors, another privilege enjoyed by all other regiments.

Having detailed the deficiencies in management and treatment of the 369th Hayward described the consequences. "During the recent offensive in which this regiment participated as the centre regiment of the 161st Division [French] and in which the heights and ridges of Champagne lying between Butte du Mesnil and Main Massiges were stormed, a large percentage of the personnel of the regiment conducted itself in the most heroic manner, standing the terrific losses inflicted without yielding. To the disgrace of the regiment, the Negro Race and the American Army, it must be said that large numbers of enlisted men of this regiment conducted themselves in the most cowardly and disgraceful manner. They absented themselves without leave prior to each of the battles, stealing away in the night, throwing away their equipment, lurking and hiding in dugouts, and in some cases traveling many, many kilometres from the battlefield. This result did not come from any condition of general panic, as the regiment was never attacked, but on the contrary itself attacked the enemy each day. The result was that practically all of the heavy casualties were suffered by the older and better men of the regiment, and of course among the officers. The situation now is such that it is not believed the remainder of the regiment can be made to attack if the cowardly offenders escape punishment. Large numbers should be tried for misconduct in the face of the enemy. There should be wholesale executions following convictions. With all reward for bravery in the form of citations denied this regiment and no punishment for gross cowardice inflicted, the unit cannot be made a fighting unit . . ."

The complaints voiced by Hayward applied to the other African American regiments assigned to the French army. Captain George Marvin, a white liaison officer from the AEF with the French Seventh Army noted, "Officers and men feel that they are being de-Americanized; the officers without any language contact and no adaptability became almost useless, and the men have shown inability to master the French rifle and bayonet; they do not take kindly to the French pack and the French scheme of equipment based upon the wearing of an overcoat. As instances of this non-working scheme, many of the soldiers had thrown away their first-aid packets, for which the French equipment had supplied no place except in the overcoat pocket. Our soldiers had on overcoats with or without pockets; they knew nothing about the use of the French mess kit. Their three blankets had been taken away and substituted by one French blanket.

"The system of requisition and supply [works] very badly. The French expect the negro officers to make requisitions based upon a knowledge of what was required and available by their own French regulations . . . the negro officers had no idea what to ask for and would always wait for someone either to tell them or to dump supplies upon them . . . The men had to haul wagons four miles by hand . . . and the horses then provided . . . were in some cases unbroken. . . . the 370th Regiment during its month in this sector has had practically no training; they have never dug a trench, had no target practice with their new arms . . ."

Unlike the 93d, the 92d functioned as an intact division but it too served under French commanders except for a short period toward the end of the war. It suffered because the top leadership showed little confidence in the ability of blacks to fight. The commanding general, Ballou, blamed incompetent black officers, the assignment of senior whites "rabidly hostile to the idea of commissioning blacks." And although he talked of equal opportunity, he regarded blacks as tempermentally unsuited for leadership or combat, particularly at night. Most of the officers responsible for preparing the 92d to enter combat during its stay in the United States did not accompany the division to Europe, an arrangement that often leads to inadequate training. Chagrined at failure which doomed his future career, Ballou savaged his black officers, convening courts-martial for thirty lieutenants and captains on the grounds of cowardice. The all-white offficers sitting in judgment sentenced four men to die for cowardice in the face of the enemy. A review board trimmed the punishment to extended prison terms.

Pershing's headquarters transferred the 92d to the American Second Army under Lt. Gen. Robert L. Bullard who met with the remaining black officers and at least convinced them he desired better communications between white superiors and those of lesser rank. One brigade of the 92d under Bullard's direction advanced the Allied line, repelled enemy attacks, and even aided a French unit in distress, but another element of the division did not push forward at the pace demanded by Pershing.

Nevertheless the Americans acquitted themselves well enough to draw praise from their commander, General Gouraud. The regimental leader of the 370th, objecting to the practice of passing his organization among various French divisions noted, "both Generals Mittelhausser (36th) and Goybet (157th) have expressed a desire to hold onto the regiments they have; the latter once told me that he could ask nothing better than to have a complete division of American troops. Gen. Mittelhausser had done everything in his power to hold this regiment with his division, but the GHQ has ruled otherwise." When Pershing decided he would like to retrieve the regiments assigned to the French for use as labor troops, Marshal Ferdinand Foch, commander of the armies in which the 93d served, demurred at the loss of "combatants." Although their American guests frowned upon distribution of honors to its African Americans, the French issued the Croix de Guerre (cross of war) to three regiments and one company.

Hayward had protested the AEF's great reluctance to acknowledge the achievements of individual black soldiers. Still, a handful managed to gain recognition. As early as 14 May 1918, not long after the 369th took its place on the front lines, a twenty-four-man German patrol sneaked through the barbed-wire emplacements in search of prisoners for intelligence purposes. They targeted an outpost manned by five Americans, including Pvt. Henry Johnson and Pvt. Needham Roberts who were on watch while the other three men slept in a dugout.

Colonel Hayward wrote a letter to the wife of Johnson and described the action. "Your husband . . . has been at all times a good soldier and a good boy of fine morale and upright character. To these admirable traits he has lately added the most convincing numbers of fine courage and fighting ability. I regret to say at the moment that he is in the hospital, seriously, but not dangerously wounded, the wounds having been received under such circumstances that every one of us in the regiment would be pleased and proud to trade places with him . . .

"We had learned some time ago from captured German prisoners that the Germans had heard of the regiment of Black Americans in this sector, and the German officers had told their men how easy to combat and capture them it would be. So this raiding party came over, and on the contrary Henry Johnson and Needham Roberts attended very strictly to their duties. At the beginning of the attack the Germans fired a volley of bullets and grenades and both of the boys were wounded, your husband three times and Roberts twice, then the Germans rushed the post expecting to make an easy capture. In spite of their wounds, the two boys waited coolly and courageously and when the Germans were within striking distance opened fire, your husband with his rifle and Private Roberts from his helpless position on the ground with hand grenades. But the German raiding party came on in spite of their wounded and in a few seconds our boys were at grips with the terrible foe in a desperate hand-to-hand encounter, in which the enemy outnumbered them ten to one.

"The boys inflicted great loss on the enemy but Roberts was overpowered and about to be carried away when your husband, who had used up all of the cartridges in the magazine of his rifle and had knocked one German down with the butt end of it, drew his bolo from his belt. A bolo is a short heavy weapon carried by the American soldier, with the edge of a razor, the weight of a cleaver, and the point of a butcher knife. He rushed to the rescue of his comrade, and fighting desperately, opened with his bolo, the head of the German who was throttling Roberts, and turned to the Boche who had Roberts by the feet, plunging the bolo into the German's bowels. This one was the leader of the German party, and on receiving what must have been this mortal wound, exclaimed in American English, without a trace of accent, 'Oh, the son of a ——— got me,' thus proving that he was undoubtedly one of the so-called German-Americans who came to our country, not to become a good citizen, but to partake of its plenty and bounty and then return to fight for the kaiser and help enslave the world . . .

"Henry laid about him right and left with his heavy knife, and Roberts, released from the grasp of the scoundrels, began again to throw hand grenades and exploded them in their midst, and the Germans, doubtless thinking it was a host instead of two brave Colored [sic] boys fighting like tigers at bay, picked up their dead and wounded and slunk away, leaving many weapons and part of their shot riddled clothing, and leaving a trail of blood, which we followed at dawn near to their lines. We feel certain that one of the enemy was killed by rifle fire, two by your husband's bolo, one by grenades thrown by Private Roberts and several others grievously wounded. So it was in this way the Germans found the Black Americans. Both boys have received a citation of the French general commanding and will receive the Croix de Guerre . . .

"Some time ago, the great General Gouraud placed in my hands the sum of 100 francs to be sent to the family of the first one of my soldiers wounded in the fight with the enemy under heroic circumstances. Inasmuch as these boys were wounded simultaneously, and both displayed great heroism, I think it but fair to send to each one-half of this sum. Accordingly, I am enclosed New York exchange for the equivalent of fifty francs. I am sure that you have made a splendid contribution to the cause of liberty by giving your husband to your country and it is my hope and prayer to bring him back to you safe and sound, together with as many comrades as humanly possible. . . . But it must be borne in mind that we cannot all come back, that none of us can come back until the job is done."

An official account suggests that the sound of a wire clipper snapping a strand alerted the pair and they fired a rocket to illuminate the area. Although the colonel makes no mention of them, the three others at the outpost were trapped in the dugout. Johnson, a former porter for the railroad depot in Albany, brought to bear his French-issue Labelle rifle with its puny three-cartridge magazine and emptied the clip. Out of ammunition he now faced a soldier with a pistol. Johnson swung his rifle against the head of the attacker who wore no helmet in order to preserve silence.

According to this version, "Some time later, during the subsequent offensive, an officer of our regiment who read German, found a diary of a German officer in a captured sector. In the diary was a description of the Henry Johnson fight from the German viewpoint. Our estimate of numbers was verified but the conclusion of the Germans was their raiding patrol had run into a superior force of Americans placed to ambuscade them."

Later, his white company commander, Capt. Arthur Little, interviewed Johnson while medics treated him at an aid station. Little, relying on his ear for dialect, reported Johnson's words, "Suh, Cap'n Suh, yoo all doan' want to worry 'bout me. Ah'm all right. Ah've been shot befo." In spite of rendering a minstrel-show patter, Little submitted Johnson and Roberts for decorations and also pushed visiting journalists like then-famous Irvin S. Cobb, to play up the story in their newspapers. The publicity helped. As Hayward wrote, Johnson was awarded France's highest military honor, the Croix de Guerre, the first African American to receive the award.

Another official citation for valor reported an incident in which eight Germans led by an officer infiltrated the American positions, surprising and capturing half a dozen doughboys and Lt. Gorman R. Jones. "Our group was forced to put up their hands and lead the way through a *boyaux* [French slang for trenches] towards the German lines. The captured officer [Jones] was in the lead and he led the party to a very advanced point where he had earlier that evening placed a small group with a *Chauchat* [light automatic rifle]. As the party advanced and approached this point, Lt. Jones called out, 'Sgt. Butler, don't shoot. It's Lt. Jones and some of our men made prisoners and being driven off by the Germans.'

"Sgt. Butler answered, 'Not yet, but soon.' Lt. Jones called, 'Right!' and leaped over the parapet. His men followed him. At that instant Sgt. Butler opened fire with his automatic rifle. A number of our men were shot as they tried to escape but the entire German patrol was annihilated." Butler and the other enlisted men were African Americans.

On 29 September 1918, Lt. George S. Robb, a black officer, led his platoon in an assault. In recommending him for a Medal of Honor, a citation reported, "He was severely wounded by gun fire. He remained with his platoon until ordered to the dressing station by his company commander, but in forty-five minutes he was back. Early the next morning he was again wounded but remained with his platoon. Later in the day, a shell bursting near him added two more wounds, the same shell killing his company commander. Whereupon, Robb assumed command of the company and organized its position. He displayed wonderful courage and tenacity at critical times. He was the only officer of his battalion who advanced beyond the town and by attacking machine guns and snipers, he contributed greatly in aiding his battalion to hold its objective." Despite the description and request for the country's highest award, Robb went unrecognized.

During the attack at Champagne mentioned by Hayward, the 371st Regiment also engaged the enemy. Squad leader Cpl. Freddie Stowers was in the vanguard of the Americans assaulting Hill 188. As the Americans advanced, the enemy ceased firing and climbed up on the trench parapets with their arms up as if to surrender. When the black doughboys crossed an open stretch of land within less than 100 yards of the German positions, the foe suddenly jumped back into their positions and resumed firing rifles, machine guns, and mortars. Company C, Stowers's outfit, incurred about 50 percent casualties.

Most of the officers and noncoms were out of action but Stowers rallied the survivors. He led a successful fight to wipe out one machine-gun position but when crawling forward toward a second a burst from that weapon fatally wounded him. Before he died, he urged his fellow soldiers on and they overran the Germans. His commander put Stowers in for a citation but not until 1991 did he gain full recognition as President George Bush awarded a Medal of Honor to his family.

The African American soldiers who came to France frequently expressed their delight at the native hospitality, friendly receptions that caused consternation among white Americans. Charles Houston, the young lieutenant with the 368th Infantry, which reached the continent well after other units had been committed to combat, wrote that the regiment was encamped about twelve kilometers from the town of Vannes with its population of 10,000. "The first weekend we were in town probably took a lot of Americans by surprise. Negro officers appeared in the two best hotels; one of which, the Hotel du Dauphin, was being operated by its French owner under contract with the American Red Cross as an officers' hotel. The ladies of the town began to show a keen interest in this new set of officers.

"By the third week, however, American race prejudice had got itself organized. Reserved signs suddenly appeared at the best tables in some of the hotel dining rooms and one or two tea rooms announced they were booked up with private parties." Houston also noted that the preferred rooms at hotels were no longer available to men of color.

During World War I, an estimated 25,000 American women sailed to Europe in support of the Allies and the AEF. The largest specialty, 10,000 nurses, worked under the auspices of the American Red Cross or in the Army Nurses Corps, both of which had drawn the line against black participation. The U.S. Army employed about 350 women, again all white, either as telephone operators for the Signal Corps or in the Quartermaster branch. These auxiliaries remained civilians throughout the war. Beyond a few other organizations that provided some technical skills, the YMCA, YWCA, Salvation Army, the Quakers, and nearly another 100 foreign and domestic agencies recruited an additional 10,000 females, to provide aid and comfort to the troops.

Only half a dozen black women, out of thousands who applied, managed to reach Europe. Only the YMCA sponsored black welfare workers overseas and these were mostly men. The most notable black women involved were Addie Waites Hunton, a forty-eight-year-old former college dean, and Kathryn Johnson who together wrote a book about their experiences, *Two Colored Women with the American Expeditionary Force.* They too endured slights, discrimination, and outright insults. With African American doughboys banned from many canteens or else denied service by the white women running them, Hunton, Johnson, and a third person, Mrs. James Curtis, widow of a former ambassador to Liberia, operated a canteen for men of color. Barred from working close to the front, the women mainly succored noncombatants, the so-called pioneer elements.

By Armistice Day, 11 November, the nonwhite combatants counted 750 dead and more than 5,000 wounded. The 92d Division remained in France after the Armistice. When it prepared for the voyage home in 1919, Pershing said to its members, "I want you officers and soldiers of the 92d Division to know that the 92d Division stands second to none in the record you have made since your arrival in France. The American public has every reason to be proud of your record." The overblown praise smacks more of public relations than an objective evaluation since the 92d's record as a division was hardly exceptional and Pershing had shown reluctance to employ it in the fighting. But although some African American units may have performed at a mediocre or even substandard level (as did some white ones) individual black soldiers and officers once again had put their lives on the line for the country that refused them the civil equality it granted all other citizens and which socially despised and oppressed them.

The harsh realities of American attitudes struck the black members of the AEF even before they landed on U.S. shores. When some members of the 92d Division arrived at Brest to board transports, the troops received orders to help load coal for the boilers of the battleship USS *Virginia*. It was assumed that when they completed the arduous, dirty task, they would remain aboard for the trip to the States. Captain H. J. Ziegmine wrote a letter of appreciation to the Company D commander, 367th Regiment, for a job well done. "I take great pleasure in commending you and the officers and men under your command in connection with the coaling of this ship and at the same time wish to express my appreciation of the good conduct and the high state of discipline of your command."

However, while Ziegmine welcomed the labor of Company D he declared the men unfit as passengers. He told the embarkation authorities, "No colored troops had ever traveled on this ship," and he intended to preserve that record. The soldiers went ashore aboard a tug and waited for a transport that would accept them. The navy carried its segregation policy for the returning army to a ludicrous extreme. On the *Siboney* the officers' mess seated a maximum of 200. The manifest for one voyage listed 399 whites, a single black. To maintain separation, the navy served 200 whites, then the remaining 199, and finally the lone black officer, shunned throughout the trip by all but a single white man, ate at a third seating.

9
Between the Wars

Hostility toward blacks intensified during the final year of World War I. The African Americans in uniform seemed less willing to accept the role handed them. That resistance infuriated whites. At the same time, the expansion of segregation by the Wilson administration may well have encouraged extremism, and the riot at Houston undoubtedly inflamed many who believed African Americans a threat. Membership in the Ku Klux Klan boomed, klaverns appeared not just in the South but in other parts of the country. The melting pot boiled over. In 1918 alone, mobs lynched seventy-eight people. In the following year, ten black men who had served their country were among the seventy-nine strung up and burned. Non-Southern cities like Omaha, Nebraska, and Duluth, Minnesota, witnessed their first lynchings. In 1919, a black youth drowned in Chicago on the shores of Lake Michigan after a gang of whites pelted him with stones, preventing him from getting to the beach. His offense was swimming in an area whites considered for their use only. The race riot that followed killed a total of thirty-eight people from both races and injured another five hundred. That was the worst of some twenty-five such melees during a single year.

The ardent supporter of black participation in World War I, W. E. B. Du Bois, observing a turn for the worse rather than the better, soured on the entire enterprise, particularly as those intent on defaming blacks continued to rant. In February 1919, at the behest of the NAACP, Du Bois sailed to Europe with the twin purposes of investigating how African Americans had been treated and to represent to the delegates, wrestling with a peace treaty, the interests of Africa.

In his autobiography some years later, Du Bois wrote, "With the Armistice came disillusion. I saw the mud and dirt of the trenches; I heard from the mouths of soldiers the kind of treatment that black men got in the American army; I was convinced and said that American white officers fought more valiantly against Negroes within our ranks than they did against the Germans. I still believe this was largely true. I collected some astonishing documents of systematic slander and attack upon Negroes and demands upon the French for insulting attitudes toward them.

"Everywhere an opportunity presented itself I talked with white officers," remembered Du Bois. "In almost every instance they [black soldiers] were referred to as cowards, rapists, or other remarks made relative to their work which were absolutely untrue, and which were intended to cause a bad impression."

One of the predictable charges against black soldiers was that while quartered in France they had embarked on a campaign of sexual assault. Colonel Allen Greer, chief of staff for Ballou and the man who signed the infamous bulletin from Ballou regarding the sergeant barred from a theater, wrote a letter to a senator in which he referred to "about thirty cases of rape." Du Bois investigated and found five convictions for attempted rape, and one execution for committing that crime. He noted that the 92d's official photographer took pictures of the hanging but two hours later did not cover the awards of the Croix de Guerre to a pair of black officers. Du Bois wrote to the mayors of a number of French villages inquiring whether they had found that African Americans encamped in their areas had attacked local women. The officials unanimously responded they knew of no such problem.

Outraged by the tenor and direction of the country, Du Bois wrote, "By the God of heaven we are cowards and jackasses if now that the war is over we do not marshal every ounce of our brain and brawn to fight a sterner, longer, more unbending battle against the forces of hell in our land."

Du Bois could muster statistics to demonstrate that the accusations of lust gone amok lacked any foundation. Much more difficult to combat were the postmortems allegedly detailing the achievements and failures of black military units in World War I, most of which were authored by those who believed African Americans unfit for fighting, much less command.

With the U.S. military once again engaged in downsizing, the general staff began to evaluate performances during World War I and the uses of available men. Allan Greer, clearly in the ranks of racists, as a member of the American occupation troops in Germany in 1919, authored a "circular letter" that deprecated the abilities of black soldiers. More influential, Maj. Gen. W. H. Hay contributed an opinon based upon his "20 years of command of colored troops of the Regular Army, officered entirely by white officers, and second on my experience in command of the 184th Infantry Brigade of the 92d Division . . . all company officers being negroes."

The former brigade leader said, "Officered by white men, negroes make excellent soldiers. . . . The failures among all the divisions, where failures have occured have been due primarily to the lack of trained leaders in the smaller units. This is true of all the white combat divisions, so far as I know. The negro needs trained leadership far more than the white man needs it . . . The negro has confidence in the white man as a leader, and granted proper initial training before going into battle, he will follow the white leader with the utmost bravery and without fear of personal consequences."

Having paid tribute to African American courage and ability to fight, Hay damned blacks, "On account of the inherent weaknesses in negro character, especially lack of intelligence and initiative, it requires a much longer time of preliminary training to bring a negro organization up to the point of training where it is fit for combat than it does in the case of white men."

He contended, "One of the peculiarities of the negro as a soldier is that he has no confidence in his negro leaders, nor will he follow a negro officer into battle, no matter how good the officer may be, with the same confidence that he will follow a white man." The general pronounced, "The negro as an officer is a failure and this applies to all classes of negro officers, whether they be men of long experience and training in the Regular Army, as noncommissioned officers or whether they be men of education who gained their commissions through the Officers Training Camp.

"The fact that a negro holds a commission, leaves him still a negro with all the faults and the weaknesses of character inherent to the negro race, and as compared with the negro soldiers, the officer has the same faults, which are exaggerated by the fact that he wears an officer's uniform." Hay accused black officers of being more concerned with personal appearance and enjoying themselves than performing their duty. He denounced them as "without moral integrity," as cowards in battle who would abandon their troops "at the first signs of artillery or machine gun fire. . . . Negroes should not be used as commissioned officers in any combat units."

Hay strongly urged total segregation. "So far as I am personally concerned, I am unalterably opposed to mixing of negro and white officers, under any circumstances, other than those which arise in the performance of military duties. One of the greatest difficulties that I encountered in handling negro officers was that they are more concerned with trying to force race equality than they were in trying to become familiar with their military duties."

He allowed that nonwhites might "be used with some safety to form combat units" but only if under white officers and trained for at least twice the length of time ordinarily afforded their white counterparts. If that were not feasible then they should be restricted to labor and pioneer battalions.

Greer continued to wage war against African American officers. He followed up on Hay's broadside with a summary of what he said he experienced with the 92d Division. He claimed all the black officers assigned to the engineers and artillery had to be replaced because of their "unfitness." "I observed the negro officer very carefully during the thirteen months which I served with the Division. Taken as an average their ignorance was colossal. I do not remember a single patrol report coming from an officer that ever gave sufficient information to base any plan thereon, . . . Nearly always the negro officer had the same attitudes, so far as veracity was concerned, as the negro soldier."

Perhaps the most damaging blow to the prospects for African Americans in the army came from Charles Ballou. He pointed to serious shortcomings in the staffing of the 92d Division. "The Secretary of War gave personal attention to the selection of the white officers of the higher grades, and evidently intended to give the Division the advantage of good white officers. This policy was *not* continued by the War Department. Many excellent officers, desirous of remaining with the Division, were, on promotion, assigned to other organizations notwithstanding the fact that vacancies existed for them in the 92d, which was made the dumping ground for the discards, both white and black. Some of the latter were officers who had been eliminated as inefficient, from the so-called 93d Division ["so-called" because it actually never operated as a division during the war].

"It took nearly five months to get white Captains of Engineers. Meanwhile the companies of the Engineer Regiment were officered by negroes who had never had an hour's previous instruction in Engineering, except as Infantry. Similarly negro officers with no artillery training were assigned to batteries of Artillery. The Field Signal Battalion suffered equally."

Ballou then began to systematically destroy the possibilities for nonwhites in the army. "In Mexico, on my examination for a Colonelcy, General Pershing asked *one* question: 'How does the negro compare with the white man as a soldier?' I replied essentially as follows: 'The colored soldier is as physically brave, strong and capable as the white soldier. He is more contented and obedient and endures hardship with less growling. On the other hand, he has little capacity for initative, is easily stampeded if surprised, and is therefore more dependent than the white man on *skilled leadership.*'"

Ballou said he now wanted "to modify" those of this remarks that dealt with bravery. "I forgot that the average negro is a rank coward in the dark, and I subsequently realized to the full how worthless this trait rendered him in the service of Security and Information [patrols for defense and intelligence gathering]."

He showed slightly more understanding than many of his associates in his explanation for what he perceived as the behavior of the black soldier. "Both his faults and his virtues are the natural result of his environment and education. Born of slave parents or grandparents, he is the child of people in whom slavish obedience and slavish superstition and ignorance were ingrained . . ." Ballou appraised his subject as a fair rifleman, artilleryman, or engineer, but very poor with machine guns, poor in signal service, "weak in the solution of problems—in fact in everything that required the exercise of judgment and arriving at a decision."

He heaped scorn on the African American troops and especially their officers as trench warfare infantrymen, criticizing them as "useless" for patrols where he said they more or less fictionalized their information. He was particularly harsh on the efforts of black officers and stressed that nonwhites could only succeed if they had even better leadership than white soldiers.

It could hardly have surprised anyone when he concluded, "It is probable that philanthropic considerations, or at any rate considerations not purely military, influenced decisions regarding the use of negro officers; but even so it is believed that the decisions were erroneous. No good came, or could come, to the colored race from imposing upon it responsibilities and burdens it could not creditably sustain. Such action was unfair to the race and unfair to the handful of white officers whose reputations were bound up with the achievements of the colored troops."

Furthermore, according to the former general—he had been dropped back to a colonel—African Americans disrespected officers of their own race. ". . . the mass of colored troops distrusted their colored officers. They had been reared under white domination, and to them a *colored* officer was simply a 'stuck-up' nigger. The negro officer therefore experiences a certain handicap in the prejudices of his own race as well as in those of the whites."

Obviously, he was well aware that his own career had suffered when his division was regarded as ineffective. That may explain the rather contradictory statements he made in the memorandum. "In attack, the negro directly reflected the qualities of the leader that he could *see* and *hear.* This trait was well exemplified in the Argonne. Some officers and their commands drifted to the rear—the officers not saying one word to prevent it . . . Yet a few other officers 'stuck'—and in every case their men 'stuck' with them."

He also recognized how prejudice affected decisions. "In the last battle of the war, the Division did some very good aggressive work, so far as the companies were concerned, and the same would have been done in the Argonne had there not been too much eagerness to get the negroes out while their credit was *bad* as many preferred it should remain."

Ballou reiterated his conviction that darkness terrified African Americans. ". . . even in open warfare there is such a thing as night; and it is then that the colored soldier, anywhere under fire, or where he is conscious of unusual danger, need capable and aggressive leadership that he respects and looks to for his salvation."

Ballou recognized a critical problem in the policy that limited blacks to no higher than company-grade-officer levels. The arrangement restricted promotions strictly to replacement of a black lieutenant or captain casualty or for some reason removed from the division. In a faint overture to fairness, Ballou declared that when the War Department prescribed less stringent requirements and lowered "intellectual equipment" for entrance to officer training, "it *gave* the colored man something *because he was black.* When it limited him to certain grades in the 92d Division it *deprived* him of something *because he was black.* Both acts were wrong."

He praised his troops for their handling of sanitation, supplies, and transportation. "The work of the Trains was excellent, and no Division in France kept its animals, harness, wagons, motor trucks, motor cars and motorcycles in better condition than the 92d.

"General Bullard [the Alabaman commander of the Second Army] said this was due to the fact that 'A niggah just likes a hawse'—but he knew nothing of the facts, or else preferred to ignore them. The negro was carefully taught how to care for transportation, and then closely observed. He soon learned that the penalty for any neglect or disobedience of instructions meant that he would be transferred on that very day to a front-line company of infantry whose captain would receive instructions to put him in front of the trenches repairing wire, under the eyes of German snipers. It was wonderful how artillery and engineer drivers and chauffeurs braced up under the example of a few from their sacred organizations thus summarily converted into 'doughboys' and given a front seat in the performance."

Ballou asserted that all of the deficiencies of African American soldiers was "deducible from our knowledge and experience" before World War I. The comment indicates ignorance of the only war experience within the memory of then-active participants, the Spanish-American War, where black soldiers performed as well as any combatants, although they were led by whites. He may have been misled by revisionist histories of the time.

Ballou sneered at his superior Bullard for ignorance "of the facts," and indeed the former head of the Second Army was, if anything, more biased than the subordinate. A veteran of the Spanish-American War where he served with the 3d Alabama Volunteer Infantry, a black regiment whom he had lauded for their restraint while abused by the local citizenry and touted as an example of soldiers who could be relied upon in an emergency, Bullard now denigrated the worth of black troops. "Poor Negroes. They are hopelessly inferior . . . If you need combat soldiers, and especially if you need them in a hurry, don't put your time upon Negroes. The task of making soldiers of them and fighting with them, if there are any white people near, will be swamped in the race question. If racial uplift or racial equality is your purpose that is another matter."

Neither Bullard nor Ballou had any experience with the four regiments of the 93d division which, in spite of the handicap of unfamiliar equipment while serving with the French, apparently fought creditably. Certainly the more than 3,000 casualties indicated a willingness to fight.

William N. Colson and A. B. Nutt, a pair of black, junior officers in the 92d readily admitted, "The 92d Division was a tragic failure. It was a failure in organization. It was a failure in morale. It was a failure in accomplishment." However, unlike their white superiors who discerned some inherent weakness in African Americans as the cause of the 92d's weak record, they described their outfit as victimized.

Writing in an issue of *The Messenger,* they noted that while expected to operate as a cohesive whole, their division trained in pieces and never assembled in one area until the final days of the war. With African Americans who had education at a premium and assigned to more technical or clerical operations, about 40 percent of the ranks of the 92d were classified as illiterate. From their observations, Colson and Nutt identified the white officers as largely drawn from the South because of the prevailing belief that men from that region knew best how to deal with African Americans. Instead they appeared unsympathetic or openly hostile.

The two black officers, graduates of the program at Fort Des Moines, remarked that the white instructors showed preference for the former Regular Army enlisted men and noncoms who behaved with the expected deference to their white superiors. Commissions went to unqualified people and even on a whim. They claimed one lieutenant earned his gold bars for singing plantation songs. They confirmed that freshly minted officers never attended special schools but went off to artillery, machine-gun, and other technical assignments without any training other than the basic infantry course. The two critics said constant shifting of white, upper-echelon staff hampered effectiveness and they spoke of inadequate equipment once the division reached France. But these African American alumni of OCS were voices from outside the military establishment and given little credence.

Colonel Vernon Caldwell, whose experience covered African American soldiers in Cuba and the Philippines, and who commanded one of the regiments of the 92d Division, offered a sophisticated and intellectual dissent from the general condemnation of blacks as combat soldiers. He began on the premise that organization of nonwhites into units of regimental or larger size was a mistake. "I think the largest unit of colored troops should be the battalion. In organizing them into the larger units the race classification fact is stressed and a condition is established where criticism and prejudice concentrates. There is created in all minds the impression that they are not selected but that they are segregated and the segregation is based on inferiority. It is a matter of every day experience that sentiment and opinion acts cumulatively as the mass increases where segregation is applied. Red light district, Nob Hill, Italian quarter, business district, etc."

Caldwell argued, "Most military men recognize that national defense is no longer a matter of a Regular Army but that it is, and always has been when correctly grasped, a matter of being able to make full use of its entire man power . . . it is fairly evident that the colored people of the United States form an important military asset and the more they are segregated, the less they will regard themselves, and the less others will regard them as an amalgamated part of the whole. In other words, the more they are separated into masses, the more they will see their interests as things apart from the interests of the whole; others will also see it the same way. This will not tend towards harmony or team work.

"As far as possible I believe that every white regiment should have either a Company or Battalion of colored troops, and that there should be no colored regiments or higher units." Although not an appeal for total integration, it was a recommendation for a much closer relationship between units made up of the two races.

Nor did Caldwell believe that only whites could lead. "I consider that the colored officers assigned to the regiment [during World War I] were probably the best qualified that could be supplied under the circumstances and that the best policy to follow was to eliminate as few as possible and to make them as well qualified tactically as possible . . . From the foregoing experience and from other experience in Cuba and the Philippines I am of the opinion that it is not objectionable to officer colored troops with colored officers, and as a matter of policy I consider it very objectionable not to do so to a considerable extent."

Caldwell analyzed the kind of training given troops and from his experience found that too often the authorities skimped on teaching tactical principles and methods to black soldiers because, "It is assumed to be beyond them." Instead, the belief that these men more readily absorbed "display features"—appearances through dress uniforms and marching—brought a focus on these noncombat activities. Caldwell argued that "a colored regiment which cannot deploy and advance into action intelligently, rather than mechanically, no matter how well it parades, turns out the guard, etc., is of little value."

After delving into technical aspects of instruction further, Caldwell returned to the theme of a more integrated army. "Personally, I think it is a waste of time to consider whether we shall have colored troops and colored officers. It is quite probable that in the future as in the past circumstances will arise to compel us to have both. . . . The National Defense problem is national and not racial. It is dependent upon citizenship rather than color. I think that colored troops will do much better where they are associated as component parts of white organizations. This idea as to its worth depends upon the fact that in civil life the colored people have done much better where there has been a certain amount of association with reputable whites." Having implied an even greater heresy suggesting the merits of a better-integrated civilian society at a time when the country was headed pell mell in the opposite direction, Caldwell's proposition for a modification of racial policy in the army could hardly have converted many decision makers.

With almost no one to speak on behalf of the black soldier from within the military establishment, except for Caldwell, and the civilian leaders of African Americans bound up with other issues, the status of the nonwhite member of the army just about hit bottom. Charles Young, in retirement, died of heart disease. Ben Davis and John E. Green, commissioned at the same moment, traded foreign legation posts, Philippine duty, and staff position teaching at Wilberforce.

The results of the treatises offered by the likes of Greer, Bullard, Ballou, and others culminated in a study on the Organization and Training of Negroes at the General Staff College at Washington, D.C., which informed students, "The negro is mentally inferior to the white in general." Citing alleged examinations of brain stems it said, "In childhood the negro is sharp, intelligent and full of vivacity but on approaching the adult period a gradual change sets in. The intellect seems to become clouded . . . animation giving place to a sort of lethargy and brightness yielding to indolence." The explanation given for the decline lay in the brain's failure to develop. ". . . education cannot create mental powers; it can only *develop* that which is innate." Mindful of the critiques of the records for the 92d Division, the paper suggested that black units should be attached to white divisions.

The African American presence in the army declined sharply after the war, even before the official pronouncments on the lack of intellectual or emotional talents desired in soldiers. The end of the war shrank the standing army down to 30,000 and in the scramble for places by the military career-minded, the first cuts lopped off blacks. The War Department in 1919 barred enlistment of nonwhites except for those who had soldiered in the Regular Army, and those admitted could enter only the infantry. Limited allowances were granted to a few special services. The policy was onerous because despite the hardships and the indignities inflicted upon them, a substantial number of black soldiers considered the army a more promising occupation than they could hope for in civilian life. Far more African Americans than whites sought to re-up.

Faced with the need to drastically reduce the total of men in uniform, the top brass sought ways to rid themselves of what they believed the least desirable units. The bean counters of the day cast their eyes upon the four black regiments created by Congress right after the Civil War. Military combat structure during the 1920s mandated two regiments to a brigade. Abolition of either the 24th or 25th Infantry Regiments, for example, would force pairing the survivor with a white outfit, an unthinkable arrangment. Prevented from doing away with any of the quartet of regiments reserved for blacks, the War Department, in its zeal to provide more slots for whites, sharply reduced their strength, enabling expansion of such all-white operations as the Air Corps. In a bookkeeping sleight of hand, black soldiers, listed on rosters as troopers from the cavalry or as infantrymen, drove trucks, worked security details, groomed horses, and tended stables at West Point for the cadets and staff, thereby creating additional opportunities for Caucasians.

As secretary of the NAACP, Walter White inquired of the War Department the restrictions upon black service, particularly with regard to the fast-expanding Air Corps. Major George Van Horn Mosely, then acting chief of staff, drew a fine juridical line. "White enlisted men are not permitted to enlist in the four colored regiments. They are kept exclusively for colored applicants. The Congress having thus expressed its will, the War Department has labored under the belief that it was the general intent of Congress not to mix white and colored enlisted men in the same organizations. Thus troops, batteries and companies throughout the service are made up entirely of white enlisted men or colored enlisted men . . . Following its long-established policy, the War Department would not feel justified in mixing colored and white enlisted men in the same squadrons of the Air Corps. [Mosely apparently felt the notion of black flight officers was too absurd even to mention.] To do so would also violate what we believe was the intent of Congress when it prescribed that four regiments should be composed of colored enlisted men." What had originally been an opening up of opportunity to African Americans after the Civil War was transformed into a limitation.

Aware of the efforts to deprive blacks of opportunities in the army, Robert R. Moton, president of Tuskegee Institute and hardly a militant, wrote to Herbert Hoover. ". . . Negro troops at Fort Benning are without arms or equipment that would be used in training for combat service. . . . It is merely a pretense that Negroes are accorded the same treatment in the United States army as are given to white troops. It has never been the case and is not so now. This applies to the rank and file, as witness the presence of the highest-ranking Negro officer in the United States army [Col. Benjamin O. Davis Sr.] at Tuskegee Institute at the present time, who by reason of his color is denied service, according to his rank and with his own regiment." While the navy faced the same pressure for downsizing, the enlistment of African Americans never entered into the calculations. With no comparable units to those designated for blacks in the army and berths for only messmen and stewards, the navy could manipulate its manpower without having to accomodate a bloc of nonwhites.

Within the warrens of the army chief of staff's section however, some individuals apparently saw a potential problem in an all-white fighting force. Although they could not countenance any diminution of segregation they foresaw unhappiness among their constituents if only whites entered harm's way. A 1922 study declared, "To follow the policy of exemption of the Negro population of this country from combat means the white population upon which the future of the country depends would suffer the brunt of loss, the Negro population none . . ."

For the next twenty years, however, who would die in the service of his country remained a theoretical issue and for the bulk of the United States a very low-priority one. During the 1920s America was at peace; its entire military force a miniscule percentage of the national population and the blacks involved with the armed forces only a fragment of that tiny segment. In the 1930s, oppression and discrimination were overshadowed by the terrible weight of the Great Depression.

The administration of President Franklin D. Roosevelt, elected in 1932, created the Civilian Conservation Corps to enroll unemployed youths in a program to build parks and public recreational facilities. Initially, the CCC integrated its camps but protests from whites led to segregation. Paid a nominal wage, given food and lodging, the recruits to the CCC lived in camps run by officers and noncoms from the Regular Army. Benjamin O. Davis Sr., posted to the inspector general's office of the army, recalled that trouble with local officials occasionally came to his attention. "I told the [camp] authorities you may be in the geographical south but you're in the Army and treat men by regulations." However, although the statutes which established the CCC banned race as a factor in signing up individuals, blacks never were represented in proportion to their percentage of the general population.

Meanwhile, the struggle within the army to provide people for what it deemed essential to national defense drew the attention of civil rights leaders. There were sporadic protests at the continued exclusion of black soldiers from the amenities such as restaurants, swimming pools, theaters, in some cases even latrines, on posts around the country.

In manipulating the numbers, the army desperately tried to discourage blacks from enlistment. African Americans could only enroll in one of the regiments reserved for them if there were an open slot, and furthermore they would need to present themselves, at their own expense, to the organization where it was quartered. A man in Georgia who hoped to join the 25th Infantry stationed in Arizona would have to pay his way west, then hope he could pass the examinations and be accepted. Whites seeking admittance to the Regular Army had only to apply to the nearest recruiting site.

Black officers in the standing army were an endangered species, although schools like Wilberforce, Howard, and Tuskegee continued ROTC classes, which is what occupied Ben Davis at Tuskegee. The Davis family now challenged the army from a different direction. Benjamin O. Davis Jr., born in 1912, and a student at the University of Chicago, won an appointment to the U.S. Military Academy through Illinois representative Oscar S. De Priest, at the time the only member of his race in Congress. The younger Davis arrived at West Point in 1932 as a member of the Class of 1936. It was sixty years since Henry Flipper broke into the long gray line, and the passage of time had not changed the attitude of cadets. In July 1932, during the first month, or "Beast Detail"—from BCT or Basic Cadet Training—several other plebes spoke to him and even indicated they might show some friendliness. But subsequently, the first-year men assembled in the latrines and Davis heard someone ask, "What are we going to do about the nigger?"

He says "I realized that the meeting was about me and I was not supposed to attend." For the four years the junior Davis studied at the academy, he, like Flipper, was shunned with never a social word spoken to him, except at the close of plebe year when a number of upperclassmen congratulated him for reaching the status of yearling.

One year ahead of Davis at the academy was John Rhoades, son of an army dentist whose four-year-assignment at West Point stimulated young Jack to apply. As a boy, he attended segregated schools. "The national policy of segregation had been the 'normal' policy ever since the Civil War. Our family accepted it as a fact of life but supported the few proposals for change when the opportunity to do so arose. Reports of Klan lynchings and other illegal actions against the Negroes were discussed and condemned in our family.

"Benjamin Davis Jr.'s barracks were the most distant from my barracks and being in the class behind mine, we shared no academic classes. I don't recall ever seeing him, but I did know that he was a cadet. I never heard of any specific action, such as hazing against him, however, I assumed that he was probably pretty much ignored, which of course would make his life very difficult."

Davis endured four unpleasant years of isolation in which he roomed alone and ate alone and in some situations was even denied an unoccupied seat at a dining table. Many years later he told John Holway, author of *Red Tails, Black Wings,* "West Point is supposed to train leaders, but there was no damn leadership at all. The commandant of cadets, Lieutenant Colonel Richardson, an old cavalry officer, was a fine gentleman but he wasn't about to interfere with what went on. The captain of cadets was William Westmoreland [later a veteran of World War II, and subsequently commander of all U.S. forces in Vietnam]. If he'd been a true leader, he would have stopped that crap. It was designed to make me buckle, but I refused to buckle. They didn't understand that I was going to stay and I was going to graduate. I was not missing anything by not associating with them. They were missing a great deal by not knowing me."

In a history class dealing with the Civil War, two cadets delivered oral talks on slavery. "Their speeches were full of 'nigras' and the like," recalled Davis, "and I was struck by the absolutely blind racial prejudice that existed in the minds of these supposedly intelligent men. The instructor, also from the Deep South, was not quite as prejudiced as some of his students and tried to convince them that some blacks were not depraved. When he said there was no comparison between the highly educated black and the poor white, quite a bit of shock registered on the faces of my classmates."

During Davis's time at the Military Academy, Congressman De Priest appointed another African American, Felix Kirkpatrick. But although Davis believed Kirkpatrick appeared able to handle the academics, the harrassment caused him to pile up enough demerits to permit his dismissal. "I had never seen nor heard anything about him except in his favor, and everyone at West Point understood the real reason for his discharge—that he was black."

Davis applied for the Air Corps while in his third year at the Point. He passed a physical examination and Gen. William D. Connor, the superintendent, summoned him to his office. "I was handed my application and a letter from Brig. Gen. Oscar Westover, the assistant chief of the Air Corps, saying that I had been rejected because no black units were to be included in the Air Corps. . . . This decision came as a complete shock to me . . ."

The superintendent then advised Davis his rejection was "only the beginning of what I would encounter in the Army because of my race, and that perhaps it would be best for me to obtain a detail permitting me to attend law school with a view to entering politics and pursuing a congressional career. It was not 'logical' for a black officer to command white troops, he said. Consequently he intended to suggest . . . that the Army send me to law school thereby solving both 'my problem' and theirs."

Davis, intent upon an army career, refused. In the 1936 graduation issue of *The Howitzer*, the academy magazine, the text under Davis's photograph reads, "The courage, tenacity, and intelligence with which he conquered a problem incomparably more difficult than plebe year won for him the sincere admiration of his classmates, and his singleminded determination to continue in his chosen career cannot fail to inspire respect wherever fortune may lead him."

The "admiration" and "respect" he supposedly earned apparently warmed no hearts among his colleagues. Upon graduation as a second lieutenant in the infantry, Davis took command of a black service company at Fort Benning, Georgia. Alan Gropman, an Air Force historian, wrote, "In the two years Davis served at Benning, the nine Academy classmates also assigned there only talked to him in the line of duty." Dick Cross, son of the provost marshal at Fort Benning, then a twelve-year-old, remembers Davis "with his new bride and a new dark green two-door 1936 Buick Special. He was assigned a set of brick quarters at the end of the street near the old Army Hospital. The only other black officer on Post was his father, Col. Davis. They could not use the Officers' Club and were left to socialize with themselves." Indeed, Davis's wife Agatha, whom he married in the cadet chapel immediately after graduation, later wrote, "From 1936, when I married . . . until 1949, I too was silenced by his classmates and their wives."

In his autobiography, Davis recalls an incident where his fair-skinned wife happened to encounter the wife of another officer who did not know her identity. The two women exchanged salutations but when the white woman learned Agatha was married to Davis, neither she nor her husband ever again acknowledged their existence.

The conditions at West Point for any African American with the courage and ability to matriculate remained inhospitable. Holt Fairfield Butt III, a Virginia-born Protestant chaplain in residence at the academy from 1938–1941 recalled some anxious moments. Butt and his wife held open house for plebes on Sunday afternoon with thirty or forty from each company attending. They would have light refreshments and play games with the daughters of officers assigned to the post."One Sunday afternoon, the girls were discussing the fact that if he [a black cadet] came up to the house, they would refuse to meet him." Butt says he saw "the colored cadet headed our way. He came to our back door and engaged our cook in conversation. I went back and asked him, as I asked many other cadets, to go in the basement to get some wood for the fireplace . . . He came up with his arms full of wood, knelt down and built a fire. I was offering a prayer that this boy would not be embarrassed in my home. He was a very intelligent young man who took in the situation immediately, stood up and brushed himself off and said he had studies he must attend to in the barracks and left without any embarrassment to any present.

"He was a star athlete in high school [from Chicago] and yet he was never allowed on any of the athletic teams. He was a lonely man who was standing for a principle of equality for his race and suffering many of the consequences of such martyrs. He once remarked to me that it was strange that he was ordered to attend chapel with the cadets but could not play football with them."

According to Butts, the campus was not friendly toward other minorities such as Jews. Noting that during his tenure there were thirty-three Jewish cadets in residence, he realized that there was chapel for Protestants and Roman Catholics but none for Jews. He approached the superintendent to ask for services for these cadets. "Chaplain, what is the precedent for this action?" demanded the superintendent, Brig. Gen. Jay L. Benedict.

"Sir, there is no precedent except the Army recognizes Protestants, Catholics and Jews. Therefore, they should at West Point."

"What is the precedent at West Point?"

"None, sir." Benedict refused to act until Butts obtained the support of a national organization, the Jewish Welfare Board in New York City, which supplied a rabbi.

After a lapse of almost four decades a black congressman from Illinois appointed one of his constituents to the Naval Academy at Annapolis. James Lee Johnson entered in June 1936 but was among 135 middies asked to resign in January 1937 because of academic inadequacies. The congressman protested to President Franklin Roosevelt but after an inquiry by the Academic Board, Johnson and the others remained dismissed. The following year George J. Trivers joined the new plebe class but he lasted only three weeks before resigning. Meanwhile, in one of the more ludicrous efforts to maintain "racial purity," the Naval Academy refused to play lacrosse against a visiting Harvard team because the opponent fielded a black student. The Marines steadfastly continued not to enroll even enlisted African Americans.

Notwithstanding the absence of nonwhite officers and the devious attempts to increase whites in the military at the expense of blacks, the planners of national defense as early as 1922 foresaw the political and military need to include African Americans in any massive mobilization. The same paper that had warned in terms of eugenics of the threat to the future of the country if only whites became combatants said, "the negro is a citizen of the United States, entitled to all the rights of citizenship and subject to all the obligations of citizenship; that the negro constitutes an appreciable part of our military manhood; that while not the best military material, he is by no means the worst."

Based upon the evidence presented to them by the likes of Ballou, Bullard, and other white field or general level officers, the authors perceived that smaller units under white officers, "either separately or in conjunction with other white troops" achieved better results. The study recommended that "Negro units should not be grouped exclusively in organizations as large as a division but smaller units should be grouped with white units. We know that white regiments and negro regiments have operated successfully side by side, and this being the case, there appears no good reason why these should not be brigaded together." This advice was rejected when the War Department considered eliminating one of the black infantry regiments and uniting the remaining one with a white outfit during the downsizing era. After World War II enveloped the nation, the recommendation against all-black divisions was also disregarded.

The paper addressed the controversy over black officers. Although allowing that the disappointments with black troops during World War I might be attributed to "the preponderance of Negro officers," the report acknowledged "the record of the Negro regiments which operated with the French is not discreditable, even though in the case of at least two regiments, the Negro officers greatly predominated." Hewing to the party line, the Army savants insisted successful achievements did depend upon "proper leadership" by "white officers or by white officers in command of principal units." But they were savvy enough to add, "it is not reasonable to expect that the negro will be willing to serve in the ranks with no hope of a commission. Moreover, it cannot be fairly stated that no negro possesses the necessary qualities of leadership to make him an efficient officer . . . Not all our white officers are selected from the ranks of the most intelligent. As a matter of fact, we commission many white officers of only average intelligence.

. . . The trouble in the past, has been that we have not demanded from the negro the same standard of intelligence grade for grade, as from the white." In this regard, the study stipulated a rigid standard for men of all races.

The plan was pure theory so far as the regular army was concerned but it had relevance for organized reserves. Corps-area commanders throughout the United States were instructed to create plans that took into account the findings of the 1922 study, putting together a blueprint for mobilization in the event of an emergency. That involved setting down on paper the reserve units of infantry, artillery, and other services with appropriate obeisance to race. However, the African American reservists, except for their time in a college ROTC program received little or no training. The other major source of troops in the case of another large war, the National Guard, under local state control, was free to adopt such elements as each locale saw fit, which meant very few black units. New York State maintained the 369th Infantry, one of the remaining National Guard organizations devoted to nonwhites. In 1938, Governor Herbert H. Lehman designated Ben Davis Sr. as commander of the regiment. In that same year, the younger Davis, who had hoped for at least a post with a line infantry outfit, was dispatched to Tuskegee Institute for an ROTC position that was in his words, "as close to nothing as it could be and still be called a job." As war clouds lowered over Europe in the late 1930s, African Americans in the regular army and National Guard combined, added up to fewer than 2 percent.

In 1937, after Franklin D. Roosevelt had sounded the tocsin to "quarantine the aggressors," the War Department revisited its mobilization strategy. The research pointed to one problem created by the politics extant in 1917. When World War I broke out, the almost total prohibition on voluntary enlistment for blacks, because of a lack of units to absorb them, resulted in 650,000 whites enrolled against a paltry 4,000 African Americans. In those areas where blacks were a large part of the population, whites expressed dismay that so many of their color had now gone to war, leaving behind what they considered a heavier proportion of nonwhites in the region. At the same time, the African Americans protested bans on their enlistment.

But when selective service began in September 1917, the percentage of blacks available for unlimited duty was much higher than that of comparable whites because so many of the latter had already volunteered. Now blacks complained they were providing an excessive amount of the draftees. They objected to these massive call-ups, as did whites who saw their agricultural workers vanish almost overnight and then surface in unwanted concentrations at military camps in the South.

Although equality of unhappiness among the races was achieved in 1917, the planners of 1937 sought more efficiency and equity. As part of a program in the interests of justice as well as to maintain the loyalty of African American voters, the Roosevelt administration in 1938 had supported legislation to guarantee the franchise in elections and to banish lynchings. Omitted was any backing for an end to discrimination in the armed forces. Both the *Pittsburgh Courier* and the *Baltimore Afro-American* expressed displeasure over the silence of the White House on this issue.

Efforts to change the statutes that excluded or limited enlistments in any branch of the military establishment on account of race, creed, or color failed. Instead the regulations were modified to read, "No negro, because of race, shall be excluded from enlistment in the army for service with colored military units now organized or to be organized for such service." So sensitive was the issue of African American mobilization that the new more liberal policy remained under wraps until 1940 when it was revealed that the quota for the army's employment of blacks would be figured as an approximate ratio of their manpower of military age to that of the pool of all Americans of the same status. The agreed-on percentage was roughly 9 percent. Segregation would continue and black officers would not exceed the number required for such units.

When the army toted up the figures to fill the different divisions, regiments, battalions, and the like designated for the race, however, the 9 percent allotment to African Americans dropped down to less than 6 percent of the expected available blacks. In addition, while the two races were supposed to field the same ratio of combat soldiers to service troops, the figures for African Americans declined even more.

There was provision for a variety of organizations—cavalry, infantry, artillery, supply, and service outfits but no assignments to the Signal Corps or Air Corps. Wyoming senator Harry Schwartz convinced his colleagues to include black institutions in a program that provided flight training for civilians that served as a future resource for the Air Corps. The bill, passed in June 1939, enabled seven black colleges to enroll students under the Civilian Pilot Training Act. Of the first 100 African Americans to avail themselves of the opportunity, ninety-one obtained pilot's licenses.

The law covering the first U.S. peacetime draft in September 1940 authorized a quota of 800,000 men and included a clause that said, "There shall be no discrimination against any person on account of race or color." But the statute neither outlawed segregated units nor opened up areas previously barred to men of color. In fact the military community continued to believe they had the power to accept or reject any individual presented for service. At the same time, to accommodate its expanded population, the president appointed eighty-four new generals, passing over Benjamin O. Davis Sr. who was superior in years of service to many. Black newspapers editorialized on the slight.

African American leaders angrily attacked the policies of the armed forces who interpreted the new selective service system as permission to discriminate against blacks swept up by the draft. The black leaders presented proposals to integrate the armed forces with the sole criteria for assignment and rank dependent upon individual abilities. Secretary of War Henry L. Stimson noted in his diary, "I saw the same thing happen twenty-three years ago when Woodrow Wilson yielded to the same sort of demand and appointed colored officers of the Divisions that went over to France and the poor fellows made perfect fools of themselves and one at least of the Divisions behaved very badly. The others were turned into labor battalions." The passage of time appears to have clouded Stimson's memory for Wilson "appointed" no "colored officers" and his description of the fate of the two divisions in the AEF is erroneous.

The pressure from the black community, against a backdrop of a national election a few months off, testing the right of FDR to an unprecdented third term, forced the Roosevelt administration to modify practices. Black soldiers would now be allowed in all areas including the Air Corps, although the question of flight-cadet status remained obscure. Officer candidate schools would accept African Americans. However, the statement issued over the signature of the president reaffirmed segregation on the grounds that this approach had been successful over a long period of time and change might be detrimental in preparing for national defense.

The minor adjustments hardly mollified the spokespeople for the black community, and a week before the voters went to the polls, Roosevelt offered further concessions. He pledged better access of blacks to the commissioned ranks and true opportunities in military specialties, and he announced the promotion of Benjamin O. Davis Sr., now sixty-three years old, to the rank of brigadier general, the first of his race to achieve that rank. Privately, Stimson voiced his unhappiness with the nomination. With retirement on the horizon, Davis headed for Fort Riley, Kansas, and command of the 4th Brigade of the 2d Cavalry Division, a unit composed of the skeletal 9th and 10th Cavalry Regiments.

Roosevelt also signed up Judge William H. Hastie, dean of the Howard Law School, for the post of assistant secretary of the army, advising on racial matters, and Maj. Campbell C. Johnson, another black officer, went on the staff of Gen. Lewis B. Hershey, director of Selective Service, for his input. Hastie, reluctant at first to accept his position, immediately posted notice of where he stood. "I have always been constantly opposed to any policy of disrimination and segregation in the Armed Forces of this country. I am assuming this post in the hope that I will be able to work effectively toward the integration of the Negro into the army and to facilitate his placement, training and promotion." Hastie's principle guaranteed that his stay in the corridors of the War Department would be relatively brief.

Following Roosevelt's victory over Wendell Willkie and as the economy, boosted by defense expenditures, quickened, the African American community renewed its pressure upon the government. A. Philip Randolph, the leader of the Brotherhood of Sleeping Car Porters, proposed to his associates a massive demonstration in Washington over the inequities for blacks seeking jobs in manufacturing war goods and the continuing discriminatory practices in the military. A series of meetings led to a major gain in the private sector. The Fair Employment Practices order banned discrimination in both government and defense industries, which covered not only jobs but vocational training programs connected with them. However, the military leaders adamantly refused to budge on integration of their fiefs.

As Benjamin Davis Jr. indicated, the Air Corps had stubbornly refused to accept men of color for flight instruction. Those in command relied on their own catch-22. The policy of segregation eliminated assignment of commissioned flight officers to fighter or bomb groups because the officers would be superior to white men. No separate units had been authorized for nonwhites. Even with the allocation of War Department funds, materials, and personnel for the Civilian Pilot Training (CPT) program to cover nonwhites, the Air Corps continued to stonewall admission to its ranks. Howard University and the NAACP now backed a graduate of the CPT, Yancey Williams, in a suit to force the Air Corps to remove the barriers.

Beyond the bureaucratic niceties, the upper echelons of the flying service, as in other military specialties, considered African Americans as incapable of mastering the technology required to pilot an airplane. They clung to their prejudice even though a handful of blacks had demonstrated that they could fly as well as whites. During World War I, an American expatriate, Eugene Jacques Bullard, enlisted in the French foreign legion. After incurring severe wounds as an infantryman he learned to fly and in 1917 joined a pursuit squadron. Unable to transfer to an American outfit because of his race, Bullard, under the tricolor of his adopted land, shot down at least one, possibly two enemy aircraft.

Like so many young whites, African Americans succumbed to the romance of flight between the two world wars. Well over 100 blacks were certified pilots by 1939. Two of them fought against fascist expansion in Ethiopia and Spain. A pair of black airmen, Chauncey E. Spencer and Dale L. White, members of the National Airmen's Association of America flew cross country to lobby for acceptance of nonwhites in all the aspects of military aviation. Two African American women, Bessie Coleman and Willa Brown, barnstormed about the United States. Coleman produced aerial circus shows and Brown operated a successful flying school.

Perhaps the best known civilian flier was Charles "Chief" Anderson. Born in Pennsylvania, where his father acted as an estate manager and chauffeur in Bryn Mawr, Anderson taught himself to fly in the late 1920s after borrowing $2,000 to buy his own monocoupe. A former member of the German air force during World War I then tutored him sufficiently for Anderson to obtain the first commercial license ever granted a member of his race. He scratched for a living, as a farmer, then sold rides and trips, piloted a local numbers racketeer anxious to save time, ran a flight school, and teamed up with Dr. Albert Forsythe, a New Jersey surgeon, on a series of adventurous long-distance excursions. Anderson explained, "Being a very, very aggressive and determined man, and an ambitious person, he [Forysthe] wanted to advance aviation among blacks. He said, 'We are going to do something to show that we can do these things, just like everybody else.'"

When approval of CPT for African Americans came, two prominent blacks, Dr. Frederick Patterson a veterinarian who became president of Tuskegee Insitute and George L. Washington put in a bid with the army to place the program in the institute's vicinity. A grant from the Rosenwald Foundation enabled Patterson to buy land and hire instructors.

Because of his extensive background, Chief Anderson was a natural choice for the Air Corps–sponsored CPT program at Tuskegee. Early in 1941, First Lady Eleanor Roosevelt traveled to Tuskegee Institute, perhaps because of an interest in the polio unit there, but she also visited the field where the CPT program operated. Said Chief Anderson, "I remember her telling me that everybody told her we [blacks] couldn't fly. Her remark was, 'I see you are flying all right here. Everybody that's here is flying. You must be able to fly. As a matter of fact, I'm going to find out for sure. I'm going up with you.'

"That caused a lot of opposition among her escorts. They were thinking of calling the President to stop her, but she was a woman, who, when she decided to do something, she was going to do it. She got in the plane with me and we had a delightful flight. She enjoyed it very much. We made a tour of the campus and the surrounding area. We came back and she said, 'Well, you can fly all right.'"

Anderson credits her with a major role in causing her husband to order the army to open up the air corps to blacks. How much influence she had on the decision may be debatable but only two or three weeks after her jaunt, came authorization for an African American pursuit squadron.

10
The Coming of World War II

With a huge amount of European real estate gobbled up by the Nazi juggernaut, the British and Soviets struggling to stave off conquest, the armies of Japan advancing in China and threatening Western interests, tens of thousands of white and black Americans wore their country's uniforms or prepared to enter military service well before the first bombs hammered Pearl Harbor. The mobilization, which began more than a year before the United States officially went to war, eventually enveloped fifteen million men and women. It was the largest the country ever experienced, covering the widest possible spectrum of social, educational, and economic backgrounds. It jumbled together illiterates and university students, zoologists, lawyers and laborers, mechanics and clerks, farm boys and city-street toughs, the sons and daughters of patricians and sharecroppers, graduates of military academies intent upon careers in the armed forces, and those reluctant to serve but swept up by the draft.

During World War I, a diversity of a similar nature had marked the white soldiers, sailors, airmen, and marines but the preponderance of African Americans, still hugely concentrated in the rural South and deprived by the malevolent hand of rigid segregation, was far more homogeneous. Except for a small core of educated and professional people, most blacks had struggled to survive in agriculture or menial labor. The demand for defense workers during World War I brought the first significant shift to more skilled, better-paying positions in cities and the North. During the 1930s, the Great Depression drove many who had remained behind from the land and the life of sharecroppers or dirt-poor farmers. Then as World War II heated up tens of thousands more heeded the calls for workers in defense industries and the perceived freedom of the North. When Selective Service started in 1940 and over the next five years, the two million blacks who put on uniforms, to a much lesser extent of course than the whites, included professional people, academicians, skilled technicians, and white collar workers along with a mass of people still consigned to physical labor, whether in urban centers or tilling the land. Whatever their parentage or their vocations, African Americans had in common the color of their skin and the attitudes and behavior of the dominant population toward them.

To contain the African American fliers, the War Department, in late March 1941, activated the 99th Pursuit Squadron. The site for training, Tuskegee Army Air Field, or TAAF, was not a part of the educational institute and its location infuriated the natives. Local whites strongly objected to a "colored aviation camp" in their neighborhood. Although the federal authorities brushed off the complaint, the citizens would continue to demean and oppose the operation.

Within the overall black community the establishment of TAAF roused considerable controversy. William Hastie, as Secretary of War Stimson's aide on "Negro Affairs" vigorously opposed the arrangements at the base. An emphatic adherent of integegration, he complained about separate barracks, drinking fountains, and toilet facilities for whites and blacks working on the base. His objections were ignored. Assistant Secretary of War for Air Robert Lovett told the air corps command, "There must and will be segregation."

The NAACP echoed Hastie's opinion as did the editors of some black dedicated newspapers which according to Ben Davis Jr., a member of the first group to report to TAAF, "ranted against Uncle Toms—blacks who were willing to serve in black units and seemed to tacitly support segregation."

Benjamin O. Davis Jr. who says he would have preferred integration believed the format imposed "could easily have sabotaged our mission." However, he says in his autobiography, he was persuaded, as many others had been in the past, "blacks could best overcome racist attitudes through their achievements, even though those achievements had to take place within the hateful environment of segregation. I believed that TAAF should move ahead rapidly and prove for all to see, especially within the Army Air Corps, that we were a military asset. The coming war represented a golden opportunity for blacks, one that could not be missed . . ."

Davis was an obvious candidate for flight training from the standpoints of ability, military background, and not least politics. The plan for the squadron listed Davis as its eventual leader. That in itself marked what would become the 99th Pursuit Squadron as a singular unit. In white squadrons well-experienced fliers commanded the outfits, but with the 99th, segregation dictated an approach that placed a novice airman in charge.

Davis, already holding the rank of captain, reported to TAAF with a dozen others of his race for what some dubbed the "Spookwaffe" to begin their primary flight instruction. On hand, in addition to Chief Anderson, were three other civilian teachers, including one who was white. There was nothing exceptional about the status of these individuals; for much of the war, cadets received their introduction to the controls of an airplane from civilians like Anderson who had operated or worked for aeronautical schools.

With the exception of Davis, the first men enrolled, although subject to the discipline of the air corps, were not actually full-fledged members of the service. Davis and four of his classmates completed the course eight months after they began. During the early phases, the wash-out rate ran about 50 percent, a figure that detractors cited as evidence of the innate weakness of blacks but that other observers attributed to a haphazard application of selection criteria or bias.

When TAAF opened for business, Maj. James "Straight Arrow" Ellison, white, served as the base commander. According to Davis, Ellison showed good faith in dealing with the blacks and did his best to ward off intrusion of the cultural practices of the hostile local white population. He was apparently so stalwart a defender of his subordinates that Davis among others believes political pressure forced a transfer. In his place, Col. Frederick von Harten Kimble, who graduated last in his 1917 U.S. Military Academy class, arrived and "immediately," says Davis, "antagonized TAAF's black population." He posted signs FOR COLORED OFFICERS and FOR WHITE OFFICERS on various facilities. He created segregated sections in the mess hall for the commissioned. Whites could not attend the officers' club or post theater because these were reserved for blacks. Worst of all, he allowed civilian authorities to harass or take jurisdiction over African American personnel off post, barring black MPs, for example, from carrying sidearms while patrolling Tuskegee or other areas. Kimble's actions stirred protests until the War Department replaced him with the white Southern-born officer in charge of operations, Maj. Noel Parrish. A former sergeant in a black cavalry regiment, Parrish stepped up to the commissioned ranks with the coming of the war. He quickly convinced those in residence that he had their best interests at heart. Parrish held the post for the remainder of World War II, rising to the rank of colonel and reaping almost unanimous praise from those who passed through TAAF.

Operation of a segregated fighter squadron obliged the air corps to train black support personnel, ground crews to service and maintain the aircraft. Unable to justify an entirely separate institution to teach the technology of engines, air frames, and weaponry, the air corps assigned those chosen to learn these subjects to its school at Chanute Field, Illinois, where they attended integrated classes while housed and fed separately.

Although Gen. H. H. 'Hap' Arnold, as head of the air corps, had resisted efforts to allow African Americans into the cockpits, he was susceptible to influence from Chief Anderson. "My daddy was a coachman for General Arnold's father who was a doctor in Ardmore, Pennsylvania, and he used to carry General Arnold to school as a kid in his carriage. So I had some connections there, and I wrote a letter to General Arnold explaining the situation here, that we wanted to see more blacks over the Army airfield—see some over there at least as flight instructors. They said none were qualified, which wasn't true. He sent a representative down here from his staff to check things out, and soon after that, they decided to accept a black flight instructor [military] over here."

As more and more African Americans entered the armed forces, the War Department assigned Benjamin O. Davis Sr. to its inspector general's office. Unlike Judge William Hastie, his civilian counterpart who was free to speak his mind, Ben Davis, with more than forty years in uniform, accepted the constraints of military protocol. In his new capacity he toured Tuskegee in August 1941, and in his report commented on the antagonism displayed toward the cadets by the local police and white military police. He pointed out a lack of hotel space for visiting families or friends. Although Davis was often criticized as insufficiently militant, and even as an Uncle Tom, he wrote, "In the development of our national defense I believe the War Department has a wonderful opportunity to bring about better race relations. Policies of discrimination practiced with the current sanction of the federal government will not make the democracy we talk about in our attempt to rally the nation to our program of national defense. The establishment of a separate flying school for colored flying cadets at Tuskegee in my opinion was a mistake. Already the question has been asked by some colored leaders why must colored officers of the Air Corps be separate . . . in a Jim Crow school. Colored infantry officers, colored noncomissioned officers attend infantry schools, and colored artillery officers attend the artillery school. I believe the time is right for breaking down the discrimination and unfair practices toward colored people. Colored soldiers must support white soldiers in combat and vice versa.

"Officers white and colored most certainly should have the same preparation. They must prepare together, live together, march together, share the hardships of the campaign. Then only will they be in a position to be mutually helpful in combat." (The same point is made today by adherents of a gender-equal military.)

Davis launched into a full-scale denunciation of the system. "Right here in Washington, the capital of the nation, approximately one-third of the population is denied equal privileges to avail themselves of the facilities making for culture. The same facilities and agencies are provided or licensed by the federal government. I have in mind the cafeterias and restaurants in public buildings, hotels, theaters and other public entertainment. The legal tender of the United States in the hands of colored citizens does not secure the same values as for other citizens or even for foreigners in our midst. I think the Department would do well to give some consideration to this angle of national defense. The induction of colored men into other branches of the army beside infantry and cavalry has had a most wholesome effect. I have, based on my long service and association with the regular army and the civilian components, great confidence in our army to meet this situation once they concentrate upon it."

As in any large corporate structure, the personal touch employed by Chief Anderson with Hap Arnold occasionally made a small difference, but fundamental systematic changes suggested by reformers like Benjamin O. Davis Sr. never found much of an audience in the halls of power. For the overwhelming numbers of GIs, sailors and marines, with all their individual backgrounds, the military machine drew few fine distinctions and frequently seemed without any logic to its decisions. But wherever their homes, the African American recruits were aware of lynchings and knew the knout of discrimination.

"I was born in a South Carolina cottonfield, in 1916," remembers Spann Watson, one of the original members of the CPT operation at Howard University in Washington, D.C. "My Daddy would not sharecrop. He said that separated the men from the boys and there was no question about who was in control. I started school when I was four years old. It was a three-mile walk, with my oldest brother Roy, two cousins and several other youngsters. We crossed brooks, walked over rocks, came upon snakes to get to a one-room school house.

"After two or three years I went on to the Reeda Branch School, with no desks or tables. You wrote on a pad on your knees. Later, when white folks wasn't going to give us a school, my Dad got with several people and located a teacher. She lived at our house rent free. They took her to school in a buggy but we had to walk. My parents started us reading when we were six or seven. He subscribed to the *Atlanta Constitution* for $1.60 a year and he'd ask you questions about what was in the paper." Young Watson endured and continued to learn under similar circumstances until his tenth birthday when his father, alarmed by a nearby lynching, moved the family to Lodi, New Jersey, where he had occasionally held temporary jobs before Christmas.

The North as exemplified by Lodi in 1927 was a revelation to ten-year-old Spann Watson. "We lived on the top floor of a house with an Italian landlord downstairs. There were bathrooms inside. My Dad asked a policeman there which was the colored school. He told him you send your children to the school nearest your home. You didn't have to buy your books. We had electric lights in school. We thought about all the dark days in the South."

The family was apparently the first of its color to live in Lodi. "The first day we went to Lincoln School in our Sunday best. The Principal, one of the grandest ladies, escorted us from class to class where she announced the rules with a civil rights speech. We were not going to be subject to any kind of slights. If we detected any, we could go to her. My oldest brother and I went right to the top of the class. The police chief lived in a small house between the school and our home. He would stop us on the street regularly and ask how we were doing, and so did his wife. It was a miracle."

About two miles from where the Watsons lived was Teterboro Airport. "Down south," recalls Watson, "Maybe you'd hear an airplane a couple of times a year. I just about lived at the airport when not in school. Dad used to take us there on weekends and we saw Wiley Post, Amelia Earhart, Jimmy Doolittle, the Gates Flying Circus. They sold rides, a Fokker single engine, $2.50, a Ford tri-motor, $5.00 and in a Jenny, $1.00. On July 4th, 1927, there must have been 15,000 people there and I saw a plane circle overhead. I had seen a stamp at the post office with the *Spirit of St. Louis*, and I said, 'That's Lindbergh.' Some guy says, 'The little colored boy says that's *The Spirit of St. Louis*, haw, haw, haw.' It was a big joke and I said, I'll show that son of a bitch.

"When Lindbergh landed, the mob went crazy, they would have torn the plane apart. They asked for volunteers to protect and roll the plane into a hangar. My Dad helped push it into place and a bunch of us actually got to touch it. Then they closed the doors and Lindbergh escaped out a back door."

The ambience changed with a move to Hackensack where Northern prej- udice showed its face, undoubtedly more visible to the young Watson as he aged and entered high school. "I had decided I wasn't going to wash cars for a living and Dad, who got a job as a machinist, wouldn't let us be bus-boys. He wanted us to work any job, except that of a flunky." There wasn't enough family money to pay for a school that taught aeronautics. Instead Watson studied mechanical engineering at Howard University. While there he obtained a private and commercial pilot license with Chief Anderson as his instructor. Among Watson's closest friends was Yancey Williams, the plaintiff in the action to pry open air corps flight programs. Watson him-self had been turned down once when he applied at the recruiting office in New York City.

He had strongly supported the NAACP's position for integrated flight training but became convinced that had the air corps done so, opportuni-ties to wash out the minority would have diminished the possibilities for African Americans. After a radio news broadcast reported that the air corps had backed off from its recalcitrance toward black flight personnel, Watson reapplied. When no word came he wrote a letter again inquiring about his status. Upon the creation of the 99th, Watson anticipated that as one of the first to complete CPT he would be chosen for the original cadet class but instead his admission was delayed several months. When he was not in the first group, Watson became unhappy about the choices. "We had been the ones who led the fight but when they admitted the first class, most of them were strangers to us. Who they knew or how they were taken puzzled me." He finally received orders to report to TAAF with the fourth class to undergo training.

"Our group had already taken ground-school and flight training and had exceptional records. The instructors, Guido, Rosenberg, Camilleri, Shelton and Anderson were excellent and there was no racism from any of them. I stayed away from the city to avoid any trouble there. When I finished the course in March 1941, I had been to Maxwell Field. I saw bigotry at its worst and fair play at its best. Colonel Parrish was the greatest guy around. He said, 'I'm a pea-shelling redneck from Georgia but we're here to do the job. While we were cadets, he was cordial, respectful, a friendly guy. You knew where you stood, that he'd do the right thing.

"The military pilots who taught us were great guys. They were strict, and gave you hell if you screwed up. But I didn't think they behaved badly. There was a final physical examination and some of the white doctors looked at a man's penis and said, 'Is that all there is?' There was a white optometrist and for the two people ahead of me, he wrote down, 'astigmatism.' When it came my turn, he said, 'Here's another one.' A white doctor, said, let me see. After he tested me he said, 'This man's perfect.' He passed me and the other two. Then he took the optometrist off the line. We went through a battery of psychiatrists. A bird colonel looked at my record, born in South Carolina and now from New Jersey asked, 'Whaddya think about niggers marrying white women?' He thought he'd blow me out. I said, 'I'm not concerned about it.' I kept my cool and he didn't wash me out."

Harry Sheppard, born in New York City in 1917, while living in Harlem, attended integrated schools. "The only resentment we felt were when we tried to use the natatorium in Hell's Kitchen [an Irish American enclave at the time] or sometimes in Yorkville [a German American neighborhood]. I didn't feel any impact of the racial situation on my personal life. We read about lynchings and my parents, who came from the West Indies, were deathly afraid of the South. None of us had ever been as far south as Washington.

"I was steeped in the English education tradition. It was very important and I was made by my parents and grandparents to study. I attended night classes at City College of New York, with an eye toward electrical engineering. Meanwhile, war clouds were getting blacker and blacker. Hitler was running over Europe and I couldn't see the U.S. staying out. When a cousin at the Manhattan School of Aviation said the Air Corps was opened up to Negroes, I enlisted at Mitchell Field in April 1941, for $21 a month. There were 275 enlisted men to be basic support for the 99th Squdron and we went to school to become prop specialists, welders, experts in electrical and armament aspects. We had excellent instructors at Chanute Field. All of us had at least high school, and many some college. We were a professional bunch who worked together, studied together, and although we later found out this was an experiment designed for us to fail, when we left Chanute Field we had the highest grades seen there.

"In October 1941 we arrived at Tuskegee and they had not finished building the field. We lived in tents and some of us were sent to Maxwell Field to be used as labor, even though they were short of mechanics there. We still had some white supervisors in armament and other specialties but we were weaned away from them. I was a prop specialist, first class, equivalent to a staff sergeant. I was hauled off to instruct in the cadet ground school and one of the students there was Captain Davis who would be in the first graduating class, March 1942."

The prospect of flight enticed African Americans to enlist before America joined the shooting war, but for many, the idea of a military career and the proximity of the draft helped them to a decision. Elliotte W. Williams, born in 1920, grew up in what New York City residents came to know as the Sugar Hill section of Harlem. "My father was a bricklayer," says Williams, "and one of the first of his race able to join the union. The area was initially integrated although most of the middle class whites attended private parochial schools. There was no real tension, until high school when people started to distance themselves. We had only about enough blacks to fill a single bus at George Washington High, where Henry Kissinger became a student and the kids laughed at the refugees in their lederhosen.

"I went to CCNY [the City College of New York] and was in the 369th Infantry of the National Guard ROTC. I had a cousin at West Point [assigned to the base housekeeping detail] and I got a discharge from the National Guard, in the fall of 1940 and enlisted in the regular army at West Point. I got on-the-job training there, a week of close-order drill, classes in customs and courtesy and they made me admissions clerk at the hospital. The medical unit was an integrated unit, one of the very few. The only segregation was in living quarters, we enlisted men shared one of the 10th Cavalry barracks. The NCO quarters were mixed. The post theater, clubs, PX were not segregated. Our AGCT [military version of an IQ test] scores were the highest on the post. We had a black 1st sergeant who later got a commission. While he was 1st sergeant, we had four or five whites in the unit but none of them were a lower rank than he.

"In February they broke us up. I took the entrance exam to be a cadet but I caught up with some of the others at Ft. Devens [Massachusetts] where they brought in about two hundred men from the 24th Infantry to start the 366th Infantry Regiment. We had all black officers except for the regimental and battalion commanders who were whites. At Devens we were put way off to the side of the post in an area that was still being built. We were fairly well restricted. I was promoted but they had a segregated barracks for NCOs. For the first time since I entered the army I saw that we had our own clubs, library and all back in the boonies."

For most whites who entered the services while the nation was on the cusp of war, the African American, in the words of Ralph Ellison was the "invisible man." DeWitt C. Armstrong III, a descendant of the Scottish clan which produced Samuel Chapman Armstrong, commander of a regiment of black volunteers during the Civil War and founder of Hampton Institute, focused on a military career from boyhood. Clare Hibbs Armstrong, his father, the son of a Minnesota banker, graduated from the U.S. Military Academy in 1917 but a bout of influenza cost him an opportunity to fight in France.

Young DeWitt reveled in the stories of a soldier's life in the Philippines, Panama, and other stations. Although intent on an appointment to West Point, he finished high school before his sixteenth birthday, too early for consideration as a cadet. To fill his time with useful enterprise, he enrolled at the Citadel in South Carolina, his mother's home state. "Memory suggests that 90 percent of my classmates were South Carolinians. All were white, and nearly all their names were Anglo-Saxon. If the question of blacks as soldiers ever arose, that has escaped my memory. Around us were some blacks, mostly waiters and janitors, and the usual gentle Southern indulgence and mutual respect seemed to prevail. Never really hearing (or wondering) how this all looked to the blacks, I simply accepted the status quo. Now it is clear to me that in those days the social standing of that student body was probably somewhat higher than it later became. In the 1930s, after all, there weren't many people, especially in the deep South, who went to college."

Subsequently, upon reaching the appropriate age, Armstrong received his ticket to the Military Academy Class of 1943. "Our class included two blacks, Tresville and Davenport. Tresville was tallish, about six feet and had an athlete's coordination and physical grace. Davenport must have been around five foot seven and seemed clumsy. Neither was in the same cadet company as I, nor ever in any of my academic sections, so I didn't really see much of how our other classmates treated them. My dim recollection is that Tresville was viewed as being, except for color, more like the rest of us than was Davenport."

Robert Bernard Tresville Jr. was the son of a soldier and an athlete with a scholarship to Penn State. When he transferred to the academy, Tresville became the first black at West Point to represent the school in intercollegiate competition. Upon graduation he achieved another milestone, the first black graduate to go directly into the air corps and gain his wings through the Tuskegee program.

Clarence Maude Davenport Jr. grew up in Detroit. "My parents were very supportive by word and by example. They also unselfishly committed their fiscal resources to the educational and spiritual well-being of their children." Like his classmates Armstrong and Tresville, Davenport also tucked into his dossier several years of college at the University of Detroit before he surfaced at West Point.

Armstrong cannot recall any guidance offered cadets on how they should relate to their black classmates. "Could it perhaps be that the authorities gave none at all, simply letting matters take their natural course? I am reasonably certain there was never any 'silence' applied, as rarely occurred with cadets thought to have committed moral violations. There must have been a fair amount of talk amongst us at some point, perhaps in autumn of our plebe year. Still, fifty-eight years later I cannot characterize how our Northern and Southern classmates may have differed in attitude. All of us were under intense pressure and trying desperately just to stay afloat. In plebe year especially, nobody wanted to rock the boat.

"My impression is that there was very little social contact by my classmates with either man. In the line of duty, of course, there was the necessary conversations, but not otherwise. A vague fragment of memory suggests that a few classmates did treat Tresville pretty much like anyone else. But it must have been an extremely trying four years for each of those two men.

"At West Point my only other contact with uniformed blacks was in horsemanship. Our horses were kept by a detachment from the 9th or 10th Cavalry. Those soldiers always seemed competent and quiet. The instructors who actually taught us were white cavalry officers. Cadets understood that enlisted men, white or black, knew a lot that we needed to learn, and the fact that we were senior to them was entirely irrelevant. Once a classmate joked about how the black cavalry troopers took care to see that Tresville and Davenport were always on good horses. But who cared? Part of horsemanship is learning to control the skittish and the wide-eyed ones, and that's even fun, on the tan bark at least."

As an African American member of the class after Armstrong, that of 1944, H. Minton Francis, a fifth-generation resident of Washington, says he regarded with "some disdain many of my fellow white officers (including some of my West Point classmates) mainly on the basis of their socioeconomic class. When many of their ancestors were just arriving in the USA as immigrants or were poor dirt farmers in Texas or elsewhere in the South, my grandfather was graduating from the medical college at the University of Michigan in 1877. His sons were sent to Dartmouth, Harvard and Pennsylvania and became lawyers, engineers, physicians and dentists.

"I was one of the offspring of a marriage between the Francis and Wormley families of the District. The famous Wormley Hotel in Washington was operated by my great-grandfather, James K. Wormley, before, during and after the Civil War. It was in the conference rooms of the hotel that the Missouri Compromise was devised and signed. So I was raised in very comfortable circumstances, proud of who I was and confident in my ability to compete with anyone regardless of race.

"My parents and elders were all very active in the NAACP and the Urban League when it was established. My uncle was a close friend of William E. B. Du Bois. So there were frequent and lively discussions of the "race question" in my home.

"All schools in the District of Columbia were segregated by race in my youth. But the Paul Laurence Dunbar High School was so well accredited by Ivy League schools, except perhaps by Princeton [possibly one more legacy of segregationist Woodrow Wilson who was head of Princeton for a number of years before he entered politics], that admission for high performing students was practically guaranteed. Most of my male elders were practicing physicians or dentists; there was therefore, the expectation that I would study medicine. I was readily admitted to the University of Pennsylvania in a pre-med curriculum. When World War II loomed on the horizon as Hitler invaded Poland, and the draft was about to begin, my father decided that I should apply for admission to West Point. You might say I went to West Point as a draft-dodger. I do not regret it. I am a loyal son of West Point—it molded my character and instilled in me a determination to overcome all obstacles to my goals."

Conditions, however, had not improved significantly since the days of Henry Flipper or Benjamin O. Davis Jr. For Francis the first conversation upon arrival at the academy included the question, "Why do niggers want to come to West Point?" After that the blanket of silence descended. During summer camp, someone put human feces in his shoes. The superintendent broke protocol to visit Francis and another black in plebe quarters, "to tell us, after we had been subjected to an egregious episode of hazing that bordered on criminal assault, that if we had been white that the perpetrator would have surely been dismissed from the Academy, but because it had happened only to a black man, the guilty party would merely be suspended for one year and turned back [forced to reenter as a member of the next graduating class]."

Harold Hayward entered the U.S. Military Academy at the same time as Francis. Born in Utah, as a youngster he lived in small towns in the mountain West. "With two exceptions, most of the people I knew and grew up with were white and had Anglo-Saxon, German or Scandinavian forebears. The two other racial groups were Native American Indians and Japanese immigrants. The children of both were fully integrated into the schools. Socially, Indian children were scorned—after all we were only one generation removed from 'the only good Indian is a dead Indian.' Indian children were not forced to attend school and most of them dropped out at an early age or were carried away by the contagious diseases that periodically swept the community. The children of Japanese immigrants were noted for the good grades they earned in school, but socially, they were ignored. However, their parents were recongized for their diligence as farm workers and their success as small business entrepreneurs.

"Until I was about twenty years old, I don't think I had ever laid eyes on more than a dozen black people—all of them men. The only times I recall their coming into our town was as part of traveling carnivals. A black man's carnival role was often to stick his head through a hole in a sheet of canvas, face the midway, and serve as a target for baseballs thrown by local yokels. I recall being told on one occasion that 'being hit in the head by a baseball didn't really hurt a "nigger" very much because his skull bones were much thicker than those of white folks.' I remember taking in that bit of information with more than a bit of skepticism.

"This is not to say that, as a youth, I was not exposed to information about black people. As a matter of fact, I was fed a lot of what can best be characterized as 'misinformation.' In school and around the piano at home we sang the songs of Stephen Foster; we read the stories of Joel Chandler Harris. We recognized the characters in *Uncle Tom's Cabin.* Local male glee clubs did song and dance acts in black face—complete with Mr. Interlocutor and jokes about 'Rastus' and 'Mandy.' We thought we knew how black people thought and spoke—we had listened to *Amos and Andy.* We weren't quite sure what to think and say about Joe Louis and Jesse Owens—they were anomalies to us. Without intending to be particularly degrading 'nigger' was the word most commonly used to identify black people.

"We learned that the Civil War, which took place in someone else's backyard, was fought over the issue of slavery. Without having much understanding of the institution of slavery itself, we also learned that Abraham Lincoln was a great president because he 'freed the slaves.' At the socio/religious level there was a pervasive undercurrent of belief that black people carried 'the mark of Cain' that they were truly inferior, and that their inferiority and subjugation by white people was punishment for misdeeds they had committed in prior existence.

"For better or worse, that was the racial baggage I carried with me as I entered West Point. While I had known people who had strong emotional feelings on racial issues—especially with respect to blacks—my attitude was primarily one of indifference. I do not know how many blacks entered West Point with me in July 1941; I can recall only two. Although 'hazing' had been officially prohibited, it was still being practiced surreptitiously and, often quite openly. From a distance, I observed that one of the blacks was 'hazed' into submitting his resignation before the end of our first week as cadets. At a closer range, and from within my own cadet company, I saw the second black getting the same treatment, but my attitude of indifference prevailed. As I saw it, he had his problems and I had mine, which for me, were sometimes almost overwhelming.

"The second black, H. Minton Francis, survived to graduate and enter the army with the rest of us. Throughout his cadet years he was 'silenced'— treated as though he did not exist. Two of the cadets, who through hazing, were trying to persuade Francis to resign, were members of the next class above mine. That they undertook their task with gusto is not to be denied, although it was commonly understood that they had the tacit approval, if not the mandate, from cadets senior to them. Someone reported them for hazing to Academy authorities."

As Francis recalled, the disciplinary board punished the offenders with a suspension from the Academy. They could return after a year as "turn-backs," reappearing at West Point as members of the next lower class. According to Hayward, in the army of today, where promotions are on merit, being turned back would be of little consequence. But in 1941, where promotions were based on seniority, the one-year setback could mean a difference of years in moving up through the ranks.

"With my sheltered background and naive as I was," says Hayward, "I was surprised by the virulence of the emotions regarding blacks as displayed by some white cadets. I admired Francis's courage and often wondered if I could have 'taken it' as well as he, although I acted as though the situation itself did not exist." Like DeWitt Armstrong, Hayward remembers the black cavalry detachment stationed at the Point to care for the horses. He notes that these men were clearly subservient to the cadets and the faculty. As the draft carried off more and more eligible males, Hayward says a special group of black, former dining-car waiters served meals to the cadets, "All of which served to reflect the traditional master/servant relationship between whites and blacks."

The same vague impression of African American presence was held by white citizen-soldiers from the North. Jim Pedowitz, from the then Jewish neighborhood of Brownsville, Brooklyn, born in 1915, recalls an occasional black family with means in the area. "There were some blacks from the Bedford-Stuyvesant area at Boys High when I graduated in 1932 but I didn't pay any attention to race relations. I thought of black women as domestics. I don't think I knew a black woman who was in any better paying job. At NYU Law School there must have been some blacks but again I just wasn't conscious of them.

" In May of 1941, I agreed to go into the service because I was single, in good health and I knew my number was coming up. All I knew about a military officer was that he was a guy who wore pink pants [The dress uniform of the period]. The Army sent me to Camp Jackson for basic training as part of quartermaster bakery outfit, although I was already a lawyer, for which they apparently had no use in the regular army." For Pedowitz during his first year as a soldier, blacks would be as invisible as they had been when he was a civilian. All that would change within a few months after the Japanese bombed Hawaii.

In the autumn of 1941, with that attack a few months off, the American Red Cross declared itself firmly on the side of segregation announcing that it would not accept blood donated by blacks on the grounds that whites would refuse plasma if they knew its origin. The army accepted the decision of the Red Cross. Major General James J. Magee, the surgeon general, wrote a memorandum to Assistant Secretary of War John J. McCloy in which he noted, "For reasons not biologically convincing but which are commonly recognized as psychologically important in America, it is not deemed advisable to collect and mix Caucasian and Negro blood indiscriminately for later administration to members of the military forces."

Within the defense establishment, the stances of the two highest civilian authorities adamantly opposed change. Secretary of War Henry L. Stimson with responsibility for the Army (which included the air corps) noted in his diary, "Leadership is not embedded in the Negro race. Yet to try to make commissioned officers to lead them in battle . . . is only to work a disaster to both. Colored men do very well under white officers but every time we try to lift them a little beyond where they can go, disaster and confusion follows. In the draft we are preparing to give the Negroes a fair shot in every service, even in aviation where I doubt very much they will not produce disaster there. Nevertheless, they are going to have a try but I hope for heavens sakes they don't mix the white and colored troops together in the same units for then we shall certainly have trouble."

An entry for 25 October 1940 notes, "We must not place too much responsibility on a race which is not showing initiative. Mrs. Roosevelt engages in impulsive and impudent folly in her criticism of our policies. The foolish leaders of the colored race are seeking, at bottom, social equality." Stimson boasted he was not prejudiced, that he was a descendant of Abolitionists at the same moment as he remarked on "those foolish leaders of the colored race who objected to segregation while seeking social equality. This was impossible because of the impossibility of race mixture by marriage."

In the summer of 1940, thirteen black messmen serving on the cruiser *Philadelphia* signed a letter to the *Pittsburgh Courier*. Describing themselves as "sea going bellhops, chambermaids and dishwashers," they wrote, "With three months of training in making beds, shining shoes and servicing officers completed we are sent to various ships and stations of the Navy. The white sailor after his training period is not only eligible for the branch of service he has chosen but he is automatically advanced in ratings and his pay is increased to $36 a month without ever having to take an examination." In contrast, they said, they were required to serve a full year at $21 a month and then pass a test, which still did not guarantee them a rating. The navy issued the entire baker's dozen discharges as undesirables. The navy also stated, "After many years of experience, the policy of not enlisting men of the colored race for any branch of the naval service except the messman's branch was adopted to meet the best interests of the general ship efficiency." Secretary of the Navy Frank Knox, whose jurisdiction extended over the marines, openly defended the policy with a remark about the impossibility of other assignments because of the close living conditions required on board ship.

Major General Thomas Holcomb, commandant of the marines bluntly refused to have any men of color in his organization. "If it were a question of having a Marine Corps of 5,000 whites or 250,000 Negroes, I would rather have the whites."

As 1941 wound down black leaders with William Hastie at the forefront lobbied for an end to segregation in the armed forces. General George C. Marshall, the army chief of staff, responded on 1 December 1941, "The settlement of vexing racial problems cannot be permitted to complicate the tremendous task of the War Department. . . . the War Department cannot ignore the social relationship between Negroes and whites which has been established by the American people through custom and habit; second, that either through lack of educational opportunities or other causes the level of intelligence and occupational skill of the Negro population is considerably below that of the white . . . experiments within the army in the solution of social problems are fraught with danger to efficiency, discipline and morale." Six days later, the bombs from Japanese aircraft rendered the discussion academic, so far as official Washington was concerned. The policy makers could and did firmly cite the war effort as precluding consideration of any other issue. A statement from the War Department dismissed any responsibility upon the military. "The army did not create the problem . . . The army is not a sociological laboratory." While the priority of prosecuting the war served as a convenient excuse for maintenance of the status quo, what began on 7 December and the shattering reverses that followed over the next few months, certainly concerned white American leaders to the exclusion of race relations as well as other social problems.

At the start of World War II the four black-only regiments were stationed in the continental United States. At Pearl Harbor, Japanese bombs and torpedoes did not discriminate, imperiling black messmen along with white sailors. Aboard the USS *West Virginia,* shrapnel mortally wounded Capt. Mervyn Bennion. Steward Dorie Miller dragged him from the bridge and then replaced a dead gunner at a machine gun. Although Miller had no formal instruction with the weapon observers credited him with shooting down two enemy planes. Awarded a Navy Cross, Miller, after the shooting stopped, continued to serve food to white officers.

When he first assumed his office as secretary of the navy, Frank Knox attempted to deal with the pressure to open up the navy by steering blacks toward the existing African American units of the army. He had claimed that any service at sea other than cooking or serving food lay beyond the capabilities of nonwhites. But because of continuing public pressure, Knox had created a committee in July 1941 to investigate whether the service should accept blacks for other duties. As a former undersecretary of the navy, Roosevelt was reluctant to roil the seas for his favorite branch of service. To a delegation of black spokesmen he proposed a gradual approach that would begin with "good Negro bands" installed on battleships, an arrangement that might lead to greater acceptance among whites and blacks. Whether the civil rights leaders were more appalled by the condescension or the absurdity they stifled their reaction. The navy's general board, composed of top level officers akin to the army's general staff, rebuffed ideas for even modest experiments to train blacks in the skills of sailors.

While the committee convened by Knox deliberated, the president discarded his musical approach and chivvied his minions for forceful action to allow more general service. Roosevelt asked the general board for a plan that would enroll 5,000 recruits. The admirals and their staffs saw no reason to accommodate the desires of the president. The board offered "regrets that it is unable to comply." In about as close to a sneer as an official report can contain, it remarked, "If in the opinion of higher authority, political pressure is such as to require the enlistment of *these people* [author's italics] for general service, let it be that." Marine corps commandant Holcomb reiterated the theme expounded by Knox, "the negro race has every opportunity now to satisfy its aspirations for combat in the Army—a very much larger organization than the Navy or Marine Corps—and their desire to enter the naval service is largely, I think, to break into a club that doesn't want them."

Two weeks after Dorie Miller manned the machine gun on the *West Virginia,* a majority report blandly declared, "The enlistment of Negroes other than as mess attendants leads to destructive and undermining conditions." Furthermore, the committee found there was no discrimination because the characteristics of blacks made them fit solely for messmen's duties. An official statement announced, "The Navy insists even more strongly that it cannot take a chance on a social experiment. Since racial integration on naval units implies much more than in any other service, the Navy feels that it cannot justly [be] expected to be so far ahead of the nation's general habits in racial matters as the advocates of full integration."

The navy's delay in adopting a less restrictive atmosphere triggered public outcry. Wendell Willkie, the opponent of FDR in 1940 and head of the Republican Party, blasted the service's "racial bias" and demanded, "Are we always as alert to practice [democracy] here at home as we are to proclaim it abroad?"

In 1942, the general board, now confronted with a wartime situation and cognizant of a less tolerant president, relented to the extent that it theoretically agreed to enlist African Americans for general service but in fact not until 1943, when the seagoing branch started to absorb draftees, was there any significant expansion of duties. At that they were almost entirely in the form of labor, stevedore, and construction tasks.

A few months later, even that most obdurate opponent of African Americans in his branch, Commandant Holcomb of the marines, issued formal directives to recruit qualified "colored male citizens of the United States between the ages of 17 and 29, inclusive, for service in a combat organization." In the main, however, African Americans were never regarded by the marine hierarchy as suitable for battle. All but a few hundred blacks who volunteered served in noncombat units. The handful that was organized to fight never saw action.

In the Philippines where both American and indigenous troops faced the Japanese, the commonwealth status of the islands looking toward full independence in a few years, separated Filipinos from the U.S. soldiers. American white officers acted as advisors to native forces and in the case of the Philippine scouts actually led them. Most of the Americans assigned to these duties regarded the local people with the same mixture of contempt and condescension employed by their brethren who supervised black troops.

Mobilization for World War II forced the military and its major source, Selective Service, to enroll physically able African Americans in vast numbers. At the time the draft began, before Pearl Harbor, many communities struggling with the burdens of the depression and clamored for military installations in their vicinity because of the expected economic benefits. In Texas, where, because of the Brownsville and Houston incidents, activation of black units was a sensitive subject, the citizens of Calverton petitioned for a base that would billet nonwhites. A letter from the local postmaster cited the large numbers of nonwhites already living in the area and bragged that good relations existed between the races. He added, "Our cotton crop on our upland East of Calvert was a failure. We haven't had a CCC Camp in our county, our town, also our country population needs something to stimulate business and employment." Citizens of Arizona also requested an installation for black troops.

For the most part, however, not even money could persuade the locals that a large number of African Americans in their neighborhood was desirable. Just as whites in Alabama complained about placement of the program for cadets at Tuskegee, other Southern states railed against the stationing of black soldiers within their precincts. The Southern Governors Conference of 1942 unanimously objected to the presence of nonwhite soldiers in their midst. Governor Homer Adkins of Arkansas warned, "The use of Negro soldiers" to guard an airfield in his state "would be a grave mistake. It would add to agitation of Negroes by subversive groups" and the "fiery Negro press." Mississippi's congressional delegation decried the as-

signment of any African American officers in their home state. Southerners argued that if it were necessary to house black troops on their turf, they
should at least be natives of the region rather than from the North. A Virginia congressman contacted native son George Marshall to ask that Camp
Lee have only a limited number of necessary black labor troops. Because
plans for Camp Lee included nearly 20,000 blacks, the army added a rifle
company of whites to the base complement in the event of a race riot. Its
services in this respect were never needed.

In Wyoming, Sen. Harry Schwartz, who championed the cause of black
airmen asked for a reduction in the number of blacks at Fort Warren because the city of Cheyenne housed so few nonwhites. As a result, 500 soldiers originally consigned to Fort Warren headed for Camp Lee. However,
the whites assigned now to replace the original contingent at Fort Warren
encountered a housing shortage. A telegram from the VII Corps pointed
out that "segregation cannot . . . be accomplished. . . . no housing available
for any increased quota of white selectees except in barracks adjacent to colored selectees . . . rather than quartering white and colored together
strongly recommend no substitution . . . of white for colored selectees." The
authorities frantically cobbled together enough temporary arrangements to
deal with the problem of the two races housed in close proximity.

Throughout the war, civilian antipathy to nonwhites engaged in the nation's defense infected many parts of the country far from the Mason-Dixon
line. The small town of Oscoda, Michigan, demanded removal of black soldiers stationed there because of fears of social and racial problems. Residents
of Spokane, Washington; Albuquerque, New Mexico; Las Vegas, Nevada; Battle Creek, Michigan; and Morehead City, North Carolina, all expressed concern at the lodging of blacks in their bailiwicks. Tucson rejected a grant of
$50,000 to build a USO for the exclusive use of black troops visiting the city.
An Arizona newspaper and a senator requested that all African American
personnel be transferred from a local airbase. The national commander of
the American Legion criticized integration of black and white soldiers in
army hospital wards and barbershops. A survey of commanders, all white,
from installations around the country indicated none wanted men of color
added to their encampments because of the inevitable complaints of the local communities.

The problem was not confined to the United States. Brigadier General
Dwight D. Eisenhower, then a member of Marshall's staff, dispatched a memorandum to his boss on "The Colored Troop Problem." He listed a series of
overseas places that objected to stationing African American soldiers for
their defense. Of Alaska he noted, "Governor Gruening states informally that
he was unfavorably inclined to the assignment of colored troops to Alaska
as he feels that the mixture of the colored race with native Indian and Es-

kimo stock is highly undesirable." (Gruening appears to have believed that the blacks were to be sent to his territory for breeding purposes.)

Australia, which since it achieved commonwealth status at the beginning of the twentieth century, employed a no-blacks immigration policy, while seriously threatened by the advance of Japanese forces, according to Eisenhower, wanted only whites. "The Australians, through Commander Harries of the Australian Embassy, advised the War Department in person that the Australian Government could not agree to the dispatch of colored units for station in Australia. Later, General Barnes reported . . . the Australian Government would agree to the assignment of a limited number provided they were removed on the termination of the emergency . . . General Brett reports that trouble has developed between white and colored soldiers; that those brawls will undoubtedly spread to the civilian population, resulting in eventual bloodshed. He *recommends withdrawal* of all *colored troops*" [Italics from DDE.]

Hawaii, Panama, Bermuda, Iceland, Trinidad, South America, and even Liberia were described as inhospitable to nonwhites. In some cases, however, the objection was voiced by the white U.S. commander for the area, rather than the local civilian officials. Army military commanders, who controlled the location of troops under their jurisdiction after March 1942, soon recognized that shipping an unwanted group of soldiers to another area only fostered complaints at the newest site. The head of the army ground forces uttered a common-sense response to the fears of civilians, noting that for the army the solution lay in military leaders, "who can forestall racial difficulties by firm discipline, just treatment, strenuous training and wholesome recreation."

A small headache for those classifying by race lay in the definition of a black. At the time of World War II, a "negro" was defined as anyone with a known trace of African American blood in his or her veins. A preponderance of white ancestry brought no release from the bondage of segregation. It was easy enough for draft boards and military reception centers to identify people with dark skins or those who presented birth certificates that described them as "negro" but light- or fair-skinned people who did not offer any evidence of the damning background could not be so easily categorized. Benjamin Davis Jr.'s wife had unknowingly "passed" when she first appeared at Fort Benning. Only identification of her husband caused a colleague's spouse to shun her. Light-skinned women who visited the Tuskegee airmen were similarly accepted in town until their connection was determined. Throughout the war, incidents of mistaken identity added to racial turmoil.

The deployment of men from Puerto Rico added another complication. The War Department attempted to segregate troops drawn from the island into separate units both for reasons of color of skin and their heavy reliance on Spanish. The authorities even designated the 245th Quartermaster Service Battalion as "colored." At the same time it labeled others from Puerto Rico as "white," although it subjected them to Jim Crow. It seemed convenient to ship the Spanish-speaking, 65th Infantry soldiers composed of Puerto Ricans to man outposts in Panama, but word came that the country did not want any blacks. The army quietly screened the regiment to remove 600 men deemed "unmistakeably colored."

The Red Cross had literally drawn a line over blood. Later, there was a compromise in which the Red Cross agreed to accept blood from blacks but to label and separate it from that of whites. Red Cross chairman Normal H. Davis agreed that the distinction had no scientific validity but declared, "the question really is whether or not the views of the majority of those for whom the blood is being produced . . . are to prevail or whether the views of the minority who wish to donate their blood should prevail." The notion that a seriously wounded battlefield casualty would rather delay his chances of survival until pints with the white label were available is hard to believe. But this separation by race continued in the Red Cross until 1963.

Painfully aware of the attitudes of their superiors, of most white GIs, and of the public, the black servicemen responded to a campaign initiated by the *Pittsburgh Courier.* It encouraged them to supplement the standard "V for Victory" sign with the fingers of one hand by adding a second V with their other hand to symbolize the triumph over discrimination at home as well as abroad.

11
Command and Control

Even as the Selective Service calls garnered large numbers of black men, a bottleneck prevented African Americans from immediate active duty. There were not enough slots open in the designated units to accommodate these recruits. To whites, aware of the impasse, it seemed unfair for African Americans to be granted a stay. To some blacks it seemed like an insult, denial of the right to serve. The problem eased with the activation of the 92d and 93d Infantry Divisions, the two units which would field black foot soldiers, although the studies following World War I had suggested segregated outfits be restricted to no larger than regimental size.

To avoid conflicts with either civilians or white units, the War Department, in the spring of 1942, located the 93d Division at Fort Huachuca, Arizona. The post had been home to black troops in the past and it was fifty miles from the nearest town of any size, effectively isolating the personnel from contact. To fill the ranks, the 25th Infantry Regiment, one of the two established Regular Army outfits, reconstituted with draftees, was joined by the 368th and 369th. The 24th Infantry was part of a hastily assembled force sent to man defenses for islands of the South Pacific, including Australia, which allegedly resented their presence.

Fort Huachuca separated officers' clubs, hospitals, and other facilities according to race. At its activation, the 93d had relied heavily on white officers, even at the company-grade level, although policy directed these positions should go to men of color. Milton Gish for the first six years of his life was a neighbor of the Eisenhower family in Abilene, Kansas. "My oldest brother Wesley and Ike delivered ice to the people in Abilene. Ike drove the ice wagon and Wesley put the ice in the homes."

The Gish family moved to Lincoln, Nebraska, where Milton attended the local schools. "There were few Negroes living there when I was growing up, although in seventh grade we had a Negro pitcher and elected him captain of the team." Gish graduated in 1932 from the University of Nebraska as an ROTC second lieutenant. Ordered to Fort Huachuca and the 93d he was assigned to instruct in the use of 60mm mortars. "But we had no mortars and had to improvise. I was transferred to command a service company. During this period, we officers had no problems with our troops and I think it was because most of the officers were from southern states, Oklahoma, Louisiana, Texas and Arkansas. We had no trouble with civilians. We were so isolated that we saw only a few Negroes [civilians] and most of them were weekend prostitutes. The only incident I recall was while I was in K Company. This young Negro was a trouble maker and for some reason I was called to check it out. I was cleaning my .45 and had it in my hand when I found him. He reported the incident because he thought I would shoot him."

On the heels of the activation of the 93d came two more large units which absorbed thousands of African Americans. The nexus of the 92d Infantry Division were the 365th, 366th, and 370th Infantry Regiments but with Huachuca occupied by the 93d, the War Department, sensitive to problems with civilian communities or antagonistic white troops, could not find a suitable camp for all 15,000 soldiers. The army, instead of training the various components together, parceled them out to a number of camps in Alabama, Arkansas, Kentucky, and Indiana, an arrangement unique to infantry division preparation. Somewhat smaller in size, the 2d Cavalry Division, incorporating the 9th and 10th Cavalry Regiments, set up shop at Fort Clark, Texas, and Camp Lockett, California, again an unusual dispersal of a single force.

Gish would remain with the 93d throughout the war, moving on to a division staff post but an influx of black officers replaced most of the junior-grade whites. During World War I the army had operated a separate officer training program at Fort Des Moines. With a greater number of options for African American service during World War II, the service schooled candidates for commissions at the same installations that instructed whites, albeit the men attended class separately, ate and slept according to the rules of segregation. ROTC programs and federalized National Guard units also supplied black officers in various specialties.

Although many opportunities to win a commission existed, the African American pool of eligible men was disproportionately small in comparison to that of whites. Entrance to OCS required a minimum score of 110 on the Army General Classification Test, as well as passing a physical examination. Separate but unequal schooling, particularly in the South, deprived many blacks of the kind of academic background upon which much of the AGCT depended. In 1940, blacks accounted for slightly less than 11 percent of the 132 million Americans, and 80,000 African Americans held a college diploma, compared to three million whites. Only fifty-four nonwhites in the entire country were qualified mechanical engineers against 82,000 whites. Three times as many African Americans came from farms while only slightly more than 5 percent of the nation's electricians were blacks. In white-collar jobs such as accountancy, bookkeeping, and that of cashier, the ratio between the races stood at forty-four to one.

Poverty, substandard housing, an inadequate diet, and lack of proper sanitation affected health and stamina. As a consequence, fewer blacks met physical standards. Furthermore, since white officers supervised or actually controlled OCS programs, candidates sometimes washed out for offenses that alienated their racist superiors rather than because they could not do the work.

Once an African American qualified for a commission he bumped against an even more resistant ceiling. Benjamin O. Davis Sr. wrestled with the issue in his office at the War Department and expressed his dismay. ". . . the interpretation by the Commanding General of the 93d Division limits colored officers on duty with the division to the grade of 1st lieutenant . . . unless the 93d Division is designated as a unit in which Negro officers can serve in all grades. Upon the promotion of a Negro officer above the grade of 1st lt., he is automatically assigned to another unit. The announcement of this policy has certainly shaken the morale of the 93d Division. Negro officers are required to meet the same qualifications, make the same sacrifices as white officers. I cannot believe the War Department is going to maintain policy that is so unjust or bad.

"I cannot see why it would be any more degrading or unjust or whatever it may be called, for a white man of lower grade to serve under a Negro officer of a higher grade than for a colored man to serve under a white man . . . There certainly should be no objection to Negroes commanding Negroes." Once again, Davis, who devoted his life to military service and hardly qualified as a radical on race relations, firmly asserted that rank supercedes the individual, making color of skin irrelevant.

The lack of formal education handicapped enlisted men in the eyes of their white superiors. According to a War Department survey published in 1944, although more than 50 percent of the army's nonwhites had completed grade school, 26 percent some high school, with 17 percent high school graduates, almost 83 percent of them who took the AGCT fell into Categories IV and V, the two lowest, while only 30 percent of the whites did so. In the eyes of whites that was one explanation for what they perceived as failure to perform adequately. To be sure, for certain duties involving technology and skills that required good comprehension of written material, book learning and study habits were essential. And even at the lowest level of military endeavor, understanding of the Articles of War and the capacity to read and absorb manuals on weapons would seem highly desirable. A significant number of men had vocabulary problems, being unable to comprehend words such as "discipline," "chevron," "sentinel," "barrage," "cadre," "counterclockwise," and other terms used commonly for military operations. Additionally, men with substandard formal education tended to be more susceptible to venereal disease or sickness through failure to observe good hygiene. They also seemed more apt to go AWOL. The War Department had directed that no more than 8 percent of any unit should be Grade V but particularly in the infantry divisions that were heavily manned by Southern blacks, the percentages ran much higher. Concerned about communication between officers and men, the authorities produced a card covering possible problems when commanding nonwhites. The materials advised the officer to ask himself: "Did I make allowances for lack of education? Did I make an effort to teach skills? Did I provide literacy courses? Did I use phrases or words not understandable? Did I use or say things that wounded men? Did I keep before the men why we fight? Did I protect their rights with other troops and the public?"

But some experts questioned the AGCT as a true test of intelligence. To serve effectively as a rifleman did not require more than a modest amount of learning. Benjamin O. Davis Sr. had recalled that some of his cavalry troopers while illiterate were highly effective soldiers. In one World War II experiment, a random group of black soldiers underwent a nonverbal type of test; 30 percent formerly consigned to Grade V under the AGCT now registered higher, with some achieving Grade I.

Whites who came from backgrounds where formal education was a prerequisite of the culture and who were disposed to see African Americans as inferior per force regarded the unschooled blacks as inherently defective. The maintenance of segregation, the pronounced differences in backgrounds and culture, even in the North and Far West, continued the practice of looking upon the black soldier as something different, a phenomenon to be held up, inspected, studied, interpreted, and above all judged. Whites, commanding blacks, filed a number of memoranda with the War Department in which they explained how they successfully handled these exotics.

A letter from an officer serving with an antiaircraft battery somewhere in the Pacific, whose recipient forwarded it with praise to Davis, read, ". . . I am sincere in my beliefs that these troops will act their very best . . . if they are properly led, which is true of any class of troops but those of the colored race have certain characteristics so different from those of other races, especially white that it makes it especially true of them. They are without doubt the most responsive of any people. They respond so readily to any type of leadership. . . . appeal to that responsiveness by those things the man can understand: pride of the individual; a deep religious consciousness; continual changing of interests; continual passing out of compliments and that good word—giving them color; always showing them an outward humanness. These are some of the ways to reach the man and the biggest of these is pure, unadulterated showmanship. You might think that such ways also apply to the white soldier. They do, but not in the greater sense they do to the colored troops.

"Some of the things I do you never have to do with white troops . . . I encourage battery commanders to buy good garrison caps, also good neckties. Names of drivers are painted on the windshields of all vehicles. Vehicles have a nice big 'safe driver' when a man drives a truck six months without an accident.

"Best way to appeal to their pride is service ribbons. I got the jaundice ribbon throughout. I had to order them airmail but we were the first to have them. They were awarded at battery ceremonies by myself. Then I got the first American area ribbon. Cost a case of Scotch but we . . . awarded them three weeks before anyone else did. I have given out Good Conduct ribbons freely. If a man just stayed out of the guardhouse for three years he got one with a big ceremony . . . I've been trying to get the authorities here [the country was not named] to award their ribbon for six months service. Officers are required to wear ribbons to set the example. You ought to see a big buck with his ribbons. You can imagine what a big shot he is with the women, their weak point. I harp on that too, encourage battery dances, well run so now we are getting the very highest strata of the native population as our friends.

"Color, I do not mean black or white but that intangible Babe Ruth had and Lou Gehrig did not. I dress the band up with white spats. I finally found the man I wanted for a drum major, big, tough, commanding, with the ability to almost prance. I hiked the beat up instead of the usual 120 per minute. I carry the biggest cane and I encouraged all grades, one and two and three to carry swagger sticks to walk in front of the battery. The best example is my baseball team. I will not let them on the field unless they have a complete uniform as a baseball team. All the other teams play in the usual conglomeration of soldier clothes. My team looks like a baseball outfit. The overall impression makes the individual soldier consciously proud of his team."

Davis must have writhed as he read on. "My own actions and conduct are funny. I have found that by applying showmanship tactics and less of the stern and unyielding West Point discipline that you and I know, the very best turns up. I pay a great deal of attention and always find something good. I always let the man know that I like it. I will stop my car any place, get out and compliment a man on his salute or dress. I find something good every place I go. I know that when I return a salute and say, 'Good morning, Walker, or Jones,' I have made him one of my men. From that time he is with me, not neutral or against. It is 'me and the cuhnel' or 'de cuhnel say to me'" [Another example of white ebonics.]

". . . Do not get the idea that all is love and kisses in a colored outfit. I have troubles and lots of them. There is never a dull moment. In such a group of men there are bound to be many morons, bums and irresponsible wrong-thinking individuals. I have my share. There are things I handle so that the men are kept out of the guardhouse if possible. Shortly after I came here, at a meeting of the senior noncoms I told them that I would refuse to handle disrespect to noncoms. These and similar cases [should] be handled behind the barracks by themselves. I'd back them up, of course. If one ever broke a jaw, the man must have attacked the sergeant and the sergeant was acting only in self-defense.

"When you have trouble in a colored outfit, it can be layed to the unit commander. For this reason, the greatest possible care should be exercized on [selection] of commanders for such outfits. I would say the type must have a flair for the dramatic. He must be a showman, must have least of all ability as an AA technician. Brains are the cheapest commodity, real leadership, the most expensive and rarest. Because even good officers cannot make the grade with colored troops, I believe that each regimental commander should have some [way] out available to get rid of those unfit for such duty without prejudice to the officers in return."

When Davis returned the note to its owner he ignored the condescension, the assumptions that pseudodecorations and a false camaraderie made good soldiers out of African Americans. Instead he focused on the idea of leadership. "It is another confirmation of the conclusion arrived at by nearly all the officers who have conducted investigations involving racial disturbances, namely that such occurences are largely attributable to mistakes on the parts of officers and commanders in charge of colored troops."

The letter from the antiaircraft battery commander was replicated in other memos that circulated through the War Department. Among these was an undated, confidential memo titled "Certain Characteristics of the Negro Which Affect Command of Negro Troops" and it enumerated them in a handy, short form: "Gregarious, extrovertive, strongly attached to group and family. Easygoing—line of least resistance, not physically 'lazy.' Very sensitive. Resentful of correction. Easily hurt by criticism in public. Mentally lazy, not retentive. Ruled by instinct and emotion rather than by reason. Has to be made to face facts, prone to escapism. Likes pomp and ceremony. Stubborn no end—Hard headed as a Swede. [Stereotypes were not limited to blacks.] Difficult to make assume responsibility. Lacks mechanical sense. Has keen sense of rhythm which can be put to good advantage in drills of all kinds (marching, gun crew). Lies easily. Can *only* be led, not driven."

Another, more formal series of instructions counseled: ". . . an officer must be additionally perspicacious to discern if a Negro soldier is just feigning ignorance, [this is] a favorite trick of the colored soldier who understands much yet appears not to understand . . . They pay only superficial attention to talks and instructions. The white soldier frequently will absorb much more of lectures because of a vague feeling of duty. The more appealing approach must be had with the colored soldier. His morale can be held at high level by combining plenty of hard work, good food, frequent drills and ceremonies with a reasonable opportunity and facilities for recreation.

"The most important factor is the first, the provision of carefully planned productive work in which he can take pride at the end of each day's accomplishments. He will not work until told specifically and exactly what to do. He will not look for work. He must be assigned a specific task that will keep him busy or else he will soon fall asleep . . . the colored soldier is extremely responsive to compliments. In directing a man, praise should be given any point warranted while requiring correction of a deficiency. 'Sergeant, these look like wonderfully tasteful cookies but I don't think I would like to eat one until you clean that stove properly.'

"Occasionally a new soldier will fail to obey or refuse to obey. The best procedure is to send him to the barracks or elsewhere and have him around in private and explain to him the need for obedience and insist upon his immediate obedience on the spot. Make an issue of it then and although this might result in a man ending up in the guardhouse, sending a man to the guardhouse does little to make him feel the shame attached to it and the loss of pay generally is not felt severely. In the guardhouse he just gets time to talk it over with sympathetic soldiers in a similar plight. He must be punished promptly for any dereliction of duty so that he gets over it and makes a fresh start. Brooding over his delinquency is fatal for him.

"The colored soldier wants to do right and continue in the good graces of his superiors. He hates very much to be repimanded by an officer whom he respects and one of the most effective ways to make him come round is to shame or to challenge him. Knowledge of the Bible or appropriate quotations now and then is helpful. The colored chaplain is extremely helpful in getting the views of the men and getting the difficult points across to them.

"Commanding officers should cope with the colored officers at great length. The colored man has a fierce pride in his race and that pride should be appealed to on any appropriate occasion. Pointing out to colored soldiers that the enjoyment of their four freedoms after the war will depend largely on how well they conduct themselves as soldiers now is appreciated by them and is effective." Like others from the past, the author does not explain why only for African Americans "enjoyment of their four freedoms after the war" depended upon the effectiveness of their military service.

"While every attempt should be made not to focus undue attention on the colored question, no hesitation should be displayed in discussing and dealing with any specific and pertinent phase of the racial problem. It may be said that colored troops require more of their leaders in the form of consideration and that conversely they may look upon their leaders more than in other organizations and in well-led colored organizations there is intense loyalty to its leaders that is sensed by them far more than is apparent to a casual observer. Greater effort is required by an officer of colored troops which is more than repaid by the loyalty he feels that his organization has for him . . . It is always necessary to avoid slights and listen carefully and understandingly to his side of the story. Never argue with colored soldiers. After sifting the evidence, make a decision and inform the colored soldiers and have no more of it. Many colored soldiers have the unfortunate faculty of convincing themselves they are right simply by repeating the argument often enough.

"In civilian life before entering the army, the colored soldier was used to obedience all his life. He will gladly continue to do so with a will when he knows what is required. Instructions to colored soldiers should be warm, fatherly and personal. They have been fathered for generations and the Army can't make completely independent individuals out of them in a brief year. It is all very well to say that they should be treated like other soldiers but it is necessary to remember that to secure them proper uniforms generally requires helping them dress. Storming at a soldier for the improper way he salutes helps little. Much more helpful is to take the time to describe in detail the proper method even though he has previously been shown a dozen times. Bawling out an individual for a dirty rifle avails little. He must be shown exactly where the defect lies and the specific methods for correcting it. It is obviously insufficient to say, 'Shoes will be shined for inspection,' when one considers some of them have never had new shoes before and they have never previously considered it necessary to shine shoes.

"While persistent firmness and strict obedience are always necessary, the hard-boiled vituperative 1st sergeant attitude famous in movies and fiction has little place in a colored unit. The instructor of colored troops must be exceedingly well grounded and well prepared and must have the ability to show how on the job. Bluff and generalities simply do not [work] with the colored soldier. All instruction must be exceedingly and deliberately specific. This applies equally with the NCO as the private. It is insufficient in a Noncom meeting to express the desire that the barracks be policed up better or that the venereal rate be reduced without telling the noncoms in detail what they should tell their men and exactly what their duties are.

"In giving instructions or issuing orders, extreme care must be taken not to stress inadvertently some insignificant point or the result may be perfection on that point to the exclusion of others. While otherwise very expressive on listening to a talk or receiving instructions, the colored soldier frequently conceals his reactions quite completely. It requires almost a sixth sense to determine his reactions.

"Much more than white soldiers, colored soldiers desire to be known by their names. It seems extremely desirable for a battalion commander to know his men by their names, even their first names. Before induction into the army, they were generally known as much by their first name as their last name and that will not change materially in this war. Occasionally, to call a man 'Corporal John' instead of 'Corporal Smith' makes him feel that the speaker is a friend of his.

"The colored soldier is extremely responsive to what is known as 'color'. He likes to stand out from the crowd, be distinctive. In the showman part, a general flair for the dramatic, a successful leader of colored troops must have full appreciation of this and direct this tendency into the proper channels. He loves to march and marches well. He likes to 'sound off' in giving commands and may be used for parades and ceremonies of all kinds. Parades should be used in great frequency.

"Supplementing uniforms is desirable as far as regulations will permit and sometimes a bit beyond. MPs and the band should have white shoulder guards, belts, leggings and etc. For the rank and file, the peak cap, formally known as the garrison cap, should be cleared for all to wear on pass. High quality neckties, garrison belts, individually tailored uniforms are items the colored soldier likes in his uniform and their adaptation should be encouraged wherever possible. A pride in the individual can be easily stimulated by the wearing of various service ribbons. Medals for marksmanship, drivers and mechanics are well within his [the black soldier's] ability to secure. The colored soldier revels in the wearing of medals. An elaborate and colorful ceremony is possible. It should be held in awarding medals and ribbons and much made of the event."

A few points could obviously apply to white enlisted men. The morale of any serviceman can be maintained with a combination of hard work, good food, reasonable opportunities, and facilities for recreation. That men in uniform do not look for work is again fairly universal; the expression "to soldier on the job" is indicative. The notion that blacks respond only to insignia and dressing up of uniforms ignores the enormous investment by white organizations in gee gaws calculated to attract everyone from high-level officers down to the lowest privates. The prospect of pinning wings upon their chests, the so-called fifty-mission crushed hat, and the appropriate shoulder patches enticed many into cadet programs. Paratroopers lusted for the symbols of their trade and high leather boots, and in fact airborne troops were known to assault any unqualified GIs sporting these unique shoes. Officers who before the war swaggered with Sam Brown belts still cut gaudy figures with their tailored dress pinks, green jackets, peaked caps, and shiny marks of rank. Those of flag rank freely improvised on their cap markings, turning the conventional "scrambled eggs" into personal statements à la Douglas MacArthur. No other country was as profligate as the United States in dishing out tangible honors and ribbons. Ground forces all relied on marksmanship medals as a means to encourage weapons proficiency. The dressed-up MPs promoted by the War Department circular as supplementing the uniforms of blacks were a standard feature of upper-echelon ceremonies. Marching bands, pomp, and circumstance pervaded military traditions worldwide throughout history and exclusive of racial considerations.

Whites promulgating special ways of dealing with African Americans assumed some inherent behavioral reactions of blacks. For example, "While otherwise expressive on listening to a talk or receiving instructions, the colored soldier frequently conceals his reactions quite completely." Few Americans were familiar with the techniques by which nonwhites coped with the slings and arrows of racism, particularly in the South where overt reactions might readily lead to disagreeable consequences. Ways of dress, patterns of speech, and means of expressing one's self often owed their form to the need of avoiding confrontations with oppressors.

An obvious stereotype was the belief that "rhythm" lay in the genes of African Americans, and a fondness for parade. White officers, therefore, frequently arranged for them to engage in more close-order drill than accorded whites. In a self-fulfilling prophecy, practice made precision, rather than racial characteristics.

None of the white authorities on African American troop control took cognizance of the biggest influence, the attitudes and actions of white civilians and soldiers with regard to black soldiers. An almost unending stream of incidents at home and abroad testified to the tension between the races. From June 1941, when Ben Davis Sr. accepted his post as advisor to the inspector general "in connection with matters pertaining to the various colored units now in service" he had roamed the country to observe and investigate disturbances. He filed a number of reports, which while differing on specifics, sounded similar themes, the poor quality of white officers assigned to black units, the absence of equal facilities, resentment toward segregation, and the treatment of soldiers off post. In dealing with the conflicts that involved massive groups, Davis also served as an ombudsman for black GIs. During his tours, he patiently listened to the questions and gripes of individuals upset about their particular case or uncertain about benefits for dependents. When he visited MacDill Field in Tampa, 600 men, one-third of the African American complement, lined up to speak with him. He had to enlist the base chaplain and some NCOs to group the petitioners based upon similar issues and then speak with a representative. Sometimes he was confronted by soldiers whose real problem was not racism but a lack of understanding of what it meant to be in the army.

At the same time, Davis was never able to forget that in spite of his august position, he was just another black man. Segregation pursued Davis even in his home bailiwick of Washington. As long as he worked there, the War Department provided no dining facilities for its blacks, and rather than eat in a segregated place elsewhere, Davis fasted at lunch time.

As early as 1941, while the nation was still at peace, the body of Pvt. Felix Hall, his hands tied behind him, was found hanging from a tree in a wooded section of Fort Benning. To African Americans, the death smacked of a lynching but Benning authorities, apparently unconvinced by the hands tied behind the back, labeled it a suicide. The circumstances behind the hanging were never discovered.

In the city of Columbia, South Carolina, near Fort Jackson, bitterness bordering on rage enveloped black 48th Quartermaster Regiment soldiers, white 30th Division infantrymen, white MPs, and the townies of both races. In April 1941, the flammable mix ignited into an exchange of rifle fire by troops, and during the following year an interracial medley of men in and out of uniform brawled in the Columbia streets.

During the summer of 1941, at Fayetteville, North Carolina, the nearest town to Fort Bragg, a large number of African American soldiers, immediately after a payday and a night in town, gathered at a bus stop for the ride back to Bragg. Many of them had been drinking. When a bus arrived, the soldiers crammed in but some sought to bar the unarmed black MPs from accompanying them. As the disorder spread, the driver refused to depart unless he received protection. A detachment of white MPs appeared and attempted to quell the disturbance by grabbing those they deemed troublemakers and slamming them with truncheons.

One soldier seized a pistol carried by an MP and fired six shots at its owner. Another MP returned fire and a volley of bullets exploded outside the bus. When order finally was restored, a white MP and a black soldier lay dead and three more were wounded. At Fort Bragg, panicky officers ordered all blacks on post herded into the stockade to join those arrested at the site of the shootings. Press reports, gossip, and the investigation of the incident which could not identify the killers angered both races.

Arkansas became another battleground as several hundred black troops, from the 94th Engineer Battalion, a Michigan unit on maneuvers, visited the small town of Gurdon, which offered neither hospitality nor any recreation. As the men milled about the streets, white MPs brusquely urged them to move on, rather than hang about. While they waited for transportation back to the bivouac area, rumors of ill treatment circulated. The soldiers picked up stones or branches with which to defend themselves if attacked. At the same time they shouted unpleasant and profane remarks about the inhabitants.

The night passed without any confrontation but the aroused citizens augmented the local police force with hastily recruited deputies and promised to use force if any trouble developed. Unsubstantiated tales of violent acts worried the VII Corps area commander enough for him to declare Gurdon off limits and shift the battalion to a new bivouac site several miles farther away. Unfortunately, no one thought to notify the civilian authorities who decided to go on the offensive. State police with drawn guns appeared at the entrance to the 94th's encampment, ordered the army sentinels off the highway and struck several of them in the process.

Two days later, as the engineers assembled on the road to hike to their new location, the Arkansas cops reported to the 2d Army headquarters that a mob of black soldiers was rampaging on the highway. The provost marshal accepted the report as fact and authorized the civilians to control matters until a military police force could take charge. State troopers, their ranks swollen with the armed deputies in civilian dress, reached the scene and with curses and epithets ordered the soldiers off the road and into a ditch and woods soggy from a heavy rain. When a white officer protested, a state trooper hit him in the face, calling him "A Yankee nigger lover."

Military police who reached the scene made no effort to interfere with the actions of the white civilians. Seeing themselves at the apparent mercy of the police and their allies, a number of black soldiers slipped away through the woods, some working their way to safety at Fort Custer while others, terrified by the danger, went AWOL.

An anonymous member of the 94th later wrote to his family about the encounter. "We were scared almost to death . . . we went on a 10 mile hike alongside of the highway off the concrete. All of a sudden six truck loads of mobsters came sizzling down the highway in the other direction. They jumped out with guns and sub-machine guns and [revolvers] drawn, cursing, slapping and saying unheard of things. . . . They took us off the highway into the woods. Daring anyone to say a word, they hit two of our white officers who tried to say something back. But the bad part of it all, the military police were among them and against us."

Referring to the earlier incident, the letter stated, "We have guards, guarding a place and the State police deliberately came off the highway, took [one's] gun (rifle) which was empty and beat Yankee Doodle on his head. These people are crazy, stone crazy. . . . Our officers are nearly as afraid as we are. They call them 'Yankee Nigger lovers,' us 'black Yankees.'"

When the War Department failed to take steps to prevent the outbreaks a high level of violence permeated confrontations. Early in 1942 a riot at Alexandria, Louisiana, involved hundreds of soldiers and civilians. Little Rock, Arkansas, witnessed the shooting of a black soldier by a white cop. In Tuskegee, the home of the cadet program for nonwhites, Alabama police surrendered, at gunpoint, a soldier prisoner to a black MP, then recaptured the accused with the aid of fifteen civilians carrying shotguns. A pitched battle was avoided only after white officers rounded up angry black soldiers in town and brought them back to camp. At Fort Dix, New Jersey, white military police shot it out with black soldiers in an argument about a telephone booth and three men died.

Affairs of this nature ultimately forced the War Department to examine the dynamics that governed the maintenance of order. Army intelligence worried whether dirty work by enemy agents aided by Communists and radical blacks might be responsible for the unrest. Investigators from G-2, however, subsequently put to bed the "outside agitators" explanation when they announced awareness of "several types of subversive groups at work . . . but have been unable to discover evidence of action by these groups in the Armed Forces . . ." The intelligence experts advised that the location of troops, the discipline imposed, the police methods, and the absence of recreational facilities all played a role in fomenting trouble. The G-2 paper fingered the basic source of discontent with a recommendation that the army mandate due deference for its members, "irrespective of the race, color or previous condition of servitude of the wearer . . ." At the same time, the authors also asked that "all possible steps should be taken to reduce and control the publication of inflammatory and vituperative articles in the colored press."

The findings of G-2 met a mixed reception. Some leaders continued to blame "Propaganda . . . being promulgated by outside agencies" and those in a position to change policies and institute new programs dithered. By the summer of 1942, after six months of war that mostly featured defeats, Washington seemed to realize that the failure to address the racial problems within the military might worsen with disastrous effects upon the national effort.

Within the War Department's power lay means to prevent much of the violence and lessen tension. One obvious remedy was better training and instruction to all military policemen. Although some effort in that direction occurred, the concentration upon producing soldiers to fight a war minimized efforts to professionalize a force designed to restrain these GIs. Added reliance upon African American MPs in camps and towns with a heavy presence of nonwhites, however, helped considerably.

Beginning with the peacetime draft in late 1940 and throughout World War II, the question of jurisdiction over those soldiers accused of breaking a civil statute or committing a crime off post produced confusion. The laws enacted to cover this period of time clearly reserved to the military commander the right to custody of a member of the armed forces if he or she ran afoul of the local regulations governing misdemeanors or even felonies. Civil authorities could only hold that person with the agreement of the commander. But in many cases, the local police ignored the restrictions and seized, beat, and imprisoned men without regard to the limitations on such behavior.

While some local newspapers and civic leaders blamed subversion or undisciplined African Americans, there were magazines and newspapers that sensed deeper causes for the problems. The black press placed the discontent squarely upon racial discrimination. The *Amsterdam Star-News,* published in New York City, said, "They [black servicemen] cherish a deep resentment against the vicious race persecution which they and their forebears have long endured. They feel that they are soon to go overseas to fight for freedom over there. When their comparative new-found freedom is challenged by Southern military police and prejudiced superiors, they fight for freedom over here."

Some white organs of opinion supported this view. The magazine *Common Sense* observed, "The leaders of the most responsible Negro organizations have said that the 13,000,000 Negroes in America are not 'wholeheartedly and unreservedly' behind this war. It is not Hitler's fault that they are not. It is our fault. Negroes are discriminated against in defense industries. They are even discriminated against by many unions . . ."

The Roman Catholic publication *The Commonweal* remarked, "The natural reaction of the colored population is to wonder just how much it is worth their while to join in a fight which is generally advertised as a fight for 'democracy' when their own share of democracy is at present so small and gives no promise of being much greater in the future."

One of the South's most prominent newspapers, the Richmond, Virginia, *News Leader* editorialized, "If Negro soldiers are to be drafted into the army or are to be accepted as volunteers, they must be treated as fellow-soldiers and not as vassals or as racial inferiors . . ." The newspaper echoed the Civil War statements, "They are entitled to the same uniform, the same food, the same facilities that other soldiers enjoy." However, the *News Leader* was hardly about to endorse desegregation. "As the South well knows upon longer and closer experience than the North has had, this does not mean that either whites or Negroes are at their best in the same company, the same branch, the same mess. They are not . . . [but] boys can be brought to see that they must fight—together and not against each other."

Such comments in the media of the day changed very little in the way of public opinion. However, the furor over the prewar racial disorders involving white and black soldiers eventually roused the War Department to begin work on programs that might dissipate bitterness and promote a more harmonious relationship among those wearing the same uniform over different-colored skins. But it would be years before a committee could decide on an effective presentation of materials. That effort may have been galvanized by the upswing of skirmishes and full blown conflicts that erupted in

1943. At some of the larger army posts which housed huge numbers of men from both races, pitched battles that employed everything from fists to rifles interrupted the preparations for massive offensives against the Axis powers in Italy, on the French coast, and in the South Pacific. Elements of the 93d Division, with morale down because of abrupt, unexplained transfers of personnel, while in Phoenix, Arizona, engaged in a shooting spree with black MPs that killed an officer, an enlisted man, and a civilian, and seriously wounded a dozen GIs. The courts-martial that followed handed out sixteen sentences of fifty years of hard labor.

When the regiment reassembled at Camp Van Dorn, Mississippi, for retraining, the GIs considered themselves being punished through the assignment to a firmly segregated area that offered neither recreation nor entertainment. The soldiers acted out their resentment by showing up at the area service club out of uniform, by breaking rules on consumption of beer, and violating closing hours. Unruly behavior turned criminal with the theft of stock from the post exchange and only the arrival of a military police officer could disperse a group about to tear up the town.

The situation deteriorated. During a confrontation between a military policeman and a black soldier outside of camp, a local sheriff intervened. The civilian authority fatally shot the GI when he tried to run away. Alerted to the killing, the regimental commander forestalled a move by the dead man's company to take revenge, as he ordered the firing pins removed from all rifles. He set an officer guard over the supply room. But in another company of the regiment, the soldiers rushed their supply room and grabbed a number of rifles. A riot squad of black MPs approached several hundred angry soldiers gathered in the camp who then charged them. The military cops fired into the throng. As the chain of events neared critical mass the regimental commander and his chaplain arrived to plead restraint. Eventually, the soldiers returned to their barracks. It took several days of intensive search to locate all of the stolen rifles. Meanwhile, the citizens in the area, having heard that the troops had been organizing to march on their town, armed themselves and demanded the regiment be shipped out.

An uneasy peace lasted for about a month before a dance on post which imported a number of young women from surrounding towns occasioned another near disaster. Far more soldiers than the premises could accommodate poured into the service club. When club officials could not clear the building the regimental guard and black MPs were summoned. Still, those in the hall refused to vacate it. Finally, a battalion of whites from the 99th Division, stationed at Van Dorn, managed to break up the crowd of 2,000. The tension between the local community and the regiment was so overwhelming that the War Department felt it necessary to remove the regiment. Since no active theater of operations wanted a separate infantry regiment, particularly one composed of African Americans, the solution was to consign the outfit to the Aleutian Islands where the men served in garrison status for the remainder of the war.

Camp Stewart, Georgia, also rumbled with discontent. There was a volatile mixture of troops from both races, with the city of Savannah as the potential battleground, since together with the African American and white GIs, mostly all white, marine, navy, and coast guard men spent their liberties in Savannah. A flurry of letters and petitions from individuals in the military as well as from civilian groups in the vicinity triggered a visit by Benjamin Davis Sr. in his capacity as a representative of the army's inspector general. Even as Davis and his associates completed their investigation and filed recommendations designed to dampen tensions, a number of altercations inflamed the African American soldiers. A tale of a black woman raped and murdered by white soldiers who also killed her husband spread through Camp Stewart. The story, later found to be false, added to the anger of the nonwhites, already aroused by several incidents such as military police accused of harassing troops at a dance and a soldier who sought water at an ice plant receiving a blow to the head with tongs instead.

On the evening of 9 June, about 100 soldiers, some bearing rifles, gathered in the African American section of Camp Stewart. Officers and military police attempted to break up the group and at least one shot was fired. In the confusion that followed over the next few hours, men broke into gun racks and supply rooms to arm themselves with ammunition, rifles, and even submachine guns.

When a military police vehicle rolled through the area, someone fired on it and more shots orginated in other parts of the camp. By the time two white battalions protected by half-tracks restored some order, five people had been wounded, including four MPs and one had been killed. The subsequent inquiry produced the usual explanations about Northern blacks unable to adapt to Southern ways, the low educational level of the African American, coupled with his "superstition, imagination and excitability" that made him particularly susceptible to rumors or agitators. The standard disciplinary actions were taken against those identified as active participants.

Similar outbreaks occured at other military encampments while military authorities struggled to control the growing penchant for mayhem. Race relations played a major role in the embroglios, but to complicate matters, with millions of young males in uniform there were bound to be some simple criminal acts. Trained in the arts of war, commanders, burdened by the racial baggage of tradition, also brought little sophistication to the need for distinguishing the individual thefts, robberies, assaults, rapes, and murders from behavior that had its genesis in the perception of maltreatment because of skin color. Adding further to the chaos, the race riots in civilian communities such as New York's Harlem, Detroit, and Los Angeles enveloped people in and out of uniform.

The attorney general of the United States, Francis Biddle, offered a casual observation on the Detroit melee. "One of the striking features of the Detroit riots was that there were no racial clashes in the plants where a well-disciplined union [the United Auto Workers] had insisted it would not tolerate the refusal of whites to work side by side with Negroes." Had the military authorities thought of looking for other models, they might have also taken a cue from the merchant marine, a civilian operation. It was totally integrated, employed some black offficers, and both races shared bunk areas and ate together.

While Gen. Benjamin O. Davis Sr., acted "the good soldier," overtly accepting the racial separation in the armed forces whatever his personal feelings, the civilian advisor to the War Department, William Hastie, fought against segregation. Assistant Secretary of War John J. McCloy, as chairman of the Advisory Committee on Negro Troop policies, told Hastie in 1942, "Frankly I do not think that the basic issues of this war are involved in the question of whether Colored troops serve in segregated units or mixed units and I doubt whether you can convince the people of the United States that the basic issues of freedom are involved in such a question."

Undaunted Hastie continued to argue for integration until early in January 1943. He was unable to abide the continuation of a Jim Crow army. He singled out the air corps for the dubious honor as the worst offender. Hastie wrote "Where handling of racial issues has been reactionary and unsatisfactory . . . further retrogression is now so apparent . . . so objectionable and inexcusable that I have no alternative but to resign in protest and to give public expression of my views."

In his farewell statement, Hastie mentioned the creation of a segregated OCS ground school at Jefferson Barracks. He pointed out that the original desegregated program at Chanute Field for mechanics worked beautifully, but in spite of the success, the air corps opened up a separate training program. He lambasted the air corps for admitting only two blacks to aerial observer school, for having no provision for weather officers, and no special training for black flight surgeons in aviation medicine. He criticized the total segregation at Tuskegee and the disarming of black MPs on duty in town.

African American Truman K. Gibson Jr., a Dartmouth College graduate, Chicago lawyer, and politician, replaced Hastie as special advisor to the secretary of war. Although less outspoken than his predecessor, Gibson, like Davis, privy to the maunderings of those who professed understanding of what motivated the African American expressed his resentment of these nostrums to John J. McCloy. "The Negro soldiers [do not] want to be fathered, pampered or treated as mentally deficient laborers." He decried "the premise that white officers to be successful in handling Negro troops, should be Bible spouting, fatherly masters who recognize the primitive and child-like qualities of their Negro soldiers who . . . should be worked hard and given a reasonable amount of recreation along with pretty uniforms, medals and pats on the back."

Gibson offered his information and impressions of the disturbances that had ripped through the army installations, and the "smoldering unrest" at other places. He mentioned use by officers, particularly junior ones, of "nigger," "darkie," and "boy." He remarked on their unwillingness to share mess facilities with their black colleagues. Gibson then delved into the deadlier aspects of race relations. "Many Negro soldiers have been shot and killed on the flimsiest of pretexts." He cited an incident in which a Louisiana state trooper killed a black military policeman and the civil authorites refused to bring any disciplinary action against the cop, even though the deceased was unarmed and on active duty.

In the way of reforms Gibson asked the top military leaders to provide adequate transportation in civilian communities and argued that "No officer who cannot subordinate race prejudice should serve with Negro troops."

General Ben Davis Sr. continued to call attention to the legitimate grievances of the African Americans in uniform. Davis drafted a memorandum to his superiors in which he noted, "During the last two months, I have, with Mr. Gibson . . . visited colored troops at the following stations, Fort Devens, Mass.; the New York Port of Embarkation, Brooklyn; and New York City; Camp Shanks; Mitchell Field, New York; Camp Kilmer and Fort Dix, New Jersey; Selfridge Field, Oscoda, Michigan. During 1941–42 and the early part of this year, my visits were made to stations located in the southeastern states . . . I was deeply impressed with the high morale and the attitudes of the colored officers and soldiers stationed in the states visited in the past two months. These were so different from those of the colored officers and soldiers at the stations located in the southern states.

"While there has been great improvement in general conditions, there is still great dissatisfaction and discouragement on the part of the colored people and the soldiers. They feel regardless of how much they strive to meet War Department requirements there is no change in the attitudes of the War Department. Colored officers and soldiers feel they are denied the protection and the awards that ordinarily result from good behavior and proper performance of duty."

Like many others of his race, Davis championed the right of the African American to fight. Noting that black combat units that had finished their prescribed training still had not been dispatched to the theaters of operations, he complained that two battalions of field artillery were transferred to service units, causing a precipitous drop in morale. He warned that the disposition of the 93d Infantry Division could have "great effect upon the morale of colored people."

Davis reviewed the most recent troubles. "The press news items and reports of investigations show there has been little change in the attitudes of civilian communities in Southern states. The colored man in uniform receives nothing but hostility from community officials. . . . The colored man in uniform is expected by the War Department to develop high morale in a community that offers him nothing but humiliation and mistreatment. Military training does not develop the spirit of cheerful acceptance of Jim Crow laws and customs. The War Department has failed to secure for the colored soldier the protection against violence on the part of civilian police and to secure justice in the courts. In the communities nearby to stations in the areas recently inspected [the North] the colored soldier feels he can secure justice in the civil courts. He has not been set upon by the civilian police; he has not been denied the privilege of occupying empty seats in public busses, streetcars. Taxicabs do serve him. This is not so in Southern communities." Davis raised a proposal, previously bruited, in which all the black troops would be removed from Southern states and stationed elsewhere in the country. He drew no support.

Cambell E. Johnson, the black officer assigned to serve as an aide to Gen. Lewis Hershey, the Selective Service chief, also touched on a sensitive area. He informed his superior, "It has been my frequent experience to see trains on which Negro soldiers and civilians are packed in inadequate coaches and on the platform of the next coach and on a number of coaches following them have vacant seats available for white soldiers and civilians which were not used.

"These were not short trips but trips which consumed hours or even days of time. Negro women have reported to me that on trips to visit their sons in camps in the South, they had to stand or sit on suitcases in the aisles. Numerous seats were available in other coaches and they had to endure this physical inconvenience which amounted to physical suffering for many hours, even overnight. Negro women of culture and education, teachers in Southern colleges told me that to their personal knowledge there is a practice of white MPs to bring intoxicated white soldiers back to the Negro coach for detention because their vile language and general actions were revolting to white passengers. [Gibson had also remarked on this practice.]

"These Negro women have had to sit and endure this situation. When they complained they were told it was none of their business, to just shut up if they did not want to be put off the train. I have been told by many civilian groups and soldiers in the South that it is the common practice of bus companies serving camps not to permit any Negro soldiers on buses until all white soldiers have been taken care of. This results in a situation of colored soldiers on pass or leaving on furlough to remain sometimes for hours waiting for transportation and finally walk off down the road in hope of hitchhiking a ride.

"In the movement of individual soldiers from one camp to another or from their home camp to training school, I understand that it is the usual practice to buy these soldiers Pullman accommodations. Negro soldiers, although they have orders and are told they have reservations for such accommodations very often are unable to secure them."

Aware of Truman Gibson's position, some black soldiers addressed their complaints to him. A GI under treatment for a debilitating ailment and stationed at Camp Shelby, Mississippi, wrote, "We have no place for recreation, except one place which is three miles away almost. We do not have any way to get to it except to walk. We are limited duty men, and all not able to hardly do any work. When we want to go to town we can hardly get a bus. Whenever we get a bus they will take five colored soldiers and sometimes we have to wait about two or three hours for a bus."

A medic at Camp Barkeley, Texas, corresponded with Gibson about his experiences. ". . . Up until a few weeks ago, we could attend only one theater out of five on the post. This theater was an open-air theater which we could only attend when the weather was favorable. By protest, we acquired the right to attend any theater of our choice but are forced to contend with being segregated. We have buses which are local and those that run to and from camp, on the local buses we are compelled to sit in the back, threatened by the drivers if we refuse. Despite the fact the buses run all day back and forth to camp at regular one half hour intervals, we have only three which we may ride . . . The camp provides army buses that carry soldiers to town but we aren't allowed to ride them."

The medic further stated that "nine companies, including our two, are forced to use a small post-exchange capable of conveniently servicing no [more] than three companies. . . . We have one service club shared by both divisions. It is poorly equipped having nothing but writing tables, a Ping Pong table and a piano. We don't have a library, a chapel or a chaplain. We conduct our own services in one of the poorly constructed classrooms. We have had Joe Louis to give a boxing exhibition and two dances in the three months I've been here. We were told that if we wanted entertainment we would have to provide it ourselves.

"It was to my amazement, a short time ago, when I had the opportunity of visiting the German concentration camp [German and Italian prisoners from the campaigns in the Mediterranean had been brought to the United States] here at Barkeley, to observe a sign in the latrine, actually segregating a section of the latrine for Negro soldiers, the other being used by the German prisoners and the white soldiers . . ."

A black officer in the air corps at Keesler Field, Mississippi, wrote the "Afro-American Newspapers" of the conditions at his base. He described a number of inferior substitutes provided on the basis of separate but equal—"a small inadequate exchange," "a day room in place of a service club," "a poor excuse for a library in the day room of a Negro squadron," all to discourage blacks from using the post institutions. "I, a commissioned officer of the United States Army, am denied the rights and privileges of an officer. I am excluded by members of my own rank and station in the Army. I am denied the privilege to use the Officers' Club."

Black women in uniform expressed similar dismay at their treatment. An army nurse stationed at an Arizona prisoner of war camp—the Army's 347 commissioned black nurses almost exclusively treated captives or black soldiers rather than white American wounded—observed, "For five months we have had to do all our own scrubbing and cleaning of quarters, while the white male and P/W officers have someone to do theirs. We are told that no P/W or enlisted man can work in women's quarters. The white nurses before us certainly had someone to clean for them. To do what we are and have been doing is against Army regulations. Apparently we are not considered officers by those in command for we are never included in the command affairs" [such as the reception thrown for the new post commander].

As a further discomfort, the nurse noted, "There is some kind of recreation on the post for everyone but us. Phoenix is a little 'South' in itself. We cannot be served in any restaurant, Kresge's, Woolworth's or soda fountain because of our color." The senior officer of the Army Nurses Corps in the office of the surgeon general insisted that nurses underwent integrated training and messing but "Negro nurses, however, are housed together as a matter of their own convenience." She denied assigments were based on race.

On 15 May 1942, the president signed the bill that established the Women's Auxiliary Army Corps. Subsequently the second word was dropped and by the end of World War II, about 150,000 women, including 6,500 African Americans wore the WAC uniform. The 122 black female officers were drawn from a few college reserve programs, OCS, and commissions issued directly to civilians. The first enlistees trained at Fort Des Moines, with a segregated mess, barracks, and swimming pool. Later four more sites featuring the same conditions were created.

A black WAC advisor warned that segregated facilities hindered recruiting. ". . . Our people are aware and fear the Army. They hesitate to join the WAC. They mistrust the principles for which the Army stands. The community . . . is keenly sensitive of democractic malpractices accorded our men and women in the Army."

Some white base commanders adamantly refused to allow black women to perform technical or semiskilled jobs even if they were qualified. The commander of the base hospital at Fort Devens would not permit black WACs to work in the motor pool at medically related tasks. Instead, he routinely assigned them to perform the most menial tasks. Six women feeling qualified for other duties balked and they were court-martialed. Four were discharged but a review board reinstated them.

A member of the Women's Army Corps [WAC] wrote from Camp Forrest, Tennessee, "I and thousands of decent girls abandoned college, clubs and friends . . . then joined the Women's Army Corps . . . to do our share to help the boys over there. We were told those qualified could be dieticians, stenographers, librarians and the less skilled would be trained at specialist schools. But they were sent to Camp Forrest, Tennessee, abused by civilians, did scut work, washing windows, scrubbing floors, working in hospital mess." The navy and coast guard, although practicing strict segregation for their males, decided to integrate the women. The reasons may have had more to do with efficiency than belief in equality for the 8,000 officers and 70,000 WAVES [Women Appointed for Voluntary Emergency Service] in World War II; the navy enrolled only 72 black women and issued just three commissions to nonwhites.

Truman Gibson alerted John McCloy, assistant secretary of war and a classmate of Gibson's at Dartmouth, to the legal injustices meted out to black soldiers. He cited several cases of soldiers handed over to civilian authorities in the South for trial and punishment involving civil laws. He cited a private convicted of possession of marijuana cigarettes who received five to seven years on a chain gang. A local peace officer killed another soldier, "At most he raised his arm in a threatening gesture after a fight with a white man."

Gibson argued, "There can be no guarantee of a fair trial for a Negro soldier in most courts in the deep South. Particularly is this true where any Negro is called on to dispute the veracity of a white witness. . . . Surrender to local authorities by a few commanders has operated to effectively deny many Negro soldiers their right to a fair trial and to deprive many more the more serious right of freedom [from] unwarranted physical attacks." Gibson observed that abject surrender to town and state police was not universal. "Large numbers of commanders in the field have been vigorous and forthright in their protection of all soldiers."

The special advisor emphasized, "Article of War 74 provides for surrender of soldiers to civil authorities except in time of war." He added that since 1942 it had been War Department policy to decline to remand to civil authorities military personnel charged with civil offenses other than very serious ones. Under these circumstances the local authorities had no right to arrest members of the army for misdemeanors. Instead, offenders should face courts-martial.

By midsummer 1943 and during 1944, some top brass appeared to develop a better understanding of what was involved. Colonel Pierre V. Kieffer of the inspector general's office addressed the issues in a speech to commanders of the Army Service Forces in whose ranks the bulk of African Americans served. ". . . the toughest problem confronting service commanders today is the one of preventing disturbances involving colored troops, since it involves some matters which are not under your control. . . . General Peterson's [the inspector general] information indicates that in too many instances commanding officers are too far removed from their colored troops; they are not sufficiently interested in their day-to-day welfare in providing them with reasonable recreational facilities within the post and in seeing that reasonable transportation is provided to and from recreation areas off the post; they are not enough concerned about the discrimination that may be practiced against Negroes in the surrounding country . . . they permit on their own posts discriminations which are contrary to the War Department policies and instuctions; they fail to maintain appropriate standards of discipline in Negro units; they grudgingly accept Negro officers assigned to their commands and thereafter spend a good deal of time griping about the unfitness of a Negro to be an officer, rather than requiring him to meet officer standards."

Kieffer went on to say "I do not want to give the impression that disturbances are the fault of the commanders, but by failing to act appropriately, they facilitate the work of groups of individuals who are attempting to create unrest and later riots among Negro troops."

Kieffer's insight was marred only in the last half of the statement where he clung to the belief in subversion or provocateurs. Serious efforts to convey to white officers useful information about African Americans in uniform would be made but the approach continued to be muddied with the flotsam and jetsam of those who sailed under the flag of white supremacy.

12
Soldiers, Airmen, Sailors, and Marines

Whatever the controversies and the disorders involving race, the nation continued to enroll and train millions of Americans including those of color. In October 1942, the air corps activated the 99th Pursuit Squadron as the vessel for the pilots trained at Tuskegee backed by ground crews who learned their jobs there and at other installations. However, although the air corps' white inspector pronounced the 99th fit, the War Department plotted to station it in Liberia, ostensibly to hunt German U-boats.

The resignation of William Hastie, protests from black leaders, and an inquiry from Eleanor Roosevelt forced the command staff, in April 1943, to ship the 99th to an active theater, North Africa. Based originally at Oued N'ja, Ben Davis Jr. in his autobiography said, "A strong bond exists among those who fly regardless of race and we got along well with men from the 27th [Fighter Group stationed nearby]." Others from the 99th report most white units in the area gave the black fliers a chilly reception peppering them with the usual derogatory names and refusing to share vital information about missions. Colonel William "Spike" Momyer, an ace with eight victories, commanded the fighter group to which the 99th was attached. His manner indicated he did not desire the 99th as an addition to his organization.

The squadron, flying the Curtiss P-40, a sturdy plane outclassed by the enemy Messerschmitt 109 and Focke Wulf 190, was ill prepared for combat. A number of units in the Mediterranean still used the Warhawk although fighter pilots operated out of England first with the superior British Spitfire and then the American P-38, P-47, and eventually the P-51. Most aircrews honed their navigational skills during cross country trips in the United States. But the Tuskegee airmen were not welcome anywhere beyond their home field. They seldom had an opportunity to learn through trial and error how to locate themselves, a problem made more severe by the trackless desert of North Africa. Nor did the 99th have veterans to teach the younger men. Their commander, Benjamin Davis Jr., was no more experienced than any others in the outfit.

Colonel Philip Cochran, the inspiration for a comic-strip hero, Flip Corkin, a training specialist on the staff of Maj. Gen. John K. Cannon, tactical air forces commander in North Africa, stepped forward, making a prodigious effort to build the skills of the 99th. He moved in with the men for a week and flew several training missions with pilots. "Cochran was a great guy," says Spann Watson, one of the twenty-six pilots of the 99th. "At Tuskegee we more or less trained ourselves. They would just send you out to practice. But Cochran helped the 99th learn how to fight."

Many of Watson's missions involved air-to-ground attacks upon Sicily and Italy. During one sortie he recalled hitting an Italian town. "I was really burning things up, when my eye flashed on a wedding party in a circle, bridal clothes around a piazza. The priest looked up right at me as I flew into his eyes, almost hitting a power line. I kicked the rudder and held my fire. It was the noblest thing I did in the war, but we did a lot of damage to trucks, trains and other equipment."

In June, the 99th participated in the raids upon the small island of Pantelleria, which surrendered even before the ground forces landed. The area commander, Col. J. R. Hawkins, offered "heartiest congratulations for the splendid part you played in the Pantelleria show."

On 2 July 1943, about one month after the unit went operational, the 99th and sixty other fighters from three more groups escorted bombers raiding Sicily. German planes scrambled after the bombers and the Tuskegee airmen engaged in a major dogfight, pitting their 280 mile per hour aircraft against enemy ships 100-miles-an-hour faster. Lieutenant Charles "Buster" Hall took on a pair headed for the bombers. "It was my eighth mission and the first time I had seen the enemy close enough to shoot at him. I saw two Focke Wulfs following the bombers just after the bombs were dropped and I headed for the space between the fighters and bombers and managed to turn inside the Jerries. I fired a long burst and saw my tracers penetrate the second aircraft. He was turning to the left, but suddenly fell off and headed straight into the ground. I followed him down and saw him crash. He raised a big cloud of dust."

With this kill confirmed, the 99th scored its first victory. Dwight Eisenhower, theater commander Carl Spaatz, and Jimmy Doolittle personally congratulated Hall. But it would be six months before the 99th shot down another German plane. Consigned to ground support, dive bombing, and strafing, the most dangerous form of aerial operations, the squadron had no opportunity to battle enemy fighters or bombers. An absence of opportunities to tangle with German aircraft hurt their reputation. In the eyes of commanders like Momyer, the only statistics that really mattered were aircraft destroyed. Momyer sneered, "Based on the performance of the 99th Fighter Group to date, it is my opinion that they are not of the fighting caliber of any squadron in this Group." Momyer added some comments about their lack of stamina, a charge that apparently originated with a request from Davis for three days of rest after a number of missions tied to the invasion of Sicily.

Brigadier General Edwin J. House, Momyer's superior, backed the negative evaluation, "the consensus of opinion seems to be that the negro type has not the proper reflexes to make a first class fighter pilot." In turn General Cannon, whom many of the 99th believed was at least neutral if not on their side, replayed the negative themes for Lt. Gen. Carl Spaatz, air commander in the theater. The Spookwaffe was further condemned by patently false claims that no white units had enjoyed as much preoperational instruction as the 99th.

Within the headquarters of the theater commander for air operations, the most benign attitude was represented by the likes of Maj. Gen. Edward Peck Curtis, a staff officer for Ira Eaker, Spaatz's deputy who recalled, "Ben Davis was a first class officer and when Ben was leading the boys, they did a pretty good job. Without Ben, they were not as aggressive or as effective as they might have been, but as I recall, when he was actually leading any of the formations they did all right. They were escorting bombers and that sort of thing. Their navigation wasn't too good. I remember their code name was Blue Moon and it started when they were escorting the bombers into Italy over some target there. The little voice came over the radio and said, "This here Blue Moon calling. Where is you all bombers?" The anecdote has the ring of apocrypha, for the airmen of the 99th were at least as well educated and well spoken as those of the white units, but the currency of the story emphasizes the stereotypical image of the black man.

All of the disparaging comments and reports suited the temperament of the air corps chief Hap Arnold, never an advocate of African American airmen. Facing demands that the Tuskegee "experiment" continue and even be expanded, he notified Spaatz, "We have received from very unofficial sources second-hand tales of the fact that the Negro tires easily and that he loses his will to fight after five or six missions . . . I am sure that you realize the urgency required for the information, in view of the fact that we contemplate building additional Negro units at once."

Withdrawal of the 99th from combat would effectively kill continuance, to say nothing of expansion of opportunities for African Americans to man cockpits. Summoned home to assume command of the newly formed 332d Fighter Group to be based initially at Selfridge Field, Michigan, Benjamin O. Davis Jr. left his squadron in the hands of Lt. George "Spanky" Roberts and used the opportunity to refute the charges. "I was furious," says Davis. "Momyer's criticism was completely unwarranted and unreasonable, and surely the details should have been brought to my attention at the time the alleged deficiencies were observed. By mid-September I had quieted down sufficiently to hold a press conference at the Pentagon. I stressed that the Army Air Corps had looked upon the 99th as an experiment that would have to prove that blacks could be taught to fly airplanes to its standards, and that blacks could operate effectively as a team in combat . . . it seems ridiculous that as late as 1943, the AAF [Army Air Corps] still believed that the utilization of black men as pilots had to be regarded as an experiment. But the same kind of backward thinking had inspired the racist 1925 War College report and many otherwise capable and reasonable senior AAF leaders continued to believe that blacks could not possibly qualify as combat pilots, in spite of what the 99th had already accomplished."

Davis was further angered by a piece in *Time* that questioned whether the 99th had proved the case for black airmen and reported plans to relegate the outfit to routine convoy cover. The classified information on the future of the 99th was an obvious leak from someone with less than the best interests of the 99th at heart.

Davis won an audience with top officials of the War Department that included both his father and Truman Gibson. He admitted to some mistakes during early missions, which he attributed to lack of experience, but then detailed examples of the unit's achievements to effectively rebut Momyer's complaints. He noted that the 99th operated with a complement of only twenty-six pilots compared to thirty and thirty-five for other squadrons who nevertheless flew fewer missions. In his presentation, which he says, "did not come near to expressing the depths of the rage I felt," Davis also challenged segregation, "If black and white soldiers can work and fight together in a common cause on the battlefront, why can they not be trained together in this country?"

A study initiated as a result of Davis's defenses concluded, "An examination of the record of the 99th Fighter Squadron reveals no significant general difference between this squadron and the balance of the P-40 squadrons in the Mediterranean Theater Operations." Talk of an "experiment" ended, and the African American segment of the Army Air Corps was established for the duration of World War II.

Indeed, even as Hap Arnold and his like-minded associates had sought material to shoot down the 99th and any new units, a growing number of black airmen were gaining their wings. Roscoe Brown, a graduate of the Dunbar High School in Washington, D.C., which Minton Francis mentioned, remembers a city of 350,000 with 100,000 blacks. "We lived in an integrated neighborhood because my father bought the house in the Depression and the whites couldn't afford to leave. But only on the ballfield was there a kind of integration, usually black kids playing against white ones."

He passed up an opportunity to attend Dartmouth in favor of Springfield College in Massachusetts. "I wanted to combine phys ed with a pre med course. In Springfield, everything was integrated, the dorms, the class officers, class leaders; it was a great experience that reinforced what I was taught at Dunbar.

"At Dunbar I was in the ROTC and went to the CMTC [Citizens' Military Training Camp] and I earned a lieutenant's commission. When I was 19, and the war started I was called to active duty. I wanted to finish college and wanted to fly. I resigned my commission and enlisted in the Tuskegee air program. I graduated from there in March 1944."

Harry Sheppard, the propeller specialist who had enlisted in April 1941, decided after servicing planes that he would prefer to fly them. He applied for cadet status and received his commission as a rated pilot in May 1943. He was assigned to the 302d Fighter Squadron, a newly organized segment for the 332d Fighter Group that was to absorb all of the nonwhite fighter pilots. "We did operational training, learning combat tactics at Selfridge Field," says Sheppard. "We had P-40s and P-39s." The newer, better-designed aircraft were not yet available for black pilots.

John Suggs, Kentucky born, grew up in the Midwest. "Terre Haute [Indiana] was segregated in a lot of ways. You couldn't eat at the dime store counter and in my time they did not allow blacks to play in any of the school contact sports. My father had a fourth grade education and my mother went through the eighth. I didn't know what I wanted to do in life. I went to Indiana State, got a degree in Industrial Arts and Science, but there were few opportunities in teaching for minorities. I worked in a foundry while attending night classes at Indiana State."

Fascinated by aviation, Suggs eventually entered the Civilian Pilot Training program and by the time he finished college he had also completed that course. He was in a position to retain a draft deferment because of his foundry job but Suggs chose to apply for the cadet program, earning an appointment in the autumn of 1942, ten days before his twenty-seventh birthday, which made him one of the older candidates for wings. Like so many others, he was an accomplished pilot even before he arrived at Tuskegee, with more hours at the controls than some instructors.

"When I headed for Tuskegee, at Evansville, you had to go to the Jim Crow cars. I always had a different philosophy; all white people are not bad. Even if there are only 10 percent who are reasonable, it's a matter of how you find that 10 percent." Like so many others, he considered Noel Parrish easily qualified for the 10 percent. "He was a very astute guy. You could ask him anything and he was not offended. He wasn't about to clobber someone just because they weren't entirely correct. But there was no social intercourse with white officers at the base. They ate separately and they didn't come to our officers' club."

Charles Bussey grew up in Bakersfield, California. His father, a railway mail clerk until the Depression, scratched for a living as a sharecropper and the Busseys worked in the fields as migratory laborers. Eventually, his father climbed out of the ruck to become a real estate broker. In his autobiography, *Firefight at Yechon,* he says, "My youth as a black in a bigoted town taught me some hard lessons—survival, resolution, reason. I took some beatings there—physical beatings, emotional beatings, psychological beatings. But the town also taught me to recover fast, prepare myself, plan and try again. It didn't allow me to quit or to recognize that I'd been beaten. It taught me to birth a baby and to shoe a mule. In a way, growing up as I did helped prepared me for being . . . in combat."

At Bakersfield High School, Bussey saw a notice advertising the Citizens' Military Training Camp. "I had always wanted to be a soldier, as far back as I can remember. One of the reasons was because my father had served in the Army in World War I. Another was the stories I heard from Old Man Caldwell when I was just a kid of about five or six. He had served as a sergeant in the 9th and 10th Cavalry Regiments along with my grandad."

Although Bussey knew from early childhood abuse because of race, he had been part of an integrated community which included his school. When he reached dating age, he saw his white acquaintances abandon him. The endorsement for his enrollment in the CMTC read, "Recommend approval for attendance at an appropriate camp for Negroes, in accordance with military policy."

Two summers in the CMTC, with a cadre drawn from the 25th Infantry only sharpened Bussey's appetite for military life. "Despite the bigotry, the Army was home." Upon graduation from high school he moved to Los Angeles to study engineering at the City College for two years before enlisting in the Army in September 1941. Determined to become a fighter pilot, Bussey, unable to break through the barriers for young men of his race, wrote a letter to Eleanor Roosevelt asking for her help. "She responded with a recommendation and an apology for the social conditions in which I lived." Accepted for aviation cadet training he boarded a train bound for Tuskegee. He earned his wings in the same class as John Suggs and Harry Sheppard.

The father of Daniel "Chappie" James, a native of Pensacola, Florida, loaded coal at the local gas plant or worked as a street lamplighter during the 1920s. Chappie James's mother, who held only a high school diploma, decided the local segregated school was inadequate and created her own institution that enrolled as many as seventy neighborhood kids, including her own. James quickly learned the Southern folkways. "There were parks in Pensacola with green grass and benches. The benches were labeled 'colored' and 'white.' To make sure I didn't sit on the wrong one, they were painted black and white. The water fountains—'colored' and 'white'; the waiting rooms 'colored' and 'white'; the latrines 'colored' and 'white.'"

Pensacola was also home to a naval air station and Chappie James quickly became enamored of airplanes. Occasional visitors to the installation—Lindbergh, Adm. Richard E. Byrd, and Amelia Earhart added to the glamour of flight. As a teenager, James hustled errands and odd jobs around the town airfield and in return pilots treated him to rides.

After he graduated from Pensacola High School, James entered Tuskegee Institute and when the Civilian Pilot Training Program formed there James was accepted. Chief Anderson said, "I could tell the first time I took him up he was going to be a good pilot. He had more guts than anyone I had ever seen!" Although somewhat oversized, and seemingly built more for a football lineman than a pilot, James exhibited such skill he became a civilian instructor. To earn money he wielded a paint brush as workers rushed to complete construction of Moton Field and the complex about it.

After Pearl Harbor, James applied for air cadet status but not until January 1943 was he accepted. As an accomplished pilot he sailed through the courses, but because of his stature, the evaluators steered him toward a newly planned black bomb squadron, the 477th. Years later after James proved he could function well in the small space of a fighter, someone asked him if he had problems fitting into the confines of a fighter cockpit; he remarked, "I don't get in it, I put it on."

Brown, Suggs, Sheppard, Bussey, and James had all become members of a contingent posted to Selfridge Field, Michigan, as the 332d Fighter Group. While just up the road Detroit grappled with the aftermath of the July riot, Selfridge writhed with its own racial turmoil. In May, Col. William T. Colman, the drunken base commander, shot his black driver in the stomach. During his court-martial the record indicated he had been drunk and disorderly five previous times, engaged in fraud and misappropriation of goods and services, and it slapped him on the wrist for nearly killing the black driver. Colman was absolved of conduct unbecoming an officer and a gentleman, convicted only of minor charges, and sentenced to a reduction in grade with promotion prevented for three years. African Americans could hardly have been reassured of equal justice.

Colman's replacement, Col. William Boyd, in direct violation of the 1940 army regulations, denied admission to the Selfridge officers' club to the commissioned ranks of the 332d. He was backed by Brig. Gen. Frank O'Donnell Hunter, the 1st Air Force commander who insisted African Americans await construction of their own facility. The situation deteriorated as Col. Robert R. Selway Jr., a West Pointer, assumed command of the 332d. Noel Parrish said, "I knew what Selway's attitude was . . . he took the position that he could not have black crew chiefs on airplanes. It was all right to have black mechanics, but all the crew chiefs had to be white. He was setting up various levels—arbitrary levels of black employment. You mentioned somebody being hostile—that's what he was."

To some members of the 332d, Selway as the head man of the 332d seemed more intent upon enforcing restrictions on their comforts than preparing the outfit for combat. Ben Davis Jr., however, credits him with "developing the predeployment posture I found when I took over the command in October."

Said Chappie James, "Brigadier Frank O'Donnell Hunter came to talk to us because we had objected to the segregated theater. They had drawn a line down the middle of the theater, even when those in downtown Detroit were not segregated and said, 'The blacks will sit on one side of this line, and the whites on the other.' So when, with the full cooperation of most of the whites who were not in authority and did not agree with this sort of enforced segregation we decided to go on what we called 'Operation Checkerboard' after the lights went out in the movie, they turned the movie off and made us go back to our segregated seats. They did it two or three times a night.

"We would go into the club at Selfridge and order a drink and the bartender would say, 'I can't serve you here. We just can't serve you here, this is the Supervisory Officers' Club.' We would reply, 'Well then, we'll sit here until you serve us. [The sit-ins at Selfridge predate those of the Civil Rights movement by some ten years.] Then they would close the bar. We would leave and later one of our white friends would call us and say, 'Hey, they just opened the bar, come on back.' We would dash up, and as soon as we walked in again, they said the bar was closed.

"I'll never forget [Hunter] with his big black mustache, standing up there, telling us that the world was not willing to accept us socially. He started out—and I am paraphrasing a bit—saying that they were willing to let us fight beside them, and they were willing to let us fly, but the world was not willing—society was not willing—and *he* was not willing to accept us socially. That what we were trying to do was ahead of the game, and not only were they not ready, but he wasn't going to stand for it, and if we didn't stay 'in our place' he had other means that could be used to keep us in our place.

"We were only spurred to go on further, and to keep pressure on him, because we knew that he had been charged by the War Department to press on with this project. At that time the 99th was already overseas and was doing well, and we were smart enough to realize they couldn't throw us out of the flying business at that time just because we weren't sitting on the right side of the theater or staying out of the White Officers' Club.

"However, that was the recommendation of some of our black senior officers—that we 'cool it.' We said, 'Cool it, hell!' and continued to do things that would embarrass [the white command] and get the attention of the media. They were trying just as hard to stop us from getting the attention of the media—because they knew that their policies could not be supported under Constitutional Law.

"We had some pretty good advice, mainly from the NAACP. We had some pretty good lawyers in our midst, young men who had come from law school.

Many of them had not passed the Bar, but were good 'guardhouse lawyers.' They knew the law extremely well and they were reading like mad to keep up with it."

The siege of the airmen was relatively mild. For black ground troops, the forces arrayed against them were far more formidable. The domestic enemies ranged from the violent to the extremely subtle. While stationed in the states, the fliers operated within a contained area and their small numbers made it much easier for them to avoid confrontation with hostile whites. At Tuskegee they benefitted from the services of a commander who respected them. The pilots were at least as well educated if not more schooled than most white fliers who frequently were younger and less prepared for the vicissitudes of military life. Black GIs whether riflemen, truck drivers, ammunition details, laborers, or permanent housekeepers numbered in the millions and, except for the rare isolation of the 92d Division at Fort Huachuca, could not avoid encounters with white civilians and soldiers, most of whom at best held them in disdain. A great many of the white superiors looked at their subordinates through stereotypical lenses. They had little confidence in their abilities and often regarded assignment to such a unit as a form of punishment. There was constant turnover as officers sought transfers.

To command the 92d Division, the chief of staff, Gen. George Marshall, selected Maj. Gen. Edward M. Almond, former assistant 93d Division CO and like Marshall a graduate of Virginia Military Institute. Although some of his contemporaries admired Almond for his intelligence—Eisenhower described him as "one of the half dozen ablest men in the Army"—they also perceived an obdurate aspect that brought trouble. General John H. Chiles, who would serve in the Korean War as a close aide to Almond remarked that he was "very proud, very intolerant . . . overbearing." Said Chiles, "He could precipitate a crisis on a desert island with nobody else around." Another associate in Korea, Gen. Maurice Holden, said, "When it paid to be aggressive, Ned was aggressive. When it paid to be cautious, Ned was aggressive."

Born in Luray, Virginia, in 1892, Almond recalled listening to his grandmother speak of Civil War days where her husband served with the Confederacy. Almond said, "Older people, especially those who knew people who had been killed in the Civil War were bitter about it. Everybody of any means had lost their businesses, their animals, their way of life due to the poverty generated by the Civil War." To an interviewer in 1975 he said his only contact with blacks had been in their work as "laborers."

Almond expected an appointment to West Point but the senator who promised him died suddenly. Almond then entered VMI on a state scholarship, graduating in 1912 from a school that continued to pump him full with the glory of the Confederacy. During World War I he led a machine-gun unit in France.

Almond remarked, "General Marshall felt that General Hall, who was in command of the 93d Division when I was there and was from Mississippi, understood the characteristics of the Negro and his habits and inclination. The artilleryman at that time was General William Spence from North Carolina as I recall, who also had that understanding and I being from Virginia had an understanding of southern customs and Negro capabilities—the attitudes of Negroes in relationship thereto."

His interviewer in 1975 proposed, "Whether it was deserved or not, the 92d had emerged from World War I with a reputation for failure. When it was announced that the 92d was to be activated again for duty in World War II, there was an air of expectant failure in some circles mixed with a hope for success in others."

Almond responded, "I knew of the failure of the 93d and 92d Divisions in World War I. I was unable to find in any library a description of the type of failure, the nature of the exercise that was being criticized . . . I decided not to make my mind up in any direction until I saw to my own satisfaction, the capabilities of the components of the 92d. I advised my officers to do likewise. My main theme announced repeatedly . . . if we work hard enough we can accomplish anything and don't admit failure before you try to succeed."

The general added that it took more time to make the outfit combat-ready—nineteen months instead of the customary ten to twelve. "Rifle marksmanship, for example, required three to four times as much ammunition for instruction practice. The men of the division being largely illiterate or Class IV in intelligence took longer training and more effort on the part of the instructors to get across the lessons being taught."

The inspector general dispatched Ben Davis Sr. in the summer of 1943 to evaluate the 92d. As early as 1942, Davis had visited Huachuca and been deluged with complaints. Officers spoke of overcrowded quarters, shortages in supplies, the segregated club, and the refusal of the officers' post barbershop to cut the hair of blacks. While sympathetic, Davis could only rejoin that the inequities stemmed from the War Department insistence on separate but equal.

On his second inspection, Davis, accompanied by Truman Gibson, described in his report the racial tensions in the division. Davis cited an unnamed general officer who objected to the presence of a black chaplain and his wife in the post restaurant, ostensibly because that would cause trouble with white officers. Only the intercession of Col. Edwin Hardy, the post commander, an old cavalry hand to whom Davis gave high marks for his efforts against discrimination, prevented the incident from becoming a cause célèbre. Davis and Gibson learned that white officers had been stoned while passing through the enlisted areas. One of them had been assaulted with a shovel while asleep in his tent. There were many men confined to the stockade for various infractions. Among those locked up were three officers accused of being AWOL or insubordinate. He was shocked by the "unusual disrespect" for Almond after he attended a dedication of a baseball field, held in the stadium at which the appearance of the commanding general of the 92d drew a raucous cacophony of catcalls and boos from the 10,000 GIs. Morale was described as very low.

Charles Brown, a teacher at the time he was drafted in February 1941, received a direct commission in August 1942. He was assigned as an aide to Davis during his expedition to Fort Huachuca. Brown recalled that Almond arranged for the soldiers to demonstrate their skills in drills and small combat simulations. The aide remembered that Davis was well aware of the "dog and pony shows" during his inspections and remarked that he was tired of being distracted from his real mission, investigating the unhappiness of officers and soldiers. Brown sat in as Davis and Almond jointly listened to complaints from some of the troops. They heard the expectable frustration over segregated facilities. A number of men grumbled about the number of drills but Davis dismissed this lament with an observation that such activities were normal. Although Davis recommended solutions to some difficulties or explanations for grievances, he did not give either the offended officers or men satisfaction by agreeing they were correct. Brown interpreted Davis as seeking to avoid undercutting the division commander.

According to Brown, Davis and Almond met privately to go over the visitor's findings. Brown overheard some of the talk. Almond, said the eavesdropper, was "luke-warm" to remedying social problems raised by his soldiers. Almond offered an explanation for the low morale and the apparent dissension. "At formation, all our officers were white. Starting in the spring of 1943, every thirty days, thirty Negro lieutenants or captains arrived as replacements and thirty white lieutenants or captains would be released." The outfit went from 700 to 400 white officers with blacks making up the difference. "We perceptibly realized a change in the attitude of the enlisted men toward authority and discipline that was required. Many Negro officers were of low caliber and inexperienced." Almond then claimed that one of them was a former bootblack with only a high school education. He said he saw no morale problem. He had punished a white officer for striking a drunken black soldier with a pool cue as "unnecessary." The main difficulty, said Almond, was some 800 or 900 malingerers, unfit for combat duty.

Almond perceived a meddlesome influence behind the entire inspection. "Mrs. Roosevelt, the wife of the President," Almond told a later interviewer, "who was very alert to Negro complaints sent an individual in the War Department to investigate." The 92d's former CO claimed that when he talked to Davis, the inspector seemed understanding. But the report by Davis is ambivalent. "There were no complaints or reports of racial discrimination. General Almond was held in highest respect by all officers. The colored officers were especially profuse in their praise of him for his fairness and deep concern for their advancement and welfare." On the other hand, Davis also wrote that Almond was influenced for the worse by subordinate white officers, although he allegedly disciplined any who deviated from his publicly stated policies of fairness.

He and Gibson agreed that Almond, perhaps because of his zeal in preparing the organization for war, ". . . has in the opinion of the inspector general overlooked the human element in the training of the men. The execution of ceremonies with smartness and precision and the perfunctory performance of military duties is taken as an indication of high morale. This is not true with the colored soldier. He can be driven to perform without necessarily having a high morale. Due to long suffering and working under conditions highly distasteful to him he has developed as a defense mechanism the ability to present an outward calm appearance. The so-called emotional attitudes which characterize his action on occasion when to the white man what seems a small incident, are due to pent-up resentment against unfairness and the inequalities suffered by him on account of his race.

"General Almond noted the disorder when he rose to address the audience in the ballpark and it is the opinion of the I.G. that he was greatly shocked. However, General Almond appears to be an able officer and it is believed that now, since he is well aware of the situation that in all cases of unfairness or misconduct involving racial issues he has taken remedial action. The causes of unrest will be removed . . . except the promotion policy." He attributed Almond's surprise at the rude greeting he received during the ballfield ceremonies to his unawareness of the typical African American reaction to oppression, "a defense mechanism, the ability to present a calm outward appearance." (The learning Almond professed he gained as a white Southerner apparently did not cover this aspect.)

Word of the tour taken by Davis and Gibson reached the black press. The *New York Amsterdam News* published a piece, based largely on letters from soldiers stationed there, that described Fort Huachuca as "Hell on Earth." Among other charges, it stated that Almond referred to soldiers as "niggers." The two black investigators said in their questioning of several hundred men that they could not find anyone able to positively confirm the accusation. They speculated that Almond, in his Southern drawl would say "Negra," which to some ears came across as "nigger." The two visitors asserted they had urged the general to use "colored" to avoid confusion. The newspaper also, incorrectly, accused Davis and Gibson of having rated conditions there as excellent. The advisors disputed this interpretation. They did deny that the troops lacked proper equipment, evaluated the mess halls as up to standards, and that whites, as well as blacks, underwent ammunition shakedowns to prevent incidents or accidents. Davis also maintained that the bulk of complaints against Almond and his staff arose from individual problems rather than any systematic discrimination. The potential effects of segregation and ill treatment by members of the upper echelons of the 92d appeared ignored.

Among the black officers assigned to the 92d Division was Frederic E. Davison, an ROTC graduate of Howard University in 1939. Called to active duty in March 1941, he reported to the 366th Infantry, activated in February. "None of us," recalls Davison, designated a heavy-weapons platoon leader, "in the company had any extended duty before we arrived. The only thing I knew about machine guns was what I read out of field or technical manuals. About a month after the officers got there, the draftees came in. In retrospect, the caliber of the white officers in the regiment was such that I could only conclude in later years that it was so designed that the regiment would fail. All the ingredients for failure were in place. For example, our equipment. Initially, we were issued the old trench mortar until it was withdrawn for the 81mm. We had water-cooled machine guns but even at that time they were probably the poorest quality kept in the Army's inventory. We had the old World War I rifles. Communications equipment was practically nil and the same holds for gas masks. Some of this, though, was common to the entire Army."

The events of 7 December 1941 brought some changes. "Some of us were sent to training schools," says Davison, "but not until I had been on active duty for sixteen months did I attend my first real course in commanding. Every black officer who went to Fort Benning, regardless of his course or his rank, stayed in one building." In contrast, whites studying communications, motor maintenance, or heavy weapons all resided with others pursuing that particular specialty. "There was absolutely no recreation one could profit from. The post theater was closed to us; the main post club was closed to us. The swimming pool was off limits to us. People looked askew if you entered the PX. You didn't go to the main chapel.We were told by the senior black officer, who was called in by Omar Bradley, the Commandant of the Infantry School, and told we were not to use those facilities and the question was, I quote, 'Do you understand?' 'Yes sir, I understand.'"

Also assigned to the 92d Division, Jehu Hunter, another native of the nation's capital, grew up in a middle-class neighborhood. "My father taught auto mechanics in the Armstrong Technical Institute which offered both technical and academic curricula. I attended the school as did my brother who was younger. My father designed a course to give interested students hands-on experience in automotive repair. Unfortunately, my father had a difficult time placing his students in the major auto-repair establishments who generally would not hire colored students even when my father certi-fied they were competent. The white owners were afraid their white me-chanics would stage a walkout. It's a situation that continues today.

"Although Washington was a segregated city in many respects, it was not hard-line segregated. There were gaps in the fence, probably because it was the capital. Once you knew the limits you would know which areas of the city to avoid. There was no segregation in public transportation but most taxi service was. Most hospitals would not accept black patients, but some very good ones did. Black patients usually were treated at the Freedmen's Hospital, built in the late 19th Century and initially funded by the federal government's Freedmen's Bureau. By the time I was 16 in 1938, the hospi-tal had been ceded to Howard University as the teaching hospital for most of the black physicians.

"My father and mother both had a few white friends. They were profes-sionals who knew my father as an educator and my mother as an active cham-pion of desegregation of public facilities and president of one of the city's parent-teacher associations. She was also active in promoting birth control to prevent women from being overburdened with too many children. She worked with Harold Ickes, then Secretary of the Interior, to de-segregate the parks and playgrounds, paid for by the taxes of *all* the citizens of the District and they won.

"I was aware of the segregation within the armed forces. Of the three ser-vices—Army, Navy and Marines, only the Army offered chances for blacks to become officers." As a graduate of Howard University with a degree in zoology, and an ROTC student, Hunter was admitted to OCS at Fort Ben-ning. He completed a thirteen-week infantry communications course. "I learned to climb telephone poles, and install overhead lines and cables. I could draw line-route maps that linemen could use to determine the most effective way to bring telephone lines to the command and observation posts of the various units that used our switchboards.

"While I was traveling in the South, I wanted to get a light lunch in the Atlanta railway terminal. I was told that I had to go to a service window in the back of the restaurant but that same hostess warmly welcomed some Ger-man prisoners of war into the dining room."

Hunter was assigned as communications officer for the 3d Battalion of the 365th Infantry Regiment, a component of the 92d Division at Fort Huachuca. "The Army segregated its officers' clubs, with minor exceptions. None of the services considered black officers worthy of the rank they held, from second lieutenant to colonel. General Edward [Ned] Almond, com-mander of the 92d established a Division Officers' Club that was open to ranks below that of major only by invitation. In the 92d, only the four black artillery officers qualified for the club, along with the Division Chaplain.

How often they used it, I don't know. I was only a second lieutenant and couldn't go but I was usually so busy I didn't have time for it.

"We had some good guys and some not-so-good guys. I am convinced that most of the white officers wished they were somewhere else and most of the black officers wished that most of the white officers were somewhere else. There were some white officers who genuinely thought of black officers as competent. I believed that General Almond was a sorry excuse for a Division commander, something he would prove in Italy during World War II and on the Korean peninsula. But I was glad I was in the 365th since Colonel Armstrong [white] was the best of the regimental commanders."

Another member of the 92d Division, Spencer Moore, a country doctor's son, was the fifth generation of his family born in Magnolia, Camden County, New Jersey. "My Dad did it all, made his own medicines, did minor amputations—children born with a sixth finger or toe—attended fire and police during emergencies. When we went to the movies in Haddon Heights, we had to sit in the balcony. In school I went out for the swimming team. The coach had heard I was a good swimmer but he had no place for me to train. The YMCA pool was closed to the colored and the Camden County Vocational School pool for which my Dad paid school taxes, was also closed to colored. We did all of our socializing with people of color, mostly in Lawnside, New Jersey, which was an all colored borough.

"I had enlisted in the First Separate Battalion, New Jersey State Militia in 1940 when I was eighteen. Being in a New Jersey militia we were trained by our officers and NCOs. I volunteered for many off hour details, cleaning newly issued M-1 rifles, learning to field strip them. I did not realize segregation was so severe in the military until we were called to active duty, March 10th, 1941 at Fort Dix. We were quartered away from the main post and were not allowed on it unless we were a labor detail. All of our officers were colored in the four rifle companies but the battalion commander was white.

"In August 1942, I went to OCS. We had the largest number of colored candidates in the history of OCS at that time, sixty men. We all slept in one barracks that usually housed forty. When I received my commission—45 of us completed the course—I was 20 years old and assigned to Company G, 370th Infantry. All the platoon leaders were colored while the CO and Exec were white. Conditions at Fort Huachuca were segregated, PX # 2, Service Club # 2, Officers' Club # 2 and Theater # 2. The white officers utilized the #1 facilities.

"About 80 percent of our enlisted men were from the South where they couldn't go to school or attended "separate but equal" schools so we had low quality in terms of education. Nor could they vote. At an officers' meeting I asked my company commander when he was going to be duty officer, since the battalion commander said *all* officers were to pull that assignment.

From then on, my CO gave me unsatisfactory ratings even though my platoon during training won third best soldier, 3d best squad and 3d best platoon in the entire 92d Division. He was Captain Orville C. Sutton and he left before we went overseas. I was transferred to Company B of the 370th."

Edgar Piggott, like Harry Sheppard, the child of immigrants from the West Indies, lived in a brownstone house on West 140th Street in New York City with an extended family that included three aunts and their husbands as well as his maternal grandparents. "When we were there in the mid 1920s, the area was interracial. My mother and her sisters were all employed at Barnard College as switchboard operators and housekeepers. My father was an elevator starter. By the time I was 10 or 11, the neighborhood had turned completely 'colored'; my little white friends had vanished from my classes and the houses in my area. We became more aware of the subtle, northern-style prejudice whenever we had occasion to travel out of the ghetto, but nothing like the lynching that was going on in Dixie.

"I was fortunate enough to attend Townsend Harris High School (a science oriented high school, predominantly white) and developed some new friends that I never mingled with socially. I did form some lasting friendships with the few other black students and one Japanese boy. Our graduation was in February 1942. When Roosevelt made his speech about the 'day that shall live in infamy,' that was the last time I saw my Japanese classmate."

Instead of following most of the Townsend Harris students to the City College of New York, Piggott chose to attend Hampton Institute to study agriculture. "I told myself and my parents who were paying that I needed to be in an academic atmosphere that accepted me socially. During the two semesters I spent in Virginia, I experienced my share of drinking from segregated water fountains, sitting in segregated movies, buses, railroad cars and waiting rooms. Driving with friends to New York via South Jersey, we would have to go 'around back' to buy any food when we stopped for gas. As the war went on, and my friends began to be drafted, I became more active in the agricultural activities at Hampton, even promising to stay during summer vacation as part of a poultry husbandry project, in hopes of getting an agricultural deferment. No such luck—I was drafted.

"Doing well on the AGCT, and being a former student, put me in line for the Army Student Training Program [the ASTP installed qualified soldiers as students under military control but with civilian educators at institutions of higher learning around the country] and I joined an ASTP platoon at Camp Wheeler, Georgia. The trainees and non-coms were all black, the officers, white. Infantry basic was a snap for our elite ASTP platoon. We were all more intelligent than the cadre. Our platoon leader, Lt. Hammond, was a decent white southerner, born and bred in Macon. We all liked him and were able to identify with him. Our Company Commander was from

Missouri and did not share our platoon leader's sentiments. One of our guys filed an application for OCS which never got past his desk. We did get into town once in a while to carouse and have an occasional but not serious brush with the local white citizenry. Because of our elite status, we'd get invited to social affairs at local black colleges, even as far away as Atlanta."

To Piggott's delight, his ASTP assignment was back at Hampton but after two three-month terms, the army abandoned its engineering ASTP programs and continued only courses for men with prior medical or dental training. "We were given the option of joining infantry or engineer units, which boiled down to combat or port battalion duty. I opted for infantry. I joined the 370th Regiment in the middle of the night while it was on maneuvers in Louisiana. I was assigned to Intelligence and Reconnaissance and took to the task eagerly. We went to Fort Huachuca where we learned the two elements of the 92d, the 365th and 370th were going overseas. Our training continued in earnest over the vast expanses of Arizona. One or two visits to Nogales and Agua Prieta were enough to convince me and my buddies that our time was better spent remaining on the post, avoiding KP and amusing ourselves."

Vernon Baker, born in Cheyenne in 1919, was raised by his grandparents after his parents died in a car crash. His grandfather held a steady job as a brake inspector for the railroad. His first encounter with racism came after he beat the drums for his high school band at a parade in Omaha. The musicians adjourned to a cafe for food, but when the restaurant manager spotted Baker and two other blacks from the group, he spoke to the white bandmaster. The group left and one of the other African Americans turned to Baker, "You know why we can't eat here? Because we're black."

After high school, an unemployed Baker attempted to enlist in the army but the recruiter turned him away with a comment that the service did not have a quota yet for his race. Later he tried again and was accepted. During the bus ride to basic training in Texas, his instruction in race relations took an even harsher tone. As he dropped his gear on the front seat of the bus, the driver snarled, "Hey, nigger, get up and go to the back." An older black man pulled Baker away before he threw his first punch.

He began his career as a soldier with the 25th Infantry, then at Camp Wolters, Texas. When a sergeant discovered Baker could type, he was appointed company clerk. He says he was shocked to discover that more than a third of his fellow GIs could not read or write and many marked the payroll with an X, just as they had forty years earlier for Benjamin O. Davis with the cavalry. Pearl Harbor opened up an opportunity to attend OCS. When he graduated as a second lieutenant he traveled to Fort Huachuca to join the 370th Infantry.

A native of Indianapolis, Frank Hodge notes, "My mother was the daughter of a Civil War veteran. She had attended public schools in Ohio and graduated from Wilberforce University. My father did not have too much formal education but had worked as a Pullman porter, a cook and at odd jobs before becoming a molder for Link Belt. While my older sisters went to integrated schools in Indianapolis my younger sister and I attended segregated ones."

After finishing high school, Hodge worked as a city park custodian, as a postal clerk, and laborer. He enlisted in the Civilian Conservation Corps for eighteen months, employed mostly in clerical duties. In February 1941, the draft called him.

"I was well aware of segregation in the army and that there were the four Negro units. I was among about 500 men assembled at Fort Benjamin Harrison and everyone went to Fort Huachuca and we formed the 1st battalion of the 368th Regiment, just activated. I was assigned to battalion headquarters and of the roughly thirty men, half of them had some college education. All of our officers were white, except for the chaplain. The cadre came from the 25th Infantry which had been permanently stationed at Huachuca. Discrimination was not much of a problem since we were all Negroes. In the period just prior to the war, quite a few men were selected to attend OCS.

"Shortly after the war began, some of us were sent to northern Arizona to guard the Santa Fe Railroad and I was stationed in Flagstaff. After a few days there, a minister opened the doors of the church for us to have a USO type of setting. That lasted about a week. Some of our guys went to the church and were told the minister no longer was there and we were not welcome."

For some months Hodge served with the newly activated 93d Division but he and many of his associates soon prepared to move over to the 92d. "Parts of the division were in a number of camps and everything we heard about their handling of subordinates was bad.We attended classes that seemed to me to teach us to be prison guards over ourselves. Morale was mighty low. General Wood and General Rowny's reputations with a Negro engineering outfit were well known to the men of the division. At the activation ceremonies of the division the speakers were all white supremacists. [The tenor of the speeches] was that it was wonderful for us to be in their state from an economic point of view, as long as we stayed in our place.

"There were several white officers with the division that I respected as gentlemen. By the end of about four months, all of them were gone. I don't know if they were able to go on their own or whether General Almond had them transferred. Anyone that had a liberal attitude towards blacks had to leave. General Almond was a racist if there ever was one. From the time the division was activated until right before we went overseas, the various officers candidate schools would send notices of opportunity for men to attend their school. Every one of these chances were turned down with the reason that there were no qualified applicants.

"While we were in Fort McClellan, Alabama, there was a secret General Order specifying the order of promotion of all white officers in a unit before a Negro was to be put in a position for promotion. Just before we went overseas, a graduate of Wilberforce, Russell Adrian of the medical battalion wrote an article in *The Buffalo,* the division newspaper, "You Belong." The article was about being proud to be members of the division. He was about the only one to get to go to OCS."

Not every African American found his World War II military experience a dismal exercise in segregation and discrimination. Already in his late twenties when drafted shortly before Pearl Harbor, Henry Williams, a native of Cleveland says, "I had experienced little discrimination while growing up. We socialized with whites. But I knew nothing about how the army was segregated until I put on a uniform.

"At Fort Huachuca I became an infantryman in the 93d Division. The cadre came from the 25th Infantry and the 9th and 10th Cavalry. Everything in our area was black and the only white folks were the superior officers. My first company commander was from Texas, a graduate of Virginia Military Institute. He instructed his subordinates to address all men as 'soldier' rather than as 'boy' since, he said, Uncle Sam saw fit to put us in uniform."

Williams advanced through the ranks to become a first sergeant. "We did not have a real problem because of men who were not educated. We had only one in my company who could not read or write. Still, he could count well enough to shoot dice."

Percy Roberts, born in the small town of Lincoln, Illinois, in 1914, remembers little racial trouble during his childhood other than name-calling. "The town was small enough that the schools were integrated. Except for church, all of my playmates growing up were white. After I went into the CCC for three years and liked it enough I enlisted in the army and rode a bus from Stockton, Illinois, to Fort Huachuca.

"My first real segregation came after the bus left St. Louis. It was back of the bus, backdoor of the restaurant and hard to find colored rest rooms. I was a peace time recruit, brown shoes and wrap leggings. My training consisted of close order drill, how to roll a pack and pitch a tent, and always the General Orders and the Articles of War. I never had any problems when I went on pass; I was good at avoiding them.

"I was in my second enlistment when Pearl Harbor occurred. The 368th Infantry and 25th Infantry were sent to guard vital installations on the West Coast, but I was part of the enlisted cadre assigned to fill the slots in the general staff of the 93d Division which was to be activated and I stayed at Huachuca." Roberts earned a commission through OCS at Fort Washington, Maryland, in March 1943. He accompanied the 93d during its maneuvers in Louisiana and the California desert but was declared a surplus officer when the division shipped out to the Pacific.

Minton Francis, the black U.S. Military Academy graduate was one year behind Robert Tresville and DeWitt Armstrong III, at West Point. He became a battery commander with the 90th Field Artillery, a unit attached to a former Florida National Guard division stationed at Camp Gruber, Oklahoma. "I was considered an instigator and a subversive when I forced them to integrate the officers' mess." Francis was one of the few African American officers with an infantry and field artillery background who did ship out to a combat zone during World War II.

Robert Powell spent his pre-army years in Port Arthur, Texas. "It was a seaport town, an international city with people from all over. I don't recall any racial incidents in Port Arthur and some of the towns like it which had a sizeable black population, black people had a lot to say and held their own. When I turned 18 in 1942 I volunteered because there really wasn't much else for me to do. I thought there might be an opportunity for me in the Army. I was assigned to the 93d Division and I was trained as a rifleman. But I left them when they were on maneuvers in Louisiana. I transferred to a quartermaster outfit. We were sent to Hereford, England where we assembled things that would be used during the invasion of France."

Elliotte Williams, the former New York National Guardsman who enlisted in the Regular Army before Pearl Harbor and served with an integrated medical unit at West Point, applied for OCS and went through a course at the Carlisle Barracks in Pennsylvania. "There were six blacks in the class and they split us up so that we were not even segregated in the barracks. The entire post was open to us except we had to go outside for haircuts. After the first month four guys washed out, including two who had college degrees. We were really concerned but they called us in for an interview and assured us there was no quota.

"When I finished and was commissioned I was assigned to the 93d Division at Huachuca. Conditions there were terrible. Everything was segregated, separate tables for black officers in the mess hall, separate BOQ [bachelor officer's quarters], separate officers' clubs, separate seating behind a rope at the post theaters. Edward Almond was then the assistant division commander.

"I got out of there. That was not for me. There was open prostitution just outside the gates. I had no confidence in the leadership and they had none in the men. The white officers all wanted to move to white organizations. The outfit seemed programmed for failure. I managed to get a transfer to the Tuskegee medical unit hospital where I became a first lieutenant and stayed throughout the war."

Black soldiers assigned to the two African American divisions initially had few opportunities to apply elsewhere. However, the clamor to provide more opportunities for nonwhites had cracked open on a small scale some specialities. A handful of armored units, tanks, and tank destroyer battalions began training blacks, under white officers but according to those in command, the African Americans labored under a serious handicap. Brigadier General H. T. Mayberry ran a tank destroyer school at Fort Hood, Texas, from 1942 to February 1944. "We trained both Negro officers and Negro enlisted men. We also had Negro candidates in the Tank Destroyer OCS. The educational background of the Negro enlisted men was very poor. At first, we sent many of them back to their units because they could not assimilate the instruction. But the COs of the battalions from which these men came asked us to keep the men, even though they were incapable of absorbing the instruction, to let them complete the course for such profit as they might be able to derive. We complied.

"In TD School there were separate messes and barracks for both officers and enlisted men. There was some protest but I took the position that we were operating in a part of the country where segregation was the custom, and it was best for us to conform to established social usage." One exception was the program for making officers where blacks and whites shared barracks and messes without difficulty.

Jack Rhoades, the white West Pointer who matriculated a year earlier than Benajamin O. Davis Jr., enjoyed his time as commanding officer of the black-staffed 459th Tank Destroyer Battalion at Camp Maxey, Texas. "In 1943, when I was informed I would soon be assigned to activate the 459th, no mention was made that it was a black battalion. Only a day or so later was I informed. I knew my first problem would be to placate my white officers in my cadre of experienced officers to the fact that they would be training, and probably later, leading a black unit in battle. While I had never served in a black unit, I knew that most white officers felt that blacks did not make good combat soldiers. My first step was to write the Librarian of the Army War College asking him to send me anything he had on black combat units, which he did with commendable speed. I was pleased to find many examples of valorous conduct in battle by well led American black units. I annotated all these excerpts and required each of my officers to read them, so they would *know American blacks* had a good history of valorous combat, when well led. I was particularly glad that our black cadremen all came from the black 9th Cavalry Regiment which was known for its black Buffalo Soldiers who had outstanding, though not well-known combat records in the Indian Wars, following the Civil War.

"I learned that the blacks preferred to be called 'black' rather than 'colored' and also found they lacked self-confidence—not surprising when you consider the effects of hundreds of years as slaves; and, following their emancipation their substandard education under the 'separate but equal' public educations, as the 'equal' was an unachieved goal.

"The arrival of our first trainload of recruits came from the Chicago-Detroit areas and I began my education as a leader of a black battalion. Most of our officers and enlisted cadremen were at the depot to pick up our recruits and take them to their barracks areas using the Post buses. I had our sergeant major with me as we watched the troops unload from the train. I noted that each Post bus had the sign, 'Blacks Only.' I noted one group of recruits gathered around another recruit who was saying, 'I wonder if they have bullets marked 'Whites Only.'

"I told the sergeant major I wanted to see that recruit in my office when we got back to camp. 'Don't tell him why. Just be sure he knows how to salute and report to me.' When I returned to my office, the recruit reported to me. I told him that I had heard him wonder if there was a sign on any bullets marked, 'Whites Only.' His eyes got big and I knew I had his full attention.

"I said, 'I'm going to put my cards on the table, so you will know I am talking straight.' I continued, 'I expect this may be your first time living in a Southern State. You have already started learning how to live as a soldier; now you have to learn about living in a Southern State. I want you to know that this battalion, the 459th Tank Destroyer Battalion, is way understrength in non-commissioned officers and higher paid specialists. We have a cadre of experienced soldiers, the men who met you at the depot and brought you to our battalion area. Their jobs now are to teach you recruits and train you to be capable of being promoted to fill some higher paid positions. Do you understand what I am telling you? In civilian life, as I am sure you know, blacks are frequently blocked from the higher paid jobs. In the Army, the color of your skin will not keep you from being promoted. If there is a better space open in your company and you are capable of doing the job, you will be tried in that position for promotion. The first thing is that you be capable of leading the men under you. You have already shown me that you have leadership potential by the way your fellow recruits on the train looked to you for leadership. Yes, we have bullets for both black and white soldiers.' He was already prepared, already started, to lead, but in the wrong direction.

"A second problem confronting me on the first day was there was no black chaplain in the camp. I felt religion is important to most blacks and I didn't believe any white chaplain could reach them effectively. I had my adjutant and sergeant major review all the personnel records to find if we had a 'shade tree' preacher, before his being drafted. Better than that, they came up with Recruit Danforth who had been a consecrated priest of the Episcopal Church in Atlanta when he enlisted. I had Danforth report to me and he confirmed he was indeed an Episcopal priest. I asked him if he was aware that as a priest he was eligible to be a commissioned officer as a Chaplain in the Army? He told me he knew that but had decided to enlist as a private because he felt that 'as just another private,' he could be more effective and do more for his people than as an officer. I told him I respected his purpose and asked if he was willing for me to appoint him as our Acting Chaplain, while he remained a private with full responsibilities and the additional duties as our Acting Chaplain. He told me he would appreciate that and wanted to have services this coming Sunday, which I approved.

"That Sunday I was met by the Deacon Jones, one of our recruits who had served as a preacher before being drafted. He conducted me to a seat in the first pew. A second of our shade tree preachers came to the pulpit, read a text from the Bible, and explained how the text applied to us all. He was followed by a another former preacher with his own separate text and explanation. Then the Reverend Private Danforth came to the pulpit and announced, 'We are honored to have our Battalion Commander with us today. Major Rhoades, will you please give us our sermon for today. I was flummoxed and totally unprepared. I had noticed that the two who had preceded me to the pulpit had drawn spontaneous Hallelujahs and Amens. I decided to congratulate the Congregation for organizing their Sunday Service so rapidly and to keep talking until I drew at least one Hallelujah or Amen, which I did."

According to Rhoades, he also believed he could stimulate esprit de corps through fife and drum music to accompany parades. "We were not authorized a battalion band or fifes and drums. I made contact with a Post Special Services officer who had spent some time working in the Texas penitentiary system to see if he could arrange for fifes and drums made by convicts could be donated. He pulled it off but since the prison did not make fifes, substituted bugles. The Sergeant Major located recruits for a drum and bugle unit. During periods scheduled for infantry drill, these men practiced and became our marching band.

"I had heard that one of my cadre, Lt. Wilson, was a remarkable rifle shot. I remembered the problems I had with my regular army recruits' tendency to jerk their triggers, causing rifle sight alignment to move and the bullet to miss the target. I asked Lt. Wilson if he would put on a show as the introduction to our rifle marksmanship program, emphasizing the importance of holding a proper sight alignment. After a day of dry firing [no ammunition in the weapons] instruction and teaching the importance of not jerking the trigger I had Wilson put on a shooting show.

"He started by tossing a dime into the air and as it fell back toward the ground, he shot the dime before it landed. For his next shot, he strapped his hunting knife vertical to a portable wood stand with the blade facing the recruits. He then fastened two light bulbs, three inches from each side of the blade. He explained he would shoot to hit the knife blade, splitting the bullet in half, with the pieces flying to the sides to break the two bulbs. He fired and broke the bulbs.

"I (loudly) asked Lt. Wilson, 'If I went down range about twenty-five feet, put a lighted cigarette in my mouth, could you shoot it out of my mouth?'

"'Yes, sir,' he answered. I now said, 'Now I am no idiot; I know that Lt. Wilson will align his rifle sights as we are teaching you to do, and will squeeze his trigger, not jerk it. I *know* his bullet will hit his target and not my head.' I went down range, put the cigarette in my mouth and Lt. Wilson shot it out of my mouth. I like to think that bit of showmanship helped our recruits to make the highest score [in marksmanship] as a battalion among the two white and the other black battalion, a National Guard outfit of several years standing.

"The time came when the 12th Tank Destroyer Group with its four battalions was to move to Camp Hood. The Group Commander thought his three recruit battalions had advanced enough in their basic training to be in condition to make a one-day full pack march, followed by trucking into Camp Hood. The 459th was the last to march the one day. We marched on a dirt road through miles of pine woods. I started by leading the column. After half an hour I pulled to the side to check the condition of the lead company's recruits. I could see that the recruits were beginning to look a little down in the mouth. I started to lead company singing, calling to a soldier named Hill, 'Let's start a song we can march to. Any song of your choice, and the rest of you join in with Hill.' It worked. Within a few minutes the first company were all singing, swinging along. I repeated the same thing to the following companies.

"I noted that 'God Bless America' was a popular march song with all companies. As we were nearing the end of the march, I saw the Group Commander standing beside the trail. I told the lead company to start up "God Bless America." I had fallen out of the lead to stand next to the Colonel to review the troops as they passed. When the last company had passed by, I saluted the Colonel to leave and rejoin my battalion. But he asked, 'Where is your slow column?' I replied, 'We don't have one, Sir. You may have noticed some were marching without their rifle, which was being carried by a stronger soldier in addition to his own weapon.' The Colonel then asked, 'You don't have *any* soldier fall out?' 'No, Sir.' He told me all the other battalions had a slow column following them by half an hour or more and most had a truck carrying those who couldn't walk any farther."

Rhoades, however, did not stick with the outfit. Instead, he was transferred and soon became the executive officer of the 4th Armored Cavalry Group as it prepared for the invasion of Normandy. Later, in France he would have a moment of reunion with his Camp Maxey recruits.

The War Department's Advisory Committee on Negro Troop Policies in December 1942 agreed to activation of a black parachute battalion, "for purposes of enhancing the morale and esprit de corps of the negro people." The gesture seemed to have less to do with furnishing an effective combat force than with pacifying those angered by the lack of choice for blacks.

Bradley Biggs, a native of Newark, New Jersey, where he hated the "ghetto" in which he grew up, was the first black officer to qualify as a paratrooper. Anxious to demonstrate that people of his race could compete with anyone, Biggs learned to fly with a club in his home state and after high school played professional football for the New York Brown Bombers. He had begun his military career as a private in the New Jersey National Guard and progressed to the level of sergeant before he qualified to attend OCS at Fort Benning.

As a lieutenant, posted to the 92d Division's 371st Regiment then training in Arkansas, Biggs, upset by what he considered an unfair order and the racism of superiors, refused to carry out a training exercise. He faced a court-martial just as Benjamin O. Davis Sr. came to the camp on an inspection. Biggs seized the chance to lay his grievances before Davis. "I told him that I was humiliated by the second-class status I received while serving my country, and bitter that prisoners of war had more rights than I did. I listened while he lectured me for thirty minutes on his career and the prejudice he had faced.

"'Your anger will ruin your hopes for a military career,' he warned me. 'So curb your tongue, quiet your temper, and remember that you are an officer, not a changer of behavior.'

"But what he said that day that most stuck in my mind was, 'Things will change. More opportunities will come to our soldiers but we must be ready for them. There are plans to give our soldiers the opportunity to serve in the air and in other branches of the service heretofore denied to them.'"

Biggs accepted the admonitions and modified his conduct. Subsequently, after treatment for a medical ailment placed Biggs in a pool of officers designated for reassignment at Fort Benning, the adjutant for parachute school then preparing to train a small group of nonwhites interviewed him. If the first blacks demonstrated they could pass the four-week course in airborne techniques, they would form the cadre of the now-activated 555th Parachute Battalion or what would eventually be known as "the Triple Nickles."

Months elapsed after he applied for paratrooper instruction. Meanwhile, Biggs served with a tank battalion attached to the 92d Division at Fort Huachuca. "One assignment at Huachuca made me want airborne duty all the more. Outside the main gate of the base was the small, unincorporated town of Fry. And one of Fry's principal industries, not surprisingly, was prostitution. With dozens of other officers from the 92d and 93d Divisions, I was on the roster to enforce the peace in the small red-light district of Fry. We called the duty the 'whorehouse watch.'

"It was degrading duty, set up by some insensitive idiot who never visited the area. Each evening following retreat, soldiers on pass would line up at the hundred or more tin, wood, and paper shacks which housed the prostitutes—and often their husbands and children as well. Fights and knifings were common, especially around pay day. The hospital emergency room was crowded nightly from the 'Fry Frolic Palaces.' So the post and division commanders agreed to supplement the military police units with teams of officers, three to a jeep usually with locked and loaded weapons. I pulled that duty eight times."

Release from the onerous life at Huachuca came with selection as a member of the test platoon for the 555th. At Fort Benning, the nonwhites lived in a segregated section of the camp but, says Biggs, "Our instructors, both officers and enlisted men, had of course, all been white. Some had grown up in the racist culture of the Deep South. They were hard driving and tough. Yet, because of the camaraderie of the airborne club, or out of respect, or simply because they were professional, we sensed no racial undertones in their attitudes or actions, no resentment that men of a different color were now entering their special world." Similarly, Biggs says he could detect no racism in the actions or words of the parachute school commander, Brig. Gen. Ridgley A. Gaither, his executive officer, Col. Harvey "Jabo" Jablonski, a football star while at West Point, or the adjutant, Major Hoover, who interviewed the first men accepted.

Along with five other black officers and sixteen noncoms, Biggs pinned on the wings of a parachutist in March 1944. The group then served as cadre for successive classes while also partaking of advanced courses in tactics and weapons. When their number totaled eleven officers and 165 enlisted men, the 555th, now up to company size, moved to Camp Mackall, North Carolina, to build itself to battalion strength. Although the post commander followed the traditional segregation policy for barracks, theaters, and most recreation facilities, the black paratroop officers, says Biggs, freely used the previously all-white officers' club and the races mixed at the post exchange.

The Triple Nickles, like the 332d Fighter Group, remained staffed by blacks from the bottom through the top. That was rarely the case elsewhere. Jim Pedowitz, the Brooklyn-born lawyer who volunteered to serve his year as the peacetime draft approached him, graduated from OCS early in 1942. In a brief effort to exploit his background, he had an assignment at the Quartermaster Depot in Washington, D.C., working on contracts. Subsequently, named commander of a black truck company which became part of the 470th Quartermaster Battalion, he was stationed at Camp McCain, Mississipppi.

"The men were almost all from agrarian Mississippi and came with minimal formal education. We had to teach reading and writing as well as other basic skills. Most knew how to handle vehicles or else they learned very quickly. Our regimental CO was a [white] veteran cavalry officer from the old school who felt we had to train very hard, with twenty-five mile marches completed in eight hours, four-mile hikes in fifty minutes. We were taught to take care of trucks the way they took care of the horses." Cavalry tradition stressed that the mounts' needs came first, then those of the troopers.

"For the most part there were not serious racial problems. The one black warrant officer in the battalion ate in the officers' mess. There was some overt discrimination from white residents in the area and one time troops fired rifles into a nearby village. We never determined who did it. In February of 1944, we sailed for England."

Neither the navy nor the marine corps relied on an ombudsman like Truman Gibson or Benjamin O. Davis Sr. to investigate, advise, and ease racial matters, although Secretary of the Navy Frank Knox had appointed a committee to review the role of blacks in his bailiwick before the attack on Pearl Harbor. The navy and the marine corps had resisted any significant change in their highly restrictive policies. Sensitive to the political climate generated by civil rights adherents, including his wife and the African American educator Mary McLeod Bethune, President Roosevelt insisted upon opening more opportunities for African Americans. A wary service proposed to add duties beyond handling food but tried to reserve for itself wide latitude in assignments, recruiting, training, and the number of people enlisted. As a former assistant secretary of the navy and a government administrator of long standing, the president recognized the potential for maintaining discrimination. He identified the escape mechanisms as "the Ethiopian in the woodpile." While his patrician Groton and Harvard background stifled resorting to vulgar racism, FDR saw no offense in a more elegant phrasing. Whatever the president's perception of African Americans, he forced the navy, beginning in April 1942, to add tens of thousands more blacks although he told Knox, "I do not think it in the least bit necessary to put mixed crews on ships."

In February 1943, as demand for manpower rose, the navy turned to the draft for personnel, potentially increasing the percentage of black sailors to the roughly 10 percent of African Americans in the general population. Although seemingly unrestricted, actually the Navy created what it called "base companies," or "composites" whose all-black enlisted personnel served as laborers, stevedores, ammunition handlers, and maintenance workers. Like the army, the navy operated a segregated service that covered billeting, messing, and units. To pacify those who demanded black officers, the V-12 program, which combined college studies with reserve-officer training, admitted some African Americans who passed the entrance examinations.

Not until 1944, after Frank Knox died and James V. Forrestal replaced him, did the service agree its WAVES should enroll black women. The marine corps' female contingent stayed all-white throughout the war and among the 11,000 navy nurses there were but four African Americans.

Gary Bell, born in Roanoke, Virginia, but raised in Cleveland, endured the life of a messman with considerable distaste. "My mother managed an insurance company and others from our family were in education, law and even business in England. I felt no discrimination because I was better off or equally as wealthy as others in the area. There were only a few African Americans in my schools. I enlisted in the navy not out of obligation to the country but being young, I felt it would be an adventure. The movies inspired me, that this was a chance to see the world. Many of my school friends had also entered the service.

"Boot camp was in Norfolk, Virginia, which we called the asshole of creation. There were no signs of discrimination on the base because the only people we were involved with were black. The highest rank of an African American in Boot Camp was a chief petty officer, nicknamed Hitler. He was a black dude with a Hitler style mustache and mean. Being from Cleveland I was immediately indignant because in the city of Norfolk were signs that said, 'Niggers and dogs keep off the grass' and there were signs in public places for separate drinking fountains, restaurants and restrooms. My greatest indignation came in our nation's capital. While in uniform, I was not allowed to eat in white establishments, the most notable being lunch counters at drug stores. It was not only insulting but hurtful because I was one of those fighting for the country. During stops at various places when we were transferred to Treasure Island, California, we were not allowed to eat in places owned or operated by whites." Bell was assigned as a messman on the USS *Cabot,* a light aircraft carrier (CVL) destined for action in the Pacific.

During World War II, about 40 percent of the navy's 165,000 black sailors did messmen's duties like Bell. Almost all of the remainder labored as stevedores, in construction work, or base maintenance. But a thousand or so gained admittance to other shipboard ratings equal to whites on the seas or at least along coastal waters. In 1943, the navy had created the Special Programs Unit with four naval officers to monitor the enlistment and assignment of its black sailors. Under prodding from the Special Programs Unit and the demands from civil rights leaders, the service agreed to an experiment that would place African American crews aboard two deepwater vessels, albeit with white officers and petty officers above them. Chosen to sail under these conditions eventually were *PC-1264,* a submarine chaser, and the USS *Mason,* a destroyer escort.

James W. Graham, as a seventeen-year-old South Carolinian, and several members of his high school class attempted to enlist for pilot instruction in the air corps. Rejected by a recruiter who told them blacks were ineligible, Graham says a navy recruiter invited him to become a sailor. In *Proudly We Served,* by Mary Pat Kelly, Graham recalls answering, "No. I'm not going to cook for anybody or clean up behind anybody."

The navy recruiter told him, "You don't have to go into that. You can join the seaman branch the same as the white guys, the white sailors." Graham accepted the offer, fibbing about his age on the enlistment papers. As a boot he went to Camp Robert Smalls, named for the slave who commandeered a Confederate ship, the area reserved for black recruits at the Great Lakes Naval Training Station. He qualified for radio school and received sixteen weeks of instruction in the field before being made a petty officer, third class and assigned to the Cape May Naval Air Base in New Jersey, eventually receiving assignment to a fishing boat converted into a minesweeper. From a white shipmate in charge, Graham learned seamanship.

Like others from the South, Graham remembers Chicago with mixed emotions. "You'd be walking on the street, and a guy would drive up in his car, with his wife and his daughter and he would take you to church or take you home and give you dinner. You could ride the bus and the El free of charge. The people there in Chicago treated the servicemen nice."

However, the largest USO in the city was exclusively for whites. After protests, a facility was opened on the South Side for the African Americans. And there were the usual incidents of discrimination and unpleasant exchanges with some white servicemen. At Cape May, the blacks again met segregation, Northern style, when an usher tried to make them move from their downstairs seats. They refused and a group of white sailors backed them up.

When he heard rumors of the navy search for personnel to man the *Mason,* Graham says he jumped at the opportunity. "But the chief said, 'You're only third class; we wanted second class.' So the communications officer told the chief to give me the radio manual for me to study." With the aid of a friend, Graham boned up on his specialty and passed an examination. He then transferred to the *Mason.*

Lorenzo DuFau, married, the father of a child in New Orleans, held a 3-A draft classification and could have avoided service for some length of time. He told Mary Pat Kelly, "I had a young son and I felt that if I could get into the service and do good, it would be an opening for him and others like him. It's just inbred in a man to want his child to be a little better off than he.

"Also at that time I was hearing in the news about what was happening over in Germany with the repression that was going on, the terrible actions against the Jews. I heard about that through the newspapers. And I said, I can kill two birds with one stone. I could take part in trying to stop this action and also open doors here at home . . . I guess some people would look at me as being kind of stupid at the time, thinking I was young and foolish to get all patriotic, knowing what ordeals I was living under. But it was *my* home being violated, threatened, and I felt it was only right to defend it. . . . You defend your family—you defend your country—because there's no other place that's home but here in America."

Even though DuFau worked in a civil service position at an army hospital making $90.00 a month, after struggling at jobs that paid as little as $3.75 a week, he says he believed that if he enlisted he might be able to get his family out of the South while "opening doors for the black man in the navy." Like Graham, DuFau attended boot camp at the Robert Smalls facility. He and some of his colleagues continued to view their service as a way to improve the image of African Americans. "At Robert Smalls we used to try to police each other so that we didn't make a bad record, a bad reputation, because you have bad eggs and good eggs in any group."

He also graduated from a service school at Great Lakes, becoming a signalman, third class. On a nine-day leave he realized his uniform meant little to white civilians. "I had to change trains in Atlanta. I tried to get a cup of coffee at the lunch counter. I was told there was no coffee, so I told the fellow, 'There are two urns going there. That's what I want, coffee.'

"'We don't *have* any coffee,' he said. And then it struck me, what he was really saying to me. I was in uniform and couldn't get a cup of coffee in the train station. It really was like an arrow in me. And I thought, 'I'm ready to go into the service to defend *this?*' But that didn't discourage me. It didn't stop me from trying to reach the goal that I was after." DuFau then spent ten months in New York harbor, serving aboard a lightship. When personnel experts sifted the records for appropriate ratings to crew the *Mason*, DuFau left the lightship for the destroyer escort.

Merwin Peters, born and raised in Cleveland, was tired of listening to his father who served in World War I as an army enlisted man. "When I learned there was going to be a draft and that sooner or later I was going to be drafted I decided that the army was not going to get me. As a matter of fact, I wasn't going *anywhere* where you had to do any marching or walking around a lot." Initially rejected by the navy and unable to immediately enter the merchant marines, he put his name on a waiting list for the navy and was eventually called up. Like Graham, Peters specialized in radio communications after his test scores indicated he qualified for several other specialties as well. "I chose radio because as a high school kid I was interested in amateur radio and this kind of fit into my plans."

At the service school he drilled in Morse code, radio theory, typing, and other aspects of the craft. Only one of the eight in his class earned a rating; Peters left Great Lakes as a striker, someone yet to be rated, for an air station near Boston. When he heard about the *Mason*, Peters says, "I volunteered for it because I wanted to be part of the seagoing navy as opposed to being landbased. There were some black navy enlisted people, most of them rated, I guess, who were serving on small ships like minesweepers. Some were on the coastal patrol, and some were on yard tugs. But I really wanted a warship. That's what I was looking for.

"I applied for a program for naval aviators. I was at an air station. There were two slots, and the two people who came out tops on the exam were to be selected to go down to Pensacola, Florida, and become naval aviators. Four of us took the exam. The two black fellows, myself and Dan Motley, came out on top on the exam. Then they changed the selection process." Instead of test scores, length of service became primary and the whites had served several months more. Peters joined the sailors on the *Mason.*

To serve as skipper of the *Mason,* the navy chose Lt. Comdr. William Blackford, son of a Seattle physician. A veteran yachtsman and two semesters shy of a doctorate in chemistry, Blackford, as a naval reservist from the University of Washington, commanded a minesweeper operating in the Aleutian Islands after being called up in 1941. Although the Navy seems to have been unaware of his ancestry, Blackford's forebears figured as prominent abolitionists. Shortly before the commissioning of the vessel Blackford wrote to his family, "The ship is coming along fine . . . am sure we will have a good crew as have some very fine reports concerning them. Can't figure out why I was picked but will do the best I can—really quite an opportunity to do something. We have a very good bunch of officers now."

Blackford must have been aware that his subordinates shared his views for the other eight officers, given the chance to opt out of the experiment without prejudice, all decided to stay with the project. In fact, they signed a paper that specifically said they could have selected other duty but chose to remain with the ship. The navy demanded hard evidence that it had not forced prejudiced officers to serve with the blacks.

Another missive home from Blackford said, "Am delighted with the colored men who are here. They know what they are doing and can really put out the work." He remarked that, "A colored society gave us enough musical instruments for the ship's band," and noted many of the sailors were musicians. "I think the crew is better than average," Blackford advised the home folks. "There has been a lot of bunk said about Negro crews. We can't see that they are any different from others if treated the same . . . They are anxious to make a name for themselves and actually work harder." He acknowledged shortcomings, due undeniably to the restrictions of service for blacks. "There is difficulty in getting qualified men for certain highly technical billets. [It is] impossible to train technicians aboard so the schools are being combed."

DuFau, among others, appreciated Blackford's approach. ". . . William Blackford was a captain indeed, and a man I will always have love and respect for. From the very beginning he was straight with us. He used to meet with the leading petty officers aboard ship. We would meet in the wardroom. There were few times you ever had a chance to be in the wardroom. That was like no man's land, except for those gold braids. But he used to call the leading petty officers from each division and sit and talk with us. This was just between him and his crew. He wanted to know if there were any problems on the ship that he should know about or that he could sort of work out. Because he didn't want any conflict on the ship.

"And he advised us that, 'As long as you do your job, what your rank calls for, you'll have no problem. I am just here to run a U.S. Navy ship. I am not here to solve a race problem.' He said, 'As long as you carry out your navy duties, you are going to get along with me. But if you cross lines, I am going to come down on you.'"

The navy not only opened up limited opportunites to serve as an enlisted man on a warship, it took a few tentative steps toward putting gold braid on the sleeves of its African Americans. Samuel Gravely Jr. says, "I was a youngster from Richmond, Virginia. I became draft eligible on my 20th birhday, June 4, 1942 and was required to register. I talked to my father who had been in the Army in World War I and I talked to other people who had been in other branches of the service and the consensus of opinion was that the Navy was probably what I would enjoy the most, primarily because the Navy had stated it would permit blacks to come in general service. I had no desire to [be a steward]. As a kid I had worked a couple of parties for tips and I didn't particularly care for that kind of work.

"I assumed that I was qualified for one of the [Navy] schools and picked the course of diesel engineering. I had been to segregated schools all of my life; going to a segregated Navy boot camp [at Camp Robert Smalls] was no change from what had happened. From there I went to Hampton Institute, which of course was set up as a segregated service school."

From Hampton Institute, Gravely shipped out to San Diego where he applied for the program. "In the V-12, a high school graduate would go to college for roughly two and a half years, then attend midshipman's school and on graduation be commissioned an ensign in the reserves. I already had two years of college so going about two semesters was about all I needed. It was not a program designed for blacks but for kids who might be high school graduates. At the time I passed the test and was permitted to go in 1943; it was before we had the first black officer in the Navy. I went to UCLA and to Columbia University. For the first time I was in a world where I had to compete with the people I would compete with the rest of my life. I think I discovered for the first time that all men put their pants on one leg at a time. No matter what the complexion is, you all do it the same way. I was commissioned in 1944." Gravely remembers being shocked to tears when sent back to Great Lakes as an ensign. Having been treated like all other midshipmen while in V-12, he reentered the segregated navy. He could only hope sea duty might provide a different atmosphere.

Graham Martin, already a college graduate, followed a different and even more unusual route to a commission. "We had a tobacco farm in Tobacco Port, Tennessee," said Martin in an interview for Paul Stillwell's book, *The Golden Thirteen*. "After my father died when I was five or six, my mother moved to Indianapolis. All the schools were 100 percent segregated. I wasn't a very good student. I was always playing hooky, skipping school, going to a movie. I belonged to a little gang, stealing a little, breaking windows. I ran away several times, was in a detention home temporarily and finally a judge put me in an orphanage.

"It was a structured environment with sports and my fourth grade teacher took a lot of interest in me. She told me why didn't I try to get some good grades and behave myself and see how I liked that. I tried for five or six weeks and I got all As and A plusses. It felt good to have a teacher praise me."

Martin became a good student and was part of a jug band organized by the school principal that peformed mostly at white segregated high schools. At Crispus Attucks High School the teachers, "all of whom had at least master's degrees and some were Ph.d.s, were inspirational. They urged the students to break through the poverty cycle." Martin, as part of the school's sports teams, traveled out of the state and was busy enough, he said, not to have time to resent segregation. On the other hand, he remembered when Joe Louis lost to the German Max Schmeling, whites drove through the streets, shouting epithets. Louis gave Martin pride in his race. "If he was inferior, why could he beat everybody?"

Becoming religious, at eighteen, he was appointed Sunday school superintendent. After his nineteenth birthday, he returned to live with his mother who earned $38.75 a month as a WPA seamstress. Martin worked for the Youth Progress Administration at a cafeteria and washed windows of a school. Granted an academic scholarship by a philanthropic foundation, he passed up an opportunity to attend Fisk University because he heard it drew rich kids. He enrolled at the University of Indiana where tuition cost about fifty dollars a year and made the football team, coached by Alvin "Bo" McMillan, a 1919 all-American and former pro coach. Martin believes, "His thinking was that blacks were normally and naturally inferior and whites were superior." The coach displayed no open racism but Martin played only occasionally.

With his diploma in hand, Martin fruitlessly applied to black colleges for a teaching position. He enrolled at Howard Univeristy working toward a master's degree. The draft board agreed to allow him to finish. He wrote a thesis on the underground railroad in Indiana and the research opened his eyes to black history.

"I considered the Army was too dirty for me, crawling in all that mud and stuff," says Martin. The announced openings in general service ratings to blacks encouraged him to become a sailor. At the Great Lakes Naval Station a white petty officer ran the training company. "The race thing never came up but I don't think he was in any way prejudiced. He never showed it, at least and was only very helpful."

During his first year at Great Lakes, nonwhites were not recruited for the football team. The following year, after the squad lost its first two games, Coach Tony Hinkle who had been at Butler University, "came to the black camp and asked if any of us boys wanted to play." Martin proved an outstanding member of the team. When Great Lakes traveled to the University of Indiana, Martin found himself assigned an alcove of the locker room while the others stayed at the athletic club. Graham informed the coach, "If this is my room then I can stay home." In spite of such incidents, the navy players racked up a 12–2 record for 1943 against top teams like Notre Dame, Purdue, and Ohio State. Martin became a permanent cadre at Camp Robert Smalls, serving as a physical training leader.

While he was so engaged, some in the Roosevelt administration became concerned that the administration's V-12 program, which included African Americans, would not produce an officer until well into 1944. Assistant Secretary of the Navy Adlai E. Stevenson, later an Illinois governor and candidate twice for the presidency, along with other influential figures, coaxed Frank Knox to open a kind of OCS for black sailors that would be the seagoing equivalent of the army's ninety-day wonders.

Knox acceded and a search for suitable candidates commenced. The archives indicate that Comdr. E. Hall Downes, the officer in charge of the Naval Training School at Hampton, nominated eight men. Comdr. Daniel Armstrong [kin to Samuel Chapman Armstrong, founder of Hampton and to Dewitt Armstrong, the West Pointer, who headed the black boot program at Great Lakes,] suggested another seven, including Graham Martin, and one more man was proposed by the Eighth Naval District. What is clear, according to Paul Stillwell's research, is that the navy chose its first candidates very carefully. All had demonstrated leadership as enlisted men. Most of them, like Martin, were athletes and background checks discovered nothing to suggest any militant civil rights advocacy. Some did not have a college education but others had, like Martin, obtained postgraduate degrees.

A classmate of Martin's in the pilot officer program was George C. Cooper, a native of Washington, North Carolina, where his father, a sheet metal worker tried to support a family of ten children. "He had only a third grade education and my mother a fourth," Cooper told Stillwell. "He was very independent, always stressed to each of us that the only thing anybody would pay for in this world was production. You've got to have an education, because without it, you're not going to make it." In fact, the senior

Cooper started his own business and did well enough so that all of his youngsters went to college.

George Cooper, possessing what he called a "very mediocre education" from a segregated high school, entered Hampton Institute as a work student. That meant a light academic load while holding a job to earn enough for more than a year's tuition. Cooper acted as a bellman and "maid" at the campus guest facility and sang with the Hampton Choir and other groups to pick up extra funds. A brother and a sister as well as his father contributed toward the financial load.

When he completed his courses he started to work with his father. "In Washington, [North Carolina], Jim Crow was the name of the game. Everything was separate; nothing was equal. The 'choice' you had was to try to make the best of it or get in trouble. Making the best of it did not necessarily mean being subservient, with your hat in your hand, but taking an unfortunate situation and trying to make something creative and constructive out of it."

In 1939, Cooper established his own sheet metal shop, manufacturing roofs and gutters for an insurance company but he gave that up to teach his trade at Wilberforce. Commander Edwin Hall Downes, United States Naval Academy 1920, recruited him to his alma mater, as part of the Naval Training Station. Downes convinced Cooper with his pitch, "We'd like to have you take the job because we need you and there aren't many of you around, white or colored." Cooper recognized in Downes someone who considered only ability, not skin color, while he says the navy maintained, "The only thing that a black man could do was serve as a steward."

When Selective Service pursued Cooper, Downes vainly tried to have him declared exempt. Failing that, Downes promised that he would guarantee Cooper a rating of chief petty officer. Cooper had barely put down his sea bag at Great Lakes before Downes, making good on his pledge, brought him back to Hampton as a CPO. In his capacity as a selector for the black officer training program, Downes picked Cooper as one of his eight nominees.

Ordered to Great Lakes from Hampton, Cooper says he guessed it was for officer training. "We knew to a man that if we failed in this endeavor, the evil of segregation in the Navy, as related to black officers, would be set back for God only knows how long. We had to do something. I think the Navy, as an institution, was making a good faith effort because it had been ordered to do so by the CINC [commander in chief]. This doesn't relate to the fact the institution is made up of people with their personal likes and dislikes. I don't think BuPers [Bureau of Personnel] said, 'Make these men fail.' I don't believe BuPers said, 'Send them through the mill, give them hell and flunk 'em.' I think it was more institutionalized racism, which in my judgement is still alive and well in this country. [This interview dates to 1987.]

All of the African Americans in the first class agreed that their chief teacher, Lt. John Dille, was exceptional. "We had some good instructors," says Cooper, "but John was the exception. He went over and above the call of duty beyond the subject matter and in being an inspiration to us. He gave us a helluva lot of support when we really needed it by being understanding and helping us think through situations that rose in the course of the training.

"When our grades were sent to Washington we came out two-tenths of a point ahead of any indoctrination class they'd ever had. They said it's a mistake. Send them back through. We started the whole thing all over again. We were serious about the business of sinking or swimming together. Graham Martin was a coach and his approach was, if you're going to be on this team, you gotta make the grade. You gotta make the grade in classroom work, you gotta make the grade out in the field, you gotta make the grade if you wanna be on this team. You're gonna have to bring it intellectually, you're gonna have to bring it physically, you're gonna have to bring it spiritually. Time after time, when you'd be down in the dumps, Graham would come back, let's get our crap together, man."

Probably the highest level achieved by any of those admitted to the officer candidate school was William Sylvester White. He had been appointed an assistant U.S. attorney in Chicago shortly before 1943, when, as a twenty-seven-year-old, he volunteered for the navy rather than risk his future through the draft. "My father was a chemist and pharmacist, a graduate of Fisk and the University of Illinois, my mother a school teacher with degrees from Fisk and the University of Chicago. During the depression, my Dad's business as a pharmacist plummeted. We depended on my mother's salary as a school teacher. They sacrificed and sent their only child [himself] to college and law school."

In 1937, new lawyers, particularly young black ones, could not count on earning a living through jurisprudence. White struggled as a law clerk for a criminal attorney with a tiny practice, did casework for a relief organization, enabling him to buy a few suits and a second-hand car but could not scratch a living in his chosen profession. He applied to be an FBI agent but J. Edgar Hoover refused to accept nonwhites. "It disgusted me that whenever they had some undercover work to do, they would take on a smart black detective [from the Chicago police] and have him work with them, eliminating the need for black agents." Civil-rights agitation ultimately brought White a measure of relief. "I got the appointment to be an Assistant U.S. Attorney in Chicago, as the token black."

Although the others chosen for the officer candidate school had been in the navy long enough to demonstrate leadership, intelligence, and skills, White had little navy experience to his credit. However, at the time he entered the service, a reporter friend had put out a press release extolling his achievements. "By the time I hit Great Lakes, they knew that Sylvester White, an Assistant U.S. Attorney, was coming to the Navy. That's how I became an officer." The Great Lakes Naval Training Station jolted him. "That was my first experience with enforced segregation, although growing up in Chicago [I knew] that white folks lived here and black folks lived over there. I remember we were marching to the chow hall. They had a double level hall. All the white recruits were marched upstairs. The black recruits were marched down in the basement. That hit me. Blacks played on the Great Lakes football team because in those days there were a few blacks playing on the college football teams. It sounds ridiculous, but blacks could not play on the Great Lakes basketball team.

"My impression of Commander Armstrong was of a southerner, aristocratic, egotistical, sincerely interested in advancing the status of Negroes in the Navy, according to his viewpoint. [In his view] we should remember we were colored officers and not do all the things that white officers do. He felt that way we would ensure the success of the program. We hated it. But I am sure he thought it best. In a sense it is rather like Branch Rickey telling Jackie Robinson in spite of his [combative] nature, don't let that show. You're a pioneer. It might hamper others who come along." Among the strictures urged by Armstrong was avoidance of the officers' club.

Major General Thomas Holcomb, commandant of the marine corps, who had suggested that blacks could satisfy their desire for combat in the army had reiterated his opposition to their wishes to become part of the few and the proud. "There would be a definite loss of efficiency in the Marine Corps if we have to take Negroes." Overruled by a presidential executive order, Holcomb directed his staff to create an African American component of his service.

A memorandum from the commandant to subordinates conveys the dubious attitude of the marine hierarchy. "Mixing of white and colored enlisted personnel within the same unit will be avoided, except as may be temporarily necessary in providing white noncommissioned officers. Plan should contemplate relief of these white noncommissioned officers as rapidly as colored noncommissioned officers can be qualified.

". . . The long experience of the army with regard to Negro military organizations indicates the importance of the following considerations:

"Successful units were commanded by excellent to superior white officers who were firm but sympathetic with their men, and who thoroughly knew their individual and racial characteristics and temperaments. These officers once assigned were not changed." The statement was absolutely false.

The paper did point out that racial disturbances often occured in the absence of adequate recreational facilities for nonwhites. It directed local commanders to try and involve civilian officials in the provision of such features. "Lacking this cooperation, the only other method of preventing trouble is by extensive use of highly trained military police, both white and colored."

Ray A. Robinson, then a marine colonel in charge of a personnel section, later said, "When the colored came in, we had the appropriations and the authority. It just scared us to death. I went over to selective service, and saw Gen. Hershey and he turned me over to a lieutenant colonel and he was one grand person [Lt. Col. Campbell C. Johnson, an African American]. I told him that Eleanor [Roosevelt] says we gotta take in Negroes and we are just scared to death, we've never had any. We don't know how to handle them. We are afraid of them.

"He said, 'I'll do my best to help you get good ones. I'll get the word around that if you want to die young, join the Marines. So anybody that joins has got to be pretty good.' And it was the truth. We got some awfully good Negroes." To make marines out of these black civilians, a tract of land at the New River, North Carolina, installation that housed whites was set aside. Known as Montford Point it was separated from the larger all-white area by twelve miles of scrub pine and the New River. The primary organization was known as the 51st Composite Defense Battalion.

In spite of Johnson's promise to supply men, blacks hesitated to volunteer for a branch that had no tradition of nonwhites. The first black recruit to report to Montford Point arrived on 26 August 1942. By October, six hundred men of color, half of what had been the goal, drilled under white noncoms, officers, and the command of a South Carolinian and graduate of the Citadel, Col. Samuel A. Woods—the belief that Southerners knew best how to deal with blacks pervaded the armed forces. Holcomb had issued a Letter of Instruction that stated it was "essential that in no case shall there be colored noncommmissioned officers senior to white men in the same unit and desirable that few, if any be of the same rank." Mindful of unfavorable publicity, the marines classified this document until after World War II. African Americans who earned stripes, like the white noncoms at Montford Point, became known as Special Enlisted Staff (SES).

Among the first African Americans who reported to Montford Point was Gilbert H. "Hashmark" Johnson. Born in Mt. Hebron, Alabama, in 1905, Johnson had served three hitches with the 25th Infantry, beginning in 1923. In 1933 he switched to the navy and assignment as a steward before he applied for a transfer into the marines. At age thirty-seven he showed up at Montford Point in his navy uniform. With his military background, Johnson quickly became a drill instructor, supervising the very platoon to which he was originally assigned. For the duration of the war, many of the men who passed through Montford Point learned under the stern, demanding eye of Johnson.

Edgar Huff, a crane rigger for a steel company near his home town of Gadsden, Alabama, signed on without prior military experience but remembered a father who died from the effects of having been gassed while part of the AEF during World War I. Huff, whose mother supported the family on three dollars a week as a houseworker for whites and raked coke from the ashes of white people's fireplaces to use for fuel at home, said, "I wanted to be a Marine, because I had always heard that the Marine Corps was the toughest outfit going and I felt I was the toughest going, so I wanted to be a member of the best organization."

His budding career nearly was nipped by an altercation during an emergency leave to visit his sick mother. A pair of white marine MPs accosted him in the Atlanta railroad depot, asking what he was doing wearing marine green. According to Huff they snarled, "There ain't no damn nigger Marines. You going to jail."

Huff says he gave the pair his furlough papers. "They tore 'em up right in my damn face. Said I was impersonating a Marine." He languished in the Atlanta city jail for five days, as various marine authorities refused to accept his credentials. Even a navy chaplain dismissed him. At last Huff convinced a marine major to telephone the Montford camp and Colonel Woods rescued him.

During the early days of Montford Point, black marines enjoyed a program of boxing matches and other performances. The overall Camp Lejeune commander, Maj. Gen. Henry L. Larsen, who had recently come back from the South Pacific, received an invitation. There has been some debate about Larsen's actual comments but the gist of what he said, and the most inflammatory phrase is contained in Huff's remembrance. "I just came back from Guadalcanal. I've been fighting through the jungles. Fighting day and night. But I didn't realize there was a war going on until I came back to the United States. And especially tonight. When I come back and I find out that we have now got women Marines, we have got dog Marines and when I see you *people* wearing *our* uniforms, then I know there's a war going on." According to Huff the first black marine riot ensued.

Huff's ability surfaced immediately and he was quickly enrolled in a drill instructor's course before getting a platoon of his own. Both Johnson and Huff achieved renown during their time in the marine corps.

The presence of a large number of African Americans in the uniform of the marines traumatized the local civilians. When the first graduates of boot camp received liberty, they walked through the front gate to Jacksonville with the intention of catching buses to towns that had a substantial black population. The natives of Jacksonville, however, apparently frightened at the sight of several hundred nonwhite marines shut down their stores and the bus station. Colonel Woods averted a potentially nasty situation by ordering the trucks of the 51st Defense Battalion to carry the men to their desired destinations and then when liberty expired to return them. Unfortunately, on other occasions, the area bus companies enforced the back-of-the-bus rules or even denied passage if whites could fill the vehicles.

Woods, whom some described as cultivating a paternalistic manner that brought him the unflattering title of "the Great White Father of everybody" accepted segregation and the mores of the white supremacist South. At the same time he strove to protect the men from oppression by aggressive white law-enforcement authorities and to salve some of the humiliations of discrimination.

Although most of the black marines avoided the hassle of Jacksonville by traveling to larger cities with a greater black population, some men on pass short of money or time tried to while away off-duty hours in Jacksonville. According to Perry Fischer, a white SES at Montford Point, "Most would go in groups for their own safety. They were confronted on almost every corner, on every street, in every public place with racism and segregation. Frequently, they had to either 'back off' or 'square off' for a fight."

Fischer says Colonel Woods sent military police into town to check places where black and white marines might clash. SES staff sometimes ran these patrols, taking with them an unarmed black marine sergeant. When fights among the marines began, if the patrol could not quell the disturbance, the local cops were called. "In almost every case," noted Fischer, "the black Marines seemed to come off the worse, even though they may have contributed little or nothing to the cause of the altercation. Also, the black MPs could not arrest or detain white Marines."

Gunnery Sergeant Perry Fischer served as deputy to Lt. John D'Angelo in command of the first platoon of the 8th Marine Ammunition Company. A native of Chicago, Fischer, says that in 1939, after three years of wrapping and packing merchandise for Montgomery Ward, "I felt frustrated that I could never rise above a hand worker unless I acquired a professional skill or higher education. We were still suffering from the Big Depression and I was financially unable to attend college." Desperate for a change, he and two friends planned a trip to Latin America for opportunities with the United Fruit Company whose benefits package would eventually pay college tuition. The trio pooled their resources, bought a twenty-eight-foot sloop, passed the coast guard requirements, and prepared to sail from New Orleans to a Central American port. But with German U-boats prowling the Gulf of Mexico, the coast guard intercepted them and withdrew their permits.

"The few weeks at sea got into my blood. While sojourning in New Orleans, trying to decide what to do next, I met a couple of seagoing Marines at a dance. I liked their uniforms. They seemed to be content with their military life—I didn't know that Marines on leave who recruited civilians for the Corps received extra leave. They convinced me that with the war in Europe I was a perfect candidate for a draft. The best and easiest job in the service was as a seagoing marine. I fell for it, enlisted in August 1940 and reported to Parris Island, South Carolina, for recruit training."

Instead of duty aboard a ship, however, Fischer, upon completion of recruit camp, served at the Washington, D.C., marine barracks and acted as field first sergeant for President Roosevelt's hideaway "Shangri-La" in the Catoctin Mountains just north of the District of Columbia. (Later, President Dwight D. Eisenhower renamed it Camp David for his grandson.) "It was one of the plushiest jobs in the Marine Corps. However, as the Marine Corps suffered severe losses in personnel fighting their way across the South Pacific, replacements were sorely needed. Since I had no combat experience, I became immediately available for reassignment and combat training."

Posted to the 8th Marine Ammunition Company, Fischer admits, "Initially, I experienced a sense of disappointment at being assigned to a black Marine unit. When I first reported for duty with the 8th I was not aware that blacks had been permitted to enlist in the Marines. Most of the other members of the white Special Enlisted Staff [the senior noncoms] were as surprised as I was. I said to myself, 'Oh my God! What have I gotten into? Was I being punished for something I knew nothing about?'"

As a Jew, however, Fischer believes he developed some sensitivity about the status of minorities. "In the first stages of my Marine career, I felt my Jewish nationality caused me some difficulty but nothing serious or harmful to me. I never was a 'practicing' Jew, and only my Jewish facial features made it obvious of my race and more significantly there were few Jews in the Marines at that time. I believe the Jews who were in the Marines were intelligent, hard working and loyal. We had a good sense of teamwork, tolerance and physical endurance. I was good at sports and participated in all of them and so generally I was considered a 'good Jew.' On a few occasions, individuals, especially those from deep Dixie—perhaps even KKK members—would belittle me but I had too many other good friends who supported me. Being a Jew never threatened me as a Marine or as a soldier [a post–World War II career] but I tried twice as hard to meet all demands and rarely ever brought undue attention to myself because of my Jewish identity." The affinity with the situation of African Americans is obvious.

According to Fischer, the CO of the 8th, Capt. John R. Blackett, a former enlisted man commissioned after the war broke out and a veteran of sea battles while serving on ships, set a standard for behavior and attitude. "Only a few moments after holding his first company formation, he spoke out long and loud about his uncompromising stand that under no circumstance would the staff or anyone else under his command support racism, prejudice, discrimination or oppression." Fischer praises several other key people, Lt. Kenneth Graham, and Lt. John D'Angelo, former enlisted men like Blackett, because of their concern for the welfare of their men. "Graham made certain he was in town when the black Marines were on pass in order to be present if any of the men of the 8th Marine Ammunition Company were unduly harassed by the local white authorities. D'Angelo spoke often of his anguish as a young boy in Pennsylvania, the son of an immigrant Italian father, being called 'Dago' and 'Wop' for reasons he never could understand. He was outspoken about his aversion to racism, bigotry and prejudice."

Fischer says he subsequently learned that the first 144 white noncoms and 84 white officers assigned to train and serve with nonwhites were chosen with care, recommended for having demonstrated fairness, leadership, ability to teach and communicate, and desire to take care of their subordinates.

It was by no means all serene. "The first weeks were rife with tension. There were many moments with a lot of shouting, a lot of threatening and a tremendous amount of explanation, cajoling, persuading and other techniques. Many mistakes were made on both sides of the color line, before the black Marines came to understand that the white staff was their ally. Open and honest communication between the two colors resulted in coordinated, cooperative, responsible results, which made what was a hell of a life at Montford Point a little easier for all."

Occasionally, white introduction to Southern mores meant culture shock. Edward Andrusko, as a child in Perth Amboy, New Jersey, says, "I didn't know any black people in grade school and I saw one or two in high school. I didn't have any racial opinions. Every nationality from Europe had its own culture and the blacks had their own ethnic ghetto area in our city and somehow we all got along. The schools, jobs and churches were the melting pots.

"I joined the Marines right after my seventeenth birthday, in September 1941, before World War II. There was little or no work available. We had five brothers and four sisters in our family. Four of us boys would join the military for employment. A Marine sergeant from my neighborhood came home on leave after four exciting years in China and sea duty. We heard his wondrous sea tales of travel and adventure. I was very impressed. It was very difficult to get into the small pre-war military. You had to be in excellent shape, both mentally and physically. I enlisted and passed.

"Then we headed for boot camp at Parris Island, South Carolina. During a stop at a railroad station in the South I walked over to a water fountain and started to turn it on and off. The Marine sergeant in charge of us asked me what the hell I thought I was doing. I said the sign said 'Colored' and I was trying to see the colored water. He yelled at me as a wise guy Yankee but that's how little I knew about segregation. I didn't know that there was segregation in the military, and I never saw a black person in either the Marines or the Navy during my first years in service. When I was on leave in the Carolinas, I was shocked at the living conditions of both whites and blacks. However, the blacks had it much worse. We were all apathetic about the race situation. There were more North versus South problems; we were refighting the Civil War. In the South, we Yankees had to be indifferent (for our own safety) to the racial situation."

As the United States became involved in the shooting war, Andrusko trained hard with the 7th Marine Regiment of the 1st Marine Division. The outfit shipped out to the Pacific early in 1942 to engage in a number of island-hopping battles.

Company E, 4th U.S. Colored Infantry at Fort Lincoln, District of Columbia, November 17, 1865. (Library of Congress)

Picket station near Dutch Gap Canal, November 1864. (Library of Congress)

Gun crew conducting "cannoneer's hop" in a garrison situation. (Tony Powell Collection)

Soldiers guarding "slave pen" in Alexandria, Virginia. (National Archives)

An infantry company, circa 1880. Soldiers are in dress uniforms. (National Archives)

Troop K, 9th Cavalry Regiment at Wounded Knee, South Dakota, 1898. (Tony Powell Collection)

Cadet John Hanks Alexander, second African American graduate of the U.S. Military Academy, was commissioned from the Class of 1887. (Tony Powell Collection)

Cavalry squadron in mounted review, circa 1886. (National Archives)

Sailors' mess on USS *Newark*, circa 1890. Note that crew is integrated. (U.S. Navy)

Steward aboard USS *Brooklyn,* serving as wardroom servant, circa 1917. After 1900 and until World War II, non-whites in the Navy were restricted to food service and valet duties. (U.S. Navy)

Company from 24th Infantry Regiment, in Cuba, 1898. (National Archives)

Soldiers on duty with the Punitive Expedition in Mexico, June 2, 1915. (National Archives)

Court Martial of 64 members of the 24th Infantry, November 1, 1917, Fort Sam Houston, Texas, on trial for mutiny and murder of 17 people at Houston, Texas, August 23, 1917. (National Archives)

Volunteers for active duty during World War I. (National Archives)

Ike Sims of Atlanta, Georgia, 87 years old, had eleven sons in service. (National Archives)

"Big Nims" of the 365th Infantry, 92d Division, World War I. (National Archives)

Many black troops in Europe in 1918 worked in the Supply Service. (National Archives)

World War I era nurses. (National Archives)

Artillerymen of the American Expeditionary Force, World War I. (National Archives)

Soldiers in barracks, World War I. (National Archives)

Troops being awarded decorations in France, circa 1919. (National Archives)

An uncomfortable bed, but not really a dangerous one. France, 1918. (National Archives)

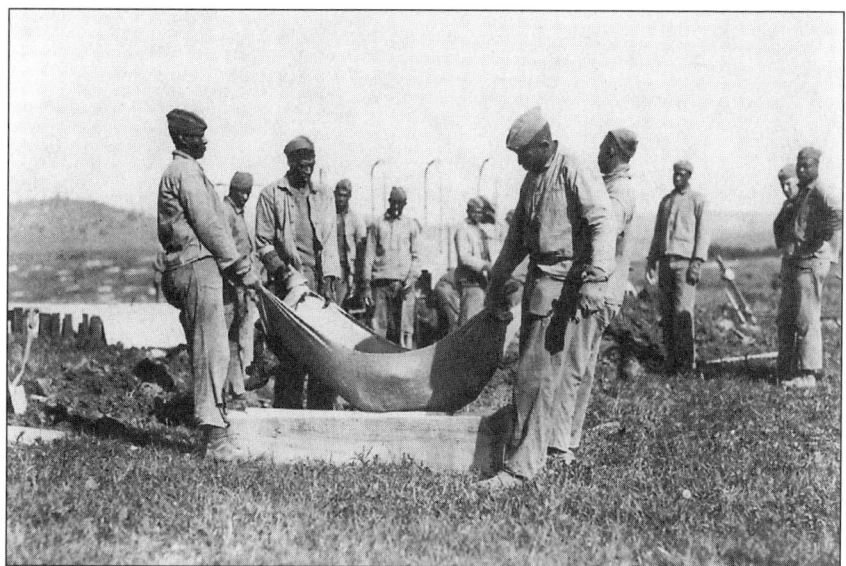

Onerous burial detail moving corpses to new location. France, 1919 (National Archives)

Artillery battery in action in France, 1918. Many American units were equipped with "French 75's" during World War II. (National Archives)

Soldiers in training learning to use the bayonet early in World War II. (National Archives)

Soldiers negotiating obstacle course, circa 1941. (National Archives)

Segregated cafeteria at the post service club, Fort Huachuca, Arizona, May 19, 1942. (U.S. Army)

Spann Watson, Tuskegee pilot, World War II. (U.S. Air Force)

Color guard at Fort Riley, Kansas, in 1942. Note the great heavyweight champion Joe Louis carrying the national colors. (Library of Congress)

Famous and talented singer Lena Horne entertaining troops at Fort Huachuca, Arizona, September 6, 1942. (U.S. Army)

The 480th Port Battalion Headquarters Company set up in Greek Temple of Neptune (circa 700 BC) in Sicily, September 22, 1943. (U.S. Army)

Officers and ladies of the 9th Cavalry Regiment at Fort Riley, Kansas, August 1943. Note Lieutenant Jackie Robinson on the left front. (Eric Saul Collection)

Soldiers of Company I, 3d Battalion, 370th Infantry Regiment advancing against the German enemy, Cascina, Italy, September 1, 1944. (U.S. Army)

On December 17, 1944, captured American soldiers were executed by Nazi SS troops at Malmedy, Belgium. These soldiers of the 3200 Quartermaster Service Company removed the bodies from the death ground for proper burial. (U.S. Army)

Pilots of the 332d Fighter Group serving in Italy in 1944 are being briefed before a mission against the Germans. (U.S. Air Force)

Field religious service for troops of the 26th Quartermaster Battalion, Jarny, France, October 29, 1944. (U.S. Army)

Brigadier General Benjamin O. Davis, USA, pins the Distinguished Flying Cross on his son, Col. Benjamin O. Davis Jr., Capt. Joseph D. Elsberry, and 1st Lt. Clarence D. Lester. (U.S. Air Force)

Captain Charles B. Hall was the first black pilot to shoot down a German aircraft in World War II. (U.S. Army)

South Pacific, World War II. Litter bearers of Company K, 25th Infantry Regiment, 93d Infantry Division struggling up Hill 290 with a wounded comrade, ambushed while on reconnaissance mission on April 7, 1944. (U.S. Army)

Members of the 92d Infantry Division drying out in shattered house near Viareggio, Italy, December 14, 1944. (U.S. Army)

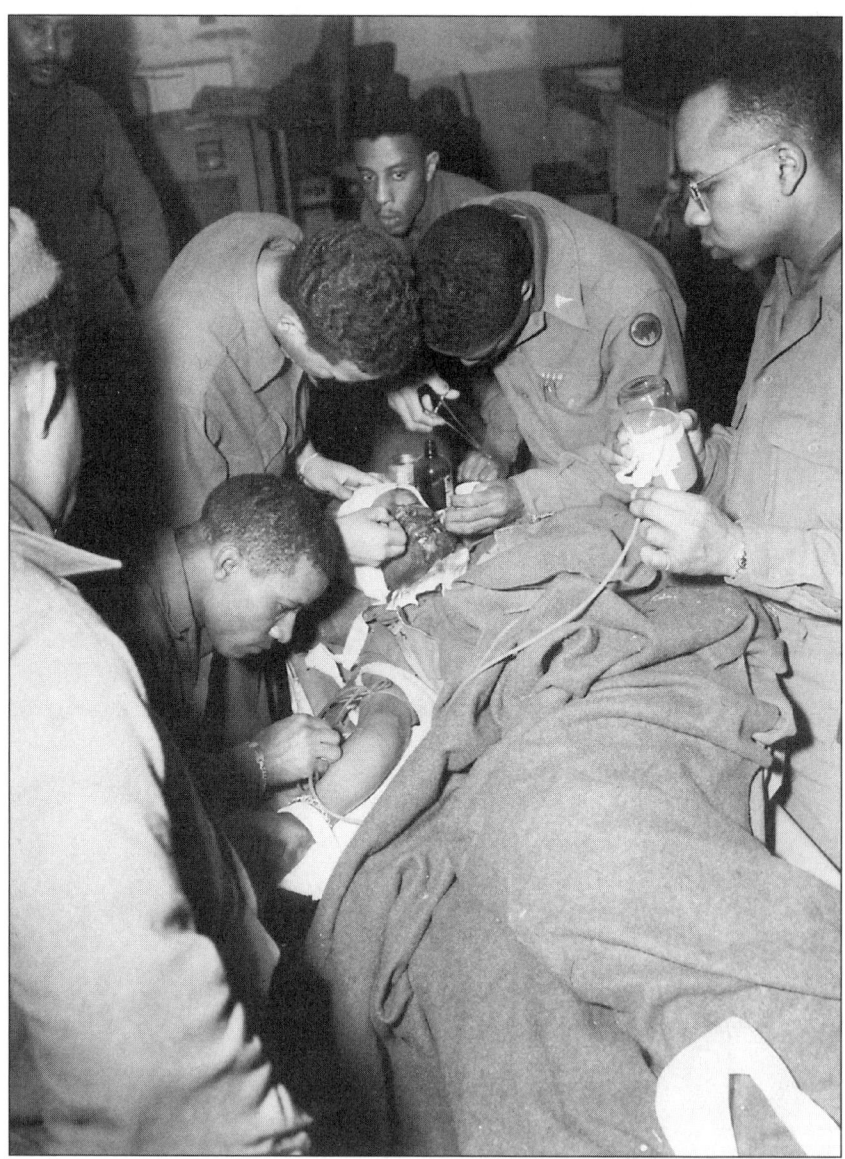

Captain Ezekia Smith, 370th Infantry Regiment, is being treated at the 317th Collecting Station for shell fragments in face and shoulder, Querceta, Italy, February 10, 1945. (U.S. Army)

Men of the 9th Infantry Regiment prepare to evacuate wounded soldiers from the area of Hill 201, Korea. (U.S. Army)

Korean War. Soldiers manning front-line outpost near Kaejun, Korea, November 22, 1950. (U.S. Army)

Mortar crewmen of Company B, 25th Infantry Regiment, 25th Infantry Division. August 15, 1951. (U.S. Army)

Vietnam War. A medical technician of Company B, 1st Battalion, 7th Cavalry Regiment, 1st Air Cavalry Division gives first aid to children wounded by grenade fragments in the An Lo Valley, April 29, 1967. (U.S. Army)

Lieutenant Colonel Donald Sims, 1st Air Cavalry Division, just having received the Silver Star for gallantry in Vietnam. (Eric Saul Collection)

Members of Company C, 5th Battalion, 9th Infantry Division cross a canal during operation "Hot Tac" northeast of My Tho, Vietnam, April 6, 1967. (U.S. Army)

Staff Sergeant Melvin G. Gaines shows the strain of serving as a "tunnel rat" after a several hour search of a Viet Cong tunnel complex, March 17, 1967. (U.S. Army)

A machine gunner of the 3d Battalion, 187th Airborne Infantry Regiment, 101st Airborne Division defending a position in the A Shau Valley. September 30, 1969. (U.S. Army)

After receiving fresh supplies, men of the 173d Airborne Brigade continue on a jungle "Search and Destroy" mission in Phouc Tuy Province, June 1966. (U.S. Army)

Brigadier General Frederick E. Davison, Commanding General, 199th Light Infantry Brigade, left, congratulates Maj. Gen. Fillmore K. Mearne, Commander, Capital Military Assistance Command, after receiving the Distinguished Service Medal, April 1969. (U.S. Army)

Wesley Brown, first black graduate (Class of 1949) of the United States Naval Academy. (Courtesy of Crystal Brown)

Chief of Naval Operations Elmo R. Zumwalt conferring with sailors during a Human Relations Council session to reduce friction and improve opportunities. (U.S. Navy)

Vice Admiral Samuel Gravely, first black Navy admiral. (U.S. Navy)

General Colin Powell, Chairman of the Joint Chiefs of Staff, 1991. (U.S. Army)

Brigadier General Clifford Stanley, U.S. Marine Corps, presently on active duty. (U.S. Marine Corps)

13
Combat and Other Battles

Honors for being the first blacks in the army to face enemy fire belong neither to the Tuskegee airmen nor the infantrymen of the 93d Division. Instead, the 450th Antiaircraft Battalion along with African American engineers, as members of Operation Torch, the Allied landings in North Africa in June 1942, received credit for shooting down two German bombers during an air raid. Later, while still aboard a ship in the Naples harbor, the 450th added another victim attempting to disrupt the invasion of Italy.

The 99th Fighter Squadron, which had survived the disdain and criticism of its white-commanded parent group and learned its trade mostly on the job, bedded down at Foggia following the storming of the Italian mainland. The unit now flew under the aegis of the 79th Fighter Group commanded by Col. Earl Bates who welcomed them and quickly demonstrated respect for the African American airmen. Previously, upper echelons neglected to adequately brief the 99th and share intelligence but Bates not only made the outfit an integral part of his group, he even flew with them.

As 1943 ended, a large contingent of African American airmen prepared to leave for Europe. The 99th was to be joined by the latest products of Tuskegee and Selfridge Field. Benjamin O. Davis Jr. was to return to the Mediterranean theater with the newly constituted 332d Fighter Group that included the 100th, 301st, and 302d Fighter Squadrons. On the eve of their departure, the airmen staged at Camp Patrick Henry, Norfolk, Virginia, for travel by sea to the war zone.

Charles Bussey, one of Davis's pilots, built up a head of steam as he contemplated the signs WHITE TROOPS ONLY at a nearby PX and the movie theater. With several allies, he plotted a small demonstration of his displeasure. While perhaps one hundred white soldiers waited to buy tickets to a Humphrey Bogart film, Bussey reached up and yanked down the sign on the theater. Then he, another officer, and some of the ground crew bought seats and entered the building.

"I didn't enjoy the movie," says Bussey. "Racial expletives could be heard coming from the white members of the audience during the latter part of the movie. It appeared that the situation in the movie theater was going to get out of hand and become violent. I didn't know what to do about stopping the violence that was on the way; hatred had set the scene for trouble."

Surprisingly, except for some seats torn up by the angry black soldiers, the theater emptied out with no fights. But later that night, gunfire sounded as the men who had been issued weapons and ammunition expressed their unhappiness. Bussey's squadron commander came to his bunk and blamed him for having caused the commotion by his action at the theater. He warned Bussey the post commander was arming infantrymen with the purpose of quelling the outbreak, at the risk of death and injury to many. The squadron commander appointed Bussey his provost marshal with the appropriate military police powers.

Donning a steel helmet, Bussey recruited a tech sergeant to accompany him through the barracks area. The sergeant explained to Bussey that most of the men really were not looking for a fight but were simply sounding off because of bitterness with Jim Crow conditions. "We walked into the first barracks. In the semi-darkness, I yelled, 'All right, men! Stop the firing!' To my complete surprise, it stopped immediately."

At the next unit, however, someone challenged Bussey. He answered, "This is Lieutenant Bussey of the 302d Fighter Squadron, Temporary Provost Marshal. I'm telling you that it is time, right now, to stop this firing. You have made your point. I'm proud of you but let's knock it off now."

The soldiers complied but Bussey remained in considerable jeopardy. His "Skipper" reminded him that Davis would expect to talk with him in the morning about his role and that Davis would probably be under considerable heat from the base commander. Bussey could only hope that Davis would recall his experiences with bigotry at West Point and during other moments of his career. Furthermore, a court-martial would complicate shipment of the group the following day. He confided the dilemma to his brother who excoriated Bussey's conduct but also prepared publicity releases for the leading black newspapers.

When Bussey reported to Davis, the senior man thoroughly reamed him. "He rebuked me for ages. He declared that I was not fit to be an Army officer and I almost believed him. I was thoroughly intimidated. He concluded, 'As long as you and I are in the same Army, you will never be promoted. I am going to run you through my Underwood typewriter. Your scars will never heal. You will not recover.'" Although Bussey's style would always contrast markedly with that of the aloof, well-controlled Davis, the junior man recognized him as "one of the most outstanding men of his time."

In late January 1944, the 332d, with the chastened but unbowed Bussey along, reached Italy where Davis was gratified to learn that the 99th had just scored impressive victories while supporting the invasion at Anzio, south of Rome. Although still at a disadvantage with P-40s versus the swifter, higher-flying, more maneuverable enemy fighters, the Americans tangled with marauders out to harass the beachhead at Anzio. They shot down eight on 27

January and added four more kills the following day. During the first tense days of the Anzio campaign, the 99th racked up a total of seventeen victories, outdoing the records for three white squadrons.

"The glamour of a quick succession of aerial victories immediately produced a wave of recognition for the 99th and other black airmen in the theater," says Davis. "No number of bombs expertly placed on ground targets or in support of ground troops could have produced comparable acclaim."

His elation evaporated on news of the 332d's relegation to coastal patrol. "The assignment," says Davis, "was a direct result of the initial Mediterranean theater assessment and the evaluation of the 99th Fighter Squadron's performance during its first three months in the theater, since the G-3 reassessment was not completed until March. To assign the group to a noncombat role at a critical juncture in the war seemed a betrayal of everything we had been working for, and an intentional insult to me and my men." In the Davis tradition, however, he kept his feelings to himself, determined to show a commitment to whatever job his outfit undertook.

The 99th continued to function separately, as a cog in the Twelfth Air Force, dueling with German fighters and exploiting the strength of the P-40 as a ground-support weapon through dive-bombing attacks and low-level strafing. Meanwhile, for three months, the 332d, housed at Montecorvino Airfield with its own mess and clubs, performed routine patrols during which the pilots encountered only three enemy aircraft.

Ira Eaker, the commander of the Mediterranean Allied Air Force ended the 332d's season in limbo with a mission to escort heavy bombers of the Fifteenth Air Force. To carry out the task, the pilots were reequipped with the faster, high altitude, longer range P-47. The group moved to Ramitelli Air Force Base beside the Adriatic Sea and the prodigal sons, the 99th, returned to the family. Amid a flurry of promotions, including Davis breveted to colonel, Capt. Robert Tresville Jr., the graduate of the United States Military Academy, stepped up to command the 100th. But only three weeks after the 332d went operational with its P-47s, Tresville, along with two pilots, crashed into the sea during a raid on Genoa. Charles Bussey charges that the restrictions at swimming pools while the Tuskegee airmen trained in the United States prevented many from learning to swim and as a result they drowned when downed at sea.

Losses like that, and rotation home of those who flew the prescribed hours of a tour, demanded replacements, and the Tuskegee program continued to produce new entries for the cockpits of the 332d. In addition, the air corps had created the 477th Bomber Group, which was to be a multiengine equivalent for the fighter planes. The graduates of Tuskegee followed the routine of moving on to Selfridge Field, Michigan, for advanced instruction, some of which came from veterans of combat with the 99th. The conditions found by Davis at Selfridge during his sojourn there, most notably the base housing and officers' club barriers to nonwhites, continued to inflame the tempers of the pilots.

The issue boiled over when a trio attempted to enter the main officers' club on New Year's Eve but were ordered to leave by superiors on the scene. On the flight line that morning, the white training commander warned against any effort counter to "Army policy." Nevertheless, the threesome tried the club again, asserting that regulations obligated them to support the club and therefore guaranteed them admission. The training CO with the approval of the base commander issued orders directing them to depart.

News of the incident reached Washington, D.C., and in the wake of the Detroit riots from the previous summer, B. O. Davis Sr. came to investigate. After hearing from all of the interested parties, Davis brought his information to the War Department. About a week later, the training commander and the base commander were relieved. The apparent victory over the forces of discrimination turned into a sour defeat. First Air Force Commander General Frank O'Donnell Hunter had assembled the men from Tuskegee and declared, "This is *my* airfield. As long as I am commander of First Air Force there will be no racial mixing at any post under my command. There is *no* racial problem at this base and there will *be* none. You are not ready—colored officers are not qualified to lead anyone. The policy of the Army is the same as the rest of the country, and that policy will be enforced to the letter."

Hunter followed up his ukase by restricting them all to the base. Two days later, under cover of night, the disgruntled fighter pilots entrained to an isolated airbase at Walterboro, South Carolina. Upon debarking, the astonished fliers faced a line of fully armed white soldiers, posted to the railroad siding because, according to one white soldier, "We had been told some bad niggers were coming in." Apparently, white officers in an absurd leap of imagination feared an outbreak of violence. The pilots calmly went about their business while the soldiers disappeared.

The discomfited fliers contested segregation at Walterboro, raising a ruckus at the theater. The camp authorities remained adamant. While payment of dues to an officers' club brought entitlement to enter, other facilities such as the theater and PX could and did maintain segregation. To cover themselves on the officers' club the white leaders arranged to build a separate one for blacks.

Spann Watson's confrontation went beyond the military authorities. Serving as an instructor at Walterboro he sought to have a flat tire on his car fixed at a local automobile dealer's shop. A dispute arose about the work and then one of the mechanics punched Watson. "The President himself isn't going to hit me in the mouth, so I floored him. He got up and I floored him again— I beat the hell out of him." Other employees came to their battered comrade's aid and Watson recruited some nearby MPs to support him.

"I said, 'This is not going to be a case where a black man in handcuffs is shot dead because he was supposedly trying to escape. You leave your holsters open; when the time comes, I'll get 'em, you won't have to.'"

The disturbance brought out the city and state police along with a mob of outraged citizens. More MPs arrived including a white officer. Watson says, "He was a redneck with a long-barreled pistol sticking out of his holster. He asked the whites what happened. They told him the nigger had beaten up the town mayor for no reason. When I gave him my side of the story, he said, 'That ain't what they're saying.'

"I said, 'You're just like them. I don't want to talk to you at all.' The deputy base commander, Colonel Lockwood showed up. He told the MP lieutenant, 'I'm in command now.' He said he'd see if he could straighten things out. While I waited he tried to talk to the mob. He came back and said, 'We can't deal with these people. I'm giving you an escort with the MPs back to the base. Get your car and go there and don't leave until I see you.' Later he said to me that I would have to ship out. He gave me a choice of returning overseas to fly with the 332d or accept a transfer to the 477th. So I became a bomber pilot."

In Europe, the 332d's first two bomber-escort excursions passed with little interference from the enemy. But on the third mission, a raid into the intensively defended area around Munich, the Luftwaffe came out to fight. Davis, who led his forces, said, "As we approached Munich, I dispatched Capt. Red Jackson's 302d Squadron to meet a threat developing at the high right rear side. Simultaneously, two ME-109s flew through the squadron I was leading. We took our best possible defensive maneuver, turning into them. In the turn, I fired a wide deflection shot at the closest enemy fighter without visible results. Captain Jackson gave this report in his debriefing. 'An ME-109 came in on my tail . . . out of the clouds behind me; a dogfight ensued until I shot the ME-109 down. Metal flew off his left side as the door flew off. The Nazi pilot bailed out over a German airfield. I hit the deck and came home. Flak was everywhere.' Including Captain Jackson's kill, we destroyed a total of five enemy fighters."

Upon landing at Ramitelli, the 332d heard from one of the bomber commanders. "Your formation flying and escort work is the best we have ever seen." Davis received the Distinguished Flying Cross for his role. Still, performance did not dent the color line. At the Ramitelli Air Force Base, the white Italian civilians employed to perform maintenance used separate toilets from the black Americans.

The fighter group continued to shield flights of bombers throughout June, and then traded in their P-47s for what was considered the most effective escort, the P-51 Mustang with its extraordinary range and maneuverability. The four squadrons chose to place distinctive markings on their seventy-two Mustangs, bright red tail sections, a red propeller nose cone with different colors on the engine cowling, rudder, and aileron trim tabs to distinguish the squadrons.

Because airmen share a special sense of flight, the barriers between black and white pilots loosened slightly during the 332d's time in Italy. Bomber crews who owed their survival to the efforts of the Red Tails regarded them with more respect. John Suggs says, "I never wanted to be part of a segregated society and when I went down to Rome, over eight or ten bottles of champagne, I made friends with British and other foreign nationals. By meeting with these other officers I got a semblance of what was going on. I felt it was important to get a sense of what was happening beyond the intelligence briefings. I even used the British type gloves and Mae West. They were more comfortable than what we were issued."

Roscoe Brown, as a replacement pilot in June 1944 who trained on P-47s at Walterboro, and was then segregated with other pilots aboard a ship, had two days to learn the P-51 after his arrival at Ramatelli. "Maybe 20 percent of the time we did ground support or attack airplanes on the ground. Otherwise we flew mainly close escort, within 500 to 1,000 feet above the bombers. We also covered P-38s on photo reconnaissance. Over Berlin I was in command of a flight and I flew as Tail End Charlie while trying out a new flight leader. The other fighter groups arrived late so we had to continue escort of the bombers while they were dropping their bombs. I noticed at nine o'clock, two jets. I said, I'm taking over, drop back.

"I dove down to straight below the level of the bombers while the enemy planes came in from the left. I made a wide turn to let my guys get behind me and make closure. After a reverse turn to the left, then hard right, I put the circle of my new gunsight around the wings of the target. The old ones you had to figure leading the target but these did the job for you. I fired. The canopy of the jet flew off and after the pilot ejected, the plane blew up. The other guys with me followed jets down and scored some hits. One of the jets went into the ground.

"I was now all by myself when I saw another P-51; I recognized it by the square wings. But then I saw that it had German crosses on its wings. It was a plane they had somehow captured and infiltrated into our formation. I went after him but as I was gaining on him I started to run out of fuel. When I landed my engine literally cut off."

Brown was the first man in the Fifteenth Air Force to shoot down an enemy jet. In celebration he took up his refueled aircraft and indulged himself with some hairy acrobatics over his base, zooming down to tent-level height, roaring up and down the company street including at least one upside-down pass, racing beneath the telephone wires that linked headquarters with other units. Another 332d pilot, Bob Williams, told author John Holway, "Brown was flamboyant, he really took chances. When we'd come in off a mission, everyone tried to make the tightest turns and real steep approaches and buzz the field—it was show-off time. Brown would always get down lower than anybody else, just barely touching the ground. One day he didn't quite make it.

"He flipped the plane over and ended up with 100-octane gasoline pouring out all over him. Richard Caesar, our engineering officer in the 100th, dug him out from under the plane. He had to dig in the ground from below so Brown could get out of the hole he'd dug." Moments after Brown escaped the plane exploded.

The hot-shot routine cost Brown. "Davis had put me in for promotion to captain but he withdrew it because of this stunt. But after a month he resubmitted the recommendation."

Although the commendation after the Munich raid and the first knockdown of a jet delighted Davis, the public face of many who dealt with his organization hid their true attitudes. Brigadier General Dean Strother, head of the 15th Fighter Command, complimented the group on several occasions and Davis felt encouraged. Years later, however, Strother was revealed as a resolute opponent of integration in the air force. Harry Sheppard recalled, "He didn't like us and had nothing good to say about us."

General Edward P. Curtis, who had politely sneered at the quality of the African American contingent, claims he sought to improve life for the black fliers. "After the Sicilian operation was over and we moved into Italy," remembered Curtis, "they started setting up rest areas for all the various components, the British and the Americans, the navy, the air force, the army. We [the air force] got ranked out of everything, and the only thing left was the Isle of Capri. Nobody wanted it because it was a horrible logistical problem. The Germans were still bombing the Naples harbor. The fellow who was running [the Capri rest area] from Naples was a Southern gentleman from Memphis, Tennessee. The first thing I hear is there is an uproar when some of the pilots in the 99th arrived to go to Capri and he wouldn't let them go out. He was sort of prejudiced about the whites and blacks as you can understand. This had all the elements of a frightful thing." Curtis asserted he informed the man that he must make accommodations for those from the 99th. The solution, according to a veteran of the outfit, banned the blacks from the hotel at the R & R camp on Capri but provided them rooms across the park in the vacation home of former King Victor Emmanuel. When the hotel held a dance, white officers barred the door because the guests included white nurses.

While the fighter pilots were proving themselves in European skies, the 477th headed to Godman Field, Kentucky. What proved particularly odious to bomber trainees like Chappie James was the installation of an old nemesis of African Americans, Col. Robert Selway, as the group commander. "We continued to press. They really thought they had it made down at Godman because we were on one side of the tracks and Fort Knox, Kentucky was on the other. They felt that in housing all the so-called trainee officers at God-man Field, we would not go to Fort Knox at night. In the evening the white or supervisory officers would go to Fort Knox because that's where their BOQs were. Our BOQs were former enlisted men's quarters at Godman Field and a little hut of a club. So it started all over again. We said, 'We are going to go to Fort Knox. If they can, so can we.'

"The Army commander at Fort Knox got upset and told Col. Selway he better keep his black air corps troops away from over there because 'his boys' (the black army officers) knew better than to come in the club and with our antics we were going to ruin the good manners of 'his boys.'"

While the African American airmen had battled abroad and at home, the first major ground outfit to move into the Pacific combat zones was the 24th Infantry, hastily detached from the 93d Infantry Division and dispatched to defenses in the New Hebrides during 1942. As the threat of a Japanese invasion faded the African Americans lost their status as combat soldiers. After training as an infantryman at Fort McClellan with the 92d Division, draftee Leon Hiers, a native of York, Pennsylvania, headed for the 24th on Guadalcanal as a replacement. Instead of performing the function for which he trained, Hiers says, "they wasted all that money." He and his fellows hoisted cargo onto ships bound for frontline positions, and unloaded supplies from the States. "Morale was kind of sluggish; when a man is put in a menial job it takes a lot out of him." Two racial incidents stuck with Hier. On the boat between Hawaii and New Caledonia, the heat drove everyone to sleep on deck. White marines tried to prevent blacks from bedding down outside, causing a miniriot. The ship's captain grabbed a machine gun and ordered the marines below deck. On Bougainville he remembered a USO club dedication at which the local women were expected to mingle with blacks and whites. When one girl started to dance with an African American GI, a white MP yanked out his .45-caliber pistol and growled, "No nigger is going to dance with a white girl." A white sailor tackled the MP and he was beaten up.

John McClary, drafted in 1940, served with the 24th throughout the war. In the Pacific, he also recalls the 24th's infantrymen were parceled out to different units, including the marines and air corps to work as stevedores and truckers. Unlike Hier, however, he reports morale as "very high" with the men determined to make the best of their situation. He heard that whites, who resented the presence of the African Americans, believed they would turn and run if caught in a tough situation. But on Guadalcanal while members of the 24th labored on behalf of the 1st Marine Division, the black GIs captured a batch of Japanese soldiers. According to McClary, MacArthur sent a letter of commendation.

The reconstituted 93d Infantry Division sailed to the South Pacific early in the winter of 1944. Just as its predecessor in France during World War I, the 93d, however, never functioned as a single organization. Instead the 25th Infantry landed at Guadalcanal in the southern Solomon Islands, the 369th Infantry took up station at New Georgia in the central Solomons, while the 368th Infantry garrisoned at Banika in the Russells.

All of the black infantry units might well have passed the entire war in the Pacific performing security details or acting as a labor pool had it not been for pressure from civil rights leaders to give them an opportunity to demonstrate their fighting ability, with the understanding that only through the ordeal of fire could the African American press the case of equality. Along with the usual standard bearers, black and white, a new sponsor, Assistant Secretary of War John J. McCloy forced the army to use its nonwhite assets for the purposes for which they originally trained.

As head of the War Department's Committee on Negro Troop Policy, McCloy signed a 2 March 1944 statement to Stimson advising, "it is the feeling of the Committee that colored units should be introduced in combat at the earliest practical moment . . . With so large a portion of our population colored, with the example before us of the effective use of colored troops (of a much lower order of intelligence) by other nations [he was referring to French and British colonials] and with the imponderables that are connected with the situation, we must . . . be more affirmative about the use of our negro troops." Any shortcomings, he added, could be corrected by more intensive training. Stimson accepted the proposal and directed implementation.

A few weeks earlier, in fact, the 1st Battalion of the 24th Infantry, supporting the Americal and 37th Infantry Divisions and other Allied units with its usual supply details, quit that work upon orders to assist in the battles with 25,000 Japanese intent on ousting the Americans from Bougainville Island. Attached to the 148th Infantry Regiment, on 11 March, the first two black infantrymen lost their lives during a grenade attack by the enemy. Under a white lieutenant, the first combat patrol of the 24th ventured forward almost a mile beyond the American positions, engaged a party of Japanese. The Americans killed one but also lost a man.

Officially, however, the strategists controlling operations declined to employ the men in an offensive role. General Oscar Griswold, commander of the XIV Corps advised his superiors that the GIs of the 24th "did an excellent job in organizing and preparing its defensive positions." He remarked, "In general, the troops of the battalion were inclined to be a bit trigger happy, but perhaps no more so than those of any other organization which has never had its baptism of fire." He might also have pointed out that while the white soldiers had been preparing themselves for combat with training exercises, the soldiers in the 24th had been employed as dock wallopers for nearly two years since they had learned the infantryman's trade. The rustiness showed particularly during patrols that were called "decidedly inferior." Subsequently, with more experience on the job, the battalion's skill in this form of endeavor showed considerable improvement. A highlight of the campaign occured in April when men from the 24th met stiff resistance from a well-entrenched force. A company from the regiment and the all-white 754th Tank Battalion coordinated an attack that swept the enemy from the field. The joint operation by whites and blacks was a first for World War II. General Griswold now described the outfit's efforts as "highly satisfactory. Although this battalion has in the past been employed largely on labor duties to the detriment of its training, its work in combat here has progressively and noticeably improved."

The 25th Regimental Combat Team also arrived on Bougainville, attached to the Americal Division. The surrogate parent introduced the novices to combat gradually, sending the African Americans forward under the leadership of the seasoned units of the division. Except for white officers, however, the troops were divided by race. The 593d Field Artillery, composed of blacks, having demonstrated an ability to lay down accurate fire and prepare strong positions, basked in a friendly greeting from the Americal artillery commander.

The 25th's reputation nose dived following a deadly mishap during the first week of April. Company K from the 3d Battalion, led by Capt. James J. Curran, a white officer commanding black platoon leaders, moved out on an expedition that included photographers from the Signal Corps, on hand to provide publicity for newspapers. The venture began with a handicap; the location of Company K the night before it jumped off prevented adequate premission briefing, supply, and inspection. As the GIs sifted through the dense jungle, an advance patrol suddenly opened fire, claiming they had seen enemy soldiers and killed a pair of them. Before Curran could investigate, volleys of rifle shots erupted among the soldiers. The Americans heard enemy weapons, including a machine gun, interspersed among their own fusillades. In the thickness of the undergrowth and bamboo thickets confusion gripped the separated platoons who lost track of each other's positions. Weapons lieutenant Oscar Davenport, a black, sought to give aid to the wounded and was hit twice, the second time fatally. A white intelligence noncom from the 164th Infantry tried to settle the rattled Americans. One of the Signal Corps photographers commented, "He walked calmly up and down carrying his carbine, telling the men there was nothing to worry about, that there were a few Japs and that if they held, everything would turn out OK." The same witness said he could not see anyone exercising control over the random shooting other than Captain Curran. The order to withdraw came, and lost were Lieutenant Davenport as well as nine enlisted men plus a number of weapons. The investigation by Americal brass determined that at best a dozen Japanese had been engaged and the bulk of the casualties resulted from the wild ambuscades unleashed by men from Company K.

The men of the 25th continued to work with the Americal Division and give a creditable account of themselves in a number of battles. Race relations between whites and blacks combining on operations were considered excellent. Private Isaac Sermon, wounded four times while doggedly sticking with his patrol, earned a Silver Star. However, rumors that Company K broke and ran spread beyond Bougainville. The gossip tainted the judgment of military organizations in the theater. Based on this false information whites concluded that they could not rely on a black unit. Even General Marshall believed the tale, describing the 93d Division after the war as an organization whose troops "wouldn't fight, couldn't get them out of the caves to fight."

In contrast, African Americans, removed from the action and the scene, spoke of a white company commander who deserted his men and the black officer who died had sacrificed himself in order to save the soldiers. World War II was replete with incidents where friendly fire by infantrymen, artillerymen, and airmen killed fellow soldiers. But the carping scrutiny applied to African American soldiers damned the race for such disasters while describing similar mistakes by whites as the inevitable errors that happen during wars.

In fact, critics seized on every mistake by personnel from the 93d. The area commanders had employed the black infantrymen as combat soldiers mainly because of pressure from Washington. Now, able to cite a number of unfavorable cases, it was easy for General Griswold to denigrate the nonwhite units as unschooled in jungle warfare and too slow to learn. He reported the combat efficiency below that of his white organizations, without noting that the latter were veterans of South Pacific campaigns. In Washington, D.C., John McCloy, who during the course of the war appears to have shifted to a more friendly stance toward African American servicemen, made a last ditch appeal to preserve the 93d's frontline possibilities. After hearing the negative reports forwarded on the 24th and 25th Infantry Regiments, he noted to his boss, Secretary Stimson, "Although they show some important limitations, on the whole I feel that the report is not so bad as to discourage us.

"The general tone of these reports reminds me of the first reports we got of the 99th Squadron. You remember that they were not very good, but that Squadron has now taken its place in the line and performed very well. It will take more time and effort to make good combat units out of them, but in the end I think they can be brought over to the asset side."

Stimson tersely responded, "Noted—but I do not believe they can be turned into really effective combat troops without all officers being white."

Aside from prejudice, the African American infantrymen bucked a need for more service troops, people to handle supplies, construct roads, and handle security. With their combat efficiency questioned, it was convenient to remove the regiments of the 93d from the battlefields and devote them to behind-the-lines duties. Occasionally, they were used for mop up details, but in the Pacific, the shooting war for the 93d basically ended by the summer of 1944.

While they rarely faced harm from the enemy soldiers, African Americans in the Pacific, as they would in Europe, brawled with the fellow GIs in racial disorders. A particularly nasty fight in the streets of Brisbane, Australia, led to a request that no more blacks be assigned to the country and those already on hand be posted to certain sparsely populated sections that were home to the aborigines. Hostility toward African Americans undoubtedly increased after a group of them were convicted of gang rape of two white nurses and the murder of a pair of officers. The court-martial condemned six men to death. Subsequent research indicates the board ignored evidence that might have exonerated some of those executed.

Segregationists in and out of uniform saw North Africa as one battleground where blacks might be deployed with the least interaction with whites. But when the 2d Cavalry Division with its major components, the old-line African American 9th and 10th Cavalry Regiments, sailed into the Mediterranean in the spring of 1944, the North African campaign was already over. Ostensibly committed to fight in Italy, once off their ships, the cavalry troopers stowed their weapons and spent the remainder of the war in the noncombatant roles of service and supply.

When the United States prepared to send its first troops to England in early 1942, the Britons debated the presence of a large number of blacks to be stationed on their islands. At that time, the total black population in the British Isles amounted to between 10,000 and 15,000. Most Brits had never been in contact with nonwhites and their image of African Americans was totally derived from Hollywood movies in which the actors played dim-witted servants or superstitious, lazy laborers. During World War I only a few African Americans in uniform had been in residence.

The NAACP complained in 1941 that the British refused to accept non-white applicants for the Royal Air Force and black American physicians who offered help. There was also a charge that blacks could not donate blood. His Majesty's government protested that it would not discriminate against blood donors because of race, agreed to drop the "whites only," at least for ferry pilot volunteers, but hemmed and hawed about recruiting black doctors, noting that patients might not accept them.

In World War II, however, problems had arisen even before Pearl Harbor through the Lend-Lease program that opened up bases for the United

States in the colonies of Trinidad and Jamaica. The *New Statesman* reported, "Quite a large proportion of the soldiers and airmen came from the Southern States. Their immediate reaction to Jamaica was to attempt to put into practice the social behavior of Georgia . . . American soldiers would go into a bar demanding to be served before 'all these niggers.' On refusal they would try to wreck the bar. In response, Jamaican youths organized themselves into bands and whenever Americans attempted to create incidents they were frustrated by sheer weight of numbers."

Eisenhower while still serving in Washington under the chief of staff had noted the resistance to assignment of "colored units to Trinidad." The source of opposition lay not in the matter of skin color, however, but in fear that the black soldiers would upset the low pay scales doled out to indigenous labor.

Once the United States entered the war, however, and England became the staging area for millions of Americans with their gear, the question of whether blacks would comprise part of the forces created a small but intense discussion among the hosts. Parliamentary committees grappled over the position appropriate for the government under Prime Minister Winston Churchill. Some of those opposed to blacks in Britain raised the specter of problems that might develop in the United States if the troops experienced the equality offered in Britain. They fretted that American whites might be offended and the relationship with the United States deteriorate. They worried that equitable treatment of their nonwhite visitors might cause them to return home in a militant spirit bound to create trouble. There was talk that British troop morale might be affected by associations of black Americans with local females. Conservative MP Maurice Petherick warned of half-caste babies. Secretary for War P. J. Grigg proposed that his nation follow the policy of the U.S. Army and educate the women in the British military to avoid socializing.

General Arthur Dowler, a professional soldier in the Southern Command, liaised with the Americans and he adopted the predominant white American attitude. In what was described as "non official policy" he issued notes to area commanders and some civilian channels that began with denigration of blacks: "They have not the white man's ability to think and act to a plan. Their spiritual outlook is well known and their songs give the clue to their nature . . . Too much freedom, too wide associations with white men tend to make them lose their heads and have on occasions led to civil strife . . . White women should not associate with colored men . . . they should not walk out, dance or drink with them. Do not think such action hard or unsociable. They do not expect your companionship and such relations would in the end only result in strife [with white American soldiers]."

Pronouncements of this nature induced some serious misunderstanding among American authorities. A general in the U.S. intelligence division proclaimed, "There are no basic factors tending to prevent sending negro troops to the British Isles. A very strict color line is maintained everywhere. The people have been accustomed to the presence of their own native troops, among them negroes. The American negro troops stationed in England during the World War [I] created no unsolvable problems and they were generally very well treated." What the general did not understand was that in World War II, the trouble would come not from the indigenous people but from the Americans themselves.

Dowler tried to keep his memorandum confidential but its content leaked and generated considerable negative comment. One member of Parliament asked Churchill if he were aware of discrimination against black troops by Americans in Britain and requested "friendly representations to the American military authorities asking them to instruct their men that the colour bar is not a custom of this country and its non-observance by British troops or civilians should be regarded with equanimity."

Churchill gracefully evaded the issue but his secretary for foreign affairs, Anthony Eden, proposed a ban or at least a limitation on the number of nonwhites imported from the States. The American strategists could not accommodate him. The build-up before the coming invasions of North Africa and then France demanded a great many service and engineer forces, the organizations to which the bulk of African Americans were shunted.

Within the home establishment, viewpoints differed. Eden's private secretary, Oliver Harvey, argued, "It is rather a scandal that Americans should thus export their internal problem. We don't want to see lynching begin in England. I can't bear the typical Southern attitude towards the negroes. It is a great ulcer on the American civilization and makes nonsense of half their claims."

Lurking behind most of the discussion and only occasionally showing itself was the flash point where race met sex. The separation questions in England almost always centered upon situations that presented an opportunity for black men to socialize with white women. American authorities considered dispatching large numbers of black women from the Women's Army Corps [WAC] but hesitated because of the implication that these females would be assigned to England to satisfy the sexual appetites of African American GIs rather than for their contribution to the war effort. Those black women who did reach Great Britain, such as the 700 WACs in a postal battalion at Birmingham, encountered the same two strains that affected the men. Welcomed by the British people, they were barred from the only local swimming pool by the American army.

Until a guiding policy came down from on high, confusion abounded. Individual British military commanders and local civilian authorities, acting in accord with the attitudes expressed by Dowler and Grigg or on their own, barred African Americans from dances or entry to the town reading room. Elsewhere, free association occurred and British Tommies displayed no reaction. As more and more blacks arrived, the host country sought a position that would not anger its ally while at the same time satisfy its home constituency and its colonies from whom support for the war effort was needed.

The American commander Dwight Eisenhower accepted a Home Office circular in September 1942, which stated there would be no discrimination by Britons in public places—restaurants, pubs, and dances. If the U.S. military wished to place restrictions on these, British police would not enforce them. A cabinet conference distributed a statement to those with the rank of colonel or above for guidance of troops under their command. It noted that British troops should be aware that American blacks were not accustomed to close and intimate relationships with whites. ". . . for a white woman to go about in the company of a Negro American is likely to lead to controversy and ill feeling."

Eleanor Roosevelt offered the War Department some undoubtedly unwelcome advice. She wrote Stimson, "I've heard that the young Southerners were very indignant to find that the Negro soldiers were not looked upon with terror by the girls in England, Ireland and Scotland." She suggested that Stimson organize, "a little education among our Southern white men and officers. Normal relationships with groups of people who do not have the same feeling they have about the Negro cannot be prevented and that it is important for them to recognize that in different parts of the world certain situations differ and have to be treated differently."

As the man in charge of the Americans in Europe, Dwight Eisenhower, a native of Abilene, Kansas, was hardly an integrationist, as his tepid response to the civil rights movement during his presidency later demonstrated. In conversation he occasionally used "nigger." According to author Graham Smith in *When Jim Crow Met John Bull*, he privately confided to actress Merle Oberon his unhappiness at the sight of black soldiers with white English women. However, he agreed with Mrs. Roosevelt that the British people differed in their attitudes on race. He issued an order, distributed to every American officer in Great Britain, which emphasized this point. Although segregation prevailed at all U.S. military institutions in Britain, he publicly declared that no official restrictions should be placed on voluntary associations. His staff may have been less generous. Commander Harry Butcher, Eisenhower's naval aide and confidant, fumed over the attitude of the British. "England is devoid of racial consciousness . . . [the English] know nothing at all about the conventions and habits of polite society that have developed in the U.S. in order to preserve a segregation in social activity without making the matter one of official or public notice."

But Eisenhower was not willing to leave the matter to ad hoc actions. He apparently believed in the meanings of both "separate" and "equal" and accepted as inevitable, enmity between GIs of different color skin. As a consequence, Eisenhower advised his subordinates, "A more difficult problem will exist in the vicinity of camps where both White and Negro soldiers are stationed, particularly with references to dances and other social activities . . . Local Commanding Officers will be expected to use their own best judgement in avoiding discrimination due to race, but at the same time minimizing causes of friction between White and Colored troops. Rotation of pass privileges and similar methods suggest themselves for use; always with the guiding principle that any restriction imposed by Commanding Officers applies with equal force to both races."

A patch quilt of off-limits places and restrictions for issuance of passes helped keep black and white American servicemen away from each other. Whole towns were set aside on a basis of race. The village of Eye hosted nonwhites, and Horham absorbed Caucasians. Blacks went to Northwich on pass while whites visited Chester fifteen miles away. Within some towns, certain pubs and restaurants catered to clientele from one race, while different establishments accommodated patrons of the other. Service clubs and Red Cross hostelries likewise drew color lines.

The arrangements did not sit well with some people back home. Truman Gibson forwarded to John McCloy a document from the provost marshal's office in England. It listed public houses "exclusively reserved for colored troops" and gave the address for a dance hall and Red Cross club that admitted only African Americans. Gibson noted the arrest by military policemen of enlisted blacks in the town of Stowmarket, which was supposed to be out of bounds for them and the attempted arrest of an officer there because the local provost marshal said, [Stowmarket], "is laid aside for whites." Gibson advised McCloy that regulations did not sanction any town as off limits to an officer. "It would . . . appear superficially at least that the Army has taken to England practices that exist widely in this country and that are regarded by many persons as constituting *the* solution for the racial problem. Segregation is not a solution to anything and certainly would not constitute one in the Army. We do not have a black army and a white army but rather an Army in which racial contacts are unavoidable in the very nature of duty assignments. Any system that attempts to keep men rigidly apart increases distrust and suspicion. Even more serious is that by recognizing and acceding to prejudice, the Army might be thought by some to approve them." (Perish the thought!)

For all of the precautions, it was impossible to prevent confrontations between the two groups of GIs. At a Red Cross dance in Oxford, some blacks showed up when it was a night set aside for whites who then started a fight over the usurpation of their prerogatives. In a follow-up, African Americans attacked several white soldiers in a nearby town. The authorities put Oxford out of bounds for blacks who then regarded Chipping Norton as exclusively theirs. When whites appeared in this village, they were assaulted. A nasty battle broke out in Lancashire at Bamber Bridge after a scuffle with white MPs over the closing hours at a pub. During the disturbance, gunfire killed one black soldier and wounded two others, and a white officer suffered injury. Courts-martial sentenced twenty African Americans to sentences of from three months to fifteen years. At Launceston, another dispute with military police ended with more wounded and fourteen black soldiers faced charges of mutiny and attempted murder. The convicted drew long prison terms. Near Leicester, members of the 82d Airborne Division challenged some black soldiers dating white women. Invectives led to the use of weapons and killed one of the paratrooper MPs.

Shortly after the 82d Airborne bedded down in the United Kingdom, a black soldier knifed but did not kill one of the paratroopers. The airborne soldiers plotted revenge but the outfit's deputy commander, Gen. James M. Gavin, who maintained close rapport with the GIs got wind of the plot and supported by the 82d's CO, Matthew Ridgway, foiled it by declaring the city of Leicester off limits.

In his diary, Gavin noted, "Several near riots in town last night. English people, especially the lower classes, do not discriminate in any way. In fact they prefer the company of colored troops. The colored troops have been in this community for almost a year and they are well entrenched. Many are living with local white women. With the advent of the white troops, frays and minor unpleasant encounters have occurred in the local pubs and dance halls. American whites resent very much seeing a white woman in the company of a colored soldier. Here they almost see them in bed with them. Last night, the 505th [a regiment of the 82d] had its officer patrols armed."

It was black against black in the hamlet of Kingsclere. Men from a newly arrived quartermaster unit wandered into town without passes or proper uniform. A black MP ordered the soldiers to return to camp and supposedly backed up the demand with a cocked rifle. Irate, ten GIs returned to camp, grabbed their weapons, and walked to Kingsclere in search of revenge. In the shootout that followed, an MP, a soldier, and the wife of a pubkeeper died. A tribunal issued life sentences to the guilty.

Great Britain had ceded to the United States the power to try GIs for crimes committed against civilians. The military courts handed out severe punishment, particularly for sexual offenses, and generally black men drew harsher sentences than whites. A bizarre case, detailed in *When Jim Crow Met John Bull,* almost cost one man his life. In May 1944, a thirty-three-year-old woman who lived in Bath claimed she was awakened by Leroy Henry, a black

GI, who knocked on her bedroom window and said he was lost. She said she invited him in while she threw on a coat over her night dress, then accompanied him down the road to help him find his way. She swore Henry insisted on accompanying her back to the house but pulled a knife and raped her. Her husband, alarmed by her disappearance, supposedly searched for her and she informed him of the sexual assault.

Military police apprehended Henry but found no knife. After interrogation, however, Henry, AWOL at the time of the alleged rape, confessed to the crime. At Henry's court-martial, a physician testified to signs of recent sexual intercourse by the woman but saw no evidence of any struggle or physical force. On the witness stand, Henry retracted his confession, declaring it had been extracted under duress. He said he knew the woman from previous encounters where he twice paid her a pound for sex but when she demanded double that amount on the night in question, they argued about the fee.

In his summary, the American officer acting as prosecutor admitted, "The action of the woman in getting out of bed and walking off with a dark, strange soldier is rather odd, but in our relations with the English they do things that we don't do and many of us will be able to teach our wives lessons. English wives do everything possible to help their husbands."

The court convicted Henry and sentenced him to the gallows. The British press featured the case and a public commotion centered on the execution for a crime that in England was not a capital offense. The uproar caused Eisenhower to have the facts of the case reexamined and subsequently he reversed the sentence and restored Henry to duty.

The bloodiest incidents usually involved military police. Those responsible for law and order in the army frequently contributed to the violence. As in the States, soldiers often performed this function as temporary duty. Commanders designated them military police, issuing brassards and pistols without screening or training them. At Antrim, in Northern Ireland, a group of African Americans assigned to a quartermaster regiment ventured into town to see a movie and then stopped at a pub. As some of them hiked back to camp, two apparently drunken white soldiers taunted them. There was a brief fistfight which ceased as the participants broke off contact at sight of a pair of white military policemen. They seized three blacks, but MP corporal Lester Davis fired two shots while in "pursuit" of Pvt. William C. Jenkins. One bullet struck Jenkins in the back of the neck, killing him. News of Jenkins's death fomented a near riot among the quartermaster soldiers at their base. They armed themselves and only intervention by the camp commander, Gen. Leroy Collins, prevented a firestorm. The day after the shooting, the quartermaster troops refused to work because the task placed them in the vicinity of a white unit and they were afraid of further assaults.

A general court-martial met to consider whether Cpl. Lester Davis, the white military policeman who fired the fatal bullet, did "with malice aforethought, willfully, deliberately, feloniously, unlawfully and with premeditation, kill one Private William C. Jenkins . . . a human being, by shooting him with a pistol." The tribunal also weighed a charge that Davis did not attempt to render first aid to a "dangerously injured" Jenkins.

During the trial, Sgt. Earl G. Edie of the MPs testified that he and Davis while on duty heard the commotion of a fight. The witness said the scuffle ended as they approached with flashlights. He said he recognized the two white combatants and, believing they could be apprehended later, chased the departing four blacks. Edie reported that he and Davis shouted for the men to "halt," "freeze," and "stop," and three of them obeyed. While Edie held his pistol on the group, Davis pursued Jenkins who had been walking ahead of the others. The witness claimed that Davis hollered for Jenkins to halt. Edie said he heard the dead man answer, "Go ahead and shoot, you've got a gun." Then he heard a shot, another cry to stop, followed by a second shot some fifteen to thirty seconds later. When he turned his light on the scene he said he saw a soldier on the pavement. Edie testified he dispatched Davis to get medical aid for the fallen man.

Three companions of Jenkins also appeared before the court. They reported that after consuming a few drinks they had been standing together talking when two white soldiers, at least one of them drunk, approached and the blacks heard a remark, "Look at the old damn niggers standing there." More words passed and then the fight started. In substance they verified the account given by Edie, although none of them could recall what, if anything, Jenkins said just before he was killed. All insisted the street brawl had broken up by the time the MPs accosted them.

One of the captive soldiers testified that the MP sergeant would not permit him to attempt first aid for Jenkins. The ambulance summoned for the victim did not reach the hospital until anywhere from fifteen to thirty minutes after the shooting, far too late for medical succor. But no definitive evidence of a malicious delay was presented.

The MP, Sergeant Edie, was listed as a prosecution witness although his account supported the behavior of the accused. A member of the court inquired, "Your orders are that you were to use whatever force, if necessary, to stop a prisoner from escaping?" When Edie agreed, the questioner continued, "And resort to shooting, if necessary to do it?" Edie responded yes. The court pursued the policy further. "What are your general instructions when you shoot?"

ANSWER: Shoot to stop.
QUESTION: What do you regard as "shooting to stop?"

ANSWER: That could be injury in the leg or it might be "shoot to kill."
QUESTION: What are your instructions on that?
ANSWER: They have never been defined other than to shoot to stop.

The sole defense witness was Davis himself. He repeated that Jenkins continued to walk away after saying "Shoot! You have the gun." According to Davis, after the warning shot, "He continued to go on in a fast cadence. I wouldn't say he was in a run and I couldn't say he was in a walk. He was in a real fast cadence—the next thing to running."

Queried on his instructions as to the amount of force to be used to arrest or stop an escaping prisoner [technically, Jenkins was not yet a prisoner], Davis testified, "My orders were to use anything, any means. To stop them, that was necessary."

The prosecutor inquired, "Whatever force was necessary or reasonable, is that right?"

When Davis assented, the officer continued, "And on that occasion, having directed this soldier to stop several times as he went down the street and having fired the first shot or warning shot, he still refused to stop? Then you considered it necessary to fire at him, is that right?"

With such a cross examination, the defense rested. The tribunal acquitted Davis of all charges. Putting the best face on the evidence presented, the murder of an unarmed soldier, who had offered no threat, by shooting him in the back of the neck for walking away from charges of the misdemeanor of a street brawl, revealed the low level of professionalism in the military police. Given the racism of the times, the authority for an indiscriminate use of deadly force was a prescription for such abuses.

When Benjamin O. Davis Sr. looked into the matter, he drew some troubling information from one of the black GIs on the scene, Sgt. Robert Horton. He had been the soldier who tried to aid Jenkins after the shooting only to be rebuffed, he said, with the comment, "There's one nigger you don't have to worry about." Horton added that racial trouble was common. After white soldiers came to the area, the African Americans resented being barred from some dances, at gunpoint in at least one case. He remarked that the local people treated blacks better than he was accustomed to in the States.

Concerned about the welfare of African American soldiers in Great Britain, Walter White of the NAACP, in the company of white U.S. officials, toured the country and discussed the sources of discontent with both the troops and their leaders. White proposed an end to setting aside separate establishments for the two races and the odd-even pass days. He called for a board of review with at least one black lawyer to oversee court-martial decisions on the grounds of probable discrimination against nonwhites. He asked for an end to segregated Red Cross clubs and more black performers to entertain the troops. Two assistant inspector generals reviewed White's findings, which were supported by Capt. Max Gilstrap, a former editor of the *Christian Science Monitor.* The IG officers dismissed most of White's representations out of hand. They refused to concede that white attitudes affected the black troops.

Ashley Bryan, the New York City man drafted out of Cooper Union where he studied art, became a winch operator for a port battalion in Scotland. "We handled everything coming in for the invasion of Europe—trucks, tanks, cars, ammunition. I knew nothing about operating a winch but learned as I worked and that gave me a rating of a tech sergeant. I could have gone to OCS but didn't want to. I thought I could concentrate on drawing if I remained an enlisted man. The British people received us well, even though some white soldiers tried to tell them we had tails." Bryan's difficulties came from fellow Americans. A white officer annoyed with Bryan's habitual use of a pencil and paper when not on duty told him to cease. "Don't I have a right to draw?" inquired Bryan.

"You have no rights. Stop drawing or I'll put you in the guardhouse."

Bryan appealed to the battalion commander. "Colonel Pierce was a decent man. He gave me permission to attend the Glascow School of Art." The white officers seemed bemused that a black was preoccupied with art. Bryan further raised eyebrows of white Americans when he attended an opera.

For some African American units, at least in the eyes of their white superiors, the sojourn in England passed without major trouble. Jim Pedowitz with a trucking outfit recalls, "There is a natural tendency to head for places where you are more welcome. Morristown was one of the favorite spots. There were lots of English girls who had no problems socializing with our men. We didn't have any racial problems in England. Perhaps it was because we were sort of isolated in a relatively small area. It was also my experience that black soldiers who came from totally segregated areas of the South, such as were in our company, were less inclined to rebel."

Naturally, incidents of strife made news, captured headlines, or triggered investigations and other forceful action. Despite all the Sturm und Drang, the two million GIs in the British Isles trained and labored on behalf of the job at hand, much of the time without racial issues becoming a factor. The day that absorbed so much of this planning and effort, 6 June 1944, placed upon the European mainland some 85,000 U.S. combat troops from all-white infantry, airborne, and ranger units. However, African American engineers, truckers, medics, and antiaircraft crews with their earthmovers, trucks, ambulances, weapons, and other gear arrived on the Normandy beaches within hours of the first waves. They dug in alongside infantrymen from the 1st and 29th Divisions during the first fright-filled hours of the invasion as enemy shells and small-arms fire blasted and peppered Omaha Beach.

Lieutenant Bob Edlin of the 2d Ranger Battalion, felled by a sniper's bullet through his right leg and then a burst of machine-gun fire through his left leg, lay exposed on Omaha Beach alongside a wounded sergeant half comatose from morphine given by a passing medic. "Because of the heavy artillery fire, people were taking cover under the seawall. They wouldn't come and help us. Finally, two black soldiers, part of an engineer battalion, came out under heavy fire and dragged us to cover. They would have made good Rangers." Edlin would remember who aided him after the war.

As the German counterfire slackened slightly, the black ammunition handlers and engineers scrambled to their tasks. They piled up stacks of ammunition with the hope an enemy hit did not explode the beachfront dump and them in one earthshaking blast; they carved openings with dozers while defensive rounds whizzed around them. First Sergeant Norman Day of the 582d Engineer Dump Truck Company won a Silver Star for directing traffic on the beach in the midst of heavy shelling.

Corporal Waverly Woodson of Philadelphia, with the 320th Barrage Balloon Battalion, earned his Purple Heart while still riding an LST through the choppy sea, already littered with bodies and shattered landing craft. When a mine exploded, shrapnel wounded Woodson. With mortar and machine guns damaging the LST further, the skipper beached it. An associate treated Woodson's wound who then continued to render aid to other casualties. The following day, on an errand to the shoreline, Woodson met a party of incoming soldiers attempting to rescue others from the water and he administered artificial respiration. After further examination of Woodson's wound, a doctor directed him to hospital care.

But the primary mission of these soldiers was support for white combat units. The 333d Field Artillery Battalion, whose black crews manned 155mm howitzers put ashore on D plus 10, making it the first and for several months the only nonwhite unit in France. The campaign to get more African Americans onto the firing line brought Ben Davis Sr. back to Fort Huachuca for an inspection to determine if the 92d Division was combat-ready. Undoubtedly feeling some of the pressure for more of his race to become engaged in the shooting war, Davis found the morale there excellent and recommended the 92d be considered for overseas service.

Again, unlike almost all of the counterpart white infantry outfits, the components of the 92d headed for battle separately rather than as a whole. First to leave Huachuca was the 370th Regimental Combat Team, which included the 370th's foot soldiers, the 598th Field Artillery Battalion, and a few special attached units. Edgar Piggott, the former ASTP engineering student at

Hampton Institute who believes his unit was properly readied for combat, says, "I rode the equipment freight train with a loaded M-1 as a guard. We usually stopped at the edge of town or went through it slowly. I recall being cheered by blacks and jeered by whites." The outfit sailed from Hampton Roads, Virginia, 15 July 1944, and by the end of the month the men debarked at Naples.

Despite the advances achieved in France and the breakout at St.-Lô by tankers commanded by Gen. George S. Patton, the Nazi resistance in Italy continued stiff and depleted the Allied ranks. The Fifth Army of Gen. Mark Clark desperately needed fresh soldiers to replace veteran U.S. divisions engaged in the Mediterranean campaign for between one and two years. As part of the reinforcements, the 370th Combat Team dug into the line on the south side of the Arno River from where strategy dictated an advance to crack the German Gothic line before another dreadful Italian winter paralyzed the Allied war machine. The 370th joined Task Force 45, a mixed bag of troops, including infantrymen only recently converted from antiaircraft crews, Brazilians, and Italian *partigiani* (partisans). An orphan outfit, the 370th had been committed to a bastard organization.

The circumstances boded poorly for the African American infantrymen. Still, in the beginning it appeared the contingent enjoyed a friendly reception. Two small teams of officers and enlisted men met with the nearby 1st Armored Division and the 85th Infantry Division, both seasoned campaigners well qualified to orient the newcomers. Ulysses Lee, an historian who served with the U.S. Center of Military History after World War II, wrote that in vivid contrast to its previous history, the 370th, whose sole contact with whites had been through its own superior officers, functioned in close contact with white units, officers at company level, and enlisted men. However, Spencer Moore, the former New Jersey militia man and OCS graduate leading a platoon in the 370th contends, "I had no interaction with white troops in combat." In a middle ground, Edgar Piggott with the regimental Intelligence and Reconaissance Platoon says, "We interacted with white troops from time to time—we would rendezvous to form combat (ambush) patrols or we'd have forward observers (air/artillery) spend time with us in our OPs. Once they proceeded beyond the relative safety of our front lines to the tenuous trepidation of the OP, they became quite sociable."

As the 370th occupied positions on the line, important visitors briefly visited the scene. Winston Churchill surfaced for a few moments. Benjamin O. Davis Sr. accompanied a film crew working on *Teamwork,* a movie to convince both servicemen and civilians that blacks were important contributors to the war effort. Mark Clark inspected his newest assets. Clark supposedly asked the 370th's CO Col. Raymond G. Sherman if he had any major problems. When Sherman complained about the slowness of promotions for his officers, Clark says he snapped, "Give me an example." Sherman summoned 1st Lt. Charles F. Gandy, who commanded Company F. "Here's a good example; this man is overdue for promotion."

Clark turned to an aide, "borrowed" the captain's bars off the man's uniform, and pinned them on Gandy. The gesture impressed those on the scene and as accounts of the incident spread through the ranks sagging morale rose.

The newly promoted Capt. Charles F. Gandy led a twenty-two-man patrol across the Arno River and in the process destroyed a machine-gun position while capturing two prisoners, the first taken by African Americans in Europe. Along with the other units for the IV Corps, the 370th advanced beyond the stream for several miles as the Wehrmacht retreated to its Gothic line. Progress toward the enemy redoubts continued while elements from the rest of the 92d Division started to reach the front. By the end of September, the regimental combat team had pushed forward more than twenty miles, punching through the Gothic line. Casualties numbered eight dead and 279 wounded, injured, sick, or missing.

Brigadier John E. Wood, assistant division commander, now on hand, soon applied the intensive study given only men of color. Wood filed a spate of mixed reviews to Almond. "They are not aggressive but will go willingly anywhere their officers take them; they will stay where led." He noted a trigger-happy tendency set off at "any noise or anything which moves, to challenge and fire at about the same time." He chafed over a slackening of basic discipline, saluting, sanitation, and other activities of a similar nature. The sources of Wood's data are unknown. However, the chief of staff for the IV Corps reported to the Fifth Army the outfit's performance matched expectations for any unit without battle experience. Colonel Sherman, the 370th's commander, believed his men felt they had proven themselves and developed confidence. Although they had yet to meet resistance in force, they had cleared areas of snipers and machine guns, and learned to cope with incoming artillery.

Although Edgar Piggott recalls amicable relations with white forward observers and troops with whom his regiment joined in small operations, he realized race relations were tenuous. "There were times when we had patrolled through a town, attempting to contact the retreating enemy rear guard, that we 'liberated' the townfolk amid cheers and well wishes, only to find, the next time we entered that same town, the cheers turned to indifference and avoidance because the main body of occupying troops, if white, had given them to believe that we would rape the women and children and eat the babies."

Almond himself took command of his regimental combat team as it prepared for its most ambitious efforts, an assault up the northern Apennines'

Mount Cauala toward the town of Massa. Jumping off in a heavy downpour that created deep, thick mud, they sought to climb rocky slopes guarded by artillery while subject to sharp, well-organized counterthrusts from the foe. A pattern of early gains followed by retreats developed. Each effort added casualties. Problems of communications, command, and control bedeviled the outfit. Spencer Moore's Company B expected to move out immediately after artillery hammered the German positions. But the order to advance arrived late, enabling the enemy to regroup and respond with its own barrage. "We were making progress," says Moore," when the enemy walked mortars in on us. I was hit by shrapnel and evacuated." Contact and coordination broke down; most of the unit fell back. Other companies also clambered up Mount Cauala and among those killed was Captain Gandy who despite a fatal wound continued to rally his forces in a vain struggle to hold their positions. Men balked when told to move out. Regimental headquarters ordered the arrest of one entire platoon for such dereliction of duty but a proposed court-martial action fell by the wayside as superiors realized it would be difficult to identify miscreants from those willing to soldier on.

Lieutenant Colonel John J. Phelan, a white veteran of six months in the Italian campaign, and transferred to the 370th to replace the original executive officer killed earlier, said, "During my period of observation, I have heard of just as many acts of individual heroism among negro troops as among white. There is no reason to believe there is any greater lack of individual guts among them," he informed Almond. "On the other hand, the tendency to mass hysteria or panic is much more prevalent among colored troops."

Phelan's analysis was echoed by some black officers and noncoms. Lieutenant Robert Montjoy, who led four fruitless tries to ascend Mount Cauala said, "They will not stay in their positions unless constantly watched and give as their reason for leaving the fact that the man next to them will leave anyway so there is no good reason for them to stay." Staff Sergeant Johnny R. Walden reported, "I asked one of the C Company men why they had left the ridge. He told me a lot of exaggerated stories." When Walden tried to convince the men they would be safer if they climbed onto the ridge and dug in at night, they refused, preferring to wait until morning in the apparent safety of buildings. Colonel Sherman, responding to the queries on whether his men measured up, seemed ambivalent, telling Almond, "Results so far—many satisfactory and many unsatisfactory—are, to my mind inconclusive at the present time."

Phelan offered no explanation for the breakdowns by blacks in groups. Ulysses Lee concluded that poor educational backgrounds and low motivation alone did not account for the behavior. The military historian suggested that a lack of trust that flowed from the top command down to the lowliest of privates and from the latter right up to Ned Almond irreparably compromised the 92d Division. While the upper echelons blamed failures on character defects in the black soldiers, the enlisted men and lower ranks placed responsibility on their leaders for indecision and incompetence.

As a member of the 370th, Lt. Vernon Baker says he never encountered much overt racism from his white equals and superiors. But they seemed to ignore him, making him feel "lower than snake doo-doo." If he offered suggestions they passed without response. No one, however, called him "nigger." "When you have a weapon, people are cautious about what they say. But I knew what they were thinking."

In October 1944, Baker fired at the silhouette of a German beside a tree. The soldier answered with a bullet that pierced the black lieutenant's right forearm. It went numb and he lost a considerable amount of blood. When he awakened after surgery, he noticed he was in a segregated ward at the hospital. "We were in the same war, yet were different."

As the campaign dragged on, the state of the 370th deteriorated. The competent leaders, officers, and noncoms, the willing GIs, because they put themselves on the line, incurred wounds or were KIA. The ineffectives became a higher percentage of the personnel. Unlike the white element of the army, no provision had been made to train replacements for the unavoidable casualties in the black combat ranks. To fill the gaps in the 370th, those in charge of personnel scraped up replacement enlisted men from disciplinary barracks and other punishment tours, further damaging the quality of the outfit.

The remainder of the 92d Division debarked in Italy throughout October, and if anything these components were in worse shape than the battered 370th. To help staff a regimental combat team, some of the better men in the other units had joined the 370th shortly before it left for Europe. When the other infantry regiments and support battalions received orders to ship out to the combat zone, many white officers sought to be relieved on the basis of a policy that rotated whites serving with black soldiers. On the eve of departure for the shooting war, the division staff could hardly acquiesce in a heavy exodus of officers, no matter how much time they had accumulated at Fort Huachuca. Knowledge that their white superiors wanted to abandon them obviously demolished any faith the enlisted men might have had in these officers.

Shortly after the last of the 92d landed in Italy, an unknown assailant wounded a white lieutenant, John T. Murphy, in the leg while he slept in his tent. Murphy, assigned to the division's 317th Engineer combat battalion, served as adjutant to the unit's leader, Col. Edward Rowney. The army investigator, in his search for evidence, painted a devastating picture of conditions in the 317th. That more than likely also described others parts of the 92d. "The

EM dislike their officers; the officers dislike each other; and they all seemingly dislike their Bn Commander [Col. Edward Rowney]. Most of the EM have no confidence in their officers which, justified or not, is bad . . . The men don't feel these officers are fit to lead them into combat. One officer, a company commander, is intensely disliked by his men and some of the members of his Co. have threatened to kill him." The investigator recounted a number of events that reflected poorly on the leadership and actions of Rowney and recommended he be relieved. The advice was not only rejected but later Rowney assumed command of a task force for what Ulysses Lee described as, "one of the 92d Division's more disastrous ventures."

Poor as the regard of the men was for their immediate superiors, they disliked if not hated the top figures in the division. Almond, his deputy Wood, the engineer chief Rowney, and the artillery commander, William Colbern, had reputations for virulent racism, and derogatory statements about African Americans. Spencer Moore quotes Wood, "to get along with Niggers is to treat them like puppies, and just pat them on the head." According to Edgar Piggott, Almond was "visually challenged" and nicknamed "One-eye," "not what one would call a term of endearment. I never met anyone that held the General in high esteem. Frank Seaforth [a fellow alumnus] reminded me that One-Eye was the one that said something about 'taking the scum of the earth and turning them into superb fighters.'" Rowney had come to the 92d after an incident in which he tried to enforce segregation aboard a transport ship bearing a black engineer outfit to Liberia. In Italy, he insisted upon separate tables for whites and blacks at the staff mess. Unsuccessfully, the division chaplain and his assistant petitioned headquarters to remove Rowney as detrimental to morale and effectiveness. Some believed that Rowney actually was the target when Lieutenant Murphy, his adjutant, was shot in his tent. He became the target of further criticism when he was awarded the Combat Infantryman Badge, and the Silver and Bronze Stars for valor. Frank Hodge who went to Italy with the 368th Infantry says, "When the powers of the division decided some of the officers at Division Headquarters should get the Combat Infantry [man] Badge, the badge was only for infantry personnel. There was a paper transfer of these officers into infantry regiments for the required time. Then they were reassigned to Headquarters."

Spencer Moore who recovered from his wounds endured and survived unhappy experiences with whites. He remembers, "I called for artillery fire and the Americans in the Fire Direction Center claimed they had fired their rations for the day. A British officer fired the mission and destroyed 15 enemy. Our company commander, a white captain named Holland hid under a table and said the men were trying to kill him. The first sergeant had to call the battalion commander to get Holland relieved."

The African Americans in Italy were without friends in high places. The situation was slightly better in France. Benjamin O. Davis Sr., upon completion of his chores in Italy, had traveled to the United Kingdom to examine conditions for black soldiers there. With so many African Americans now in Europe, particularly as the Allied armies moved beyond the Normandy beachhead, Maj. Gen. John C. Lee, head of the Special Services, which contained the bulk of the African Americans in Europe, requested that Davis be assigned as special advisor based in England. Davis, impressed by Lee's efforts to see fair treatment in spite of segregation, was delighted to accept the post.

14
Forward Movement and Reversals

Although they sorely needed an infusion of reinforcements and additional support troops, the marines preferred that African Americans serve in somebody else's neighborhood. Major General Charles F. B. Price who commanded American forces in Samoa wrote an "unofficial" letter to Gen. Keller E. Rockey, director of the Division of Plans and Policies, in which Price remarked on the dangers of mixing African Americans with the natives of his turf. "While the mix of Polynesians with the white race produces a very high class half-caste and even the mixture with the Chinese . . . produces a very desirable type, the mixture with the Negro, however, as evidenced by the few types of cross breeds with individuals of the Melanesian types in the islands . . . produces a very undesirable citizen." Price claimed that Europeans, New Zealanders, and Australians voiced similar fears about blacks. He suggested they be sent to the Micronesian zone "[where] they can do no racial harm," and he believed they might even "raise the physical and intellectual standards."

Although many may have agreed with Price, such fine distinctions were overridden by the needs of those under fire. On 15 June 1944, Brooklyn-born Leroy Seals as a member of the 3d Ammunition Company landed on the Saipan beach in support of assault forces attacking the Mariana Islands. Recalled one officer in command of black leathernecks, "Mortar shells were still raining down as men unloaded ammunition, demolition material and other supplies from amphibious vehicles. They set up security to keep out snipers as they helped to load casualties aboard boats to go to hospital ships. Rifle fire from the Japanese defenders was thick as the black marines rode guard on trucks carrying high octane gasoline from the beach. A squad leader killed a Japanese sniper that had crawled into a fox hole next to his. The men at the beach stood waist deep in the pounding surf, unloading boats as vital supplies . . . were carried ashore. Even as they worked, they were exposed to several Japanese snipers shooting from concealed positions on the beach." Only a few hours after debarking, Seals was fatally wounded, the first of his race in the marines to die from enemy fire.

African American marines subsequently waded ashore on Tinian, Guam, and then on Peleliu in September 1944, where Edward Andrusko encountered the Black Angels. Following the conquest of Saipan, Gen. Alexander Vandergrift, who had replaced Holcomb as commandant of the corps declared, "The Negro Marines are no longer on trial. They are Marines, period."

The 8th Marine Ammunition Company loaded onto a ship that also carried white marines. Roped-off compartments separated units by specialty and color. The men ate at segregated messes. All the kitchen workers were black, with many assigned from the 8th Ammunition Company to work with the African Americans in the ship's crew.

As Ed Andrusko indicated, the whites were bewildered by the sight of blacks in their uniform. Some thought the corps had developed "night fighters" whose skin color would make them hard to see in the dark. In Hawaii, the African American leathernecks faced the barrier of a color line. There were areas closed to them, including streets that featured houses of prostitution. Some felt themselves tolerated only for their money.

The 8th Ammunition Company handled cargo and received additional training as infantry while stationed in Hawaii. The outfit then boarded a landing ship for a forty-day voyage to Iwo Jima. En route the black marines worked in the kitchen, disposed of garbage, and cleaned latrines while a white howitzer unit spent its time basking in the sun.

Although they had been told they would reach Iwo Jima during the cleanup operations, they arrived at a scene marked by constant small-arms gunfire, blasts from artillery, and the distinctive roar of flame throwers hurling napalm at bunkers. Marines were busy flushing out Japanese soldiers from holes and caves using grenades and pack charges.

Perry Fischer was with the 8th Ammo Company as it made its way to the Iwo Jima beachhead on D plus 2, 21 February 1945. "Landing craft carrying supplies from the ships to shore had to be literally pulled by hand through the rough surf. Many capsized before reaching the beach. Some of the men of the beach parties had to jump into the surf to pull boxes and crates from capsized boats, then wade back to shore. Strong backs were essential and so was coolness and courage in performing these tasks while fighting the elements and dodging exploding antiaircraft shells. The battle lines were everywhere. Black marines were intermingled with white marines on the beach where unit integrity was sometimes lost for several hours. The black marines may have been regarded as laborers rather than combat troops, but artillery from Japanese guns made no such distinction."

The ammunition dumps, manned by units like that of Fischer, served as tempting targets for Japanese gunners. According to Fischer, "Sgt. Tom McPhatter [a black marine] again continued to display the leadership qualities that made the operations of the dump run smoothly and efficiently." Shortages of high-explosive mortar shells brought a parachute drop of this item at the edge of an airfield not yet fully under marine control. "Lieutenant D'Angelo and Sergeant Tom McPhatter led a crew of the black ammo handlers to the airfield to chase down the parachutes and to load the ammo on trucks for return to the dump. During the hunt for the parachuted ammo, they came under sporadic rifle and mortar fire from snipers, but this did not deter the men." Although no one was hit in this episode, a number of people from the 8th Ammunition Company in other skirmishes won Purple Hearts.

After more than a month and a half, Iwo Jima was officially declared secure. The marine conquerors evacuated the island, leaving the final mop up to soldiers from the army. Black aviation engineers from the army moved in and men from the 8th Ammunition Company enjoyed the kinship of color with them. A group of Japanese soldiers suddenly emerged from a hillside cave and assaulted the engineers and some army pilots in their tents. Members of the 8th Ammunition Company along with blacks in the 5th Pioneer Battalion, some Seabees, and even army ground crewmen engaged the roughly 250 to 300 enemy.

Says Perry Fischer, "In the darkness, the fighting was confused and terrible. The chief difficulty, that of distinguishing between friend and foe, was compounded [because] many of the attackers were armed with American BARs, M-1 rifles, U.S. .45-caliber pistols, even an American bazooka. Several of the Japanese soldiers wore Marine uniforms." Some 250 dead Japanese littered the contested areas while more than fifty Americans lost their lives and more than 100 were wounded with three casualties suffered by the 8th Ammo Company. That brief encounter ended the outfit's moments in harm's way. They returned to Hawaii scheduled for their next mission, the invasion of Japan itself.

During the furious battles for places like Peleliu and Iwo, race seemed to become irrelevant but once the common threat, the Japanese, departed the scene the tensions between whites and blacks resurfaced. Ed Simmons, a white officer from New Jersey with a degree in journalism from Lehigh, participated in the marine efforts to retake Guam and then settled in there as an adjutant to the commanding officer of a field depot unit on the island.

"I don't think I ever saw a black Marine until Guam and we began fighting there. The two ammunition companies we had were much better than the depot ones. The ammunition companies had better officers and NCOs, with all the noncoms from platoon sergeant up white career marines. The blacks had separate camps, because of race and because they were responsible for the ammunition. They had good mess halls, a fine officers' club with a bartender and general factotum named Columbus Jones, a onetime Pullman porter who knew how to run things. Morale there was good. The CO for the 4th Ammunition Company, Russell 'Frenchy' La Pointe, whom

I knew from Quantico, had enlisted in the mid 1930s and was a first sergeant who had served in China before he got his commission. He had ideas on how an officer should behave, with flair.

"The depot commanders were not the best. Generally speaking they were middle-aged men, originally expected to be aviation specialists but now given administrative duties. Some were alcoholics. The lieutenants were a mixed bag, not happy to be with the depot companies and all of the noncoms were black. Most of them were not very good. The Marines had not been taking blacks long enough to have a pool of educated ones for noncoms.

"There was trouble on Guam with black men and white men fighting over brown women. The 3d Marine Division regarded themselves as the conquerors of Guam and entitled to set the ground rules. They tried to keep blacks, marines and sailors, from visiting the main town, Agana. The Navy port companies [black sailors] were in sad shape. They were not given good administrative support."

Animosity mounted during the month of December 1944. Major General Henry L. Larsen, the island commander, cognizant of the tense atmosphere, issued a statement, ". . . the present war has called together in our service the men of many origins and various races and colors . . . All are entitled to the respect to which that common service is entitled." His remarks poured no oil on the troubled waters. Whites, riding trucks, showered the black cantonment of the Naval Supply Depot with rocks and smoke grenades. In an argument over a woman, a white sailor shot and killed a black marine. White marines from the 3d Division taunted a black sentry on post at his supply depot. When one of the tormentors crossed the restricted line, a guard fired a fatal bullet. In both cases, the shooters were convicted of manslaughter but apparent evenhanded justice did not lessen the hostility. A rumor of another killing set off a posse of black sailors armed with automatic weapons in commandeered trucks. White MPs drove them off before serious carnage ensued.

"I was having a Christmas dinner with La Pointe," says Simmons "when word came that blacks were invading a white area. It became known as the third battle of Guam. We made a frantic attempt to see that all of the marines returned to their bases. Most of the bad stuff involved the Navy port companies." The scrap involved forty-three black sailors using knives and clubs. When it was over, courts-martial disciplined not only those identified as rioters but also some whites judged guilty of having provoked violence.

"Fragging," says Simmons, "was not invented in Vietnam. Blacks, more often than whites, used the fragmentation grenade as the weapon of choice, rolling it into the tent of authority, perhaps a staff noncom, not necessarily a white man." Others suggest fragging originated with white soldiers.

The black marine support units came under fire during a number of the corps' island campaigns. But the African Americans on hand primarily were present to service white combat units. There were two outfits, the 51st and 52d Defense Battalions, staffed by black enlisted men with white officers, ostensibly designed for more direct involvement in the shooting. But both were used to relieve white marines after territory had been secured. Occasionally, they encountered enemy holdouts or fought off an air attack but they played no offensive role.

Ed Simmons remarked that the marine ammunition companies seemed a cut above the other service units. The accounts of men like Perry Fischer point out the special training given to those charged with handling ordnance. Lack of such technical instruction and racial distinctions lay behind one of the terrible disasters that befell the navy during World War II, and in the aftermath what was described as a mutiny by black sailors.

To feed the guns of the Pacific fleet and arm the aircraft seeking to destroy Japanese shipping and fortification, the navy operated a gigantic supermarket of explosives at Port Chicago, a naval ammunition base located on the Sacramento River near its entrance into San Francisco Bay. Many of the officers detailed to supervise the work, like Lt. James Tobin, had neither previous training nor experience in arranging the transport of bombs, shells, napalm, or other hazardous materials before assignment to Port Chicago. Said Tobin, "It was my duty to go down to the dock with the division for the purpose of loading ships with ammunition. What I learned about ammunition came through the . . . ensuing months." Other officers at Port Chicago, aware of the lack of knowledge among the commissioned ranks talked of developing an instruction course but nothing was done before the disaster.

Like many of the enlisted men Cyril Sheppard was a draftee. According to an interview by Robert L. Allen for his book, *The Port Chicago Mutiny*, Sheppard says, "I wanted to go into the Army. I think about thirteen of us went down to the induction center at the same time . . . we were all trying to stay close so we could be together. No two went to the same place. When they got to me, they just sent me over to the Navy officer and the next thing I know I'm in the Navy. I didn't want to be in it."

Joe Small worked on his family-worked but not owned farm in New Jersey until he joined the CCC where he drove a truck. At his draft physical, the doctor asked whether Small or a friend with him wanted to go into the army. "Neither of us answered. He just grabbed a stamp and went bam! He looked at it and then said, 'All right, move out soldier.' My buddy happened to be ahead of me and so he got the Army, and I got the Navy."

Sheppard, Small, and almost all of the black enlisted men in the labor force at the Port Chicago facility never attended any classes or lectures and did not receive any manuals on the care and handling of munitions earlier while at the Great Lakes station. They too learned on the job, taking their cues from the very few who had experience or a background in the work.

Just as Ashley Bryan in the army educated himself on operation of a winch, Joe Small at Port Chicago randomly volunteered for this highly skilled and critical function without any previous acquaintance of the machinery. According to *The Port Chicago Mutiny*, the longshoreman's union warned the navy it courted catastrophe if it continued to employ untrained seamen for loading ammunition. The union barred any of its winch operators from dealing with explosives unless they had years of experience with less-dangerous cargo. The longshoremen even offered to send trained volunteers to school the sailors but the navy refused help.

The enterprise was also jeopardized by a hodgepodge of safety measures. The navy itself never produced a loading manual to guide its personnel. Instead officers relied on regulations designed for the peacetime shipment of small amounts of explosives. At that the installation neglected to promulgate basic safety procedures among officers. The Port Chicago commander, Capt. Merrill T. Kinne, did not even bother to post any stipulations in the enlisted men's barracks because he did not believe they were capable of understanding them. Then there was an internecine dispute between the navy and coast guard about which organization enforced rules.

The racial atmosphere at Port Chicago was almost as volatile as the substances in transit. Captain Nelson Goss, in command of Mare Island and whose jurisdiction covered Port Chicago, objected to nonwhites. He complained that they functioned at only 60 percent of what whites achieved, and lacked discipline. Goss griped that they "arrived with a chip on their shoulder, if not indeed, one on each shoulder." He spoke of subversive influences upon them on the peculiar grounds that many, having been rejected after volunteering for combat assignments, resented the role of laborers. Goss also disdained civilian workers, alleging they might be saboteurs or of enemy-alien descent.

Goss arbitrarily set a questionably high quota of ten tons of ammunition per hatch per hour for loading crews. The officer in charge of Port Chicago, Capt. Merrill T. Kinne, a U.S. Naval Academy 1915 graduate, had last worked with ordnance some twenty years earlier, having been recalled from a civilian career in 1941. To meet Goss's target, Kinne created a competition for the loading divisions, posting data daily in the dock office. The tactic goaded junior officers, who were anxious for better efficiency reports and promotions and who wagered money with rival units, to push their petty officers. They in turn applied the scourge to the men, with the inevitable sacrifice of prudent action for speed.

For the enlisted men the only reward for efforts above and beyond the norm was a free movie and sometimes a pennant to fly over the barracks. Losing in the competition brought threats of punishment or the loss of privileges. Segregation annoyed them. They were unhappy at being relegated to hard physical labor. They felt that as blacks they had to work harder than whites assigned to the same duty. They could not hope for promotions, certainly not to the exalted level of the commissioned. The base itself offered few amenities. The town of Port Chicago might just as well have been in the deep South as its residents regarded the nonwhites with considerable hostility, and with no military busses, travel to San Francisco or Oakland cost hard-earned sailor's pay.

On 17 July 1944 it happened. According to Allen's book, Cyril Sheppard was in the barracks. "I was sitting on the toilet—I was reading a letter from home. Suddenly there were two explosions. The first one knocked me clean off . . . I found myself flying toward the wall. I just threw my hands up . . . then I hit the wall. The next one came right behind that. Phoom! Knocked me back on the other side. Men were screaming, the light went out and glass was flying all over the place. I got out to the door . . . the whole building was turned around, caving in. We were a mile and a half away from the ships. . . . I said 'Jesus Christ, the Japs have hit!' . . . But one of our officers was shouting, 'It's the ships! It's the ships!' So we jumped in one of the trucks and we said let's go down there, see if we can help. We got halfway down there on the truck and stopped . . . there wasn't no more docks. Wasn't no railroad. Wasn't no ships."

Winch operator Joe Small, lying in his bunk, said of the two explosions. "I didn't know what the first one was—and the second one just disintegrated the barracks. It picked me up off the bunk—I was holding onto my mattress—and flipped me over. I hit the floor with the mattress on top of me. That's why I escaped injury. The glass and debris that fell hit the mattress rather than me. I got one minor cut.

"Other fellows were cut and bleeding all over the place . . . One fellow's feet were bleeding and I gave him my shoes. Another fellow had a cut all the way down his arm and I put a tourniquet on it to try to stop the bleeding. There were no medics around; it was chaos."

An enormous explosion had instantly wiped out the lives of more than 320 American sailors, 202 of whom were black. It blew up a pair of cargo ships tied up at the pier, devastated the base itself, and even battered Port Chicago more than a mile away.

Immediately, the navy imposed a program to train men in the art of handling ammunition and mandated procedures designed to lessen the risk of another disaster. A court of inquiry heard testimony about the competition for tonnage honors, defective bombs, problems with winches and other equipment, and the rough handling of cargo by the enlisted men. With no evidence to support sabotage, and no one who might have witnessed what set off the blast, the navy's grand inquisitor, the judge advocate, while accepting the possibility of a bad piece of ordnance as a contributing factor, offered a vague diagnosis of an unknown "overt act" that triggered the explosion.

What he left unsaid and unexamined was whether the race to load hazardous materials by men untutored in the potential problems could have been the source of the "overt act." In fact, the judge advocate blamed the matter on the deficiencies of African Americans. "The consensus of opinion of the witnesses—and practically admitted by the interested parties—is that the colored enlisted personnel are neither temperamentally or intellectually capable of handling high explosives . . . These men, it is testified, could not understand orders which were given to them and the only way they could be made to understand what they should do was by actual demonstration . . . It is an admitted fact, supported by the testimony of the witnesses that there was rough and careless handling of the explosives being loaded aboard ships at Port Chicago." The judge advocate did not criticize the white superiors responsible for supervision and presumably in a position to halt any "rough and careless handling."

The full court listed a number of possible causes for the "overt act"—a supersensitive explosive element, rough handling, a breakdown of equipment, and other mechanical or human failings. Except for a mild rebuke of the officers who created a competitive situation, those in command and control were not deemed responsible.

While the navy deliberated on the causes of the Port Chicago disaster, repaired the damage, and began to review procedures, its ships and men in the Pacific needed their bombs and shells more urgently than ever. To supply the demand, "the colored enlisted personnel . . . neither temperamentally or intellectually capable of handling high explosives" were ordered back to the task. Unhappy because of all of the indignities of a Jim Crow service, but now frightened by what had happened to so many of their comrades, groups of black enlisted men discussed their situation. They gathered for informal meetings where they exchanged views. Later the navy would argue that a conspiracy built up which led to a refusal to work when ordered.

Some officers pleaded with the men to return to duty. Others threatened dire punishment, long prison terms, or even execution for mutiny. When the showdown came, 258 sailors would not return to the assigned jobs. Fifty men, including both Cyril Sheppard and Joe Small, were charged with the seagoing service's most serious crime, mutiny. The defendants claimed this was not an organized resistance against lawful authority but simply the reaction of a group of men in fear of their lives.

The trial, which began in late September, covered thirty-two days of hearings, and on the thirty-third day, the panel deliberated only minutes before declaring every defendant guilty. The board hardly considered each individual—the time taken to consider the cases works out to one and a half minutes per man. Everyone drew a fifteen-year term, with the exception of a seventeen year old granted clemency because of his youth. A review of the court's decision reduced sentences for some, including Cyril Sheppard, to twelve years, but for Joe Small, along with others tagged as ringleaders, the long years at hard labor remained. In all cases a dishonorable discharge, which denies any veteran's benefits, was part of the packet. The other 208 sailors involved in the work refusal went through summary courts-martial, which hit them with bad-conduct discharges and forfeiture of three months' pay.

The Port Chicago Mutiny reaped as many headlines and public attention as the disaster that preceded it. Black newspapers in particular questioned the navy's justice. The NAACP Legal Defense Fund took on the obligations for a legal appeal. Thurgood Marshall led the attorneys into the thickets of naval jurisprudence while orchestrating a public-relations defense through such organs as the NAACP's *Crisis* magazine, and questioning Secretary of the Navy Forrestal about the circumstances that preceded the explosion and the reaction to it. Despite Marshall's efforts, the navy board would not reverse the convictions. Only after the war ended did the navy relent and commute sentences.

Undoubtedly many of the black sailors granted sea duty, albeit as messmen, chafed at the general restrictions placed upon them by reasons of race. But some remember their tour with a good deal of pleasure. Gary Bell, well aware that he was a servant in a navy uniform, says, "In spite of this, many white sailors envied our job because we had access to all the commissary products, which meant we had the choices of food, plus outstanding liberty."

Assigned to a light or fast aircraft carrier, the USS *Cabot,* Bell immersed himself in activities. "I was involved in Armed Forces Radio, played any sports, participated in Navy Relief Carnivals where I sang or was master of ceremonies, going from island to island to promote the shows. We worked with personalities like Bob Hope, Bing Crosby and Jane Russell.

"I never felt like a second-class citizen and I didn't have any real racial troubles. There was no friction or open hostility on the *Cabot.* We were all brothers. When we were at general quarters because of a kamikaze or other action, my station was in the ready room where the pilots were briefed. I had to comfort some officers before they took off on a mission. I did have one fight with an officer who felt himself superior. Because he swung first, he was confined to quarters while I was restricted for 30 days. Being restricted while you were at sea was bullshit, because there was no place to go. Later the officer and I became friends.

"I had a commanding officer who recognized that I could be something other than a mess attendant. Unfortunately, due to naval and military practice I never had a chance to go to an OCS program or be other than a steward. Ernie Pyle [the most famous war correspondent of World War II spent several weeks on the *Cabot*] and I were friends. He called me a boy, but that was not racial. I was a boy. He asked me a lot of questions and about my postwar plans."

Pyle did not write about Bell but in one of his columns he gave an inkling of the atmosphere on the ship. The correspondent wrote about a white sailor, Jerry Ryan, a boilermaker, first class from Davenport, Iowa. "Ryan's oil shack was a social center, somebody was always hanging around. You could get a cup of coffee there, look at seashell collections, see card tricks, or find out the latest rumors that had started on the bridge five minutes ago . . . Some nights we popped corn in the oil shack. The boys' folks sent them corn in cans, and they begged butter from the galley, and popped 'er up in a skillet on the grill. One of Ryan's friends who came to eat popcorn was a Negro— a tall, athletic fellow from his home town of Davenport. They were on the ship together for a year before they found out they were from the same place. The colored boy's name was Wesley Cooper and he was a cook. He had been a star athlete back home and was the best basketball player in the whole crew. He had a scholarship waiting for him at the University of Iowa.

"Wesley came down to the shack almost every night after supper. He smoked a curved-stem pipe, holding one hand up to it and listening and grinning and not saying much. We were popping corn one night. One of the boys said, 'Wes, how about getting us some more butter?' And another one said, 'Wes, bring some salt will you?' And a third said, 'And bring me a sandwich when you come down, will you, Wes?' And Wes grinned and his white teeth flashed and he said, 'I suppose you'd like for me to go up and cook you a whole meal?' He never made a move."

When the navy opened up its modest officer-training program at Camp Robert Smalls of Great Lakes Naval Training Station, the first class listed sixteen men. The predicted rate of washout was 25 percent but to the amazement of those in charge, everyone passed. The Bureau of Personnel, according to historian Bernard Nalty, could not bring itself to award commissions to all and arbitrarily made ensigns of twelve with a thirteenth individual rated as a warrant officer. The three not chosen remained enlisted men with assignment elsewhere. The commissioned referred to themselves as "the Golden Thirteen."

Elevation to the status of "Officers and Gentlemen" brought little acceptance from their peers. Members of the Golden Thirteen were not welcome at the officers' club at Great Lakes and at most installations overseas. Off base the black ensigns encountered the same hostility as African American civilians. When Graham Martin took his wife to dinner in a Chicago restaurant, unfriendly stares greeted them and the meal served brought on an acute attack of diarrhea. However, one of the group, John W. Reagan, remembers fondly an incident in Oxnard, California, where a waiter in a restaurant refused to seat him at a regular table. Reagan called his base and they sent over an officer who announced, "You know, most of your business is with Navy people, and if you don't serve this gentleman, you're not going to serve anybody else. You're off-limits. Sorry."

Having manufactured its first black officers, the service seemed puzzled about what to do with them. There were only two deepwater ships, the USS *Mason,* a destroyer escort vessel, and the subchaser *PC-1264* crewed by African Americans. On the subchaser was the only place where a berth for a black officer did not put a black man permanently in command of a white. Sam Gravely, upon completing his V-12 course, had joined the subchaser, which previously had only white officers while the *Mason* could hardly be expected to absorb the Golden Thirteen. Most of them had little or no background in seamanship, which further limited their possible assignments.

Graham Martin, the "coach" with his great athletic and teaching background, was appointed a battalion commander for the black boots at Camp Robert Smalls. "I didn't need to be a battalion commander, really. Some of the battalion commanders before that time had been chief petty officers, so they didn't need to waste an ensign." Following a period in that capacity, Martin went to San Francisco where he joined with another member of the Golden Thirteen, Frank Sublett, on a yard-patrol boat. "This was another made-up job because they didn't need two officers. But I said to myself, 'Even though I resent it, I'd better go ahead and do a good job because if I don't, that will give them something to talk about.' Another factor in that duty was that the crew of the patrol craft was white when we reported. As we learned how to handle the patrol craft they were allowed to go on to other duty. And then we finally got a totally black crew."

Martin progressed to skipper of a yard oiler along with Sublett, who says that vessel didn't need two officers; it could have been run by a first-class boatswain's mate. Martin and Sublett moved on to duty in Hawaii and Eniwetok in the Marshall Islands. At the latter they acted as straw bosses for the black stevedore gangs unloading ships and both also became involved in the recreation and physical fitness programs for the sailors. Martin remarks, "Naturally, I was well qualified for that kind of duty, but it still didn't seem like a real assignment. Again I felt that the Navy didn't know what to do with us and they were just trying to make sure that we weren't pushed into situations where we couldn't extricate ourselves. I don't know whether they were trying to protect us or hold us back. I'd rather be positive and think that they were trying to protect us."

Upon George Cooper's graduation, his mentor, Comdr. E. Hall Downes, arranged to retrieve him for further service at the Hampton naval training school. "Downes made me his personnel officer. At the time, all of the trainees were black while the preponderance of ship's company were white. All of the officers except me were white. Many members of the ship's company simply refused to salute me. If they would see me coming, they would cross the street. You can't go to the skipper and say, 'I want to resign.' I developed a technique. If I ran into difficulty with you and you were either an officer, a petty officer in ship's company, as personnel officer I would develop something that would require us to be together. I did that time and time again in the hope that as we sat down man to man to solve your problem you would recognize me as a human being.

"For example, if a guy needed to go on emergency leave, he didn't have to come to the personnel officer. It's routine, if his mother's dying he's gotta go home. I made it so he would have to come through me to get that leave. Sitting down and talking with him about his mother who is dying, you start empathizing with this guy and he begins to see you as a human being and not a son of a bitch black with a shingle on his shoulder. It would work almost invariably."

Cooper admits his techniques failed to soften some bigots. While walking on a street in Newport News, a sailor accosted him and snarled, "You black son of a bitch. I read about you guys but I never thought I'd meet one." Only the intercession of Cooper's wife prevented a street fight.

On another occasion, as officer of the day he picked up a captain arriving to assignment at Hampton. "He looked at me and said, 'You obviously are assigned to the school.' I said, 'Yes, sir.' He asked 'Where am I going to stay tonight?' You are going to the BOQ [bachelor officers' quarters]. He asked, 'Where do you stay?'"

When Cooper answered he had an apartment, the captain said, "Good. But before I go to bed I want to see the skipper." Cooper advised the newcomer that would not be possible until quarters the following day. "'I am not going to call him tonight.' The newcomer said, 'Well, I've got a problem.' I said, 'Can I help you with the problem?' He said, 'You are the problem.' I told him, 'There's nothing I can do about it, then. But I'm sure not going to call the skipper tonight, sir. You'll have to see him in quarters tomorrow morning.'

"We all had to go to quarters the next morning. This guy got there early. Commander Downes was the kind of guy who always got to work 45 minutes or an hour before time. He was always in his office. When I got there, the captain had already seen the skipper and was gone. Downes said, [to our staff] 'We had a new officer come in last night. George [Cooper] met him and he came in early this morning to see me and told me that if he had known there was a colored officer on this base he would have asked not to be sent here because he never wanted to see another nigger as long as he lived. He said he'd been in touch with BuPers and he would not stay here. He shipped out to Alaska.'

"Two or three weeks later, the skipper came to quarters and asked 'Do you remember that captain who came in here and said he never wanted to see another nigger and we sent him up to Alaska. He never saw another one, because he died yesterday.'"

Cooper felt no disappointment at missing shipboard duty. "I enjoyed my work at the school. I had a young family and I was not that anxious to leave them. It was a way of being able to serve and be with them, of having your cake and eating it too."

The senior officials for all of the armed forces frequently complained about the black press, charging it with printing erroneous accounts of situations or incidents. When the marine commandant issued his memorandum on the introduction of blacks to the corps he emphasized this aspect. "Every possible step should be taken to prevent the publication of inflammatory articles by the Negro press. Such control is largely outside the province of the Marine Corps, but the Marine Corps can, by supplying the Negro press with suitable material for publication and offering them the cooperation of our Public Relations Division, properly encourage a better standard of articles on the Negro in the military service." A basic problem lay in the failure of the services to accredit reporters from the African American media. Unable to tour bases or accompany troops, the newspapers relied on letters from black servicemen or their families. Without trained correspondents to interview and investigate, the accounts concerning conditions for blacks in uniform obviously were subject to distortion. In 1944, official Washington, aware of the deficiencies in this area and importuned by the newspapers, began to issue credentials to blacks and to attempt to influence the nonwhite outlets. However, the distance between the military establishment and a media whose interest lay in conditions for black servicemen was enormous. William Sylvester White, with a minimal naval background but an in with the hurly burly of Chicago politics, drew assignment to public relations for the navy in his native city.

"Secretary of the Navy Forrestal picked an old chum, Lester Granger, who was black to make the rounds of shore installations with goodly numbers of blacks, to see to what extent the Navy's integration policies were being implemented. We went to New Orleans and asked the commanding officer if they sent any releases to the Negro press and he said, 'No, and we don't send anything special to the Jewish press, the German press, the Japanese press. We just send it to the general press. The only time they ever come over here is when they hear that something is wrong.' We asked did you ever ask them to see something right? He said, "No, I don't do that.'

"We talked to the black newsmen and they said we have a lot of things to cover and we presume when they've got something good, they'll call us and tell us. Part of my job was to talk a language that would be understandable by both sides."

In July 1944, Benjamin O. Davis Sr. toured the European theater of operations. He brought with him newly accredited reporters from the black press. The War Department public relations office exploited his presence. Davis attended an awards ceremony in Italy where he pinned a Distinguished Flying Cross on his son's breast, a sure-fire coup for those concerned with managing the air corps image with blacks. A press release of 10 August quoted Davis, "I'm thoroughly pleased with the performance and conditions under which Negro troops are operating here, especially the performance under fire." A black newspaper carried a Davis statement, "There appears to be more harmony and lack of racial friction in the combat zone than is found behind the lines." Unfortunately, the 92d Division would not undergo its baptism of fire for two weeks, making Davis's statements premature. At that, others from both races on the Italian scene, never shared the viewpoint. White officers who had always expressed unhappiness about the 92d Division would become more vociferous and the undercurrent of gossip denigrating the 332d Fighter Group had not ceased. The attitudes of white officers and fellow enlisted men remained an irritant if not a downright outrage to black soldiers and airmen.

The movie production that brought Benjamin O. Davis to the site of the 92d Division on the front lines was part of a major public-relations effort of the Morale Services Division. Earlier, Col. Frank Capra had directed a thirty-nine-minute film, *The Negro Soldier,* which offered a condensed history from Crispus Attucks to Robert Brooks, the first African American soldier to die in World War II. The narrator said, "In each of our great wars he [the Negro soldier] has fought for the land of his adoption. [A peculiar description of people brought in chains and sold as slaves.] . . . and the Negro has gained a little more freedom than he had ever before enjoyed." The voice-over did remark on the failure of the Declaration of Independence to apply to slaves or freemen.

The historical section of the script noted the presence of blacks with Perry at Lake Erie, the Massachusetts 54th during the Civil War, the Buffalo soldiers, San Juan Hill, and the Croix de Guerre awards to Henry Johnson and Needham Roberts in World War I. Then the film focused on a black enlisted man as he went through basic training, and concluded with footage showing African American soldiers in a number of the different war zones. Although the issue of segregation was never challenged, the production portrayed the black soldier with respect.

The Morale Services Division aimed the film not only at servicemen but also sought distribution in civilian theaters. Benjamin O. Davis Sr. traveled to Hollywood to screen *The Negro Soldier* to moving-picture executives, people whose product reinforced the worst stereotypes of African Americans. Davis impressed the studio heads by his demeanor and they were also quite enthusiastic about the film, which they pledged to play in the theaters under their control.

The press praised the picture and so did blacks, although some said it told only part of the story. Although its overall influence upon white attitudes is unknown, this author recalls an incident involving *The Negro Soldier.* In 1944, during basic training, my company of infantry replacements, as part of what was called "orientation," attended a showing. After the movie ended, we shambled back to our barracks with little display of proper military bearing. Our training commander turned livid and he dressed us down, "You guys marched like a bunch of godamn niggers!"

A week or so later, during a break, my company, almost entirely teenagers from the Northeast, ragged a young lieutenant from Wisconsin as being from a hick town. He snapped, "Well, at least we don't have any kikes or niggers there." *The Negro Soldier* apparently had not won the hearts and minds of at least two white officers.

On another front, the War Department on 29 February 1944 distributed a pamphlet concerning "Command of Negro Troops." It flatly stated, "The same methods of discipline, training and leadership apply to Negro troops that have proved successful with other groups. Nevertheless, the Negro in the Army has special problems. This is the result of the fact that the Negro group has had a history materially different from that of the majority in the Army. His average schooling has been inferior, his work has been generally less skilled than that of the white man. His role in the life of the nation has been limited."

For the first time, the army officially placed the reasons for difficulties, not on inherent defects, but on culturally imposed burdens. "Soldiers are made, not born. It is alleged by some that the Negro cannot be reliable in battle because his race lacks the necessary qualities. It is a matter of heredity. Many Negroes, like many other people, do lack soldierly skills. But insofar as this belief assumed that there is some mysterious inborn factor— courage, fear of fighting—whose presence or absence is a matter of racial inheritance, there is no scientific evidence to support such a view. All people seem to be endowed by nature about equally with whatever it takes to fight a good war if they want to and learn how."

The authors took dead aim on the self-appointed "experts" who claimed to know how to handle nonwhites. ". . . commanders can ill afford to lean too heavily on the advice of good officers or civilians who profess a special insight into the Negro mind. It is entirely unlikely that such advice will be a better basis for judgement . . . A sure sign of inaccuracy is the tendency of such experts to depend on generalities. It is just as untrue to say that 'all Negroes believe such and such' as to say that all Negroes have certain mental and physical traits.

"Commanders are advised Negroes resent any word or action that can be interpreted as evidence of a belief that they are by birth inferior in ability to members of other races. 'Boy,' 'Nigra,' 'darky,' 'coon,' 'Mammy,' 'Auntie,' and 'nigger' are generally disliked by Negroes . . . Colored and Negro are the only words that should be used to distinguish Negroes from soldiers who are white."

The instruction from the War Department warned officers that if they acted on the theory that little could be expected of their nonwhite subordinates they would indeed reap minimum results. Indeed, it suggested that the men had been known to take advantage of such superiors. Furthermore, the pamphlet dismissed some cherished beliefs, observing that no scientific evidence found blacks born with a special sense of rhythm or muscular control that enabled them to dance or make music. The achievements on these areas were attributed to an interest in the activities because of history rather than race.

The material even challenged the basic structure of American society, particularly in the South. "To many people who have come to accept the formula of separate but equal facilities, it seems that protesting Negroes are unreasonable or that all that is lacking is something vaguely defined as social equality. The protesting Negro, on the other hand, knows from experience that separate facilities are rarely equal and too often racial segregation rests on a belief in racial inferiority."

For all of its civil rights import, the document still sprang from a segregation-entrenched establishment. "The Army accepts no doctrine of racial superiority or inferiority. It may seem inconsistent, therefore, that there is nevertheless a general separation of colored and white troops on duty. It is important to understand that separate organizations [are] a matter of practical military experience and not an endorsement of beliefs in racial distinction."

To justify this position, a recent poll was quoted. It found that a great majority of white soldiers, including men from the North, supported peaceful separation in the service. "However sound their reasons may or may not be, this mass sentiment cannot be ignored."

"Command of Negro Troops" pointed out the special difficulties endured by African Americans in uniform. It remarked on their problems in transportation and urged local commanders to confer with local authorities and bus companies to avoid trouble. "We have not only to enforce good behavior by the troops but also to protect them from unwarranted discrimination." Officers were advised "A long, widespread tradition [is that] both civilian and military police are not impartial and this is an obstacle that must be overcome to make sure of the best behavior and proper disciplining of Negro troops. The Army is concerned that the civil rights of all men wearing a uniform be respected not only by the police but by all civilian authorities and private citizens as well. There is no excuse for the officer who allows his men to be maltreated without the utmost strenuous legitimate effort to provide them with protection." The commanders were reminded that in time of war the military authorities had a paramount right to custody of a soldier charged with a civil offense. No one should be turned over to the civil system without the approval from the commanding general of the area.

The War Department in October 1944 followed up with a manual that covered ten periods of instruction for officers, made up of lectures and discussions based on reading matter. The classes recapitulated the history of blacks in the military and their current status. The manual delved into education, health (with a focus on the prevalence of venereal disease), living conditions in African American communities, occupational limitations, and the possible expectations of blacks after the war ended. Again there is no way to measure what if any effects these seminars had upon race relations. But at the least, someone in the War Department was trying to bring a more sophisticated and reasoned approach to the subject.

Although James Forrestal, unlike his predecessor Frank Knox, seemed wholeheartedly in favor of opportunities for African Americans, the seagoing service never developed much of a head of steam on the issue during World War II. By V-J Day, only 60 blacks held commissions, in contrast to the air corps which issued almost 1,200. The experiments that had placed black crews aboard deepwater navy ships, like the Tuskegee program for airmen, demonstrated the ability of qualified African Americans to perform any duty, except that the navy could not bring itself to give complete control to a nonwhite. On both the *Mason* and subchaser *PC-1264,* the top command remained in white hands although on the *Mason,* almost the entire complement including a number of officers were blacks. On the subchaser most of the commissioned were white.

Forrestal understood that the stationing of the races was destructive to the morale of both whites and blacks. "The Negroes resent the fact that they are not assigned to general service billets and white personnel resent the fact that Negroes have been given less hazardous assignments ashore." The same unhappy dichotomy affected morale in the army. In one of the more egregious manifestations, Han Rants, then a wireman of the 24th Division in the Philippines recalled, "One of the things that was very upsetting was that we had visitors who were being punished. We were racially segregated and there weren't any blacks in the fighting units. [Again, the symptom of the invisible men since there were African Americans in the Philippines but not in the sectors involving Rants.] Once in a while we would have two black guys brought in from the rear and left with us overnight or for a couple of nights. We were told these were people who had been stealing supplies, like the cigarette ration and other items and selling them to other outfits or to Filipinos. We were told they were being punished by having to spend two or three nights at the front.

"It was very frightening for them, and of course this didn't make it with us. We were wild-eyed angry, because if this was a punishment, why were we there every day and having to go through years of it."

In Europe, Jack Rhoades, now the CO of the 4th Armored Cavalry Group, was in a jeep returning to his command post when he passed a truck bearing a group of soldiers. "I heard a loud, happy voice, 'That's the Major!' I saw an excited black soldier waving. I had my driver get into the column, just ahead of the truck, slow down and I signaled its driver to pull over and stop. I jumped out of my jeep and saw a black soldier getting out of his truck. Sure enough, he was one of my former 459th Tank Destroyer Battalion soldiers. He told me that the TD Bn had been declared surplus and they were converted to a Port Battalion. That was all the time we had to talk before he had to get back in his truck. We were still engaged in heavy fighting and our advance had stopped to get needed supplies from the Normandy beach supply dumps.

"I was particularly disappointed, as while in command of the 459th, giving them their initial military training, I had repeatedly pointed out to them, as a black combat arms unit, this war gave them the opportunity to show the world that black combat units could fight just as well, if not better than white ones. I sensed that for most of them, they accepted that their service in combat was of particular importance to black Americans. Is it any wonder that blacks put little faith in what whites tell them?"

15
The End of the War and Return to the Past

In the second half of 1944, the Allies began to smell victory. The 6 June invasion on the Normandy beaches, the breakout by the 3d Army at St.-Lô, the second invasion of France in August, signaled the decline of the Nazi armies, falling back in France, Italy, and on the eastern front. One of the significant contributions to the advances toward the German border lay in the Red Ball Express, a river of trucks hauling gasoline, munitions, food, and other supplies to the swiftly moving Allied troops. About 60 percent of the personnel in the Red Ball Express belonged to African American quartermaster units. On the other side of the world, the island-hopping campaign in the Pacific accelerated with the return of U.S. forces to the Philippines in October, the Japanese air armada reduced to deadly but futile kamikaze attacks, the Imperial Army hunkered down to await inevitable defeat.

Critical to the support for the Allied armies penetrating inland after the landings on the coast of France was continued control of the Atlantic Ocean over the German submarines that in the early days of the war threatened to shut down the lines of supply. When the keel of the USS *Mason* was laid in October 1943, U-boats sank eleven merchant ships in the North Atlantic during the month. The *Mason* entered the campaign against the enemy marauders in July 1944, as part of the escort for a convoy with the first European port of call, being the Azores. As a possession of neutral Portugal, the Azores played host to all comers, and to the astonishment of the sailors on the *Mason,* tied up nearby was a German submarine.

Merwin Peters, the Cleveland youth who joined the navy largely because he tired of hearing his father boast about his World War I army service, says, "I was fortunate to learn to read and interpret the German code. Because of this, I became a real key factor in the radio communication part of the ship. The wolf packs, German submarines that ran in packs would surface at night to do their communication. I was able to intercept their messages and, in some respects, was able to break those messages to find out exactly where they were and what they were doing.

"I can recall one time when I copied some German messages, and because they were so close to us, we put in to the Azores Islands, and we sat there for about a week, I believe. The German submarines *came in* while we were there.

Watched them come in; they were on the surface. And they just waited us out. But then we slipped out and slipped away from them." The ship escaped harm; torpedoes blasted other DEs in convoys ahead of the *Mason.*

At the first port of call in the United Kingdom, Belfast, Northern Ireland, the crew wondered how the local people would greet 160 black sailors. Lorenzo DuFau, the New Orleans native with a wife and child that had entitled him to a 3-A draft deferment, recalls, "This was like another world to us because never in my life until that day had I been treated like that. Never in my life had we received such greetings from people—perfect strangers." A shipmate adds, "The Irish people didn't look on us as our skin color. They looked on us as Americans—as American fighting men."

On its second trip to Europe, the *Mason* shepherded a fleet of tugs towing barges intended to serve as temporary piers at French ports. Roughly the length of a football field, the barges, made of iron and wood, reacted poorly to high winds and mountainous seas, nor were their tugs designed to deal with the North Atlantic when it turned ugly. The thirty-day voyage at an excruciating pace of less than five miles per hour presented tempting targets to the wolf packs. A huge storm blew ninety-mile-an-hour gusts and forty-foot waves that sank three tugs, eight steel car floats, and five cargo barges with the loss of nineteen lives.

Along with a sister escort, the *Mason* sought to sink a capsized barge with 20mm incendiary ammunition and machine guns. But the wooden hulk refused to go down. Nevertheless the convoy commander radioed, "I may have forgotten to give you and your excellent gunners a well deserved 'Well done!' for their effective shooting. The *Mason* has performed each task assigned in a most commendable manner. Please convey my appreciation to your excellent crew."

The gale battered the smaller vessels until all but one dropped their tows. British navy vessels came out to assist but abandoned the battered convoy because of rough seas. For three days, the DE battled the elements, rescuing tugs in distress, recapturing barges, and assisting other naval vessels. By itself, the *Mason* guided twenty small craft to the first available port without charts and from buoy to buoy through a treacherous channel to safety. The convoy commander recommended that every crewman aboard the *Mason* receive a letter of commendation. Captain Blackford also wrote a letter to the Navy Department requesting that his crew be so honored. But the authorities refused any tangible recognition for the efforts made.

When at last relieved of its responsibilities, the *Mason* dropped anchor in Plymouth Harbor. DuFau says, "We went ashore because we had heard about a Red Cross canteen. The word was out among the sailors that they served Coca-Cola and hot dogs and mustard. We hadn't had Coca-Cola and hot dogs and mustard since we'd left the States. About three or four of us were together, found the canteen and went up the steps, excited about getting hot dogs. This lady told us, *it wasn't our canteen,* that our canteen was a few blocks down. It was such a slap in the face. All we wanted was hot dogs and Coke, and we ran into this.

"So she directed us to a canteen that was operated by a black woman who was a USO lady. They had this canteen, and what it consisted of was a pool table, and, for refreshments, cookies and Kool-Aid, lemon-flavored Kool-Aid. The USO lady apologized to us for offering something like this." When the sailors traveled to London they also found a segregated USO.

On a subsequent voyage, bound for Hampton Roads, Virginia, from Oran, Algeria, shortly after midnight, sonar picked up a contact at about 3,000 yards with all of the characteristics of a submarine. All hands manned battle stations. Merwin Peters in the radio shack could hear through speaker phones the communications around the ship. "Then, all of a sudden, everything just went crazy. Guns started going off. Depth charges starting going off. We had one kid in our radio shack who had just come aboard for that trip. He had never heard a gun. We hadn't had any gunnery practice with him aboard. He went berserk. He wanted out of that radio shack. We had to restrain him."

A heavy shock rattled the *Mason*. The ship had rammed an object big enough to bump the bow into the air and ripped off the sonar, the pitometer log that gauges speed in the water, and damaged a propeller. Momentarily slowed by the impact, the *Mason* now reeled from the explosion of its own depth charges and its stern rose out of the water.

Peters notes, "We had slammed into something and everything got quiet. The lights went out, and it was completely silent. Then, eventually, the skipper came on the PA system and said, 'This is your captain speaking. I think we got red-dog.' We referred to the German wolf packs as 'red dog.' So we were all jubilant. We had sunk a German submarine!"

Because another U-boat might make them a target, the warship briefly flashed lights to observe the wreckage and then moved on. There was no time to confirm what the *Mason* hit. The navy never confirmed a submarine kill, suggesting instead that the destroyer escort may have encountered a derelict, possibly a wooden barge. Some sailors from the *Mason* believe the authorities declined to give credit to a black unit but others accept the official version.

Despite humiliations ashore, the *Mason*'s captain, William Blackford, wrote, "Morale has been on a gradual upswing for several months now and I understand we have an excellent reputation for operations. The job is becoming increasingly more pleasurable."

On the ground, to capitalize on the retreating foe, the U.S. forces marshaled almost all available assets. Among those added to Gen. George S. Patton's armor in France was the 761st Tank Battalion, with black enlisted men and junior officers and commanded by Lt. Col. Paul Bates, a white New Jersey native referred to by his subordinates as "the Great White Father."

According to one of his staff, when Patton was told he could add the 761st to his arsenal, he remarked, "If you give those niggers the best equipment you've got, give 'em good food, I'll take 'em." A member of the 761st, William McBurney, recalled his words on their arrival in November 1944. "Patton came down to Saint-Nicolas-de-Port, France to welcome us into the 3d Army. We'd been there about two days. We could hear fighting at the front line, heavy artillery. We were in a state of nervousness. So Patton came down to greet us and said, 'I don't care what color you are as long as you go up there and kill those Kraut sons of bitches! The whole world is looking at you. Your people are looking at you and I'm looking at you. So God damn it, don't let me down and don't let them down.'"

From that date until V-E Day, the 761st fought the Germans while attached to half a dozen different infantry divisions. Their exploits, perhaps somewhat misreported in *Liberators* by Lou Potter, William Miles, and Nina Rosenblum, nevertheless earned them 11 Silver Stars, 69 Bronze Stars, and 280 Purple Hearts that cover thirty officers and men KIA. Advancing on the town of Guebling, France, the Sherman tank commanded by S.Sgt. Ruben Rivers, part Cherokee, part black, and a native of Oklahoma, struck a mine disabling the vehicle while gashing Rivers above the knee, laying the leg open to the bone. He refused morphine or evacuation but hobbled to another tank at the head of the column to fight on, despite the urging of the company commander to seek medical help. Less than two weeks later, his wound stitched, Rivers saw the battalion's lead tank knocked out by a German 88 [artillery piece]. Rivers ignored orders to pull back and, spotting the enemy emplacement, radioed, "I see 'em; we'll fight 'em." He directed his tank toward the foe and engaged the antitank gunners in a duel. A shell exploded on his tank turret killing him. Rivers won a Silver Star, and his company commander, David Williams, a white Yale graduate, tried to nominate him for a Medal of Honor. The acting battalion commander greeted the idea coolly, and after Williams submitted the proper paperwork, the documents disappeared. More than fifty years later, Rivers was one of the seven African Americans awarded a very posthumous Medal of Honor.

In his autobiography, *War As I Knew It,* Patton maintained, "Individually they [the 761st] were good soldiers but I expressed my belief at that time [when the outfit joined his organization] and have never found the necessity of changing it, that a colored soldier cannot think fast enough to fight in armor."

The Patton of George C. Scott never mouthed these words nor the subject's other noxious comments: "Everyone believes that the displaced person is a human being, which he is not, and this applies particularly to the Jews who are lower than animals. Either the displaced person never had a sense of decency or else they lost it during their period of internment by the Germans. My personal opinion is that no people could have sunk to the level of degradation these have reached in the short space of four years." And a man who saw the concentration camps firsthand could still write his wife, "Actually, the Germans are the only decent people in Europe."

Other small, black outfits entered the lists in Europe. The 614th Tank Destroyer Battalion, committed to battle late in November, worked alongside white units attacking the German Siegfried line. Early in December, when a counterattack threatened to smash through the U.S. lines, a platoon of Company C, of the 614th beat off the enemy while taking more than 50 percent casualties. The valor displayed brought a DSC to Lt. Charles L. Thomas, badly wounded during the battle, with four soldiers, a pair posthumously, given Silver Stars, and nine Bronze Stars awarded. The platoon was recognized with the Distinguished Unit Citation, the first black outfit to win one and also the first for men attached to the 103d Infantry Division. Thomas also was posthumously given a Medal of Honor in 1997.

In Italy, the brass reorganized the 92d Division. The official histories of the late fall and early winter of 1944 indicate difficulties in maintaining the line, with Almond reporting to Gen. Mark Clark at the Fifth Army the phenomenon of "melting away" from the assigned positions. To replace casualties or people deemed inadequate, Almond gained a fourth regiment, the 366th Infantry, previously engaged in guarding the Fifteenth Air Force. While the 92d's components occupied fronts against an enemy content with a defensive stance, the brass from Clark through Almond and lesser senior people said they reserved judgment on whether the division would acquit itself well.

On behalf of the Advisory Committee for Special Troop Policies, Truman Gibson arranged for Maj. Oscar J. Magee to personally gather information on the combat quality of the 92d. Magee interviewed Almond, then met with those responsible for supply, intelligence, personnel, and operations, and a number of white officers. His report on paper spoke guardedly. He described its work as "satisfactory with two exceptions, patrol and assault. In regard to assault by the infantry and observance of the rule, 'Close with the enemy and destroy him with cold steel' the 92d has yet to prove its courage and tenacity." Magee employed the standard cavil, the tendency to "melt away." He noted that even though the infantry had been "nursed along" the results were disappointing. In his opinion, the only real test however would come when the soldiers entered into either an all-out assault or faced a fierce attack.

Gibson forwarded the findings to McCloy, with the caveat that there was a tendency toward prejudgment in all studies of black soldiers. They were either assumed incapable or excellent. The special advisor suggested that evaluations which started with a conclusion rather than facts had little value.

Gibson was bothered by what Magee did not insert into his report. The investigator confided to Gibson during an informal conversation that white, field-grade officers expressed dissatisfaction with their posting to the 92d, had no confidence in their men, and believed the black soldier doomed to fail in combat. [They exemplified the dire equation of low expectations mentioned in the War Department circular "Command of Negro Troops."] According to Gibson, one of them said to Magee, "I don't like my assignment because I don't trust Negroes. White officers who work with them have to work harder than with white troops. I have no confidence in the fighting ability of Negro soldiers."

The special advisor warned McCloy "the conclusions reached [by Magee] completely overlooked the effect on the men of the attitudes of the officers. Soldiers generally know how their officers feel. If they know that their officers dislike them, have no confidence in them or feel that they will not stand up under combat, the likelihood is that they will fail." For Gibson the promise of "low expectations" was a foregone conclusion. He scheduled his own inspection of operations in Italy.

As winter smote the northern Apennines in December 1944, intelligence indicated a counteroffensive by the enemy. The Allied command shifted about its forces placing cheek by jowl a patchwork of international units—Americans, Britons, Brazilians, Indians, and Italian partisans. The black GIs faced formidable German forces in the Serchio Valley: flooded-out fields, iced-over roads, subfreezing weather, a commander who kept his cards so close to the vest that except for his immediate staff no one knew the play, particularly in the event of delays or reverses. All this would take place while back in the States reports belittling the outfit circulated through the War Department.

The opposing forces struck one another the day after Christmas. As the battles raged and men and machines advanced, retreated, slid right or left, Spencer Moore says, "We were surrounded at Molazzana. We fought our way out."

German infantry battalions swept over African Americans from the 366th Infantry. Lieutenant John R. Fox, a graduate of Wilberforce and the forward observer for the regiment's Cannon company, peered from the second floor of a house in the village of Sommocolonia. Fox called for artillery, giving coordinates that would rain shells down on the attacking enemy. When one exploded nearby, Fox told the operator at the other end of the line, "That last round was just where I wanted it, bring it in 60 yards more." The man at fire control warned that would be right in Fox's backyard. Supposedly, Fox answered, "There's more of them than there are of us." Several days later, American soldiers recaptured Sommocolonia and discovered the body of Fox and those with him surrounded by the many Germans also killed by the rain of artillery. Fox's widow received the obligatory Purple Heart for the death in action of her husband, but not until 1982, as it sought to make amends for oversights during World War II, did the army award a posthumous Distinguished Service Cross. Fox was named a Medal of Honor winner in 1997.

Frederic Davison, who was moved from his original Company H to becoming the plans and operations officer of the 1st Battalion, places the onus for the death of Fox and fifty-three others upon the entire chain of command involved in the strategy and tactics at Sommocolonia. "I was very much concerned at the time because Fox was a Cannon company observer with the platoon which I had initially commanded when I first came on duty. I was not there and everything is second-handed but somewhere along the line someone should have required a redisposition of the weapons, there were all the indications that things were boiling. It was not that difficult [for a division commander] using their assistant division command and staff to check in critical areas. The responsibility begins with General Almond and went all the way down the line to the Company and Platoon Commander or someone.

"Fox was there with the company commander and was the type of individual who was obsessed with being the best. He was that way when he was an anti-tank commander—terribly competitive. 'I am going to be a better anti-tank officer than you. I'm going to fire better.' He would try to outshoot the gunner. Fox didn't know fear. [From the reports] my guess would be that he probably counseled the company commander to get the hell out of that house and set up elsewhere, not to pull out of position. I would believe it in character that John Fox would call artillery in on his own position. I believe it in character that John Fox would do that knowing, not thinking it wouldn't hit him, but that he was fully conscious and expecting to be killed. It was the trade off, to be killed by them, surrender or get ourselves killed."

To add to the confusion amid the fury of the fighting, Nazi soldiers disguised themselves in the garb of the Italian partisans. Command coordination collapsed as a battalion from an Indian brigade that was expected to back up the 370th refused to submit to control by the Americans. An intensive attack wrought a gap in the American lines, forcing a hasty reorganization. On the following day the 2d Battalion of the 366th went into positions without entrenching tools. Unable to dig in, they succumbed to heavy pressure from the foe, withdrawing in disorder. Just as in the Ardennes of Luxembourg and Belgium, where a pre-Christmas blitz smashed a huge bulge in the Allied lines, the smaller-scale thrust in the northern Apennines petered out, but not before, as in the case of the Battle of the Bulge, the Americans had been bloodied and certain units accused of cowardice and poor leadership. But in the case of the Italian fiasco, the talk in Washington and in Fifth Army circles was of the unreliability of black troops as a group, while in the Ardennes, the reverses were attributed to individuals.

During February 1945, the 92d began an offensive designed to improve and strengthen its grip on a sector facing the northeastern end of the Gothic line, employing all four regiments aided by artillery and the 758th and 760th Tank Battalions, units manned by African Americans with a few senior white officers. Early gains achieved against heavy resistance eroded as counterattacks inflicted substantial casualties. After ten days of intensive combat, the 92d occupied basically the same territory it had before it attacked and mourned the loss of a number of officers and enlisted men. Perhaps the greatest casualty, however, was any belief that the division could maintain an offense. Ordinarily, divisions that absorbed the pounding endured by the 92d could be restored to combat readiness with a fresh infusion of replacement troops and officers. Unfortunately, unlike the manpower situation for whites, where thousands of soldiers were available, only several hundred existed to fill African American ranks. There were few black infantrymen coming through the training pipeline.

Along with a Brazilian Expeditionary Force and an organization of Italians volunteering to help free their country of the Germans, the 92d was considered useful only for defensive purposes. General George Marshall, who had always doubted the reliability of black combat soldiers, happened to be in Italy when the February attack broke down. To fulfill the Fifth Army's need for offensive power, he proposed to Mark Clark, now elevated to head the Fifteenth Army Group, a recipe in which, said the chief of staff, "[Clark] could take those three regiments of the 92d Division and form one regiment out of them, take the one regiment [473d Infantry] made up of AA troops [antiaircraft battalions] who had already been converted to infantry and I would bring back the Japanese regiment [composed of American-born Japanese, or nisei], the 442d from Southern France. He was to put the Negroes in front and the Japs in reserve behind them. The Germans would think the Negro regiment was a weak spot and then would hit the Japs. The Japanese regiment was spectacular."

Almond distanced himself from the arrangement. In a letter to Clark, he said, "Considering the characteristics which have manifested themselves in the infantry combat activities of this Division, I do not visualize that the combat reliability of the newly vitalized 370th Infantry will be greatly raised. I had no part in this matter . . . I do think that the divisional potentiality will be greatly increased by the use of the 442d and 473d Infantry Regiments . . ."

Available for combat, theoretically, was the 65th Infantry Regiment, a unit composed of Puerto Ricans. Many of them would have been listed as "colored" had they gone through processing centers in the States and had they spoken English rather than Spanish. Originally maintained to provide defense of the home island, the 65th when it reached North Africa went to work as laborers and housekeepers for the air corps. Almond chose not to request they be attached to the 92d.

The deployment plan for the reconstituted division included public relations. General Lucian Truscott Jr., Clark's successor as Fifth Army chief, recommended any attack use the 370th "at least in part, otherwise we are bound to occasion comment and draw unfavorable publicity at least in the Negro press."

During the shuffling about of units and men, Truman Gibson, invited by Clark and recommended by McCloy, flew to Italy for a personal look. He began at the Mediterranean theater headquarters with a critique of the discouraging reports filed on the 92d. Gibson observed that the authorities placed all of the blame for alleged lack of achievement upon black officers and enlisted men. The prevailing opinion held that everything possible had been done to achieve success but in spite of this the 92d failed. He noted that the reasons behind the visible facts [territory gained, retreats, missions accomplished, casualties, damage to the enemy] needed scrutiny.

Gibson interviewed hundreds of soldiers, senior commanders, company-grade officers, and enlisted men in search of information on why as well as what. He analyzed the phenomenon of "melting away." "It is a fact that there have been many withdrawals by panic-stricken Infantrymen. However, it is equally evident that the underlying reasons are quite generally unknown in the division. The blanket generalizations expressed by many, based on inherent racial difficulties [a rare euphemism by Gibson], are contradicted by many acts of individual and group bravery. In the 365th Regiment, before large numbers of men were transferred to the 370th, certainly the generalizations do not hold." Gibson might also have cited the rout of U.S. troops in the first days of the German thrust through the Ardennes, two months earlier. No one sought to racially stigmatize the white officers and men who fled their positions or surrendered some 7,000 soldiers to forces inferior in numbers and weaponry.

The civilian aide identified a familiar list of factors which he believed weakened motivation and consequently performance. Among these were the denial of promotion opportunities, the separation from their black counterparts insisted on by white officers, and the high number of men who scored toward the bottom of the AGCT. He added that most of these individuals came from civilian backgrounds where there was little opportunity for "an inculcation of pride in self or even love of country," a soft punch at deep-dyed discrimination.

Gibson warned his hosts that their restructuring of the 370th, which replaced all the black company commanders with white ones, discredited commissioned nonwhites. If the division and Fifth Army staff had no confidence in black officers, how could it expect the enlisted men to respect them?

At a mid-March press conference held in Rome, Gibson spoke frankly of his findings. To his dismay, some of his constituency back home chose to concentrate upon the negative "facts" and scalded him for his acceptance that black soldiers "melted away" and his admission of generally low levels of literacy. The *Chicago Defender* chastised him, "Negroes have fought bravely and valiantly in all American wars without the generalship of Truman K. Gibson Jr. . . . no sooner does Truman Gibson Jr. come upon the scene, the Negro troops start 'melting away' in the face of the enemy . . . It is enough our boys have to fight Nazis and Dixie race haters without having to face the venom and scorn of 'Uncle Toms.'" Columnist George Schuyler, writing in the *Pittsburgh Courier*, said, "He has been an appeaser and one of the nouveau Uncle Toms since taking office. He should resign at once." Congressman Adam Clayton Powell Jr. labeled Gibson's remarks as a "smear." The critics ignored Gibson's comment, "if the division proves anything, it does not prove that Negroes can't fight. There is no question in my mind about the courage of Negro officers or soldiers and any generalization on the basis of race is entirely unfounded." He also remarked, "not all the straggling and running has happened in the 92d Dvision."

Other voices in influential organs such as the *Baltimore Afro-American* as well as some of the black newspaper correspondents in Italy defended Gibson for stating painful truths placed in an insightful context. Gibson offered no apology. "It is hard for me to see how some people can, on the one hand, argue that segregation is wrong, and on the other hand, blindly defend the product of that segregation."

Two months after Gibson's Rome appearance, Lt. Col. Marcus H. Ray, commander of the 600th Field Artillery, part of the 92d Division's big guns, and one of the most senior black officers engaged in combat operations, wrote the special advisor a letter with a fine, microscopic diagnosis of what ailed the 92d Division. "It is my considered opinion that the 92d at the best was doomed to a mediocre performance of combat duties from its very inception. The undercurrent of racial antipathies, mistrusts and preconceived prejudices made for an unhealthy beginning. The failure to promote worthwhile Negroes and the giving of preferred assignments to white officers made for logical resentments. I do not believe that enough thought was given to the selection of white officers to serve with the 92d and further, that the common American error was made of assuming that Southern white men understand Negroes.

"Mixed units as we have known them have been a dismal failure. In white officered units, those men who fit into the Southern pattern are pushed and promoted regardless of capabilities and those Negroes who exhibit the manliness, self-reliance, and self-respect which are the 'sine qua non' in white units are humiliated and discouraged. In the two Artillery Battalions of the Division, officered by Negroes, it was necessary to reduce large numbers of Non-commissioned officers because they held their rank only because they fitted the 'pattern.' Their subordinates resented and disrespected them—justly so. I was astounded by the willingness of the white officers who preceded us to place their own lives in a hazardous position in order to have tractable Negroes around them.

". . . I don't believe the junior officers guilty of faulty judgment or responsible for tactical failures. Soldiers do as ordered but when plans sent to them for execution from higher headquarters are incomplete, inaccurate, and unintelligible, there is inevitable confusion." Noting that OCS usually weeded out the unfit, Ray argued that the refining of an officer's skills after receiving a commission was the duty of his seniors in the division but that had not been done in the 92d. Again he blamed this upon "mixed units" because the whites at the top were either unable or unwilling to fulfill this responsibility.

On the ground, however, the record of African American soldiers in Italy remained spotty. The Allied strategists scripted a spring offensive called Second Wind with the 92d deployed along the western coastal front while the main attack aimed at Bologna was well to the east. Under the reorganization, the division's black artillery units supported the racially mixed combat foot soldiers, nisei from the 442d, whites from the 473d, and blacks from the 370th, albeit the men were segregated into their own regiments. Black and white tank and tank destroyer battalions also participated. The other original infantry regiments of the 92d, the 365th, and 371st were assigned to follow up and hold captured territory.

Company C, from the 1st Battalion, spearheaded the 370th's advance and rapidly moved forward two miles, gaining positions in the vicinity of the objective, Castle Aghinolfi. The outfit had pushed forward farther and faster than expected. When artillery fire control was finally convinced of Company C's achievement, it served up excellent support, enabling the GIs to bore deeper into the enemy positions, engaging in hand-to-hand fighting with impressive results.

Lieutenant Vernon Baker, the weapons platoon leader and the only black officer in the company, participated in the attack. "I was ordered to set up my machine gun section to cover the approach of the riflemen to the objective proper. Upon moving forward to reconnoiter for a position, I observed two cylindrical objects point out of a slit in a mound at the very edge of the hill overlooking the flatland. At first I took these objects to be machine gun barrels. Crawling up under the opening, I stuck my M-1 into the slit and emptied the clip into the aperture and discovered an [artillery scope] which I had mistaken for a machine gun and two men, one of whom was slumped in a chair and the other wounded, trying to crawl into a corner where some 'potato-masher' grenades were piled. Seeing this, I moved to the rear of the OP and pulling the pin from a hand grenade, tossed it into the rear entrance. After the explosion, I went into the position and discovered a powerful telescope and two telephones. I cut the telephone lines, placed a hand grenade in the cradle of the scope, pulled the pin and moved out.

"Moving to another position in the vicinity, I stumbled on a well camouflaged machine gun position, the crew of which was eating breakfast. I shot and killed both of the men and ordered my machine gunner to set up his gun at the same position.

"Meanwhile, the second rifle platoon was moving up a small hill to the right flank of the castle to wipe out any enemy there. While they were in the process, a machine gun opened up on the crest of another hill opposite. With two men, Lt. Botwinik, Executive Officer of Charlie Company advanced on the position and destroyed it with hand grenades and rifle fire. Up to this point in the attack, we had killed an estimated twelve Germans, one enemy officer, destroyed two machine gun nests and an OP, without suffering any casualties."

Between the Americans and their objective lay a draw from where the Germans could see them as they came over the crest of a hill. Artillery fire, summoned by the forward observer, prevented the enemy from exploiting the advantage. Says Baker, "While Captain Runyon [John, the company commander] and I were discussing the best possible way of getting into the draw unobserved to clear it out, an enemy soldier appeared just below us and threw a hand grenade at the two of us. The grenade missed us, and failed to explode. The enemy soldier tried to duck back into the concealed entrance of a dug-out, but before he made it, I shot him in the back, twice. He fell just inside the entrance. Borrowing a sub-machine gun from S/Sgt. Willie Dickens, I followed the path down to the entrance where the 'Jerry' was lying and looked inside. There was a single room with a few grenades scattered about but it was unoccupied. Following the path around the hill, I came upon another concealed entrance which was fashioned from an automobile door. I was unable to open it, so retracing my steps, I acquired two German hand grenades. I went back to the second position, pulled the pin from one of the grenades, placed it at the bottom of the door, took cover and waited. After the explosion of the grenade I moved to where I could see the entrance of the dugout. A German soldier, half-dressed, came to the door, stuck his head out to see what was going on. Immediately shooting him in the head with the sub-machine gun, I moved quickly to the entrance and tossed the other 'potato masher' inside. [Then] I stepped inside and emptied the remainder of the thirty round magazine into the dug-out. Replacing the magazine with a loaded one, I stood inside, out of the light to one side until my eyes became accustomed to the semi-gloom. After approximately three minutes I could see an overturned table and food on the floor. Also, there were three bodies on the floor indicative of the fact they had been eating.

"I returned to the top of the hill, joined the Company Commander and related the occurrences to him. He informed me that during my absence the other men had been engaged in a hand grenade battle. Casualties had been suffered by the enemy. While we were in the midst of this discussion, the enemy began to zero in on our position with heavy mortars. As the first three rounds fell, Lt. Botwinik was injured by a fragment of one round which fell less than five yards to the rear of his position. The mortar position could not be located at the beginning of the barrage but, as the firing continued, one soldier, glancing up into the air happened to see what he thought at first was a flock of birds. It was soon discovered that the flock of birds was instead a barrage of mortar shells which had just been fired from a position behind a demolished house on the hill. The soldier informed the artillery FO who in turn called for fire to be placed on the hill to neutralize the mortar fire and aid the medics in caring for our casualties. Before the artillery could be placed on the position, another barrage of mortars fell in the area, killing three men and wounding three others severely.

"The FO, Lt. Walker was instructed to call the Regimental CP for reinforcements; the call was made and our position was reported by him. The answer received said that reinforcements were on the way. The call for reinforcements was made at 1300 hours. At 1430 hours, a heavy mortar barrage fell in the area, preceding a counter-attack by approximately a platoon of enemy soldiers disguised as medics and litter bearers who approached our position under the protection of a Red Cross flag. Nearing our forward line, the disguise was dropped and from the litter was taken a machine gun which was set up in plain sight in preparation to cover the advance of the riflemen upon our position. S.Sgt. William Boswell killed the three men setting up the machine gun before they could fire while the others of our riflemen inflicted so many casualties upon the attacking force that they withdrew, leaving their dead and wounded upon the southern slope of the Battalion objective.

"At 1515 hours, no reinforcements had arrived and our casualties were very heavy. Later it was learned that Major Haines, Regimental S-3 [a white officer], had stated that he would not take an artillery FOs word on the company's position. Hence, no reinforcements were forthcoming."

According to the army's official history of the campaign by Ulysses Lee, "Reinforcements from the remainder of the units supposedly behind the lead company were called for. At first the regimental S-3 refused to accept the forward observer's word for the company's position; the 370th had not been changed enough by reorganization to believe that one of its units could move out as planned and once again Company C had to convince the regiment that it had moved as far as it had. Then the regimental executive officer informed Captain Runyon not to expect reinforcements for a long time, perhaps for days."

In the 1st Battalion, the leaders of the two other rifle companies were both KIA, "their companies were straggling away." There were no reinforcements on the way and the hard fighting around the castle inflicted 60 percent casualties upon the most advanced troops of Company C. Runyon ordered a withdrawal to prepare a defensive position.

Baker says, "I told him that I would remain and help to get the wounded out and follow him and the executive officer later. Eight men stayed with me and the wounded while I covered their evacuation. Being the last man to leave the area, I destroyed several rifles and carbines that had been the property of the killed and severely wounded.

"As I left the area and started out to catch the rest of the men, another mortar barrage fell in the area and four enemy soldiers appeared on the crest of the hill. I shot and killed one from my place of concealment behind a bush and the other three took cover. I waited for a few minutes and as the men did not reappear, I moved out and joined the eight men and the wounded.

"Nearing a demolished house, we were spotted by an enemy mortar crew and were the recipients of a barrage of light mortars which wounded one of our members, cutting our party down to seven. Going on for another 300 yards, a sniper shot and killed the only medic with us, decreasing our number to six. Private James Thomas located this sniper and personally killed him with his BAR.

"Moving up to Hill B-4, we encountered two machine gun nests that had been by-passed earlier in the attack. Covered by the fire of Private Thomas I crawled up to the positions and destroyed them by the use of white phosphorus grenades. Thus, safely clearing the way for our small party to evacuate our casualties to the bottom of the hill and to the Battalion Aid Station."

The enemy, caught by surprise during the initial stages of the assault, rallied, pouring shells and small-arms fire upon the exposed soldiers. Casualties mounted, the unit lost radio communication, and the men pounded by mortars while trying to dig foxholes became disorganized, according to Runyon. He reluctantly decided to fall back to the battalion lines.

It was another defeat for African American troops whatever the reasons. Runyon argued that if the other rifle companies had come forward as originally promised, the outfit could have held the ground captured. The division command nominated the white company commander Runyon for a Medal of Honor and Baker received the Distinguished Service Cross. Runyon's award was reduced to a lesser medal, while in 1997, Baker became the sole living black soldier from World War II to be given the Medal of Honor.

Company C and the 1st Battalion resumed the offensive the following afternoon. Baker was on hand with 71 GIs, half the previous day's force of 142, to respond to Runyon's orders. As they struggled to gain ground, Runyon shifted to temporary duty with the 473d which now passed through the African Americans. In combined operations with the 442d and other units, the fresh infantrymen eventually routed the Germans entrenched around Castle Aghinolfi in the process capturing a set of strategic hill masses. During the following week, the African American outfits rather successfully engaged the enemy in patrols and skirmishes but the heavy duty fighting was mostly relegated to the two nonblack regiments assigned to the division. By the end of the month German resistance collapsed.

Truman Gibson in his comment that panicky retreats were not exclusively confined to the 92d did not specify other culprits. But the Ardennes salient created by the Germans in mid-December, partially attributable to an unorganized, pell-mell pullout, inflicted severe losses on the U.S. forces. Casualties from battle and accidents cost the Americans more than 125,000 men. Desperate for replacements, the army rushed to France 30,000 soldiers, mostly men who had barely completed basic training, some of whom died before anyone in the unit even knew their names. The shortage put a premium on riflemen. As supreme commander of the Allied forces in Europe, Eisenhower offered a deal to thousands of GIs serving time inside prison stockades. If they would pick up a rifle to go into battle they would receive a pardon and a clean slate. The results were disappointing, as the only recruits were those with fifteen-year or longer sentences at hard labor. Certainly a substantial number of those incarcerated were there precisely because of a desire not to bear a rifle in harm's way. Jim Pedowitz, serving with a black truck regiment, says, "We were never asked for volunteers. But as a lawyer, I sometimes acted as defense counsel for soldiers accused of crimes like black marketing. Some already in prison and others when convicted were offered the option of going into the infantry rifle platoons instead of serving their sentences."

The commander of service troops in Europe, Lt. Gen. John C. Lee, whose first two initials and religiosity led some to an unearthly nickname, consulted with Eisenhower, those in charge of ground forces reinforcements, and Benjamin Davis Sr. on another potential source of fodder. On 26 December, ten days after the opening rounds of the Battle of the Bulge, Lee offered "to a limited number of colored troops who have infantry training, the privilege of joining our veteran units at the front to deliver the knockout blow."

The original plan as described in a circular prepared by Lee for distribution to base and section commanders for confidential presentation to black troops, boldly promised assignment "without regard to color or race to the units where assistance is most needed." Eisenhower initially approved the proposal but his chief of staff, Gen. Walter Bedell Smith, realized the import. He objected strenuously on the grounds that it contradicted War Department policy. When Smith could not convince Lee to recall the memorandum, he appealed to Eisenhower. According to Russell E. Weigley in *Eisenhower's Lieutenants,* Smith said that Lee "believes that it is right that colored and white soldiers should be mixed in the same company. With this belief I do not argue, but the War Department policy is different." The chief of staff remarked that Lee's move would stir a tempest in the States. "Every Negro organization, pressure groups and newspapers will take the attitude that while the War Department segregates colored troops in organizations of their own against the desires and pleas of all the Negro race, the Army is perfectly willing to put them in the front lines mixed in units with white soldiers and have them do battle when an emergency arises."

In the words of biographer Stephen Ambrose, "Eisenhower was no more ready to promote a social revolution than Smith." With a fine bureaucratic machination, a new circular bearing the same date, file number, and subject as the earlier one appeared with a cover note ordering all copies of the original returned and destroyed. The revised announcement sounded a generalized call for volunteers for combat service drawn from the Communications Zone troops. An italicized sentence specified that the offer "extended to all soldiers without regard to color or race but preference will normally be given to individuals who have had some basic training in Infantry."

The document also stipulated, "In the event that the number of suitable Negro volunteers exceeds the replacement needs of Negro combat units, these men will be suitably incorporated in other organizations so that their service and their fighting spirit may be sufficiently utilized." There were no black infantry organizations in the European theater (Italy with the 92d Division was in the Mediterranean theater) and to clarify its plan, SHAEF (Supreme Headquarters Allied Expeditionary Force) announced that the first batch of black infantrymen, after training, would enter the African American tank, antitank, and artillery units. Any surplus beyond what these outfits required would form separate infantry organizations, such as a battalion. Subsequently, headquarters quietly revised its notion of distributing candidates to the armored and artillery units because the training program only covered infantry.

Eisenhower stepped back further, directing that these replacements would not be inserted into units in the fashion ordinarily employed for whites. Lee argued "that we should afford the volunteers the full opportunity for infantry riflemen service. To do otherwise would be breaking faith in my opinion." He persuaded his boss that "these colored riflemen reinforcements [should] have their training completed as members of infantry rifle platoons and then be made available as platoons to army commanders who would provide officers and NCOs."

The authorities were overwhelmed by the number of applicants when 2,500 men volunteered immediately and by February the total hit 4,562. Because of the taboo on blacks in command of whites, only privates and privates, first class were to be enrolled. Many of the recruits accepted a reduction in grade from sergeant to the lower ranks.

By 1 March, the first 2,253 graduates of the retraining course, which was minimal in its breadth, were organized into thirty-seven overstrength [to compensate for expected losses] platoons and distributed through the Sixth and Twelfth Army Groups, which then parceled them out to divisions. In the Twelfth Army, each regiment added one platoon to a company as a fourth rifle platoon. None of the volunteers went to the Third Army of George Patton, whose sentiments about African Americans apparently were well known.

The veteran 1st Division, the Big Red One, whose combat days stretched back to North Africa, absorbed three platoons during a period when there was little time to impart the wisdom of experience. Nevertheless, the novices showed little or no hesitation upon being thrust into combat. If anything, they were described as "over-eager and aggressive." For one unit that zeal led to so many casualties that instead of their own platoon the men served as a squad in a white one.

Headquarters of the 99th Division advised the XII Corps that its commanders deployed the reinforcements in the same manner as any other troops. "[They] performed in an excellent manner at all times while in combat. These men were courageous fighters and never once did they fail to accomplish their assigned mission.The platoon assigned to the 393d Infantry is credited with killing approximately 100 Germans and capturing 500."

The assistant division commander, Brig. Gen. H. T. Mayberry, later said, "True, we had the Germans on the run but we had to cross several rivers and fighting at the crossings, particularly the Danube was hot. The Negroes participated in some intense fighting. They were subjected on occasion to some artillery and mortar fire. All-in-all, the fighting in which they took part was of such character as to give them a pretty good test.

"They would go anywhere their leaders would take them. Their performance was consistently good. I watched their casualty list. They each had a strength of about forty-three when they came to us. When hostilities ceased, they were down to about thirty-two. We thought they fought very well. One of the platoon leaders said to me, 'I'll take these people anytime. They'll go anywhere I want to take them.'" A history of the 393d Regiment captioned a photograph, "The Colored Platoon of Easy Company—one of the best platoons in the regiment."

The 104th Timberwolf Division took in some of the platoons and veterans of the organization provided added instruction. "We wanted to make sure they knew all the tricks of infantry training," said Brig. Gen. Charles Trueman Lanham, assistant division commander. "I watched those lads train and if ever men were in dead earnest, they were."

General Terry Allen, CO of the 104th, pinned a Silver Star on Pfc. June Jefferson with the 414th Infantry. When an enemy tank smashed through a road block to enter a recently captured town, Jefferson rushed across open, fire-swept ground in the face of direct fire from the tank. He located the armor, tossed incendiary and fragmentation grenades into its open turret. As the crew stumbled out, Jefferson killed them with his rifle. Jefferson returned to his platoon and organized a successful assault on the grenadiers who had supported the tank.

Claude Pierce sprinted through intense enemy fire to reach an American tank ablaze from an artillery hit. Knocked from the tank by concussions from near misses, he climbed back on the burning hulk, extinguished the fire, and pulled out the crew. After administering first aid, he carried the most seriously wounded man 200 yards while exposed to bullets and shells. He too earned a Silver Star.

When Allen presented the awards, he remarked, "We're all proud of you for your fine record." Lanham added, "I've never seen soldiers behave better in combat than you. I want you with us when we go after the little yellow devils." The African Americans committed to the 104th dubbed themselves "Black Timberwolves."

Robert Powell, formerly an infantry soldier with the 93d Division who transferred to a quartermaster outfit that supplied gasoline for armored forces, traded his three stripes as a buck sergeant to carry an M1. "We all volunteered but nobody was beating any drums or holding parades for us. I wanted to be a combat soldier. I was trained as one, I knew I could function in that capacity. They gave us a five or six week refresher course and then I was assigned to a platoon placed with the 47th Infantry Regiment in the 9th Division.

"In a combat situation just about everybody accepted you if you functioned up to par." The 104th happened to be in reserve when it took on the volunteer platoons and had the luxury of schooling their additions. But the 9th Division with Robert Powell immediately thrust its newcomers into battle as it crossed the shaky Remagen Bridge over the Rhine. Within days of his arrival on the line, Powell had retrieved his three stripes to become a squad leader.

"Near Hartzrode, Germany," remembers Powell, "we were the lead-off platoon. I was on one flank, the platoon commander on the other. I came upon a barn and realized there were enemy troops there and we'd be crossing an open field in front of them. We had three Browning Automatic Rifles with us and I told them not to let any heads come up." Powell led an assault that eliminated the threat from the barn. For his cool handling of the problem he won a Silver Star, to go with his Bronze Star and its cluster.

Vincent Malveaux, married, the father of two children, with a law degree and a job in the statistics section of the surgeon general's office, gave up his first sergeant's rank for a chance to be a private in a rifle platoon. Malveaux joined the 78th Division just east of the Rhine. His platoon was greeted by a white lieutenant who offered the blacks a share in all the privileges and hardships that the company would face. During chow the first night on the line, Malveaux recalled, there were not enough mess kits for the entire company. There was no water to wash the used ones but they were passed from one man to another without discrimination as to race. He said the off-duty relations of enlisted men in the white and black platoons were marked by "mutual respect and tolerance based on performance in combat." From his viewpoint the platoons went on missions without any regard to race. The white company officers provided excellent positive leadership and the white platoon sergeants who led black platoons were all highly regarded by Malveaux. Both his platoon leader and his sergeant came from the South.

During the first day's action, his platoon lost ten men, with a pair killed by a German mortar barrage. By the end of the war, the unit fielded only seventeen able-bodied soldiers. After two weeks on the line, the blacks started to receive NCO ratings. Malveaux declined an offer to become the platoon sergeant with a tech sergeant's stripes because he did not want to replace a combat-experienced white NCO. Malveaux refused to apply for OCS because he heard that the applications of other highly qualified blacks had been rejected.

His company commander announced that orders issued by black noncoms would be respected by the white enlisted men. When the CO's white radio operator went down with a wound, he selected a qualified black as the replacement, elevating him to sergeant and in charge of a white assistant.

Major General Edwin F. Parker of the 78th told the senior Davis he would like more black riflemen. Terry Allen's G-1 likewise complimented the recruits, reporting to Davis on Company F's experience. "Morale: Excellent.

Manner of peformance: Superior. Men are very eager to close with the enemy and to destroy him. Strict attention to duty, aggressiveness, common sense and judgment under fire has won the admiration of all the men in the company . . . When given a mission they accept it with enthusiasm, and even when losses to their platoon were inflicted the colored boys accepted these losses as part of war . . . all agree that the colored platoon has a calibre of men equal to any veteran platoon. Several decorations for bravery are in the process of being awarded to the members of colored platoons."

The deployment of the African American volunteer infantrymen, through the Sixth Army Group into the Seventh Army under Gen. Alexander Patch followed a different pattern. Instead of being attached to white rifle companies as extra platoons Patch formed them into provisional companies with roughly 240 soldiers under white officers and noncoms and dispatched them to the 12th and 14th Armored Divisions. Notified of the imminent arrival of these reinforcements, the 12th Armored vigorously objected, having recently had an unhappy experience with the 827th Tank Destroyer Battalion, a black unit. Later, the division's personnel chief modified his attitude, remarking the newcomers made a "good" impression.

The provisional units given to the 12th Armored labored under two severe handicaps. In their refresher course, the men had been trained only in platoon operations rather than as a company. Worse, they had neither instruction nor experience as armored infantry, working with tanks, half tracks, and the other motorized accoutrements of the 12th and 14th.

Because of these deficiencies and the problems with the tank destroyer battalion, the 12th Armored was slow to assimilate Provisional Infantry Company No. 1. Nevertheless, some black soldiers rode a tank near Speyer, Germany, on 23 March. *Panzerfausts* and small arms greeted them. Staff Sergeant Edward Carter scrambled off the tank and led three other soldiers toward the source of the fire. Within minutes a fusillade from the enemy killed one of the patrol. Carter ordered the two survivors to seek shelter and cover him while he advanced alone. Gunfire from the Germans killed one of the soldiers and seriously wounded the other. Carter continued forward by himself only to be hit three times in his left arm by a machine gun. Doggedly pressing on, the sergeant staggered and fell from a fourth wound in his left leg. As he lifted his canteen for a drink, a bullet knocked it from his grasp and pierced his hand.

Carter started to crawl toward the enemy position under heavy fire, then lay behind a dirt embankment. When eight German infantrymen approached with the intention of making him a prisoner he shot six of them dead and captured the survivors. They provided valuable intelligence on the disposition and number of enemy troops in the area. Carter was another belated recipient of the Medal of Honor in 1997.

DeWitt Armstrong III, the Military Academy graduate posted to the 94th Cavalry Squadron of the 14th Armored Division, had taken no more notice of African Americans in uniform than he had of the two blacks at West Point during his years there. In April 1945, his outfit was the only Allied force east of the autobahn between Munich and Berlin. "We thus became the target, under the eyes of German Field Marshal Kesselring, Commander-in-Chief in the West, of the final major counterattack by the German army in Bavaria. On April 15 the depleted 17th SS Panzer Grenadier Division reinforced by fifty tanks and other troops struck the 94th. We had concentrated in the road-center of Creussen, about ten kilometers south of Bayreuth. Well beyond the range of our supporting artillery, we were quickly surrounded. Five or six distinct assaults were made against us, from almost all points of the compass by tanks and infantry. We took losses but we held our ground, inflicting much heavier losses upon the attacking Germans.

"This was the only time I saw an all-black unit in combat. This formation we knew as the CCR [Combat Command Reserve] Rifle Company. It stormed the little village of Gottsfeld, a couple of kilometers west of Creussen in the late afternoon. There was a great deal of small-arms fire, all friendly I believe, which gave way to dead silence."

Two platoons of the 25th Tank Battalion bearing black infantrymen had headed for Creussen. Antitank guns in Gottsfeld opened up and scored four hits on tanks, destroying two. The remaining armor pulled back but the African Americans dismounted and wiped out the enemy in the hamlet.

"They advanced no farther," says Armstrong, "but perhaps they had been ordered not to do so. By that time the battle of Creussen was over, and we had decisively won. The main mission of CCR that day was to advance toward us far enough to let the following artillery be within supporting range of our cavalry squadron." For the next few days, the provisionals prowled the area around Gottsfeld and Creussen, capturing a number of prisoners. The journal kept by one platoon in Armstrong's 94th commented, "And were those guys good!"

Although this particular effort was an outstanding success, evaluations of the performance of the companies established in the armored divisions fell below that of the rifle platoons deployed by the 12th Army Group through the First Army. When Gen. Alexander Patch commander of the Seventh Army complained to Benjaimin Davis Sr. about the blacks given to his forces, Davis explained that the newcomers had never been instructed in either company or armored tactics. Before any adjustments could be made in the Seventh Army, the war ended.

Ben Davis Sr., on hand for the ceremonies at which a bevy of medals went to the Black Timberwolves, said, "You have been given a chance and you won the respect and friendship of your comrades. The Army doubted white and Negro soldiers could serve together. I knew they could. They had served together before the first World War and I knew they could fight together. You have proved I was right."

How many whites were convinced remained questionable. A white South Carolina platoon sergeant remarked, "When I heard about it, I said I'd be damned if I'd wear the same shoulder patch they did. After the first day when we saw how they fought, I changed my mind. They're just like any other boys to us." A white Indiana noncom said, "I didn't think it would work at all. I think more of them for it but I still don't want to soldier with them in garrison." However, with a million GIs engaged in Europe, the exploits of a few thousand African Americans, late in the war, escaped the notice of most men in uniform.

In the skies over Italy, the 332d Fighter Group continued to fly missions with a mixed reception from others involved in the air war. The critics argued that the outfit lagged behind in the homerun department, enemy airplanes shot down. The black airmen rebutted that the primary mission established by their commander, Benjamin O. Davis Jr., was to protect the bombers. Actually, Ira Eaker, the Mediterranean theater commander for air operations, when he held the same post for the European theater, had mandated bomber escort as the prime priority. He had been scorned for the policy by fighter pilots with the Eighth and Ninth Air Forces based in the United Kingdom. After Gen. Jimmy Doolittle replaced Eaker in England, Doolittle loosened the reins governing fighters, gradually expanding their ability to seek and destroy enemy aircraft until his airmen felt it was open season. According to the junior Davis, when the 332d was relieved of its coastal patrol duties, Eaker "pointed out the contribution the 332d could make to reducing heavy losses of B-17s and B-24s" and Davis's group would "join the escort mission."

"Davis let it be flatly understood," says Harry Sheppard, "that your job is to protect the bombers enroute, over the target and home. Even bomber crews who were not our customers liked us. When there were stragglers, we broke off a couple of guys to stay with them."

The exploits abroad brought no end to the continuing friction between the white establishment and the black airmen in the States, some of whom were preparing for battle and others who had rotated home, having completed the prescribed hours of flying combat sorties. Along with the replacement fighter pilots, the program for African American fliers trained the 477th Bomber Group in the twin-engine B-25 Mitchell medium bomber. The development of the bomb group had fallen well behind schedule because of an acute shortage of navigators and bombardiers as well as multi-engine pilots, largely due to the inevitable bottlenecks of a segregated system for schooling people. By the beginning of 1945, when the pipeline had disgorged sufficient aircrews for combat training, winter weather had reduced flyable hours, delaying the readiness of the outfit even further.

The facilities at Godman Field, less hangar space, shorter runways, and poorer flying weather than Selfridge forced the air corps, in March 1945, to shift the unit to Freeman Field near the hamlet of Seymour in southern Indiana. The natives were less friendly than those around Godman with some grocery stores and restaurants unwilling to admit black officers or their wives. In spite of the problems that had arisen at Selfridge and continued at Godman, Col. Robert Selway Jr. remained the CO of the unit and he fueled the fires of resentment with notification to the African Americans that there would be two separate but allegedly equal clubs for officers at Freeman. But instead of predicating admission on the basis of race, one club would serve the supervisors and permanent party while the other would be reserved for trainees.

Since all the supervisors appeared to be whites while the black flight officers of the 477th were still training for overseas, the distinction sidestepped War Department regulations on equal access to such facilities. When the men of the 477th arrived at Freeman, they immediately protested the arrangment. Selway conferred with General Hunter who reassured the colonel that he had complied with policy, since he did not make color, race, or creed a criteria for admission. According to Alan Gropman in his book *The Air Force Integrates, 1945–1964,* Hunter added, "I'd be delighted for them to commit enough actions [illegal protests] so I can court martial some of them."

Selway confided to Hunter that he had spies within the 477th who would keep him informed and the general, through his intelligence section, dispatched a white agent to Freeman Field. The investigator's report alarmed the white hierarchy. "The primary location of discontent and most likely location of any possible uprising is at the Freeman Air Base. The colored officers and colored enlisted men located there are in the majority thus giving them the psychological feeling of superiority over white personnel, and the white personnel . . . resent [this]." The agent quoted remarks heard from whites at the officers' club, which included threats of killings as well as the standard complaints about blacks insisting upon equality.

The unrest at the site surfaced in the African American press which carried stories about the confrontation over segregated facilities. On 5 April, some 100 black officers reported to Freeman Field to begin combat crew training. Selway, alerted that the newcomers intended to enter the white club, instructed the provost marshal to arrest anyone who insisted on admission. The first four who appeared retreated when barred. But shortly before 10:00 P.M. nineteen black officers pushed their way past the provost marshal. All of them had their names taken, were arrested, and were confined to quarters. During the following two hours another forty-two entered the premises with the same consequences.

Apprised of the situation, Hunter conferred with the deputy chief of air staff, Brig. Gen. Ray L. Owens in Washington. The latter backed the separate facilities principle. "They can't claim discimination . . . one officers' club is student and the other is permanent." In spite of such niceties, both generals referred to the club in question as "white."

The judge advocate, however, advised Selway to release all of those arrested except for three who physically forced their way into the club. Selway complied and temporarily closed the club to prevent more trouble. He promulgated a new set of regulations governing the place, again distinguishing between command, supervisory or instructor personnel, and trainees. However, in order to maintain segregation he designated all members of two permanent base support squadrons whose complement included several black officers, as trainees.

Selway and Hunter arranged for the directive to be communicated to all personnel and required the men to sign a paper stating they had read and understood it. All whites and some blacks appended their signatures but more than 100 black officers declined, even after Selway commanded them under pain of breaking the 64th Article of War, willful disobedience to a lawful order. Under arrest, 101 men were shipped to Godman Field. When the white club at Freeman opened again, word that blacks would attempt to enter convinced Selway to shut it down. Chappie James happened to be on a cross-country training mission during the latest confrontation but says when he returned he learned he was under arrest.

Hunter rounded up allies from the inspector general's office and the air force's judge advocate who backed his approach. While claiming the separation of the clubs on the bases of supervisory and training categories, Freeman Field was the only installation under Hunter's command that made this distinction. Moreover, Hunter and his supporters argued they operated according to War Department policy, which endorsed segregation. A written opinion from the judge advocate, authorized by Air Corps Chief Hap Arnold, agreed that it was permissible to make "a reasonable division of club facilities where circumstances make such division necessary or desirable from a practical disciplinary, or morale standpoint." Arnold was quoted as saying "we are perfectly pleased and happy with his [Hunter's] actions."

The black officers also gathered reinforcements, Truman Gibson and John McCloy's Committee on Special Troop Policies. The NAACP telegraphed President Roosevelt about the deleterious effect of the Freeman Field situation upon morale among African American civilians and servicemen. The Chicago Urban League asked a congressman to investigate the problem. Walter White, as executive secretary of the NAACP, wrote to Secretary of War Stimson pointing out that Selway even designated a black doctor as a trainee.

The heat of protest singed the top brass. Chief of Staff Marshall approved a plan to release all of the arrested officers and drop the charges, except for the trio seized because they employed force. Hunter was outraged, insisting he held court-martial jurisdiction within his command. Resolution of what was becoming known as "the Freeman Field Mutiny" fell to the McCloy Committee, which received a summary sheet from the air corps. The statement abandoned the pretense of apartheid for supervisors from trainees and flatly identified its guiding principle as the policy of segregation by race.

Truman Gibson denounced the paper as a "fabric of deception and subterfuge." The McCloy Committee agreed with Gibson's reasoning if not his language. The staff recommended the language of War Department literature, which stated that racial policies carry specific bans on segregated clubs. McCloy himself advised his boss, Stimson, that the actions taken by Selway and Hunter did not follow army regulations. Although top air corps leaders vigorously dissented, arguing strictly on the need to socially segregate by race, McCloy noted the issue had been decided in the Selfridge Field disturbance.

Nor did Selway, Hunter, and their adherents gain comfort from the eventual courts-martial of the three officers charged with the capital crime of forcibly disobeying Article of War 64. None of the accused were trainees but instead officers of air base units and therefore under Selway's rules entitled to use the club. Furthermore, testimony indicated the gatekeeper said, "colored officers are not allowed to enter the club whether they are base personnel or not." That further damaged the prosecution. The men were all acquitted of the most serious charges but one who shoved the provost marshal received a $150 fine. Hunter, forced to endorse the outcome, signed off, "the sentence, although grossly inadequate is approved and will be duly executed."

When the war in Europe ended, the 99th and 332d had flown 1,578 missions and more than 15,000 sorties. Four hundred and fifty graduates of the Tuskegee program flew combat missions and sixty-six were killed. The official accounts list 136 enemy aircraft destroyed or damaged in the air and another 273 hammered on the ground. The Red Tails victimized a considerable amount of enemy locomotives, rolling stock, and trucks. The scorecard for the Black Eagles, compared to that of other fighter groups, places them somewhere in the middle in terms of the amount of destruction visited upon the enemy. One statistic, however, stands above all others: a zero for the number of escorted Allied bombers lost to enemy fighters. With the European career of the 332d concluded, General Arnold replaced all of the white officers in the 477th Bomber Group, now back at Godman Field, and brought home Col. Benjamin Davis Jr. to serve as commander. James remarked, " I feel that Colonel Davis was really with us but he couldn't come out publicly and say so. And by the time Davis checked in, the base commander had dropped his opposition to use of the officers' club by the men of the 332d."

As news of the Battle of the Bulge circulated in the United States, the Triple Nickles at Camp Mackall had continued to hone their skills, improving marksmanship, practicing small-unit operations, studying judo and other types of hand-to-hand combat, certain they would be summoned to aid the embattled troops in Europe. Months passed and instead of crossing the Atlantic on a ship, they boarded trains bound for Pendleton, Oregon, to perform a highly classified mission, eventually dubbed Operation Firefly.

When they reached their destination, paratroopers learned they had been converted to smoke jumpers, their enemies forest fires, some of which were ignited by balloon bombs launched by the Japanese. The devices and the damage could hardly have been expected to save the Imperial Empire from defeat but they were more than a nuisance and in fact killed a woman and five children who happened on one just as it exploded.

According to Bradley Biggs, Pendleton Air Force Base and the surrounding environs proved no more friendly than previous locations. Of the colonel in command, Biggs says, "a man who would quickly make it clear that he disliked having an all-black unit at his station. He was careful that we did not mix with his officers, that our area was inspected with undue meticulousness. We didn't give a damn about all of that because we enjoyed eating with our men and our areas were always clean and well policed. But we disliked the fact that we had to serve again under a prejudiced post commander. We had just left one at Mackall. And before that at Benning.

"In Pendleton, then a town of about twelve thousand and famous as the home of the Pendleton Rodeo, the black soldiers who were helping Oregon save its forests, and possibly some of its people found it difficult to buy a drink or a meal. Only two bars would serve them anything.

"The general atmosphere was similar to the white 'cracker corps' of the Deep South. One night Lieutenant Ford and I were standing in the hotel lounge to get out of the rain when a white racist, in conversation with another of his color and kind said loudly, 'Once a friend of mine said that he had a meal with one of his nigger workers; he is no longer a friend.'"

As firefighters, the Triple Nickles underwent a three-week training regimen that tutored them in tree climbing, descent into wooded areas, Forest Service maps, and firefighting techniques. They traded in their steel helmets for football helmets with wire-mesh protectors. Their gear now included a fifty-foot length of rope in the event they needed to lower themselves to the ground after a chute snagged on a tree.

For three months the 555th fought blazes, disarmed a number of balloonborne incendiaries and even helped school navy fliers in proper tactical ground support for troops. It was tough, dangerous work and over the course of thirty-six missions one man died falling from a tree, others suffered spinal, leg, and arm fractures. While most military units around the world stood down after V-J Day, 14 August 1945, the Triple Nickles kept at their task as smoke jumpers until the forest-fire season petered out in October.

For the African Americans aboard the destroyer escort USS *Mason,* their responsibilities ended earlier, but on a somewhat sour note. Captain Blackford skippered the ship on several more convoys, finishing off with three expeditions to North Africa. In June 1945 Blackford was promoted and given an excellent performance evaluation from his superiors. That did not prevent the Bureau of Naval Personnel from a brief and perfunctory comment about the ship and its crew. "The USS *Mason* served in Atlantic convoy duty [and] operated satisfactorily."

In fact, the African American–manned vessel's reputation may have suffered because of Blackford's replacement. The new captain, Norman Meyer, a graduate of the U.S. Naval Academy in 1937, and recalled to service after Pearl Harbor, volunteered for the position. Meyer had spent most of his naval career at shore installations but he says, "I am from Minnesota and really had never known Negroes. A few janitors we had in Annapolis, that's all. But I had never seen any talented Negroes.

"I heard about the [Gunnar] Myrdal book [*An American Dilemma*], and so I sent away for it. And when I read it, the complete story about Negroes and how they were treated, I was incensed and outraged." He wrote the navy and asked to be assigned to a ship with a black crew. According to Meyer, the response was "We have one [there were two including the subchaser] and the reputation is, 'it's a terrible ship'—the professional reputation." Meyer claims that as a reservist he was not fearful of damaging his career by serving on a ship with a dubious history.

Meyer made few friends when he took command, even though he adopted a militant stand when it came to equal rights for his officers and crew. He had the impression that many of his crew were illiterate and announced he would teach them to read and write. The men were outraged; a number had been to college and the navy had taken care to screen the sailors before assigning them. Meyer was perceived as a bit of a martinet, a result of his conviction that Blackford ran a slack ship. He squabbled with the men over the music played on the loudspeaker; he scissored shirttails that hung out. "When I walked on board the *Mason* I could see that it didn't perform well. It got along, but it just wasn't a top-notch ship. For example, when it's time to get under way, the exec will say to the captain, 'Captain, the ship is ready to get under way.' And it is. It wasn't so on the *Mason*. There was always some rope tied to the dock, or somebody hadn't completed some routine. It was just poor organization." Nothing in the navy archives justifies his statement and none of the crew, officers included, support his assertions. Meyer would continue to belabor his predecessor many years later, going so far as to describe him as "a drunken slob."

Whatever the state of affairs when he assumed command, Meyer damned himself before the crew with inept seamanship. In the New York harbor he ripped a hole in the ship beside his at the dock. In Bermuda, the sailors say he almost navigated onto a shoal. These final misadventures of the ship added no glory and perhaps misled those looking at her record. The war ended with big bangs over Hiroshima and Nagasaki but for most African Americans, like those aboard the *Mason*, it seemed to peter out.

16
Postmortems and Pullbacks

Regardless of the medals for valor or the relatively smooth mixing of the races on combat operations, once V-E Day came, the provisional platoons quickly disassociated from the white infantry divisions. Some soldiers who qualified for an immediate discharge [through a point system that credited individuals for months of service, months overseas, medals, and campaigns], elected to become civilians and traveled to a processing center to come home with other blacks. The African Americans with insufficient points went through reassignment that placed them back in fully segregated units.

For many African Americans who had served during World War II, peace and reentry into civilian life raised issues suppressed by their military lives. The pilots and ground crews for the 332d Fighter Group embarked on ships for the voyage back to the United States. "We had talked about what would happen when we got back," says Roscoe Brown. "Many of us had illusions of how things would be. The Fair Employment Practices Act meant that whites and blacks had worked side by side in defense plants. During summers before I went into the service I taught white kids chemistry. But when the ship reached Boston and we came down the gangplank, there were signs to indicate white troops this way, black troops that way."

Brown quickly opted for civilian life, where he discovered skin color also still mattered more than qualifications. "I went to Eastern Air Lines to apply for a job since I had some double-engine experience. The clerk threw the application in the basket. He said, 'We don't hire colored.' I decided that education was the way to open doors in the professions." He pursued an advanced degree and began a career in education.

Harry Sheppard also remembers how infuriated he became as the ship docked in Boston and he saw the split between "white" and "Negro" as they landed. "They selected me to be a twin-engine instructor on B-25s, since the 477th Bomb Group was to be readied for combat in the Pacific, although nobody wanted us there either." Aware of the refusal of the civilian airlines to accept the veteran pilots from the Tuskegee program—"They used the excuse that the public wouldn't accept black pilots"—Sheppard chose to remain in the service. Similarly, John Suggs and Spann Watson, in spite of the low status accorded African Americans in uniform, chose to make the military their careers.

Charles Bussey had rotated back to the States a month before V-E Day and served as a flight instructor at Tuskegee. He separated from the service as quickly as he could, in February 1946. Using the GI Bill, he attended night school at the University of Southern California. He also joined the California National Guard in an engineer unit.

Gary Bell never entertained any notions of remaining in the navy, which still relegated its blacks largely to the most menial positions. His efforts with Armed Forces Radio steered him in another direction. "I felt I had better opportunities in civilian life, working in the field of broadcasting."

Sam Gravely, having successfully served as the first black officer on the subchaser *PC-1264* which, like the *Mason,* was decommissioned shortly after the Japanese surrender, says, "I didn't expect to stay in the Navy any more than I had to. I got enough points to get out in April 1946. I had planned to go to college and then I would coach and teach. In 1948, when I applied for a job and had a couple of opportunities, coaching and teaching paid considerably less than the railway mail service or the postal service. My father had preached federal service. I took an exam and all of a sudden I was a railway mail clerk, and I enjoyed it."

Of the Golden Thirteen, only one man, Dennis Nelson, received a commission as a regular officer when the navy began its reduction in force in 1945. During his final months on active duty, Graham Martin worked on public relations. Upon discharge he returned to teach and coach, settling down at his old high school, Crispus Attucks in Indianapolis. As a civilian, George Cooper counseled students at Hampton, directed the trade school there, and then involved himself in various municipal and community operations in Ohio. William Sylvester White resumed his life as a lawyer and held several state governmental positions before being appointed a judge.

With his high point score—his Silver Star put him over the top—Robert Powell left the army shortly after V-E Day. "A soldier was looked on as a hero if he had medals on his chest but still it was the back of the bus for us." Powell became a merchant seaman and then started a career in private security.

As a member of a quartermaster supply organization Ashley Bryan headed home via the port of Le Havre. "When I saw the total devastation, the food drops for people who were starving, I came home completely spent. I went to college as a philosophy major trying to figure out the why of war." Bryan chose to teach and create art.

Ed Piggott, the former ASTP student, quickly sought to further his education. "After three years of service, a CIB [Combat Infantryman Badge], and three battle stars, I didn't think anyone would doubt my Americanism. I was free to exercise my rights as an American. I was wrong. I did utilize my GI Bill to get an education, buy a house and get veteran's preference on job obligations." The government hired him, first as a cartographic draftsman for the Army Map Service and later as an employee of the Social Security Administration.

Spencer Moore, another alumnus of the 92d Division could not discern any improvement in the status of African Americans who fought for their country. "I still couldn't get a good job. I attended Temple University for a year but gave it up because I was having nightmares from the mortar concussion and seeing so much death, bodies blown apart." He labored in a cinder block plant and later secured a slot in the U.S. Postal Service.

Jehu Hunter, the communications officer with the 365th Infantry in Italy, accepted an honorable discharge but enrolled in the reserves while he worked first as a graduate assistant in zoology at Howard and then as a medical biology technician at the National Cancer Institute.

Frederic Davison recalls, "I applied for a Regular Army commission before the war was over but I wasn't good enough to make it." Rebuffed by the service, Davison used his GI benefits for medical school. Involved with an Italian woman, Vernon Baker who earned a DSC, decided to remain in Europe. He would not return to the United States for three years.

Jim Pedowitz, the white officer with a truck organization staffed with blacks, came home with no regrets about his assignment. "I was proud of our guys. I thought they were as good as any other truck outfit. When I became a civilian I did not become involved in the civil rights movement but my attitude towards black people was that they should be treated as equals."

While individuals confronted their future, the military examined the past in preparation for planning ahead. The shooting had not actually halted in the Pacific theater before the army singled out African American GIs for study, to determine how well they handled their responsibilities. The adjutant general of the army, James Ulio, right after V-E Day in May 1945, announced an evaluation by the Army Service Forces, Army Air Forces, and Army Ground Forces, of all black units in preparation for their role in the army after the war.

The approach, which would assess performances under segregation, signaled to Truman Gibson that the army intended to maintain separation of the races. Indeed, all three major components of the army had reaffirmed segregation as the best way to use black manpower and to harmonize with the sentiments of civilian communities. He protested, pointing out that because of poor educational backgrounds, 83 percent of the blacks scored in the bottom categories of the AGCT. Because of segregation, the disposition of nonwhites concentrated men with lesser skills and knowledge, making them less likely, as a group, to function effectively.

In July 1945, with the Japanese still in the field, the War Department started to collect a dossier on the 92d Division. Brigadier General William Colbern, the organization's artillery commander, offered his appraisal of his four battalions, two of which were staffed by black officers, and two of which had a mix among the commissioned ranks.

Colbern asserted, "The performance of the 92d Artillery compared favorably with any other Division Artillery in the Mediterranean Theater." Colbern reported that the guns were as accurate as any other outfit's although they may have been a bit slower. He claimed they took better care of their weapons than most. Colbern attributed the artillery battalions' superior performance to that of the division's foot soldiers because they were under direct control of the parent organization rather than dispersed under separate commands as happened to the infantry regiments. In his view, they also benefitted from not coming in close contact with the enemy and because of rigorous training before reaching Europe.

Colbern addressed the factor of race. "I was highly pleased with the performance of the battalions having all Negro officers. They did much better than I expected them to do. It doesn't make a nickel's worth of difference to the general run of Negro enlisted man whether his officer is white or black, just as long as the officer knows his job, is a good disciplinarian and has the welfare of his men at heart. Maybe the Negro officer has to know his job a bit better than the white to command the same amount of respect from the Negro private. The morale of Negro officers was better in battalions having only Negro officers. Less conflict . . . less suspicion."

Colbern thought the relationship between officers improved overseas. "I saw white and colored officers in Italy playing cards together around the billets. In Rome I saw them drinking together, occasionally. The one place where they drew the line was in functions involving women."

The artillery commander sketched his two black battalion COs. "One old time coal black Negro [Lieutenant Colonel Derrick of the 597th] who had pulled himself up by the bootstraps. He was a very strict disciplinarian . . . the officers he brought from the old 184th [Field Artillery Battalion] were black, not good educational backgrounds; the batteries slower firing."

In contrast, Colbern portrayed Lt. Col. Marcus H. Ray, CO of the 600th Field Artillery Battalion, as "A well educated, light skinned, polished officer who surrounded himself with officers of similar background. His battalion shot as well as any battalion I ever saw . . . very well trained and very fast." Colbern, whom Jehu Hunter believed less racist than Almond or his second in command, Brig. Gen. John Wood, however took issue with Ray's letter to Truman Gibson in which the black officer contended that blacks who conformed to the patterns of life under segregation drew promotions without regard for their effectiveness as soldiers.

A month later, a board appointed by the Mediterranean theater commander reviewed the final efforts by the elements of the 92d Division. Since white commanders supplied the evidence to the panel the conclusions were foregone. ". . . the divisional supporting elements were excellent but the achievements of the 370th Infantry were disheartening despite the excellent leadership . . . the unreliability of the Negro infantry, its lack of will to fight." The account sprinkled phrases such as "badly disorganized," "panic-stricken," and "sneaked off" throughout the text. At the end, Almond was quoted, "I am now convinced that the great majority of negroes cannot be made into good infantry soldiers or even satisfactory ones."

No testimony was taken from the likes of Lt. Vernon Baker who scoffed at those who denigrated the black soldiers. "In my unit there were no cowards. We fought and men in my platoon died, and I never had to shoot anybody in the back because they'd turn tail and run. We went up [the hill before the castle] enthusiastically, for a bunch of cowards."

Baker remarked that white officers leading black "was just a promotion thing. You'd see a new bunch of white officers come in, go out on a patrol once or twice and next thing you knew they'd be gone, and in comes another batch."

The evaluations of African American effectiveness covered almost all units. For example, there was a brief review of the 999th Field Artillery whose white commander, Lt. Col. M. T. Watson, labeled the work of his black enlisted men during combat, "excellent." He also noted that the venereal-disease rate was less than that in the United States. His only complaint was that three-quarters of the personnel came from the two lowest categories of the AGCT.

The appraisal of an officer from the 17th Armored Group on the 761st Tank Battalion was less than a rave. Lt. Col. Hollis Hunt, who served as commander during a period in which the regular leader, Lt. Col. Paul Bates was hospitalized, said the enlisted men performed well when properly led, but that outstanding performances were few and that African American officers did not show the same initiative as whites in similar positions. The evidence from official accounts of the campaigns in which the tank battalion participated indicates the outfit fought with valor and effectiveness, but that sort of material disappeared into the archives while the negative summary by Hunt, confirming the traditional prejudices, remained readily accessible.

Those charged with reviewing the use of black troops also anatomized the provisional rifle platoons made up of volunteers from rear echelons. They interviewed Brig. Gen. H. J. Mayberry, assistant division commander of the 99th Infanrty Division. According to Mayberry, "A large percent of the men in the three platoons that served with the 99th were NCOs who took reductions in order to serve with the infantry. They were high type personnel. Many of them were mulattoes." [Apparently Mayberry believed the presence of white blood might account for superior quality.]

The former Tank Destroyer School chief professed relations with white soldiers were "harmonious throughout. They [African Americans] were served in the same messlines and they bivouacked in the same area. I never heard of any manifestations of resentment on the part of white troops at serving with Negroes. There were no 'incidents.' These factors must be considered: We were living under combat conditions. There were no mess halls or barracks. Men slept in foxholes or haystacks. There was a degree of what you might call 'natural segregation.' Colored men serving in these platoons were of an exceptional type. Most of them had been NCOs."

These and other summaries on the role of blacks in World War II were gathered by theater commanders initially without any specific idea for their usage. But in the fall of 1945, Robert P. Patterson who had succeeded Stimson as secretary of war approved a proposal for formal assessment on the future use of African Americans troops. Lieutenant General Alvan C. Gillem Jr. was named to chair the committee, which interviewed some sixty witnesses and studied thousands of pages of reports, such as those filed by Colbern, Watson, Hollis, Mayberry, and others.

Other minorities, Jews, Native Americans, Asians—in fact if one makes ethnicity the criteria, every American belongs to a minority—were not examined for their military proficiency nor did anyone include the shade of their skin color à la Colbern, or elements of physiognomy if such seem to have a common reference. Questions about the venereal-disease rate were never attached to any other nationality or background. But then only the African Americans, the Puerto Ricans, and the one nisei regiment served in segregated units. While race-based, the Gillem study bore on the larger issue, the deployment of resources in a peacetime era. With the Cold War still several years off, radical cutbacks required those in charge of defense to make critical decisions on manpower and to a lesser extent, woman power.

General Almond advised the Gillem Committee on his experience with black soldiers. "They seem concerned with racial aspirations to the extent which impedes their military mission. They do much good work when not in immediate danger but freeze up when under fire. One mortar squad which could put twenty 60mm shells in the air at once in training, ceased firing and started to pray when enemy artillery opened up on the company they were supporting. There are instances of individual heroism but there is no evidence of pride in making a good racial showing. Initiative and determination are low by white standards, so was responsibility. Negro troops are easily led and with enough supervision can accomplish anything. Without supervision they will disappear. Negroes are afraid at night. They lack confidence in each other and they lack leadership. They perform well in all capacities behind the regimental command post, artillery and etc."

Almond pronounced the idea of a Negro division as a failure and advised use of black GIs in combat platoons which might be expanded gradually. Otherwise he thought it prudent to restrict blacks to service and support units. He rated the 370th Regiment, after it culled the best men from its brother units, as only 10 percent improved. Almond called for broadening of the officer base, through admission of more blacks to the United States Military Academy and retention of the best wartime officers. He asserted that at one time, 93 percent of the enlisted men in his division fell into classes IV and V of the AGCT, but then remarked that "Negro higher education seems aimed at development of racial equality as their principal objective."

The opinions of Almond were more or less echoed by two of his white officers from the 92d. Colonel Harry Semmes declaimed, "A soldier fights because he will not let his buddy down but Negro soldiers did not seem to . . . have standards of duty that help to give pride in performance." However, Semmes added, "The educated Negro makes a very good soldier" and he cited a valiant officer, a college graduate, who died while leading his troops in battle.

Colonel George O. Weber who served with both the 370th and 371st Regiments testified, "Negroes in the 92d did not fight very well. As individuals they seemed backward and deficient. The more education Negroes have, the more dependable they become as officers. Negro troops lacked the pride and sense of responsibility to stick under fire." He sounded a popular theme. "They don't run; they melt away."

Frederic Davison, who spent considerably more time under fire, retorts, "There was little question in most of our minds. We didn't have friends back in division headquarters." As far as a remark by Mark Clark is concerned, that the 92d was the worst of his divisions, Davison snaps, "The 92d did not disintegrate as did so many of the divisions in the [Ardennes] Bulge. I know of no wholesale surrender. [Two complete regiments did so in the Ardennes.] I know that in the 366th units that were surrounded, they were wiped out. General Clark was either a victim of misinformation or misrepresented the facts."

The Gillem Committee heard from Maj. Gen. Virgil L. Peterson, the army inspector general during World War II and Benjamin O. Davis Sr.'s immediate superior. He informed the committee that no one wanted black officers during the war and there were very few good ones. He believed that "Negro master sergeants could be converted to good second lieutenants." Peterson said black units would fight if the men were educated, if they received the training that instills combat attitudes. "The Negro officer will not disappoint if he gets equal training to whites. Negro units [in World War II] were cadred to death. They would have fought better if they had better officers who served with them for a longer time."

Ira Eaker spoke for the air corps. He mustered his points against mixing the races. "White and colored individuals do not do their best work when so integrated. There would be difficulty in getting white volunteers. Civilian life is not organized on such a basis in this country. Negroes should be segregated in their own units, which should be held to the same standards as white soldiers. The War Department should not conduct a social experiment. [He did not consider the possibility that integration of forces could be considered a military matter.]

Eaker contended race did affect skills, insisting the 332d did its best work as long-range bomber escorts, and that other types of aerial endeavor required more training. He testified, "Negro pilots will not go to the same schools as white pilots since they require more training and would not graduate from the school run by white standards."

Benjamin O. Davis Jr. rebutted Eaker. He doubted if all black pilots take longer to train than white pilots. He favored everyone attending the same schools and he believed he could select thirty good flying officers from those of his group to remain in the air corps who could match the abilities of whites. He recalled his experience at West Point where he was shunned. He warned, "That attitude, that there is no place for a Negro officer still exists in the Army."

The Gillem Committee listened to Capt. J. H. Porter, the commander of the Triple Nickles, the paratroop battalion in which Bradley Biggs served. Porter recalled his experience at the OCS program for paratroopers at Fort Benning and observed there was no discrimination shown to blacks nor was there trouble between races. He favored integration of whites and blacks within paratroop battalions. His was a lonely voice.

When it finished gathering all of the testimony and seemingly digested the huge pile of reports, the Gillem Committee issued findings predicated upon changes in the premises of War Department policy. "Leadership qualities had not been developed among the Negro, due principally to environment and lack of opportunity. These factors had also affected his development in the various skills and crafts." No longer did the army maintain, as after World War I, that the "smaller cranium" of the African American limited his ability to serve. On the other hand, the board declared that service in World War II had added greatly to education skills and health, on a parallel track with civilian activities.

Focusing on infantry battle situations, the Gillem Committee accepted as fact "the least proficient performance has been derived from combat units which were required to close with the enemy to accomplish a prescribed mission." It found that the "relatively slight losses inflicted on the Negro infantry should not have resulted in the habitual 'melting' which seems to have been the final phase of almost every action." However, "Negro platoons in white companies when led were eminently successful even though relatively heavy casualties were suffered." As a result, the board pronounced itself convinced that black soldiers could execute combat duties in a satisfactory manner in a supporting unit—that is, an artillery battalion.

The Gillem Committee softened its criticism with an admission that the weaknesses might have been due to inadequate preparation of blacks for combat units which, it commented, only came about after pressure from the African American community. Furthermore, the adverse findings of those judging the black fighting men did not reflect "the many factors that contributed to sub-par efforts." In particular, the study mentioned failures of junior officers and noncoms to provide good leadership.

The Gillem Committee endorsed the continuing presence of African Americans in the Army. It proposed establishment of "all types of Negro units," tank, tank destroyer, artillery, along with other combat outfits, and that there be "equal privileges and opportunities for advancement." Iterating a theme from the 1920s the assessment cautioned against massing blacks in organizations of division size. It preferred experiments in grouping black units with white ones in composite organizations as a way to stimulate efficiency through competition. Gillem and company recommended that black units of the postwar army be stationed where communities' attitudes were most favorable and in numbers where they would "not burden local facilities."

The War Department stamped its imprimatur upon the Gillem Committee, issuing its report as a directive. To the dismay of some, that meant acceptance of segregation, which invariably blocked equal privileges and promotions. Furthermore, the Gillem study endorsed a quota system, keeping the percentage of blacks in the army in proportion to that in the general population. The board repeated a standard line, "The Army is not an instrument of social reform," and insisted it "focused directly and solely on the problem of the most effective military use of colored troops." Unexamined was the presumption that segregation was the most efficient deployment of manpower.

Both Truman Gibson and John McCloy objected to continuation of a segregated service, even though the Gillem Committee remarked that with the passage of time separation by race would disappear. Benjamin O. Davis Sr., in retirement, shedding the burden of acceptance of army policy, informed a church group in Columbus, Ohio, that segregation was destructive of morale and "there was no such animal as separate but equal." Within the military establishment itself, reception of the Gillem findings was mixed. General Brehon Somervell, the commanding officer of the Army Service Forces had already objected to any publicity about the effectiveness of the black provisional rifle platoons drawn from his command. ". . . One thousand volunteers [there were 4,500] can hardly be a conclusive test . . . Organizations like the NAACP might try to use pressure for similar experiments with troops in training in the U.S. and operating in the Pacific . . . Many members of Congress, newspaper editors and other leaders who have given strong support to the War Department are vigorously opposed to mixing Negro and white troops under any conditions . . . might alienate support of a universal training program."

Ira Eaker as deputy commander for the air corps remained opposed to interracial composites, placing black units with larger white organizations, contending that African Americans could not compete with whites when it came to the intelligence, skills, and education required in the air corps He extrapolated that since they were not functionally equal to whites, they did not deserve equal access to officers' clubs, theaters, and post exchanges at bases located in segregated communities. To do otherwise, he warned, could turn public opinion against the air corps and invite disturbances.

In the navy, Secretary James Forrestal, who had signed up Lester Granger, an executive with the Urban League to serve as his Truman Gibson, dispatched Granger on a tour of ships and bases to survey race relations. Granger returned with encouraging news. During the last months of World War II, conditions for blacks had improved in a limited number of situations, and 200 ships now operated with racially mixed crews that included machinists, yeomen, and seamen as well as messmen.

Emboldened by a modest integration policy that seemed to be working, Forrestal, concerned for efficiency as well as justice, attempted to expand the practices. The Navy Bureau of Personnel advised the service that "all restrictions governing types of assignments for which Negro naval personnel are eligible are hereby lifted." To ensure against the usual means of separating by race, the navy also directed that no ship or base could have a complement in which more than 10 percent of the sailors were black, matching the figures for the African American proportion in the U.S. population. That was policy; practice was quite different. The percentages and numbers did not apply to messmen assigned to the Naval Academy. Furthermore, the enlistment ratio of African Americans to whites hovered around 5 percent, making it quite easy to shunt blacks into the backwaters of naval careers.

For all of the favorable word brought by Granger, some congressmen inveighed against the new navy. Georgia representative Stephen Pace talked about "a very distressing letter from a young friend of mine, now stationed on the USS *Wyoming,* advising that Negro seamen have been placed on this ship and the white boys are being forced to sleep with these Negroes."

After V-J Day, the Marines had disbanded the 51st and 52d Defense Battalions, although in November 1945, one leatherneck from the 51st, Frederick C. Branch, graduated from the platoon commanders course at Quantico. He became the first officer of his race in the marine corps. Operating under the same rules that Forrestal had forced upon the navy, the marines made little or no effort to attract African Americans. Aware of the attitude of the hierarchy toward them during World War II as well as the limited opportunities in the service, blacks declined to volunteer for the marines during the postwar era. With the advent of more downsizing, the percentage fell to about 2 percent. It became difficult to staff segregated units, but in the eyes of the top brass the most critical shortage was stewards. Headquarters went so far as to propose that even senior black NCOs must sign a statement that they would accept assignment as stewards or else receive a discharge. Opposition by blacks killed the notion.

African Americans socializing with, even marrying, white European women caused considerable uproar among GIs stationed in the army of occupation. Early in 1945, the issue of interracial marriages troubled Benjamin O. Davis Sr. "I have discussed the question of marriage with a large number of Negro chaplains. They have all been opposed to their soldiers marrying foreigners, even one of their own race. You will find that Negro chaplains, who are rightfully keen against discrimination are double keen against marriages of this type."

However, Davis could not accept a ban on such unions as that promoted by the white European theater chaplain L. C. Tiernan, who announced, "It is the opinion of the Theater Chaplain that in cases where a miscegenous [sic] marriage is invalid in the home state of the soldier . . . permission for such marriage should not be given. The permission to marry in such a case would be to create a state of concubinage which is definitely bad for social conditions and does reflect discredit on the service."

Davis demurred at the familiar export of home prejudices or restrictions abroad. ". . . race or domicile of the member of the armed forces at the time of application should not enter into consideration . . . [the soldier is] a free agent when he leaves service, privilege to marry is the same as any other privileges." It was not an academic issue since the commanding general of the U.S. Strategic Air Forces in Europe, Carl Spaatz, refused blacks under his command permission to wed.

The mere presence of blacks in postwar Europe aroused controversy. A report by counsel George Meader from a Special Senate Committee on Military Government in Occupied Areas of Europe bleated, "A major difficulty with troops in Germany has been the proportionately large number of Negro troops used not in military government but in the Army's occupational duties. There is a question whether Negro troops should have been used at all for occupational service because the race question was bound to be encountered since no Negro population is to be found in Germany."

Obviously the legislators and their staff meant the absence of black German females would result in African American involvement with white women. Indeed, one of the abuses Meader mentioned was of a black soldier who lived in a house with his white English wife. Meader also accused the nonwhite GIs of buying the favors of German women through their access to supplies. Unproven charges of excessive venereal disease, black marketing, and crimes marked the Congressional inquiry and inflamed adherents of white supremacy and segregation who viewed returning African American servicemen as a potential threat to the status quo.

After seeing photographs of black soldiers dancing with German women, a former commander of the American Legion, Alvin M. Owsley, wrote to Eisenhower, still supreme commander of the Allied forces in Europe. "My dear General, I do not know . . . where these Negroes come from but it is likely if they expect to return to the South they very likely are on their way to be hanged or to be burned alive at public lynchings by the white men of the South."

The prophesied fury consumed even those innocent of anything remotely similar to what Owsley saw in pictures. In 1946, Sgt. Isaac Woodard boarded a bus in Georgia for a furlough home after fifteen months in the South Pacific. The driver raged at Woodard for taking too much time in the "colored only" rest room at a South Carolina stop. When the bus reached the next town, the driver called for the local sheriff who arrested the sergeant for drunkeness, although he did not drink. The lawman and at least one associate beat the prisoner with a blackjack and nightstick, poking him in the eyes before locking him in a cell overnight. Convicted the following day and fined fifty dollars, Woodard entered an army hospital in Spartanburg, South Carolina, where doctors discovered so much damage to his corneas he was diagnosed as permanently blind. The case aroused a storm of publicity that shook President Harry Truman who said to the NAACP's Walter White, "I had no idea it was as terrible as that. We've got to do something." The courts of the state acquitted the sheriff of any wrongdoing. Two years would pass before the president actually took action.

Meanwhile the assaults continued. In Monroe, Georgia, four black people, including a veteran, were murdered by a mob. Mississippi whites assaulted a group of men riding in trucks. Again Truman reacted, ". . . my very stomach turned over when I learned that Negro soldiers just back from overseas were being dumped out of army trucks . . . and beaten." The behavior was hardly surprising since the leading political figure of the state, Sen. Theodore Bilbo, had publicly demanded that "red-blooded Anglo Saxon men stop Negroes from voting."

Lunch counters, restaurants, hotels, theaters, and other public facilities remained segregated. Of the 32,892 Southern Baptist churches 90 percent refused admission to blacks seeking to pray in their pews. While the civilian population attempted to maintain inequality, similarly, most military authorities either disregarded or even sought to evade the spirit behind the calls of Forrestal and the Gillem Committee for improvements in opportunities for blacks.

One memorable exception was Gen. James M. Gavin, CO of the 82d Airborne Division, triumphantly returned from Europe to its home base at Fort Bragg, North Carolina. Gavin boldly stepped out in favor of integration. Gavin, an orphan who entered West Point after a stint as an enlisted man, recalled, "The first black man I ever saw was a Pullman porter who allowed me to go through his car selling newspapers when the train stopped in Mount Carmel [Pennsylvania]. He was very kind and helpful to me." Gavin says that after his graduation from the Military Academy, "I served with the all-black 25th Infantry on the Mexican border near Douglas, Arizona. I enjoyed my service with this hard-driving, well trained regiment. Its members often talked about the histories of black units in the Spanish-American War that made clear their effectiveness in combat, providing they were well-trained, well-armed and well-led. The NCOs knew their business and of course with long service, we had a Sgt. Bilko or two, who knew how to take every advantage of the system."

According to his biographers, Michael T. Booth and Duncan Spencer (*Paratrooper: The Life of Gen. James M. Gavin*) "racial prejudice among his men annoyed Gavin intensely." In 1946, the Triple Nickles, following their tour as smoke jumpers, after a brief attachment to the 13th Airborne, joined the 82d. Said Gavin, "I first encountered the Triple Nickles when I took the 82d Airborne Division fresh from a victory parade up New York's Fifth Avenue to Fort Bragg. In spite of the fact that the 555th were volunteers and jumpers, outstanding athletes, there would be two kinds of soldiers at Fort Bragg. The 82d Airborne were housed in well-maintained barracks with good swimming pools, gymnasiums and chapels and so forth. When I toured the facilities [of the 555th] with the battalion commander, I was appalled. Our new friends, the Triple Nickles were billeted in old tar-paper-covered shacks. Their swimming pool was not much more than a mud puddle and their bathhouse was a scandal. It was obvious that these black troops were going to be second-class citizens in the 82d if living conditions were not improved."

General Melvin Zais, a veteran of the European theater with the 517th Parachute Regimental Combat Team, Gavin's brother-in-law and a member of his staff, described the conditions at Fort Bragg. "There was an area called Spring Hill which was for blacks. That's where black truck companies, black quartermaster companies and the Triple Nickles were located. They all lived in the Spring Hill area, used the black officers' club, the black theater, the black noncoms' club and the black lake in which they swam."

Elliotte Williams, as a medical administrative officer in the 555th, echoes their memories. "The first year we were at Fort Bragg we were physically sep-

arated from the rest of the division. Everything, social or cultural was segregated. We Catholics had a separate religious instructor to teach catechism
to the kids. The priest came from town."

"Recalling my own experience with black troops," said Gavin, "I knew the
time had come for a change. The 555th had to be integrated into the 82d.
This was a serious problem, not to be taken lightly, for our Army had been
a two-colored Army for a long time, just as was our own society. I was concerned that if I asked for a letter of authority to integrate the Triple Nickles into the 82d there certainly would be opposition. Tradition in the Armed
Forces is very strong and I was certain to get a rejection. So I decided to grab
the issue and go directly to the Department of the Army staff. I called on
the Chief of Plans and Operations in the War Department at the Pentagon.
I was aware that the 82d was going to be part of the Army's Strategic Reserve
[ASR] and that if the 555th was integrated into the 82d Airborne Division,
it would become part of the ASR and that meant the 555th would be superbly
trained and equipped and have the highest priority for the newest equipment and weapons.

"The G-3, Lt. General Hull, had but one question, 'General, do you in-
tend to give all those fourragères and medals that the 82d won in Europe
to the 555th?'

"'Yes, General,' I replied, 'I will and they will earn them. I'll see to that.'
There was no further discussion. I returned to Fort Bragg and the integration order followed." Many paratroopers who came to the 82d as replacements after combat in Europe were entitled to garland their uniforms with
these unit awards but only when that honor was extended to blacks did the
question arise.

Zais adds, "General Gavin didn't command the post so we had to have
the cooperation of the post commander. Gavin really pushed the business
of 'Let's get the blacks out of the Spring Hill area. Let's not have one area
for blacks. Let's allow blacks in our officers' club and in the noncoms' club.
Let's get this moving.'

"You had true integration then because the personnel were spread
through the 82d Airborne Division. I had Bradley Biggs on my staff when I
was G-3. That was the first black officer on the division staff. I had General
Gavin's permission and his encouragement. I told General Gavin he [Biggs]
was also going to join the mess and come to the general officers' mess. Gavin
said, 'By all means, of course. Mel, do you think you will have any trouble
with this?'

"I said, 'No, I won't have any trouble at all.' He asked why not and I said,
'Because I'm going to take him over there myself and he's going to eat with
me.' We didn't have any trouble."

The 555th or Triple Nickles disappeared under the new organization and
instead the men became the 3d Battalion of the 505th Regiment. It was not,

in spite of Zais's assertion "true integration" since the mixture was by units rather than by individuals.

How to deal with mandated reductions in force preoccupied all of the upper echelons of the military more than what to do about matters of race. Programs such as that of Forrestal or the recommendations from the Gillem Committee became secondary, if not irrelevant, in the minds of those charged with management of appropriations and maintenance of national defense. Certainly the supreme commander of the Allied forces in Europe provided no encouragement for blacks in the military. Eisenhower told a Senate Committee on Armed Services, "I do believe that if we attempt merely by passing a lot of laws to force someone to like someone else, we're just going to get into trouble." While hardly a speech against integration, the words presaged the attitude of a powerful figure already vested with a political future.

The issue of manpower was further complicated by the suspension of Selective Service in the immediate post–World War II years in favor of open enlistments. Lack of economic opportunity, particularly as veterans with preferences and previously developed skills entered the job market, encouraged less-educated, inexperienced young men to turn to the military. The army believed it faced a glut of poorly educated, unqualified black recruits. A good many white newcomers also tested low on the AGCT. In Europe, the commanding general found it necessary to provide remedial military training as well some basic education on a high school level.

Marcus Ray, the artillery commander who had his own perspective of the problems of the 92d Division, had replaced Truman Gibson as special aide to the secretary of war. To cut back to the authorized strength of the army, Ray proposed a discharge for anyone in the lowest category of the AGCT. But that covered 92,000 soldiers, and because whites with weak educational backgrounds could be distributed throughout the forces, they did not cause whole units to be substandard. But the few outfits available to blacks resulted in concentrations of less-qualified people with greater deleterious effects.

The War Department adopted a modified version of Ray's prescription. The process shook out many of the men incapable of adequate performance. To prevent further enlistment of risky volunteers, the War Department placed a ceiling on the number of blacks it would accept and in a nod to racism added a requirement that they score thirty points higher than the minimum for whites. Through this gambit, the army expected to avoid overload of incompetents in its black outfits.

The new rules sharply trimmed the percentage of African Americans in the army, but while the higher test scores may have improved the functioning of the black organizations, they also angered civil rights adherents who criticized the imposition of quotas and unequal demands upon blacks.

The army defended itself, explaining these were temporary measures. At the same time, obedient to the advice of experts, rather than create divisions for its black contingent even on paper, the service assigned the 24th Infantry Regiment as an organic part of the 25th Division and committed a pair of infantry battalions to what had been all-white regiments. Segregation remained within the smaller organizations.

The vision of an independent air force branch, first voiced by Gen. Billy Mitchell, during the 1920s, became a reality in September 1947. A few months before, the 477th Composite Group, which included both fighter and bomb groups, had been deactivated and replaced by the 332d Group with the B-25 component removed. The multiengine pilots like Chappie James underwent retraining in fighters. However, the expansion plans of the air force added no new black flying units.

Politics and principles suddenly intruded upon the largely internecine struggle between the minority and the white military establishment. They appeared in the form of President Harry Truman. His history hardly marked him as a likely candidate to confront the forces arrayed against integration of the military. He grew up in a part of Missouri where during his senior year in high school, the *Jackson Country Examiner* observed, "The community at large need not be especially surprised if there is a Negro lynching in Independence [Truman's hometown]. The conditions are favorable at this time. There are a lot of worthless young Negro men in town who do nothing. They do not pretend to work and stand around on the streets and swear and make remarks about ladies and others who may pass by. They crowd into the electric cars and become offensive."

During Truman's years in Independence, blacks lived in a section known as "Nigger Neck." They were unwelcome in most stores, could not use the town library, and attended segregated schools. The bias virus coursed through the future president's veins. Referring to an uncle, Truman wrote, "He does hate Chinks and Japs. So do I. It is race prejudice, I guess. But I am strongly of the opinion that negroes ought to be in Africa, yellow men in Asia and white men in Europe and America." (He offered no opinion on where redmen or Native Americans should live.) In 1918, Truman described New York City as a "kike town" with "wops."

Still, as a U.S. senator in 1940, he declared his belief in at least civil equality. "I believe in the brotherhood of man; not merely the brotherhood of white men, but the brotherhood of all men before the law . . . If a class or race can be permanently set apart from or pushed down below the rest in political and civil rights, so may any other class or race when it shall incur the displeasure of its more powerful associates, and we may say farewell to the principles on which we count our safety.

"Negroes have been preyed upon by all types of exploiters, from the installment salesman . . . to the vendors of vice. The majority of our Negro people find but cold comfort in shanties and tenements. Surely, as freemen they are entitled to something better than this." He opposed the shameful evacuation of Japanese Americans to internment camps early in World War II, recalling how his grandmother and mother, along with many other Missourians, had been moved by federal troops to a kind of concentration camp during the Civil War. Truman's mother refused to sleep in the Lincoln Bedroom when visiting her son in the White House. Author J. Robert Moskin in his book *Mr. Truman's War* credits the experiences of his family during that conflict with shaping his mature views against loyalty oaths, in favor of civil rights for blacks, and for programs to heal the damaged countries of Europe.

Even as he uttered his condemnation of prejudicial acts, Truman displayed his inbred racism during casual conversations where he lapsed into "nigger," "coon," "bohunk," "Dago," and "chink." When some old associates questioned his loyalty to the traditional values, his sister Mary Jane said, "Harry is no more for nigger equality than any of us."

Through the winter and spring of 1948, Truman seemed a sure loser in the coming presidential race. Petty corruption within his administration, the growing Red scare that targeted his Democratic Party as infested with Communist agents and sympathizers, and concern about the power of unions boosted the hopes of the Republican Party. A phalanx of Southern politicos, ordinarily supportive of the Democrats, threatened to bolt if the party and the president showed any inclination to encourage the incipient Civil Rights movement.

Politically sensitive, Truman might well have been expected not to rile the vital bloc from the South but he had always been proudest of his time as an artillery captain during World War I. The crimes and humiliations visited upon black servicemen outraged him because these denied and even dishonored military service. A board headed by William Green, who supervised the building of the Ledo Road in Burma, in 1947 had reported to Truman on the condition of minorities in the armed forces. Green, impressed by the performance of the black soldiers who worked on the Ledo Road, supported an end to discrimination in the military. The study produced nothing concrete at the time but it registered with the president.

In June 1948, as the Cold War grew more intense, a new Selective Service law went on the books. A. Philip Randolph, the head of the Brotherhood of Sleeping Car Porters, had warned the Senate Armed Service Committee "that passage now of a Jim Crow draft may only result in mass civil disobedience." Although Marine Master Sergeant Gilbert "Hashmark" Johnson through a letter to the president took issue with Randolph, a great many African Americans agreed with the union leader.

On 26 July, Truman issued an executive order, "It is hereby declared to be the policy of the president that there shall be equality of treatment and opportunity for all persons in the armed services without regard to race, color, religion or national origin. This policy shall be put into effect as rapidly as possible and having due regard to the time required to effectuate any necessary changes without impairing efficiency or morale."

In a second part of the statement he announced the creation of "The President's Committee on Equality of Treatment and Opportunity in the Armed Services which shall be composed of seven members to be designated by the President." The committee was to be more than another public relations effort and empowered to ensure implementation of the policy enunciated. He named Georgian Charles Fahy chairman and the other active members included Dwight R. G. Palmer, an industrialist and active member of the National Urban League, William E. Stevenson, president of Oberlin College, Lester Granger, the former advisor to Forrestal and now head of the Urban League, and John H. Sengstacke, publisher of the African American *Chicago Defender.*

When an old batterymate from World War I and businessman from Kansas City wrote to Truman advising him, as a Southerner, to soft-pedal civil rights, Truman responded. "The main difficulty with the South is that they are living eighty years behind the times and the sooner they come out of it, the better it will be for the country and themselves. I am not asking for social equality because no such thing exists, but I am asking for equality of opportunity for all human beings, and as long as I stay here, I am going to continue that fight. When the mob gangs can take four people out and shoot them in the back, and everybody in the country is acquainted with who did the shooting and nothing is done about it, that country is in a pretty bad fix from a law enforcement standpoint.

"When a Mayor and a City Marshal can take a negro Sergeant off a bus in South Carolina, beat him up and put out one of his eyes, and nothing is done about it by the State Authorities, something is radically wrong with the system . . ." Whatever Truman's views on racial integration, he believed both in equal justice and opportunity, particularly in government agencies such as the U.S. military.

17
The Walls Begin to Tumble

The services interpreted and reacted to the presidential decree in their own fashion, keenly aware that political wisdom predicted Truman a sure loser in the November 1948 elections. Some may have been understandably confused by the meaning of Truman's order. Although it did not specifically outlaw segregated units, unlike previous statements concerning equal opportunity, it omitted any sanction of the old all-black outfits. There was even some ambiguity in the president's understanding of the consequences as evidenced by his statement that he did not seek social equality because in his mind it didn't exist. Truman could be understood as a believer in the concept of "separate but equal" with an insistence upon true fulfillment of the second adjective. His harsh reaction to lunchroom sit-ins after he left office indicates he did not think in terms of total integration of society. However, logistical and logical analysis of the military and its use of people under the Truman rules rendered maintenance of parallel forces a non sequitur.

Opponents recognized the threat to their two-tier system, particularly as the Fahy Committee made clear that its mission was to ask each branch of the military for a blueprint on how it would meet the mandate. Senator Strom Thurmond of South Carolina, who headed the ticket for the so-called Dixiecrats, defectors from the Democratic Party, labeled racial integration of the armed service as "un-American." Senator Richard Russell of Georgia, chairman of the Armed Forces Committee, publicly deplored any lessening of segregation as a threat to military effectiveness.

Even after Truman shocked the political, military, and media establishments with a victory over the Republicans in spite of the Dixiecrats schism, the services, with one exception, the air force, balked at any substantive effort to meet the presidential order. The marine corps struck a defiant pose. Commandant Gen. Clifton D. Cates huffed, "The problem of segregation is not the responsibility of the Armed Forces but is a problem of the nation. Changing national policy in this respect through the Armed Forces is a dangerous path to pursue in as much as it affects the ability of the National Military to fulfill its mission. . . . Should the time arise that non-segregation, and this term applies to white as well as negro, is accepted as a custom of the nation, this policy can be adopted without detriment by the National Military Establishment."

The navy congratulated itself for having preceded the directive with widespread reforms designed to guarantee equal opportunity. In fact, the navy had done so little to implement change that the number of general-service seamen had declined while more than 60 percent of its black sailors still acted as valets, cooks, and waiters.

Bill Thompson, a young ensign in 1949, saw firsthand the evidence of the resistance toward the top of the chain of command. As a boy growing up in Escanaba, Michigan, during the 1920s and early 1930s, Thompson remembers only Caucasians in the population of 10,000. When the family moved to Green Bay, Wisconsin, with 42,000 citizens, he saw a single African American shining shoes at the train station but did encounter a sizable representation of Native Americans from the Oneida tribe. He had some contact with the handful of them who attended his high school. As a track athlete he competed against blacks from other schools but he says he was ignorant of racial problems.

After uneventful World War II service in the navy, where he remained unaware of the history of segregation in the military, in 1949 he held down a desk dealing with public information at the Pentagon. "When things slowed in the office or I was eating my lunch, I occupied my time reading newspapers published for black communities, such as the *Chicago Defender, Baltimore Afro-American,* and the *Norfolk Journal and Guide.* I would pick them up from the desk behind me, occupied by Lt. Dennis Nelson, the first black officer in the regular Navy [a member of the Golden Thirteen]. The Navy was severely segregated at that time; Dennis was the token black. It wasn't a good move because he was at least 35 years old, probably pushing 40, so had to be made a lieutenant. Also, he had little or no sea experience so he couldn't be put aboard a ship to compete with seagoing officers. The leadership, acting in good faith, I'm sure, decided to make him a Special Duty Only Officer in Public Information. Dennis had been a professor at Fisk University in Tennessee and had no experience in journalism or public relations. Everyone handled Dennis with kid gloves because he could and did get in to see Secretary of the Navy John L. Sullivan. With 20–20 hindsight, Dennis should have been assigned to Community Relations where he could work with the NAACP and other black oriented organizations and been an asset to the public information effort.

"The Secretary of the Navy had a 'cruise program' in which influential civilians were invited to *cruise* with the Navy to learn more about the sea service and the people who run it. The annual summer midshipmen training cruise in which Naval Academy and Naval Reserve Officer Training Corps midshipmen spent about six weeks in fleet ships learning the trade is an excellent time to embark civilian guests. Dennis recommended that the Secretary include some black guests. As a result the 1949 Midshipmen Training Cruise had a manifest of twelve civilians to be embarked on the battle-ship, USS *Missouri,* three of whom were black, two newspaper editors, Julius Harper, *Chicago Defender,* Bernard Young, *Nashville Journal and Guide,* and James C. Evans, Deputy Assistant Secretary of Defense for Minority Affairs. [White editors and university dignitaries filled out the roster.] For obvious reasons, Dennis was not designated to be the escort officer but he appar-ently recommended me for the duty.

"I was excited about being aboard *Missouri* on the fourth anniversary of the Japanese surrender ceremony. My introduction to Rear Admiral Allen E. Smith, Commander Battleship Cruiser Command, Atlantic Fleet was an extraordinary event. To begin with, Admiral Smith was not pleased with hav-ing an ensign assigned as escort officer and PIO for the Midshipman cruise. He said he deserved at least a lieutenant commander. Smith was also beset with the problem of having blacks (Negroes) aboard *Missouri* for the cruise. He lectured on the possibility of a mutiny, a revolt in the ship's wardroom because it was carrying three blacks, even though two were newspaper edi-tors and the third an official from the Defense Department.

"Smith's chief of staff, Captain Ferdenall Mendenhall, was adamant that a mutiny would occur if the "niggers" were allowed on the cruise and were assigned quarters in the same spaces as officers of the Navy. Typical of field commands, Admiral Smith and Captain Mendenhall thought that those in the ivory towers in Washington were not in sync with the real world and were forcing the fleet to solve the social problems of the nation.

"As it turned out, we could not have asked for three better guests than the three blacks. They were gentlemen befitting their professional positions, knowledgeable in their fields and intelligent. Julius Harper was an excellent raconteur and had a story or joke to tell for any and all occasions. By the time the cruise was over, he was regaling the wardroom at each evening meal with his stories. There was no mutiny."

Subsequently, Thompson drew an administrative post aboard the aircraft carrier *Midway.* He believes that word of his role as an escort for the black visitors aboard the battleship spread through the network of African Amer-ican sailors because a number of them sought him out for counsel. "Al-though I was not prepared for the task, I did the best I could. Most of the complaints had to do with assignments and promotion opportunities. I gave an inordinate amount of time to helping them in proportion with their num-bers in the entire crew but I thought it was the thing to do. My immediate boss was the Executive Officer who hailed from South Carolina and a strong advocate of segregation. His successor was much more open minded and we seem to have accomplished more although the Navy itself did not seem to be organized to enforce the policies announced and implemented by President Truman."

Still there were at least small signs of change. Burt Shepherd, son of a Kansas City newspaperman and a secretary at a B-25 assembly plant, grew up in a city that was racially diverse but separated as much by class as color. "I recall few blacks or other minorities in our high school. I believe they attended [a different one]. I did not notice any problems of discrimination from teachers, coaches or other students. I was too busy trying to 'make the grade,' 'keep up,' and 'grow up' to notice any discrimination except that directed toward me because we were poorer than most of my class. The races came together at packing and assembly plants to work their shifts and then went home to whatever community homes they were able to afford. The feeling that 'they' (whoever 'they' might be) were out to get 'my job' was the most important issue. In a community of mostly whites, the black person was more easily identified as 'they.'"

As an eighteen year old facing the draft in 1945, Shepherd, who always dreamed of flying, enlisted in the navy. Because he had some junior college background he qualified for flight training. Before he ever sat in the cockpit of a plane, however, he endured life as an apprentice seaman at Great Lakes where he cleaned planes, hangars, and barracks. "It was evident there was segregation in the Navy. Blacks and Filipinos served only as stewards in the galley and officer's mess. I was naive enough to believe that this was an improvement from other possible employment for 'them.' I assumed that if they had the education and motivation they could also compete in other fields. I was so busy trying to succeed in my very demanding flying arena that the racial issue seldom entered my consciousness. The priority was to get my wings, fly with the fleet and get promoted."

Shepherd met his first black equal while a student flier. Jesse Brown, the first of his race to enter the program for naval pilots, was still learning the skills at the same time as Shepherd. "[Jesse] got his wings a few months before I did and we were stationed together at the Quonset Point Naval Air Station in Rhode Island, in 1949–50. He was in a different squadron but we lived in the same B.O.Q. We roomed together on at least one deployment aboard ship. I admired Jesse because he was, seemingly, able to survive with grace the routine scrutiny of a junior officer coupled with the massive attention accorded "the first." He was a good friend, a pleasant companion and just one of the guys. He flew the latest fighter aircraft, the FHF Bearcat off small deck carriers along with others so qualified. He did everything everyone else did and he was black.

"I knew that then and I saw him as a fellow achiever and a shipmate and a friend. I saw him as an individual—not as 'one of the blacks.' There were some who resented his presence among what they felt was an elite corps. These 'aginers' were a small minority, in my view, who made more noise than their numbers warranted. I believe Jesse and others who had the requisite education and physical skills to fly, got a fair shake in their training. Those who did not measure up, whatever their background, did not succeed."

Emmett H. Tidd, another young naval officer during the transition years, while growing up in Palestine, Texas, remembers a black nannie supported and retained as part of the family by his grandparents in her old age. "She was loved by all of us for the care and love she had given so generously to all of us." Well into the 1930s, his family operated a general store. "Many of their regular customers were black to whom they extended credit during bad crop years and especially during the depression. They lost a lot of money doing this, but the black community knew of their trust and generosity.

"The segregation was typical in Texas for that era. I never remember any violence. I learned the 'N' word early but I never liked to use it. I had an inherent feeling it was an offensive, unnecessary word. Why? Probably by the demeaning and mean tone with which it was used. It just seemed like one of those 'bad words' that we were taught not to use. My grandparents treated everyone with respect and kindness. That word just did not sound kind and respectful. We referred to them as 'colored' and I was comfortable with it, because our black friends used it. Later, in grade school and junior high in Tyler, Texas, with segregation in schools, restrooms and busses, I had less contact with minorities. I accepted segregation as 'normal.'"

The family moved to Oklahoma City where the separation of races continued. At the dinner table, Tidd recalls, "There was talk of discrimination but never of lynchings or violent acts. But my dad had a negative attitude toward the black race in general. Maybe that is why he pointed out the 'good' blacks. There was an implication that some were not 'good.' By then I had observed that not all white kids were 'good.'

"After I was a young adult, I realized that dad was so intolerant that when my wife and I had our small children (from age 4 up) we would find reasons for not letting them spend holidays or summer visits alone with my parents. These were good, fine and gentle people but they had not progressed socially through those difficult years of integration to accept blacks as equals. It hurt me to realize this, just as it hurt my wife to realize the same thing of her own father. In that respect, they were hardly unique white citizens of their age."

Tidd attended the University of Oklahoma and enrolled in the Naval ROTC program. There were no African American students and the subject of blacks sailors never arose. When he graduated and started active duty aboard a destroyer preparing for the invasion of Japan in 1945, the only men of color occupied billets as stewards and cooks.

"I became uncomfortable with the realization that blacks and Filipinos were the only ones that had to sleep in those overflow berthing areas in the maindeck passageway, traversed by all hands going fore and aft when weather decks were closed by weather conditions or blackouts at night. These were always hot, narrow places. The bunks, hinged at the bulkhead side, had to be closed up during the day to permit traffic to pass more easily. At night the bunk occupants were often jostled, sometimes unavoidably, because of the rolling decks and limited clearance. These physical interruptions, plus the clamor of an adjacent busy galley operating most of the night, and an open engineering hatch emitting steam and fuel oil odors, made for miserable sleeping conditions. All living spaces on these World War II destroyers were over-crowded but it did not seem right that these minorities, as humans and shipmates, had to be the only ones given the worst of available berthing locations. The executive officer and other seniors passed it off as the only solution for the extra number of personnel assigned for wartime conditions. I don't believe it was ever considered that those spaces could and should be rotated periodically. I was as guilty as the seniors in accepting it."

Secretary of the Army Kenneth Royall argued that the history of black soldiers in two world wars demonstrated that they were better qualified for manual labor than combat duty. He believed that desegregation would impair national defense. Those in uniform and in command took their cue from him.

While its brothers vacillated or resisted, the air force plunged ahead with plans for complete integration of its personnel. Almost immediately upon establishment of the service as an independent duchy, a small chorus of scholars in uniform had called for change. Noel Parrish, the erstwhile white head of the Tuskegee program, while attending the Air Command and Staff College, wrote a thesis in which he said, "Any limitation on a man's equal right in the service of the nation tends to destroy the equality of his responsibilities." Lieutenant Solomon Cutcher in his paper under the aegis of the same institution dismissed the belief in white superiority, arguing that any limitations of blacks were "scientifically proven to be products of environment and not characteristic of race." Other students at the college noted that segregation was wasteful of human resources and lessened effectiveness.

Amid the confusion of the moment, Secretary of the Air Force Stuart Symington demanded that his generals proceed swiftly. A central figure was Gen. Idwal Edwards, who had been assistant chief of staff for training and organization during World War II. Edwards had represented the air corps on John McCloy's committee. Edwards recalled, "Ben Davis was a brigadier general who had a very fine reputation throughout the whole Army, and I liked the old man very much. I was quite impressed by the old man and his temperate approach to our problems and that was my first association with the Negro problem. He told me that the only place where he could get a decent meal in Washington, and he was a brigadier general in the Army, was at the Union Station, the only restaurant that would let him in."

According to Edwards, he had been commander of the air force in Germany when summoned home to become deputy chief of personnel. "I got a call from Mr. Symington and he said, 'Come down and see me.' He had a directive from the White House, from Mr. Truman, saying that the forces would be integrated. Symington said, 'Now I don't want any shopping around on this. If we're going to integrate, we're going to integrate. We are going to do it properly and we are going to do it thoroughly and there will be no more Negro units.'

"I said, 'I am completely in accord on this business.' I had been convinced for years that it should be done. It wasn't sensible to try to run two different kinds of armies or air forces or anything else." Edwards added, "I was convinced of the justice of the thing. It was a sound decision, the right decision [but] I was not evangelical about it."

Edwards, looking back almost twenty-five years later remembered no opposition within the air force brass but Jack Marr on Edwards's staff in the Pentagon reported an almost cloak-and-dagger operation in order to get the integration plan accepted. Marr had done a study of what would be involved even before Truman issued his call for equal opportunity. "General Edwards approved it [the study]. Then it was held in my safe for several months because General Edwards was waiting for Gen. Fairchild [air force chief of staff Gen. Hoyt S. Vandenberg's deputy] to go on leave so he could take the paper to Gen. Vandenberg, because all these things had to go through Gen. Vandenberg. I suspect that they [Edwards and Fairchild] had talked it over and that Fairchild told Edwards that he could not approve of this, and that he would go on leave and then General Edwards was to bring the subject up and Vandenberg probably would approve it.

"The next thing that happened Vandenberg gave it to Symington and then it had to go through the Secretary of Defense Personnel Policy Board. This consisted of the Secretary of each service plus his personnel man. All personnel policy—Army, Navy and Air Force—had to be pretty much alike. When this paper was presented . . . Kenneth Royall hit the ceiling. He said we, the Army could never go along with anything like this, that it would never go along as long as he was Secretary of the Army. It was brought up more than once, and somebody told me that in one of those meetings, Symington was sufficiently disturbed so that he called Royall stupid. It was not ordinarily the way Secretaries get along.

"Our action leading towards integration was stopped completely. We couldn't do it until it was approved by the Secretary of Defense Personnel Policy Board. I suspect, and this is pure speculation on my part, that Stuart Symington was from Missouri, Harry Truman was from Missouri, and Stu

Symington went to Harry Truman and said, 'Look, if you will put out an executive order, if the Navy and the Air Force are ready to act, then the Army will have to act."

Marr recalled that the first drafts of the proposal contained a paragraph which allowed commanders to segregate their barracks. "Gen. Edwards and I took it out. It was put in to satisfy Gen. Fairchild and we never expected that particular statement to remain. When you write a regulation you have to go around the halls and get coordination on it. You visit a whole bunch of people and unless everyone concurs you are in tough shape. We slipped that in there to get concurrence."

The director of military personnel, the officer charged with seeing that any orders issued by Edwards were executed, was Gen. Dean C. Strother, who had denigrated the role of the 332d in Italy. Strother, according to a colleague regaled companions "with the funniest stories in the world about the 332d." Marr remembered Strother as against the plan from the start. Marr adds, "I mentioned this would never get any place if I had to trot up and down the halls getting coordination on it, because there were enough people already who had surfaced and had heard about it, and were voicing their opposition. General Edwards said, 'Leave the coordination to me,' which meant that it was never coordinated throughout the air staff. It went directly from Edwards up. General Strother stopped me in the hall one day and told me to be sure he coordinated on this. I knew then that he was intending to block it, so I took General Edwards at his word not to coordinate with anybody.

"I never heard General Strother used the word 'Negro' or 'colored person.' It was always 'ape,' or 'coon,' or 'eightball,' or some other such expression when he referred to a colored person. And the discussion I had with him on the subject led me to believe that the study would never get any place as long as he was in the personnel business."

According to Edwards's long-term memory, there was little Sturm und Drang. "We put out orders of course but the only direct personnel contact that I had was with Ben Davis's [Jr.] group which was at Lockbourne Air Force Base at the time. I found Davis very, very serious about the thing, but also trying to avoid any trouble. It worked very nicely. None of the people in my office, as far as expressing themselves to me, showed any antagonism to integration."

Edwards recalled his superior, air force chief of staff, Gen. Hoyt S. Vandenberg as having "no leanings one way or the other. He was not enthusiastic about it, but he was not averse to it." According to Alan Gropman in *The Air Force Integrates, 1945–1964,* Vandenberg, immediately after World War II, had denigrated blacks as lacking in intelligence and leadership, making them undesirable candidates to train as officers or technicians. But in 1949

Vandenberg understood political realities and may well have been more concerned with building an organization capable of meeting the perceived threat of the Soviet Union rather than a much lesser issue of separation of the races.

Whatever Vandenberg's views were previously, he impressed Chappie James with his desire to see that integration occurred smoothly. "I had a variety show called *Operation Happiness*. I led a group of USAF entertainers, a great band, singers and dancers with a lot of talent. I was appearing at Mitchell Field [New York] and when we finished we flew on a C-54 from there to Washington. I rode with [Vandenberg] to Washington. He talked to me on the order of 'What do you think of the plans we have for integrating the Services.' We talked generally and when he walked off the plane, he came back to shake my hand. I never will forget that. Not just that gesture, but how really interested he was. There were other military leaders who obviously were not interested in the conversation at all. They couldn't care less." To James, that a four-star general would ask the views of a humble first lieutenant, indicated a touch of "soul."

For the most part, top white officers understood, just as Ben Davis Sr. had, that whatever their personal inclinations, military discipline obliged them to follow orders. During the first year after the air force introduced its integration policy, the Strategic Air Command's Eighth Air Force maintained segregation in the barracks. SAC boss Gen. Curtis LeMay, who after retirement ran as the vice-president on a ticket headed by the then-avowed segregationist George Wallace, summarily commanded the Eighth Air Force head to take immediate steps "to billet and mess Negro troops with the white units . . ." When Edwards heard that a white officer at Maxwell Field made a fuss about a black officer at the officers' club, he reminded everyone involved of the new policy.

Marr notes, "The major commanders were given to understand in no uncertain terms that this policy was to be implemented immediately, without any dragging of feet. The attitude of General Edwards was expressed at the bottom of one of the letters that I prepared where he added a sentence that read, 'Failure to implement this policy will be considered a failure of command.' This caused each major commander to realize that his job was in jeopardy."

Like Edwards, Marr insists that the steps taken were not due to pressure from blacks or whites. "Our action was taken to try to give the public more Air Force for their money, and there was no doubt that having a white Air Force and a separate small black Air Force was not the most efficient way." From his study of earlier troubles like those at Selfridge, Godman, and Freeman Fields, Marr recognized that the root cause lay in separation of the races. "We have no history of any sort of a riot where our people were working together in an integrated situation. All of the riot information that we had was in our highly segregated situations."

The decision to fully integrate the air force spelled the end for the 332d Fighter Group and a number of its members opposed the changes. Screening boards were created to review qualifications of those who would be reassigned. Ben Davis Jr. wrote, "Many blacks at Lockbourne were angered by the mere existence of screening boards, and I sympathized with them. Considering the far greater good of discontinuing the existing system and integrating, however, I thought the critical initial stages of the program warranted caution." Davis tempered his endorsement with the comment, ". . . the Air Force wanted the board to recommend reassignment to white units only when the individual is first, of such temperament, judgment, and common sense that he can get along smoothly . . . in a white unit, and secondly that his ability is such as to warrant respect of personnel of the unit to which he is transferred." Davis was bothered that personality counted for more than ability but said he accepted the need to avoid incidents that might jeopardize the ultimate goal. Clearly, once again the onus fell on African Americans rather than whites who faced no discharge from the service if they lacked the "temperament, judgment, and common sense" to get along smoothly with those of color. On the other hand, Davis himself, as president of the board that screened members of the 332d, had a vested interest in retaining the best of his people.

Mindful that their ranks had been hit hard when the air force discharged many competent fliers because of reduction in force demands, the Tuskegee airmen speaking against the new policy did not favor separatism. But they believed they would be better served if some white fliers joined their organization rather than having themselves scattered throughout the many more white outfits. Spann Watson, who argued against a separate black air unit in 1942, was one who now plumped for retention of its descendant, albeit with an infusion of white pilots into the 332d. "It seemed to me that if we were spread throughout the Air Force it would be much easier for them to get rid of us anytime they had an excuse such as a reduction in force." Watson with a group of like-minded individuals presented their views to the Fahy Committee. "Roy Wilkins went to bat for us but Lester Granger said he was surprised to hear opposition to integration from a bunch of officers. We said integration means we're out. We're not trying to keep segregation but to make integration work. We said it would happen and it did." When the process ended, 168 officers of the 242 in the group were distributed to various air force units. Although dispersed worldwide, not a single black officer received a post that involved command over whites. Watson despaired, "We had Lewis Johnson, the Air Force gunnery champion and they sent him home."

Even hard-earned amenities vanished. According to Harry Sheppard, "When they integrated us at different places we went to the bottom of the family housing lists. There was no place for our wives and children." John Suggs, assigned as a check pilot with the 35th Fighter Group, along with his white compatriots watched anxiously as the Defense Department swung its down-sizing ax, but he survived.

Even those retained often found themselves shunted to the less prestigious duties which lessened opportunities for advancement. Harry Sheppard flew military air transportation, then with air-rescue units, and in research development projects. "I was a captain for ten years, a major for eleven more." When the air force seemed uncertain what to do with him, John Suggs filled the vacuum by attending a variety of higher education courses including one in foreign affairs at Cambridge University.

Spann Watson drew an assignment to a radar control station which he says was in dire condition. Watson shook up the outfit, transferring racists and brawlers, whites and blacks, many of whom protested loudly and in one instance solicited Alabama senator John Sparkman to intervene on their behalf. Watson held his ground; the outfit's effectiveness picked up but in the air force he gained a reputation as a troublemaker.

Integration opened up a huge opportunity for Benjamin O. Davis Jr. In the summer of 1949 he attended the Air War College, a prerequisite to advancement beyond the rank of colonel. Obviously the first of his race accepted for the course, Davis, upon graduation, moved to the Pentagon for the customary position at air force headquarters. In his new position, he supervised white officers and enlisted personnel.

For Chappie James, restructure also boosted his career. At Clark Air Force Base in the Philippines he flew with the 12th Fighter-Bomber Squadron. Many of his new associates and their wives resented the black presence. James worked hard at his job and at winning friends. His skills at practice bomb runs and gunnery persuaded the squadron executive to make him a flight leader, putting him in command of whites. His talents as an athlete and entertainer delighted and charmed some associates who began to accept him as one of the guys.

The Tuskegee airmen were veterans of the segregated service, but men who signed up after World War II had little experience before they plunged into the transition. Robert Gaylor, a white youth, born in Iowa in 1930 but raised in Indiana, was the son of a factory worker. He completed high school in 1947. After working as a stockroom clerk for about a year, Gaylor along with several close friends approached the navy, which rejected them because of no quota for the moment. Gaylor says, "We went right down the hall in the same building to the Air Corps recruiter, he said, 'Sure I'll take you tomorrow.' We joined on a whim; we had decided we wanted to get away from Mulberry, Indiana, and grow up."

Originally sent to Texas for his basic training, Gaylor "volunteered" for military police and headed for Camp Gordon, Georgia. "I rode a bus for three days across the South. It was my first exposure to segregation. I had never tasted it in Indiana. I was removed from it in the small community. I'll never forget seeing the different water fountains, the different rest rooms, the different sections in restraurants and bus stations."

Upon completion of the six-week course he returned to Lackland Air Force Base in Texas. "It was about then that they integrated the Air Force. Until then blacks went through a separate basic training, with a section of Lackland all to themselves. They had their own motor pool, their own guard-house, their own dining hall, their own PX, their own clubs. And their jobs consisted of working within their own activities. I remember we'd be out-side of our barracks on smoke break. A flight of blacks would march by. They would catch everyone's attention. First they marched very smartly, much bet-ter than we did. Man, they had a cadence and a strut about them that was very impressive. I never questioned why they were not integrated with us. It was a way of life; you accepted it; you took it for granted.

"In mid-1949, the rumor began to spread they were going to move the blacks in with the whites. Then, again in rumor fashion came word that if anyone felt because of upbringing he could not live with a black person, all they had to do was go to the orderly room and ask to be discharged. The rumor held, 'We're not going to force anyone if it goes against your grain, black or white, you can get out.'

"That rumor ended very quickly. Our commander, Capt.V. E. Griffiths Sr., who had a red mustache which twitched when he got mad, called the 70 of us in the unit together. He said, in words to this effect, 'Anyone who can-not live with a black, or does not attempt to get along with them, will be court-martialed and severely punished.' That put a stop to rumors.

"Some guy asked, 'I heard you could get out?' [Griffiths] said something like 'You'll get out, but with a dishonorable discharge.'

"In a few days they moved in. In our open-bay barracks, right across from my bed began to appear some black airmen. I must admit, there was a bit of tension, no question. On both sides, there was an adjustment, a feeling out, a getting-acquainted with. The music in the barracks changed. We had our own little single-record playing system for an old 78 rpm record. The music of the day was Tommy Dorsey, Glenn Miller, and the country and west-ern—Ernest Tubb, Hank Snow and Lefty Frizzell. Suddenly, we added Cab Calloway, Billy Eckstine, Count Basie, Dinah Washington and things we'd never heard.

"I made friends with some very quickly. I found a couple of guys who were very decent, very enjoyable to be around, to talk with and to get to know. It was an education for me because the only time I had seen a black person up until then was from a distance or at a sporting event, like the Indianapolis Clowns and the Kansas City Monarchs when Jackie Robinson played for them in 1945.

"There were some who weren't too straight, but I'd found some of the whites fitted that category. That began my education and the Air Force's into integration. It was appropriate and it needed to happen [although] it was not without problems. We had our rednecks and I can empathize with them. They had grown up in environments where segregation was very strong, mostly in the South. My buddies from Alabama, Mississippi, Georgia and the Carolinas had never tasted integration. They had difficulty accepting it. There were fights. There were [even] more arguments. There was a lot of voice raising, yelling, swearing, especially in the open-bay dorms. A lot of the fights were over the music. There were new scents in the barracks. The black men used colognes and creams on their bodies and faces we didn't use. On the softball team at Waco, we began to win more games because we inherited the talent upon integration."

According to Gaylor, the fistfights struck him as more a matter of man against man, rather than what he says later became known as a "racial incident." He remembers that at the time, while "nigger" provoked an angry response, African Americans in those days preferred "colored" to "black" which again ignited fights.

Subsequently assigned to James Connally Air Base, Gaylor found that the nearby city of Waco clung to the old pattern. "We still had separate, segregated town patrols because all the black airmen went to East Waco and all the white airmen went to downtown Waco. I became a Baylor University football fan, went to every football game and never saw a black there from 1950 to '52." Gaylor found conditions at Laredo worse. "There were no blacks there. Black airmen had to go across the river to Nuevo Laredo [Mexico] to get a haircut."

Among those present at the transition to integration in the infant air force was an enlisted man, Thomas Barnes an African American who grew up in Chester, Pennsylvania. "There was a great mix of people, Italian, Polish, Irish, black. I went to an all black elementary school but from junior high through high school it was integrated."

While a student he worked part-time at a shipyard and upon graduation continued as a steward for maintaining linens and dry stores during shakedown cruises on the first supertankers. Intent on entering the navy, Barnes fell ill the day before he was to be sworn in at Great Lakes. His hospitalization put him on a wait list for the next Navy class and when the air force recruiter said he could begin right away he enlisted.

He traveled to Lackland Air Force Base near San Antonio to start his career in the air force in mixed racial company. Barnes says, "I got the shock of my life, being picked up from the train station and trucked out to Lackland and ran into a segregated basic training. The friends that I had gone with I lost. They were on the other side of US 12, the loop that runs through Lackland. White trainees were on one side and black trainees on the other.

"The TIs [training instructor] were tough. I think these guys were selected sadists in their job [but] they were good. They gave no slack. I thought it was the most grueling, cruel situation in the world for a time. I had to wait for more blacks to come to make a flight of fifty before we could actually begin basic training. In this waiting time, which is termed casual time, hell, you can't imagine the things we were called upon to do. I planted lots of trees, and I pulled up lots of trees. I painted many rocks, and I put railroad ties in and built a few parking lots along with the others while waiting for my flight. When it finally filled up, there was great cohesiveness and a great desire to move on and get into what was later a very fruitful career.

"Since the TIs were black, we were black, there was no discrimination. All you could say was, 'This guy was the meanest bastard I ever saw.' They were sharp. They wore blue helmets with white stripes. They wore white gloves, and some of the starched, most perfectly pressed fatigue uniforms and highly polished shoes I ever saw. They could instill rhythm in a marching group. They could instill great pride."

Barnes, who had studied automotive mechanics in high school, moved on to Chanute Field's Aircraft and Engine School. "Training was mixed [for races]. I worked on P-47s and one F-80, an early jet. It had some damage, so they class 26'd it [declared it salvage] and brought it there. We learned the ejection system on the F-80. There was a lot of classroom work, a lot of academic exposure. Everything was in the old lockstep method of technical training at that time, irrespective of the capability of the students to grasp it and go ahead. It got to the point that if you were abreast of what was going on and you did your studies at night, class could get a little bit boring." Subsequently the air force adapted a method where individuals in technical fields could progress ahead of fellow students.

Upon completion of a course in hydraulics, Barnes shipped out to a replacement depot, Camp Stoneman, California. While waiting what seemed an extended period for an overseas position that matched his qualifications, Barnes whiled away time in a supply room, issuing items to those already ticketed for a foreign base. "Little did I know the reason for the delay. The effect of President Truman's integration order had taken place. Up to that point, many of the overseas assignments were to what were formerly black outfits. Things [were] kind of dissolving.

"I went to McChord Air Force Base, Washington, the 4th Troop Carrier Squadron. I went as the first black in the Squadron, which was an experience. The commander [white] was one of the finest men I ever knew. My shop chief was Roy Arquello. Roy was a staff sergeant and probably one of the sharpest hydraulic mechanics the Air Force ever had. He taught me an awful lot about the system. He is another person from my Air Force career for whom I have the highest regard."

Barnes received an assignment to Great Falls, Montana. "It was an abominable place. It was cold; it was windy. There were only two places that black personnel could go off the installation. The base itself was an abomination. The quarters were single-story, open bay, little wooden buildings covered with tar paper, no insulation, no water inside. There was a street of dirt and an outside building that was the latrine. There was a need to fire a coal-burning stove to get hot water and heat. When it snowed, the snow would come through the windows. The food was bad, the worst I have ever eaten. The little club was without ventilation and everybody smoked. You had to develop the art of looking down under the smoke layers to see. The only issue was who could drink the most beer. Cold as it was outside, it made for togetherness. The guys got together and did things mutually."

What is significant about Barnes's description of his life at the time is the absence of any racial strife during these first months of full integration within the air force.

The Fahy Committee, delighted with the Air Force plan and implementations, dispatched its white executive secretary, E. W. Kenworthy, on a tour, escorted by Jack Marr, of the service's installations for an eyewitness report on actual conditions. In the main, Kenworthy discovered a high amount of compliance of "Negroes working with whites." He observed a racial mix of instructors, students in radio repair, jet training, movies, athletic teams, and officers' and noncoms' clubs. There were a few instances where commanders refused to schedule Southern-based teams who would not play against integrated squads. In off-duty activities, however, considerable separation continued, with what he called "tacit, though incomplete and unenforced segregation" in service clubs and pools and the races tended to stick to their own color at dances.

The air force achievements influenced few civilians. Those areas that restricted access of blacks to their eating places, entertainment, and other amenities by law or by custom ignored the example of the local military.

The good faith and swift execution of the air force so impressed the Fahy Committee that it pointedly inquired of the other services what prevented them from achieving similar results. The navy, which had retained Lt. (jg) Dennis Nelson, one of the Golden Thirteen as a replacement for Lester Granger, to assist the secretary of the navy in racial matters, responded to the demands of the committee. In June 1949, the secretary of the navy, Francis P. Matthews, issued a statement of policy that spelled out basically the same regulations promulgated in the air force. The seagoing service agreed to emphasize equal opportunity to recruits, open up transfers to any available slots, and improve the status of chief stewards, giving the blacks in those posts petty-officer rating commensurate with their responsibilities. The directive also applied to the marine corps. Montford Point shut down as black leatherneck boots began to train alongside of whites and the corps even welcomed black women to its small female contingent.

The army, under Kenneth Royall, stubbornly stuck to its old guns. Louis Johnson, as secretary of defense, informed the Fahy Committee that the ground forces expected to maintain some all-black units. Johnson explained that qualified personnel would receive assignment to positions without consideration of race and not all African Americans would wind up in the black organizations. The army doggedly held out until the Fahy Committee grudgingly accepted the arrangement. Critics faulted the policy because although it spoke of assignment without regard to race or color, it did not specifically ban segregation. The committee did force the army to abandon its 10 percent quota. Gordon Gray, who succeeded Kenneth Royall in June 1949, had insisted this was the best means to ensure that the army signed up only the best black recruits. In 1950, the percentage of blacks, enlisted and drafted, hovered at slightly more than 8 percent; by April the figures ran from 22 to 25 percent. To cope with the large number of African American recruits, the army, still maintaining modified segregation, bulked up its black units until they were overstrength, while white outfits struggled with manpower shortages. At army headquarters the solution to the influx was a request for reinstatement of the quota.

While the United States Military Academy barely cracked open its doors to African Americans, in spite of recommendations from even such pro-segregationists as Ned Almond, there were signs of a slightly more civil atmosphere at West Point. Ed Howard, the child of a high school teacher of English and an attorney, passed through the Washington, D.C., segregated schools. His only interracial encounters occurred in two Soap Box Derby races dominated by whites. At Dunbar High School, Howard actively participated in the military cadet program, and while he started college at Dartmouth in 1943 he also applied to the Military Academy.

"The appointment [to the Class of 1949] came when my deferment from military service was running out and came from Congressman Dawson of Illinois. I knew several earlier graduates of Dunbar who had made it through West Point. They helped me prepare for cadet life with a good background for what could happen in an environment of segregation and discrimination.

"I don't recall any exceptional treatment by faculty. I do not remember having been singled out. There were cadets who were aloof or in avoidance demeanor. Only recently, I was told by a school mate, one year my senior about an incident he handled following new table seating for meals. A cadet one year behind me objected to being at the same table. The bottom line was he would either accept the seating or go hungry.

"Those were the days of segregated rooming arrangements. In beast barracks, the first plebe training, I roomed with the other African American who started in July 1945. We survived that part of the training together. He suffered more than I perhaps because I had the edge on posture and presenting the appearance of trying, or as was said, 'putting out.' When the academic year started, a returning African American who repeated a year because of scholastic problems was with us. At the time that meant three of us. But the cadet who began with me had academic problems [and left permanently]. When the class of 1950 arrived in 1946 there were two more A-A cadets. One was near my height and the other close to the size of my repeating classmate. Because companies were sized by height so that military formations and parades would appear uniform, I roomed with a cadet a year behind me and my classmate who was shorter, lived with the other man. The arrangement continued until the two of us in '49 graduated. But for the segregated rooming policy, I know there were classmates [white] who would have roomed with me. There had been no A-A cadets in the classes immediately senior to us, none started in 1947 and five in 1948 during our senior year.

"In contrast with the Academic Department there was an incident with an officer in the Tactical Department. At the time, plebes remained at the academy during Christmas holidays. The lieutenant colonel who was the tactical officer commented to my classmate, who as a returning plebe had more privileges, "I don't suppose that you will take a date to the hops during the holidays, will you?' Thus he suggested that he not go to dances open to plebes."

After graduation, Howard attended courses at Fort Riley, Kansas, and Fort Monmouth, becoming a specialist in signals. "Both were integrated and I don't remember segregated officer clubs. Certainly towns and eating places were limited."

Detroit native John Costa was a classmate of Howard at West Point but as a white man from one of the most racially charged cities in the North he was well aware of the hostility toward people of color. While the depression occasioned hardships on the family, the coming of World War II saw his father employed as a labor-relations specialist at Packard Motor Car Company. "He brought tales from work about his experience with the workers including blacks. He seemed to have a good relationship with them and even perhaps affection for them although his terminology for blacks and other ethnics included all the politically incorrect terms.

"As the city received and absorbed a flood of workers, black and white from the South, the racial climate changed for the worse and exploded into the bloody race riot of July 1943. My mother called her 'cleaning woman' who lived in the neighborhood where violence was rampant. She offered sanctuary, assuring her of her concern and affection. The offer was declined but it made an impression on me of the heart displayed by my mother, not only in that incident but in arguments within our extended family, aunts, uncles, grandparents, which exposed me to the latent animosity, hatred or fear in people of my own family. There was a definite division of attitudes and a lot of arguing about what was happening, and what to do about it. One of my uncles, a true Michigan redneck, was a police officer in Detroit. His deep-seated animosity towards the blacks was a shock to me as he related stories of how the 'niggers' were being taken care of.

"I had turned 18 in May, a month or so before the race riots. When I was drafted in July, the train which transported us draftees to Fort Custer was organized with a rail car filled with MPs in the middle of the train, cars with white recruits on one end of the train and cars with blacks at the other end. These experiences made a deep impression on me. I couldn't get over the fact that blacks who were so mistreated by Americans of the majority, still submitted to being called to military service and so far as I could tell were serving honorably. The feeling led me years later to join the NAACP, an organization which I viewed as dedicated to racial harmony, something I felt our country desperately needed."

Black servicemen disappeared completely from Costa's horizon as he passed through basic training in the air corps, then attended training and schools that qualified him as a navigator and second lieutenant. He applied for West Point and as the war ended, became a member of the Class of 1949. Like his prewar predecessors, John Rhoades and DeWitt Armstrong, the nonwhites were out of sight. "I had minimal contact with black cadets, although two of our classmates were black and I must have shared classroom time with one or both of them. I did not see any discrimination but I would be very surprised if it didn't occur. I don't recall any classes that dealt with handling of minorities in segregated units. We had an active social life during the cadet years, both at West Point and while on class trips to bases in the Deep South and elsewhere. I don't recall any tension because of participation of black cadets in these affairs which leads me to think they probably avoided or were strongly encouraged not to mix in." He thus confirms Ed Howard's memories.

In 1937, George J. Trivers had accepted an appointment to the Naval Academy but quit after a stay of only three weeks. His sponsor, a black congressman from Illinois, A. W. Mitchell, investigated the circumstances and said Trivers resigned because he "could not do a midshipman's work." Eight years later, Congressman Adam Clayton Powell Jr. of New York nominated Wesley Brown, a student at Howard University, to the Naval Academy.

Born in Baltimore in 1927, Brown grew up in Washington, D.C. Remembers Brown, "My mother was a presser in a laundry and then a clerk in the War Department. My father drove a truck that delivered meat and fruit to hotels and restaurants. It was a good job in the Depression because when he was finished with his deliveries, whatever food was left over weekends and which wasn't worth saving, he was able to bring home. Large numbers of people were waiting for him to return and he gave a lot of those commodities away. I recall as a youngster people would knock at the door and ask for a piece of bread. If you put butter on it, you were a hero."

Brown's widowed grandmother lived with the family in a rowhouse at Thirteenth and Q Streets. She was, like many of her generation, according to Brown, a neighborhood watcher. "They took an interest in making sure the kids were properly disciplined and raised as they should be. If you were doing something you shouldn't be, chances are someone up the street who saw you would let your grandmother know."

As a boy, Brown sold magazines, helped sort clothes for a dry cleaner, boxed, and swam at the YMCA. He knew Jim Crow, with restaurants shut to his race and observed pockets of people separated by color in the neighborhoods. Because of segregation, he rode a school bus for which his family had to pay the fares. Keenly interested in his background, "a voracious reader," he joined the Association for the Study of Negro Life and History, which published material on black personalities and history. He attended Dunbar High whose graduates provided the showcase blacks admitted to Massachusetts Institute of Technology, Radcliffe, and other prestigious colleges.

Brown started a career with the government at age fifteen, handling registered mail at the Navy Department, working the four o'clock to midnight shift five nights a week. As a Dunbar student, he enrolled in the Cadet Corps, a program originated by the Civil War soldier and historian, Christian Fleetwood. The cadets drilled in the morning from 7:30 to 9:00, which meant that twice a week Brown returned from the Navy Department after midnight and then rose at 6:00 A.M.

African American congressman William Dawson of Illinois, a friend of the Brown family, knew his colleague Adam Clayton Powell Jr. wanted to nominate a black to the Naval Academy. Powell briefly interviewed Brown and then submitted his name. Listed a third alternate from New York, Brown, like a number of black Military Academy nominees from Washington, used a fake address; in his case a vacant lot.

"I spoke to George Trivers [now a teacher in Washington] who had been at the Academy and he said he was not prepared for the hazing or the isolation, not being able to talk with anyone or get help." The chat helped prepare Brown for what he faced and he credits the confidence instilled in him at Dunbar. "If anybody's ever done it, then I can do it. If no one's ever done it, then I'm going to be the first one to do it."

The atmosphere at Annapolis was slightly more benign for Brown than that which eight years earlier buffeted Trivers. "Initially, there were two or three fellows who offered to room with me. I wasn't sure I wanted them to share my burden. I might feel I was responsible for their getting chastised or whatever." He chose to live alone but felt free to visit the other rooms and he entertained visitors in his quarters.

There were a few bigotry-driven acts. After he left for class one day, an inspecting officer found Brown's bedding and belongings strewn over the floor. It was obvious what had happened and Brown did not receive any demerits. However, he picked up 140 of a maximum of 150 demerits during his first semester, allegedly for marching out of step or talking in ranks. Occasionally an upperclassman paddled him. "I never knew whether it was because I was black or just a plebe." Years after he graduated in 1949, Brown learned that then-Comdr. John Bulkeley, an instructor in steam at the Naval Academy, had been charged by the secretary of the navy with preserving his personal, physical safety. (Bulkeley had earned a Medal of Honor for his exploits in the Pacific during World War II, which included spiriting Douglas MacArthur from Corregidor to the safety of the Philippines aboard his PT boat.)

Early in Brown's plebe year at the academy, his benefactor, Adam Clayton Powell Jr., complained to Secretary of the Navy Forrestal of a plot to dismiss his protégé through undergrading his academic work. Brown knew nothing of such efforts and after he graduated, Powell, who liked to stir the pot, admitted he fabricated the charges. Although the conspiracy was a gossamer of imagination, other nastiness was quite real. Several senior midshipmen proffered the usual insults, "What are you trying to prove?" "Who's going to want you on board ship as part of the crew or as part of the officers' mess?" "Don't you understand how people feel about this?"

Others offered friendship. "There were a number who were very supportive, protective. They would even tell me, 'Hey, watch out for this guy.' They were not just in my class, but in the senior classes." One of these, a midshipman from Louisiana, gave Brown an inkling of how Southerners felt about his presence. Brown quotes him, "I have the advantage of seeing you just about every day. I know what you're up to, and I know how things are coming. But the other guy over there who's never seen you—all he knows is you're here, and he doesn't like the idea of you being here. If I was over there, I might be the same way. I'm not going out of my way to help you do anything. I still have my prejudices; I'm under enough pressure as it is from the other guys."

Perhaps more of a revelation to Brown was his discovery of bias beyond his race. "I found out there were other kinds of prejudices that were just as irrational, against Italians, Polish , Catholics, Jews, people from certain parts of the country. I did learn that everyone from the South wasn't prejudiced and everyone from the North wasn't a raving liberal. You couldn't tell by the way a person looked or talked. You really had to get to know the person to find out whether they had one extreme or the other in mind."

Brown says that while in high school he developed the ambition to be an engineer. He focused on this area while at Annapolis and when, in 1949, he became the first of his race to complete the course at the Naval Academy, the navy assigned him to its civil engineering services. The color line at the academy had finally been broken but would not be breached again for three years until Lawrence Chambers graduated in 1953.

As part of its commitment to opening up opportunities and attracting more black recruits, the navy reached out to some of its African American alumni, including John W. Lee. Like Graham Martin a graduate of Crispus Attucks High School in Indianapolis, Lee remembers his parents telling him the local schools were actually integrated when they attended before World War I but the 1920s brought separation by race. "There were fiery crosses burned in our neighborhood but race wasn't a big deal with kids. I never heard my parents or grandparents talking too much about those things. We listened to Amos and Andy on the radio and I don't think anybody in my little world thought badly of that program. It wasn't a matter of some white guys talking like black people. It was an entertaining show. We had one theater in our neighborhood we could attend and see vaudeville and musicians."

As a student at the University of Indiana, where because of barriers to blacks in the dormitories he lived in a boarding house, Lee held a deferment until 1943. "My brother joined the Navy and gave me a copy of *The Blue Jackets' Manual* [a nautical bible for naval recruits] and it was interesting. Instead of waiting to be called up in the Army I joined the Navy. Mainly it was the matter of hot food and clean sheets versus being in the mud and eating K rations. Units of the 92d and 93d had trained at Camp Atterbury in Indiana. Those guys were pretty rough."

At boot camp, Lee was surprised to find many of his associates could not read, write, or even tell time. Because of his academic background, he became an instructor in a remedial school for the illiterates. The notice for the V-12 program, which had enabled Sam Gravely to become an ensign, drew an application from Lee. Sent first to DePauw University, Lee then graduated from midshipman school at Northwestern at the end of July 1945, with peace only a few weeks off. An officer at Northwestern had counseled him, "Learn everything we've got and then more. Forget the social information. Don't worry about the officers' club. Don't do that. Not that you can't go but that's just some advice until you really have joined the club."

Lee learned that BuPers, before dispatching him for sea duty, had sent his dossier ahead and asked the commander whether he would accept a black officer. When he reported there was no problem at his initial post. The only unpleasantness occurred with insults from a drunken officer at a restaurant. In a display of solidarity, the other navy people at the scene left with Lee. Mustered out after a year at sea, Lee entered the reserves. In 1947, under an augmentation program that converted reservists, he became the first of his race to hold a commission in the Regular Navy. According to Lee, Capt. Roland N. Smoot, director of officer personnel in BuPers, spoke frankly about his situation. Captain Smoot said to me, "Congratulations, you're going to be the Navy until somebody graduates from the Naval Academy." [Wesley Brown was then still two years from completing his studies.] Lee admits he was so naive that he had never realized that the small "n" which appeared on his orders meant Negro. However, as he discovered, "The Bureau of Naval Personnel was receiving a great deal of static because there were no commissioned black officers in the Navy." With his rank established, Lee began a full-blown career as a naval officer.

Sam Gravely, who had won a commission and sailed on the subchaser *PC-1264,* received a letter. "We are planning on increasing our training programs for blacks in the service and we plan to bring back on active duty several young black naval officers and put them in various recruiting stations. Would you be interested?"

Gravely abandoned his job as a railway mail clerk and accepted the position. "I went to Washington, D.C., and was in the main recruiting section there for two years. I sort of sold myself on the Navy during my two years of recruiting." According to Gravely he also realized that he would need to go to sea if he wanted to "make or break it," becoming a regular rather than a reservist. He spent two years as a recruiter, then eighteen months aboard the battleship *Iowa* and another two years on the *Toledo* before he achieved a Regular Navy commission. The extended time as a reservist suggests that while the navy followed the letter of the directives promoting integration, the spirit was less than willing.

Charles Bussey, the pilot with the 332d Fighter Group, had left the service and on the GI Bill earned a degree in political science. To boost his income, Bussey, now in a second marriage and the father of several children, joined the California National Guard whose nearby unit was an Engineer Combat Group. "Civilian life was full of frustration for me. The service had been filled with young men of integrity, but integrity was a quality totally lacking in the civilian populace. Military relationships were strong and meaningful. One could rely explicitly on the character and strengths of one's military associates in all matters. Not so with my civilian associates. I didn't enjoy civilian life."

Unable to find work as a teacher and desperate for work, Bussey volunteered for the police but says he was turned off by assignments to work vice in the black ghetto. In 1948, he applied to reenter the army. "Even going back into the Brown Shoe, Jim Crow Army was preferable to what I'd seen on the streets." Although he wanted to be a fighter pilot again, the army assigned him as a platoon leader with an all-black engineer unit in Kentucky. After a year and a half at Fort Campbell, he shipped out to Japan for occupation duty.

"An obvious effort was made to quarter American black troops as far from civilization as possible with as little transportation as feasible. All aspects of Jim Crow were practiced. White Americans resented blacks associating with and marrying Japanese girls. A positive effort was exerted to preclude marriages to Japanese girls. This effort came from the military and the State Department. As a result there were hundreds of half-breed babies at the end of the Korean War. Many, many men who were not allowed to marry sired kids and became casualties. The Japanese government was less than sympathetic toward those kids.

"Sure, President Truman . . . had issued an executive order in 1948 that banned segregation [the directive did not specifically eliminate it]. But the president's order was not followed, and he could not see all the way from Washington, D.C., to what continued to take place in the Far East." In Japan Bussey became restless at his duties, largely defenses of men at courts-martial. He sought a meeting with his battalion commander who, says Bussey, advised, "You don't like it? Take a jeep. Go down to Eighth Army Headquarters. Tell the G-1 to move ya. Ah didn't want you or no other nigra offisas heah in the fust place." [Blacks can also imitate dialects.]

Eighth Army Headquarters moved him to the 77th Engineer Combat Company, attached to the 24th Infantry. At the time Bussey arrived in Japan, the congressionally established African American 24th Infantry, with whites still in the top posts and some company-level commands, was part of 25th Infantry Division whose two other regiments were understaffed with whites.

Charles Bussey's comment about the inability of the president to see the condition of the American army in Japan could also have applied to the generals and their staffs at the Pentagon. Quite apart from their reluctance to implement Truman's directive or the subsequent interpretation by the Fahy Committee, those back home plotted global strategy unaware of how weak and unprepared were their forces.

Bussey describes an army convinced that atomic blasts eliminated any possibilities of war. "Training was conducted accordingly. It was slipshod and routine—not a serious or focused professional activity. . . . Perfunctory training meant an occasional spell of maneuvering at the Gotemba Training Area beneath the majesty of Mount Fujiyama. Training was not designed nor apparently intended to maintain or even create a 'fighting' Army. The night training was farcical, cold-weather operations, and counterguerrilla tactics were not only not emphasized, they were not even considered.

"Troop units were commanded by white officers almost exclusively. That proved to be the downfall of the performance of black units in Korea. The [combat readiness of] the 24th before Korea was 'piss poor,' pitiful even for a Boy Scout Troop. [The Americans were] untrained and up against the finest physical specimens in the world, plus the North Koreans had tremendous Communist indoctrination. The U.S. morale was 'pigshit.'"

"The senior officers were there essentially to get their tickets punched for promotion to higher rank or pass the time until retirement . . . A large number of lower-ranking enlisted men were products of the 1948 draft and the general intelligence level was low. They loved their fat, tomcatting life, and reenlisted in overwhelming numbers. Any U.S. private could afford to share his bed and board with a native lady. . . . The general physical condition of the troops was poor. The blacks were denied promotions on the basis white soldiers enjoyed. Moreover, many blacks knew they could not vote in their home states such as Mississippi, Georgia and others. Serious drug problems had begun to be manifested . . . Heroin and alcohol ran rampant through veins, just as venereal diseases ran rampant through the ranks. The black market was a significant factor. Many, many soldiers routinely (but illegally) supplemented their pay through transactions, which they hardly bothered to hide, on the money market."

Joe Kornegay, a child of the 1930s, whose family supported itself through seasonal labor on the North Carolina tobacco farms, says, "The town where I lived is located near military installations so I was aware of segregation in the Army before I put on a uniform. Most of the men who came home from the war could not find jobs and there were veterans in our high school classes. We'd listen to war stories and other adventures. The military needed men very badly and the draft was off so the ninth and tenth grades were targets for recruiters. Soon we had answers to all the recruitment tests floating around the school for enlistment—whom to see for any branch and guaranteed to pass the tests. They promised I would not fight a war, that I could finish high school in the military and graduate with my school class."

Kornegay accepted the premise. After only eight weeks of basic training, he boarded a train that traveled through Mississippi with the curtains shut for coaches containing blacks. "We were not allowed off the trains to buy from the concession stands. We had to ask whites, if they would do it for us." In Japan he became a member of Company C in the 24th Infantry where he observed a steady worsening of relations with the native people who, according to Kornegay, "understood the relationship between American blacks and whites."

Racial conflict simmered in the cities of Tokyo and Kobe. Jerry Johnson, a private serving with the 24th Infantry, recalls, "The 1st Cavalry wouldn't let them [blacks] in some of the clubs and fights broke out. There were two

MP companies in Tokyo, one black and one white. When a fight started, the black MPs would wait until the white MPs arrived before they broke it up. At Kobe the clubs were also segregated; blacks could go on the east side of town but not on the west."

Bradley Biggs, the former paratrooper with the Triple Nickles and then the 82d Airborne, through routine assignment overseas, became Company L commander in December 1949. He remembered that the base at Gifu was quiet with few housekeeping chores for the troops. Japanese workers cleaned the barracks and handled the KP chores. The troops, bored with training exercises, frequently quit around three in the afternoon in favor of sports. Although Biggs thought morale high because of the freedom and easy life, he felt the preoccupation with venereal disease demoralized the outfit. The company with the most cases of VD carried a guidon advertising their infection. Any GI leaving the post for downtown automatically received "a penicillin cocktail."

Race discrimination, said Biggs, hampered unit effectiveness and promoted disharmony. Neither he nor one of the enlisted men's favorites, Capt. Richard Williams, although senior to whites, were considered for the top staff jobs. He recalled his battalion CO, Lt. Col. Samuel Pierce, as yearning for Europe and unhappy over serving with "these people."

Colonel Michael Halloran, known as "Screaming Mike" because he habitually shouted, had commanded the 24th from April 1947 to August 1949. Halloran led parts of the 92d Division in the early days of World War II but did not go to Italy. Most of the junior black officers considered him color-blind, perhaps paternalistic, but genuinely concerned with the welfare of the troops. If a white officer had to be in charge, they regretted losing Halloran. His successor, Col. Horton V. White, U.S. Military Academy 1923, also previously commanded black soldiers, but as Biggs and others contended, he never developed any real rapport with the men of the 24th during his time with the organization. White told Biggs that it was a shame when people crossed the line, referring to black officers with white women and vice versa. White kept a distance between himself and the soldiers at company level.

Others also reported on the dismal level of the occupation army. The 24th Infantry, which had become a dumping ground for black newcomers, suffered from a large number of poorly schooled GIs. Many possessed only a fifth-grade education, and the head of the personnel section in 1947 noted that only four enlisted men in headquarters had completed high school. One platoon sergeant could neither read nor write. A program to improve academic skills helped but peacetime service in the immediate post–World War II period fed upon the less educated. Captain Sam Adams Jr., an OCS graduate in 1942 who fought with the 84th Division in Europe during World War

II, considered the 24th Infantry, of which he became the communications officer, neither well-trained nor motivated to enter combat immediately.

White officers regarded duty with the 24th as undesireable. Houston Mc-Murray, a 1949 Military Academy graduate, when ticketed to the outfit recalls being told, "Just forget about any training you had. When you finish this assignment, you can go back to the Army." He had a classmate who upon docking at Osaka refused to serve with the regiment.

Jasper Johnson, a white officer who served as a platoon leader with the 80th Division in Europe during World War II, recalls an unwillingness to face hard truths. "I was required as company commander to make quarterly combat readiness reports. Based on a lack of equipment and the lack of speedy repair I rated my readiness as unsatisfactory. It was returned to me by battalion headquarters for an upgrade to satisfactory. I refused and predicted if an emergency happened I would be proved correct. Not just my company, but other companies proved to be in the same boat."

The 24th as well as other units depended heavily upon reserve officers. To accumulate experience that might qualify them for permanent, regular-army status, both whites and blacks opted for a program designed to rotate them through a series of different slots. Although the choreography afforded officers opportunities to acquire new skills, it sacrificed continuity in command for the enlisted men. Kornegay recalls that his unit lost 85 percent of the trained officers and enlisted personnel through rotation in May 1950.

Although the 24th in contrast to most outfits mustered a full complement under the table of organization, like all units it worked with World War II weapons and gear, much of which was damaged by wear and tear without an adequate supply of spare parts.

The 24th Infantry was the largest of the all-black outfits in the army. On a lesser scale, veterans of the 25th Infantry and some other black units manned the 3d Battalion of the 9th Division. The commander and his executive officer were whites. The 64th Heavy Tank Battalion was a black armored outfit with a white in charge. The 159th Field Artillery Battalion and Bussey's 77th Engineer Combat Company were composed of African Americans. The latter two organizations were both attached to the 24th.

In its operations, the Eighth Army allowed black lieutenants and captains to serve only at platoon and company-grade levels. Field positions starting with major and through the highest echelons belonged almost exclusively to whites. In fact, the manipulations of the service during cutbacks in personnel enabled the Eighth Army to reduce the percentage of black officers in the 24th from more than 50 percent to 40 percent.

White combat units guarding the frontiers in Japan, Okinawa, and Korea were hardly in better shape than the black ones but they were free of internal racial problems. And they had the license to remove or shuffle offi-cers and noncoms among many organizations in order to develop greater effectiveness. Aimless, unready for combat, poorly disciplined, accustomed to a soft, corrupting garrison existence, all the American forces in the Far East were an army ripe for conquest and the test would come in June 1950. For the African American GIs, the war in Korea would strike a traumatic blow and at the same time smash the official sanctions of segregation.

18
Korea

While the three branches of the armed forces attempted to sort out their racial policies with varying degrees of good faith, the matter abruptly became secondary on 25 June 1950 as the North Korean People's Army (NKPA) invaded South Korea. Although belligerent talk had ruffled the diplomatic atmosphere for weeks before the border breach, the United States was still surprised by the outbreak of war. Within two days, President Truman progressed from a policy to protect Americans and their dependents in South Korea to an authorization for the U.S. commander in the Far East, Gen. Douglas MacArthur, to unleash his air and naval power against the North Koreans. What Truman called "a police action" was ratified by the United Nations Security Council.

Unfortunately, South Korea could mount precious few assets for a defense against the well-armed, battle-hardened enemy which had fought with the Communists during the Chinese civil war. Although the South Korean forces counted 154,000 men in uniform, they were poorly trained, lacked ammunition, operated no tanks, and manned a modest amount of American 105mm howitzers backed by a few heavy mortars. The U.S. presence consisted of only 482 military advisers.

American warplanes from Japan struck at the foe while the indigenous ground forces sought to halt the aggression, but after only four days, the capital city, Seoul, fell into enemy hands. Truman signaled MacArthur to deploy American ground forces. The Far East commander dispatched the 24th Division, an understrength, substandard outfit, to meet the onrushing North Koreans. Within one week, the 24th had lost more than a quarter of its 15,965 GIs and had not halted the advance.

As part of the 25th Division, the all-black (except for white officers) 24th Infantry Regiment was ordered to the battlefields along with the division's two white regiments who packed their ranks with men from other units. The 24th itself scooped up a number of its GIs from men who labored at a variety of tasks unrelated to combat. Some of these soldiers only dimly recalled their basic training from years before. Shortly before embarking, a flurry of reassignments shifted many officers in and out of the 24th, adding to problems of confidence and smooth coordination.

"Our move to Korea," says Joe Kornegay, "was not a smooth one. Before leaving our garrison, the unit became demoralized and at times uncontrollable. There were changes in superior officers, rearrangement of enlisted personnel , new COs, platoon leaders. That made a morale problem because men did not get promotions that were due for their good work before the war, since the new platoon leaders were not familiar with one's skills and cared less. Everyone became an individual because they were strangers who had never worked together. The provost marshal, who was white, was attacked and wounded in the head when he tried to stop armed and unruly soldiers determined to see their girlfriends and children before shipping out. He also referred to the women as prostitutes, causing near riots. He apologized for that remark and allowed the women to enter the camp. We had trained as riot control troops because of the May Day demonstrations in Japan. We were assured we would have time to train the new people because we would only be guarding supplies."

The regiment and other African American units embarked for battle with one other significant handicap. Serving as MacArthur's chief of staff was Ned Almond who after World War II had pronounced blacks unfit for combat. According to historian Clay Blair, who did exhaustive research on the Korean conflict, both the Eighth Army chief, Gen. Walton Walker, and the 25th Division commander, Gen. William B. Kean also subscribed to the theory that African Americans were unreliable when under fire. These attitudes permeated the upper echelons, trickled down to subordinates, and sapped the trust of other outfits that would fight alongside of the 24th.

Because Truman used the phrase "police action," some enlisted men in the 24th naively believed their duty would consist of riot control or security at the docks. Censors and poor reporting hid news of the rout of South Korean troops and the first Americans, members of the 24th Infantry Division. Colonel Horton White, the CO of the 24th, at a meeting with his officers told them they would be in Korea only a short time and they should be sure to pack their "pinks and greens," the dress uniforms, for "a big parade."

During World War II, White had been an intelligence officer for MacArthur and never served in combat, unlike the two commanders of the other infantry regiments in the 25th Division. Furthermore, at age forty-nine, he was physically unfit for an arduous campaign in the heat, humidity, and mountainous terrain. Reality hit him shortly after the regiment reached the town of Kumchon. Charles Bussey says White told him, "I'm too old for this. I didn't realize it until this morning, but soldiering is for young-uns. Mine is all behind me. I'll do the job as required while I'm here, but I'll have to pack it in soon."

Shortly after sailing to Korea, his second in command, the white executive officer, Lt. Col. James B. Bennett, collapsed at the train depot in Kumchon and medics evacuated him as a victim of a heart attack. Bussey sneers, "He walked down . . . belly flopped onto his sleeping bag and clutched at his chest. I looked at him with sickening disgust. He made a soft place to flop on and continued with his 'heart attack.' Others also questioned the nature of Bennett's ailment, with one officer swearing that Bennett openly avowed never to enter combat with a black unit and others suggesting an emotional breakdown.

Company L under Bradley Biggs debarked in Korea without light machine guns, bazookas, automatic rifles, or mortars. Several men said their rifles did not have firing pins. Because the sharp, hard rocks at the Japanese training site ripped up the soles of their boots, a number of men tramped to war in sneakers or dress shoes. Almost immediately a shortage of rations and water led the men to sell their blankets, fuel, and other items to the local civilians in return for edibles.

Only two of the four 75mm recoilless rifles issued to Company M's heavy-weapons squad worked, and even one of those required cannibalizing a broken one. When the soldiers of the 25th Division dug in for their first night in hostile territory, the anxious troops, spooked by sounds, lights, and shadows, excessively exercised their trigger fingers. White GIs from the other regiments behaved in similar fashion.

For a week the 24th held its ground while the ROK (Republic of Korea) army gamely tried to halt the enemy, but when the NKPA overran the defenses and seized the strategic town of Yechon, Eighth Army headquarters ordered a counterattack. The assignment fell to the 24th. Military historians and participants disagree on what actually happened during the operation. According to the official U.S. Army history by Roy Appleman, there was no firefight and the NKPA fled before the Americans came within range. However, Bradley Biggs says that when the 3d Battalion of the regiment, spearheaded by Company L under Biggs marched on Yechon, it encountered opposition. He deployed three platoons to attack all abreast.

According to Biggs, "As I approached the outskirts of the town in my jeep, with a .30-caliber machine gun which my driver Pfc. Burke had scrounged and secured on a pedestal riveted to the jeep floor, we came under fire from a hut in an open field about 200 yards to our left. At the same time we came under heavy small arms fire from a large cluster of trees at the entrance to the city.

"I told Burke to stop the vehicle. I took a position behind the machine gun and laced the hut with five or six short bursts. The firing from the hut ceased. I then turned the machine gun onto the cluster of trees from which we were drawing sniper fire. I ordered Burke to move the vehicle to the left side of the road and to take cover near some huts. I ran forward to Redd's [Lt. Vincent] platoon, which was now under fire from the same cluster of trees. I could see that we had to move north faster, and not try to clean out the tree cluster. To attempt to fight through Yechon house by house, street by street, would have been wasteful and foolhardy. The best tactic was to rush down the main street of the town, driving out anything that was in our way.

"We moved out on the double, down the main street, firing at anything that fired at us. We came upon two sandbag positions, both deserted. We did not bother to search any huts or go up any side streets. Any North Koreans in the town would be sandwiched between L Company on the north end of Yechon and K Company coming behind us for the mop-up operations. There was no artillery support except for three rounds dropped on the cluster of trees from which we drew small arms fire. Midway through the attack, tank support arrived in the form of four M-24 light tanks.

"Later an official South Korean interpreter reported that citizens of the town said that the North Korean forces retreated into the hills when they saw an attack coming at them from three directions. The attack was over in about an hour. Lt. Col. Pierce drove up to my CP to tell us we had done an extremely fine job and extended congratulations. Yechon was, again, in our hands."

Black Soldier, White Army, published by the Center of Military History in 1996, describes a messy engagement. ". . . enemy mortar fire from the hills north of Yechon began to hit the road, separating Biggs' unit from the remainder of the task force . . . Pierce [Lt. Col. Samuel, 3d Battalion CO and an ROTC instructor throughout World War II] replied by ordering his own mortars and artillery to silence the enemy's weapons. The mortarmen . . . responded almost at once, but the artillery had difficulty moving into position because the road was jammed with the infantry's vehicles. In the end, the artillery commander cleared the way only by instructing his men to push many of the vehicles into surrounding rice paddies. Once the artillery was in position in a dry, sandy riverbed about three thousand yards behind Biggs and prepared to fire, Pierce added to the confusion by questioning the commands the unit's officers were issuing . . . Pierce relented and apologized but the episode sat poorly nonetheless . . . Company K advanced, checking the huts in the small villages and wounded one of the unit's platoon leaders. Even so, part of Captain [Thurston] Johnson's force [Company I] moved on ahead and managed to enter Yechon."

During the assault, Charles Bussey, as commander of the 77th Engineer Combat Company, and his jeep driver drove toward the battleground with mail for one of his platoons. Bussey says, "My jeep was prepared for combat. A .30-caliber machine gun was mounted on a post on the right side, immediately in front of my leg. I kept a Browning automatic rifle close at hand in the back seat for use if we had to leave the vehicle to fight." About a mile from Yechon his jeep stalled behind a line of vehicles halted on a narrow levee. "Hell was breaking loose in the town up ahead at the end of the levee. I asked a sergeant where the 77th Engineers were, and he replied, 'They're spearheading the attack, sir.'"

Bussey writes that he became fearful of an attack on the rear of the column, which because of the scant width of the levee would be unable to turn to face a firefight. He climbed a nearby hill and examined the terrain with binoculars. "About a kilometer to the north I noticed a large body of men coming out of a defile and heading toward the rear of our vehicle column. I scuffled down the hill, commandeered a dozen of the lollygagging infantry soldiers, and had them carry a .50-caliber machine gun and ground mount, plus one of their water-cooled .30-caliber machine guns, and all the ammo we could carry in two trips, up the hill. I set the guns up 100 feet apart and watched the group of white-clad men moving purposefully toward my position . . .

"The group of farmer-soldiers came ever closer and I reckoned that farmers scatter and run if you send a long burst of machine-gun fire over their heads, but soldiers flatten out like quail and await orders or signals from their leader . . . I sent a burst from the .50-machine gun dangerously close above the heads of the approaching group, which was moving in a loose, hustling, route-step, doubletime column astride the levees in the gigantic mire of the rice paddies. True to the form of soldiers, they flattened into the paddy as the bullets flew past them. A whistle was sounded and an arm raised to signal a movement . . . My next burst was not just dangerously close. The signalman and those close to him were broken up like rag dolls in the mouths of bulldogs. The .30-caliber machine gun joined in. Bullets raked and chewed them up mercilessly.

"The advancing column was under tight observation from somewhere on the mountain because large mortar rounds started barking at us like a giant dog—long, then short, then overhead. I was nicked by a fragment. The gunner on the .30-caliber was hit badly and his assistant killed. The enemy mortar was accurate. The shells were bursting about twenty to forty feet overhead, showering us with shell fragments. And we were now drawing small-arms fire from the rice paddies below.

"I was locked in and totally committed, but at intervals I wished I was almost any place else. I was hunkered over that gun. My assistant gunner was damned good and I chopped the North Korean troops to pieces. I called to the sergeant to bring up a lot more ammunition but he was cowering behind the trucks and pretended not to hear me. I still had ammunition and I continued to depress the trigger, systematically sawing down the levees and turning the area into a bloody mire."

Because the weapon overheated, Bussey says he moved over to the .30-caliber machine gun where he pushed the dead assistant's body away. "The young gunner was paralyzed, hunkered in his place, struck dumb and rigid by the events around him. I kicked him hard, twice, three, four times, until the glare left his eyes. I moved him over to the assistant gunner's place.

"'Feed it,' I told him and he did. . . . I continued firing. I fired bursts of two rounds, of three rounds and sometimes of four rounds . . . It seemed like eternity plus eleven days, whereas it was only a few minutes . . . Finally there was no more movement, and the carnage ceased. There was nothing left to kill."

His wound bandaged, Bussey rounded up "lollygaggers and stragglers." He handed them a bandolier of ammunition as they advanced to where a few of the badly wounded enemy lay. "There was no doctor or hospital within thirty miles. I saw indescribable pain and misery in the rice paddy. With great pity and sorrow for the enemy and myself, I did the merciful and the only human thing that I could; we shot the nearly dead." Bussey says he and his companions counted 258 dead and arranged for a bulldozer to bury them in mass graves.

A day after the Americans occupied the town, Associated Press reporter Tom Lambert filed a story that described a firefight to drive out the North Koreans and said it was "the first sizable American ground victory in the Korean War." Even if the conquest of Yechon were a minor triumph it would seem that Eighth Army Headquarters and the Far East Command might have celebrated the event. However, overshadowing the success was the news that to the west, enemy soldiers overran white infantrymen of the 24th Division and among the missing in action was the outfit's leader, Maj. Gen. William F. Dean, who incautiously ventured into territory controlled by the NKPA. The defeat and loss of a member of the military establishment either disturbed the MacArthur staff so much it failed to recognize the work of the black regiment or perhaps no one was inclined to credit them. Charles Bussey received a Silver Star from the 25th Division CO, Gen. William Kean, who reportedly remarked that the medal was a "down payment" on a higher award.

The events around Yechon became the subject of heated controversy. As much as anything the uproar sounds a cautionary note for all readers of military history. Both official and popular descriptions depend upon the retelling of eyewitnesses—people caught up in the hurly-burly of deadly exchanges—and whose viewpoints may be distorted by self-interest or flaws of memory. The recorders of history bring their own biases; they choose whom to interview and whom to believe. Often the officer responsible for the after-action report or the combat narrative took no part in the action, may have gotten his information from the first available soldiers, and colored the information with his own preconceptions. Although the variations in observations may be influenced by prejudice, discrepancies in reports also may be due to the separation of units over several miles of mountainous terrain where soldiers often hardly know what is happening to men in other platoons, to say nothing of other companies and battalions. The complaint about Appleman's coverage of the 24th Infantry is that he relied on senior and staff officers, white men, the likes of Almond, Walker, and Kean, all of whom harbored prejudices against African Americans. However meticulous Appleman was in accumulating information, he, like most military historians, appears not to have tapped the men who did the fighting. In the case of the 24th Infantry they happened to be largely African Americans.

David Carlisle, a black 1950 graduate of the U.S. Military Academy, recalls walking by a newsstand while on graduation leave and noting a heading, NEGRO TROOPS SCORE FIRST KOREAN WAR VICTORY AT YECHON. Little more than a month later, Carlisle joined the 77th Engineer Combat Company under Bussey. In 1975, Carlisle and Bussey sought to correct the errors of Appleman. They collected interviews and researched other information that related to the Yechon story. Although Appleman had remarked, "Whether there were North Koreans in the town on 20 July is something of a question." Carlisle noted the casualty lists reported two Americans killed and eleven wounded, which certainly indicates a malevolent enemy presence. According to Carlisle, some soldiers from the 77th told others that their CO had "killed half of the North Korean Army."

On hearing of the exploit, says Carlisle, 1st Sgt. Roscoe C. Dudley, "Investigated his soldiers' reports thoroughly." On the basis of their statements he prepared a formal recommendation for the award of a Medal of Honor to Bussey. In accord with the rules for the nomination, he secured sworn corroboration from two eyewitnesses. Carlisle located Dudley in 1983 and he confirmed his effort to gain recognition for Bussey. Carlisle also found one of the original eyewitnesses, LeVaughn E. Fields, who signed an affidavit that repeated his observations of having seen the first ten to fifteen enemy drop when Bussey started to fire. Additionally, Carlisle contacted a veteran from the 77th who said he operated the bulldozer that dug the mass graves for the several hundred corpses.

Despite all of Carlisle's efforts, the army's Military Awards Branch refused to grant a Medal of Honor to Bussey. But, says the retired West Pointer, "I became aware for the first time that the Office of the Chief of Military History (OCMH) had grossly misrecorded the quality of the 24th Infantry's Korean War combat performance." Carlisle was disturbed by the frequent use of such adjectives as "faltering" and "stampeding," the phrase "a tendency to panic," and harsh descriptions of behavior without acknowledgment that the 24th put in more than fourteen months of frontline duty, "longer service, virtually unrelieved, than other American regiments."

The evidence presented persuaded the OCMH to authorize a revised history of the 24th's experiences in Korea with the first original researcher, a black colonel, John A. Cash. Unlike Appleman, the researchers interviewed black as well as white GIs. Because a major question concerned Yechon, special effort went into an investigation of the events of 20–21 July 1950. Among the sources was Bussey himself who traveled with Cash and Col. Tom Ryan to Korea in an attempt to find evidence supportive of his story. Unfortunately, thirty-nine years after Yechon, Bussey could not pinpoint the mass grave site. Nor could local civilians recall anything of the incident. None of the survivors of the 24th or the 77th Engineer Combat Company were able to provide facts to prove or disprove Bussey's account.

Clay Blair's book accepts Bussey's description of the slaughter at Yechon. The OCMH text quotes Biggs on his unit's actions at the town but tersely summarizes the account from Bussey. A footnote adds that the source is the war diary of the engineers.

The facts about the Battle of Yechon were academic for the men fighting for their lives. On 28 July, a week after he entered Yechon, Bradley Biggs led a patrol that took him along some treacherous shale cliffs. The ground suddenly crumbled under his feet and he fell a considerable distance, fracturing his spine. Shrapnel from an enemy grenade added a head wound. From an aid station he traveled to Japan for several months of recuperation.

The NKPA's forces, while temporarily dislodged from Yechon, attacking from the west and northwest battered both ROK and U.S. troops, overwhelming three battalions from the newly arrived 1st Cavalry. In the vicinity of Sangju the relentless attacks engaged the entire 25th Division, undermined by the collapse of the South Korean soldiers manning the right flank. Again, the accounts of what occurred differ markedly. Appleman's book, relying on his white sources, wrote, "The tendency to panic continued in nearly all the 24th Infantry operations west of Sangju. Men left their positions and straggled to the rear. They abandoned weapons on positions. On one occasion, the 3d Battalion withdrew from a hill and left behind twelve .30-caliber and three .50-caliber machine guns, eight 60mm mortars, three 81mm mortars, four 3.5-inch rocket launchers and 102 rifles."

Roger Walden, a colleague of Biggs from the Triple Nickles, and the CO of Company F while still a lieutenant, vigorously disagrees. "On the attack to the northwest from Sangju we had been assigned a line of departure (LOD). We headed up the road in a column of companies, E Company in the lead. Long before reaching the LOD, E Company ran into an enemy roadblock. The men held up for thirty to forty minutes and the rest of the companies deployed to either side of the road to await developments. Shortly thereafter we were withdrawn to the rear, not in a state of panic— there was no panic whatsoever—to carry out a new task." Walden vigorously denies any wholesale abandonment of arms or gear.

However, several other individuals, blacks as well as whites, reported a disorderly retreat. The 2d Battalion commander, Lt. Col. William Cohoon, whose disposition of his headquarters during the attack left him out of touch, appeared to have lost control of the situation and himself. Regimental commander Horton White temporarily restored order. But instead of giving the men a breather he directed them first on a five-hour hike to new positions, and then two hours later shifted them another fifteen miles by foot and motor where the exhausted men dug in for defense. White made no attempt to replace or transfer Cohoon or those officers, white or black, who allegedly failed to provide leadership. Those who observed the regimental commander in the following critical days spoke of him as if he were losing his grip—"extremely nervous, shaky . . . at a loss of what to do"; "looked extremely old, haggard"; "He was on the verge of a nervous breakdown."

The OCMH chapter on Sangju points out that although a company in the all-white 35th Regiment fled after their South Korean compatriots vanished, their commander, Lt. Col. Henry G. Fisher, immediately procured a hot meal for them, provided new equipment, and fresh leaders to replace deficient officers and noncoms. Unlike Cohoon, Fisher also wrote up award citations for GIs who performed well. Furthermore, he immediately arranged for a brief retraining program before returning the company to the fighting. Its confidence restored, and with belief that their commander cared about their well-being the outfit subsequently performed well.

On 5 August General Kean, the division commander, relieved White and replaced him with a veteran of combat in both world wars, Col. Arthur S. Champeny. The new leader possessed energy, dedication, and sound strategic and tactical knowledge, but he immediately destroyed any hope of building goodwill with his troops. The day after he took charge he harangued members of the 3d Battalion and James L. Hicks, the correspondent from the *Baltimore Afro-American,* heard the speech. As Hicks later told a subsequent investigation of the 24th Infantry (another study that singled out black soldiers), "He got up and told them . . . that he had been in . . . Italy, and at that time had an element of the 92d Division attached to him, and he said that this was the outfit that had a reputation for running, and they ran all over Italy, and he said that his observations had proved that colored people did not make good combat soldiers, and that his job down there was to change the frightened 24th into the fighting 24th." Champeny later explained to Hicks that his remarks were intended to get the men mad enough to fight harder. He only succeeded in digging a deep pool of resentment among the black soldiers. He further antagonized his troops by having a wire enclosure constructed around a hill position to prevent them from running. A white intelligence officer, Capt. Gustav Gillert, later said Champeny's statements "appalled me and others, who had put our anatomies on the line over the previous two months and were working hard at motivation and personal leadership."

The North Koreans continued to hurl men and machines against the three Americans divisions, the 24th, 25th, and 1st Cavalry. When the 24th regrouped after falling back from Sangju, it formed a line almost ten miles in length, at least double what military manuals prescribe for a defensive position. Battalion, company, and platoon commanders shuffled through the officer deck almost constantly over the following months. Eighth Army commander Walton Walker attempted to rally his forces with a bombastic "stand or die" speech to subordinates. Not only did they regard the words as foolish but they believed an orderly pullback would enable them to set up a strong defensive line. Despite Walker's harangue, a general retreat ensued, occasionally resembling a pell-mell flight. *Black Soldier, White Army,* although noting the problem of stragglers and the inability of the 24th to maintain its positions, says, "It was thus hardly unusual for units of all races hurriedly withdrawing through rugged terrain to lose individuals or small groups who would drop back because they could not keep the pace. Later, the survivors would appear in rear areas with perfectly honest stories of being separated from their units. That shirkers would use the same excuse was of course to be expected."

In the vicinity of Haman, a platoon from Company C, led by white Lt. Leonard H. Kushner, became pinned down on a hill. Joe Kornegay regarded Kushner favorably, not only because he had a reputation for defending men in courts-martial but because, "You were either with us or you wasn't. We knew he was with us, fair. He would even shoot craps with us. There seemed to be a mix-up of orders which caused us to get caught there at Haman. Kushner got wounded. We stuck with him and eventually they got him out, strapped to a tank."

On 31 July an event rattled the entire regiment and besmirched the reputation of all African Americans in Korea. Major Horace Donaho, the white commander of the outpost line of resistance (OPLR) for the 24th Regiment at the moment, ordered 1st Lt. Leon A. Gilbert, acting commander of Company A, to return to the front with a group of his men. The purpose of an OPLR is to delay an enemy attack until establishment of the main line of resistance (MLR). Obviously, it can be a very dangerous, if vital, assignment. In this instance, Gilbert refused the direct order and according to a black enlisted man, the regimental executive officer, Col. Paul Roberts, pleaded with Gilbert, "Don't you know what they'll do to you?" Gilbert allegedly responded, "No, I'll get killed." Afforded by Horton White [still in command 31 July] an opportunity to change his mind, Gilbert remained adamant.

Gilbert was arrested and charged with desertion in the face of the enemy, a capital crime. At the time, Gilbert had been a soldier for more than ten years. A former waiter, he entered the army as a private, graduated from OCS in 1942, and served on the Italian front with the 92d Division. After Gilbert embarked for Korea with the regiment, his pregnant wife and two children remained in Japan. On the morning of 31 July, the day of the incident, he had been appointed temporary CO for Company A.

The authorities convened a general court-martial little more than three weeks after the incident with Major Donaho. Gilbert was charged with violation of the 75th Article of War, "misbehaving himself before the enemy at or near Sangju." When the trial began, the defense asked for a dismissal on the grounds of "lack of mental responsibility." The U.S. Army manual for a court-martial allowed for such a ruling if a reasonable doubt existed over whether a person was able "to distinguish right from wrong and to adhere to the right." After examining Gilbert, the three physicians reported he suffered from "anxiety reaction, acute, severe, while cognizant of right from wrong, may well have been unable to adhere to the right."

The prosecution summoned Lieutenant Colonel Roberts as its first witness and he described the accused. "He looked like a man that was in combat . . . I think anybody being shot at is a little bit jittery." Roberts did not observe any differences in the demeanor of Gilbert from other soldiers in the area. On the stand, Major Donaho and Colonel White also testified they detected nothing in Gilbert's behavior or responses to suggest that he had become unhinged. For the defense, three members of the regiment, a pair of junior officers and the platoon sergeant, said that Gilbert was not his usual self but seemed "depressed," "stunned," "confused," and barely responsive. The court's law officer denied the motion of what it labeled an "insanity" plea.

The prosecution called Donaho again and led him through the steps that preceded Gilbert's refusal to obey a direct order. The witness reported the lieutenant offered as an explanation for his action, "I cannot go back, I have a wife and two children." Roberts then explained to the court his encounters with Gilbert. The regimental exec said he explained to Gilbert the route to take and that tanks would accompany his group. Roberts admitted automatic fire from the enemy could be heard but believed "his people could go through . . . unmolested." He too remembered Gilbert mentioned his family as an explanation of why he balked but he did not quote Gilbert on his fear of being killed.

When Horton White reappeared as a witness he noted that he was the first to question Gilbert about his absence from the OPLR. "He stated that he and half of his company had come down because he was afraid that they either would be or had been cut off. I told him to get a hold of his group and get back up to the out-post line and rejoin the rest of his company." White said he then became distracted by action taking place on a hill where tanks were firing white phosphorus while some 81mm mortars blasted the foe. "About twenty minutes after I had returned to the command post, Lieutenant Gilbert came in and stated that he desired to report that he wasn't going to obey the order which I had given him." White testified he warned Gilbert that his behavior could lead to a court-martial that carried a death sentence or life imprisonment. Gilbert acknowledged he was aware of what he was doing and although White enlisted Roberts to plead with the lieutenant, Gilbert remained firm.

Under cross examination, White admitted he knew nothing of any tanks that might assist the GIs to reach the OPLR nor was he aware of the disposition of the enemy who would confront the Company A soldiers. The defense offered three witnesses, none of whom could appear in court because the dire situation of the Eighth Army required their presence in tactical operations. Two platoon lieutenants from Company A signed affidavits that described an onslaught of shot and shells upon the OPLR. Both said Gilbert advised them that he wanted to set up a roadblock. Lieutenant Albert Barnes explained the idea was "to secure the road for members of Company A who might be forced to withdraw from their positions which the enemy had partially penetrated." When Barnes attempted to set his platoon in place, however, fire from the North Koreans "dispersed and disorganized the platoon. To reassemble the platoon, it was necessary to go to the river bed at the bottom of the hill in front of the MLR . . . I was unable to do this myself as I was pinned down by enemy automatic fire." The two colleagues implied that the accused had left the OPLR for tactical reasons rather than out of fear. They credited him with being a good officer as did his former company commander.

Disaster in the field frequently encourages draconian punishments by courts-martial and this was no exception. The board convicted Gilbert and sentenced him to death. Roger Walden who at one point led Company A considered Gilbert, then a platoon leader, as very knowledgeable. He believed Gilbert was used as an example, just as during World War II, Pvt. Eddie Slovik was the sole GI executed for desertion.

Charles Bussey says he happened upon a scene involving Gilbert a few days earlier and witnessed a confrontation of White and Gilbert. "There was small arms fire coming off the hill and White said, 'Gilbert, take a squad out there and put that fire out.' Gilbert said, 'Sir, you don't want to get me killed. That's suicide. [It's] 110 in the shade and those sons of bitches are firing down on us. No. I ain't going up there.'

"And the man said, 'Let me say this one more time, Gilbert. I'm giving you a direct order. Put that fire out.' Now we're not talking about great big sheets of fire. We're talking about a couple of guys that was blinking at us. And Gilbert reiterated his position." Bussey recalls that another officer, Lt.

Ransom Holt, then led some men up the hill but the North Koreans had already left. Bussey and David Carlisle, who became his executive officer, believe the first offense was simply ignored. Bussey dismisses Gilbert as a "loudmouth" and "a poor soldier."

Word of Gilbert's behavior and the findings of the court-martial circulated throughout Korea. White soldiers talked angrily of the incident and disparaged black GIs. Said Bussey, "That was the brush that they tarred the 24th with."

In a statement recommending a reduction of sentence from death to fifty years, the surgeon general while agreeing that Gilbert was not eligible for acquittal because of not being "mentally responsible," noted that in 1945 while in Italy, Gilbert had been evacuated with a diagnosis, "Exhaustion, mild, manifested by fear, fright, instability and nervousness and was sedated because he was jumping at slight noises." Justifying clemency, the statement also noted that the convicted man's psychiatric examination after the offense in Korea reported, "Anxiety reaction, acute, severe." The same army psychiatrist, Lt. William Krause, said he observed over a fifteen-day period, approximately 200 cases with similar symptoms in enlisted men and officers.

As word of Gilbert's trial and conviction reached the United States, a number of organizations rallied to his support. The *Pittsburgh Courier* challenged the findings and the process. Civil Rights groups petitioned the army for review. Senators and Congressmen weighed in with their requests for justification of the punishment, and private citizens wrote to the authorities including President Truman. In November 1950, Truman knocked the sentence down to twenty years.

The original punishment decreed for Leon Gilbert was the most extreme, but the military tribunals dealt harshly with a number of soldiers judged derelict in their duty. Master Sergeant Peter Paulfrey Jr., a twenty-eight-year-old native of Louisiana, and a regular-army noncom, stood in the military dock accused of "wilful disobedience of lawful command of his superior officer," at Haman, Korea. He too faced the maximum authorized sentence of death for the alleged offense.

Paulfrey had entered the service in 1941 and during World War II was a member of the 96th Engineer Regiment, attached to the 32d Infantry Division in New Guinea and the Philippines. He sampled civilian life for a bare two months in 1945 before reenlisting for a full six-year term. Married, he was the father of three children.

As a sergeant in Company C, Paulfrey had been among a group of soldiers who spent several days traversing a group of hills capped by the largest one, Battle Mountain. His unit frequently came under intense fire from the enemy. Joe Kornegay, working a .30-caliber machine gun with Company C, remembers "We didn't have any food, because we were so high up. Sergeant

Paulfrey seemed to be cracking up. He'd been out of it for close to a month. We all saw he was falling apart. He was pitiful. Captain [Laurence] Corcoran, the Company Commander was not in much better shape. He wasn't an infantry man but from signals." Although Corcoran was listed as an infantry officer, he had worked mostly in communications and Kornegay insists he would make remarks such as "I know about radio but I don't know anything about leading infantry."

Kornegay, a sergeant himself, recalls that in an effort to improve their position, Lt. Donald LaBlanc announced he could lead the company to an improved position. "The guys told him he was taking us in the wrong direction. LaBlanc went ahead and then we had to get him out of an ambush after he was wounded. He got a Silver Star for that." Company C regrouped and subsequently worked its way up Battle Mountain where strong opposition pinned it down.

The version presented to the court-martial board began with the testimony of Lt. Prince A. Williams Jr., a black adjutant from the 1st Battalion, and white Maj. Eugene Carson, the battalion executive officer. Williams testified that at the time in question, Company C commander Capt. Laurence Corcoran called asking if any men from the outfit could be found and sent back up on Battle Mountain. The foxhole population for Charlie Company showed fifty-seven unaccounted for. Carson and his adjutant corralled a number of GIs from the outfit, including First Sergeant Paulfrey. When Prince Williams ordered the group to take its equipment and return to Battle Mountain, Paulfrey who had been on sick call for headaches and an inability to eat or sleep, refused to obey the orders. Carson testified to the same effect and another noncom backed up the two officers. Paulfrey's reaction, in the words of his fellow sergeant, "If I go back, I'll only be a detriment to the organization." Carson noted that physicians had marked him as fit for duty and offered Paulfrey a chance to change his mind, but Paulfrey answered, "I refuse to go back on the hill."

Both officers said they detected nothing in Paulfrey's demeanor that would suggest emotional difficulties. In his defense, Paulfrey described how three days earlier, an enemy assault penetrated deeply enough to split Company C in half, forcing a portion into the ranks of adjoining Company B. With communications lines destroyed, Corcoran, as company commander, ordered Paulfrey to take two men, make their way back to the battalion headquarters, and inform the staff of the predicament. Paulfrey said the group fought its way through the foe's positions and as instructed he reported the situation to Major Carson.

During the trial, the prosecution agreed to a pair of stipulations. The first accepted that the accused had a regiment-wide reputation "as an unusually competent and reliable first sergeant and noncommissioned officer." The second noted, ". . . in action against the enemy prior to the incident for which the accused is being tried, he functioned efficiently and capably as a first sergeant. That . . . C Company withstood two severe attacks during which time, Sergeant Paulfrey obtained reports from the platoon sergeants; relayed the orders of the company commander back to the platoons; and in all ways conducted himself creditably as a first sergeant. . . . Sergeant Paulfrey did not leave the position until ordered . . ."

Testimony revealed that on reaching battalion headquarters, he sought help for his physical and emotional symptoms. The doctors told the court they believed his complaints were real. The battalion surgeon prescribed medications, belladonna, antihistamines, and phenobarbital and agreed that if Paulfrey downed the pills indiscriminately he might well have been, as was pleaded with Leon Gilbert, aware of right and wrong but unable to "adhere to the right." A psychiatrist thought a motorcycle accident sustained while Paulfrey served in the Pacific could have caused injury that might explain the severe headaches rendering the sergeant unable to perform his duties.

Actually, Paulfrey told the court he had attempted to rejoin his outfit on Battle Hill twice. On the first occasion, he and other men were instructed to wait because their battalion was moving to new positions. He tried again a day later even though he still felt quite sick. As he started back up Battle Hill with another sergeant, James Williamson, Paulfrey testified he vomited and felt weak. According to Williamson, as they hiked up the mountain, "He [Paulfrey] fell out . . . he fell down. He passed out." Williamson recruited two men from Company C to help Paulfrey back to the aid station. That evening Paulfrey rebuffed orders for him to head back up Battle Mountain. After deliberation, the court pronounced Paulfrey guilty and sentenced him to twenty years at hard labor, and a loss of all benefits.

On Battle Mountain the situation indeed had turned desperate. Kornegay recalled that the men were determined to fight their way out, although a lieutenant from a field artillery unit attempted to usurp Corcoran's authority, urging they give up. "I said to him, I'm not going to surrender. Then this North Korean started up the hill toward us with a white flag and talked to that officer." But the Americans refused to yield. In fact, says Kornegay, as the emissary started toward his lines, a North Korean officer and several aides appeared at the top of the hill. Kornegay says, he whispered to the sergeant at his side, 'I got 'em in my peep sight. Let's get them.'" After a short burst of fire, the enemy soldiers, including the one with the truce flag, lay dead. Kornegay cut the officer's mortar boards from his uniform and carried off a briefcase with maps. The beleaguered men of Company C then shot their way back to safety with Corcoran promising medals for all of those who had remained on the hill to fight.

"Corley [Lt. Col. John then 3d Battalion CO] met us as we were coming back," says Kornegay. "He told me to give him the case with the maps. I refused. I wanted us to get credit for them and said I'd give 'em to the regimental commander. Corley told me I was insubordinate but I would not give the stuff to him. I presented the maps to Champeny. But when the story came out in the Associated Press, they left out my name."

During the period the remnants of Company C under Corcoran hunkered down on the hill, an air strike showered the area with rockets and napalm. Years later, Corcoran claimed, Carson told him that Paulfrey had reported all of them dead and the air force struck the site on the basis of this intelligence. Peculiarly, there is no mention whatsoever of Paulfrey carrying a false report to Carson in his court-martial. It is difficult to believe that if the sergeant had misled Carson the major would not have reported this to the court.

Again, civilians in public and private life petitioned for a review. Senator Russell Long and Congressman James Morrison, from Paulfrey's home state of Louisiana wrote, to the army. The NAACP filed an appeal. Paulfrey himself asked several times to return to combat but General Kean rejected his services.

Sergeant Nathaniel Reed of Company E in the 24th also faced the death penalty for his unwillingness to go back to his outfit. Reed said he had endured a series of attacks upon his outfit as it clung to a hill. According to Reed, after a firefight, he discovered that only eight GIs and four Koreans remained. Reed said he heard wounded men outside his pillbox groaning through the night. "The next morning, when I went out and looked around I saw the tops of their heads had been beaten in. I could tell somebody held them up by the fatigue jackets and beat their heads in. I was nervous and upset and the Battalion Surgeon gave me a slip and I was given a rest of two days. After I came back . . . when I would go to sleep at night, I could not stand it. When I would go to eat, it would look like I could see blood. I tried to tell my company commander I couldn't take it anymore." The charges against him were preferred by a black officer and Reed drew a fifteen-year prison term.

The severe, peremptory actions taken against perceived malingerers is partially explained by the climate of the Korean War's first months. Importuned by Eighth Army and division headquarters, desperate to halt the enemy and perhaps fearful even for their own survival, the officers of the 24th frantically sought to muster every able body. General Kean, CO of the 25th, set a tone with a letter to all units in which he directed commanders to take action to punish men guilty of misconduct before the enemy. During Paulfrey's trial the defense entered into the record a statement by the battalion surgeon, "At that time the doctors were sending all patients who were not warranted for treatment of other than actual wounds or anything that there was not a logical answer to, they were marking them all 'duty' and sending them back to the front lines." Although the evidence indicates a fair number of the junior officers who brought charges themselves were black, it is not difficult to believe that the subsequent vigorous prosecutions stemmed from upper echelon prejudices about the African American soldier and assumptions on how best to control him.

For example, Maj. Eugene Carson, the white acting battalion commander who confronted Leon Gilbert, told an inspector general shortly after the trial, "I think that when [the men of the 24th] . . . become scared they react with an animal instinct, which is to run. I am not saying that all the men are like that. Five or ten percent are not, but I am saying that there is about 85 or 90 percent that do react this way . . . These people are different in instincts."

During the period in which Gilbert, Paulfrey, Reed, and the others were accused of dereliction of duty, the units of the 24th drew mixed reviews from black and white leaders. Captain Charles Ellis, a black officer, offered a scathing critique. Ellis reported to an inquiry board in 1950, that after some shelling from what he believed were enemy tanks, "I heard quite a bit of noise on my left. I ran over . . . and it was my 3d platoon pulling out of position. The platoon leader, Lt. Wright [black] who had no previous combat experience, was leading them. I asked him where he was going. He said the enemy was attacking them in force. I knew it was a damn lie because no small arms was fired. I threatened to kill him if he did not get back in position. I fired a shot between his feet just to scare him. He went back into position. My right flank was also pulling out of position. I went down to the Korean captain who was in charge and asked him why he was pulling out of position. He said, 'Enemy coming.' I said you cannot fight them if you run. He tried to get them back in position. The South Koreans killed him and it left my second platoon with an exposed right flank. That night everyone pulled off the hill except myself and eleven men."

Ellis said he and his small cohort stuck it out on the hill against seven assaults and strafing by U.S. Air Force planes unaware that friendlies still held the turf. Yet all but one of them survived. Of those who fled, some were killed by North Korean machine-gun fire, others were hit in the back by bullets from small arms and a few were killed in U.S. minefields. The platoon lieutenant whom Ellis halted by threatening to shoot him surfaced on the casualty list with a back wound.

The Company E commander blamed much of the weakness of his company upon the quality of replacements. "I have men in my company that cannot break down a rifle. They are cooks, clerks, etc. I have had little opportunity to train them." Ellis added, "This unit as long as it operates as an all

Negro unit may or may not succeed." He added, "If you are going to maintain a complete combat Negro unit, then you should maintain adequate trained replacements." He offered his ultimate solution. "Integrate them into white units in small scale, where there would be competition. Integrate them in small proportions, that way they could get accustomed to the white and the white accustomed to the Negro. Each race has its own traits. It would be unfair to cram the traits of a white person down the throat of a Negro all at one time. Or the other way around."

GIs in his company denigrated Ellis as career-driven and so inclined to the white point of view that Cpl. Joel Ward said, "We think he had an identity crisis. Everyone had a distaste for him. He tried to show everyone up, even in Gifu [Japan]." Corporal Ward insisted, however, that the original soldiers with the company did not run away. "They wanted to prove they weren't cowards." But casualties thinned out the ranks of the trained infantrymen as well as the officers. "We were losing officers so fast that we told them to use camouflage paint or dirt to disguise themselves; do an Al Jolson."

During one of the attacks, Ward shot a replacement he saw running away. Then Ellis put a bullet between his legs when he mistakenly assumed the noncom was also fleeing. Ward had actually left his position to stop an American tank that fired on the GIs, and says he thought he would kill the lieutenant if the officer wounded him. With a BAR, Ward and several others worked their way toward the tank. The corporal saw whites manning the machine gun and convinced them they were firing at Americans. Unfortunately, a machine gun wounded Ward who then spent almost three days in a ditch before he could be evacuated.

In an interview with Clay Blair, Roger Walden as the CO of Company F rebutted the description by Roy Appleman of a 1 September attack in which the official army historian said "most of the 2d Battalion . . . fled its positions, [and was] "no longer an effective fighting force."

During the battles, the regiment suffered 500 casualties and Walden says, "The North Koreans attacked down the road and (I assume) penetrated G Company, then continued on the road to overrun the battalion CP area. My F Company *did not flee.* It never evaporated or disappeared, nor did it panic. We stayed put and engaged the enemy all night long and suffered heavy casualties. My left platoon was badly mauled . . . During the night we lost all communications with battalion headquarters.

"Previous instructions had stated that [in event of NKPA penetration] we were to move rearward to the next high ground. At daylight we did so—*on my order.* But the North Koreans were in our rear and now held that ground. Having only fifty to seventy troops with me and no communications with battalion, I figured an attack on the hill would have been disastrous. I believed it more important to move north and tell the 35th Infantry that its left flank was now exposed, we did so—again *on my order*—giving them a complete report of the North Korean penetration. On my order we then marched several miles rearward to the 25th Division CP where we manned a perimeter while the second battalion was reorganized. On about September 4, the reorganized battalion moved back into its original positions."

Buckner M. Creel III, a Virginia-bred white, descended from a military family that stretched back to the Civil War and a highly decorated combat veteran with the 77th Division on Leyte and Okinawa during World War II, took command of Company K in the 24th Infantry in mid-August. "The unit had not achieved any successes. Nor did the men of Company K have a sense of belonging. Morale was not particularly good. During the two weeks I first commanded the company, some men fell back during attacks without orders, offering one excuse after another. I made a practice to keep my executive officer in the rear to turn people around.

"When a man straggled, he traveled light—leaving much of his equipment behind, but often would take his weapon with him. They normally [fled] in ones and twos—no mass bug-out. One night I heard a whispered voice say 'TT-TL.' I was told by a soldier next to me that meant 'tam time, travel light.' He said earlier that the code-word for taking off was 'hat [tam] time.' At daybreak, most who left would be found at the bottom of the hill, waiting to be told to return. The climb back up, I suspect, may have helped to decrease the 'bugging-out.' Word had been passed that straggling would cause offenders to spend long years in prison or possibly be put to death. Eventually, when the troops found that threat was being enforced, straggling dropped off."

Creel also sought to prevent soldiers from sleeping on guard and to develop the sense of camaraderie that keeps men at their post. To keep men from dozing off, he instituted the three-man foxhole. "Once the men realized that we were all in this together and that we might not get out alive unless we worked together, sleeping on guard was not that serious a problem."

The Company K commander, who would be wounded only three weeks after he took over the outfit, praised the 159th Field Artillery Battalion, black soldiers with a mix of officers, the similarly constituted heavy mortar company, and the heavy weapons company as solid performers.

Aside from the basic complaints about the alleged inherent defects of black combat soldiers, a number of on-scene observers provide other explanations for any self-inflicted failures of the 24th. Charles Bussey whose engineer unit frequently worked alongside the outfit says, "The troops were very bitter. They felt they were stupid to risk their lives unduly because when they got home they didn't have the rewards citizenship should have provided . . . such as voting."

A frequent complaint about the 24th was the breakdown of command and control among junior officers. Another oft-repeated comment centered on the inability of the soldiers to execute basic tactical operations, a sign of inadequate training. Although many of the veterans of the 24th attribute problems to racist attitudes by junior and senior white officers, Ed Howard, the black West Point graduate and specialist in communications, a replacement with the 24th, says, "I cannot recall race related comments with battalion or regimental commanders in Korea."

The savagery of the North Koreans frightened some GIs. Joel Ward saw a captured replacement tied to a truck and tree. When the vehicle drove off it tore the rifleman's body in half. While on patrol, Pvt. Jerry Johnson said he had seen a bonfire into which the enemy threw wounded along with the dead and he and his colleagues could do nothing to interfere with the activities of a large NKPA unit. In his court-martial defense, Nathaniel Reed mentioned helpless, wounded soldiers, beaten to death. Later came reports of prisoners, shot through the head with their hands bound. The Americans, said one officer, began to retaliate in kind and the hatred he had seen among GIs fighting the Japanese during World War II now prevailed in Korea.

The triumph of the NKPA over the U.S. and South Korean forces during the first two months of the war led to an investigation of the 24th Infantry Regiment, first by the inspector general of the Far East Command and then his counterpart with the Eighth Army during August and September of 1950. Although the 24th had obviously given ground and a substantial number of men abandoned their posts or retreated against orders, the focus on the black regiment ignored the defeats absorbed by other organizations. The 24th Division's three regiments, the 19th, 21st, and 34th all wilted under the assault of the enemy. Clay Blair reports that "[General Walton] Walker believed, perhaps unfairly, that the regiment lacked a will to fight and was beyond repair." Of the 2,000 who landed at Pusan at the beginning of the war, only 184 remained. The inspector general did not conduct an investigation into why the whites of this particular regiment failed to perform adequately. Instead, some top officers were quietly relieved, the regiment deactivated and replaced with the 5th Infantry. The 19th Infantry beefed up its ranks with some 100 African Americans, volunteers or draftees from Eighth Army service organizations. According to Blair, the regimental commander, Col. Ned Moore, scattered them throughout his rifle platoons where they acquitted themselves as well if not better than their white associates. Ironically, Moore told Blair that when he first reported to General Walker for assignment, "He wanted me to take over the all-black 24th Regiment. Nobody, including me, wanted command of the 24th."

Other organizations newer to battle than the 24th also achieved less than signal success. In an early August operation, the 1st Battalion of the 5th Regiment incurred heavy losses and the two artillery battalions in support were virtually annihilated, losing all of their pieces and half their people.

The Eighth Army sweated over proposals to desegregate its forces. But in the States the weight of Truman's directive, and the subsequent demands for implementation of the Fahy Committee, affected efforts to fill the pipeline with recruits. Eli Bernheim, a paratrooper who fought in the Philippines during World War II, had retained his commission in the reserves. Called up, at considerable cost to his fledgling business, Bernheim reported to Camp Breckenridge, Kentucky, with the 101st Airborne Division. It is apparent that word of the desperate plight of the GIs in Korea had not filtered down to his new command.

"I reported to Division Hq in Class A uniform; pinks and green with my pants bloused in my boots and was promptly chewed out with the advice that the 101 was not on jump status and was strictly a training division. They assigned me to the 502d Infantry and I took my orders into the colonel's office. He was wearing his hat and reading a newspaper. I saluted and began to report when he interrupted me and asked what I did in civilian life. I said I was a business executive and he said, 'Fine, I need an executive officer and brushed past me out the door, told the adjutant to call division and tell them to assign Bernheim as a regimental executive officer. The colonel had a [desk job] during World War II, no combat experience and was totally incompetent to command anything. I as a captain on my first day of active duty since World War II was second in command of a 4,000 man regiment. There were battalion commanders who were lieutenant colonels and took a dim view of a captain telling them their messhall and area police, etc. were not up to standard. Each battalion had four companies, three all white, and one all black. I don't recall any black officers. The 101 was commanded by a major general who had no combat experience and was the most incompetent officer I ever served under or even heard of."

Eventually, a series of shifts in command dropped Bernheim without prejudice several notches lower to a battalion exec. "In the fall of 1950, Truman's order to end discrimination in the Army reached Camp Breckenridge. I was assigned to command the first integrated training company, perhaps because I was highly decorated from World War II or maybe because I was Jewish.

"Before the troops arrived from the replacement center, I was summoned to a meeting with the division command and several senior officers. I had to listen to more than an hour of all types of advice, most of it bad, after which I lost my cool and said I was going to command the company based on my experience, judgement and published training doctrine and, I hoped, without interference from senior officers and politicians. I said they could ship me overseas, send me back to my business, or even court martial me for insubordination. They let it pass and to be fair, although there were some obstacles there was little interference from higher authority.

"The Army screwed it up from the start. The troops arrived at the railhead in four sleeper cars; three each held fifty white soldiers and one car held 50 black soldiers. Someone had decided the seventy-five, twenty-five percent ratio was the correct one. Most of the blacks and whites were from the south but a few came from elsewhere.

"We assigned blacks and whites to barracks in alphabetical order. If there were any serious racial incidents I was not aware of them and very little that went on escaped me. You could sense that the blacks were afraid and tended to segregate themselves in the barracks, the chow lines, the mess hall, the PX and on pass."

"On the Friday before the start of training I was directed to march the company to the theater where the division commander stood up on the platform and had the gall to tell these men they were the future leaders of the Army and when they finished their sixteen weeks of training, most of them would be sent to specialist schools. When we returned to the company area, I had the men assembled in the messhall. I stood on a table, wearing boots, jump wings, a few rows of ribbons, captains bars and I suppose made an impressive sight. I told them everything they heard from the General was bullshit. That in sixteen weeks, ninety-nine percent would go to Korea as infantry replacements, to look around the room because in six months someone in the room would be dead because they didn't learn while they had the opportunity. I had their attention for the rest of the sixteen weeks."

Only two of Bernheim's pupils did not get orders for Korea upon completion of the course. One was a trainee whose father had considerable political clout. Bernheim refused to give the recruit any special privileges but orders from above assigned him to an intelligence school.

"We had one man who obviously had previous military experience that he was unable to conceal, but his records revealed nothing. In a conversation in my office with the 1st Sergeant present, he finally revealed he was a sergeant in the Counter Intelligence Corps and his assignment was to uncover any possible Communist influence directed towards the black soldiers. I was upset but agreed to refrain from exposing him upon his promise to go through me if he felt any incident should be reported. Nothing was ever reported and after his sixteen weeks he was the other soldier who did not get orders to Korea."

"We had a black soldier who was a total eight ball—left the Post on weekends without a pass; almost never saluted, almost always was out of uniform and so on. Everything we tried failed. The sergeants asked permission to take this man into the Supply Room and work him over. I said it was okay but no permanent marks or injuries. To my surprise, it worked and he became an acceptable soldier. Many years later, at my office, my secretary said, 'There's a Reverend——— to see you. It was him, wearing a beard and ministerial garb and seeking a contribution, which he got but only once."

Toward the end of Bernheim's term as a training instructor, an experienced veteran of the Korean War replaced the fumbling commander of the 101st. "Within days the changes were obvious. Training went from low to top priority."

At about the time that Bernheim showed up at Camp Breckenridge decked out in his paratroop finery, on 6 September, while inspecting his regiment's positions, Colonel Champeny was wounded and Lt. Col. John Corley, a highly decorated soldier from World War II and a Military Academy graduate, took command. Before Corley could have any influence upon the actions of the outfit, General Kean, sorely displeased by what he perceived as the ineffectiveness of the organization, wrote to the Eighth Army chief Walton Walker requesting that the 24th be inactivated and its personnel scattered throughout other units. "It is my opinion that the 24th Infantry has demonstrated in combat that it is untrustworthy and incapable of carrying out missions expected of any infantry unit." He heaped further insult upon the outfit with the comment that if there "are a number of individuals in the 24th Infantry who have been and are performing their duties in a creditable manner, [the efforts of that minority] have been completely nullified by the actions of the majority." Walker was hardly ready to institute so radical a solution that disbanded and integrated the army's largest unit of black GIs. Instead, Kean's letter only triggered an investigation by the Eighth Army's inspector general.

Philip Harper, who knew Corley as an instructor at West Point, had checked in with the new CO of the regiment. According to Harper, Corley warned him, "Remember, Harper, you're not leading white troops. If you're ever wounded, you're dead. These men will never bring you down off the hill." (Corley apparently ignored or was not aware of Company C black GIs whom Joe Kornegay reported stayed with their wounded white officer until he could be evacuated.)

Harper then reported to a company as a platoon leader that also placed him in charge of sixty-five South Korean recruits. By sign language, Harper managed to instruct them to dig in but he was taken aback when one of them asked him in badly broken English, "You show me how to load carbine." However disorganized and shaky the Americans, the Korean citizen soldiers, says Harper, were getting "on-the-job training in a live combat environment." He adds that in spite of their ignorance of the tools of war, not a single man withdrew to the rear during attacks that killed a number of them in their foxholes.

To revive the flagging fortunes of his new command, Corley recruited Lt. Col. Melvin R. Blair, an enlisted man who began his career with the the black

10th Cavalry Regiment during the 1930s and won a commission in 1942. Blair volunteered for Merrill's Marauders in Burma during World War II, and picked up a Distinguished Service Cross for his performance there. His record in Korea with the 24th Infantry generated considerable controversy.

According to Blair, Corley warned him of the unreliability of the 24th and their tendency to leave positions and avoid combat. Corley spoke of "tired, scared" troops with poor morale, a habit of firing weapons indiscriminately day and night. The new regimental commander said that with Blair's help they would rebuild the regiment. Under Blair, the battalion struggled to maintain its place on Battle Mountain. While bedding down with a platoon occupying a critical defensive spot, Blair and the GIs were hit by a strong night attack. A platoon sergeant, Curtis Pugh, helped Blair rally the men until they were forced to fall back. Enemy fire wounded Blair and Pugh risked his own life to rescue the battalion commander. Blair wrote Pugh up for a Distinguished Service Cross, which MacArthur pinned on the sergeant a few months later.

Blair earned favor by pushing through the paperwork that recommended Pfc. William Thompson for a Medal of Honor. Thompson had sacrificed his life, holding off an enemy force with a machine gun while his fellow soldiers escaped. Initially, the Medal of Honor had been reduced to a Silver Star but Blair personally located witnesses who attested to the soldier's valor. He resubmitted the information and Thompson became one of two African Americans in the 24th to earn the country's highest medal.

While the 24th and other outfits coped with their problems, a daring strategic stroke, the Inchon landing on the western coast of Korea 15 September, plotted by MacArthur and Almond, relieved much of the pressure. To mastermind the operations at Inchon and the offense from that beachhead, MacArthur created the X Corps, on paper a subset of the Eighth Army, but in actual practice an independent suzerainty under Ned Almond, who retained his hat as MacArthur's chief of staff. If X Corps wanted supplies or reinforcements, it had an inside track.

Already spent from the severe losses in trained soldiers and equipment, the NKPA now reeled backward. Fresh UN forces, as part of an army of 150,000, attacked across the entire Korean peninsula. Home by Christmas seemed within grasp.

19
Integration Begins

As the North Korean troops broke and retreated under the force of a three-pronged assault, the Americans outfits, including the 24th, recovered a number of their former positions. John Corley, in a story featured by the *Pittsburgh Courier,* spoke of his men as "in good formation and in good spirits." Casualties continued but the black and white GIs swept forward. What began as a measured advance swelled into a breakout. The entire 25th Division, after participating in the first days of the attack, stayed behind to deal with numerous but unorganized enemy groups composed of stragglers, guerrillas, and bypassed soldiers.

The limited operations enabled Corley to install a program designed to remedy whatever deficiencies in leadership, discipline, tactics, and weapons familiarity he felt had plagued the 24th. Part of his problem lay in a flood of replacements, more than two-thirds of the regiment's 3,663 GI enlisted complement. Former truck drivers, heavy equipment operators, cooks, engineers, and communications specialists checked in, but not many trained infantrymen. In the short time allowed, Corley complained he could not instill the necessary skills before these GIs faced fire.

Turnover also seriously diminished the effectiveness of the commissioned corps. Almost three-quarters of the rifle company officers joined the regiment after it went into battle in July. Only two of the nine rifle company commanders still on their feet in November had come with the 24th from Japan. At that, one of the pair, wounded at Sangju in July, had returned only in October. Two of the three battalion commanders also had changed and Corley was the third regimental CO.

The flow of officers in and out reached such a peak that the most cherished rule of segregation crumbled. Black officers received commands that put them over white lieutenants. At the same time, the heavy losses cost the outfit enlisted and commissioned people with Korean battle experience. One constant remained, the reputation of the 24th. Awaiting assignment in Korea, white lieutenant Adolf Voight while still in San Francisco heard a warning from a fellow officer, "Man, you don't want to go with them nigger bastards. You'll get yourself killed." Another prospective replacement remembered fears about their loyalty, given what he'd been told about inadequate training, poor education, and other deficiencies.

Voight, however, says he was pleasantly surprised to join the 3d Battalion in late September and find high morale and an absence of the predicted malingering. Others also discovered the situation much improved and the credit was attributed to the vigorous efforts of Corley.

Because it was the largest segregated outfit committed to the fighting, the 24th drew a disproportionate share of the publicity and has continued to be the major subject of discussion when historians or journalists revisit the role of blacks in the Korean War. But there were thousands of other minorities or men of color engaged in the conflict, with about 100 units bearing an asterisk on documents to designate them as African Americans.

Puerto Ricans and a smattering from the U.S. Virgin Islands staffed the 65th Infantry Regiment. When the outfit had deployed to the Mediterranean theater during World War II, the command put it to work as a service organization rather than attempting to capitalize on its infantry background. At the time of the Korean War, a West Pointer, Col. William Harris, commanded the 65th. His World War II experience had been limited to a staff position in the Mediterranean theater. When handed the assignment to lead the 65th in 1949, he says, "I was outraged at what I considered being sent to pasture for two years to command what the Pentagon brass referred to as a 'rum and Coca-Cola outfit'. . ." However, Harris grew to admire his soldiers and encouraged pride by rescinding a previous standing order from his predecessor that anyone speaking Spanish would be court-martialed. Harris fought to allow his Puerto Rican officers entrance to the Infantry School at Fort Benning as well as the Command and General Staff College. Big on discipline and field training, Harris developed a tactically sound and effective battalion.

When the 65th debarked in Korea, Almond, who knew the background of 65th during World War II, looked the outfit over, and said he "didn't have much confidence in these colored troops." Harris conceded his force included some "colored Puerto Ricans and Virgin Islanders," but protested his troops were not "colored"; "they were mostly white." Almond mated the 65th with the all-black 58th Armored Field Artillery Battalion and attached both to the 3d Infantry Division. Another minority outfit in Korea, the 64th Tank Battalion, worked with the 2d Armored Division.

The 65th remained in reserve until the advance of the NKPA forced the strategists to dispatch it on a combat mission. Almond, according to Clay Blair, prescribed a trek north and then west across the Korean peninsula. Friends of Harris warned him it was suicidal for such a relatively small number of men to engage in the expedition. Their predictions were not far off the mark as the entire battalion of foot soldiers, along with the black-manned 999th Field Artillery had to be rescued through air drops and ground support from the air force.

The color line also crumbled in previously all-white organizations greatly depleted by casualties. The 9th Infantry Regiment, a component of the 2d

Infantry Division, which attempted to ford the Naktong River on 7 September, absorbed heavy losses. Critically short of GIs, Lt. Col. Cesidio "Butch" Barberis, named to take over a battalion of the 9th in the wake of the disaster at the Naktong, says, "I was very, very low on men—less than half strength—and raised hell to get more troops. The division G-1 [responsible for personnel] called and knowing that I had previously commanded a battalion of black troops in the 25th Infantry said he had almost 200 blacks from labor units in Pusan that had served in my battalion who would transfer to the infantry if they could serve with me. I agreed. In fact, I was proud to have them. Keiser [Brig. Gen. Laurence B.] asked me if I realized what a can of worms I was opening up, to which I said, 'So what? They are good fighting men. I need men.'"

On 16 September, when the 9th Infantry had not only crossed the Naktong but developed a significant salient in the North Korean defenses, Barberis's battalion with its new black recruits, reports historian Blair, "fought well and aggressively. In the process it suffered harsh casualties." The black and white GIs overcame strongly dug-in defenders superior in numbers. The white executive William Frazier was killed and replaced by a black officer, again slating an African American over commissioned whites.

In his account of the battle in the Naktong Bulge, Blair writes "Leading his platoon with awesome courage and determination, Julius Becton was wounded in three places." Becton, a black officer from the 93d Division during World War II, received a Silver Star.

The crossing of the Naktong signaled the brief United Nations triumph over the invaders from the north. The White House, the joint chiefs, and the state and defense departments at first vacillated on just how far the forces under MacArthur should go. With a few exceptions, the policy makers encouraged the invasion of North Korea, the destruction of its Communist government. Some went so far as to suggest creating a buffer zone ten miles inside China. Foreign Minister Chou En-lai repeatedly warned that his country would not permit the conquest of its neighbor. But at a meeting with President Truman at Wake Island, MacArthur assured him the Chinese were unlikely to intervene. And if they did so, the general boasted, he possessed sufficient ground forces and air power to crush them. With a tacit signal from the authorities in Washington, whose intelligence about the strength and attitudes of the Chinese was as flawed as that of MacArthur and his chief of staff, Almond, who as one critic had noted, acted aggressively even when the situation mandated caution, the Americans pursued the foe toward the 38th Parallel, the original border that halved the Korean Peninsula.

In the waning days of October, Chinese soldiers, allegedly "volunteers," started to engage first ROK soldiers but eventually Americans. Air force reconnaissance detected massive numbers of men and equipment along the border of North Korea and China. The United Nations military high command, particularly MacArthur and Almond, discounted the presence of the Chinese, although many American allies urged caution. The offensive to the north rolled on.

By November, 118,000 soldiers of the Eighth Army girded themselves for an all-out offensive to the Yalu River bordering Manchuria and North Korea. Although the troops already shivered during wintry nights, most GIs were poorly equipped for frigid weather. They lacked clothing to protect themselves against subfreezing, even below-zero temperatures. Shortages of grenades and rounds of ammunition hampered assaults. An absence of entrenching tools compromised the ability to dig in. Not all were so poorly endowed. Reginald Sapenter, a black lieutenant, recalls that winter gear— sleeping bags, parkas, Arctic headgear, and "Mickey Mouse," or thermal boots, were issued in November. Melvin Blair as commander of the 3d Battalion likewise insists the outfit had received cold-weather items. On the other hand, Charles Bussey as CO of the 77th Engineer Combat Company says, "The 77th ECC was still dressed in summer clothing, wearing leather shoepacks." Speaking of the campaign a few weeks later he says, "My God! I had lost the equivalent of a platoon to frostbite in one night, despite the officers' and NCOs' best efforts to keep their men awake and blood circulating."

Decoyed by the skillful, hidden movement of massive numbers of the enemy, the U.N. forces marched ever deeper into hostile territory, spreading themselves thinly and abandoning any pretense at a defense in depth. Supply lines stretched for many miles, vulnerable to interdiction as they wound through the unfriendly terrain. According to Bussey, "We moved up without reconnaissance, plans or coordination. The move northward . . . resembled the great land rush into the Oklahoma territory." When the organized, hostile reaction of the Chinese was confirmed through contact and from the air, MacArthur first listed only 30,000 Chinese across the Yalu. Intelligence soon hugely enlarged the figures of the opposition to total as many as 203,000, including surviving elements of the NKPA.

On 25 November, two days after Thanksgiving, as cruel, cold winds cut through the garments of the thinly clad GIs, the Chinese—Chicoms in the vernacular of the day—sprang their trap. Hundreds of thousands of well-clothed, well-equipped, and determined soldiers fell upon the U.N. forces. The first blows slammed ROKs, the U.S. Army's 24th and 2d Divisions, and surrounded the 1st Marine Division.

The attack struck hard the 1st Battalion of the 9th Infantry, liberally sprinkled with African American replacements, and part of the 2d Division. Military historian S. L. A. Marshall credited Company B as the last unit to yield its forward ground. Lieutenant Ellison Wynn, an African American, threw rocks and canned C rations at the foe after he ran out of ammunition. Next to him, a white enlisted man swung his rifle like a club. A grenade tore a chunk of Winn's face off, but he managed to stagger back to the rear and for his valor earned a Distinguished Service Cross. He later returned to action.

For a first-hand look at the developing struggle, MacArthur flew over the battleground for seventy minutes with a P-51 escort. Although potentially vulnerable, nothing untoward happened and for this feat, the general added a Distinguished Flying Cross to his medal collection.

Everett Copeland began his combat tour in Korea with the black 73d Engineer Combat Battalion. Son of a Memphis bricklayer, Copeland grew up in an area where, while the housing was integrated, as a black youth he attended separate schools and churches. Drafted in 1945, he scorns the white officers running his rigidly segregated outfits. "White officers and NCOs were assigned duties of training blacks as punishment. The trainers rotated weekly and we never even learned their names. Most all of them were persons of low intelligence who disliked their command responsibilities."

After he completed basic training, Copeland was sent first to Italy, for a brief period with the 92d Division, and then to Wheeler Field in Hawaii where some Soviet troops, before the Cold War, were stationed as part of a Lend-Lease program. "They hardly ever socialized, except on a limited basis, primarily with blacks in sports training and sports events. I found them mostly to be very open and fun-loving. Our white commanders went to great lengths to preserve the caste system. During the period of 1945–50 practically all blacks in the Pacific Theater were used for menial labor." In this capacity, Copeland temporarily labored in the Marshall Islands during atomic-bomb tests. He had occupation duty with the 24th Infantry in Japan until honorably discharged in 1949.

As a reservist, Copeland was recalled in July 1950. "I went straight into battle in Korea, hardly any training, about thirty days from recall. "I was a replacement and had no real close attachments, so I didn't feel the stress as much as later on. Morale was rock bottom, fear of the enemy was dominant. New guys in the unit were expected to be used for the most difficult duties, longer hours on outpost without relief. The white officers didn't care, so long as they were not at risk."

Everett Copeland was with his unit in the eastern mountains of Korea. "Troops had not been issued winter clothing; we wore whatever was available. All American troops in the nearby area were utilized to cover the withdrawal through the one mountain pass. Hundreds of thousands of ROK troops and civilians poured through, day and night. People fell out of a column, lay by the road, froze and died hourly. No fires were permitted, as we were told they would give away our positions. There was no movement in our lines.

"The CO rotated half our company on the mountain pass each night while the other half remained in the village at the base of the mountain. Each morning, jeeps—two and a half ton trucks could make the climb—brought up food and supplies, took back down, wounded, dead, sick and those with frozen body parts. I remember when my patrol returned from outpost duty, a jeep with two frozen white bodies in sleeping bags lashed across the hood, another frozen body laying stiff across the lower seats. We were in the positions for two to three weeks, covering the retreat of the 6th ROK Division."

From the start atrocities marked the Korean War and the brutality, particularly of the NKPA, was well documented. The U.N. forces had responded in kind. Everett Copeland learned that war brutalizes regardless of race, creed, or color. "While I was with the 73rd Combat Engineers, the Company C commander pulled his sidearm, shot and killed a young Korean child whose only crime was retrieving garbage scraps thrown away in the company dump. Members of a tank crew during withdrawal from the village of Maji-ri when told to take a North Korean prisoner to the rear, kicked him from the tank chassis and rolled over him near Wŏnju. Soldiers of the Belgian Battalion manning a roadblock near a village on the Imjin River a short distance up river from Wŏnju [amused] themselves cutting off the ears of NKPA prisoners entrusted to their care, prior to their being taken to PW stockades. A black soldier assigned to one of the rear service units was regularly used by local ROK officials to execute civilians accused of being spies and having been removed from fleeing refugee columns."

Copeland, like others desperately trying to survive, speaks of being "caught in a meat grinder. In the attack, of the first wave, the enemy would drive captive groups of civilians before him, groups of women, children and elderly. They were driven straight into our mine fields to blow a path with their bodies right up to our double open barbwire fences.

"Those who were fortunate enough to breach the mine field were certain to die on the fences, but not before the weight of their stacked bodies collapsed the fences, allowing the enemy assault squads to fight their way into our perimeter. Once they breached our last defenses, all rifle and machine gun fire was lifted. Everyone fixed bayonets and closed with the enemy in hand-to-hand combat. Our people were working on a road for the escape route and I had a machine gun when a renegade unit, a band of North Koreans or maybe Chinese hit us. I was wounded and sent to a hospital in Japan to recover."

As part of the 25th Division, the 24th Infantry in the Kunu-ri area occupied a section not immediately challenged. But as other units in its vicinity staggered back from the impact of all-out attacks, the 24th too reeled under punishing blows of mounting intensity. The onslaught eroded command

and control as communications broke down. Company C of the 1st Battalion lost contact with headquarters and belatedly learned of orders to withdraw. Under fire, groping through the rugged terrain, Company C lost coherence with platoons and squads splitting away. Enveloped by the foe, most dropped their weapons. The Chicoms bagged four officers and 136 enlisted men as prisoners.

Joe Kornegay, who had been wounded 12 September and recently rejoined Company C, remembers the heavy assault that struck them on 27 November. An explosion of a mortar or grenade knocked him unconscious. "When I awoke, they were all gone. I was alone. Using my map-reading skills I worked my way back until I reached a white company in the 2d Division. The commander who had some new recruits didn't want me around, telling stories about how we had been wiped out. He fed me but kept me isolated."

Kornegay says that when he rejoined the 24th and reported to headquarters, Corley, with whom he'd had a run-in at Battle Mountain, wanted no part of him. "I got off on the wrong foot with him. I respected his rank but I stood up for myself like a soldier should. If I stayed in the outfit there would be trouble. I'd been listed as an MIA and I needed medical attention. I had battle fatigue, I was broken down. They gave me a paper to sign and I went to Japan to a quartermaster outfit."

A large enemy force similarly almost overran Companies E and G from the 2d Battalion of the 24th. They fought their way out, slipping off to find refuge with parts of the 9th Infantry. The latter played host, fed the survivors of the two companies, supplied them with weapons and ammunition to replace what was lost, and evacuated about 150 casualties, many of whom suffered from frostbite.

The GIs from the 24th repaid the hospitality over the next few days. The commander of the 9th Infantry informed Corley, "After the Chinese had over-run the forward elements of my 3d Battalion, they were surprised upon running into and coming under fire of your E and G Companies. As a result of their action, the Chinese onslaught for the time was halted. It was by this action that my 3d Battalion was able to hold this temporary defense line for a sufficient period of time to permit the 23d Infantry to occupy a new defense line further to the rear."

The 24th's own 3d Battalion was betrayed by either faulty communications or dereliction of duty, perhaps a combination of both. John Corley, learning that the adjacent units were pulling back, called the battalion leader Melvin Blair at his command post. As the two discussed the move, a burst of machine gun through the window sent Blair diving under the table. Those in the battalion CP scrambled to return fire. A grenade exploded, killing the sergeant major, and knocking the executive officer unconscious while an enemy burp gun riddled the clothing of Oliver Dillard, the intelligence officer.

Most of those at the command post, including Blair, fled, without bothering to convey orders for their units to retreat. Enemy attacks overwhelmed some like a Company M platoon led by Adolph Voight, where fewer than half the thirty-eight GIs, including Voight, scrambled to safety. When Corley met up with the remnants of the 3d Battalion command and Melvin Blair, he excoriated the officers, "You had the best battalion in the regiment and you went off and left them!"

Corley directed Blair, 2d Lt. Levi Hollis, recipient of a battlefield commission only a short while earlier, and Capt. Edwin W. Robertson, a white air force forward air controller to contact the hapless 3d Battalion. Robertson could then call in air strikes to stop the enemy pursuit. "Corley had not been gone more than ten minutes," remembers Robertson, "when Blair turned and said that he was going to the rear to establish his CP and that Robertson and Hollis should get word to the 3d Battalion to withdraw. Blair added that his company commanders were experienced officers and could handle the withdrawal without him."

Robertson and Hollis learned that hundreds of Chinese troops blocked the route to Blair's line companies. The air force controller summoned a spotter plane to drop a message to the GIs, informing them of the situation and advising the best route to evade the trap. Robertson says he observed an orderly withdrawal, one company covering the other, and then he turned loose the fighter aircraft awaiting the signal to strike. As the Chinese surged forward, the planes, from a South African squadron, dove and strafed. There were so many of the enemy that Robertson felt obliged to call in a wall of napalm aimed at cordoning off the main Chinese force from the Americans.

Even that tactic failed to save groups of GIs, for many of the Chicoms penetrated far enough to mingle with the fleeing Americans. Through binoculars, officers of the 24th Regiment, unable to bring their own guns to bear for fear of hitting friendly forces, watched a wild melee of rifles, pistols, clubs, and even fists as the black soldiers and their attackers fought hand to hand. Some of the Americans simply ran for their lives, throwing away their weapons and helmets. Others organized into small groups to man automatic weapons and cover the withdrawal of comrades.

Among those trapped at Kunu-ri by the rampaging volunteers out of China was Lt. Philip Harper, the West Pointer in charge of a heavy weapons platoon. "Just prior to the final assault by the Chinese," said Harper, "I told my white platoon sergeant, SFC Meyers, to move out and that I and Sgt. Cross my section leader of the 60mm mortar section would cover him. When I turned to tell Sgt. Cross to go next, he had already gone. Shortly thereafter, I was wounded by what appeared to be a concussion grenade, which resulted in my becoming confused, disoriented, and in a state of shock. About thirty yards to my front towards the enemy, I saw one of my men standing up with his hands raised above his head and when he saw me, he yelled, 'It's too late, Lieutenant.'

"I looked over my shoulder and saw approximately forty to fifty Chinese soldiers completely covered from head to foot with pieces of green foliage running in a crouch position towards us. They were armed with .45-caliber Thompson sub-machine guns and were chanting in a loud sing-song. I yelled to the soldier to 'move out' and then slowly staggered toward the rear. At that point, a black sergeant, whose name I regret to this day I do not know, was in a dry irrigation ditch and saw I was wounded, about to be overrun by the enemy. The Chinese by now had taken the American soldier to my front a prisoner and were dragging him off.

"The lead elements of the enemy assault force were only about twenty yards from me when the black sergeant who had neither a weapon nor a helmet, grabbed me by the arm and yelled, 'Come on, Lieutenant, you can make it!' The sergeant and I locked an arm around each other's waist and as though running a three-legged race, made a mad fifty yard dash to another ditch. With the adrenaline pumping harder and faster with the sound of each enemy bullet whistling past our heads, and without either of us saying a word, at a point about ten feet from the edge of the ditch, we both did a flying somersault through the air and rolled in the bottom of the ditch." In that trench Harper found fourteen men, including a white West Point officer, senior to him, but apparently so traumatized that he could not issue orders. Harper and three others who had taken shelter there slipped out the back end of the ditch while the others became captives. Again, the warning from Corley that if wounded black soldiers would never aid Harper was proven false. He was evacuated for his wounds and for him the war in Korea was over.

Reginald Sapenter, a graduate of Prairie View A & M, a black school in Texas, served as platoon leader in Company I, one of the rifle units of the 3d Battalion being led by Melvin Blair. Sapenter recalled that Thanksgiving Dinner was dished up a day early because of the scheduled attack intended to carry the regiment to the Yalu River. Company I made no contact on the first day [25 November], traveling several miles forward. The next day, the advancing companies had to be resupplied by air since there were no roads in their sector.

According to Sapenter, the next morning, after the 3d Battalion pulled back to the next ridge, they saw large numbers of Chinese soldiers to their front. The Americans in the line companies learned they were cut off. Sapenter says his instructions were to get out the best way they could, on their own.

The trio of rifle companies and some GIs from heavy weapons set up a battalion perimeter in a large rice paddy. They dug in for the night and awoke, says Sapenter, to the sight of about a thousand of the enemy on a nearby ridge. An air force plane, the one mentioned by Robertson, dropped a message instructing them to withdraw as the Chicoms moved toward them. Artillery and mortar fire pelted the enemy and an air strike dumped thousands of gallons of napalm, but the Chinese continued to advance. Fluid lines, vegetation, and the breakdown of communications conspired to dump friendly fire on the GIs.

Sapenter, his platoon, and several hundred from the hard-hit 3d Battalion escaped to a road where Levi Hollis directed 24th Infantry units to vehicles. Sapenter saw a tank close by Hollis, acting almost as a rifle, blasting single Chinese soldiers with each shell. The enemy continued to advance, but Sapenter believes many of the GIs took heart from the effort. He and his platoon briefly added their rifle power to the tank's cannonades but soon, he says, almost all of the U.S. forces from the 25th and 2d Divisions were running toward the rear. Sapenter and his men located trucks that bore them away from the foe. At a brief stop, he spotted his battalion commander Melvin Blair warming himself by a fire.

Several days elapsed before Robertson located Corley at the regimental CP. Only then could he tell him how Blair abruptly left the expedition to contact his units. According to Robertson, Corley immediately relieved Blair, listing him as a victim of battle fatigue and in need of hospital treatment.

Several months later, Blair, while recuperating from a wound in Tokyo, met with magazine writer Harold Martin. The journalist interviewed Blair for a piece on the performance of black soldiers in the war. In the 16 June 1951 *Saturday Evening Post,* Martin quoted an anonymous battalion commander—obviously Blair—"All three companies broke at once. The men fled like rabbits across the great open field, and the commander could see them fall." The text also described a scene where the battalion commander encountered a group of his black soldiers huddled around a fire and singing. When he inquired about the song, the men told him it was "the official song of the 24th Infantry," the "Bugout Boogie." The lyrics began, "When them Chinese mortars begins to thud, the old Deuce-four begin to bug."

When published, the story, "How Do Our Negro Troops Measure Up?" heaped more opprobrium upon the 24th, already tarnished, in the eyes of the white hierarchy for yet another collapse at Kunu-ri. That everyone in the path of the Chinese juggernaut, white marines, seasoned soldiers in white army units took to their heels or vehicles in varying degrees, counted for little. Only the 24th could be singled out for its distinguishing characteristic, skin color. Quoting unnamed white officers almost entirely, writer Martin focused heavily on complaints that the black soldiers would not remain in their positions, they could not be kept from falling asleep, and they were inordinately fearful at night. The only black officer interviewed spoke of low morale because of discrimination back home. Nowhere did Martin refer to racism in Korea and in fact indicated that Champeny was not antiblack. Martin softened his critique of the 24th with a conclusion that black soldiers fighting within all-white units performed on a par with their white associates. He suggested full integration in the armed forces would solve the problem of how to use African Americans in the military. That hardly mollified advocates of equality. The consequences of segregation and low expectations were not explored by Martin. The article implied that African American soldiers only succeeded under the right leadership, white men.

Years later, Blair insisted Martin put words in his mouth. The erstwhile 3d Battalion commander claimed he had never watched the enemy attack on his battalion and therefore could not have described their actions. That he was not on the scene seems indisputable. Robertson's account, buttressed by others, places Blair in no position to act as an eyewitness. Either Martin, who had a reputation as an accurate reporter (although there are several significant factual errors in the piece), or Melvin Blair made it up. Blair also denied telling the writer that he heard "Bugout Boogie" at the time of the Kunu-ri debacle, but said the ditty dated from the Battle Mountain period when Corley issued an order banning it. Some members of the 24th say they never knew of the song while other sources note that organizations like the 2d Division and 1st Cavalry used it to mock themselves.

Thomas H. Pettigrew Jr., black, a warrant officer who won a battlefield promotion, disputed Melvin Blair. In an interview with Clay Blair, he described the battalion commander as "hysterically and incoherently giving orders to defend the Command Post. Few of the battalion officers responded. Some were trying to escape on vehicles which congested the one entrance and exit." Pettigrew added that Melvin Blair and staff panicked and provided no direction. "The personnel of the 3d Battalion . . . would not have 'fled like rabbits' in the face of the onslaught, had there been leadership in the battalion command post at Kunu-ri." Pettigrew said he never heard the "Bugout Boogie" in either the battalion or regiment.

Blamed by some for much of the misfortune that befell the 3d Battalion at Kunu-ri, and supported by others, Blair defended his conduct, criticizing Corley's handling of the regiment, and charged that black accounts were part of a conspiracy to defame white officers. He denied Robertson's story and noted he was nominated for a Bronze Star for his actions during this campaign. When he closed out his military career Blair owned two DSCs, a pair of Bronze Stars, and a Purple Heart. In 1958, Blair engaged in a bizarre attempt to pull off an armed robbery of the Bing Crosby golf tournament in California. After his arrest he served fourteen months of a five-year sentence.

The marine corps, on the date the war in Korea began, counted just over 1,500 African Americans in its ranks with almost one-third, 427, consigned to the role of stewards. When the war ended, more than three years later, 14,731 blacks dressed in marine green and only 538 still served meals to officers. As part of its desegregation program, the marine corps had eliminated much of the internal reporting on the disposition and activities of black members. The absence of a paper trail detailing racial assignments, say official marine historians, makes tracking the experience of nonwhites in the Korean War difficult. A white marine lieutenant, Herbert M. Hart, wrote to his college newspaper, the *Daily Northwestern,* "It doesn't make any difference if you are white, red, black, green or turquoise to the men over here. No record is kept by color. When we receive a draft of men they are assigned by name and experience only . . . There's no way we can find out a man's color until we see him and by that time he's already in a foxhole, an integral part of his team." According to Hart, one of his leathernecks remarked, "After you've been here a while, you'll see that color doesn't make any difference." As in previous wars and those to come, when a man's life is at risk in a war, he discards his prejudices, at least temporarily.

Although a substantial portion of the minority leathernecks would eventually directly engage the enemy in battle, the initial black presence in Korea was mostly in the form of service troops. These were already in the Far East in June 1950. Among the first of the African Americans to ship to the combat zone was M.Sgt. Edgar R. Huff, a behemoth of a man, six-feet-five inches tall. When he checked in with the 1st Marine Division, Huff found he was the only one of his race in the company.

As the struggle with the NKPA and then the Chinese intensified, the trickle of blacks to marine units under fire swelled to a thick stream with men employed in all of the crafts of the combat soldier. Major General Oliver P. Smith, who commanded the 1st Division, which spearheaded the Inchon landing, later said, "I had a thousand Negroes, and we had no racial troubles. The men did whatever they were qualified to do. There were communicators, there were cooks, there were truck drivers, there were plain infantry—they did everything and they did a good job because they were integrated, and they were with good people. . . . Two of these Negroes got the Navy Cross. There was no fooling; they were real citations and there were plenty of Silver Stars and Bronze Stars. And I had no complaint on their performance of duty."

Michael Spiro, a white native of San Francisco and a graduate of Stanford University, remembers a city of ethnic enclaves rather than integrated neighborhoods. Born in 1929, Spiro says, "With the relocation of the Japanese at the outbreak of war in December 1941, blacks moved into what had been the Japanese neighborhoods." Until that time he recalls contact with people of Japanese, Chinese, and Hispanic backgrounds but few contacts with blacks. "There was little family discussion regarding race or minority issues. However, my parents insisted that all individuals be treated with respect. Bigotry was not tolerated."

In college he majored in Asian studies, learned Japanese, and during his senior year captained the rugby team. "The Marine Corps appealed to me because of its elite reputation and physical demands. I was not surprised by the lack of real integration, as it seemed that while there were not a large number of minority Marines, those who were Marines were treated as such. I knew Frank Petersen and Ken Berthoud, among the first two black officers in the Marine Corps, and as any self-respecting infantry officer, considered them only slightly inferior, not because of race, but because Frank was an aviator and Ken a supply officer. In fact, both were friends and superb officers.

"As a junior officer, I was proud of anybody who could qualify as a Marine and there was no room for thoughts of discrimination. I can't remember any discussions on the part of my fellow junior officers that was any different. The only discrimination that I can recall was Marine versus those that were not Marines.

"In the replacement company that I took to Korea I had two black Marines, both from Louisiana. They had been drafted; they didn't want to be in the Marine Corps, and most of all, they didn't want to be going to Korea. However, once they got there and saw that their best chance for survival and eventual return to the States was to do exactly as they were told, they performed well. A Marine Corps trained individual was a Marine, not a white, black or brown Marine, just a Marine and somebody you could rely on. There were a lot of unfavorable comments about the Army but it was certainly not racially oriented."

A. C. Clark, a Louisiana native, a black, automatic rifleman, had both a Silver and Bronze Star pinned on him for two separate actions as the marines sought to hold off the Chinese. He earned the former for aggressively covering the evacuation of a pair of wounded marines from his combat patrol, while killing three enemy soldiers and shutting down a machine gun, even as he was wounded twice. His earlier award of a Bronze Star came for the rescue of his wounded platoon leader.

Although the marine corps could cite an integrated presence of enlisted men, it still mustered only a few black officers for the ground fighting and but a single pilot, Lt. Frank E. Petersen, who was only the fourth of his race to complete the Naval Aviation Cadet Program. He reached Korea in April 1953 during the stalemate period, but squeezed in sixty-four combat missions in a Corsair before the truce.

The cycle of successes and failures, battle casualties, and the emotional stress of brutal campaigns wrought changes in leadership. But a 23 December automobile crash that killed the Eighth Army chief, Gen. Walton Walker, did more than simply change the name at the top of the command. Lieutenant General Matthew B. Ridgway, an outstanding figure during World War II, who led the 82d Airborne in Sicily and Italy, and all the airborne forces during the Normandy drop, was the choice of MacArthur to replace Walker. In the tradition of the paratroops where the generals jumped along with everyone else, Ridgway had a closer kinship to the GIs and, unlike his predecessor, seemed to lack any bias toward African Americans.

Their particular problems were not a priority when he first assumed command. Instead, he set about to restore order to the U.N. lines and revive saggy morale. Under Ridgway, the Eighth Army halted a renewed Chinese offensive below Seoul, once again in the hands of the invaders from the north. The winter and the heavy casualties inflicted by the defenders produced a stalemate, marked only by sporadic engagements, and during which time the Eighth Army refurbished itself. The niceties of PX sales, new clothing, and other equipment, church services and even movie shows lifted spirits. Replacements stocked units, including the 24th Infantry. Ridgway also terminated the independence of Ned Almond's X Corps.

As Ridgway plotted strategy for the new year, MacArthur received a letter from Thurgood Marshall, legal counsel for the NAACP. He wrote that following a visit to Korea, after interviews with a number of people, and a check of the court-martial records, he wondered "why there should be such a high percentage of charges and convictions for violations of the 75th Article of War [desertion] among Negro troops." Marshall observed that in the 25th Division, "sixty Negro and eight white soldiers were charged." He noted of the only two white soldiers convicted, one was given three years and the other five. In contrast, the punishment for the thirty-two blacks ranged from the death penalty to Leon Gilbert, through fifteen life terms, hard labor for others that added up to from ten to fifty years with just two black GIs remanded for five. Many of the accused saw their defense counsels for the first time on the morning of the trials and there was little opportunity to discuss the case or seek defense witnesses. Speed rather than righteous jurisprudence marked the tribunals which handed out life sentences in four trials that lasted from forty to fifty minutes.

Marshall cited the absurdity of four men accused of violating the 75th Article of War for being absent from the mess hall, then sent up to the front line where they remained for twenty-one days and nights. At the end of that period, the quartet were suddenly subjected to trial for the alleged mess-hall offense and convicted. In his bill of particulars, the NAACP attorney also included the injustices of the Paulfrey and Reed cases. [Paulfrey's sentence was remitted in 1952 with the stipulation that he would serve out his term of enlistment. Reed was released in 1953 and Gilbert was released in 1955.]

Marshall concluded, with a recommendation that "all units under the Far East Command be integrated without regard to race. The men I talked to in the 24th Infantry all made it clear to me that several of the white officers assigned . . . made it known they would have preferred not to be commanding Negro troops. There was considerable lack of understanding and mutual respect in many of the companies of the 24th. These men made it clear that their complaints were based on the period before Col. Corley became the commanding officer. If the 24th had been completely integrated, I am sure that there would not have been this disproportionate number of charges and convictions of Negro troops under the 75th Article of War." To buttress his argument, Marshall said the air force, through complete integration had achieved "a terrific increase in efficiency . . . The same is true of the Navy."

Considering that Ned Almond was his chief of staff and Walton Walker his choice to head the Eighth Army, the appeal for MacArthur to integrate his troops was futile. Although he disdained the traditional colonial attitudes toward Asians, MacArthur told close associates after V-E Day that army chief of staff George Marshall urged him to add to his forces through the use of the African American platoons but he rejected the notion as "too controversial." Indeed, MacArthur, six months later, when asked about segregated outfits, responded, "They were created in Washington and sent to me as already organized Jim Crow units. I did not ask for men by race. I did not ask for Negro or for white men. In my command, if segregation exists, . . . it exists as it may have been dictated from Washington." But as his successor in command of the U.S. Far East forces would demonstrate, the power to integrate lay in his hand.

Ridgway commenced an offensive in February 1951 and, against steady opposition, the U.N. forces pushed toward the Han River that lay in front of Seoul. Reginald Sapenter and his Company I platoon participated in the attack. Aided by artillery fire, Sapenter and his associates captured an enemy-occupied hill. During a counterattack, however, he was wounded. As he was being evacuated Sapenter could see the frozen Han River with Chinese soldiers retreating over its solid surface.

As elements of the 24th Infantry positioned themselves for pursuit, the division commander, Gen. J. Sladen Bradley, came forward to examine the deployment. He became embroiled in an argument about the tactical soundness with John Corley. The discussion ended with an unchastened Corley stalking off and the executive officer, Lt. Col. Paul F. Roberts, temporarily assuming the mantle of the regiment.

Concern that relief of a leader generally respected by enlisted men and officers might damage the morale of the organization generated a silent pause before official recognition of Corley's departure. He surfaced at a hospital in Japan trailing explanations of a bad back and ulcers. *Black Soldier,*

White Army says that of the more than 400 interviews conducted during research for the book, only two individuals disparaged Corley. His most outspoken detractor was Charles Bussey who says that he and Corley initially enjoyed swapping stories of World War II, while sharing whiskey. Bussey paid tribute to the deposed commander. "Corley led the regiment through cold, hard intimidation, but he led it better than his predecessors. He was also an opportunist. He was highly decorated, and he knew how to exploit the awards and decorations system. He'd sacrificed a lot of men. In fairness, I have to add that he also jeopardized himself."

But, says the former engineer captain, one day as they plunged ever deeper into alcoholic candor, Corley confided that although Maj. Richard Williams, an outspoken black officer, was far more able than several of the whites in command of battalions, he could not turn over one to Williams, since policy restricted men of color to company-level command. Bussey says he protested Corley's cowardice, arguing the bias decreased the effectiveness of the regiment, the division, the entire war effort.

"He told me, 'I only recommended you for the Silver Star for the job you did at Yechon, and I only recommended a Bronze Star for your rescue of Lieutenant Lenon and his people. [Bussey, disobeying orders, led a patrol that saved Lenon and the others trapped behind enemy lines.] The Distinguished Service Cross was appropriate for the Lenon rescue and well deserved. So was the Congressional Medal of Honor for Yechon. If you were white you'd have gotten them both. You'd be a hero in song and fable, because a nation, a people, are only as strong as its heroes. You will note that there are no black heroes, except maybe Jackie Robinson in baseball. Small matter . . . The Negro newspaper would lionize you . . . But, you see, we can't allow it. It was always meant to be a white man's world, and I, like all others of my station in life, am obligated to maintain the control of Negroes in my sphere of activity. I cannot allow you to become a hero, no matter how worthy. You'd be an inspiration to every young Negro in the country. Through men like you, Negroes would effectively rise above their current state in our socio-politico-economic society.'"

Reading Bussey's account, one may be troubled by several aspects. The sentiments allegedly expressed by Corley have a quasi-sociophilosophic quality hard to associate with a boozy bout in a combat zone. Recollected quotes or reconstructed conversations are always problematic. On the other hand, Corley was known to have a fondness for the classics—a black lieutenant described him as "a man of culture"—and alcohol sometimes induces florid rhetoric.

Many of his associates, white and black, deny that Corley ever displayed prejudice. Buck Creel, who led a company for him, insists, "There wasn't a racist bone in his body." Reginald Sapenter, a black officer, thought so highly of Corley that he would not believe his former commander ever told Philip

Harper not to trust black soldiers. Again, a man in his cups may utter ideas which when fully alert might never occur to him.

Whatever his underlying attitudes, Corley had been the 24th's most effective leader while under fire, as Bussey grudgingly agreed. That impression was seconded by George Shuffer Jr., a heavy-weapons platoon leader. An African American, Shuffer, rated Corley a capable commander who showed concern for his soldiers, making it his business to see and talk with privates as well as officers. Shuffer believed the GIs fought better after he assumed command.

Never officially confirmed as the CO of the regiment, Roberts, the immediate successor, rotated home to the States. Headquarters named to the post Col. Henry Britt, who had served with the 92d Division in Italy. Unlike Corley who always came forward to observe the situation and confer with battalion commanders, Britt preferred to operate well behind the front lines. Nor did he attempt to know his troops. Neither his subordinate officers nor the GIs regarded him as a worthy successor to Corley.

Lieutenant Colonel William Mouchet had replaced Blair as CO of the 3d Battalion, and in his case there was evidence of bias. A capable commander, he struck Oliver Dillard, the black intelligence officer, as striving for fairness but paternalistic toward blacks. Dillard recalls hearing the battalion leader sitting with other white officers discussing black soldiers in derogatory tones. Later he learned that Mouchet rated at the bottom all performance reports on black officers.

George Shuffer, originally a member of Company G and first of his race assigned to that company, recalls no racial prejudice displayed by any of its white officers. As the regiment prepared to cross the Han, Shuffer switched to Company F where he was in close contact with his battalion commander, Lt. Col. George Clayton. Although some soldiers considered Clayton a racist, Shuffer never heard any remarks that indicated prejudice.

Beginning on 7 March, the three regiments of the 25th Division, preceded by a massive artillery barrage, launched attacks that carried them across the Han River. Shuffer's Company F led the 24th Infantry and secured a beachhead, enabling engineers to construct a footbridge and start to float barges across the river. Although a counterattack forced the 2d Battalion back a few hundred yards, the GIs resumed their offensive and the defenders withdrew.

The Eighth Army ground forward, never quite catching up to the Chicoms who retreated across the Hant'an River. Britt chose an extremely difficult spot for crossing the stream. When Britt issued the plan dismayed officers could only salute and grouse to one another. In the predawn hours, the attackers waded through waist- even chest-deep, swift-flowing water for 125 feet, while a well-entrenched defense poured shot and shell down from steep hills that overlooked the river. Although exposed to punishing fire, GIs from the 1st Battalion forded the river and successfully assaulted machine-gun emplacements, which nearly foiled the entire operation. The 3d Battalion, clutching at ropes strung from shore to shore, also struggled to the other side, although several soldiers stepped in holes and the current carried them away.

Unfortunately, on the second day of the offense the opposition hurled a fierce counterattack at the Americans and a Turkish brigade on their flank. The 3d Battalion fell back across the Hant'an River in disorder. Sladen Bradley, the 25th Division head, became furious not only at the reversal but also at the inaccurate information fed him by the regimental staff. The success of the 1st Battalion in holding its ground while inflicting substantial losses upon the enemy received little notice.

The defenders, however, continued to put up formidable resistance. While the 1st Battalion gamely attacked under withering fire, the 3d Battalion crossed the stream again but could not achieve the heights overlooking the water. Mouchet figured his position on the side of the mountain untenable in the event of another counterattack and received permission to withdraw. A third maximum effort by the regiment finally convinced the enemy to retreat. In the three days of fighting, casualties among GIs amounted to 112 with significant losses in company-grade officers.

Lieutenant Beverly Scott, with Company A, participated in a battle to retake a sector. "We were in a very severe fight one evening. We lost a high proportion of troops in one company. We had 25–30 KIAS and 60 or 70 wounded and failed to take the top of the hill, a very difficult fight. We were visited that day by the correspondent from the *Saturday Evening Post,* Harold Martin. He watched us fight and saw the casualties and the hard times we were having and we didn't succeed. That night the battalion was so decimated they decided to pass the 27th Regiment through us the first thing the next morning. During the night, the Chinese had withdrawn and the 27th went right to the top of the hill and didn't lose anybody. Yet, when [Martin's] article appeared, he excoriated the 24th as ineffective, inefficient, and the 27th regiment as so much more efficient that they took the hill with no casualties. During all of my tour, we attained all of our objectives right alongside the 35th, 27th and the Turks who were part of our division. You could discern no differences between the regiments."

The Eighth Army slogged forward, the 24th under heavy pressure from Britt, who advised Mouchet, "Your personal future is dependent upon your efforts to accomplish assigned mission." The Chinese fought for every yard of ground. When the 3d Battalion could not achieve the prescribed goals, Britt relieved Mouchet.

On 23 April, just under two weeks after the crossing of the Hant'an, the Chinese launched a huge spring offensive, mobilizing 270,000 soldiers backed with heavy artillery. Both the 24th and its brother regiment, the 27th, bent but did not break, as they yielded ground at a fearful cost to the attackers. In the 77th Engineer Combat Company, David Carlisle, U.S. Military Academy, Class of 1950, had replaced Charles Bussey, who had been evacuated for a kidney stone, then returned to the States after 205 days, mostly in the front lines. Bussey had nominated Carlisle for a DSC on the basis of his valor at Kunu-ri, but it was denied by superiors; Carlisle recalls the 77th's fight at the Hant'an. "Reinforced with a platoon from the 89th Medium Tank Battalion and a platoon of the 21st Anti Aircraft Battalion [.50-caliber machine guns] the 77th under me, engaged several hundred enemy while we were assigned as part of the 24th's rearguard and managed to delay the enemy and to disengage without losing a single soldier to enemy action."

Unfortunately, the Turkish brigade on the western flank collapsed and as its soldiers abandoned their positions, the Americans became vulnerable to envelopment. The battered, weary Americans retreated back across the Hant'an. By the time it passed into reserve and received some respite, the 24th's rosters showed a total of 381 killed and wounded.

Settled into defensive positions north of Seoul, the U.N. forces awaited another major offensive. But the enemy forces, punished severely by the Americans and their allies, lacked supplies and their morale dropped. Constant pounding from the air and by long-range artillery further diminished the capacity for any sustained attacks. At the same time a monumental shake-up in command had occurred. When MacArthur appeared to openly challenge the policy of Truman, the president fired him, and Ridgway, in April, replaced him. Lieutenant General James A. Van Fleet, another doughty World War II leader, took custody of the Eighth Army.

The ebb and flow of battle brought an erosion of segregation during the spring of 1951. Everett Copeland, who as a replacement had been wounded while with an all-black engineer company, along with half a dozen others of his race, returned to Korea for duty with the 7th Cavalry Regiment. Integration, however, did not sit well with his new leader. "Upon reporting for duty, the company commander in the traditional slavery manner, assigned me to duty as his personal radio communications man, to accompany him into battle carrying a pack radio strapped to my back. His first advice was, 'Boy, I don't know why they sent you people here. Now, when the going gets tough, you throw that radio and weapon down, put up your hands and surrender. Don't try to be no hero. The enemy will recognize a nigger and go easy on him.'"

In spite of such remarks, Copeland says, "The overall quality of life improved greatly. People in general in our company, regiment and division that I came in contact with, though clearly racist, and held a low opinion of blacks, would meet them half way. We knew then, as now, that outside of combat we could never depend on whites for support."

Bradley Biggs returned for another combat tour but drew the role of a company commander in the 64th Heavy Tank Battalion, a unit with African American enlisted men, and mostly white officers. "All of the platoon leaders under me were white but we had no racial problems," says Biggs. "We had a white battalion commander whose attitude made all the difference, unlike what I had seen in the 24th Infantry."

Van Fleet organized another offensive and the 24th troops returned to the front lines. Some ten days after operations began, Company C of the 1st Battalion attacked a hilltop. There Sgt. Cornelius H. Charlton led an advance against heavy fire. One of seventeen children of a West Virginia coal miner who had enlisted in the army at seventeen, Charlton had come to Korea with an engineer service unit, but volunteered to be an infantryman with the 24th. When his lieutenant went down, Charlton took charge of the platoon and although wounded in the chest, refused to seek treatment. Private First Class Ronald Holmes recalled, "He got the rest of the men together and we started for the top. The enemy had some good emplacements . . . we couldn't get to him. Grenades kept coming at us and we were chased back down. Again we tried but no luck. Sgt. Charlton said he was going to make it this time and yelled, 'Let's go,' and we started up again. We reached the top this time. I saw the Sergeant go over the top and charge a bunker on the other side. He got the gun but was killed by a grenade." Charlton and his comrades wreaked heavy casualties on the enemy while saving the lives of many imperiled GIs. He became the second soldier of the 24th to earn the Medal of Honor.

When new defensive positions were established, the 24th dropped back into a reserve status. The black soldiers had doggedly contested for ground with the enemy but after almost a year on the line, with very little respite, word then, confirmed by survivors years later, indicated a malaise gripped the entire outfit. Discipline declined among both enlisted personnel and officers.

The 24th soon trekked back to the front but a white artillery observer, Lt. Gaston Bergeron, witnessed a painful display of the continued antagonism to the African Americans. As the regiment walked forward along a narrow dirt road, the white unit they were replacing hiked down the other side. Bergeron heard the whites bombard the blacks with racial slurs and insults while their officers made no attempt to quell the slurs. Bergeron had noticed on other occasions verbal abuse heaped upon the African American GIs by whites.

Still another regimental commander, the seventh since the 24th landed in Korea, appeared. Lieutenant Colonel Thomas D. Gillis, an armor specialist rather than an infantryman, on 15 September, wrote in his diary about the final operation of the regiment. "Today was heartening and a concrete example of what coordination and good leadership can accomplish. The 24th Regiment CAN [sic] fight when properly led . . . at 1330 we got things really rolling: a superb mortar concentration was followed up right away by the lead platoon and in no time a squad was near the top. Then there followed the damndest hand-to-hand grenade fight I've ever seen."

Although Gillis in subsequent entries mentioned some minor failures in succeeding days, he inscribed for 28 September, "General [Ira P.] Swift [25th Division commander] while touring the MLR [main line of resistance] this morning made the statement that this regiment has the strongest line in the entire Eighth Army. Only a little over a month ago when I took over command, he told me it was the weakest."

Gillis's plaudits notwithstanding, time ran out swiftly for the 24th. From division headquarters on up to the highest echelons of the Eighth Army, the regiment bore a reputation for failure. With fresh troops flowing into the country, most of the veterans of the 24th qualified for rotation to the States. The insertion of African Americans into a number of combat units, as in the case of Everett Copeland in the 7th Cavalry, and the experience of the marines demonstrated integration was feasible. Ridgway agreed to deactivate the 24th.

In *Colin Powell, Soldier/Statesman-Statesman/Soldier* by Howard Means, Michael Lynch, a pilot on Ridgway's staff, claims the order to integrate originated not with Ridgway but the secretary of defense, George C. Marshall, who as army chief of staff during World War II successfully stifled pleas to meld the races. Lynch flew Marshall to a meeting at a small airstrip behind the front lines where, says Lynch, "There was a conversation between the two of them. Marshall said, 'Let's finish this black thing. Let's integrate blacks in the fullest sense and not put them in separate units anymore.'" Many years later, Lynch searched out in Marshall's papers a memo that mentioned the trip to South Korea and completion of integration in the armed forces.

Whether the decision was based upon a belief in equality and a wish to end discrimination or reflected a purely military conviction that segregation reduced efficiency and effectiveness, Ridgway issued the orders that ended the life of the 24th. Those soldiers who had not completed the full tour received assignments to other regiments. The policy of integration applied to other all-black organizations such as the 64th Tank Battalion, the 3d Battalion of the 9th Infantry, and the 65th, formerly made up of Puerto Ricans and Virgin Islanders. Rather than deactivate these units, they simply swapped men with all-white outfits. The only change in their designation was the removal of the asterisk that denoted a black unit. [Official documents had used an asterisk to indicate an African American outfit.]

One of those dispatched to the 14th Regiment was the black officer Beverly Scott who had joined the 24th as a communications specialist two weeks after the Han River crossing. "The 14th was not nearly as efficient as the 24th, of course, but they were new. Later they [improved]. Then there was no distinction between them."

Ridgway's ukase affected more than the 24th and the handful of other black-based units. Homer Jones, a paratroop lieutenant during World War II who had jumped in Normandy on D-Day, commanded a formerly all-white rifle company at Fort Benning that received its first African American officer and noncom. "The officer was okay but the sergeant first class was worthless. The other enlisted men, or at least some of them poked fun at him, talking loudly near him but not to him, with derisive comments."

Jones then went to Korea. "I had a company with 50 ROKS attached and many Puerto Ricans from the 65th Infantry in the ranks. When the company was together, which was not often, and I gave a talk or an order, about 100 of the 250–300 in the company, could not understand me. Fun!"

Eli Bernheim, who had schooled the first integrated training company for the 101st Airborne Division, received assignment to the 187th Airborne Regimental Combat Team. "To my surprise," says Bernheim, "this unit, the most elite in the Far East Command was totally integrated. They had eliminated the Ranger units and incorporated all personnel, since they were airborne qualified, into the 187th to bring the RCT up to strength after heavy combat losses. There were many black paratroopers. In my 3d Battalion we had two black officers, former Rangers, who were highly respected and good leaders. During my eighteen months in the 187th we had considerable combat and garrison experience. I know of no racial incidents."

Initially, the ground forces, whether separated or mixed, staggered under the thrusts by the North Korean army, but the U.N. troops recovered and pressed forward to engage in a carnage-strewn campaign with the legions of Chinese soldiers. The air force met substantial opposition from the enemy air arm, which brought to bear the Soviet-made MiG jet fighters, piloted by a mix of North Korean, Soviet, and Chinese pilots. Spann Watson says, "The war in Korea saved blacks as part of the Air Force. They needed us and we had first lieutenants, [in grade] for as long as eight years, men with more experience and flight time than their commanders." During a respite, Charles Bussey had met briefly with former members of the Red Tails, now integrated into USAF squadrons and several were killed in action.

Chappie James flourished in Korea. "There was much controversy on how effective jets were vis-a-vis prop-driven airplanes. Many expressed negative opinions, i.e., 'What do we need these fancy jets for, when they can't spend enough time in the target area before they're out of fuel. They aren't effective. We have these old World War II planes that are doing a better job.'

"They set up a cameraman in the back of the photo planes with a motion picture camera and we had forward shooting cameras in front that I operated. We would go in behind the F-80s and F-84s to take combat and battle-damage assessment photos. We were right in with the strike force. It was kind of sporty and a lot of fun.

"A white sergeant from Clearwater, Florida, was assigned as my cameraman and he didn't bat an eyelid. We never even discussed it. I didn't know how he felt and didn't care, just as long as he showed up with the camera. I think he felt the same way about me flying. As we flew together, we talked a lot, but never mentioned racial problems. One day while the sergeant was cleaning his camera a newsman approached him and asked, 'How do you feel about flying with Captain James?' 'What do you mean?' The reporter said, 'I would just like to know how do you feel about flying with him. You know what I mean.'

"The sergeant said, 'No, I don't know what you mean. He is a good pilot. He is fine.'

"[The reporter:] 'Yes, but I mean, he's uh, colored.' And the kid just said, 'Is he?' That was the end of the conversation. The kid didn't tell me; the reporter did later. I think it was typical of the attitude of the men who flew together, the real professionals that we had in the Air Force who had to fly in the back seat."

James also flew P-51 Mustangs, mostly interdiction raids that hammered enemy ground positions, tanks, and supply lines with rockets, napalm, and bombs. He led a mission near Namchonjom in October where in a devastating attack he personally killed more than 100 of the foe. His superiors, appreciating his skill and leadership, awarded him the Distinguished Flying Cross.

James completed a stint as a spotter and forward air controller. In that capacity, he said, "Got about three jeeps shot from under me." Back in the air, he folded his six-foot-four-inch frame into the cockpit of F-80 jets. Completing a 100-mission tour, he returned to stateside duty and among his satisfactions, he noted, "Over a few beers, I've even had white guys say they like me, but you can keep all those others. They respect me. They've seen me roll in on that target when the flak was heavy, just like they did, and come scooting out the other side. They respect me."

Benjamin O. Davis Jr. reached the battleground toward the tail end of the war as he assumed command of the 51st Fighter-Interceptor Wing based in South Korea. Davis bossed thousands of airmen, most of whom were white. Again the air force detected no discernible effect by placing a man of color in charge. While in the Far East, Davis became the first African American in the air force to pin on the stars of a brigadier general.

American naval forces fought no sea battles with the enemy but provided the transportation for the Inchon landing and when possible bombarded shore installations. Emmett Tidd, as an officer on the destroyer USS *Frank E. Evans*, says, "While on the firing line off the east coast of North Korea [black sailors] performed their regular duties, menial as they usually were, as well as anyone on the ship. In the main, they were assigned to the lower ammunition magazines at General Quarters, passing five-inch shells and powder or 20mm and 40mm ammo, to the upper guns. Some were on 20mm and 40mm guns, and a few on extra lookout positions, topside. My recollection is that a black was the only person aboard this ship to earn a Purple Heart during this deployment. He had a sky lookout position on the starboard side of the signal bridge when we received several holes in our forward stack from near misses of enemy shells during heavy counter battery fire with the North Korean large guns on Kalmagak Peninsula in Wŏnsan Harbor. He received a minor, but qualifying flesh wound."

Major support for ground forces came from navy and marine pilots flying from aircraft carriers. Jesse Brown, the first black naval aviator, and a friend and former roommate of Burt Shepherd, while on a mission from the USS *Leyte* was shot down and killed early in the war. Shepherd himself did not reach the war zone until 1953 as a pilot aboard the USS *Boxer.* "I don't recall any squadron minority presence but there were minorities in all the enlisted ratings who advanced to the highest rank, Chief Petty Officer. I don't remember any racial tension on the *Boxer* but there was the usual separation of personnel during shore leave. The engine crew would not lower themselves to go on liberty with the 'Airedales' and etc. The groups who worked together usually played together. There were bars and hangouts that catered mostly to blacks, but there were more of them that evolved into places where a particular division—whites and blacks together with others—gathered to relax after the rigors of weeks or months at sea."

With his tour finished, Chappie James returned to a stateside air force where, at his level, race relations were at least civil. Some GIs painfully learned that comradeship on the battlefield ends beyond the firing line. On his voyage home after Korea, Everett Copeland happened upon a white soldier in a card game on deck. "I recognized him as a man from another unit whom I had helped carry off a battlefield while working as an emergency litter-bearer with our aidman. We looked at one another and I thought he may not have remembered me, so I spoke up. He replied, 'I know who you are, boy.' Then he resumed playing cards with the other whites."

With a quartermaster unit in Japan, Joe Kornegay says he suffered from anxiety attacks and nightmares reflecting what he had experienced in Korea. His term of service had been extended one year and he learned that unless he reenlisted, he would lose his stripes. After he signed the papers, he says, "I was pipelined right back to Korea, to the 1st Cavalry Division. It was a mixed up, horrible situation. I was still sick. They got a board together and I had no one to counsel me. I was given a discharge as an undesirable and was shipped home. My records were wrong. They didn't show that I had been with the 25th Division. It took me many years to get my papers corrected."

Bradley Biggs, bearing a background as a paratrooper, combat infantryman, and tanker had reported to the Advanced Armor school at Fort Knox, Kentucky, even before the war in Korea ended. "Most of my classmates refused to team up with a group I was in for study or work. However, John D. Eisenhower, and George S. Patton III, [sons of the generals] were not of that ilk and we were on good talking terms." But as the only black officer in the program, Biggs found those at the top not ready to accept equality or integration. The personal equation, rather than Defense Department policy, would now increasingly govern race relations in the military.

20
Policy and People

Although the Korean War groaned on for another fifteen months after Ridgway ordered full integration, the U.S. armed services grappled with racial problems. As the Civil Rights movement accelerated in the face of often violent resistance, the quest for equality by those in uniform also met opposition. Unlike civilian life where in many areas the law prescribed segregation in the military, de jure segregation no longer existed. It became a question of behavior by individuals, overt and covert.

Elliotte Williams recalls an incident at a 1951 New Years Day reception held at the officers' club. "Three or four of us on the staff were invited and we got a cool reception until Col. Charles W. Rich, the division chief of staff, stepped forward and shook our hands. Once he broke the ice, people came over, one by one."

The navy, unlike the army, appeared to have fully complied with edicts that ended separation by race. All specialities, all forms of duty, all ratings and ranks were open, theoretically. In actuality, discrimination claims roiled the personnel waters. Following his sea duty during the Korean War, Emmett Tidd worked for several years in the Bureau of Naval Personnel (BuPers) Recruiting Division. While in Korea, with the navy embarking on its process of integration, he says he had begun to hear contemporaries express their opinions, "usually by those that had very biased views." In charge of an administrative section at BuPers, Tidd bossed more than 100 black, low-level civil servants, mostly female. "The issue of equality of work assignments and promotion opportunity did not long remain dormant. There were three to four claims filed in my section about discrimination. These were all thrown out by the special administrative judge hearing them. The most serious case was dismissed on the recommendation of the NAACP lawyer, following numerous testimonies by blacks in the section, fully supporting the positive nature of the equality of treatment and promotion opportunities in my section.

"Because of the onerous nature of the detailed Civil Service regulations, implementing President Truman's directive, it was easy for those not happy about the President's order to complain and silently resist. These cases made more news headlines than did the quiet progress being made in the majority of the government." What Tidd did not see were the more subtle instances of discrimination percolating through the service.

In a sharp reversal from previous actions, the marines rewarded Edgar Huff with the rank of sergeant major for his combat service in Korea and subsequent performance as guard chief at the detachment in Port Lyautey, Morocco. A white master sergeant, passed over in favor of Huff, had informed the commandant of the Port Lyautey barracks he would rather retire than serve under a black. Marine Headquarters swiftly arranged for the man to return to the States and leave the service. Again, overt bias was not tolerated but the corps was not wide open for minorities.

Elmo Zumwalt Jr., who entered the U.S. Naval Academy in 1941, witnessed the period of absolute segregation and then the transition phase. "My parents, who as practicing physicians," says Zumwalt, "worked not just professionally but personally with people of all kinds, bequeathed me their knowledge that color of skin or racial origin provided no clue to a person's character or worth." However, the subject of race relations was of minor concern in Tulare, California, where he grew up. "There was little talk about it at home, except my parents expressed their abhorrence at stories of lynchings. The elementary schools were segregated because of the housing pattern. The high school football and track teams of which I was a member had blacks and there was some socialization around these activities."

As an Annapolis graduate and a junior officer during World War II he heard about the Golden Thirteen, the USS *Mason,* and *SC-1264,* but the subject of race never came up either while he crammed four years of study into three at Annapolis or during his sea duty. On his ships, the black stewards manned battle stations as did other people such as storekeepers not directly associated with weapons. In these responsibilities, he saw no differences between the abilities and actions of Caucasians and blacks.

"Shortly after World War II," remembers Zumwalt, "I served as executive officer on the destroyer *Robinson.* A Filipino steward on board wanted to be an electrician's mate. He was very able, so I sent his request up the chain of command, strongly recommending that it be approved. Each time it reached a new level, I had to fight for a favorable recommendation. After the request arrived at the Bureau of Naval Personnel, I had to call five different departments to gain approval, which was finally granted but only as a special exception. That episode taught me a healthy contempt for bureaucracy and institutional racism in the Navy."

Zumwalt progressed to a pair of commands on a destroyer escort and a destroyer, with duty at the Pentagon sandwiched between. He encountered more troubling signs of discrimination. Again he met opposition when a second Filipino sailor asked for help transferring from the stewards' department into the line navy. For a second time, Zumwalt bucked the resistance of BuPers. "Considering the reasonableness of the request, I found it embarrassing and uncalled for . . .

"By far [the] most troubling instance [of discrimination] occurred when I was about to take over the job of detailer for lieutenants in BuPers in 1957. [Detailers, officers of intermediate rank, channeled their juniors to stations where their talents and navy needs presumably would be best matched.] In the course of briefing me on my new duties, the officer I was relieving told me that the routine for assigning minority officers was to send them to dead-end billets so that their promotion beyond middle rank would be unlikely. If you were assigned a black officer, which was rare, we were supposed to order him to become a recruiter, considered to be the least desirable type of duty. [Sam Gravely, John Lee, and Dennis Nelson all were saddled with that duty.] When he finished two years, his posting was extended an additional year. If he was promoted, we sent him to sea but put him on the worst ship for professional experience you could find, either a tanker or an auxiliary ship. By that time, he was bound to be passed over for promotion and you were rid of him. I did not follow these verbal orders even though it was clearly winked at or even encouraged by the captains and admirals and in effect became a Navy policy."

Zumwalt doubts that the civilian authorities in the Pentagon were aware of the shenanigans of the BuPers staff since they were covert. "The briefer instructed me not to let anyone know I was doing this." Zumwalt refused to discriminate. Since the malicious mischief was supposed to be hidden, no one could prevent him from assigning lieutenants as he saw fit. The ships that received these officers remained ignorant of the circumstances that brought them. Not surprisingly, Zumwalt recalls no slate within the navy at the time to promote equal opportunity or to lessen racial tensions. The only effort to remotely improve race relations came from a chaplain, Lt. (jg) John O'Connor, later to become Cardinal O'Connor and head of the New York archdiocese, who persuaded the secretary of the navy to start a program on moral leadership, encouraging all ranks to act in concert with true religious ideals.

On 1 March 1950, George Allen was one of six black youths from Boston who enlisted in the army. "When we arrived [at Fort Dix, New Jersey] and although integration was supposedly implemented in 1949 [he is incorrect; it was not yet army policy] five were sent to a training area called Range Road at the very end of the post. I being light skinned was sent to another area that consisted of all white recruits. I asked why I was separated from my friends and was told they were being sent to the 'Negro Training Area.' I convinced the sergeant that I was 'Negro' and subsequently was transferred. This was the 365th Infantry Regiment [formerly part of the 92d Division in Italy during World War II] and everyone was black, from a lieutenant colonel (chaplain) to the recruits.

"Training was uneventful other than sporadic fist fights between white and black soldiers now and then when they confronted one another at the bus stop. Blacks had a separate service club, separate church and most facilities were separated from those of whites. We were never told we could not use the other facilities but it was unspoken that we should not or else risk a confrontation."

In 1951 Allen became an MP assigned to a battalion in Germany. "We were separated from the white soldiers by platoons and even our designated areas of patrol with the cities were separated. Most of the blacks would go to Mannheim for recreation whereas the white GIs went to Heidelberg. Patrols were assigned on the same basis, with black MPs responsible for law and order in Mannheim and the white MPs in Heidelberg. [Prejudice] was so pervasive that the German women discriminated against one another based on their choice of soldiers. A woman would call other German women 'Niggers' if they were dating black soldiers and those dating blacks called those with white soldiers similar insults."

Two years later, with the military supposedly fully committed to integration, Allen was on duty at Fort Gordon, Georgia, his first time in the still rigidly segregated South. "On my first trip to Augusta I thought I would take in a movie. I did not know that I was supposed to go to a black theater that showed old movies. I went to the white theater, just to see what was showing, not to go in, but to make a comparison. While looking outside I was approached by two white policemen. One said he was king of the street and if I wanted to look at pictures outside the theater, I would have to do so from the gutter. I spotted a pair of white MPs in their car across the street. Being a fellow MP, I thought I was relatively safe, since I wasn't doing anything wrong. I told the cop I was not going inside but only looking to see what was showing.

"I turned and walked away. I was apparently struck from behind and knocked out because I awakened in jail. One of the policemen approached me with my wallet in his hand. He showed me my mother's picture—she appeared to be white. When I told him she was my mother, he took a pen and colored her face with black ink.

"After about an hour, my commanding officer, a white, showed up at the police station, wearing guns on both hips and demanded my release. He had about ten patrol cars with him. I was released in his custody and advised I better leave Augusta as soon as possible for my own safety. I immediately volunteered for Korea and was gone within twenty-four hours.

"As the Korean conflict ended, the personnel from my unit, 3d Division Military Police, were sent to Japan. All units were integrated and discrimination was prevalent only in promotional opportunities. Whites moved up faster and in much greater numbers than black soldiers."

Jack Rhoades, who schooled black tank destroyer candidates during World War II before departing to lead a cavalry outfit against the Germans in Europe, once again found himself commander of African Americans. "In 1951, I was assigned to the 2d Armored Division's (black) Heavy Tank Battalion. It was an experienced outfit, not a just activated unit but misnamed. The Army does not want or require a heavy tank. Their motor parks had not been built for tracked vehicles and heavy rains reduced them to mud holes. During these periods it was not unusual for parked tanks to sink far enough into the mud for their tracks to be covered, creating many major maintenance problems. This was compounded by difficulties the Battalion had in getting black tank maintenance personnel into and through the Ordnance Tank Maintenance schools because of inadequate public schooling before the men entered the Army. Once in, they had an inability to keep up with their white classmates, flunking out and returning to their unit as untrainable. It was not a racial problem in the sense of blacks being mentally incapable of learning but a lack of effective public education before they went into service.

"Finally the Division Commanding General arranged for the Ordnance schools to accept the students we sent to them and keep them in classes even though they could not pass the course. Our contention was that even those of our students who had not been able to keep up, flunked out part way through and returned to us, were significantly better mechanics than they had been before.

"I found that our black soldiers' attitude was more contentious than that with those from 1943 and the 459th Tank Destroyer Battalion. For the first time in my experience, I began to hear complaints about discrimination. When the decision was made to integrate all units in Germany, my tank battalion was the first combat black unit involved. My orders were to keep ten percent of our soldiers and receive white replacements from other tank units. I was given no guide lines for selecting my ten percent retained blacks.

"I decided to keep my black battalion sergeant major, and each company would keep [some] of their problem soldiers and ten percent of the best black non-commissioned officers. After four to six weeks when we had received all our incoming whites, it was apparent that my ten percent black non-commissioned officers were more competent than before and my retained problem soldiers were less of a problem. I concluded that my retained noncoms had exhausted all their own ideas, but were quick to pick up new ones from the white NCOs in their own company. The bad actors, now even more than before, were a minority and felt less free to 'goof off' on their new white NCOs. I decided overall that integration was a win-win operation.

Our better NCOs (black) got better and our problem black soldiers were less trouble. The more contentious attitude I noticed had no relation to integration."

Raymond Battreall, born in 1926, grew up in Omaha, Nebraska, where his father supported the family as a traveling salesman for dyes that colored clothing. "I wasn't much aware of racial discrimination until the first grade where there were only one or two blacks in my class. I recall both my parents saying, 'There's nothing wrong with a good nigger as long as he knows his place.' Omaha blacks lived in a segregated neighborhood which we mostly avoided. Restaurants, drinking fountains and waiting rooms of the railroad station were segregated. I recall my mother being absolutely scandalized when a black woman sat down next to her on a trolley.

"I elected to attend Central High, where most blacks were assigned because of geography, because of its excellent academic and college-prep reputation. Blacks and whites mostly ignored one another although on one occasion, a black boy, much larger than I, deliberately shoved me on the stairs. I responded, 'Watch it, Nigger!' to which he replied, 'What's that you say, white boy?' For the next several weeks I carried to school a loaded .32 revolver."

Battreall, an aviation enthusiast since he saw the Graf Zeppelin fly overhead, figured that since his father could not afford to send him to college, he would enlist for aviation cadet training and apply to West Point. After basic training and the surrender of Germany, the commanding general of the air training command "praised our patriotism but allowed as how he had two wars worth of Air Force cadets and only one war left. Because of my pending appointment to the USMA I was assigned as barracks chief. One day I was detailed as a telephone communicator between the firing line and target pits on a carbine range where blacks were firing. I gathered from their conversation they'd been told that all who qualified with the weapon would be sent to the South Pacific as snipers. The result was wild shots in the air, even backwards over their shoulders where I was seated. I took my phone and self into a foxhole!"

At the Military Academy, there were two black cadets [Ed Howard was one] in Battreall's 1949 class. "Although I was not in the same company with either of them, I was not aware of any hazing or shunning beyond that endured by the white cadets. I don't recall any discussion of the possibility of serving with blacks after graduation."

Designated for armor, Battreall took up residence with the 14th Cavalry Regiment at Fulda, Germany, where in the spring of 1953 he commanded Company B. "My battalion commander, Lt. Colonel DeWitt Armstrong III, called me to his office to advise that we would be swapping troopers with the 26th Heavy Tank Battalion and the 373d Armored Infantry Battalion.

We were in the habit at the time of referring to these units as the '26th Heavy Razor Battalion' and the '373d Double-Clutchin' Armored Infantry, You Call, We Haul.' The 373d really named itself by answering the phone, '373 Armored Infantry, You call, we haul. Suh!'

"I advised Col. Armstrong of my fears of rape, murder and pillage in the barracks, to which he replied, 'Very well, Lieutenant. Whom do you recommend to take command of your company and who will carry out his orders?' I saluted, about faced, and fled.

"I've always wished I could have been a mouse in the corner listening to those black 1st sergeants briefing their troops just before the exchange. It must have been something very much like, 'Don't you dare go over there and say, 'Nha, nha, Honkey, look what we've done!' Go over there and show that I can soldier as well as the next guy.' For that is exactly what they did! A week later my company was patrolling the East-West German border from a field bivouac north of Fulda. There was still snow on the ground when I observed two of my troopers sharing a blanket to watch the movie being projected on a white sheet spread over the side of the kitchen truck; one GI was black and the other a white from Tennessee. I knew then that integration had worked without a hitch, and I've never since judged a man by the color of his skin."

DeWitt Armstrong remembers the brief conversation with Battreall. By way of additional background he explains that after World War II he supervised an Armed Forces Special Weapons Project (AFSWP) team that transported, tested, and assembled atomic bombs. "The officers and men were rigorously selected, highly responsible, quite intelligent, utterly devoid of disciplinary problems—in other words quite unlike a normal troop unit." Promoted to a Pentagon job in AFSWP, Armstrong, on the advent of the Korean War and the Chinese intervention, asked for release back to a ground-gaining unit, armor or infantry. Although the request from what was considered a cutting-edge assignment was unusual, his superiors granted his wish. But because of secrecy concerns, he could not go directly to the war. He had to spend a year at the Armor School and even then would not receive a post outside the continental United States. Following the mandated term at Fort Knox, the requirement of stateside duty only fell by the wayside, and in 1952, Armstrong assumed command of the 1st Battalion of the 14th Armored Cavalry in Fulda.

"With troops deployed literally along the Iron Curtain, face-to-face daily with Soviet soldiers," says Armstrong, "we guarded the main avenue of approach for the Soviet Army into Western Europe. Into our undertrained, understrength battalion, with about half the officers and NCOs of the Table of Organization, began coming some blacks. A very few had origins in the old 9th and 10th Cavalry and really understood soldiering. Most were converted infantrymen who had fought in Korea and were ready for a rest. Somewhat to my surprise, the blending of black and white, the recreating of a competent battle-ready outfit worked out rather well.

"I believe there were two main reasons. First the chain of command above us prepared the way. We were left in no doubt that integration, smooth integration, was second only to our combat mission. The matter having been decided and ordered by the Commander-in-Chief [Truman] it was going to happen and it would be done well. Resistance to it would simply *not* be tolerated. Every leader was to be constantly alert to detect emerging problems and deal with them in common-sense ways. Ray Battreall was not the only troop CO whose instinct resisted it. He was just more open about it. Old noncoms were, as usual, more set in their ways, so strong leadership, continuous and close-up was essential.

"At one point, it became clear that some senior NCOs were allowing misbehavior among their draftees, so I broke a few rules. I gathered together all my first sergeants and platoon sergeants, with no officers present. I spoke allegorically and descriptively, without issuing orders. I told them about the Old Army, the pre–World War II Regular Army in which my father had long commanded a battery or a company. [Back then] when a disciplinary problem arose and words were not enough, it was handled by a strong, tough sergeant, a senior sergeant, reinforced if necessary, who took the bad actor out behind the stables and forcibly impressed upon him the need to reform. Would there ever be a complaint, what company or battalion commander would ever take the word of a known bad soldier over that of a respected, proven senior NCO? They left the meeting amused and cheerful, confident that the chain of command would back them up when some white private from the Tennessee hills insisted that the old racial rules he learned as a kid still applied. Whether anybody was ever taken out behind the motor shop, I never heard. But our problems cleared up fast.

"The second reason why integration worked well was in late September 1952, we had extraordinary success operating against the 2d Armored Division in the first large-scale NATO maneuvers. The crack force had suddenly broken through other cavalry and infantry perhaps 30 miles northwest of us and was rapidly moving toward the Rhine. With no prior plan, nor even a warning order, my battalion made a 60-mile march across the face of the 'enemy' and advanced into contact as a covering force to delay them while preparing defensive positions. Stopped cold, the 2d AD launched two successive, powerful, coordinated attacks. We repulsed both with severe loss to them and very little to us. Instead of reaching their Rhine objective, that division, about eight times our strength, never got within 40 or 50 miles of it. Nothing so invigorates a troop unit as a brilliant victory over a far superior force, won by doing what they were trained to do. Morale and cohesion reached record heights. As an integrated team, they had proved themselves to be superior."

John Costa, following his last year at West Point, reported to the officers' courses at Fort Riley, Kansas, and Fort Benning. "I was vaguely aware of tension surrounding the use of the swimming pool at the officers' club—would the black officers go into the pool? What would the reaction be? But I don't recall anything specific. There were rumors of racial disturbances or fights involving black and white servicemen in Columbus, Georgia, Phenix City, Alabama and on the Chattahoochee River bridge. Given the state of race relations country-wide and the social climate it is probable that black officers avoided 'provocation.'"

Consigned to the all-white 1st Infantry Division in Germany, Costa recalls his 18th Infantry Regiment depended upon all-black truck companies for supplies and transportation. Although there were no incidents, he remembers the abundant "tasteless humor from enlisted and commissioned personnel pointed at blacks. They were referred to as 'double-clutching m-fers' and generally bore the brunt of ethnic jokes, much as it had been back home. The reputation of the black units was poor but I can't say there was any foundation for this. There was the story of poor performance of the 92d Division in Italy with the words, 'The 92d conducted an offensive yesterday; everybody just leaned forward.'

"Then one summer day in 1951 we became an integrated unit with a percentage of black soldiers and NCOs. I don't recall any black officers in our battalion or even in the regiment. My recollection is that instant integration went better than anyone had expected. On duty we got along reasonably well. Off duty the troops drifted apart, to their own social gathering spots. Some *gasthauses* were soon identified as for whites only or for blacks. This was a de facto segregation, certainly not sanctioned or official. There surely were fights but the GIs were always fighting because they were always drinking and because they enjoyed fighting. It took the boredom out of their lives. I don't remember it being essentially because of racial tension. I distinctly recall comparing notes with fellow officers and concluding that the integration of Hispanic soldiers which came after the overnight integration of blacks, presented more challenges and problems than we experienced with black soldiers. The language barrier was real and communication with soldiers newly arrived from Puerto Rico was a problem for NCOs."

The testimony of Rhoades, Armstrong, and Battreall indicates something of the benign influence a commander could have upon life after integration. Bradley Biggs, having weathered his serious wound in Korea and a disagreeable tour at the Fort Knox Armor School, experienced the baleful sway imparted by a malignant leader. "I was assigned to the 82d Airborne Division with General [Edwin A.] Walker as deputy CG. When Eisenhower sent the 82d to Little Rock because of the school integration crisis, Walker tried to have every black trooper removed. From 1954–1956 at Heidelberg, I was the only black on general staff status [with the 24th Division] in Germany. Did I get snubbed, ignored and rejected? Hell, yes, not only by the people in my division but also by the Germans I had to deal with. Their prejudices stemmed from their Aryan concept and being brain-washed by Americans re black people. To marry a German woman, a GI had to obtain permission from the commanding general. Walker refused to grant it to any black soldier." (Edwin A. Walker after retirement "outed" himself as a virulent proponent of white supremacy.)

Jehu Hunter, with the 92d Division in Italy during World War II, after accepting an honorable discharge, remained on reserve status while teaching and doing research. Recalled during the Korean War, he spent his first months back in uniform at a leadership course and then instructed in wire communications to desegregated units. Shipped to the 28th Infantry Division in Germany, he reported to a chief of staff, who was obviously unhappy to deal with a black officer. "He would come into a room," recalls Hunter, "and speak to everyone but me." Still, Hunter says other than this individual he had no problems with white officers and the club was fully desegregated."

On the enlisted-man's level, relations between the races at the 28th Division were less harmonious. Bill Gladstone, a Brooklyn native, a draftee with two years of college and some National Guard experience, raised eyebrows in 1950 when he innocently sat in the back of the bus while in Fayetteville, North Carolina. Assigned as a supply sergeant to a tank company, he discovered his captain disliked Jews so much that he arranged to transfer out Gladstone and a dozen others of that religion. Gladstone received a posting to the 112th Infantry of the 28th Division on occupation duty in Germany, near the town of Heilbronn.

Gladstone observed the efforts of his company commander to maintain a white organization, turning away qualified Regular-Army blacks in favor of poorly educated whites who could not learn to read a compass. Assigned to manage an enlisted men's service club, Gladstone says, "The black soldiers were never rowdy. They obeyed orders and didn't seem to have an attitude about integrating the army. Between Christmas and New Years, we had mini race riots almost every night, with forty or fifty men fighting. It was all over German girls. We had to post armed guards at the door to keep people from breaking bottles to attack someone. You had to stop selling beer at certain hours. We did not have any programs concerned with racial relations."

Another white who sought to deal with the clash of races was Perry Fischer, the white marine gunnery sergeant for a segregated ammunition unit during World War II. Discharged in 1946, attracted by a recruitment bonus, he enlisted in the army a year later. Although on active duty, Fischer soon obtained a first lieutenant's bars in the reserves. The army activated his commission in 1952, detailing him as an administrator for the 571st Ammunition Company, an all-black outfit stationed in France. "I was the first and only white soldier in the outfit, at a time when all units were supposed to be integrated. That means I was in charge of black troops for more than thirty months with the Marines and the Army."

Even as integration spread, Fischer reports there were few whites in the service units, mostly senior-rank enlisted men and officers. "The working units had their own first sergeants and below and [the breakdown by race] was 800 blacks, 200 whites. The blacks stayed on their side of the post, the whites on the other. There was very little fraternization and the blacks did not want that to change.

"Off post in France there was little racial trouble among the military personnel. In France, the blacks were welcomed by the women, for the most part. French men resented them and were very anti-black because of problems with Moroccan men brought to France to work. Some blacks got into trouble for theft, drunkenness and sexual misbehavior but there were many similar incidents among whites, maybe more. Socially, emotionally, morally, blacks and whites in the military reflected the same local weaknesses and strengths."

According to Fischer he personally strove to break down the traditional hostility through a policy of "honesty, complete instructions, understanding and trust, giving men an opportunity to learn, supervise and provide full support when deserved." He engaged in open discussions to reconcile problems, listened to complaints and played no favorites. He says he found black NCOs proud, demanding, jealous of their authority but responsive. "Black officers during the 50s and 60s were still persona non grata in the clubs and at parties. It was hard for them to acquire respect from the black ems [enlisted men] when white officers and NCOs made no effort to conceal their disdain."

As an Oklahoma City boy, Dick McDonald, born in 1931, attended segregated schools. The son of a farm-raised bank teller and a mother educated at the Chicago Conservatory of Music, McDonald recalls, "We had little family conversation about race, did not socialize or otherwise associate with blacks, the predominant other race in Oklahoma City. I think my parents had a feeling that blacks were inferior but this didn't surface because we simply had no contact with them. Both my parents were eminently fairminded and their example enabled me to take a more pragmatic view of race relations when circumstances brought me in close contact with people of other races.

"My most vivid recollection of a family-associated racial contact concerns a very old black lady who lived in so-called servants quarters connected to my grandmother's garage. She did a little housework in exchange for rent on the very squalid space and earned money working for nearby neighbors. I remember my grandmother once commenting that Lulu was hardly better than an animal. The remark was not made maliciously but as a rather sad observation reflecting the prevalent belief of black inferiority at the time. Otherwise, my grandmother was a kind woman."

McDonald quit college after a year and a half in 1951 to enlist in the marine corps because, he says, of "an affinity for military life which surfaced in ROTC. There were a few blacks in my recruit platoon as well as two American Indians and one or two Latinos. There were no problems dealing with race relations." As an enlisted man, McDonald worked at the Camp Pendleton, California, supply depot, but unlike the army, the marines still had so few blacks they did not predominate in service units. "Access to on-base clubs and recreation was fair but off-base housing was a serious problem, particularly in the Southern states."

His subsequent officer-training class contained no blacks. "Officer candidates in 1952 gave little, if any thought to racial relations. I doubt that there was more than a passing thought by our immediate seniors. The Marine Corps was run by a cadre of generals, predominately southerners, who perpetuated institutional bias. This sounds like a condemnation but it isn't. These were honorable men brought up in prejudice who had not had the opportunity to pass through the evolution of enlightenment which the civil rights movement provided to my generation.

"I had become aware of what seemed to be a cadre of black NCOs who were staff sergeants for the most part. These guys seemed to be take charge types and were the bosses of all blacks in their units. Most of them became first sergeants and sergeants major, and with a few exceptions were regarded very highly by many Marines. We had a black first sergeant in the 2d Infantry Training Regiment named McCargo. He was a horse, respected by officers and enlisted of all races and very determined to push qualified black Marines up the promotion ladder and run the slackers out. McCargo was just as hard on white slackers. There was a similar group of Samoan senior NCOs. These two groups might be viewed as Uncle Toms by many minorities today but at the time they enjoyed wide support within their own race."

With no direction from above, McDonald, like all in his position, handled racial problems on his own initiative. "As the CO of a company in the 9th Marines, I had a bigot first sergeant who singled out minorities for the least desirable assignments. We had about twelve blacks and a bunch of Latinos. The first sergeant was hardest on blacks. We had a black staff sergeant who waited for me to figure out the situation which did not take long because of its blatancy, rather than to come right in as soon as I arrived. Staff Sergeant Calhoun then was willing to alert me to any unfair treatment. A lot of commanding officers relied on a savvy minority NCO. That of course did little to rectify institutional bias or control a CO who himself was prejudiced."

Tom McPhatter, the black marine sergeant with an ammunition company during World War II, who became an ordained minister after receiving an honorable discharge, had enlisted as a navy chaplain. He testifies to similar experiences while attached to other marine organizations. "Two or three men came to me about being called 'nigger,' hearing the word used freely in the battalion. I reported this to the battalion commander who called a formation in full combat dress. The major stated very clearly that the Corps was interested in one color and would promote one color—and that color was the Marine Corps green. He would tolerate no one who had a different opinion."

As in the army, the climate depended upon the attitude of the man in command. There were marine officers who accepted the official policy and stressed that the corps was interested only in the color of marine corps green. At Camp Pendleton, California, some African Americans and white sympathizers complained about bias when it came to promotions. They also protested against the Confederate flag that hung over the paymaster's office. To get their money they were forced to come to attention and salute what they regarded as a symbol of slavery. While the issue of prejudice and promotion was not clearly resolved, the Confederate flag was removed.

The mixture of the races crossed the gender lines as well. Jeanne Hershey Murray while an Indiana coed, enlisted in the WACs in 1943 "for patriotic reasons. I had just completed my sophomore year in college and was working through the summer and decided to take a break from school. I was not aware of segregation in the Army."

Her basic training and first assignments naturally were in all-white units. When she volunteered for overseas, she traveled to Cairo, as a member of a forty-woman group. Closely supervised, with little contact with local people and restricted in where they could go in the Egyptian city, she does not recall ever seeing any black members of the U.S. military.

Upon cessation of the war, Murray completed her college education and then reenlisted with an assignment as a recruiter in Kansas City, Missouri. "At the time every three months a company of black female enlistees was recruited and sent to the WAC Training Center, Fort Lee, Virginia. I was involved in filling a small quota of those women. A high school diploma was required of all enlisted women and I had no trouble [finding] well qualified black women."

As a second lieutenant she transferred to Sioux Falls, South Dakota, with similar responsibilities. "I had no quotas for blacks because few lived in that state then. Native Americans often applied and were enlisted into both the Army and Air Force. Quotas were filled without regard to race. My next assignment in 1952 was at the Separation Center at Fort Custer, Michigan. I was not informed I would be integrating the WAC contingent and even after a lengthy conversation with the Post Commander on my arrival I still had not been told. Not until after he and his driver had escorted me to my BOQ, unloaded my car and got me settled. We were met by a black woman in civvies and I thought she was a maid. She invited me to her room and I saw all these pictures of black girls in uniform. Only then did it dawn on me that all the other WAC officers returning from work to the BOQ were black. Within a few weeks, five more white officers reported.

"It was the end of the Korean conflict and my assignment was Officer in Charge of a typing pool of fifty civilians, all black men and women, responsible for processing the paper work to discharge 800 men per day. I found them loyal, hard-working people. I don't remember any problems with absenteeism or other personnel problems. I was in the minority and my success or failure on that assignment depended upon them keeping up the rather strenuous pace of turning out those documents on time. We had mutual respect for each other." Over the following years, Murray worked at a number of posts with integrated units and does not recall any racial problems.

Not everyone in the military establishment accepted the policy of the Defense Department. Bob Edlin, the white Ranger lieutenant, whom a pair of black sergeants aided after a bullet cut him down on D-Day on Omaha Beach, recovered, and returned to the fighting to win a Distinguished Service Cross after he led a handful of Rangers and captured a force of 800 Germans. He also won a pair of Purple Hearts and a Bronze Star. After the war, Edlin had become a captain of the New Albany, Indiana, police and also commanded a company of the state's National Guard.

"I fought along with colored troops in the 2d Infantry Division [during World War II]," said Edlin. "At first they were in all-colored platoons. Later when a patrol was formed, two or three colored soldiers would be put into the patrol and that worked out better." After authorities discouraged four or five blacks from New Albany who tried to join the National Guard, Edlin says, "I talked to quite a few and tried to enlist them. My idea was to bring them right into my company. Colored and white play basketball together, now—they go to grade school and high school together in New Albany— why shouldn't they be in the National Guard? They will be together under the new policy when they get into the Federal service—so why not train together in the Guard."

"Higher ups," citing guidelines of National Guard headquarters in Washington, D.C., that forbade integration, requested Edlin's resignation. Only four states then opposed Jim Crow organization of the National Guard, and the Indiana commander declared, "I don't think the time is ripe for such a forward step in Indiana." Following Edlin's forced resignation, his brother and several others quit.

Some newcomers to service in the 1950s knew nothing of the traditional deployment for people of color. William De Shields, an African American born in 1932 in rural Maryland, grew up poor, the family supported by his father who held an unskilled job with an automobile dealer, money chipped in by a grandfather who worked as a waterman in Chesapeake Bay, and by growing some of their food. "I had very little contact with people of other races due to strict segregation policies," says De Shields, " and I was not aware of segregation in the military before I put on a uniform."

De Shields bootstrapped himself through Hampton Institute, picking up an ROTC commission as a second lieutenant in the army. In 1954, when policy outlawed discrimination, he chose to try for a career in the service because of "an affinity for military life, uniforms, drill and the like. There were very few problems with white officers and enlisted men during summer exercises." After assignment to an antiaircraft unit, De Shields applied for training as an army liaison pilot. "It was my first experience with overt discrimination in the Army. No matter how many blacks entered the Army Flight School, no more than two would graduate. Classes like mine began with 15 or 20 blacks and people would be washed out for no good reason. I made it through basic but I quit in disgust when I was in advanced. The experience caused me to question for the first time the integrity of the military. In my subsequent experiences, I had little problem gaining respect of enlisted men, white or black, the problems, if any, came from white officers, especially older ones."

William Murray [husband of WAC Jeanne Murray] grew up in pre–World War II Illinois with no particular feelings about race. "I don't recall any racial discussions or attitudes since in my younger years I had no contact with other races. Rockford, Illinois high school was integrated and I played football and ran track with a fine black player. I saw no discrimination but probably was blind to it." A volunteer for the draft in 1941, Murray earned a commission through OCS and while assigned to an antiaircraft group in the South Pacific saw black soldiers laboring as stevedores but had no contact with them.

"When integration occurred," says Murray, "I had no direct involvement in the process. I probably noted their [blacks] beginning to use the clubs and messes but had no personal reaction." He was aware of the presence of blacks in class where he taught tactics and the effects of nuclear weapons. Later, however, in another assignment he recalls an outstanding white officer, a graduate of West Point who seemed late in receiving a promotion from captain to major. "He explained [to Murray] that his wife had advised him that the spouse of a black lieutenant did not attend officer wives' affairs. The captain then asked the lieutenant about it and he answered that his wife had been told she was not welcome. The captain then went to the battalion commander and discussed it. His superior told him it was none of his business and the captain believed he received a low efficiency rating because of raising the issue. That explained the delay in his promotion."

Whites with no experience in discrimination were not the only military people to leave a sheltered background and suddenly discover racism. The descendant of Jamaican-born parents, Colin Powell had also traveled the ROTC route to start his military career, but with the advantage that his was an integrated unit. He grew up in a section of the Bronx, New York, that to many symbolizes the struggle to roll back urban decay. But in the early 1950s there was still a mix of race, ethnicity, and a spectrum of economic class. Family finances influenced Powell to enter the City College of New York, which was then tuition-free. Although conventional wisdom regards New York City and CCNY as bastions of liberal, antimilitary thought, the ROTC program at the height of the Korean War, says Powell, enrolled 1,500 cadets, the biggest contingent in the country. At the same time, he recalls, the majority of the student population barely tolerated them, and the campus newspaper called for dissolution of the reserve operation. Nevertheless, as the Korean War ended, Powell pledged the Pershing Rifles, a military version of a fraternity.

Powell and the ROTC in the form of the Pershing Rifles meshed smoothly. "The discipline, the structure, the camaraderie, the sense of belonging were what I craved. I became a leader almost immediately. I found a selflessness within our ranks that reminded me of the caring atmosphere within my family. Race, color, background, income meant nothing. The PRs would go the limit for each other and for the group. If this was what soldiering was all about, then maybe I wanted to be a soldier."

He learned that race meant something in the army after all during a summer training camp at Fort Bragg. After he finished second as Best Cadet for the entire encampment, a white supply sergeant took Powell aside. "You want to know why you didn't get best cadet in camp? You think these Southern ROTC instructors are going to go back to their colleges and say the best kid here was a Negro?"

Powell, in his autobiography, says he was more stunned than angered. "I did not want to believe that my worth could be diminished by the color of my skin." The trip back to New York, in the company of a pair of white noncoms from the City College ROTC unit, drove home the presence of racism as he dealt with gas-station restrooms reserved for men, women, and colored.

For Chappie James the air was quite smooth after he completed his missions over Korea. A forceful, ebullient personality whose aviation skills were proven, James received assignments that added responsibility and promotions. He passed through the gateway to the highest echelons after a nine-month stay at the Air Command and Staff School, followed by a Pentagon post where he plunged into problems concerned with personnel, airplanes, and operations. He learned administration and organization and later commented, "Some guys [African Americans] stalled out as Majors and Lieutenant Colonels because they stayed in the cockpit too long. Can't put [them] on [the] air staff. Never took care of [their] military education . . . how to be staff officers."

As a veteran of aerial combat, and by dint of his personality, James had acquired a cachet that made it more difficult to deny him his due. But while the principle of equality had been set down on paper, practice confounded even those who had paid their dues in education and staff work. Hughie Matthews, a black air force personnel specialist who climbed from his first-sergeant status into the commission ranks, upon implementation of integration became a conduit for grievances of African American airmen. "They would have problems when someone would try to force them to sit in a certain section of a theater and all it took was going to the right guy, the commander or theater officer, tell him what had happened and it usually got straightened out. I had men who said they didn't get promoted because they were black and I would attack this problem. Black enlisted men and officers too were kept out of areas like finance, intelligence, the Inspector General. The IGs were not responsive unless it clearly involved blatant unfairness. They were not interested in any progress. Nobody was out there plowing new ground."

Personally irksome to Matthews was the shortage of off-base housing for black officers and their families. Local commanders displayed no inclination to apply pressure on the local communities that refused to rent to African Americans, in one instance perhaps because the white superior hoped Matthews would require assignment elsewhere.

He also realized that with his experience and previous responsibilities, he merited assignments that went to people who had worked under him and had a weaker background than his. "I know that the policy for sure in the Strategic Air Command and in training commands was that there weren't going to be any black officers in those headquarters. I was selected to go the 8th Air Force Headquarters in 1958, put on orders and at the last minute they attempted to cancel. My household goods and everything had departed, so while en route they changed my assignment to the headquarters of the 57th Air Division. Two weeks after I arrived, I met the officer who had selected me for the job at the 8th Air Force and he told me that General Sweeney had become very upset because a black officer had been selected to come to his headquarters. He ordered the assignment cancelled. The officer told me it upset him so. His boss almost got fired over it and he was ashamed to be part of the organization."

Speaking of the period of 1948–1954, James said, "I'll be the first to admit that the Black enlisted man was not as well equipped to fight it [discrimination] and I didn't provide much assistance to him. At that stage I was too busy moving ahead with my own career. I did talk to those who came to me. When I could put in a word for them, I would and whenever I would walk into an NCO or Airmans' Club I would make it a point to chat with them. But I didn't try to set up some sort of organized session where I'd make myself available to them at all times to provide advice. Most of us were busy forging ahead at that time—trying to solidify our new found gains."

Although military protocols removed barriers, those in command wrestled with some racial problems seemingly beyond their control. Off-base housing remained a persistent sore issue for nonwhites particularly in regions with a history of segregation and discrimination. Not until the 1960s did the Department of Defense seriously address this situation. The difficulty in finding adequate housing for the families of black personnel lowered morale and even interfered with the ability to assign people on a basis of military need.

Elliotte Williams, while with the 82d Airborne at Fort Bragg, recalls the pattern in nearby Fayetteville. "There was housing specifically designated for use by captains and higher ranks. But none of the black officers were able to rent these units. When we protested we were told the housing authority 'had misplaced our applications.' The Division [General Gavin was now off the scene] and Corps commanders held some responsibility and advised us to be patient, that our applications would be reconsidered next year."

Even closer to home, on-post schools for armed-forces dependents usually relied upon local communities to fund and operate them. At Fort Bragg, says Elliotte Williams, "Our children were being bused to town to black schools at Fayetteville State College. The local school superintendent promised to blackball any teacher who taught integrated classes on the post. But when the Department of Defense took over total funding for schools on the post, they were integrated."

At Fort Bliss, Texas, in the period of 1951–1953, William Murray, recalled to duty from the reserves at the outbreak of the war in Korea, instructed at the Army Air Defense School. "Blacks were using the officers' mess, officers' club swimming pool and gym. My wife at the time and our ten-year-old son became friendly at the swimming pool with a black major's wife and ten-year-old daughter. When school started, the girl could not attend the post school which was part of the El Paso school system. She would have to be taken—there was no school bus offered—to a downtown school, ten to fifteen miles from the post. The 'powers that be' arranged for the major to be transferred to San Francisco."

President Dwight D. Eisenhower and his secretary of defense Charles Wilson wrestled with the issue of segregation of children at military installations where such separation was prohibited. If the president ordered integration of the schools in areas where the laws forbade it, the government might be forced to pay for them, teachers might quit, and accreditation might even be at risk. Because the elementary school at Fort Benning, unlike others, relied on federal funds, Eisenhower mandated desegregation shortly after he took office in 1953. Although Eisenhower himself never vigorously endorsed desegregation, Alan Gropman, the author of *The Air Force Integrates 1945–1964*, notes, Defense Secretary Wilson directed that all schools should be fully mixed by the start of the 1955 term. If the local governments refused support, then the money would come from Washington. Wilson issued his order eight months before the Supreme Court decreed integration in *Brown v. Board of Education*. That decision apparently encouraged the Defense Department to speed up the process, for some of the schools abandoned segregation ahead of the due date. Murray, back at Fort Bliss for a second tour in 1956, remembers that the school on post and in the El Paso public system were now integrated.

In the mid-1960s, Lyndon Johnson, exploiting the memory of murdered John F. Kennedy, encouraged by the swelling clamor for equality, twisted Congressional arms to pass civil rights legislation. In a parallel course the Department of Defense grappled with discrimination against its African American personnel by business and real estate enterprises.

Commanders, particularly those sensitive to the situations faced by their subordinates, recognized the effects of racial barriers upon morale and effectiveness. As a colonel, Richard Ault headed the 2,200-airman complement at Craig Air Force Base in Selma, Alabama, from 1962 to 1966. Ault, a California native, says, "I am not by upbringing or by anything else, race conscious." A delegation of three African Americans called on him at his office and asked him to place Selma off limits. "Boycott the town, nobody would trade there, none of my people would be allowed to traffic through the town, which was ridiculous. A majority of my people lived in Selma and had to rely on the town for their shopping and everything else. I told them I had neither the authority nor the inclination to put the place off limits. But for practical reasons I would be happy to help them in any other way. And I tried to insist on equality of opportunity on my own base and I tried to intervene with the town to achieve the same degree of acceptance for my black troops."

Complicating Ault's situation, along with the 45 African Americans and their families stationed at Craig, about 10 percent of the 330 foreign students at the base had dark skin. They encountered problems from the locals who insisted on treating them like African Americans. Ault won his first victory at the adjacent Nathan Bedford Forrest housing project, a county-built development restricted to military families. "Prior to my arrival," says Ault, "occupancy had just been whites only. I made it a point to insist that it be mixed and they [the local bank which administered the project] finally acceded." Ironically, the site honors the Confederate cavalry general who sired the Ku Klux Klan.

Ault also initiated a multiracial committee at Craig to serve as a sounding board for those with grievances. According to him, the tactic lessened tensions on the base but filled his ears with complaints about treatment in stores. "The old mayor was a dyed in the wool southern traditionalist, pretty set in his ways. He had this sadistic sheriff, Jim Clark. I didn't get very far with those people, but I tried. I was instrumental in bringing about a series of meetings between some of the more progressive citizens of the town, the top staff of the town, the principal of the black school, a couple of black clergyman. I got them to sit down with this old, rather reluctant mayor to talk about the possibility of some concessions. I can't say we had any real, single success but it was a step upward. When we finally got into office a much more progressive and modern young mayor, Joseph Smitherman, and Wilson Baker, the sheriff that replaced Jim Clark, we started making some progress."

Prior to the change in officials, however, even as Martin Luther King Jr. led the famous marches upon the Edmund Pettus Bridge in Selma, Ault was summoned to Washington for a conference in the office of Attorney General Robert Kennedy. Ault had been an eyewitness to a fracas in the street in which a news photographer's camera was smashed during an attempt to register black voters. In Kennedy's office, surrounded by a flight of generals, including Curtis LeMay, and Kennedy subordinates, Ault related what he had seen, remarking the incident had been "all blown out of proportion." Recalls Ault, "He [Kennedy] got very huffy about the whole thing and finally wound up stalking out and shaking his finger under General LeMay's nose and saying, 'General, you could do something about this if you would, if you would just put the base off limits.' He was, I thought, a little petulant, childish about the whole thing. It wasn't a very realistic approach.

"Later General LeMay called me to his office and said, 'Ault, you're doing a fine job of walking a tight rope down there. Just keep up the good work.' That was about the extent of the guidance that I received in that town. As I told Mr. Kennedy that morning, which seemed to rile him considerably, I thought my primary mission was a military one, training pilots, and not a social one of trying to bring about a social change, although I was trying to achieve equal opportunity for my people."

Upon passage of the Civil Rights Act in 1965, the air force directed commanders to oppose and overcome the barriers to access in housing, restaurants, barbershops, and other areas. How strong the action remained within the discretion of the senior staff. Ault recalls putting off-limits several establishments, mainly for their behavior rather than for refusal to serve. He drew some support from the local chapter of the Air Force Association, a national alumni group that backed the interests of the Craig people, and he credits a number of private citizens, clergy, businessmen, and progressive officials for improving the lot of black airmen.

By 1970, directives from the services took a firmer stand, "Commanders will impose off-limits sanctions against all business establishments . . . that discriminate against military personnel and their dependents."

21
Vietnam

In 1959, Benjamin O. Davis Jr. finally gained the permanent rank of brigadier general. Because of a series of overseas postings, he had viewed from afar the Civil Rights movement start to rip and reweave the tapestry of the country. Transferred in 1961 to a desk at the Pentagon, Davis was much closer to hand as President John F. Kennedy was assassinated, and Martin Luther King Jr. addressed the nation with his "I have a dream" speech.

Davis says he was deeply moved by King's speech, life, and philosophy. "We followed the events of the civil rights movement closely and with deepening interest. The hatred and senseless violence that characterized many of those events struck close to home when Samuel Young Jr., the son of a close friend of ours, was murdered in Tuskegee for daring to use the white men's room in a gasoline station. In the murderer's eyes, the act was justified because the boy was breaking the law.

"President Lyndon B. Johnson's civil rights program, with its emphasis on voting rights, aimed at improving the lot of all downtrodden people in the United States. We [he and his wife Agatha] strongly supported it, although active military duty was still so far removed from the political process in the 1960s that the idea of our campaigning for such legislation was beyond comprehension. Not until much later did it become appropriate for military people even to vote, and I can remember the shock experienced by older personnel when the policy was officially endorsed." Davis himself, who grew up as an "army brat" and was already in the twilight of his career with more than thirty years in uniform might also have wondered about the role of a soldier participating in the civil government process.

Ironically, Davis in 1965 worked directly under Lt. Gen. Dean C. Strother, who opposed racial integration in the military and as late as 1974 still contended that the armed forces moved too swiftly on the matter and "almost ruined the services." According to Davis, the subject never arose during his stay in the Pentagon and he believes Strother was no different than most of his peers. "We left the United States again in 1965," recalls Davis, "before the height of the violence by white reactionaries, and returned in the summer of 1968, when some of the major actions by black activists had already taken place. When news of the happenings in the States did reach us abroad during those years, often on Armed Forces Radio, it was sketchy and out of date. For this reason only the major events came to our attention, and we felt detached from many developments."

The messages from Washington, whether from the White House, the Defense Department, or Martin Luther King Jr. passed unheard in some military circles. Several navy transports included disagreeable instances of racism in their cargo. On the bulkheads of passenger lounges of two vessels, large maps of the United States had drawings indicating what each state was known for. New Jersey schools were indicated by a person in cap and gown and a university building. Texas had a picture of longhorn cattle, a bucking bronco, and some cowboys.

For some Southern states, the artisit depicted blacks picking or chopping cotton, a pigtailed girl dancing and African Americans playing music. While whites in Florida were seen water skiing, Georgia showed blacks eating watermelon in one hand and holding a hoe in their other hand.

The films to entertain those aboard were World War II vintage or earlier. Some included Willie Best, an actor who portrayed a stock 1940s lazy, superstitious black, or Manton Moreland as the sterotypical black stealing chickens. African Americans resented these movies and asked for other fare. Their requests were denied. The ships' commanders refused to believe that such films could heighten racial tensions. On one transport, however, when a white soldier, mimicking a line from a Bob Hope movie, uttered a racist sentiment to a black serving chow a fight broke out. In spite of the incident, the same films continued to be used on the grounds they had been approved as appropriate entertainment.

At marine encampments on Okinawa and then Vietnam, the Confederate Stars and Bars fluttered from vehicle antennas, huts, and buildings. White enlisted leathernecks, officers, and even chaplains by and large resisted attempts to have the offensive emblems removed. One wonders what the reaction would have been had the unhappy African Americans flown the black power insignia from their hooches. Complaints to the marine hierarchy usually branded an individual a troublemaker and subject to official reprimand.

While on occupation duty in Japan, Elliotte Williams saw commanders unhappy with integration use whatever leverage they had to rid themselves of African Americans. "Disciplinary actions were designed to keep soldiers in line but also to reduce the number of black troops. At Yokohama, two VD infections would be grounds for a court-martial. Failure to salute, speaking out, returning after curfew were delinquencies and a lot of blacks were put out of the service quickly." Other officers serving in Yokohama during the same period insist multiple VD cases did not result in court-martial for an individual.

For Harold Hayward, who graduated from West Point in 1944, along with H. Minton Francis, the sole African American to survive in the class, black soldiers continued almost invisible for nearly twenty years. During World War II, as a member of the 13th Airborne Division he encountered blacks only behind the wheels of trucks. In 1951 when Hayward began a twelve-year period as a student, then teacher in infantry school, followed by advisory and staff positions he did not deal directly with soldiers.

"In 1963, I returned to troop duty, as an infantry battalion commander in Korea. The Army was as fully integrated as it ever would be. My organization included blacks in all ranks, officers, NCOs and soldiers of the line. Proportionately, the mix was similar to that of the country as a whole. In the work place, the integration was complete. If there was friction on the job it was minor and seldom surfaced to my level. However, we sometimes had serious race-based problems concerning relationships between U.S. and Korean soldiers.

"Because of a shortage of U.S. military personnel, my unit, like many others, was augmented by Korean Army sergeants and soldiers fully trained in their military specialties and with a smattering of knowledge of English. They were fully integrated into the squads and platoons. Occasionally, an inability to communicate across the language barrier led Americans white and black to turn abusive toward their Korean counterparts. They would threaten to quit but through intervention by a Korean Army liaison officer, we were always able to restore order.

"Off duty, there was a tremendous gulf between white troops and black troops. On our military installation, recreational facilities were scarce and quite often those that were available did not appeal to 'red-blooded' American soldiers. At the end of the work day, ignoring the pleas of chaplains and the advice of doctors and commanders, a steady stream of soldiers decamped for the evening into the adjoining Korean village. In the 'ville' as it was known, they availed themselves of the bars, dance halls and other forms of 'recreational services' provided by Korean entrepreneurs.

"The most stringent forms of segregation prevailed in the ville—all self-imposed by the soldiers themselves. Korean providers of 'services' catered strictly to one race or another, either black or white, but not to both. The town itself was separated geographically into two ghettos, one white, one black. Ordinarily, peace and quiet reigned in the ville. Violence erupted only when, from ignorance or bravado, a soldier ventured into turf associated with the other race. On those occasions, our military police were usually called to restore order.

"I have seen the situation replicated, usually in all of my assignments overseas, both before and after my tour in Korea. I know many Americans find such behavior by American soldiers offensive. The point is that latent prejudices exacerbated by those off-duty relationships cannot be suppressed. They surface in the official business of the Army in subtle ways. Because white soldiers have the power in the strength of their numbers, black soldiers often suffer from discrimination and are denied equal opportunity."

Hayward donned his jump boots again with a year as a brigade commander for the 82d Airborne at Fort Bragg. He found a disproportionate number of black noncoms, men who had enlisted at the birth of desegregation because of the career opportunity. "Professionally," says Hayward, "they reflected the spectrum of abilities. Some were good, some marginal. I do not recall any particular problems with respect to race. It was tacitly understood that the senior black NCOs would 'take care' of any black soldier who showed signs of being a 'trouble maker.' Those black soldiers knew they had a good thing going for them and they were not about to let some black trooper upset their apple cart."

John Costa, who attended the Military Academy after winning an air corps navigator's wings, spent 1963 to 1967 with the 82d Airborne. He commanded a battalion from the 508th Airborne Infantry, stationed in the Dominican Republic. For the most part the troopers dealt only with the shoeshine boys, women who laundered their clothes, and an active cohort of prostitutes. "Sexual encounters of our soldiers," says Costa, "were impossible to control. We did what we could to protect our troops by offering medical examinations to the natives who wanted to enjoy the privilege of being admitted to the enlisted mens' club.

"I think we had a good feeling among ourselves with regard to race relations within the battalion. [He estimates about 40 percent of the GIs in the 82d were black.] The war in Vietnam was heating up but being already deployed outside the USA in Santo Domingo, we enjoyed a most unusual situation, stability. Officers and men were frozen in the battalion until we returned to Fort Bragg in September 1966." Others in the military believe a major source of trouble was the destabilization of units that followed the massive shipments of replacements to Vietnam, beginning after 1966.

"I had a black battalion executive officer who was my strong right arm. When we had returned to Bragg, racial tension was present, though not yet a serious problem. One of the black soldiers was on the carpet for some incident. I can still hear Major Harold Garner bellow to the soldier, '. . . in this battalion there is no black power except me! I am the black power here, and don't forget it.' I had several black officers in the battalion, and relations among officers were very good, honest friendships, mutual respect, innocent banter and I had good feelings about this aspect of my command experiences.

"In December 1966, I broke my leg parachuting during an exercise. I had to give up my command and having exceeded the normal command tour length, I left the 82d in June 1967. I was home on leave and watched TV coverage of the deployment of the division to Detroit where serious racial disturbances had broken out. Through it all, I don't think the division had any formal programs to deal with race and associated matters. But it was a highly disciplined organization and I didn't feel any great strain, training and leading the battalion during those troubled years."

While Benjamin O. Davis Jr. toiled at the Department of Defense, and Harold Hayward and John Costa experienced integration as practiced in the 82d Airborne, by 1966 U.S. involvement in the Vietnam conflagration had deepened. It began with a modest infusion of "advisors." Among the first Americans engaged in the Vietnam War, Colin Powell in 1962 served as an advisor with the Army of the Republic of Vietnam, the ARVN soldiers. Most of his associates were indigenous people and Powell, in his autobiography, makes only one reference to race about his first tour in the country. He speaks of his U.S. superior, Maj. George B. Price, "He became a mentor in my career, a black officer, one career generation ahead of me . . . and was generous in helping younger blacks along the way." Significantly, Powell does not mention any racial tension during this first tour. At that point the U.S. presence in the war-torn land was still too limited for there to be any serious confrontations of blacks and whites. Furthermore, the civil rights struggle had only begun to generate serious resistance outside of the South and militancy had not surfaced.

In the United States, following his Vietnam tour and watching television, Powell suddenly saw an old mate from the Pershing Rifles, killed after Powell returned to the States. "There was Tony [Mavroudis] in jungle fatigues driving home the program's message. 'Race did not matter out here,' Tony said, 'It doesn't exist . . . We're all soldiers. The only color we know is khaki and green. The color of the mud and the color of the blood is all the same.'"

When Powell went back to Vietnam in the summer of 1968 he faced a radically different situation. It was now a full fledged war for the U.S. military. Where in 1964 some 15,000 Americans served in Vietnam, by 1968, 550,000 were involved. On the homefront the attitude remained guns and butter, an unwillingness to fully commit resources. In fact, neither pursuit of the war nor satisfaction of homefront needs received their due according to their champions. Martin Luther King Jr. increasingly critical of the adventure in Southeast Asia said, "The promises of the Great Society have been shot down on the battlefield of Vietnam." Meanwhile, Gen. William Westmoreland, commander of the American forces on the scene demanded reinforcements and an expanded war effort.

Like Powell, naval airman Bill Norman was among the early batch of Americans engaged in the war. As a youngster in Norfolk, Virginia, he grew up under "the separate but equal doctrine. I lived in a neighborhood that was all black except for some Filipinos and Puerto Ricans. We didn't think about them as such. It was white people and the rest of us."

The son of a shipyard carpenter, Norman says he was not a conscious crusader against segregation. But he would test the system, sitting toward the middle of the bus and not moving when whites boarded the vehicle and the driver shouted at him, "Hey, you. Get to the back." He would sit and wait for someone to throw him out, but because he was a youngster, no one made an issue of it.

As the president of his class, president of his student government, and a senior in high school, in 1955, Norman entered the recruiting station and asked for materials on the Naval Academy. "He simply wouldn't give me any information. And he said he didn't want me to waste my time going through the tests. I was irate." At the time Norman was unaware of the fact that few blacks had entered the U.S. Naval Academy.

Norman earned a degree in mathematics and chemistry from West Virginia Wesleyan College, did a student-exchange tour in the Soviet Union for six months, and settled into a high school math teacher's job. Drafted in 1961, he opted for the navy and qualified for the flight-training program. The only black in his class at Pensacola, Norman, like Powell, says he experienced no "terrible overt racism" from his peers. He told writer Wallace Terry, in *Bloods,* "At least at the officer level, the Navy was priding itself on being ahead of what was happening in society. But the discrimination was still there, just not so open." The insults included exclusion from the band when it played at Mardi Gras in New Orleans, a mass exodus from the swimming pool if he showed up by himself, although if he came in a group his presence was tolerated. When local police harassed him off-post, the base authorities refused to intervene.

In 1963, while aboard the carrier *Ranger,* in the South China Sea, Norman as an airborne controller directed the first sorties of lightly armed planes against routes and supplies from the North. Recalled Norman, "When the intelligence people briefed us, we were told that we were trying to stop quote Communist insurgency unquote. That was the battle cry, and there was no real questioning of that. . . . When I went back in January of 1965, we had a comparatively major situation. We were regularly assigning carriers to Southeast Asia. It was taking on the atmosphere of a combat zone. . . . When I returned in 1969, I began questioning the rationale for what we were doing and the effectiveness of our efforts. It was no longer a war in which a few people were being killed. Large, large numbers of people were being killed. And everybody knew about it. It was in the papers, on television. And there were demonstrations against the war back home."

In his account to Wallace Terry, Norman does not talk about any particularly racial opposition to the war or organized antagonism toward the military. His tours roughly coincide with the period that Burt Shepherd, then a lieutenant commander, led Attack Carrier Air Wing 16 off the USS *Oriskany*. "During the wartime cruise aboard *Oriskany*," says Shepherd, "there may have been, and probably were racial tensions in the Air Wing and the ship, but they were either handled effectively by enlightened leaders or were too minor for me to remember thirty years later. Racial, family, promotion-pay problems murmurings were usually lower on the priority list when we were working up, training for a combat deployment, and during that deployment. Then, when we returned to the States and relaxed a little, with time to look for something that was 'wrong' the things that had been submerged and unaddressed surfaced with new emphasis. This happened with race relations, family living conditions and pay—especially for the enlisted personnel—length of deployments, promotion and training opportunities. 'Outside agitators' did not seem to me to be a significant problem. In the early days of our Navy, the American sailor was less educated and more susceptible to such outside influences."

But as Norman indicated, for the young men engaged, the struggle had reached savage extremes, and coupled with political assassination at home, violence, as black militant H. Rap Brown remarked, had become "as American as cherry pie." Whether or not 'agitators' influenced people, increasingly angry confrontations about the desirability of continuing to fight and the efforts of African Americans to expand their roles in society spilled over into the military. Says Powell, "Our men in the field, trudging through elephant grass under hostile fire, did not have time to be hostile toward each other. But bases like Duc Pho were increasingly divided by the same racial polarization that had begun to plague Americans during the sixties. The base contained dozens of new men waiting to be sent out to the field and short-timers waiting to go home. For both groups, the unifying force of a shared mission and shared danger did not exist. Racial friction took its place. Young blacks, particularly draftees, saw the war, not surprisingly, as even less their fight than the whites did. They had less to go home to. This generation was more likely to be reached by the fireworks of an H. Rap Brown than the reasonableness of the late Martin Luther King Jr. Both blacks and whites were increasingly resentful of the authority that kept them here for a dangerous and unclear purpose. The number one goal was to do your time and get home alive. I was living in a large tent and I moved my cot every night, partly to thwart Viet Cong informants who might be tracking me, but also because I did not rule out attacks on authority from within the battalion itself."

He adds, "As a young captain and thereabouts, I have no recollection of any specific directives concerning racial integration. We just did it at the unit level although I suspect there were probably some directives at higher levels to implement Truman's executive order." The word from Truman of course far preceded Powell's time of service but it is clear that although some abstract instruction may have been issued to the top brass, there was neither at company level nor at the highest echelons any substantive thought given to how to cope with the deteriorating state of race relations.

African American Joe Anderson, son of an employee for the Santa Fe Railroad, grew up in Topeka, Kansas, and attended the school system that served as the defendant in the landmark Supreme Court decision, *Brown v. Board of Education,* which integrated such institutions. "When I went to junior and senior high, the schools were integrated. That was also true for sports and other activities. I was an A student, and as an athlete socially acceptable."

He participated in an American Legion program, Boys' State, designed to acquaint students with government at an intimate level. The adolescents went to Wichita, the state capital, and then Anderson was one of the six blacks among 200 to attend Boys' Nation, which traveled to Washington, D.C., for a closer look at the federal apparatus. Another in the program, although from another state, was a youngster named William Jefferson Clinton.

"I got a post card from the USMA that congratulated me and enclosed an application along with information on how to secure an appointment." Originally a second alternate, Anderson entered West Point in 1961 as one of six blacks in a class of 950 cadets. "Four of us graduated, which is about the same rate of attrition as for whites. I didn't experience any overt racism. Nobody ever called me a black nigger. We had white roommates; lots of visibility. But when I took the opportunity to go to Africa for Operation Crossroads the institution had a chance and excuse to pass over me for a top cadet position. None of us got one of those."

Upon graduation in 1965, Anderson says, "I chose the infantry and wanted to be the best qualified infantryman so I went to the Airborne Rangers at the 82d Division, Fort Bragg, North Carolina. I was exposed there to race in a way I never before saw. While there were no overt experiences on the base, when we went into town, we were told, 'Don't go down that street. Blacks don't go there.' I stayed in camp."

Three weeks after he married in 1966, Anderson received orders for Vietnam. As a replacement he took over a platoon in the 1st Cavalry, 1st Airborne Brigade. "The platoon was completely integrated although I was the only black officer in the company. The CO was a West Pointer and race was never an issue. You didn't worry about color; you only wanted someone to cover your back.

"Throughout the Cav, the black representation in the enlisted ranks was heavier than the population as a whole in the United States. One-third of my platoon and two of my four squad leaders were black. For many black men, the service, even during a war, was the best of a number of alternatives to staying home and working in the fields or bumming around the streets of Chicago and New York."

Shortly after he got to the country, he and his men received orders to search for another platoon dropped by helicopter in the Central Highlands and now missing. "This was my first operation," Anderson told Wallace Terry in *Bloods*. "I'm new in-country. People didn't know me. I don't know them. They have to be thinking, Can this platoon leader handle it? I was only a second lieutenant.

"We went into a forced march all day. When it got dark, we pulled into a clear area like a landing zone and put our perimeter out and set up for the night. Headquarters wanted me to keep moving and keep searching through the night. I knew it wasn't the smartest thing to do, because you could get ambushed. You can't see what you're doing in the dark.

"Around ten or eleven o'clock, they opened up on us. They were still there. We fought all night long until six in the morning. I learned very quickly how to call in artillery, how to put aircraft over me to drop flares and keep the area lighted up so they couldn't sneak up on me. I was calling the artillery in within 35, 40 yards of my own people, as tight as I could without hitting us. I don't remember wondering if I was ever gonna get out of this. I just did not have time to think about it. I was just too busy directing fire to be scared."

The Anderson platoon had been up against an entire Vietcong battalion, outnumbering his force by ten to one. But the enemy eventually retired and when his GIs spread out they found only a few badly wounded survivors of the ambushed brother platoon. "For rescuing the survivors and driving off the VC battalion, I received a Silver Star. But most importantly, the action served as a bond between my platoon and me. It was my first chance to react under fire and it had gone well. My men knew I could handle the responsibility.

"Usually, when we had R and R," says Anderson, "I left the country and was not in the rear echelons where there was racial trouble. When there were arguments, it wasn't about sex; the prostitution system was not segregated. But race came into play over music, the troops fought over soul versus country and western."

It was while Anderson led this unit that a French television journalist, Pierre Schoendoerffer, himself captured at Dien Bien Phu when the French fought against Vietnamese independence ten years earlier, shot a documentary that took as its title, *The Anderson Platoon*. Schoendoerffer climaxed his film with a firefight that enveloped the entire company. The black soldier and the white GI shown comforting him served with another platoon.

Anderson, who completed one tour, returned to Vietnam in 1970 to lead an infantry company. Asked why he and other African Americans volunteered or persisted, he responds, "You're either living in America or else you're going to leave it." He adds, "It was like the Tuskegee airmen, we wanted to prove we belonged by doing what was asked." Anderson won two Silver Stars and five Bronze Stars, among other decorations. General Mike Davison who commanded the U.S. and Army of the Republic of Vietnam forces that included Anderson's unit says, "Joe Anderson was a superb company commander; he generated respect from white and black soldiers."

Like Anderson, Sgt. Maj. Edgar Huff of the marines, with a sleeve full of hashmarks marking service back to the early days at Montford Point in World War II, did not think in terms of color when under fire. He occupied a bunker of the 1st Military Police Battalion across from the main airstrip at Da Nang when the Tet Offensive threatened to envelope the area. Alerted to a massive assault, Huff and a colonel rushed out of their emplacement. "At the time," Huff told Wallace Terry, "I carried a shotgun, a pistol and a grenade launcher. And two bandoliers also. And when we got to the scene, you never saw a fire fight more horrifying in all your life. The boys were in a spot as hard as it could be, but they were holding it.

"I looked up and the best radio operator you ever saw—name was Rick—was hit and pinned down out there maybe 50 yards. They saw him out there in this field, and they were trying to finish him off. They were shooting with automatic fire . . . Every time Rick'd move a little, they would fire . . . just tryin' to finish him off.

"Rick was hollering, 'Mother. Mother.' I could stand it no longer. I started out. And the colonel said, 'No, No. Just wait. Just wait.' I said, 'Sorry, Colonel.'

"This wasn't a black boy. He was a white boy. I knew I might get killed, saving a white boy. But he was my man. That's what mattered.

"And I took off. Ran through an open field. They was firing from a tree line. And I got maybe 20 yards and I was hit on the head. It hit my helmet. And it spun me around, knocked me down. And I got up and started again. And another round hit on the side of the helmet and knocked me down again. And I started crawling. And it seemed like round after round was kicking at the dirt all around me.

"And I jumped up then, and I started running. Then I got to him. Then they opened up everything they had right there into that position. And I fell on top of him to keep him from getting hit again, and this fragmentation grenade hit us and ripped my flac jacket all into pieces. And it got me in the shoulder and arm.

"Then our people opened up all they had. And the Cong started moving back. And the colonel came out to help me with the stretcher to bring Rick back. . . . They gave me the Bronze Star for pulling Rick out. And Rick wrote me this letter. It says, 'Sergeant Major, I thank you for my life.' Hell, he was one of my men. Black or white. I would have done the same even if I got shot to hell in the process."

In 1967, Harold Hayward commenced an eighteen-month tour in Vietnam. As a staff officer at army headquarters he says, "I had about 60 or 70 people working for me—mostly commissioned officers. The racial mix was about par for the course and I got a lot of work done without any racial friction." During the evening hours, his white, female civilian stenographer was replaced by "a well educated, intelligent, thoroughly reliable black soldier whose home was Chicago. When talking with me, I observed nothing to indicate his racial or ethnic background. However, during breaks in our work, he often had opportunity to talk on the telephone with friends in other places in Viet Nam. I could not help but overhear his conversations. I found that when talking to his black friends, he spoke in a language that was almost incomprehensible to me. For the first time I realized the dual roles that blacks had to play to get along with the Army establishment on one hand and their 'brothers' on the other."

Hayward had a clearer picture of the separation when he next commanded a brigade from the 101st Airborne Division. "The unit had been in Viet Nam for eighteen months and was fully integrated. It is often said, 'there are no atheists in foxholes.' Almost the same can be said about 'no racists in foxholes.' However, race made a difference in one situation. Where I was located, the war was mainly fought by company size units—each operating independently in the jungle for ten days to two weeks at a time. On completion of each foray into the 'boonies' the company was extracted, usually by helicopter and taken back to base camp for a three to five day stand down, spent in rest, recreation, cleaning up and preparing for the next mission.

"Befitting their positions, the NCOs would collectively set themselves apart during a stand down. But I was somewhat surprised to observe the line-soldiers self-segregated immediately. Blacks staked out their territory in one part of the rest area while whites occupied another. Perhaps I was in error, but I sensed that the segregation was instigated primarily by the black troops and that the white soldiers were on the whole, indifferent to the arrangement."

The kind of separation seen by Hayward provided an atmosphere conducive to outbursts. Always away from the battlefields bubbled the growing signs of dangerous unrest that should have alerted authorities, as the Vietnam War consumed more and more men. Newspaper reporters who interviewed troops indicated worsening morale and in particular the bitterness of African Americans over their perception of discrimination. In 1968, black prisoners in the marine brig at Da Nang rioted. Shortly afterward, in a similar incident black soldiers at Long Binh attacked guards and someone clubbed a white prisoner to death. There were numerous arrests and casualties. Lesser eruptions disrupted air force operations and navy ships.

During the next five years protest and action-oriented groups sprang up wherever U.S. forces served. At Ford Hood, Texas, 100 African American soldiers openly denounced racism in the army after a so-called love-in aimed against continuation of the war. In Germany, the "Unsatisfied Black Soldiers" issued flyers against further combat in Southeast Asia. The Black United Soldiers, the Black Action Group, and the People's Freedom Party all staked claims against racism and particularly in the military. None of the organizations led a long life and the number of active members never amounted to many. But they made a lot of noise. GIs showed up for their demonstrations and commanders felt obliged to take notice of them.

The Defense Department dispatched operatives who reported serious racial tensions. The leader of the investigatory group, a black man, L. Howard Bennett, noted that although men under fire ignored skin color, the situation in rear echelons posed a threat of violent confrontations. Bennett warned that whites and blacks returning to the States, "agitated, hostile, and in conflict," posed tremendous potential trouble for home communities. The Defense Department all but ignored the findings, only belatedly developing a modest program to improve race relations.

In Vietnam, commanders grudgingly admitted to the worsening polarization. General Creighton Abrams, who succeeded William Westmoreland as head of the U.S. forces in South Vietnam, set up watch committees designed to open up communication among the troops and develop forums and discussion groups. The programs were of limited success. Those engaged in combat were too concerned with mission accomplishment and survival to deal with the problem. White rear-echelon officers and enlisted personnel either felt no military urgency about the matter or saw no reason to discard their prejudices. African Americans regarded the effort as insincere since, by their perception, discrimination ran unabated. According to *The Military and the Media, 1968–1973*, issued by the Army's Center of Military History, the inspector general of the Military Assistance Command, Vietnam (MACV) declared that of 2,628 race-related complaints, only 146 actually qualified as such. "The remaining cases are partially substantiated, in that there is *evidence that race is a factor but discrimination or prejudice were not causes*" [my italics]. Although seemingly intended to dismiss the charges of widespread bias-related incidents, the statement speaks megabytes about attitude and understanding in official circles. African Americans hooted when asked by Defense Department investigators why victims of injustice did not approach the inspector general. There was no confidence in the hierarchy by lesser-ranked blacks and whites.

Chick Rauch, then serving as a staff member for Adm. Elmo Zumwalt, commander of the U.S. Naval Forces in Vietnam, recalls, "I was in Saigon or Washington when the problems of the military and in the Navy were happening and did not see it first hand at any command. But my guess is that the growing civil rights movement in the U.S. gave the African-American Navy personnel courage to fight some of the gross racist practices of the various services. The growing questioning of authority that was occuring nationwide, gave these same people courage to seriously push authority in their fight for equality.

"I am sure that all of the services had racist issues to deal with. But the Navy had somehow gotten into a culture that could hardly been more racist if somebody had sat down and planned it. Stewards who were then all black or Filipino had their own separate uniforms and pay scales and were consistently referred to as 'boys' by their 'employers.' There were no hair care or cosmetic products in the Navy exchanges for non-whites. There were no NROTC units at predominantly black colleges."

The system of assignment and promotions in the navy cordoned off the handful of African Americans. Dennis Nelson, the Golden Thirteen graduate, strained against huge burdens. He was into his thirties before the navy granted him a regular commission. His deskfaring posts cost him the best credentials for advancement and he forcefully championed the cause of fellow blacks in the navy. "He was the kind of a guy that a lot of us went to for some type of advice," remembers Sam Gravely. "Nelson did not hesitate to state his opinions and seek support from secretaries of the navy. That hardly endeared him to superiors."

John Lee succeeded in obtaining berths on ships of the line. Nevertheless, he was passed over twice for the crucial promotion from lieutenant commander and forced to retire. "Being passed over for promotion was the most shattering thing in my life," said Lee, "even more than my parents dying. That really upset me."

Lee remarked that he believed he was the victim of a quota. "Sam Gravely and Dennis Nelson, along with a number of other more junior black officers were on active duty then. The three of us were lieutenant commanders in the regular Navy. My supposition is that the Navy Department decided that only one of the three would be promoted, and it was to be Gravely. I don't know whether that's true or not. I have no facts but it certainly seems a plausible explanation."

Not even the Naval Academy ring could lift Wesley Brown. Late in his career while stationed in Hawaii, his commanding officer bluntly told Brown he was not in favor of black naval officers. He backed up his opinion with a poor fitness rating that may well have derailed Brown's career. As a shore-based engineer he too lacked seagoing experience. When Brown failed to get the nod for commander, he submitted his retirement papers.

Absent any sustained, coordinated programs or directions for dealing with tensions, the problem solving in the services devolved to local commanders.

African American Fred Black, born in 1946, son of an officer who was recalled from the reserves after World War II to the 24th Infantry, through the assignments of his father had lived in Japan, France, Liberia, as well the United States before he completed his education at Howard University in 1968. "I was accepted by several colleges, including the University of Michigan but I went to Howard because I wanted to attend a historically black university. As my father and brother had before me, I entered the ROTC which was a good deal. I received a scholarship that paid tuition, fees, books and a $100 a month stipend. The draft was not an issue until I was in the advanced program and that made it moot. My plan was to serve my commitment, get out and be a lawyer. Next thing I knew it was time to retire."

After Howard he qualified as a paratrooper and attended the Ranger School before reporting back to his unit, the 82d Airborne. "About one third of the enlisted men were black and a high percentage of the NCOs. On duty, people worked together. There were few racial incidents. Off duty it was a segregated situation. I got along fine with my peers, subordinates and superiors. I had some advantages, a father who was one of the dozen black colonels in the Army and known by many of my superiors. Having spent my life in the military environment I understood the subtleties of the system and especially the social aspects. I felt comfortable with troops of all colors and seemed able to communicate with them. I never saw resentment from anyone.

"There was an incident that first year. My CO told me I had to see the Criminal Investigation Division and I assumed it was about a case in the company. When I got there, they read me my rights and asked where I was on a particular night. I asked why and was told it was in my interests to cooperate and not 'make trouble.' I refused to answer on principle and left the office. Outside, a black agent told me that a white officer's wife had been raped by a black man, described as 6' 2," dark skin and 200 pounds. I was 5' 9," light skinned and 159 pounds. The CID was interviewing all blacks to find a suspect! I took this matter all the way to the Division commanding general and he got them to stop the process. The Army of 1969 was still uneasy in questions of race.

"The 82d Airborne had done riot duty in Detroit [1967] and instituted programs to deal with race relations. Some pre-dated official ones by the Army. One set of courageous decisions placed housing, stores and other public establishments off limits because of their discriminatory policies. The Army, in effect, was making desegregation a reality in town through economic pressures. The orders never created harmony but they reinforced what was acceptable."

After a year of active service, Black reported to Vietnam in July 1969 for the standard one-year tour. "We had very few racial problems in the combat units and those occurred when we stood down in the rear. In the field people depended on each other because they wanted to go home in one piece. In the rear, they drank and became less guarded about revealing their feelings about different races. This cut both ways. Three black guys told a white guy in their squad he could not sleep in their bunker because they declared it 'black only' territory. We got on that real fast and the ring leader was disciplined. In another incident, we had a group of white guys put up a Confederate flag and a black guy burned it. A fight erupted. The guys who trusted each other in the boonies were trying to kill each other with whatever weapons they could quickly grab—entrenching tools, rifle butts, etc. The fight was broken up and we sent several off to the stockade. Once we were back in the woods, the troops soldiered without regard to the incident."

Jesse Brewer III, the son of a soldier with the 92d Division, was born in Dallas shortly after V-E Day in 1945. "My father told me how his unit had been segregated and that he received a Bronze Star after being wounded and staying with his men rather than accepting evacuation. Both my parents were college graduates of Tuskegee University. My father drove a city bus while he awaited acceptance to the Chicago Police Academy and my mother, a registered nurse, worked for the Public Health Department in Chicago."

The family moved to Los Angeles where Jesse Brewer II started a career with the city's police department, eventually retiring as a deputy chief. Jesse III says, "I attended Catholic schools grades 1–12, and then became an undergraduate at UCLA. My experiences with discrimination were practically nil, until high school. I had been exempt from the draft due to a student deferment but in 1966 I lost it. I decided to enlist in the Navy to have a choice of training rather than the infantry of the Army.

"There were no other blacks in my recruit class of November 1966. My first incident involving discrimination occurred at the San Diego Naval Training Station and prevented me from becoming the honor graduate who was chosen on a demerit system. These were issued for any infraction of the rules during basic. I had the fewest for the entire training period going into the final inspection which covered quarters, locker, bunk and so forth. It was conducted by the platoon and squad commanders out of the presence of the squads. The inspection team discovered all sorts of extraneous items in my locker, things which didn't belong to me. My gear was out of order and there were several other discrepancies. I received enough demerits to keep me from being the honor graduate. I complained to my drill instructor who thought it odd that suddenly I forgot how to pass an inspection. But the results stood."

Following his basic training, the navy sent Brewer to its hospital in San Diego to learn the skills of a corpsman. "There were two blacks in my class, myself and James Ogleby. We were pretty much isolated and hung out together. Grades on all exams were posted by ID numbers. We had some pretty tough courses—microbiology, pharmacology and etc. The white boys used to crowd around the bulletin board checking out the test scores. The top two or three knew each other's ID numbers. So they were always checking out each other. And here was one ID number tucked between number one and number three. Imagine their shock/surprise when they found out whose number that belonged to! Quite a buzz went around. Afterwards, everybody always wanted to know how I came out on an exam. They were visibly disappointed every time I came out high in the postings."

Brewer accumulated six months of experience as a ward corpsman in a hospital before assignment to Company C, 1st Battalion of the 9th Marines, located at Khe Sanh. "I joined them the end of March 1968. On the 1st of April came the Tet Offensive. This was my first experience of being in a unit with more than one black. In fact, we were suddenly in the majority. Most of the individuals were either black or Hispanic. A common theme seemed they had a choice between jail or enlistment in the Marines. All of my senior enlisted and commissioned officers were white. Marines, black or white, treat their corpsmen deferentially for obvious reasons. Most of my fellow Marines were shocked and surprised there were black corpsmen. The brothers, black and brown, were proud. The whites came around after my first fire fight and I performed well.

"I was on my first patrol when we came under intense hostile fire. There were many casualties and I was the only medic available. I set up a triage and attended to the wounded. There were several out in the open. I made it my business to get to them no matter what. At the end of the day, when I thought all the wounded had been carried out or escorted out of danger, I prepared to leave. It was pretty dark and I heard moaning. I found an injured Marine who reported he couldn't feel anything from the waist down and therefore couldn't stand or walk. He asked me to leave him and save myself. I refused. I picked him up in a fireman's carry and proceeded to get us both out of there. We were on the side of a rather steep mountain and it became obvious I was not going to be able to walk out of there with him on my back. I sat down and we literally slid down the mountain to the bottom, inch by inch. While taking a break, we both heard movement coming towards us. It seemed like an eternity waiting to find out if we'd be prisoners or rescued. By the grace of God, a squad from my unit was out looking for stragglers. We made a stretcher and got back to base camp. The soldier was white. I never knew his name. To this day, I think it would be wonderful if we could meet again."

For his deed, Brewer received a Silver Star and the citation declared, "Repeatedly exposing himself to the intense hostile fire, he made numerous trips across the fire-swept terrain and ably directed the removal of the wounded Marines . . ." Some thought he merited a higher award. Later, when his outfit was pinned down, a burst of shrapnel struck his leg. "I didn't realize I had been hit until someone pointed to the bleeding. Once the adrenaline gets going . . .

"Acceptance was pretty much based on performance under fire. It's how you respond when the ———— hits the fan. Fortunately, God gave me the courage to do my job and do it well. Word goes back to the rear area very quickly and no one ever gave me problems. We got along very well on the front line. Any problems or attitudes were straightened out in short order. Most of the racial problems occurred in the rear. People had too much time on their hands in the rear. When Martin Luther King Jr. was killed, things back there were really tense. At times, it was more dangerous in rear areas than out on patrol. There were no programs of which I was aware, designed to develop good relationships between people of different races."

William De Shields had chosen to remain in service in spite of some unpleasant experiences as a black officer in the United States. While in command of a Nike missile battalion stationed in Wiesbaden, Germany, he remembers, "This was an Air Force area with liberal policies, housing facilities and an environment that lacked the discrimination in the States in 1956. It felt like Utopia and I extended my tour so I could share it with my family. I would have been content to stay there for the rest of my military career rather than return to a racist homeland."

Instead, De Shields drew a variety of assignments, abroad as well as at places like White Sands, and Oklahoma before a posting to Vietnam in 1970–71 as commander of the 1,200-man 27th Composite Maintenance Battalion located at Quang Tri, just south of the North Vietnam border. De Shields was responsible for a number of subordinate units that handled ammunition, transportation, fuel storage, and other vital adjuncts to the combatants.

"Prior to my taking command, the enemy had blown up a 75-acre ammunition dump twice. My primary problem was to maintain morale. Morale and discipline were so bad that my instruction upon taking command was 'forget about performing the mission of the battalion, concentrate upon the people.' The basic troubles were racial, drugs, fraggings, lack of respect for officers and NCOs. Black soldiers were again fighting two battles, the so-called enemy in Vietnam and discrimination at home. For the first time in the military history of this country, blacks, realizing they had nothing to prove, decided they were not going to tolerate America's hypocrisy and many rebelled.

"I noted many of the front-line soldiers tended to be blacks, Hispanics, Italians, low-income whites. During the initial phases of the Vietnam War, casualties among blacks far exceeded their number [percentage] in the population." Martin Luther King Jr. stressed the same point. During the early years of combat, the official figures report 20 percent of the KIAs were African Americans, as against a percentage of 11 percent in the overall population. For the war as a whole, black casualties totaled 12.5 percent.

Racial tension in the military tightened as the antiwar movement coalesced with the civil rights drive. Martin Luther King Jr. criticized the war on the grounds of his commitment to nonviolence, his support for the sovereign right of indigenous people to govern their own lands, and for its devastating effects upon American poor, both white and black. Antiwar spokespeople argued that funds that might have been spent on housing, education, and health care were diverted to the Vietnam conflict.

Martin Luther King Jr. delivered powerful speeches that yoked the second-class status of African Americans with their combat service. "We have been repeatedly faced with the cruel irony of watching Negro and white boys on TV screens as they kill and die together for a nation that has been unable to seat them together in the same schools. So we watch them in brutal solidarity burning the huts of a poor village, but we realize that they would never live on the same block in Detroit." On another occasion he noted, "We are willing to make the Negro 100 percent of a citizen in warfare, but reduce him to 50 percent of a citizen on American soil. Half of all Negroes live in substandard housing and they have half the income of whites. There is twice as much unemployment and infant mortality among Negroes . . . at the beginning of 1967." His attacks on the war as inimical to the interests of African Americans certainly fueled resentment among blacks in the military.

Although leaders like King decried the war and argued that African Americans had become the most favored cannon fodder, others enthused over the roles of blacks. *Ebony* magazine praised the participation of the race and spoke of greater opportunities in the military. Whitney Young as head of the Urban League justified the high rate of casualties as due to "the simple fact that a higher proportion of Negroes volunteer for hazardous duty." As Fred Black observed, black troopers accounted for one-third of the 82d Airborne. But of all modern American wars, the one in Vietnam most definitely bore an economic and social-class character. The decision to allow deferments to college students eliminated from the manpower pool a largely white, better educated, affluent segment of the population. Even without the pass granted to this element, Defense Secretary Robert McNamara's Project 100,000 flooded the military with recruits drawn from low-income elements, which included a disproportionate number of African Americans.

To some the turmoil of the late 1960s and early 1970s played out sinister, scripted scenarios rather than happening because of collisions between uncontrolled movements, frustration, opposing demands of groups, and reactions to a climate of violence infecting the streets of America. It played against a backdrop of assassinations of political and social figures, and a bloody war in rice paddys eight thousand miles away.

DeWitt Armstrong, following his tour with the 14th Armored Cavalry and immersion of the troopers in integration, had pursued higher education at the Command and General Staff College, Fort Leavenworth, Kansas, and for three years in the Woodrow Wilson School at Princeton until he earned a Ph.D. His academic credentials and combat experiences led to staff positions in various policy-planning operations. "I became known as the most persistent advocate of a 'program of mounting pressures' as the alternative to early, abrupt use of nuclear weapons. Soon this new strategy proved to be just what the incoming JFK Administration wanted."

Subsequently, after a year at the National War College, Armstrong surfaced in Vietnam as the chief planner for General Westmoreland. "In early 1966 I was appalled to see Secretary McNamara and President Johnson reject—because it would require mobilization—the strategy that I had proposed and which Westmoreland and the Joint Chiefs had accepted."

Whatever the merits of the proposals, Armstrong returned to Fort Hood, Texas, to command troops and pin on a brigadier's star. "Those were years of wild turbulence for the Army. The nation was coming apart, and revolutionary hot-heads were doing their evil best to destroy our polity and our Army as well. The academic world irresponsibly led the way in resistance to the draft. Riots were planned, and the Army was obliged to divert attention to training for handling civil disorder. In this atmosphere, enlisted men and officers were rapidly shifted around, owing to Vietnam requirements. Continuity and unit integrity were very hard to sustain. No longer did a company have solid, experienced NCOs (many just dropped out) nor the unit cohesion which they bring. Discipline declined; rabble rousers pursued their own goals. And all this was just when a surge of black nationalism was under way. It is amazing that there were not riots among the troops.

"One of my most vivid memories is from the spring of 1968, when the CO of the 2d Armored Dvision, where I was ADC, spoke to me of the 'hatred' he saw in the eyes of black soldiers. To me it didn't look like hatred but rather bluster. The black soldiers were just as dutiful as the whites in doing or training for the Army's chores of restoring order and suppressing violence in the city streets. No doubt there were agitators among our black soldiers and lots of wild talk, but our junior leaders and the common sense of our troopers sustained the emphasis upon colorblind handling of our men. An adequate level of unit cohesion survived despite disruptive efforts by mostly white draft-dodgers and war-resisters. Our men seemed to hold those scruffy people in pretty high disdain and would probably have been delighted to beat up on them. But our rules of engagement were tight and firmly enforced. The Army attitude toward control of civil disturbances is one of strong distaste, but if we had to do it, then tight control and efficiency minimizes the harm to people. I saw no difference at all in how black and white soldiers performed."

In late 1970, Armstrong was delighted to return to Vietnam, first as a deputy advisor to the III Corps and then in charge of a force numbering 22,000 soldiers, principally from the 187th Airborne Brigade and the 17th Aviation Group deploying more than 500 helicopters. He also held some responsibility for another 50,000 men operationally commanded from Saigon. "Among the latter group," says Armstrong, "the only racial problem involved a few score blacks in service units near Cam Ranh Bay who in effect mutinied. My impression is that those people, who had done something like calling themselves an independent republic, were sort of allowed to get hungry and after a few weeks, to turn themselves in and get court-martialed. We were attentive to the possibility of contagion among my units, but none occurred."

"My deputy chief of staff was a very black, 6'3" colonel who had earned a battlefield commission in Korea in the infantry. Soon, I made him my chief of staff and then gave him command of the brigade-sized Task Force 19 at An Khe. Our critically important, frequently beleaguered posts of Pleiku and Kontum were absolutely dependent upon keeping Route 19 clear for supply traffic. The An Khe area was always at low boil, owing both to the North Vietnamese Army and the drug-riddled, ill-disciplined U.S. Forces. A black trooper who had shot and killed his first sergeant was still there unconfined. When I took command, my first action was to send him off at once to the stockade on the seacoast and second to announce that anyone charged with violence against authority would immediately be confined. There were other appalling conditions in and around An Khe, not least the brisk trade in heroin, which I made a major effort to reduce if not eradicate.

"That colonel faced a real challenge and had every right to be as nervous as he was. I made a point of stopping in to visit every three or four days to reassure him. Each time he greeted me with warm relief and spoke of his trials and tribulations but he never eased up on his efforts to educate and lead his younger officers. They responded well to his leadership and in a very dangerous situation, his losses were exceptionally low. His perimeters were never penetrated. When we were relieved I pinned onto his jungle fatigues a U.S. Legion of Merit. I tried hard to get him promoted to brigadier general but his age was against him."

John Suggs, with the knowledge gained at a number of higher-education programs, and management posts for the air force, served as squadron commander of a combat support group for a year at Tan Son Nhat Air Force

Base in Saigon. Like others he too was dismayed by the flaunting of the South's Civil War banner. "The first thing you saw when you entered the mess hall was a huge Confederate flag displayed behind the chow line in the mess hall. I thought, how ignorant can these people be."

In some situations, participants believe the basic problem was one of spirit rather than skin color. Michael Spiro, as a marine officer first worked with a battalion landing team assigned to the Sixth Fleet as Landing Force Mediterranean. "We had no problems resulting from racial tension or race-related incidents. We did have morale problems, however. These were caused by assigning personnel to a deploying unit without allowing them to have the fully authorized stateside time following their return from Vietnam. It was not unusual to have Marines, who just 45 days before had completed their second tour in Vietnam, assigned to a unit that was going to be deployed for six months or more. Med deployment was the one that stood the best chance of being extended and one that had the poorest living conditions caused by the age of the amphibious shipping and neglect of troop berthing spaces."

According to Spiro, the Naval Forces Vietnam tended to be small in size, operating with specialized teams of SEALS, underwater demolition and salvage teams, coast patrols, and riverine missions. "Individuals identified with their units and considered themselves as part of a team or crew, to which they had a strong bond. As a result, we had no racial problems or incidents that I can recall."

Chappie James reported to the 8th Fighter Tactical Wing, operating from a base in Thailand. Serving under Col. Robin Olds, James functioned as deputy commander for operations. Administrative duties prevented him from occupying a cockpit for the eighteen to twenty missions per month deemed necessary to maintain the skills required for the hot F-4 Phantom. James led a limited number of flights against the enemy but now in his mid-forties he recognized, "The less you fly, the more it takes to get your proficiency back in a combat situation and that's a quick way to the graveyard." After a raid on Hanoi, his Phantom rocked from antiaircraft shells that knocked fifty-six holes in it, shutting down one of the two engines. He radioed his second element leader, a white from Louisiana, to take over leadership and guide the others to a rendezvous with a tanker.

Instead of leaving him, however, the rest of the flight hovered around James, prepared to drive off any enemy MiG fighters. James repeated his order but the pilots continued to guard him, pretending their radios had failed. Even the highly vulnerable tanker crew risked themselves by taking the fuel to James and his colleagues. He was gratified at the response by the mostly white airmen and later said, "We don't hate each other after all. It's really not necessary and we can't afford it."

On another sortie, North Vietnamese gunners damaged his ship so badly he made an emergency landing. As he discussed what happened to him, a visiting reporter questioned him about the growing fury of the civil rights struggle in the States. James answered. "Look, friend, I'm really not interested in all of that, really. See I consider myself damned lucky to have been able to land my airplane at this emergency strip in one piece."

Subsequently, being questioned about comments of militants like H. Rap Brown and Stokely Carmichael, which implied blacks ought to fight at home rather than in Vietnam, angered James, who spoke out against ". . . the lawlessness, rioting, men like Stokely Carmichael acting as if they speak for the Negro people. They aren't, and set civil rights back 100 years!" The argument between people who favored direct, physical confrontation and those who sought change through nonviolent pressure, split African Americans and whites. James removed the black panther emblem he had worn on his fighter pilot's helmet now that it had become associated with a movement he deplored.

The statements by James in which he repudiated the most militant point of view endeared him to many concerned whites, including President Lyndon Johnson who tendered him a White House reception when James returned to the United States. Immediately following the murder of Dr. Martin Luther King Jr., and even as riots erupted in several areas of the country, James addressed a gathering of Air Force Association officers. He declared that in spite of events and the resistance to progress, "I'm not disgusted—I'm a citizen of the United States of America and I'm no second-class citizen either and no man here is, unless he thinks like one and reasons like one and performs like one. This is my country and I believe in her and I believe in her flag and I'll fight for her and I'll serve her and I'll contribute to her welfare whenever and however I can. If she has any ills, I'll stand by her until in God's given time, through her wisdom and her consideration for the welfare of the entire nation, she will put them right."

The fury of civil disorder, triggered by the murder of Martin Luther King Jr., shocked the Benjamin O. Davis Jr. family, which visited Washington, D.C., toward the end of the 1960s. After they drove through areas of the city shattered by riotous outbreaks caused by racial turmoil, Davis professsed astonishment at the extent of unrepaired damage. "It was difficult for Agatha and me, so used to the relative racial calm of our lives overseas, to understand this tragic violence that seemed to dominate both blacks and whites in the U.S." Writing in 1991, Davis remarks, ". . . the country was fortunate to have a leader [Lyndon Johnson] with his vision and courage."

A black navy chaplain, stationed on Okinawa at the time of the assassination, recalls that while at Camp Pendleton he had heard a white officer wish for "troublemaker" King's death. Angry African Americans on Okinawa broke up the local Airmans' Club and flashed black-power salutes. When the senior chaplain was asked for permission to hold a memorial service, the request was denied. However, the Episcopal bishop for the Far East granted permission for a religious ceremony in one of the civilian churches.

Chappie James, despite the favor of the president and the approval of many of his concerned associates, endured racial insults and rebuffs during his assignments and travels. But his most dangerous challenge came from a foreign source, Col. Mu'ammar Khadafy, the Libyan dicatator whose coup preceded the assignment of James to command Wheelus Air Force Base, which was established before Khadafy seized power. In 1969, Khadafy led a column of halftracks that overran the main gate at Wheelus where, in a *High Noon* scene, the dictator faced James, both men packing pistols on their hips. James says he told the Libyan, "Move your hand away from that gun!" Khadafy complied and the halftracks subsequently retreated. James later said, " If he had pulled that gun, he never would have cleared his holster. They never sent any more halftracks."

Unable to reach an accommodation with Khadafy, the United States agreed to vacate Wheelus well before the expiration of the lease agreement. During the final negotiations, a team of Libyan officers brought along a soldier with a submachine gun into James's living room. Again, the American asserted himself. The soldier vanished. The Libyans demanded all valuable equipment be turned over to them, but in a stealthy coup, a fleet of air force cargo planes descended on Wheelus overnight and carried off all high-priority items. James's adroit leadership during this dangerous period brought him a promotion to brigadier general.

The Pentagon dispatched James to respond to the antiwar demonstrations on campuses around the country. He encountered chanting mobs, denunciations of the expansion of the war into Cambodia, sneers that he served white interests, and statements that blacks had no reason to fight in Vietnam. He defended the strategy of the war as necessary for victory, and in his best, compelling oratorical style, invoked patriotism. He gamely endured hecklers when he met with all-black groups of students while continuing to argue that the military led in the struggle against racism. How many of his opponents he converted is unknown, but there was no question of the sincerity or energy he devoted to the task.

To James many of his adversaries seemed headed down the wrong path. In 1973 he observed, "Now younger Blacks tend to distrust, as do young people generally—the other side of the generation gap, as they call it—and too often they accuse anyone who has prospered within the system of Tomism. Too often this is a cop-out . . . for people who have not performed well themselves. They are reluctant to throw away the crutch: 'They did it to me because I am colored.' There are too many people today retreating into separatism. Young Blacks come to us from a ghetto, with a heart full of hurt and a fistful of hate. They don't want to come to me for advice. They would rather go to the most militant of their peer group they can find and say, 'What do you think I might do, man?'

"When they come to me, often it's too late. I get many letters from men who have been busted or are in jail and they seek my help because their lawyer or somebody said, 'Why don't you, as a last resort, try General James, maybe he can get your case reviewed.' Too often, when they are making the decision to go out and create the offense or to resist the authority outside of the limits of the regulations, they don't seem to ask me for advice. The majority of the NCOs are making it anyway, and want to move up faster. These will send letters saying, 'I've read an article by you,' or 'I heard you on TV' and want to say I agree with you and would like you to give me some advice."

"More often than I like, I'll get a letter from a young man who says, 'Hey, man, I heard you on TV the other night and you are an Uncle Tom. You talk like the whites want you to talk . . . we don't think we can identify with you.' By and large I consider the source but I don't write them off. When they do come to me for advice or I get a chance to communicate with those who have made up their minds not to like me, I never miss an opportunity to do so. I talk to all of them from ROTC to units I visit which have problems, to the enlisted men and junior officers in the field. I also talk to Black students on many university campuses. In every case when I get a chance to communicate, when they get to see where I am really coming from, I've come off with handshakes, with a better understanding, and almost without exception they say, 'I had you wrong, man. I really had you wrong.'"

With the Vietnam fighting over, James returned to high positions in the running of the air force. He ascended to four stars, the first of his race in the military to achieve that exalted level. He had barely retired when a heart attack at age fifty-eight killed him.

Shortly after Lyndon Johnson won the 1964 election for president, he appointed Lt. Gen. Benjamin O. Davis Jr. as chief of staff for the U.S. forces in Korea as well as chief of staff for the U.N. Command. The American military maintained a significant military presence in South Korea to guard against any thrust south by North Korea seeking to exploit the situation in Vietnam. The host nation volunteered a 20,000-man division to fight in Vietnam, adding further to the ethnic mix of the battle lines, although the ROK troops fought as a unit.

Davis moved on to command the Thirteenth Air Force, based in the Philippines. Although not engaged in the actual combat, the Thirteenth's role was to support the operational bases run by the Seventh Air Force in Thailand and elsewhere. Visiting various sites and units involved with his command, Davis conferred with Gen. William Momyer, the Air Force theater boss and the 99th's nemesis during World War II. He also met with the overall chief in Vietnam, William Westmoreland, the West Point colleague whom Davis remembers for an absence of leadership when cadets shunned him. In keeping with his reticent nature, Davis, in his autobiography, makes no reference to his previous encounters with either man. For that matter, unlike James, Davis, apparently detailed overseas as much for his diplomatic skills as for his direct air force duties, seems not to have directly engaged in the race-relations problems or in defending policy.

William Murray was among those stationed in Korea during these years. He took command of a missile battalion. "I had many black enlisted men, one of them, a missile-launching sergeant I considered the best man in that particular job in the whole battalion. I had others and saw no difference between them and the Caucasians in the battalion, some good, some average, some not so good. I don't recall any materials, programs, or advice specifically pertaining to race relations."

By the late 1960s, the basic civil rights legislation had been enacted, restoring the franchise to African Americans where it had been denied, fair employment and housing laws passed, and school desegregation mandated. But laws did not change hearts and minds. The more subtle forms of discrimination remained in operation and the military mirrored life in the greater society. Passage of the antidiscrimination laws for civilians did not immediately affect the embattled military.

22
Rough Seas, Turbulent Air

In 1970, for reasons that had nothing to do with race relations, President Richard M. Nixon's secretary of defense Melvin Laird reached down the list of admirals to name Elmo R. Zumwalt Jr. as chief of naval operations, the top job in the navy, jumping him over the heads of thirty-three of his seniors. At the time, Zumwalt, who had previously served several tours at the Pentagon and been a member of Secretary of the Navy Paul Nitze's staff while Lyndon Johnson occupied the White House, commanded the naval forces in Vietnam. That role did not include the planes flying from carriers but mostly involved shallow-draft craft patrolling coastal waters, rivers, and canals.

"In Vietnam," Zumwalt recalls, "the small vessels with integrated crews had no serious racial problems. The men all knew one another by first names, although when on liberty they tended to separate by race. In the field, during engagements, war with its common purpose has a way of bringing people together."

Zumwalt recognized retention as an immediate problem because the high rate of turnover in personnel impacted, for the worse, on training and efficiency. The service set a goal of 35 percent reenlistments after the first hitch but by 1970 the figure stood at a paltry 9.5 percent. The problem was exacerbated as the war demanded more and more naval assets. Zumwalt diagnosed as a major source of discontent the "Mickey Mouse" aspects of service. Sailors chafed at restrictions dictating length of hair, beards, and sideburns. They resented rules that obligated them to change out of dungarees for a trip to the commissary or don a uniform for an evening meal. Other abrasive and unnecessary regulations, familiar to army GIs as 'chicken shit,' annoyed them. As a first step, Zumwalt wiped out the petty limitations dealing with grooming and uniforms. His predecessor, Adm. Thomas Moorer, had in fact written to commanders liberalizing the standards on hair and clothing. But although Moorer specifically requested that the changes be kept quiet, Zumwalt went public, to the displeasure of many of his subordinate admirals, already unhappy with rule relaxation.

Zumwalt then instituted a number of reforms designed to relieve the stress on family life and to make a seagoing career more enjoyable. "They required," says Zumwalt, "much prodding and tweaking of long-established regulations, routines, and mind-sets and constant monitoring of the system to make sure the prods and tweaks were having the intended effect, but they presented no attitudinal problems to the great majority of the men and women of the Navy."

However, when he then focused on the specific issue of how to boost the retention rate for African Americans, Zumwalt says, "a far higher order of difficulty and importance was to bring the Navy's treatment of members of ethnic or racial minorities, particularly blacks, into conformity with stated national policy and the law of the land, not to say common fairness and decency . . . this presented profound attitudinal problems to many people, including some at high levels of authority."

Several years had passed since the urban riots of 1967–68 and the subsequent Kerner Commission report that had warned of a nation splitting into two separate societies. A flurry of financial grants, experimental operations, and introspection had originated in the civilian sphere, as people began to realize the gaps between races. Zumwalt admits he brought to the post of CNO little practical experience in race relations or even the suspicion that it would be among his most important duties. Bill Thompson, who operated the navy's Office of Information, says, "I personally doubt that Admiral Zumwalt knew of the severity of the abuse of equal opportunity in the Navy until he became CNO and I say the same for most of the other officers of the staff." But the people Zumwalt gathered about him sensitized him and supported his initiatives in the face of considerable opposition. On the highest levels these included the navy's Burt Shepherd, Horace Robertson, Bill Thompson, Chick Rauch, and Emmett Tidd, along with marine officers, Mike Spiro and Dick McDonald. He also took on board Lt. David Halperin as a special assistant. Profoundly influential was Bill Norman, the black air controller who completed three tours in the Vietnam struggle.

Horace B. Robertson Jr., a few years younger than Zumwalt, in contrast, grew up in the rigidly segregated society of North Carolina, in Kannapolis, a town about thirty miles north of Charlotte. "We knew a large number of black persons but did not socialize with them," recalls Robertson. "There were several Chinese families in the town who were fully integrated into the educational, economic, and social structure of the community. There were no Jewish families; most everyone was Protestant of Scotch-Irish and German stock. Even a Roman Catholic was a rarity until after World War II."

Robertson depicts his textile-executive father and his mother as "human persons and often ill-at-ease about the segregated system of the South. But it was the 'system' and they (and I) went along with it. My father was chairman of the local school board and presided over a segregated system. I often heard him remark that the principal of the black (then it was called 'colored') high school who had a Ph.D. was the best qualified man in the system."

As a 1945 graduate of the Naval Academy Robertson was aware that the only black personnel were mess attendants. His tours on destroyers and antisubmarine development, specializing in communications, and then the CIC before entering law school in 1950, brought little contact with African Americans who did not serve in these billets.

During his training as a Navy law specialist and then in the judge advocate's division, he says the topic of discrimination and equal opportunity seldom arose, if at all. However, Robertson plunged into a multiracial atmosphere, albeit mostly Asian, during his tour in Hawaii from 1958 to 1960. But in 1963–64, he directly encountered the question of bias while on the legal staff of the 5th Naval District, Norfolk, Virginia. "A number of black employees of the Naval Supply Center brought an employment-discrimination action against the Center. The essence of their complaint was they had been denied promotion to positions to which equal- or less-qualified white persons had been promoted. I was designated to represent the Center, its CO and personnel officers." Robertson successfully defended against the charges but notes that with appointment of a new personnel officer and new procedures, the complainants ultimately gained their promotions. Robertson continued to deal with legal aspects of naval administration and during 1970–72 he functioned as special counsel to CNO Zumwalt.

Among those Zumwalt describes as critical to the programs he initiated was Adm. Charles "Chick" Rauch. A native of southeastern Ohio where his father practiced as an osteopathic physician, Rauch says, "I believe there were two African American families in Logan but I did not know any of them personally since there were none of the children in my high school class of 117. The issue of race relations was never a question with my classmates. The only thing along racial lines involved my nickname. Somehow I acquired the nickname Chick early in high school. One of the members of the black families went by Chick. And I grew up in a culture where the kids frequently chanted 'Eenie, Meenie, Mynie, Moe; catch a n—— by the toe' And we made slingshots that at the time went by the name of n—— shooters but when we made that kind of weapon we were going to catapult stones at birds, wild life at the worst, and most probably old bottles or some other target. We certainly did not conjure up a picture of an African American human target. But the terms were commonplace and that says something about our society.

"I had only one experience with black folks in my high school years. I was a counselor at a scout camp and the scouts were all white Anglo-Saxons. However, we had a special week in which several all-black troops from Columbus had exclusive use of the camp and some of the white counselors stayed on to help out. We worked closely with the troop leaders who came along as well as the scouts themselves. I recall I had a great time but it was decades later that I realized how racist we were to have a separate week for only black scouts while the rest of the time we were all white."

As a member of the U.S. Naval Academy Class of 1947, Rauch was one year ahead of Wesley Brown. "He lived on the other side of Bancroft Hall from where I did so I had no occasion to meet him. In my part of Bancroft Hall and in my class I do not recall that the racial issue was ever raised in the two years I was there while he was a midshipman. Had I been asked, I am relatively certain I would have been *very* supportive of him. The other issue that was never raised was to question why we in our class and those before us were all white.

"My first tour of duty out of the Naval Academy was on the cruiser USS *Huntington*. The Navy had just been integrated in the enlisted ranks. By the time I came aboard in October 1947, the ship had black petty officers who were not stewards. We had a whole division of stewards who were black but there were a handful of other divisions with black enlisted members. During my tour on the *Huntington* and then on a minesweeper I do not remember any racial issues and I was unaware that our non-white sailors were having any kinds of trouble. However, African American and Filipino stewards were still completely set off from the rest of the enlisted men with a separate uniform, a different pay scale and their own living compartment. Furthermore, stewards who had shore duty working in base commanders quarters—many in their 40s and 50s—were called houseboys. It was truly racist but most of us at the time were not aware enough to realize how bad it was." Attached to Zumwalt's staff, after duty as a submariner, Rauch joined the team that concentrated upon improving the rates of retention and as a consequence issues of concern to minorities.

Rauch's association with Zumwalt predated this assignment. Previously he had headed a small group of naval officers brought to Vietnam by Elmo Zumwalt as part of his command. Zumwalt, says Rauch, had orchestrated a three-pronged strategy for the waterborne forces. First on the agenda, the navy was to become directly involved in the war, rather than limit itself to inspections of river junks and sampans for contraband. Second, the U.S. and Vietnam navies would gain control of the Rung Sat Zone, a mangrove swamp through which ran the ship channel to Saigon, and, finally, to establish and implement a plan to turn over the entire operation to the Vietnamese.

Rauch spearheaded the planning which required very close association of American and Vietnamese naval people at all levels. Says Rauch, "There were several kibitzers hanging around Saigon in those days and a couple of them told me we could avoid almost certain disaster if we took time to work on the cross-cultural problem. We had to get the U.S. people to feel comfortable living in a very unfamiliar culture, and we had to get the U.S. folks to respect and understand the Vietnamese and vice versa." Advised and abetted by some individuals experienced in this sort of liaison, says Rauch, "We set up a 'Personal Response' program that we forced virtually every U.S. Navy person in Vietnam to go through. It worked relatively well, and our turnover program was also successful. Thus, when racial issues surfaced dramatically in the other services, and finally in the Navy, we had a *little* bit of experience in dealing with cross-cultural issues and since I was then a special assistant to Admiral Zumwalt, I was involved in working on our Affirmative Action and Equal Opportunity programs."

Rauch notes a common theme, "While I was in Vietnam, I was not aware of any problems in the Navy between black and white personnel. I am sure there were serious problems but we had our hands too full with the war and the inter-racial between Vietnamese and U.S. personnel to see much of the intra-Navy racial problems."

Emmett Tidd, still in Vietnam after Zumwalt acceded to the office of CNO, saw conditions deteriorate. "Ethnic differences became issues. Music in the clubs; facial and hair care products and qualified ethnic barbers were not as available for blacks as for whites at PXs. But in the intense combat conditions in the muddy/bloody waters of Vietnam, the Navy personnel worked and fought as a team. Survival depended upon performance as a close team." Tidd grasped the same insight as Rauch. "I soon realized that the 'Arrival Cultural Indoctrination' lectures we required be given each new arrival in Vietnam, had a remarkable relativeness to our black/white cultural problems that were caused by a *lack* of awareness of cultural differences. We needed to be more aware of how sensitive blacks were to words in the vocabulary we heard and used when growing up with not the slightest intent of offending blacks."

Bill Norman had begun to question the American involvement in Vietnam and had written a letter of resignation. David Halperin, as an assistant to Zumwalt, brought Norman and his letter to his boss's attention. The CNO asked Norman to postpone his departure and work for him on minority affairs. In the course of their conversation, Norman related to Zumwalt a number of discouraging experiences. As a young officer he rarely received a voluntary salute. The CO of a naval air station requested him not to come to the officers' club one night in Mississippi because his presence might embarrass some local citizens invited as guests. He told Zumwalt of a particularly nasty encounter in which a white petty officer abused him while he was in civilian clothes and continued to disrespect him even after Norman showed his ID. Norman summoned the shore patrol and placed the man on report. But he was disheartened by the attitude of his ship's officers who adopted a permissive approach toward the offender.

Norman arranged for black officers and enlisted men and their wives to talk about their experiences in front of their seniors on Zumwalt's staff. Norman recalled for Wallace Terry, "One of the admirals listening in began to talk about how much he loved his stewards as if they were his own children . . . 'This boy that I have working for me is just like a son and a close friend.' One particular wife said, 'Admiral, how old is this *boy* that you're talking about?' And he says, 'Oh, he's almost 40.' Zumwalt heard that."

"Bill Norman," says Chick Rauch, "is very bright and diplomatic and has a tremendous amount of confidence and common sense. [Norman considers himself boldly outspoken and some superiors bridled at the comments and questions of a mere lieutenant commander.] He was well aware of every aspect of inequality that was built into the Navy structure. In very short order he taught all of us close to the CNO many aspects of racial awareness that most of us had never thought of."

The CNO, through the talk sessions, heard his white colleagues snicker when African American enlisted men griped about the lack of their kind of hair products in the navy exchanges, and the regulations on hair length. According to Norman, Zumwalt expressed outrage. The CNO later noted, "I came to realize for the first time that the Navy did even worse things to its minority people than give them demeaning jobs and stunt their careers. Day after day it inflicted upon them, sometimes without even knowing it was doing so, personal slights, affronts, and indignities of a peculiarly humiliating kind. . . . I took it as symbolic of the Navy's pervasive uncaringness for its minority people by the fact that Navy exchanges did not carry any of the lines of cosmetics black women used, or the styles of clothes young black people wore, or the records and tapes young black people listened to."

Zumwalt, already famous for messages to all commands known as Z-grams, issued on 17 December 1970 Z-66, "Equal Opportunity in the Navy" which he calls "probably the most important and certainly the most heartfelt of the 121 Z-grams." In Z-66 the CNO declared, "We must open up new avenues of communication with not only our black personnel, but also with all minority groups in the Navy . . . all of us in the Navy must develop a far greater sensitivity to the problems of all our minority groups."

He pronounced himself, "particularly distressed by the numerous examples of discrimination black families still experience in attempts to locate housing. This situation and others like it are indicative in some cases of less than full teamwork being brought to bear by the whole Navy team in behalf of some of our members and failure to use existing authority and directives to enforce their rights."

Backed by Secretary of the Navy John Chafee, Zumwalt asked for an investigation and proposals to ameliorate if not solve the problem. Toward that end he required every base, station, squadron, and ship commander to appoint a minority group officer or senior petty officer to serve as a special assistant for minority matters. Shore-based commanders were to see that a minority-group wife served as a member of the navy's spousal ombudsman concept.

Z-66 directed that navy exchanges stock items desired by blacks, including cosmetics, grooming aids, and foods. Libraries were to carry books, magazines, and records that appealed to African Americans. He put the commanders on notice that he would be checking their compliance by dispatching Bill Norman to visit all sites and meet with everyone concerned. The final sentence of Z-66 read, "There is no black Navy, no white Navy—just one Navy—the United States Navy."

Racial tensions had flared into open conflict among sailors at two major Philippine installations. An investigation produced a document that bluntly limned the deplorable conditions. Just outside the gates to the Subic Bay base, Olongapo City divided into "The Strip," a whites-only section of bars and whorehouses, and "The Jungle," similar establishments catering exclusively to blacks. Subsequently, when Zumwalt toured his Pacific domain, he briefly inspected Olongapo City and found it as advertised, "brothels in every other house, filthy places that were segregated. The same was true for the seedy bars." However, the shore patrols did not attempt to enforce separation of the races. Narcotics and alcoholic beverages fueled a volatile ambience. The widespread discontent of minority sailors threatened ignition.

With a degree of frankness that Zumwalt appreciated, the inquiry dismissed the premise that the root of trouble lay in a few, militant malcontents spreading dissension. "This would have been a felonious assumption." Instead, it quoted a black chief petty officer who said, "Just being black is the biggest problem." And it seemed clear that younger blacks refused to tolerate their situation as a fact of life. Aware of the subtle as well as the grosser manifestations of prejudice and discrimination, they wanted "to be treated like a 'human,'" and for changes to occur and at a quicker pace.

The whites, according to the Naval Investigative Service Office, believed African Americans preferred to associate among themselves and they resented "Afro haircuts, Afro costuming and the black power salute." Whites found the way blacks talked among themselves "difficult to comprehend." Few of them read literature dealing with black experiences and most disdained to discuss racial affairs with their black counterparts. They criticized commanders for yielding to pressure, setting up dual standards that allowed blacks to govern their appearance and behavior. To Zumwalt the report defined an agenda upon which the navy was "morally obligated and pragmatically obliged to act."

According to Norman, "In less than three years, we instituted some 200 programs. . . . The first ships were named after black heroes. The first black [Sam Gravely] was promoted to admiral. Ten percent of the NROTC units were set aside for predominantly black colleges. We guaranteed that blacks would be on promotion boards, assignment boards, and would make their way to the command colleges." According to Thompson, another important move created a Minority Affairs Office, which publicized internally as well as to the public what was being done to open up all avenues of job and career opportunities.

"While I was still a special assistant to the CNO," recalls Rauch, "I started a Human Resources Development program to deal with some of the leadership problems [such] as senior petty officers who could not talk effectively with some of the new sailors, drug rehabilitation and control, alcohol abuse rehabilitation and control and an attempt to spread the cross-cultural program we had used in Vietnam to many places throughout the Navy where personnel were living in somebody else's culture. It was appropriate to add race relations to the programs.

"With the help of one of the young African American officers who had been a member of the black retention study group and a Navy chaplain, we started a Race Relations program which we tried to give everybody from the CNO and Secretary of the Navy on down. This required the better part of a day for each participant and was somewhat controlled—none of that touchy-feely stuff that was then around—sensitivity training. My feeling was that maybe a quarter of the Navy did not really need this and another quarter would not change. However, perhaps half of the Navy like myself simply had never thought about what we were doing or were omitting which were purely and simply putting obstacles in the way of our black shipmates. If we could get this half to become aware and change their attitudes and behavior, we would make great headway. Then we'd have three quarters of the Navy working on affirmative action and the remainder would pretty much have to go along or at least not resist.

"This monumental task required numerous well-trained and well-selected trainers. By and large we had good ones but occasionally you'd get somebody too zealous, too emotional or too arrogant and we'd have bad sessions that may have been of questionable value. Of course, we had to order everybody to participate. Frequently, we'd get one of those folks from the carved-in-the rock quarter who'd rather be in heavy combat than engage in these kinds of discussions. Most of them were more disruptive in their body language and refusals to participate than in trying to provide eloquent reasons why we should not bother. But the greater part of the Navy tried to do their best; they went along with this program whether or not they wanted to be involved. There were a handful who wrote to their congressmen and this resulted in some problems.

"It is amazing how emotional hair can become. Z-grams had a sentence in them stating that these were changes of standards and not lessening of them, that we expected all personnel to continue to look their best and to uphold the high standards of the Naval Service. The problem is many did not read that particular part of the Z-gram and looked like hell. There were some commissioned and non-commissioned officers either confused or in opposition to Admiral Zumwalt who looked the other way and allowed this. That was true for both black and white sailors.

"There should not have been any divisiveness due to the Afros when whites were getting away with excessively long hair. But the nature of the Afros was such that a person could grow an astonishing bush of hair that rendered wearing a hat atop a ridiculous look. But I don't see that as giving one person a privilege another did not have. Those who were against beards claimed that they would compromise oxygen breathing apparatuses or other safety devices that had to fit closely about the face. Therefore, they would outlaw beards. What they should outlaw is anything that would make a breathing apparatus ineffective. If I could use my mask successfully with a well-trimmed beard, what difference does it make whether or not I have a beard?

"One destroyer was actually put out of operation for a period of time due to a 'race riot' when the commanding officer issued an order that banned the use of dap handshakes. What was happening was that a few black sailors would meet and shake hands in one of those routines that goes on and on and block a passageway. What should have been prohibited was obstructing a passageway. Who would care if two sailors back on the fantail, out of everybody's way, shake hands for an hour. This kind of insensitivity got us into trouble."

Samuel Gravely had risen to command of a number of destroyers and in that capacity become the first black promoted to captain. About a year after Zumwalt's programs altered the course of the navy, Gravely in 1971 achieved a landmark by becoming the first of his race to gain the status of admiral. He believes some of the resistance to the Zumwalt innovations stemmed from jealousy. "[He] was appointed as CNO and actually selected from below a considerable number of officers. Any guy who is selected under that set of circumstances will find that there is going to be some dragging of the feet from other people who are seeing him and thinking they should have gotten the job instead.

"I think [he was] a very, very sharp guy, very smart, very impressive. I think he may have made a couple of mistakes. The normal way things happen in the Pentagon is that the CNO comes up with an idea, checks it out with his deputies and they sit around and chew the fat [until] the CNO says, 'Well, I don't give a damn how you feel about it, but this is the way I am going to go.' And he does it and these guys try to back him to the fullest. [I believe] some of the things that the CNO felt strongly about had never been tried on some of these deputies before they heard, 'here comes a program.' The automatic thing was to resent that.

"Admiral Zumwalt did a tremendous job while he was there. I think he realized and part of the problem was he felt, if you've got only four years in the job and you are going to get things done, you have to start pushing your programs hard. He pushed hard, pushed fast, pushed furiously. It might have caused a little confusion at the top with guys who had to implement these." The sensitivity training sessions bemused Gravely. "They were pretty hard for me to swallow. There was a young group up there telling me that I was to blame for all of the Navy's problems. It got to me a little bit. In fact, I wondered why I even was sent."

As Rauch and others indicate, the reforms under the Zumwalt regime met an armada of opposition. In addition to all commanders on active duty, Zumwalt, as a courtesy, kept his predecessors and senior figures in retirement informed. Some of these individuals sniped at him or surreptitiously sought to sabotage his reforms. His immediate predecessor as CNO, Adm. Thomas Moorer, had become chairman of the Joint Chiefs of Staff. When Zumwalt as CNO and the heads of the other services met with the chairman, Zumwalt says, "Moorer, who is from Alabama, wasted few opportunities to comment sarcastically on my 'blackening' of the Navy." According to Zumwalt, retired Adm. George Anderson who served as chairman of the president's Foreign Intelligence Advisory Board, "was reportedly on the telephone tirelessly, urging retired officers and I was told, active duty officers as well, to do something to stop Bud Zumwalt's permissive programs before it was too late." Zumwalt adds, "Several of my immediate predecessors were from the South and had different attitudes than I had. My insight was more relevant to that period of time." His detractor, Moorer, actually had taken the first steps against "Mickey Mouse" regulations and created Human Relations Councils on ships and at bases in order to combat the falling retention rate. But these efforts were not concerned with correcting discrimination against African American sailors.

Zumwalt's head of public information during those turbulent years, Bill Thompson, does not wholly agree with his former boss's assessment. "The resistance did come from the old guard, most of whom were Naval Academy graduates and the Academy's history of handling minorities is well documented. They were comfortable with the status quo. Naturally geographic background had a lot to do with attitudes and compliance. Southern-bred officers were adamant and what surprised me was the number of Northern-reared officers, especially from big cities, that were not sympathetic. Navy leadership, both uniformed and civilian, had definite racist attitudes. The advocates were a mixed bag of Naval Academy graduates, officers with non-academy backgrounds and different ethnic backgrounds and gender. I did not perceive age as a factor, but I did experience the pressures and exhortations from young Caucasian liberal arts college people.

"One factor in favor of desegregation was that commensurate with the equal opportunity drive regarding ethnic groups, gender was pulled into the fracas and overshadowed race at times. This allowed the ethnic programs to mature and develop. There was more opposition within the Navy to Admiral Zumwalt's programs for equal opportunity for women."

Emmett Tidd, nominated by the CNO to head the Navy Recruiting Command, says, "I was greatly disappointed in seeing a lack of loyalty by those who had received the opportunity to fully state their views to him, but then supported the CNO's decision with at best silent contempt, and at worst covert criticism to subordinates in the Navy, to retired flag officers, and members of Congress. Some of it was the result of childish resentment at being passed over for selection as CNO. Others were the result of long years of ingrained conditioning to the old ways of harsh, unwavering discipline, with decreasing concern for the welfare of enlisted personnel, and having little touch with, nor understanding of the societal changes of the youth of the 1960s and 70s.

"There were shining exceptions to the delaying obstructionism of many older, senior officers still on active duty. Superb exceptions were Admiral Chick Clarey [Zumwalt's second in command and later head of the Pacific fleet], Admiral Horatio Rivero, and Rear Admiral Draper Kauffman. They always could be counted on to offer him [the CNO], in private their frank views and recommendations. Once they knew of his decision, they saluted smartly, and supported both the spirit and letter of the decision."

Shortly after the initiatives innovated by Zumwalt, racial explosions rattled the navy. The pro-Zumwalt forces argued these resulted from pent-up frustrations. The anti-Zumwalt faction blamed the disorders on the "permissiveness" of his programs. The opening salvo occurred 12 October 1972 aboard the carrier USS *Kitty Hawk*. On the night before the carrier headed back toward its Gulf of Tonkin station, black and white sailors at an Olongapo enlisted-men's club traded punches. Riot control from the shore patrol sprayed tear gas and arrested five black and four white sailors. After the ship left the Philippines, an investigating officer summoned African American sailors as part of his inquiry. An argument broke out and the blacks stalked out. The group then beat up a white mess attendant (according to Zumwalt) and sporadic fights rocked the vessel. When a semblance of order was restored, more than forty individuals required medical treatment and the authorities charged twenty-seven blacks with various offenses. No whites faced punishment. Civil rights groups protested that the accused would not receive justice if tried at sea. With the agreement of the navy, twenty-one sailors who requested civilian counsel flew to San Diego for their day in military court. The remainder accepted justice aboard ship.

Four days later another disturbance on a fleet oiler, the USS *Hassayampa,* docked at Subic Bay, pitted officers and whites against black crewmen. A marine detachment quelled the fights and assaults. Again only blacks, eleven of them, were charged with violations. Particularly troubling to Zumwalt was that leadership on the two ships differed considerably. The big ship boasted a good minority-affairs program, in contrast to a "virtually nonexistent" one on the oiler. The *Kitty Hawk* command included a promising black executive officer, while the *Hassayampa* apparently was skippered by a "not very conscientious" captain, a "not very competent" exec. Also living conditions seemed irrelevant. "Clearly racial animosity was not confined to an overcrowded or overworked or insensitively commanded ship but was a condition that afflicted perhaps unavoidably the entire Navy . . ."

While Adm. Chick Clarey, commander in chief of the Pacific Fleet (CINCPACFLT), immediately took steps to investigate the grievances of African American sailors in his area and at the same time meted out justice to those guilty of assaults, Zumwalt convened a new minority-officers' retention group for a progress report on his reforms. "It was a shocker," says Zumwalt. "Its four general findings were that the Navy had failed to accept the racial situation as its problem, that being a member of a minority and a member of the Navy were incompatible; that only blacks, rather than all minorities, were represented in current policies and programs; and that the Navy's classification, advancement, and placement systems selected out minorities."

The CNO was further discomfited by another report, this one from a Department of Defense inspection in Europe. It noted, according to Zumwalt ". . . if the Navy's race relations programs in Europe were compared with those of the Air Force and the Army, the Air Force could be said to be in college, the Army in high school, and the Navy in elementary school."

Even as he pondered these discouraging appraisals, racial troubles flared aboard another carrier, USS *Constellation,* during a training cruise off the California coast. While Zumwalt attributes the events on the other two ships to ineffectual handling of racial injustices which triggered spontaneous outbursts, he traces the disorder aboard the *Constellation* to a complex of elements. The exigencies of the Vietnam War had forced a sustained rapid turnaround during repairs at San Diego, at substantial hardships to crewmen. "During that period," says Zumwalt, "the ship was all but uninhabitable. The air conditioning was out for most of the time; there were regular shutoffs of water and steam . . . cooking and dishwashing and bathing were sometime activities." Civilian workers dictated schedules and sailors often could perform their duties only after midnight or on Sundays.

New additions to the "Connie" complement included a larger percentage of blacks ineligible for advanced schooling who were automatically relegated to the less-attractive berths. Many of the new recruits, hastily and inadequately trained, felt themselves unfairly assigned and the blacks perceived themselves as victims of discriminatory discipline. Zumwalt insists that subsequent investigation found no evidence of bias in either the captain's masts that dished out punishment for minor offenses, or in assignments. However, he says the ship paid only perfunctory attention to minority matters.

A large number of black crewmen met aboard ship and discussed what they considered racist behavior by superiors and the best means to obtain relief from Capt. J. D. Ward, who had assumed command only a month earlier. Alarmed by the signs of tension and disaffection, the skipper sought to issue administrative discharges for a group of black sailors identified as "agitators." At least one of those chosen had a clean record and was a skillful, popular barber. Rumors circulated that an additional 250 sailors would be handed the same less-desirable discharges. The blowoff on the carrier began with black crewmen harassing whites at mess and a sit-down demanding an audience with Ward. "We wanted to air our views," said Radarman Third Class Lonnie Brown, "and tell the captain what was actually happening. We had to get the word across to the man who runs the ship." Ward, however, refused to face the sailors but instead insisted complaints should first go to the vessel's Human Relations Council.

The session with that panel, according to Zumwalt, deteriorated into a name-calling exercise punctuated by a demand from the blacks for an audience with Ward. He refused to leave the bridge, particularly since air operations were in progress but also because he may have believed he would only expose himself to tirades rather than constructive dialogue. A kind of stand-off followed, with a large number of men occupying the mess decks and refusing to disband. At one point, marines in riot dress and with fixed bayonets appeared but they were withdrawn.

Without notifying the dissidents, Ward decided to send ashore all of them and then continue the training exercise. A group of senior officers met the ship at the dock. They suggested instead that the sailors remain aboard and that the *Constellation* officers and men work out their differences. However, Ward, intent on readying his ship for duty in the South Pacific, stuck to his position. He informed the sit-ins of that fact. A total of 130 sailors, 8 of them white, left the carrier under the supervision of a black lieutenant and 9 black petty officers. The ship weighed anchor to continue its training operations.

At this point, Zumwalt says he placed himself on "the hottest spot in the Navy," because he "was being paid to sit there." Three days had elapsed since the *Constellation's* troubles began and Zumwalt was anxious to resolve the matter before either the press or the politicians took notice. He drew in his circle of advisors and confidants such as Admiral Clarey and Bill Norman, but Secretary of the Navy John Warner, who had succeeded John Chafee, kept his distance. "Both as Under Secretary and as Secretary," says Zumwalt, "Warner, in an effort to keep peace in the family, had been in constant touch with the senior retired officers and their supporters on Capitol Hill who opposed the changes in personnel administration . . . Though he favored integration, he had urged me a number of times to go very slowly with it. I, of course, believed that going fast was essential." Zumwalt says he was informed that during this crisis, his foe, Admiral Anderson, stayed in almost daily communication with Warner.

Zumwalt accepted that Captain Ward thought in terms of his ship and its mission. However, as CNO it was incumbent upon him to act in terms of the entire navy, rather than consider only the control of sailors on a single ship. He hoped to avoid a clash between those concerned with equality for all navy personnel and the forces fearful of a breakdown in discipline. Whatever his sentiments, Warner also trod lightly. He told his CNO he did not want a confrontation.

Neither the black sailors nor Ward, however, appeared inclined to yield. The drama played out during the moments when President Richard M. Nixon, a navy officer in World War II, won reelection in a landslide and the media subsequently picked up on the story. In that stormy context, Zumwalt sought to navigate through tricky shoals: Ward's prerogatives, the positions of the dissenters and their supporters, the desires of Secretary of the Navy Warner, the opponents and proponents of a more open service. After protracted negotiations within the naval establishment, Ward offered the disaffected an opportunity to board the ship where he said their complaints of racial discrimination in work assignments, discipline, and in discharges would be addressed. However, he refused to grant blanket amnesty. Two black sailors and all eight whites accepted his terms. The remainder opted for dockside duty while civilian lawyers wrestled with impending disciplinary proceedings. Ward then accused the dissidents of "not seeking to air grievances [instead] trying very hard to create a violent situation."

Emmett Tidd observes, "Perceived discrimination was a root cause of the ship's problems. McNamara's 'social experiment' that forced the Department of Defense to accept a large group that were in the lower mental group of the Armed Forces Qualification Test directed the Navy to take a significant quota of these. Many were blacks. The black recalcitrants in the ship incidents that staged the AWOL demonstration in San Diego were the non-rated sailors. Their anger grew out of continously 'seeing whitey going off to Class A technical schools and us blacks going nowhere but to mess cooking duty, laundry and bilge cleaning!' They were forced onto the Navy during Admiral Moorer's watch as CNO and Admiral Zumwalt's Navy inherited them. The problem was their test scores indicated they were not capable of completing the technical courses."

Tidd adds, "[There were] delays in getting more blacks into the special 'BOOST' programs that RAdm. Chick Rauch and Admiral Zumwalt established in 1971 to raise education levels of potential minority leaders by raising their knowledge of math, science, and reading comprehension so that they would be qualified to compete and succeed in the various Navy college programs leading to a commission. It is little wonder that the pot did not boil over sooner, given the horrendous back-to-back combat deployment schedules for these ships. They were undermanned and undermaintained because of the Vietnam requirements, which by 1972 were falling more on Naval air and surface ships than on any of the other Services, who by then had been mostly withdrawn."

With the "shore party" seamen identified as unwilling to compromise, Zumwalt himself had concluded that the affair had reached a point where there was no more wiggle room and the refusniks must face the consequences of their behavior. However, he also saw an obligation to confront the larger issues. Although his ally Admiral Clarey, CINCPACFLT, sharply reprimanded fleet and shore commands for a neglect of minority grievances, Zumwalt chose to formally address the situation at a meeting with Washington, D.C.–area-based flag officers in what was ordinarily an informal discussion.

The eruptions of disorder connected with the *Kitty Hawk, Constellation,* and *Hassayampa* were," says Bill Thompson, in charge of public information, "of such magnitude that they were national stories, commanding attention from Washington and particularly my office. At the recommendation of the Assistant Secretary of Defense for Public Affairs, Admiral Zumwalt made a major policy speech on equal opportunity. He had scheduled a periodic meeting with all local flag officers and that was the platform chosen for his statement. It could have been to a Navy League Audience or Local Rotary Club."

In the speech Zumwalt summed up his first insights into the nature and extent of racial tensions that led to the introduction of two hundred programs aimed at the problems. However, upon receipt of a fourth account on retention studies, he concluded, "It was immediately clear to me from this report that the Navy has made unacceptable progress in the equal opportunity area. And that the reason for this failure was not the programs, but the fact they were not being used." Without recapitulating the details on the *Kitty Hawk, Hassayampa,* and *Constellation,* the CNO declared, ". . . these incidents are not the cause of racial pressures; rather they are the manifestations of pressures unrelieved . . . What we are talking about here is not a call for permissiveness, or a direction to coddle . . . discipline necessary for good order will and must be maintained."

He went on to decry a number of self-deceptions, belief that attitudes can be legislated, that a program is a reality, that Navy personnel arrive unstained by the prejudices of the society which produced them, or for that matter that all incidents involving black and white sailors stem from bias. He defended his innovations insisting, ". . . these current racial incidents are not the results of lowered standards, but are clearly due to failure of commands to implement those programs with a whole heart."

Zumwalt concluded with a promise that he would use every instrument of his office to ensure that the Navy achieved the goals of equal opportunity and an end to discrimination. He placed the responsibility for carrying out the mission upon the leadership, a challenge to those in command. His remarks triggered a firestorm. Newspapers played his speech on the front pages; network evening news shows headlined it and, says Zumwalt, "Some of the George Anderson crowd were storming about the admirals being 'chewed out' in public."

Recalls Thompson, "Dissidents labeled his talk as a public chewing out of his flag officers, which was a natural story for the media—a guy to be the target of the *guilty* finger. Many of the racists in uniform, some retired, and others in the Congress charged Zumwalt with being responsible for the incidents. Eddie Hebert [a Louisiana congressman] Chairman of the House Armed Services Committee announced hearings on Zumwalt's competency."

Samuel Gravely was among those in the audience. Although he held a Pentagon berth (concerned with satellite communications) Zumwalt had not consulted with him on race matters. Gravely laughingly confesses some chagrin—"What did I do to rate this kind of whipping?" Gravely, while applauding Zumwalt for his eventual accomplishments in reform of the Navy, wonders whether he might not have had smoother sailing if instead of relying upon the coterie around him for advice and support, he had tried harder to quietly convert the larger naval establishment. He also sees Zumwalt's battles as reflecting the hoary conflict between the tradition-bound Naval Academy graduates and the less conservative people whose pathway began with the reserves.

Serious counterbattery fire came from the White House. Henry Kissinger, Nixon's national security advisor, telephoned Zumwalt the following day. "Kissinger all but shrieked at me. [He] really had only one thing to say: the President (as Commander in Chief) wanted the *Constellation* protesters to receive dishonorable discharges immediately if not sooner. [Not even the alleged offenders at Houston in 1909 had been dealt with so summarily.] Since under the Uniform Code of Military Justice [UCMJ]—the law of the land—a dishonorable discharge was an impermissible penalty in the absence of a long-drawn-out general court-martial and in any event could not result from being AWOL for a few hours, the conversation began on a note of unreality. I learned a little later that what had first put Mr. Nixon into a fury was seeing the 'Connie' sailors giving the clenched-fist salute on the dock on the Thursday evening news . . . he tended to view all disagreement, not to say opposition, as mutiny. Therefore, he interpreted my speech as an expression of support for mutineers."

The notes taken by Zumwalt of this conversation indicate that as they talked, Kissinger's tone of voice gradually sank, and while still passing along the president's demand for drastic action, allowed that "You must follow the UCMJ." Still, the CNO grasped that his job hung in the balance and he later learned that Kissinger had actually ordered Secretary of Defense Melvin Laird, a stalwart supporter of Zumwalt's policies and programs, to fire him. Laird refused and as a former Congressman packed enough political strength to disregard Kissinger who had neither the standing nor the power to issue orders to a cabinet member.

Elements of Congress now opened fire on Zumwalt. F. Edward Hebert of Louisiana, chairman of the House Armed Services Committee and when it came to money a treasured friend of the navy, had named a three-man subcommittee to investigate alleged racial and disciplinary problems. "Eddie," says Zumwalt, "did not think long hair and beards were consistent with good discipline, did not favor women going to sea, and preferred to maintain the Navy's traditional policies towards minorities. [In fact, Hebert had always resisted civil rights legislation.] I made no bones about disagreeing with Eddie on those issues, but we remained personally friendly."

Zumwalt was appalled at the tenor of the investigation, which by the very language it used seemed to prejudge matters. During a telephone call, Hebert expressed antipathy to the CNO's "so-called equality business," which the Louisana Congressman interpreted as a quota system. Unable to deter Hebert from plunging ahead, Zumwalt rallied support for his programs. He contacted all former CNOs except George Anderson and secured backing from that quarter. A number of senior admirals publicly approved his course. When he approached John Stennis of Mississippi, the chairman of the Senate Armed Forces Committee, Zumwalt says that Stennis "offered this helpful comment: 'After all, you got to realize they came down from the trees a long time after we did.'"

The all-white subcommittee, headed by Representative Floyd V. Hicks assisted by Representatives W. C. Daniel and Alexander Pirnie, refused to allow a black congressman the right to audit the hearings. One member of the panel, Virginia's W. C. Daniel, a former national commander of the American Legion, previously had expressed fear that large numbers of

African Americans as sailors threatened the future of the navy. Pirnie, recalls Zumwalt, "apparently had no interest in conditions of shipboard life or in the problems racial attitudes created or indeed anything except whether punishments he considered sufficiently stiff were being meted out to offenders."

Against the advice and wishes of Defense Secretary Laird, the CNO arranged to address the subcommittee, which to him seemed reluctant to hear him. Meanwhile, as the investigators began to interview witnesses, Zumwalt visited eighty-nine-year-old Carl Vinson of Georgia, the former chairman of the House Armed Services Committee, whom he believed, from behind the scenes, was pushing Hebert, a protégé. Zumwalt came away from the meeting convinced he had softened Vinson's ire. Slowly, powerful figures from the military and political establishments reinforced Zumwalt. He firmly contested the assumptions that seemed to govern the inquiry. The CNO took the tack that racism existed in the navy, that it was damaging and relevant to the inquiry, but that discipline had not broken down in the overall seagoing force.

For all of his efforts, considering the makeup of the three congressional inquisitor-judges, their conclusions could have been written before anyone recorded a word of testimony. Their report read, "The members of the subcommittee did not find and are unaware of any instances of institutional discrimination on the part of the Navy toward any group of persons, majority or minority." Zumwalt comments on that statement, "This 'finding' could have been reached only by ignoring the mass of evidence to the contrary the Navy presented."

The Congressmen called for an end to gestures such as "passing the power" or "dapping" on the grounds that they enhanced racial polarization. Zumwalt snaps, "Presumably rebel yells, on the other hand, simply prove that boys will be boys."

They came down hard on "permissiveness," "appeasement," and "a tolerance of failure," all of which they detected in the attitude and behavior of senior and junior officers, particularly in dealing with the *Constellation* dissidents "for what was a major affront to good order and discipline."

The solons demanded a sterner effort at recruiting levels "to screen out agitators, troublemakers, and those who otherwise fail to meet acceptable levels of performance." To Zumwalt, the trio themselves were guilty of incitement by using the buzz words of "agitator" and "troublemaker." A personal rebuke to Zumwalt cited his public admonishment of subordinates to solve the racial problems and offered "regrets that the tradition of not criticizing seniors in front of subordinates was ignored . . ."

Although most congressmen preferred not to take a public position for fear of alienating a block of voters, there was ample resistance to change among the legislators. Chick Rauch remembers a Congressman's legislative assistant, after his boss was out of earshot, remarking, "Don't you believe that the best way to handle all these problems with blacks is a sort of benign neglect?" [A phrase that originated with Democrat Patrick Moynihan who had been in the Nixon cabinet.]

Painful, even "outrageous" as it was to Zumwalt, the product of the subcommittee drew little attention within or outside of the service. The main battle lay with antiwar, extreme militant civil-rights forces. "With the help of Rear Admiral Chick Rauch," says Emmett Tidd, "we received quality black personnel from the fleet to train as recruiters in the new environment. They had an enormously unpopular job, going out in the community that neither respected combat veterans of Vietnam nor black recruiters they considered to be 'Uncle Toms.' They soon proved their skill and mettle. We were having recruiting offices vandalized and bombed, recruiting vehicles burned and one attempted hostage case. The intended victim was a burly Navy recruiter who promptly ended the fiasco by skinning his knuckles on the chin of his not too smart protester. Our black recruiters, enlisted and officers, eventually helped us gain a new entrée into the black communities that would help us obtain qualified recruits, eligible to go on to technical schools and prove their ability to learn and perform the most challenging jobs in the Navy."

Along with the poorly educated, potential enlistees whose history indicated a disrespect for authority were barred. Zumwalt is persuaded that despite the opposition his message had been absorbed. Commanders took the right steps. Impressed by a sincere effort to deal with problems, dissent among African Americans diminished. As the navy embarked on an era of relatively smooth sailing in racial relations, interest by the media swiftly waned.

The steps taken by Zumwalt notwithstanding, the navy still pitched and yawed through a number of disturbances that threatened to sink Zumwalt and his reforms. Harry D. Train, a 1949 Annapolis graduate, had attended a Jesuit high school in his hometown of Washington, D.C. "We had Hispanics, Asiatics, blacks, Hindus and Moslems and a lot of Irish kids. I have to say I was color-blind. I did not think anything about racial relations." At the Naval Academy he was a classmate of Wesley Brown. Again Train recalls no discussions related to blacks.

Commissioned less than a year after the first directive from Truman prohibiting discrimination in the armed forces, Train went to sea first on destroyers and then submarines. "There were no black officers in submarines but quite a number of fine black petty officers. I would not have countenanced discrimination or put downs of non-whites. Actually, I did not realize that the Navy in which I served had been segregated. In destroyers and submarines, blacks and whites occupied the same berthing spaces, ate in the same mess facilities, used the same heads, and neither had precedence in lines at the mess hall, mail call or waiting to go ashore.

"My first awareness of racial problems occured when I was a Carrier Battle Group Commander on the USS *John F. Kennedy*, Capt. Robert Hugh Gormley commanding, in the Mediterranean during 1971–72. A series of high visibility incidents involving blacks suddenly began occurring in Greek ports where we visited. Examples would be destructive behavior in bars, with the black perpetrators then as they departed, shouting they were from the *Kennedy*, tire slashings and automobile vandalism with graffiti indicating they were performed by blacks from the *Kennedy*.

"My Naval Investigative Service agents informed Captain Gormley and me that there was a black power group of non-navy people following us around the Eastern Mediterranean, deliberately creating racial incidents. This culminated at sea when the ship's executive officer, Capt. Ted Fellows, was informed by notes and posted notices that if he went below decks, the blacks would kill him. Captain Gormley, Captain Fellows and I met and Captain Fellows said we had to let him go below decks because if he did not, his authority would be destroyed. We agreed that it was the [proper] course of action and we would support it and bear responsibility for whatever might happen. We made it clear we were not ordering him to do this.

"Captain Fellows went below at 2000, alone, with no orderly and no master at arms. He emerged at 0600 without incident—except for getting lost on several occasions. That ended the problem abruptly. To the best of my knowledge and that of my staff and the NIS agents, neither Gormley nor Fellows had ever said or done anything that would have caused our black sailors to believe they were being treated unfairly. The NIS early evaluation of the incidents ashore, kept the command from acting as though it believed these really were *Kennedy*-perpetrated events.

"The first identifiable programs (other than 'leadership' per se) of which I was aware to ameliorate racial antagonisms and to teach officers and enlisted men that acceptance of blacks was in the best interests of the nation and the Navy were Admiral Zumwalt's initiatives. I believe they were enormously successful."

Train says, "Moorer and Zumwalt were the two best CNOs the Navy has enjoyed since I became a part of the Navy in 1945. While Admiral Moorer was not proactive in the field of racial relations, racial tensions had not really built up to recognizable proportions during his stewardship. He was certainly not racist. He was a firm, but benevolent leader who lived comfortably within his own skin. Zumwalt might have had an uncomfortable feeling that Admiral Moorer had let the side down. Admiral Zumwalt became CNO when racial problems were becoming a serious challenge to the Navy. Prefacing my next comment with the observation that I do not believe the Marines ever had a racial problem [that would contradict even the Corps' own official account of its history], I will say that Zumwalt's leadership placed the Navy ahead of the other services in dealing with racial inequities in the military."

Like many others, Train cites McNamara's Project 100,000 as the major cause of trouble. "Was it a racial problem or a problem of having a high percentage of thugs—of all descriptions—in the military. Talk to the then-Army captains who had to wear sidearms when they entered the barracks in which these people lived. Talk to the staff sergeants who had to man positions on the tops of barracks with shotguns. The drug use problems, the AWOL problems, the desertion rates in those days were not products of racial unrest. They were the products of trying to cure the problems of American society with the military."

Zumwalt pronounces himself grateful that he did not have to fight on a third front, with the marines. "I had a superb relationship with General [Leonard] Chapman, the Corps Commandant. He told me, 'Do what you gotta do. We won't give you any trouble.'"

Contrary to Train's observation, white and black marines engaged in fights and assaults upon one another within and outside the continental United States. In Vietnam, fragging of rear-area tents and huts of white officers and noncoms was the subject of a number of courts-martial. Aware of the ferment within his command in Vietnam, Ed Simmons says, "The Marine Corps was damaged by the Vietnam War but not as much as the Army. We had de facto segregation in the mess halls. In the huts everybody had a boom box and one played soul music and the other country. The blacks had organized into things like the Mau Maus, which had recognition signals, a towel around the neck, braided bracelets. Young marines were coming from a very upset society. We'd been driven off the campuses of big schools. We were getting younger officers, already alienated from their own generation. The Armed Services weren't doing a much better job than the universities in dealing with dissent and racial confrontations. Certainly, during the war, we couldn't take time off, give cans of beer to the protestors and talk.

"We had tent camps at China Beach where the men had five-day rests, some entertainment and better chow. In the mess hall, I'd talk to corporals and buck sergeants, fifty or sixty of them with a gaggle of blacks among them. There was an obvious polarization that we hadn't seen in '65–'66. We started out trying to soft-pedal the situation but by the end of the war we had human relations councils at all levels."

Michael Spiro, as a marine aide to the CNO, says, "I had no direct input into his efforts to change things for non-whites. However, in compliance with his clear instructions, we made sure that his Minority Affairs Officer, Bill Norman, had easy access to the CNO, traveled with us whenever and wherever feasible and ensured that there was always time on his schedule to meet with minority groups and to be briefed on minority affairs. This same policy extended to Mrs. Zumwalt who always met with minority groups while traveling with her husband."

For his branch of the service, Spiro asserts that rather than racial tension, matters of postings depressed morale for all marines. "This was caused by assigning personnel to a deploying unit without allowing them the fully authorized stateside time following their return from Vietnam. It was not unusual to have Marines who, just forty-five days before, had completed their second tour in Vietnam, assigned to a unit that was going to be deployed for six months or more."

Dick McDonald dates racial troubles in the marines to the late 1960s, citing "McNamara's Project 100,000 which directed the services to take a certain number of non–high school graduates and individuals with criminal records. McNamara's idea was to take advantage of the military's touted ability to turn a bad boy into a productive citizen. Noble in their intentions, but the problem was defining what constituted a bad boy. Just another example of McNamara's incredible ineptitude as Secretary of Defense. In essence, we took in a bunch of felons and, unfortunately many of these were blacks who were smart militant leaders or dumb militant followers. There were guys who had three-page rap sheets and convictions for aggravated assault and homicide. We had loosely organized gangs that were inter-base, including overseas. One I recall was named Da Mau Mau."

McDonald focuses on the lawless character and unstructured personalities of the Project 100,000 recruits but equally, if not more critical, was their poor educational backgrounds. The bulk of the men inducted fell into the two bottom categories of the classification tests at a time when warfare increasingly demanded a certain level of knowledge and technical skills. They were more difficult to train and imbue with a sense of the military's perception of the mission.

He characterizes the period of 1970–72 while he was provost marshal at Camp Pendleton as "very difficult with respect to the combined anti-war, racial distress. We were in the midst of dealing with a crime wave that included murders, bad, bad assaults, intimidation typical of gangs, racial unrest which included setting fires in barracks. In one incident that typified the worst a group of dumb militants occupied a barracks, threw everything out of the windows—furniture, bunks, foot lockers, wall lockers and personal property and then attempted to torch the place. My MPs prevented the fire by getting into the building and capturing the bad guys. I deliberately avoid using the term arrest or taking into custody. It was a combat action which fortunately had no serious casualties. Police all over the country were engaged in this kind of combat. The guys who actually did the deed were not smart enough to organize it, but they took the hit and never named the leaders. We had some intelligence which gave us a good idea who they were, but no evidence. The anti-war demonstations aimed at Pendleton came in the form of peaceful demonstrations at the entry gates.

"There was never any doubt that we were in control. During this entire period, President Nixon was a frequent visitor to the base to play golf or go to the beach. My MPs, many of whom were black, peformed wonderfully as members of the Presidential Security Platoon. The same platoon also acted as our tactical (SWAT) team.

"Our base commander was a very southern talking major general, George Bowman. On more than one occasion, after a night of violence where whites were beat up or robbed by blacks, General Bowman suggested to me, with a smile on his face, that I order the next pick-up load of black arrestees be pushed out at high speed, or that the MPs visit some other type of immediate retribution on black suspects. I obviously never followed those suggestions, but always wonder[ed] if he were serious. General Bowman was very southern, but also very smart."

McDonald admits the changes in mores shocked him. "In spite of my 'enlightenment' in the area of race relations I vividly remember as Battalion CO receiving officers at home for official calls and opening the door one evening to a handsome and highly qualified black lieutenant accompanied by his equally handsome white wife. I was speechless, an obvious reflection on my upbringing when I never saw a black man with a white woman, much less married to one."

McDonald criticizes the revised hirsute regulations. "Our own Commandant, General Chapman, added some fuel to the fire by authorizing black Marines to wear a form of 'modified' Afro haircut, which defied practical definition. It was an unfortunate decision which fueled racial polarizations at a time when solidarity was badly needed. Chapman added to the problem by directing that Navy Corpsmen attached to the Marines could follow the more liberal grooming standards which had been recently established by Admiral Zumwalt, the new CNO. We handled incidents in one way: legal action. It was a tough time for the good-guy minority who wanted to be a Marine. The peer pressure by the criminal militants was enormous."

Edgar Huff finally signed his retirement papers in 1972, after thirty years as a marine. At the ceremonies he said, "The Marine Corps has been good to me and I feel I have been good to the Marine Corps." Indeed, he had swallowed his pride on numerous occasions when superiors denigated blacks, referred to "niggers," or joked about watermelons. Local dignitaries and marine brass celebrated his retirment at a party which drew 750 people, entertained by a twelve-piece orchestra, barbecue pits for four hogs, a 'soul pot' with stewed chicken, and copious amounts of alcohol. Three weeks later, four white marines, said Huff, lobbed white phosphorus grenades at his home and car. A white friend noted the license number on the car with the assailants and all were arrested. According to Huff the marine corps let them off with no worse punishment than a discharge or transfer. The marine corps pamphlet on blacks in the corps reports on Huff's career and dedication to duty but makes no mention of this incident.

Ugly disturbances pitted soldiers against one another at Fort Bragg, Fort Dix, and overseas. At Travis Air Force Base in California, black airmen accumulated a number of grievances involving housing, the operation of an NCO club, recreational facilities, a perception that more severe disciplinary punishments were handed to men of color, as well as a fiat by the base commander that banned the clenched-fist salute, a feature of the 1968 Olympic Games which disturbed many white Americans.

On 21 May 1971, a squabble over a loudly played phonograph during a party burst into a fracas that enveloped the base with hundreds of airmen from both races engaged in a series of battles. Air police resorted to high-pressure fire hoses, even summoned aid from civilian law-enforcement agencies in a protracted struggle to squelch the brawling. The authorities arrested a total of 135, including 25 whites. More than 30 individuals required hospital treatment for their injuries. Airmen fought one another at Chanute Field, Illinois, and in the subterranean corridors of the Goose Bay, Labrador, base where they assaulted one another with fists and handy objects like desk lamps.

Individual air force commanders, aware of the ferment in the ranks, experimented with solutions. Bob Gaylor, an eyewitness to the integration of black airmen into his previously all-white unit at Lackland, Texas, recalls his experiences while senior NCO for the Second Air Force. "We were just beginning to realize that we were having drug problems. Heroin for the most part, and marijuana. At that time, our drug abuse program consisted of a chaplain, maybe a legal officer who would go in front of a group of airmen and more or less tell them, 'If you smoke marijuana, you'll either get sick, go to jail, or go to hell. So don't do it.' The airmen were thumbing their noses, audiences laughed.

"At Castle AFB, California, then-Colonel Colin C. ("Hambone") Hamilton found Cal Espinoza, an ex-convict who had spent years in prison for use and sale of drugs and now worked for the state in rehabilitation programs. Hamilton [brought] this guy in front of the airmen and let him tell it how it really is, what happens to you when you use drugs and when you get to prison. It went over so well that he called General [David] Jones [Second Air Force CO] and said, 'I think it's worth a trip out here for you to hear this guy.'"

According to Gaylor, the talk, generously larded with four-letter words and prison savvy, impressed the entire audience including Jones who even tossed money in the hat to pay for the speaker's gasoline. Jones arranged for Espinoza to deliver the message throughout his command. Gaylor recalls criticism of Jones for this step. "That's just what we need! Some ex-con telling our airmen how to behave."

But as Jones discerned the extent of racial antagonisms in his fief, he drew upon the drug-awareness protocol. He created a team that included Cal Espinoza, Gaylor as the senior noncom of the Second Air Force, and others to tour installations. "We had to begin to educate people in the racial problems, bring them to the surface. They had been suppressed long enough. Whenever we'd head out to one of the bases, we were looked upon as both a threat and as somebody who could help them."

Others in the air force hierarchy wondered whether their organization faced the troubles of the other branches of the armed forces. The generals gathered a group of officers to determine whether there was any justification to complaints of widespread discrimination in terms of equal opportunity. Hughie Mathews, the black personnel expert, was one of two members of his race on the committee. "We did all kinds of investigations. We went through the Army, the Navy and the Air Force, called all kinds of witnesses, did all kinds of studies, got statistics. They [the others] came up with the conclusion that there was no discrimination in the Air Force. That was everybody but me. I refused to go along. I told them that if they wrote that I was going to write my own report. I argued for three days to get a statement there was discrimination in the Air Force. I finally convinced the guys, one by one, pointing out the areas where there was discrimination by using the statistics, showing [African Americans] don't get assignments, don't get promoted, the black officers and black enlisted men don't get promoted in the numbers they should, aren't getting promoted."

According to Mathews, the result was a modest effort to revitalize the equal-opportunity office. "It wasn't a very serious operation except that the guy who was in there, Colonel Lou Delaney was beginning to make a lot of waves, trying to get things done. Consequently, very few people up there liked him. They hated him as a matter of fact. He told me his contemporaries—branch chiefs, division chiefs, called him 'nigger lover' to his face, their poor idea of a sick joke."

Beyond the efforts of a few like David Jones, Hughie Mathews, and Lou Delaney, the disorders at Travis and other installations ultimately convinced authorities of shortcomings in the effort to create an effective, fully integrated service. Too much reponsibility lay upon the shoulders of individual commanders. There was no clearly defined policy nor any mechanism to ensure equal opportunity. As remedial action, all airmen, regardless of rank, were required to attend programs in race relations which stressed that friction interfered with mission accomplishment. The equal-opportunity office, a one-man operation at the time that trouble boiled over at Travis, expanded rapidly to implement the policies for which it was designed. Hughie Mathews notes, "We got across the idea that the job wasn't just responding to complaints and answering correspondence. The Equal Opportunities Office was to see that a problem in housing, assignments, or promotions got solved." Indeed, officers could now expect ratings in this area on their efficiency reports.

The turbulence throughout the armed forces persuaded Pentagon authorities to take a more aggressive stance. One 24 June 1971, a month after the Travis tumult, the Defense Department announced creation of a Department of Defense Race Relations Institute at Patrick Air Force Base, Florida, which would train military personnel to become instructors in race relations, collect research on programs, and conduct classes throughout the armed services. Those in charge realized that some of the earlier "instructional" efforts actually triggered nasty confrontations when led by inadequately trained, overzealous leaders, and that the Patrick program sought to develop more skilled missionaries.

With the media focused on the fighting, the morale, and the discipline difficulties in Vietnam, events in Europe received far less attention. Nevertheless, racial turbulence there also hovered near the flash point. Harold Hayward, on completing his tour in Vietnam, took command of the 3,500 GIs in the U.S. Army Berlin Brigade. "Rather than being quartered in the same relative positions as they served in their units, soldiers had self-segregated—white soldiers on one floor of the barracks and blacks on another. When I issued an order to integrate their living arrangements, the black soldiers more strongly resisted the move than the white ones. Seating arrangements in the mess halls followed the same lines. Off-duty recreation was also segregated although not as rigidly."

Serving as Hayward's deputy brigade commander was the former 82d Airborne battalion chief, John Costa, who had seen only modest signs of unrest in his previous posts. "In Berlin," says Costa, "we had good quality soldiers because troublemakers were generally screened out or ejected if their conduct in Berlin wasn't up to a high standard. Nevertheless, the polarization between blacks and whites in the units was apparent to anyone who looked for it or was unwilling to ignore it. I remember a softball game between two rifle companies. Although we had a goodly percentage of black soldiers and although they were usually very active in athletic activity, I saw a company team playing without a single black soldier and there were no black spectators. I mentioned this to the 1st Sergeant of the company as rather strange. He was immediately very defensive, saying words to the effect, 'Oh, sir, we don't have any problems like that in this company.'

"In fact, even as we were speaking there was a special meeting somewhere in McNair Barracks under the leadership of an outside black agitator. He worked in the barber shop and we had been alerted about him by a concerned black soldier who said that he saw trouble coming. I believe Doc Hayward and I were far more aware of what was brewing than any others, officers or NCOs. Sure enough, within a week we were both enjoying a party at my quarters, dressed formal, because it was the weekend of Doc and his wife Margaret's daughter's wedding to a young captain in the Brigade. We got a call from the duty officer that there was a disturbance at McNair Barracks. We high-tailed it out there, dressed as we were, and helped sort out a very messy affair that involved a number of assaults. The trouble started at the movie theater and spread out to the caserne streets. Fortunately, a rifle company coming in from night training made an appearance and we were quickly able to restore order."

Hayward remembers that Costa and a young civilian educator suggested he meet informally with some of the more outspoken blacks. "One, a junior NCO, delivered an emotional diatribe that didn't sit well with me or most of the black soldiers present. He was already in trouble for some infraction, went AWOL a few days later and disappeared for several months. However, another of the other black soldiers delivered a dispassionate account of what he perceived as discrimination against him with respect to promotion. He had graduated at the top of his high school class, was number one in basic and individual training and had no disciplinary problems in Berlin. Yet he had not been selected for promotion while lesser-qualified whites had. He concluded he had been 'passed over' because of his race. A subsequent informal inquiry on my part convinced me that the soldier was correct. I had a discrimination problem on my hands."

Hayward, like a considerable number of those committed to a military career, understood that a certain level of harmony and cohesiveness was vital to combat readiness. These depended upon loyalty to the unit and fellow servicemen. Racial tension was destructive of these qualities.

"I observed, as had my civilian education advisor, that the discrimination was not malicious and perpetrated by evil men but stemmed from ignorance and insensitivity. Naive as I was, I assumed the problem could be solved through educating, sensitizing, and indoctrinating the officers and non-commissioned officers of the Brigade. I expected that logic and a sense of fairness would prevail, creating an atmosphere of equal opportunity and non-discrimination. To that end, I engaged the service of a white professor from the University of Maryland. Pete Daniel, Ph.D., an authority on race relations, came to Berlin and delivered a half-dozen lectures on the subject to the officers and noncoms.

"The reaction to Dr. Daniel's introduction to the Brigade was mixed; much of it not particularly favorable. I don't regret having brought him to Berlin. He carried out his part of his contract and I liked him personally. I found him informative and helpful. However, he had a full beard and wore his hair cut long—anathema to most of my hard-nosed officers and NCOs, black and white. I suspect the message was overwhelmed by the medium. I also suspect that word got around that 'the Brigade Commander is soft on blacks.' That may have had some bearing on subsequent events.

"In August of 1970 at McNair [Barracks], we had an 'incident' one evening that amounted to a race riot. No lethal weapons were used and no one was seriously injured. Still, it took a couple of hours to get the situation under control. The most significant insight I had developed since Dr. Daniel's visit the year before was that change could not be brought about solely by education and indoctrination. This had been crystallized in my mind by a film clip showing Martin Luther King saying to some close advisors, 'We cannot hope to change people's *attitudes* in this country. What we have to do is change their *behaviors* and hope that a change in *attitude* follows.'"

Hayward translated his 'insight' into organization of a Human Relations Seminar, which in reality amounted to eight two-hour sessions. The material covered black history, prejudice, poverty, education, psychology, military history, and other themes related to race relations. With an emphasis upon discussion rather than lectures, the groups were led by two-man teams, with a black paired with a white. "The purpose," says Hayward, "was to *inform*, not to *persuade*."

The Berlin Brigade commander talked candidly to his officers, bluntly noting the pervasive presence of prejudice and discrimination. He identified the source as America's long tradition of white-controlled institutions that failed to provide blacks with the means for "adequate education, a voice in the political process, the right to economic self-determination, just treatment under the law or decent health care." He labeled incidents like the McNair outburst "an effect, not a cause" that occurred because "the young black citizen, whether he is a civilian or a soldier, is fed up and he is committed to doing something about the situation."

From Berlin, Hayward moved to Heidelberg, West Germany, headquarters of the U.S. Army in Europe (USAREUR). He now commanded the Combat Support Command, a conglomerate of troops with various specialities and considerably more soldiers than in the Berlin Brigade. "I soon learned that racial tensions and confrontation were quite common." He introduced efforts based on his Berlin Brigade experience to ensure equal opportunity and to "inform" the GIs under his jurisdiction.

From the Combat Support Command, Hayward shifted to deputy chief of staff for personnel at USAREUR headquarters. "In that role race relations was one of my primary responsibilities and I pursued the same basic policies I had developed as a commander. Fortunately, I found my approach dovetailed neatly with that of General [Michael] Davison who had become the new CINCUSAEUR."

Like many commanders responsible for fighting the war, Davison admits he devoted little attention to issues of race while in Vietnam. Asked about discrimination during his tour there he had advised his superiors that while he opposed discrimination, he found it difficult to separate fact from rumor, and without specific evidence of untoward behavior could not take action. However, when Davison completed his tour in Southeast Asia, he assumed command of the U.S. Army in Europe.

An army "brat," Davison, a United States Military Academy graduate, Class of 1939, knew of segregated units only through recollections of his father who commanded a troop in the 10th Cavalry while Davison was a child. "During World War II," recalls Davison, "news came of the so-called Panther Platoons [provisionals made up of volunteers] and someone who had experience with them said what great combat soldiers they were. In an attack, the Panther Platoons would get out in front and you'd have to work like hell to catch up.

"As CINC in Europe," says Davison, " starting in July 1971, I found things were really a mess. That was true of race relations, discipline, standards of training. The root problem lay in the extreme turbulence at the replacement centers for Vietnam. Whole battalions would turn over. There were second lieutenants in charge of companies. There was a great drain on company- and field-level officers as well as noncoms.

"Blacks were tremendously unhappy. They had segregated themselves in barracks, the mess halls and there were four or five underground newspapers feeding their discontent. Just before I got there, a huge demonstration occurred at Heidelberg. It was a very bad situation. My instructions from Creighton Abrams, now Army Chief of Staff, was if you've got a problem, then fix it. I was used to him giving orders that way from my time in Vietnam. I had input from Harold Hayward, Fred Davison, a black general who preceded Hayward as DCSPER [Deputy Chief of Staff for Personnel] and George Price, another black general. I got Abrams to make every effort he could to stabilize personnel. He did this [undoubtedly the gradual 'Vietnamization' of the conflict lessened the need for GIs]. I wasn't worried about the undergound newspapers. I figured that if I corrected the situation, the newspapers would have nothing to write about and disappear.

"I believed leadership was critical. I assembled my chain of command, down to brigade level into race-relations councils. I arranged for officers and enlisted men trained at the Army's Equal Opportunity school in Florida to be placed throughout my command. We brought general officers to my personal council room and an Equal Opportunity officer conducted a course in equal opportunity in order to get the message across to them.

"I brought back captains who had taken the Fort Benning Advanced Course to command the companies. I put all incoming captains through a five-day program so they understood matters like race relations and drug enforcement as well as their other responsibilities for logistics, maintenance, and so forth. The idea was so successful that battalion and brigade commanders called General Hayward and General Davison and said 'I need some of that myself.' It was a great help. My deputy, Lt. Gen. Art Collins, could devote himself solely and totally to training. The result was a satisfying effect. Soldiers understood why they were there. I had one brigadier general and one corps commander who resisted because they didn't think it was necessary. They were relieved. I even heard from Admiral Jerry Miller of the Navy who said he had a problem on one of his ships and needed some help. He had run into one of our teams and came back and asked if he could borrow them. He took an Army team below decks to talk with sailors."

Hayward, who describes the policy as "a vigorous, pro-active approach," says, "The chain of command in USAREUR, while it had not lost control, had suffered a significant diminution of its power to influence the behavior of troops with the command. I felt in a sense we were being held hostage by black soldiers who had the potential to create widespread disorder such as that experienced in Watts, Detroit, and Washington, D.C. Many commanders favored 'getting tough' but except for dealing with criminal behavior, for us to have taken harsh steps would have precipitated disastrous consequences, not only for USAREUR but for the Army and nation as well. We could ill afford repeating the Army's experience in Houston, in 1917.

"Our approach was to restore control slowly and deliberately. Our main thrust was to create a climate of trust and to make non-discrimination and equal opportunity a reality. We made our policies clear through all the information media we had available. We conducted periodic two- and three-day race relations conferences with senior commanders and their senior enlisted advisors. At these conferences we had small group discussions, feedback reports and usually a guest speaker. It was in that role that H. Minton Francis [formerly Hayward's classmate at the Military Academy and then an assistant secretary of defense] visited us. Fortunately for me and my conscience it gave me an opportunity to apologize to him in public for my behavior toward him in our days as cadets at West Point."

"I organized within my office, a 'flying squad' headed by my deputy, that investigated any racial incident where violence was involved. General Davison became a 'pen pal' to many black soldiers who inundated him with letters of complaint. It devolved upon me and my office to deal with these letters and to prepare replies for General Davison's signature. Where ever credible, serious breaches of policy were alleged, my flying squad looked into the situation. Many of the letters consisted of gripes about command policy or matters not associated with race relations. At times I felt as though we were being intimidated by the whims of black soldiers. The disciplinarian in me wanted to answer many of these letters by saying in effect, 'Sit down! Shut up! Get on with the business of soldiering!' My better judgment prevailed.

"Externally, we were taking a lot of heat from the black press, black civil rights organizations and several hot spots in the Pentagon and elsewhere in the government. At the suggestion of Army Personnel in the Pentagon, we invited influential people from the press, business, state and local governments to visit USAREUR and assess the situation. About every two weeks, a delegation of three to six people, usually black, selected by the Department of the Army showed up in Frankfurt, prepared for a seven to ten day tour.

"My staff arranged itineraries and our guests were escorted to any place they wished in USAREUR. They participated in 'no holds barred' interviews with people of their own choosing. As a finale they had dinner with my wife and me in our home and an exit interview with General Davison. I was most favorably impressed by those who participated. We received useful suggestions from participants, but only infrequently. Usually, we received good marks for our approach and for the progress we were making. I do not recall ever receiving significant criticism from any of them, either while they were in Europe or after their return to the States."

As a kind of point man for the army establishment in Europe, Hayward often spoke on the subject of race relations to conferences and ceremonies, including a holiday commemoration of the birth of Martin Luther King Jr. He was disappointed that most of the audience there was white, not black.

After duty on the headquarters staff at Heidelberg, John Costa received command of the 1st Brigade, 8th Infantry stationed in and around the city of Mainz. Initially designated as airborne, the brigade lost its jump status and became a pure "leg" organization. According to Costa that significantly depressed morale. The troopers lost their incentive pay, jump boots, and cap flashes [parachute insignia]. "The process of this transition," says Costa, "was begun before my command tenure and includied forming and deploying to Vicenza, Italy, a full airborne battalion combat team. The soldiers who made the switch to Vicenza were considered the elite, the lucky ones. The best of the noncoms and junior commissioned officers also went 'south.'

"Those who remained behind in Mainz either had too little time remaining on their overseas obligation or else were identified as not the best, with more disciplinary and other problems. What did this have to do with race relations? Lowered spirits and self-esteem, poor morale and the disciplinary problems associated with drugs and alcohol abuse were also reflected in tension between the black and white soldiers. Unhappy soldiers found it easy to take their frustrations out on each other, across racial lines. We were in the process of building new mechanized infantry battalions to go with the tank battalion that made up the 'new' brigade configuration. Added to this were the tensions and hostility of many in the German community which our black soldiers felt.

"I spent a lot of time addressing problems that arose with our German neighbors and these often enough had a race component. A common complaint from our black soldiers was that some owners of *gasthouses* did not want the patronage of black soldiers, saying that this reflected the desires of their German clientele. In these cases we would notify our soldiers, black and white, that this or that establishment was off limits because of their policy of discrimination. White soldiers would still go to these places sometimes, because there would be no blacks and they found this to their liking. Keeping tabs on the matter was tricky. If black soldiers saw we looked the other way, we were then not protecting their rights and interests.

"Many black soldiers found the larger cities, especially Frankfurt, more congenial. That led to another problem and threatened a major incident. In the wee hours of one summer Sunday morning, soldiers returning to base found the Mainz taxi drivers had decided not to pick up blacks looking for a ride back to their caserne. There was a near riot at the *bahnhof.* I was called by the chief of police and I summoned all battalion commanders to meet me at the railroad station where they would pick out their own men and get them back to barracks, using our trucks or buses.

"The [situation] gave cause for black soldiers to gather at the flagpole on Sunday afternoon. They wanted to talk to me about their grievances. The situation was very sticky. I told them that I was very aware of what was happening and would take all necessary steps to see they were fairly treated. The ensuing discussion with civil authorities was profitable. This kind of incident did not recur during my command tenure."

In line with the responsibilities of all commanders, whether in the States or abroad, Costa also sought to ensure adequate off-post accommodations for the families of NCOs and junior officers. To see that his people were decently housed and that they in turn maintained their residences, Costa decided to rename the largest nearby area occupied by the military. "It had been known officially as MUHA (Mainz University Housing Area), because it was adjacent to the campus of Johannes Gutenberg University. I asked permission to rename it as the Martin Luther King Jr. Housing Area, since a high percentage of the residents were African Americans. Heidelberg withheld permission, citing the policy that these installations were named for distinguished soldiers or soldiers who had given their lives for their country. I reminded them that they were sitting in the midst of Mark Twain Village, which I found to be quite a stretch from their policy. It happened that the main thoroughfare on which the housing area sat years before had been named for Dr. King after he was awarded the Nobel Prize for Peace. I proceeded with my plan, commissioned a sculptor to design a handsome bas-relief image of King and made the renaming a major event in the MLK Jr. birthday celebration which had become an annual affair in USAREUR.

"To build the new brigade, in addition to the training, wartime planning, maintenance of our equipment, etc., we devoted time and resources to put into operation a good solid race-relations program, small group—20–25 soldiers—seminars and discussions led by trained facilitators and supported by syllabuses supplied to us from higher headquarters. I believe these programs which everyone had to attend—soldier, NCO and officers—lasted a week. I made it a point to drop in on every one of these sessions where I would listen for a while and then speak of my personal feelings about race relations in the brigade and racial harmony in the army. I felt that this program helped us greatly and I know that my efforts were read as a serious commitment to fair treatment, sensitivity to the anxieties of soldiers black and white and improved attitudes on the part of German civil and police authorities."

From the Second Air Force in the United States David Jones moved to the U.S. Air Force in Europe. There he succeeded to the top position and retained Bob Gaylor as his senior enlisted man. In Europe, Jones innovated with a drug and alcohol abuse center and then courses that would enable an enlisted man to earn a high school diploma during duty time. "He established a social actions branch," says Gaylor. "As you can imagine, the majority of people who ended up in it were those who had axes to grind—the black who had caused problems, the one who didn't want to get his hair cut, a couple who were alcoholics."

A more systematic approach involved the mandatory, twenty-hour race-relations training. "General Jones and his staff were the first ones to go," says Gaylor. "Some of his generals didn't want to go. But you had to go, all over Europe, England, Germany, Spain. It wasn't totally black oriented, but about 99 percent, maybe an occasional Eskimo got to say, 'What about us?' But it was black training, black-related training.

"The training consisted basically of how to live and get along with a black man. Let me tell you, some of the people stormed out of there. I heard one say, 'I wasn't prejudiced till I went to that course. Now I can't stand them.' There were near fights. There were some serious problems because for the first time, things were being said, things were coming out that had never been said or come out before."

One flap centered on the dap. "Some discussions were, 'Why do blacks do that?' 'We're seeking our identity.' 'Hell, you're wearing your name tag; we know who you are.' 'No, we want to be proud; it shows pride.'"

Gaylor notes that not everybody welcomed the race-relations and leadership trainers. "They knew they were going to go back and report to Jones, 'This is what I found . . .' There was some consternation and some concern. A couple of people on Jones's staff got fired because they misplayed it by abusing and misusing the authority they'd been given." Others were relieved because they failed to deal effectively with their racial situation.

After the army's De Witt Armstrong left Vietnam he was assigned to Fort Devens, Massachussets. "Word had reached me," says Armstrong, "that there were significant black-and-white problems at Devens. I wanted a composed, steadfast black lieutenant to be my aide-de-camp, arriving a few weeks before I did. At An Khe I had seen what appeared to be an admirable candidate, and the colonel warmly endorsed that choice. Speaking privately to the lieutenant, warning him of the difficulties, I found him ready for the challenge. His arrival at Fort Devens was an early, silent message to the officers and men, both white and black. Fort Devens promptly joined the rest of the Army in a properly professional state of integration, without my ever having to do anything dramatic. Six months later, the lieutenant attended the advanced course at the infantry school, earned a captaincy, finished college and became a clergyman.

"There were at Devens, a few blacks who wanted to push things a bit too far, although they were usually cordial and good-humored about it. Their ideas, in 1972, had to do with asserting a status for 'the black nation' on a par with the American nation. The black activists proposed directly to me a number of local steps toward that end. Each of the advocates accepted my explanations of how inappropriate that would be and how the rights of us all would be served by the one great nation which together we served and had sworn to support."

At the request of the Continental Army Command's CO, Armstrong also fought to restore the reputation of the army in the six New England states. He undertook an active public-speaking campaign, which including interviews with the media. At a girls' prep school, Concord Academy, he arranged for a highly decorated colonel, a seriously wounded Vietnam veteran, to confront the charges by the linguistics expert Noam Chomsky, one of the foremost foes of the military effort in Vietnam. Armstrong claims the colonel overwhelmed Chomsky and converted the audience with a calm rebuttal drawn from personal experiences. "Among the topics covered, of course, was Chomsky's mistaken charge about racial bias among our fighting units and the disproportionate sacrifice of black men in battle. The colonel had been among those troops as a major and lieutenant colonel. He described the reality of mutually supportive racial integration. He had too often been in the hospitals with other wounded soldiers to allow those lies to remain unrefuted."

Although directives from on high, the creation of seminars, programs, and materials could not immediately change hearts and minds, they had signaled awareness of serious problems of a racial nature which jeopardized the ability of the armed services to carry out their missions. Quite apart from the simple issue of fairness, prejudice and discrimination reduced effectiveness. In this respect, the military now stepped out ahead of the civilian sector.

23
Shifting Sands, Settling Down

Upon the end of the American involvement in Vietnam, not only did the antiwar movement die but also racial tension diminished. The stress of mortal danger undoubtedly had been a major factor in the generation of antagonism and resort to physical violence. The mood of the nation had also changed. Political and some civil rights previously exclusively enjoyed by whites were at least grudgingly accepted by the majority as the birthright of the minority. The fields of strife shifted. Demands in the workplace, in housing, and in competitive areas such as admittance to institutions of higher learning, all of which impinged on the privileges once reserved for whites, now met stiff resistance. Voters reacted against the outbreaks of urban violence and the defiance of authority on campuses. The white majority and some from the minority called for "law and order," a tocsin that often covered dissent.

Within the military, unfinished business stirred some grumbles and rumbling. Disciplinary actions and courts-martial against the sailors from the *Kitty Hawk* and *Constellation* handed out justice that ranged from simple transfers to other ships to six months at hard labor and dishonorable discharges. Some of the black crewmen complained that although Zumwalt focused upon prejudice and discrimination, the weight continued to fall on them. They reported that on the *Kitty Hawk* no more than four blacks could gather in a group before being ordered to disperse while no one questioned twenty white sailors sitting down together. There were charges that white officers referred to them as "boys" or even "dogs." African Americans on the *Kitty Hawk* maintained that superiors discriminated when they meted out punishment for tardiness or for a fight between men of different races.

Behind the scenes, members of the military establishment, like the subcommittee created by Hebert, criticized what they labeled a breakdown in discipline and insufficient penalties for infractions. Marine Dick McDonald says, "My opinion at the time was that the anti-discrimination programs were entirely too liberal, encouraged disobedience, fostered a disdain for the well established chain of command, and were destined to create an inferior Navy. I think in fact those things, except for the last one, occurred. The incidents on the ships were mainly the result of the Admiral's racial policies, which to many COs and sailors replaced the commander with Human Relations Councils and ombudsmen. He painted the incidents as mainly the result of deployment fatigue, but that is a spin which only a master of the Washington political scene, like the Z, could pull off. I think the policies would have had a better chance of success if the senior officers of the Navy had been brought along carefully but firmly into traces, firing those who continued to resist the principles which underlay the policies. Admiral Zumwalt said as much in his book, *On Watch.* In the long haul, the Zumwalt policies did result in a racially integrated Navy, and it probably would not have happened without the drastic change of course which he ordered. He came close to the shoals but did great service to the Navy in the process."

Referring to the three shipboard disturbances, Emmett Tidd, for one, argues, "Mass draconian punishment would have been the very worst and most inflammatory thing that could have been done. It would only have inflamed a highly volatile situation that was still without violence. Fortunately, the calmer heads of Admirals Zumwalt and Clarey won out and history has proven them correct."

Military justice, often a sore point with minority servicemen, drew an investigation by the defense secretary's interracial task force. Cochairmen, Nathaniel R. Jones, general counsel of the NAACP, and army general C. E. Hutchin Jr., led a twelve-person panel that included representatives of law enforcement, civil rights groups, the legal profession, and the military services. The inquiry relied on four separate sources. Members of the task force interviewed personnel from command level through various enlisted grades at a number of installations in the United States and abroad. They also questioned lawyers, psychiatrists, and chaplains at the bases and toured the Defense Race Relations Institute at Patrick Air Force Base.

A second approach compiled and analyzed statistics dealing with the military justice system. Third, a professional research organization collected personal interviews of servicemen to produce an "attitudinal survey" which was compared with similar previous polls. As a fourth element, the group considered written material covering military justice and listened to a number of speakers who possessed experience or expertise in the subject.

Although it dealt extensively with its designated topic, the report reviewed a number of issues and phenomena associated with racial affairs in the armed services. Along with the traditional concerns about the numbers of black officers, off-base housing, and recreation it considered some relatively new items. There were several paragraphs about the practice of dapping, the involved hand-shaking, slapping gestures that seemed to provoke white anger and triggered orders that forbade such gestures. The task force observed the emergence of self-segregation, a "hostile separation," and noted efforts by concerned commanders to increase and improve communication as an "antidote." "Reverse discrimination," which would become a torrid matter among civilians in the 1990s, was briefly discussed in the context of more lenient treatment of nonwhites because of fear of being associated with white racism.

The main thrust remained whether military justice was applied equally, without regard to race or ethnic origin. (Although the study mentions the possibility that those with "a Spanish surname" or Native Americans may also be victims of discrimination, the task force said it did not have sufficient data for inquiry into their situation.) In the army, a sampling of incidents indicated that although blacks comprised 21 percent of the population at the installations involved, slightly more than 26 percent of those charged were black. In the marine corps, where the minority totaled 16.2 percent, they were the alleged violators in 23.3 percent of the cases. In the types of offenses for alleged crimes, aside from drugs, black GIs accounted for more than 35 percent. They were also supposedly responsible for more than 31 percent of the incidents of a confrontation or status nature questioning authority. On the other hand, the army reported African Americans were involved in only 16 percent of the narcotics cases and 18.7 percent of the AWOLs, both figures well below their 21 percent representation among the GIs covered.

One of the more telling comparisons lay in the disposition of incidents. Overall there seemed to be no disparity by race but when broken down into the handling of soldiers accused of a variety of military/civilian crimes, 23.3 percent of the whites received counseling instead of judicial punishment but only 8.3 percent of the blacks were so treated. In the marines, under the same category, the figures for whites was 19.2 percent but only 10.4 for nonwhites. A significantly higher percentage of minorities—39.8 percent compared to only 15.4 percent for whites—endured pretrial confinement for offenses. Although African Americans represented only 11.5 percent of the entire armed forces population, 34.3 percent of the servicemen tried by court-martial were black. Although punishment for general and special courts-martial hit both races about the same in forfeiture of pay, confinement, restriction, and extra duty, 23.4 percent of the blacks were given punitive discharges as against only 16.9 of the whites. A random sampling of those incarcerated at the U.S. Disciplinary Barracks at Fort Leavenworth, Kansas, showed 47.3 percent were black enlisted men although the race represented only 13.1 percent of all noncommissioned personnel. They also received longer terms at hard labor.

In an effort to explain the sources for disparities, the task force recognized that weaker educational backgrounds could make nonwhites more likely to enter the military justice system. It noted the baleful influence of "coerced induction"—enlistment as an alternative to civilian jails. The investigators also remarked on factors that fostered discrimination—language used by blacks that was other than the majority's idea of standard English and probably more to the point, the continued reliance upon the initial Armed Forces Qualification Test. As a screening device for those entering the ranks, the paper-and-pencil test could be viewed as culturally biased and of dubious relevance to many military assignments. Furthermore, superiors used the AFQT to determine eligibility for advanced instruction and promotions even after an individual had worn a uniform for a considerable length of time and demonstrated competence in military skills.

After an eight-month inquiry, the task-force report unreservedly accepted the need for discipline in the armed forces, but in stark contrast with the House Armed Services Subcommittee, asserted that African Americans were the victims of some intentional but largely systemic discrimination in the dispensation of military justice. The study while lauding programs in human relations and equal opportunity said these did not include instruction in the racial problems involving military justice.

The report offered a number of recommendations for changes within the administration of the military justice system and what falls under the wide umbrella of human relations. In regard to the former, these suggested stress on greater uniformity of discipline, better application of nonjudicial punishment, reforms of court-martial procedures that would improve the standing and practices of defense counsels, fostering the participation of minorities in the judicial process, standardization, and procedures to limit abusive discretion at correctional facilities. The panel's discussion ranged from improving educational opportunities for people before they enter the service, through the buzz-issue of haircuts, to full-scale equal-opportunity programs that would be supervised by an assistant secretary of defense specifically assigned to the matter. The task force observed that Americans of Spanish descent now stood as the second-largest minority in the population but that ethnic tracking for this group was unsatisfactory and called for efforts to deal with their problems.

The findings were not unanimous. Maryland federal judge C. Stanley Blair, Maj. Gen. George S. Prugh of the army, RAdm. Merlin H. Staring of the navy, and James V. Bennett, the retired director of the federal prison system, tacked on an "addendum" in which they proclaimed "racial discrimination is but *one* cause of demonstrable disparities—and we see such discrimination reflected far less frequently in the military justice system than the majority concludes." The quartet, however, said, "We are in complete accord that racial and minority discrimination is present in the military establishment, just as it is in the civilian society." In the main, however, they accepted the recommendations presented by the majority.

Brigadier General Clyde R. Mann of the marines dissented even more vigorously. He agreed that discrimination based upon racial or ethnic origins existed within the armed forces but asserted "such discrimination results from the action or inaction of individuals. I also believe that minority service personnel perceive that such discrimination is more widespread than it is in fact." Mann charged the task force with having overstepped its charter and having leaped to conclusions without proof or sufficient expertise. Citing budgetary and manpower requirements, he dismissed the suggested reforms, "The recommendations of the Task Force were made without regard to the real life problems for implementing them."

Horace Robertson, who had earned his law degree while in the navy, also regarded the report as seriously flawed. His caveat lies in the study's covering letter to Secretary of Defense Laird, which read, "Assumed as facts, based upon your charge to us, were the existence of racial and ethnic discrimination in military justice, and the disparity in punishment rates between minority and majority servicemen." Robertson notes, "This assumption was never put to the test by the Task Force, and much of the support for it is anecdotal." He recalls that while he was the 5th Naval District's reviewing officer for the General Court-Martial Convening Authority, "I was struck by the objectivity and fairness of both the lawyers and line officers involved in the process. I saw no examples or specific cases where I could identify that a minority individual was unfairly treated—either in the determination of guilt or innocence or in the severity of the sentence."

As a result of his experience, Robertson agrees with the dissenters who refused to accept that "systemic discrimination" led to "demonstrable disparities" in the administration of military justice to black and white servicemen. But he concedes that military justice was not administered as well as it should have been. He counters that one of the most important remedies to ensure fairness lay in the provision for a diligent, adequate defense. As deputy judge advocate general, he helped reorganize the navy's uniformed legal service by splitting off the Navy Legal Service from line commanders. "Both trial and defense counsel reported only to other lawyers and not to line officers who might attempt to influence their performance as defense counsel through the mechanism of the fitness report." In addition, line commanders received training and directives that emphasized impartiality and fairness in their involvement with the military justice system, whether at the lowest level of the captain's mast or the higher court-martial proceedings. Robertson hastens to add, "These changes were not initiated because of allegations of racial discrimination but rather were a part of the ongoing effort to improve the efficiency of the organization and remove any perception of command control over court-martial proceedings. They may have had some incidental effect of removing the perception of racial discrimination."

Obviously aware of the importance of perception, Robertson said, "We did a full-court press in trying to increase the recruitment and retention of minority lawyers in the JAG Corps. We had some success in recruitment but very little in retention. During that period every legal organization in the country (law firms, government, corporate legal departments) were making efforts in the same direction and we couldn't compete in terms of compensation, life style and prestige."

With all but one of the military men on the committee voicing objections to the accusation of systemic racism, and in line with the sentiments of the population at large, the Department of Defense declined to accept the charge. In one form of rebuke, the official responsible for equal opportunity within the office of the secretary of defense, rather than being named an assistant secretary, was accorded the much less influential status of simply a staff member. Ten years would pass before the Defense Race Relations Institute at Patrick Air Force Base would offer material on how to overcome systemic discrimination. While the theme of the task force was temporarily discarded, there remained on record acknowledgement of the deficiencies in what was supposed to be a color-blind military, particularly its justice system.

Marine Dick McDonald, who supported Zumwalt's reforms even if not enthusiastic about haircuts, remembers, "When I went from the CNO's office to Headquarters, Marine Corps in 1974, there was an ongoing program to create and direct human relations training which was almost totally oriented to improving race relations. I can't attribute this move to Admiral Zumwalt's efforts in the Navy. In fact the Navy programs were viewed by most Marines as the way not to do it. Our Commandant at the time, Maj. Gen. Robert Cushman, for whom I had been aide-de-camp in 1962 went along with the program without real enthusiasm, decreeing only that there would be no 'touchy-feely' courses. Things seemed to improve in spite of his cool reaction and continued largely under local control during the subsequent tenures of Generals Wilson and Barrow. There were never any programs to my knowledge that suggested career threat for failure to implement and practice racial equality, but there was no doubt that a CO who had major racial problems could look forward to being passed over and early retirement.

"My last tour in the Fleet Marine Force, racial problems had been reduced to relatively minor incidents, almost all off duty, off base. There was still de facto segregation in many liberty ports overseas and to some extent at home, but the resulting confrontations were back to the fist fight and rare knifing. On-base facilities were totally integrated and generally without racial strife. As CO of the 31st Marine Amphibious Unit and at Camp Pendleton where I was Provost Marshal (1978–81) I noticed a crime rate that indicated to me that the all-volunteer force was not of the high quality that was being advertised. General Barrow, the Commandant at the time, was incensed when I said this during his visit to Camp Pendleton. By that time, crime was as much committed by whites as by blacks, given the racial makeup. We still had a few blacks who tried to stir up racial trouble, but to little avail. Most of the black Marines now saw opportunity within the system."

Following his duty on CNO Zumwalt's staff, Burt Shepherd commanded the carrier *America*. He says, "There were several occasions in 1972–73 when racial tensions required meeting with groups of blacks to hear and attempt to resolve complaints. My personal style was to find someone who could communicate with the disaffected group and with me. Then, through that person who had credibility with 'them' and with 'me' communicated problems and resolutions where it was not possible before. At times it was difficult and challenging but in hindsight, the problem usually was that the people wanted to be heard, that the leadership was aware of their situation and was trying to help. Once they were assured that 'someone up there' cared, the problems were mollified."

In the years immediately after his two Vietnam tours, Colin Powell gained the background that would make him eligible for his eventual position as chairman of the Joint Chiefs of Staff. He studied at George Washington University for a master's degree, drew a slot at the Pentagon where he became a member of an "old-boys' network" known as the Rocks, in memory of a black brigadier general. The Rocks acted as mentors who encouraged and assisted young African American officers up the career ladders. Named a White House Fellow for a year, Powell put on his uniform again as a battalion commander of the 2d Infantry Division in Korea.

"We were in transition from the draft to the all-volunteer force," says Powell. "As we dragged ourselves home from Vietnam, the nation turned its back on the military. Most of our troops, in Army shorthand were 'Cat Four' Category IV, soldiers possessing meager skills in reading, writing and math. They were life's dropouts, one step above Category V, those who were considered unfit for Army service.

"General [Henry E. 'Gunfighter'] Emerson was determined to turn around this slack, demoralized operation . . . He had begun a program for remaking the 2d Infantry Division which he called, 'Pro-Life,' not to be confused with the anti-abortion movement. Emerson's Pro-Life program, as he put it, 'was to provide the soldier opportunities to become a winner rather than a loser in life.'" Powell adds, "General Emerson's Pro-Life program was certainly formal as it dealt with racial discrimination. There was not to be any! If he found any, you were relieved." Indeed, Powell recalls an unusually capable officer on Emerson's staff who reportedly referred to the African Americans as 'darkies.' After Powell substantiated the man's use of the word, Emerson immediately relieved the offender, even though he had been one of his favorites.

Powell observed that while white officers acted forcefully when whites caused trouble, they backed off on blacks who shirked or were disruptive for fear of appearing racist. He took it upon himself to rid the unit of a recent acquisition who held meetings where he preached race antagonism while using drugs to gain a position of control. According to Powell there were proportionately more disciplinary problems among the blacks than the white. "Less opportunity, less education, less money, fewer jobs for blacks equaled more antisocial behavior in the States and these attitudes traveled." He diagnosed part of the behavior to the minority's lack of ability to manipulate the system compared to whites, and as a consequence they resorted to defiance to demonstrate black pride. That exposed them to punitive proceedings, for challenges to authority have always been viewed by the military establishment as a greater crime than many other derelictions of duty.

The race friction Powell observed in Vietnam fermented at the 2d Division's station, Camp Casey. "The whites wanted rock and country-and-western. The blacks wanted soul, Aretha Franklin and Dionne Warwick. The issue got so testy that we summoned Tong Du Chon [the town next to the base] bar owners to division headquarters to see if we could work out a fair formula. They finally agreed that they would feature roughly seven 'white' songs for every three 'black ' songs. As a result of this compromise, the whites were unhappy only 30 percent of the time and the blacks 70 percent.

"The soldiers had worked out their own solution. White troops gravitated toward bars in a certain part of town and black to another. The line of demarcation became known as the Crack. A white crossed the Crack at as much peril to himself as a black trying to enter a white Birmingham [Alabama] bar before the Civil Rights Act. To Gunfighter, the situation was anathema. The idea that one group 'owned' part of Tong Du Chon was unacceptable. The thought that an American soldier had to fear for his safety at the hands of other American soldiers was intolerable. 'Racism is bad,' Gunfighter told his assembled senior officers. 'Race tension is not Pro-Life. I will not permit racism in my division.' We half expected him to say, 'Racism will end by zero seven hundred tomorrow morning.'"

Emerson ordered Powell as part of a mixed-race group to walk both sides of the Crack, visiting the dance halls, bars, and other public enterprises. He stationed a special detachment of MPs and other soldiers in the town with orders to clean out any place where a racial incident occurred. "I can't say that our march on the Crack produced integrated bliss. We had not achieved that at home, much less in a honky-tonk town halfway around the world. But General Emerson's gutsy solution broke the color line. Thereafter, no group owned any part of Tong Du Chon."

On another front, Jesse Brewer, the black corpsman in Vietnam discovered that position, even a commission, carried little weight with whites above and beneath him. "After my twelve months overseas I was assigned to Camp Pendleton. There were only two black corpsmen in my unit. Because of my rank, I was NCOIC [noncom in charge] of one clinic. Everyone under me was white. They didn't like it one bit. Again reputation, being a combat-experienced corpsman and medals made them afraid of me. Also being 6'3" and weighing 225–230 didn't hurt. Unfortunately, they went along with the program due to intimidation instead of it being the right thing to do."

Brewer used an Army Health Professional Scholarship to attend dental school. After graduating he was required to give the army four years. "My first assignment was the four-man dental clinic in Fulda, Germany. I was attached to the 92d Medical Detachment, headquartered at Hanau. Our CO was a racist. It was rumored that he made a statement that blacks and women had no place in the Dental Corps or the Army. At the end of your three-year rotation, the next senior captain would assume the position of officer in charge. When it came my turn to become OIC, they made the slot a major's. The major who became OIC was from Georgia and mentioned to me he hadn't had too much contact with blacks who were educated. Some of my patients warned me I should be careful around him, that he was asking questions about what kind of dentist they thought I was. He didn't seem as interested in the other guys. The NCOIC in the clinic was black, E-6 Daniel Brunner who ran the clinic very well. The major questioned everything and every decision Sgt. Brunner made. Brunner had regulations on the tips of his tongue to support every action. This antagonized the major and the headquarters 1st sergeant. I overheard them plotting how to deal with Sgt. Brunner. He was brought up on bogus charges and had a hearing. I testified on his behalf and indicated the conversation I had heard. The charges were dropped. The major told me he wouldn't forget this.

"My last Officer Evaluation Report (OER) from the major was an average one. He didn't say anything derogatory, he just gave me an average evaluation which is the kiss of death. When I returned to the States my assignment was Fort Huachuca. It was nearing the end of my obligation and a decision needed to be made by the Department of the Army whether I'd be retained another four years. Since I had only been at Huachuca a short time, the basis for the decision would be my last OER received in Germany. The decision was not to retain me. My OER after sufficient time at Huachuca was a walk on the water. If there were a series of good to excellent evaluations and a mediocre one and then an excellent there should have been some questions raised concerning the accuracy of that one [average] evaluation."

Even before the Vietnam War ended and the military no longer required huge masses of manpower, a commission appointed by President Nixon proposed that the nation would be better served by an all-volunteer force, backed by a standby draft, than one that mixed enlistees with conscripts. The study predicted that the volunteer service would not attract a disproportionate share of African Americans. The Institute for Defense Analyses disputed the view, holding that the military in 1970 offered blacks who held a high school diploma an opportunity to earn more in uniform, to say nothing of those lacking such an education. Whites with poor prospects for employment would also find the armed forces more attractive. The IDA supported its findings with data drawn from enrollments during the Vietnam War.

The first statistics on the new all-volunteer service validated the Institute for Defense Analyses prophecy. In the army, the percentages of black enlisted personnel rose steadily. In June 1972, 3.9 percent of the officers and 17.1 percent of the enlisted personnel were black. (Approximately 11 percent of the population of the United States was African American.) By 1981 while the percentage of officers rose above 7 percent, 33.2 percent of the enlisted personnel were African Americans. The other services saw similar spurts in minorities. The 1972 navy with 7.3 percent enlisted and less than 1 percent officers, a decade later upped its quotient to 12.2 enlisted and 2.7 officers; the marines which had reported that blacks represented 13.7 of its enlisted strength and 1.5 percent of its officers, by 1981 raised its figures to 22 percent enlisted and 4 percent officers. The air force over the same period went from 12.6 percent enlisted and 1.7 percent officers to an enlisted proportion of 14.4 and 4.8 officers.

Current statistics, however, reveal that the African American presence had finite limits. Once the draft ceased, and downsizing followed, the services could set higher standards of education, physical, and technical abilities for admission. Recruiters became more selective and at the same time as the clamor for more minority participation in the civilian sector increased blacks began to find other careers more attractive. The marine corps in its last census covering 1996, counted 174,883 as its "few good men (and women)." Of these, the 27,777 African Americans figured as 9.8 percent, a drop of nearly 4 percent from what it was in 1981. Black marine officers were 1,106 or about 6.5 percent, more than quadruple that of sixteen years before. Three African Americans held the rank of general. The numbers for leatherneck officers show that a black increase in the lower echelons peaks at captain (245). Among all enlisted personnel, the 26,671 men and women marines of color amounted to 16.4 percent of the total. They were well represented in the upper echelons of noncommissioned officers with more than 25 percent of the top sergeants' stripes sewn on the sleeves of African Americans.

The 1997 figures for the demographic ethnic data of the navy separate personnel into six racial or ethnic groups. Whites or Caucasians number

279,781, or 68.26 percent of the 409,896 total naval forces. The 71,296 blacks comprise 17.39 percent. That is 5 percentage points higher than in 1981. Hispanics add up to 7.63 percent, Filipinos are 3.76, with Native Americans, Alaskans, Asians in lesser percentages, and a small fraction of "other" or "unknown." Although the minority, particularly blacks, are represented in much greater proportion than their 11 percent of the general population, the commissioned ranks indicate a sizable disparity. Whites account for 85.5 percent of the 58,815 officers as against 5.91 percent of the blacks. Still, that more than doubles the percentage of officers reported in 1981. From 12 percent black enlisted sailors in 1981, the current total is 19.32 percent against the 65.37 percent of the whites. Hispanics, incidentally hold 3.56 percent of the commissions. The differentials increase markedly in the upper echelons. With 96.89 of the flag-rank white, only 2.22 percent of the blacks are in the admiral class, and .44 percent of the Hispanics. As one moves down the ladder, the ratio of blacks increases, from 2.51 as captains to 8.79 as lieutenant, junior grade. For some reason, the figure slumps to 7.66 percent among ensigns and then grows through the chief warrant officer grades. Among enlisted men the pattern is similar, with E-9s (chief petty officer) as 7.12 percent compared to 77.95 of the whites. This is the one rating where the 10.17 percent of Filipinos surpasses both blacks and Hispanics. At the bottom, E-1, 20.75 percent of the sailors are African Americans while 59.45 percent are white.

In terms of specialties, black officers were least represented in such areas as submarines, special warfare, and special operations, with slightly higher figures among pilots. Nonwhite officers were more abundant as members of the supply corps, chaplains, line surface duty, and fleet support. Whether a smaller pool of educationally qualified candidates or some subtle racism determined the differences in assignments is an unknown.

The breakdown by race/ethnicity for enlisted personnel does not fall into the same categories. However, smaller percentages of African Americans work in electronics and "precision equipment" than in administrative functions [clerks, etc.], deck jobs, aviation, and engineering and hull.

Of the men and women granted an honorable discharge, 66.76 were white, while 19.8 were black. Of those given general, or other than honorable separation papers, the figures for blacks averaged close to 25 percent, while whites ranged from 60.57 percent for general to 63.45 for other than honorable. Because so many factors may be involved, the higher rate for blacks ousted does not necessarily mean they are held to higher standards or are victims of a discriminatory system.

In retention rates, the issue that originally concerned Zumwalt, black personnel reenlisted at a far higher rate than whites—36.02 to 23.68 percent at the end of the first term, and 46.49 percent to 40.72 in the cumulative career reenlistment category. The only group to re-up more intensely were the Filipinos, whose rates went well over 50 percent.

Air force demographics show that of the 298,482 enlisted men and women, 52,071, or just under 17.5 percent, were African Americans, an increase of a bit over 3 percent from the 1981 numbers. Hispanics accounted for just about 4 percent, with whites as more than 73 percent of the airmen. The percentage of commissioned blacks stands fairly steady at 7 percent for lieutenants and is pegged at 6 percent up through lieutenant colonel. In 1997, just 3 percent of the air force African Americans wear the silver eagles of a colonel, which means the pool from which generals will be nominated is small. Currently blacks with that rank represent 3.5 percent.

The army calculates that as of February 1997, its total active duty force was 495,000. Among the 57,922 male officers, whites held 81.7 of the commissions, blacks 10.2. The roster for the 9,904 female officers reports 69.7 percent white, and 20.6 percent African American. In the same categories, Hispanics are respectively, 3.4 and 3.6 percent. The residue is classified "unknown" or "other." Overall, African American officers are 13.1 percent of the army's commissioned personnel, an increase of more than 5 percent over 1981. In the ranks of the 307 generals there are 277 whites (4 of them female) and 26 blacks (1 female). Among enlisted personnel, 60.2 percent are white males, 24 percent black, and 5.9 percent Hispanic. White women account for 45.2 of their gender while blacks are 43.2 percent, the greatest percentage by far in all of the armed forces. It would appear that the army has been the most attractive of the armed forces to black women, if not all females looking to the military for a career.

The shifting demographics have resulted from a number of forces within and outside the military. Although granted the power to reject the poorly educated and the troubleprone, the services seem to have made a good-faith effort to attract minorities. Policy setters have demonstrated an intention to prevent the dismal patterns of discrimination that have blighted civilian life. Affirmative action, a tendentious topic in civilian life, is part of the current military. The army encourages its enlisted personnel by offering Functional Academic Skills Training. The classes, conducted over a period of 180 hours, aim to improve standard reading, writing, and mathematical skills, along with instruction tailored to the particular occupational specialty of a student seeking promotion. It is an affirmative-action campaign which enlarges the pool of eligible candidates for advancement, while not setting hard quotas for the numbers of noncoms from a racial or ethnic group.

The percentages of all African Americans in uniform outweigh their proportion in the general population. Still, the officer corps representation is low except for the army, which also stands well above the others in minority occupation of top brass positions. However, if the military is compared with civilian enterprises, it is obvious that minorities in the armed forces have done better, with more of them in the better jobs of their "business." Private enterprise can hardly match the army whose African Americans are 8.5 percent of its generals, the equivalent of chief executives for very large companies. Nor do the boardrooms even match the lower percentages of the other services.

The marine corps has maintained the reputation of being the least amenable to changes. General Carol Mundy Jr., marine corps commandant, when interviewed on the CBS TV program *60 Minutes*, remarked, ". . . in the military skills, we find that minority officers do not shoot as well as the non-minorities . . . They don't swim as well . . . And when you give them a compass and send them across the terrain at night . . . they don't do as well." Mundy subsequently apologized for his remarks but the marine corps released records purportedly supporting his assertions. A statistics expert from Carnegie Mellon University countered that the numbers did not indicate significant performance differentials. The controversy forced Mundy to resign. However, a senior Defense Department personnel official noted "one bit of data that is bothersome to us . . . minorities and particularly blacks appear less likely to get promoted from captain to major than are whites."

The marine corps' African American segment is the smallest of the services and it has the lowest percentage with the rank of general. One of the three top officers, Clifford Stanley, a native of Washington, D.C., born in 1947, attended segregated schools until 1954 when the Supreme Court decision mandated a change. His father's income from a position with the CIA enabled the family to move into an all-white neighborhood in 1955. "In two years," says Stanley, "white flight turned the area into a black one."

After graduating from South Carolina State, Stanley chose to enlist in the marines. "I was always pretty idealistic and I took Army ROTC in college. But I didn't see the same kind of disciplined approach as in the Marines. At the time I was pretty sure I was going to be drafted. When I entered the Marines I never saw a black officer except in the recruiting office." Stanley plowed ahead, earning a commission for himself. "Occasionally, there were people with attitudes. Once I was marked down on a fitness report. However, a reporting senior told this man that if he ever did that again it would be his career." The issue of race is painfully personal for Stanley. His wife is a paraplegic because of a racially motivated sniper attack.

Stanley missed assignment to Vietnam and elected to change from a support staff officer to the infantry. "When Desert Storm came they thought it might be a long protracted affair and I was told 'We need to get you some blood time' [a combat command as a prerequisite to further promotion]." He handled battle assessments and became a regimental commander. Stanley left the field forces as a one-star general in charge of public information.

According to Stanley, "The Marines have equal-opportunity advisers, enlisted men, assigned through the Corps. They handle formal and informal problems, sexual as well as racial. We have a lot of classes on values and ethics. The Commandant uses the word ethical often and stresses you can't be ethical if you're racist. There is a good environment. There are standards of accountability, for what you do or say. We have human relations training, but when it was the touchy feely stuff it was more divisive. Eventually we changed it to leadership."

Meanwhile, private companies reacting to pressure for racial diversification at the upper echelons or realizing they have overlooked a source of talent, now actively solicit minorities with a strong military background. They are particularly attracted to academy graduates who understand discipline and leadership. Retention of the most capable blacks has become a challenge to the services. Joe Anderson, the West Point graduate who performed so well as a leader in Vietnam, retired before his twenty years (minimum for a pension). "It wasn't anything about the Army or discrimination but I had an economic opportunity with a large corporation [General Motors]."

In its affirmative-action bid for minority officers, the army encourages applicants to join ROTC programs at what are known as the Historically Black Colleges and Universities with special scholarship allotments. In addition, the Army Cadet Command offers special classes for black ROTC students to compensate for written, verbal, and mathematical deficiencies.

All of the armed services academies actively seek to attract minorities. At West Point the outreach operations over almost thirty years has boosted black enrollment nearly tenfold. Where in the mid-1960s, only 7 or 8 African American cadets had entered in a freshman class, 45 arrived in 1969, 40 more in 1970, and then 51 in 1972. The numbers have continued to climb, a direct result of aggressive recruiting, the introduction of black recruiters able to talk with prospective candidates, families, and high school advisors.

To make up for educational weaknesses, the USNA, USAFA, and USMA all operate preadmission schools to raise candidates up to snuff, and to enhance the racial/ethnic mix African Americans are sought. The navy preps people at its Newport, Rhode Island, station, and the air force runs its school at Colorado Springs. The U.S. Military Academy Preparatory School (USMAPS) at Fort Monmouth, New Jersey, for example, tutors promising youngsters before they actually wear dress gray. The course, essentially a fifth year of high school, lasts ten months. Originally founded in 1916 to aid enlisted men nominated by the army to West Point, the mission of the prep school was enlarged to include civilians who might otherwise not meet academic requirements. About 40 percent of the African Americans who matriculate at West Point pass through USMAPS. The blacks who reached the

Military Academy by this route have a higher graduation rate than whites who come directly from their civilian high and prep schools.

The academies recruit intensively. The Military Academy Minority Outreach Committee, composed of faculty, alumni, and other individuals also seeks to attract females, Hispanics, Asians, and Native Americans. Some candidates attend the USMAPS course. The Naval Academy routinely asks midshipmen to speak at their hometown high schools.

During the 1970s, enrollment of blacks in the academies rose steadily but it has tailed off in recent years as other minorities have been attracted. The air force institution which reached a peak of about 8 percent black is now running closer to 5 or 6 percent, as is the Naval Academy. The Army leads with between 8 and 9 percent currently.

Among those involved in bringing minorities to West Point is Fred Black. After his tour in Vietnam, Black accepted a post teaching political science at the Military Academy. "In the introductory political science course, we studied the political process. We didn't deal with race relations other than through topics like court decisions, constitutional amendments. In one of my electives on policy making I dealt with affirmative action policies. It is hard to tell whether perceptions changed. The students probably learned how to think and analyze complex issues better. Most had very shallow familiarity with the failures of segregation and the desegregation of the military. By the mid-1990s, one thing different was that more black cadets were likely to have attended school with whites. Cadets in general accepted integration as natural but were more likely to feel that self-selected grouping was the problem, not policy. If six black cadets sat together, some whites saw meaning in that. If six whites sat together, white cadets would not see it meant anything."

As a member of the outreach program designed to attract qualified African Americans to West Point, Black says, "We tried to bring highly qualified cadets into the system by ensuring they understood their options, had their questions answered. The program also hopes to reassure parents, many of whom had no familiarity with the military. It filled in the blanks, targeting impressive candidates who needed to better understand what West Point had to offer. I also found some school counselors lacked ability in this area and some area admissions officers either didn't have the time or inclination to do this."

Routinely, an officer at West Point is designated as an advisor to the students. In 1996, Maj. Edwin Tifre, a qualified helicopter pilot, had the duty. The son of Honduran-born parents, Tifre grew up in a Canarsie (Brooklyn, N.Y.) housing project. "It was 90 percent Caucasian during the early 1960s. There were no problems about race and when I went to Catholic schools and Stuyvesant High there were no real racial problems for me. I concentrated on my academics. My younger brother, who got in bad company, was shot in Harlem. He didn't have it as easy as I did."

Tifre remembers that from 7 to 8 percent of his class of 1985 at the academy was African American. "I had an easier time because I grew up in a mixed community. It is difficult because there's not only the challenge of the academics but plebes are apt to see their first year as a hostile environment. After the first year, when you have done several semesters of academics, it gets easier. As a black person you don't want to use race just because things aren't in your favor. If you get a bad grade, is it necessarily a matter of discrimination?"

"I found things much different for me in the deep South after I graduated when I was one of two blacks out of 100 in the aviation program. We decided to room together and the realtors took us to the worst section of town." At West Point Tifre praised a course, heavily promoted by the commandant, which discussed issues such as sexual harassment, date rape, and race relations. "It provided a forum for talk about things relevant to the nation and the Army." He admits race remains a concern. "Some still feel they were not accepted in the Corps of Cadets. Others worry how they might maintain their identity as African Americans within the Army."

Fred Black responds, "Some fear that a large institution like the Army might do that. Some cadets feel hostility from their home communities on one side and the institution on the other. To what extent the Army lets one 'practice' identity is often a subject of debate. Like many things, perception is reality. I see a lot of room to be who you are and still be 'acceptable' in the institutional sense. The real problem is one of expectation in the mind of the officer, not identity."

Colin Powell says he doubts that the question of an African American preserving his identity is unique to military life. "The Army and other services are not isolated test tubes. Every problem in civilian society is brought into the military with every group of new recruits."

While some African Americans grapple with the issue of identity in a white-dominated world, the rise in position and status of blacks also confuses some whites. There are those who unconsciously compare a nonwhite with others of his race, rather than the society as a whole. Colin Powell grimaces at the types of compliments he would receive—"'Powell, you're the best black lieutenant, I've ever known.' 'Pleased to meet you General Powell. You know I once served with Chappie James.' Or Ben Davis, or Roscoe Robinson. Why didn't they ever tell me they served with George Patton or Creighton Abrams. I recognized their behavior as a gesture to establish a friendly link to me. Instead it underscored a separation."

As the war clouds gathered over the Persian Gulf in 1990, Powell, from his post as chairman of the Joint Chiefs, responded to both questions of self-identity and the oneness of military service when he addressed fears about the percentage of African Americans in the combat zone. Powell said that although he would regret the death of any American in battle, black or white, it would be offensive to exclude blacks from the same duty as whites in an all-volunteer force. He quoted Benjamin O. Davis Jr. "Combat was not easy, but you could only get killed once. Living with the day-to-day degradation of racism was far more difficult."

A key difference in the dampening of racial tension lies in the motivation of those who join up. Unlike reluctant inductees, the current servicemen and women do so with a career in mind, economic and social prestige, rather than civil rights, separatism, or so-called black power issues. Whites who choose to enlist also are better educated, and they come knowing in advance they will serve in fully integrated units.

Tom LaMothe, born in 1957, grew up in Flushing, New York, long integrated in its schools although his immediate neighborhood was all white. "Both my parents adamantly favored racial equality. They were very progressive people who met at a lecture sponsored by the *Catholic Worker*. My father, who was a French teacher, had studied for the priesthood and done a student ministry in Harlem. In my school we played together but there was no social interaction between the races.

"I dropped out of high school and enlisted in 1975 because of a lot of family strife. I was on the fast road to self-destruction and the day I went to join up, the Army recruiter was closed so I signed up with the Air Force. One of my two drill sergeants was a black New Yorker and the other a white Southerner. On the first or second day, the black sergeant got in the face of a kid from Alabama and said, 'I bet you'd just love a nigger getting up in your face.' 'No sir, no sir. I'm not prejudiced.' The white sergeant said, 'We're all green, no black or whites. You help the guy on either side of you, help your buddy.' They made it clear they would not tolerate any bigotry. We realized the worst crime would be to use a racial epithet. One kid got in trouble by writing a post card. Before it hit the mail, one of the DIs saw it and the boy was in a lot of trouble with extra details.

"When I was assigned to a Strategic Air Command base in North Dakota the blacks and whites were close. We all hated the cold and didn't get along with the cowboys downtown. My closest buddy and I were into Motown, Soul music, and we socialized with the blacks constantly. We'd open up a bottle of wine, listen to James Brown and the black guys were pleasantly shocked to find two white guys jamming to James Brown.

"In Germany, there was tension over women. Somehow while there was plenty of black and white dating in North Dakota it was not as much an issue as in Germany. In Germany there were clubs for blacks, and you'd hear someone say, "that's for the niggers." We had two battalions of [army] antiaircraft attached to our base, and the air force percentage of blacks was close to 10 percent while the army was around 30 percent. Most of the racial tension was among the army troops. The air force, hung together more. We had a class in race relations once a year with films, discussions, lectures. They were not a revelation to me. It was nothing new. They only reinforced what my mother taught me as a child. I slept through them.

"When I left the service and came home I was discouraged by the racial tension I saw. If it existed in the Air Force, it was not a significant problem where I was."

At the inception of the all-volunteer force and the fear of a flood of black applicants, some officials used the buzz word of "tipping"—a term used originally to designate at what point the percentage of blacks taking up residence in a white neighborhood would cause the remaining whites to flee—in the case of the armed forces, for whites to shy away from a military career. General Michael Davison scoffs, "There is not a problem of too many blacks." The steady rate of enlistments by whites confirms his viewpoint.

Every one of the services has established lengthy protocols to prevent discrimination and provide access for investigation and redress of grievances. Military personnel are issued detailed information on the kinds of remarks and conduct that is considered biased and unacceptable. Literature on such sensitive subjects as equal opportunity, race relations, and sexual harassment is routinely distributed with instructions for action by individuals who believed themselves abused. Despite such efforts, all is not racially serene. As Powell remarks, the military is subject to influences outside the base or ship. There has been talk of white-supremacy units surreptitiously forming at military installations. In 1990, five air corps military policemen from Carswell Air Force Base, Texas, involved in Ku Klux Klan activities were discharged. Although members of the armed forces ordinarily possess the same freedom of association as civilians, the code of military conduct forbids membership in hate organizations.

In 1995, two white soldiers at Fort Bragg with a third man as their unwitting chauffeur, murdered a black couple. The GIs were found guilty but the incident revealed the infection of a small but virulent strain of racism. One of the convicted men had previously been observed wearing a Nazi medallion and engaged in a fight with a black soldier that cost him his security clearance. At the same base, after the arrest of the trio of gunmen, someone painted swastikas on the doors of rooms occupied by black soldiers in a Special Forces barracks.

In two separate lawsuits, African American civilians, employees of the U.S. Army Corps of Engineers testified to verbal humiliations, practical jokes, and physical harassment. The Corps of Engineers, although denying it condoned such behavior, settled for $1.8 million and promised to revise its policies. Timothy McVeigh, sentenced to death for the Oklahoma City bombing, while a soldier, had encouraged his buddies to read *The Turner Diaries*, a racist novel that advocates armed overthrow of the government. McVeigh, however, left the service of his own volition and with an honorable discharge.

When sexual harassment, assault, and even rape charges were leveled against a number of army sergeants, the defendants and some political figures said the procedures smacked of racism with all of the accused black and most of the witnesses white. Some of the women reportedly claimed they had been coerced to act for the prosecution, but for the most part, the men in the dock were convicted on the testimony of black and white subordinates.

Bernard Nalty, a preeminent authority on the subject wrote, "In the services and in civilian life, victories remained to be won but in the mid-1980s the vestiges of racial discrimination in the armed forces formed a minor issue." The major battles for the minority military rights appear to be over.

24
After-Action Critique

With President Bill Clinton sponsoring an introspection on race, what insights does the experience of the armed forces offer the country as a whole? Up to a point, the history of African Americans in the military provides a rough microcosm of race relations overall in the United States. In the armed forces they were either totally excluded or, when the exigencies of war required black manpower, the majority walled them off. That mirrors their place in civilian society where people of color existed as laborers, menials, politically and socially impotent, and out of sight. It is hardly surprising that white cadets at the U.S. Military Academy, like DeWitt Armstrong and Harold Hayward who grew up accustomed to the invisible presence of African Americans, do not recall the handful of them who passed through West Point at the same time. The attitudes of the white majority were guided by the prevailing sentiments and actions of an intensely discriminatory society, as typified by Raymond Battreall, before they put on uniforms. Negative feelings about the minority were reinforced by their seniors, themselves also infected with the venom of racism. Colin Powell's onetime boss, Gen. Henry "Gunfighter" Emerson, remarked, "The Army never admitted it had racial problems, but you had a hell of a lot of racists."

Denial by white Americans reached extremes. After World War II, Ed Andrusko, the marine who spoke of the "Black Angels," says, "Seldom if ever did wounded survivors from our company bring up the Peleliu black marine heroics. This epic was denied by some, ignored by others." Perry Fischer, the white marine sergeant in a black ammunition company, attended a 1990 reunion of the Veterans of Iwo Jima at Camp Pendleton. He says, "After being in attendance for over three hours, I did not see any black Marines. I spoke with over 150 of the white Marine veterans of Iwo Jima, both officers and enlisted. I asked each one, the same question. 'When you were on Iwo Jima did you at any time see a black Marine performing duties there?' Every single one responded: 'No, never!' Finally I spoke to a white colonel who readily acknowledged their presence. It turned out he was the executive officer of the 8th Field Depot, the parent organization of all the black units at Iwo."

However, the colonel refused to ask permission to speak about the role and action of the African Americans at the island and the chairman of the reunion committee would not allow Fischer to address those present. Fischer appealed to the Camp Pendleton commander to apply his influence since the get-together coincided with Black History Week. He begged off on the grounds he was not connected with the reunion other than providing facilities.

The publication in 1996 of *Black Soldier, White Army* revealed a continuing schism between soldiers who fought with the 24th Infantry. Three years after Truman's order against discrimination, the army still fielded segregated units, of which the 24th Infantry Regiment was the most prominent. Neither the armed forces nor the rest of America seemed prepared to accept equality. Michael Lynch, who retired as a major general and is the source for the meeting between Matthew Ridgway and George Marshall that ended segregation as well as the 24th Regiment, recalled, "In Korea, there was all this anti-black business. It was kind of token integration. We said we were doing it, but we really weren't. We said the black wasn't worth a damn and damned him with faint praise at the same time. We said they could be worth a damn as soldiers only if they had white officers in charge."

The record of the 24th Infantry stands as a case in point. The black veterans of the outfit, outraged at the treatment of their organization by the official army historian, pleaded, petitioned, and argued for a second look at their organization. They were bitterly disappointed by the revised account, *Black Soldier, White Army,* which stated "the 24th's record in Korea reveals an undue number of military failures particularly during the early months of the war." What angered the regiment's alumni was the emphasis upon failure rather than what was accomplished under terrible circumstances. Their unhappiness was not mitigated by the book's explanation, "a lack of unit cohesion brought on by racial prejudice and the poor leadership it engendered at all levels was mainly at fault."

Confronted by protests, the researchers and writers stuck to their word processors, citing as sources the more than 500 individuals interviewed and the official narratives to support their memoir. Apparently disgusted by the criticism, one white officer associated with the final product allegedly remarked that the entire enterprise had been a $3 million waste. But for all the interviews the military historians collected, the authors, as in all official annals and many nonofficial ones, depended upon the After-Action Reports, Combat Narratives, 25th Infantry Division Operations Reports, war diaries, and other papers. Under any circumstances these have their weaknesses. Frequently, the authors are not up front but back at a headquarters where they produce the documents. The sources may be questionable. For example, one may rely on individuals wounded early in an engagement and evacuated to the rear. These men are aware only of what occurred up to the moment that they left the stage. Furthermore, eyewitnesses offer their own limited vantage points. In some instances ambition influences their tales or they spin self-serving stories. Particularly at a time when bias and discrimination was accepted, when so many Americans grew up with negative attitudes about minorities, the sources of official accounts are suspect. They are not significantly more authoritative than the anecdotal versions of what happened.

The 24th like other segregated organizations before it, inspires mixed feelings among those who served with it. Typically, Charles Bussey says, "The Army and most historians assert that Negro soldiers in black units did not fight very well in the early days of the Korean War and were prone to run away, or 'bug out' in the jargon of the time. That is true, but white soldiers in white units also did not fight very well at that time. It was desperate combat. Bugging out was common for troops of all kinds and colors." (No less an authority than Matthew Ridgway confirms Bussey. "Sometimes . . . it just gets to a point where a man can't take it anymore, that's all.") Bussey admits reverses. "The Chinese Army had stomped the hell out of us . . . They'd eaten us up in battalion-size bits. We'd been humiliated, debased, overwhelmed—routed." At the same time, Bussey cites exceptions, like his own 77th Engineer Combat Company. He most resents the earlier narratives as well as *Black Soldier, White Army* for an unwillingness to devote equal space to achievements, such as he claims in what he calls *Firefight at Yechon.*

Outspoken and harshly critical of the white, field-grade officer corps and above, Bussey is not an apologist for the failings of men of his own race. He denounces blacks who malingered, who committed atrocities. But, he comments, "If we were so poor then [in Korea], why did black soldiers get such high marks in the Vietnam War, only fifteen years after Korea? I have some ideas. When the Army began to respect its black soldiers and give them responsibilities, perhaps the Army in return received respect and responsible soldiers."

From the earliest investigations into the performances of black units from World War I up through *Black Soldier, White Army* there is little or no attempt to delve into the egregious failures of command. A few examples: The black soldiers with the American Expeditionary Force in France, 1918, not only were poorly trained but the casual attachment to the French army added an enormous handicap. The fault lay at the top. During World War II, a number of Tuskegee airmen lost their lives simply because they could never learn to swim, a direct result of being denied use of swimming pools at air bases. Commanders preferred to maintain segregation rather than preserve the lives of American aviators. Neither during nor after the war was there any investigation of such scandalous behavior. Any reading on the Korean War reveals that the military command, from Gen. Douglas MacArthur, through his chief of staff, Ned Almond, on down to the white regimental and battalion commanders, never prepared the men to fight. In addition they did not procure the proper equipment, causing troops to enter battle with faulty weapons, inoperative radios, inadequate clothing. With the Cold War already in full swing and ample signals of bellicosity emanating from North Korea and its allies, those nearest the scene abysmally failed their soldiers, black and white, as well as their country. No one in the Pentagon certainly, nor on the various congressional committees charged with overseeing the armed forces, ever challenged the white men responsible for the deplorable state of the U.S. services when North Korea struck.

The sins perpetrated before the shooting began were compounded when the Chinese overwhelmed the Americans streaming toward the Yalu. Marines and army GIs, blacks and whites, were routed because of poor intelligence, a failure to provide winter equipment, a lack of training for the kind of warfare dictated by the terrain and climate. But again, the white leadership at the top escaped unscathed while reporters like Harold Martin and historians like Roy Appleman blistered the black soldiers.

Black Soldier, White Army, whatever its faults, diagnosed the major weakness in segregated units, "a lack of unit cohesion brought on by racial prejudice and the poor leadership at all levels." Under the rubric of "unit cohesion" lies a desire not to let one's comrades down. Most who have been in combat articulate this feeling as the principle reason those on the line expose themselves to injury or death. Although at a certain level of battle almost everyone is tempted to flee, the soldier ordinarily is reluctant to abandon his fellows. Unit cohesion arises from intensive training, working in groups ranging from squad size to perhaps an entire company, and leaders who demonstrate ability while showing respect for their subordinates and morale. The history of segregated military outfits indicates pieces of the equation were often missing. In the case of the 24th Infantry, as in all previous incarnations of segregated units with white officers, not only had they not received the proper preparation but also competent, concerned officers, the glue to create cohesion, were absent. That is evident from the tremendous rate of turnover from platoon leaders through battalion commanders.

For black servicemen, unlike their white counterparts, their status as second class soldiers, sailors, marines, airmen, and above all citizens, further eroded morale. Indeed, even after the armed forces committed themselves to integration, the struggle for civil rights at home affected some blacks who understandably might wonder why they should risk their lives while people of color were abused or denied equality at home. All of these deficiencies, some from within the military and some from the civilian sector, jeopardized the achievement of missions for segregated organizations from World War I through the Korean War. Even after the implementation of integration, insofar as discrimination in the armed forces and deprivations on the home front afflicted the individual in uniform, performance of duty was threatened.

Any study of racism must recognize that it can become an excuse. During the time of segregation, there were incompetent black officers in the African American units (just as there were white ones), but because of the limitations on assignments it was more difficult to slough subpar blacks off to areas where they could do less harm. There were black servicemen who lacked the abilities to do the job or were unable to accept the discipline of military life, and when passed over for promotion, they charged discrimination. While it is expected that established organizations would blame "outside agitators" or "troublemakers" for disturbances, it is true that a number of individuals with an agenda unconnected with military matters sought their own goals. However, their appeals to their fellow men of color would have fallen on barren ground had there not been the fertile soil of discontent. In the current era, which promises equal opportunity, any diminution of prospects will again plant the seeds of conflict.

Perception, which tends to supercede reality, played an important role and continues to do so in race relations. Whether Charles Bussey, Joe Kornegay, Dick McDonald, Elmo Zumwalt Jr., et al., are accurate in their recitation of "facts" is of course important, but at the same time, people act on what they believe happened. Only a fool dismisses this "reality" from consideration of a situation. Who says what to whom in which context makes a difference in perception. Among themselves, blacks may casually use the word "nigger," but from the mouth of a white it is an obvious insult. Noncoms, captains, admirals, and generals sometimes address their lower ranks as "you boys." [In turn the company commander or skipper will be called "the old man," although he may not even be thirty.] But when exclusively applied to a group of African Americans, "boys" offends. Indeed the virtue of sensitivity sessions is that they can reach into the depths of racism where the slur or discrimination is inadvertent.

Whites reacted negatively to the dap and the Afro haircut. To them it was an insult, an "in-your-face" statement defiant of good military discipline. To African Americans these were simple declarations of pride in their race. The contention over these phenomena is another example of how perception colors race relations.

Perception, a child of memory, harkens back to parentage. The Tuskegee airmen, so able to perceive the reality of the challenges, so resolute in the face of adversity, almost all sprang from high achieving families. Even where circumstances denied a father or mother, as in the cases of Spann Watson or Charles Bussey, economic or professional success, the strength of will and character of a father or mother influenced the son.

Judging from the small sample of whites, it is less easy to isolate what inspired them to fight for color-blind armed services. Elmo Zumwalt and Michael Spiro grew up in homes intolerant of bigotry. Jack Rhoades, DeWitt Armstrong, and Emmett Tidd came from families that at best represented a plantation attitude. Yet from their differing brews of nature, nurture, and environment emerged a willingness, even eagerness, to conquer discrimination.

Strong, effective company, platoon, section, flight leadership for the rank and file is a prerequisite for success in any military endeavor. Matthew Ridgway remarked, "I have seen individuals break in battle and I have seen units perform miserably. The latter was always because of poor leadership." But to ensure the right people occupy the slots at this level depends upon the upper echelons. Frequently, those willing to concede that an African American could be molded into a competent combat soldier added the caveat, "if led by white officers." Too often people assigned this duty were not qualified to command. They either lacked ability or disrespected their subordinates, destroying any willingness to follow.

The evolution of the military into an integrated service dedicated to equal opportunity owes much to the actions of leaders, white and black. Because the military establishment habitually kept African Americans out of top posts, the handful of senior black officers like the Davises, father and son, Chappie James, Frederic Davison, and Samuel Gravely lacked the power or influence to radically change conditions. Some African American civilians like W. E. B. Du Bois, A. Philip Randolph, William Hastie, Mary Bethune, Truman Gibson, and Thurgood Marshall pushed hard for redress and reform. They exerted influence upon political powers. Without the unrelenting pressure from African American military and civilian individuals and groups nothing would have happened. But white officers and civilians occupied the seats of power, and they, perhaps reluctantly in some cases, led the way.

Whether by conviction of the justness of the cause, the need to bolster military effectiveness, or bowing to public pressure, cabinet officials, James Forrestal, Eugene Zuckert, Stuart Symington, John L. Sullivan, George C. Marshall, Louis A. Johnson, Dan Kimball, and the top military men, Idwal Edwards, Hoyt Vandenberg, Matthew Ridgway, Clifton B. Cates, Elmo Zumwalt Jr., and Michael Davison stepped out, breaking with tradition, with history, and in some cases, rejecting the perceived wisdom of their youth. The air force got a head start on the other services because its people at the top, in the infant days of its independence, chose to establish and implement integration forcefully. The new leadership of the post-Vietnam era has enabled the military to occupy the forefront in dealing with race.

A retired general who graduated from the Military Academy remarks, "In hindsight it is easy to say that mistreatment of blacks at West Point in the 1940s and earlier was 'wrong,' because from the standpoint of fairness and justice, it was undeniably 'wrong.' It does not follow that the institution itself was 'evil,' or that the perpetrators of these injustices were 'bad' people.

The way blacks were treated at West Point reflects the prejudices and norms of our society as a whole. This same perspective is reflected by the senior senator from South Carolina, Strom Thurmond. His position on racial issues today is, as it has been for several years, one of tolerance and support of black people. When asked to explain why he was so intolerant and prejudiced when he led the Dixiecrats out of the Democratic Party, he simply says, 'It was the law.'"

It is an argument that was used by Nazis who sought to avoid punishment at Nuremberg. The previously named leaders, subjected to the similar influences as those experienced by Strom Thurmond, rejected intolerance and prejudice even when sanctioned by law. They confound the general's judgment that the perpetrators of injustices were not really bad people. The advocates of segregation undoubtedly had their virtues but fell far short of good when dealing with minorities, and by their actions they hurt the overall military posture of the country. If they talked like racists; if they acted like racists; the odds are that they were racists.

Among many whites, whether in the military or outside it, the reaction to the issue of discrimination is a form of denial, a desire to mitigate the evil by describing it as part of one's upbringing and therefore understandable, even excusable. Although the cultural environment may explain the reasons for conduct, the actions are still accountable. A spousal abuser can offer a defense that he himself was beaten as a child or saw his mother mistreated. But we still regard him guilty of assault. A drug abuser may blame his crime on his addiction; that may explain his thievery, but in court that does not qualify him as innocent. In a civilized society, citizens are expected to meet certain standards of conduct; murder is not acceptable, nor is slavery, nor is oppression through discrimination. We can understand why people engage in heinous acts but that does not grant an automatic pardon.

Early in World War II, George C. Marshall as army chief of staff, rebutted advocates of military desegregation on the grounds that the services could not ignore the social relationships set by Americans [whites]. Although Marshall shifted his viewpoint a decade later, members of the armed forces and politicians argued that the military mission was too important to risk in any "social experiment." In a democratic society, however, the services are not separate from the rest of the country but part of the whole. If they were not involved in the solution, then they were, as was painfully apparent, part of the problem. (Without judging the merits of gays in the service or the roles for women, debate should begin on the same basis.)

As an African American, Fred Black remembers the segregated army of his father, but fought in Vietnam in an integrated organization. He taught at West Point during the flowering of equal opportunity and sees his experiences as instructive for all of America. "We in the military learned a long time ago that we had to force people to communicate initially, then you had to find a way to cut it off. Talking reveals the misunderstandings and misperceptions and we eventually realize we are not that different. Requirements for teamwork focuses that [realization] in the military. When in the everyday workplace people understand the limits and the priorities, interesting things happen!"

Fred Black is not alone in declaring that the armed forces seem well ahead of the rest of America in terms of equal opportunity and interracial harmony. Some people have misconstrued how this has been accomplished. A 1997 letter to the *New York Times* from Mackubin Thomas Owens, a professor of national security affairs at the Naval War College, says, ". . . the military has eschewed affirmative action when it comes to race." In fact, the equal economic opportunity programs of the armed services were created to ensure that minorities had the academic skills and training that would enable them to compete with whites. Although the classes are open to everyone, it is obvious that the origins lay in the realization that the pool of blacks eligible for promotion needed to be enlarged if the race was to be adequately represented in all strata of the military. Affirmative action, contrary to the understanding of Professor Owens, does not necessarily mean a quota or set asides on the basis of race. The debate about making race one consideration among many others when, for example, admitting applicants to a university, is another issue.

Colin Powell enunciated his own viewpoint. "The present debate over affirmative action has a lot to do with definitions. If affirmative action means programs that provide equal opportunity, then I am all for it. If it leads to preferential treatment or helps those who no longer need help, I am opposed. I benefitted from equal opportunity and affirmative action in the Army, but I was not shown preference. . . . If a history of discrimination has made it difficult for certain Americans to meet standards, it is only fair to provide temporary means to help them catch up and compete on equal terms."

During one of the town meetings on race relations that President Clinton held, he confronted a noted critic of affirmative-action programs, Abigail Thernstrom, and cited Powell as an example of one who was able to show his worth through affirmative action. Clifford Alexander, secretary of the army from 1977 to 1981 subsequently wrote, "There was no affirmative-action program that promoted Colin Powell's promotion to brigadier general in 1978." He then explains that although Powell was a colonel, as secretary he had held up a list of those proposed for general officers, "because no black colonels had been promoted . . ." He directed the General Officer Board to look again at the records of the black colonels to determine whether any of their ratings had been influenced by prejudice or discrimination. When the board resubmitted its recommendations, "Black people with sterling records emerged on those lists. Yes, Colin Powell was like his white fellow generals—no better, no worse—but more important his white colleagues did not get anything extra either."

Abigail Thernstrom crowed that Alexander's statement supported her position, "Racial preferences were not responsible for Colin Powell's splendid career." Neither Alexander nor Thernstrom seem able to grasp the sense of affirmative action, choosing to define it strictly as a matter of set asides or quotas. By recognizing the existence of bias and the tradition of discrimination, Alexander did engage in affirmative action. He had ordered the General Board to reexamine the files on African Americans to find any untoward reports. Whites who might also have been subjected to unfair or discriminatory evaluations because of ethnic, regional, or just plain personal dislikes were not given the benefit of a second look. The new promotion lists were specifically resubmitted because of an absence of African Americans. It is clearly a result of the affirmative-action process.

Powell himself notes, "I benefitted from the environment created by equal opportunity and the affirmative action needed and used to implement equal opportunity. Affirmative action fills the reservoir from which you could select on the basis of performance. I was not aware of any specific affirmative action selection applied to me. There is a story, now repeated by Abigail Thernstrom, that my name was added to the Brigadier General's list. [That would seem to contradict Thernstrom's reaction to Alexander's statement.] Not so. I got an accelerated promotion along with four other officers on that list. We were the first officers promoted to Brigadier General from year group 1958. In those days, the list was in 'order of merit' and I was number one of the five. The selection was done by the board and I was not added by the Secretary of the Army or by a second meeting of the board."

It is fair to inquire where were those who opposed affirmative action, particularly that version in the armed forces, when "disaffirmative action," or discrimination, prevented people of color from jobs and education, produced unequal military discipline or justice, denied minorities promotions or career enhancement? Without arguing the educational merits of the matter, they remind one of the vehement opponents to school busing for integration who said nary a word when black children traveled long distances to their segregated schools while a school for whites lay only a few blocks from their homes.

African American Glenn C. Loury, professor of economics at Boston University, in the camp of conservatives, but hardly of a mind with the hard-shell whites like Norman Podhoretz or blacks like Thomas Sowell and Clarence Thomas, points to the army version of "affirmative action" as the most just and effective route to equality. "Some program that does not lower standards but concentrates on finding and promoting qualified blacks—is probably the single, most effective way to eliminate informal barriers to black advancement."

Sociologists Charles Moskos and John Sibley Butler, authors of the 1996 book *All That We Can Be,* cited by Mackubin Owens as proof of his point, actually endorse affirmative action as practiced by the army. "Good affirmative action acknowledges that members of disadvantaged groups may need compensatory action to meet the standards of competition. Bad affirmative action suspends those standards." Quite logically Moskos and Butler approve of pre-military development classes to enhance scores by would-be recruits on the armed services' entrance test. They favor the courses for personnel facing NCO examination. They praise the special help for ROTC and Military Academy candidates. All of these depend upon government funding.

By promoting equal opportunity, Moskos and Butler suggest, "The most effective way to improve race relations in this country is to increase the number of blacks who have access to the tools necessary to compete on a level playing field and to bring whites and blacks together in a common cause . . . Focus on black opportunity, not on prohibiting racist expression. . . . It would be foolhardy to consider the absence of white racists as a precondition for black achievement."

Indeed, the stress upon unit cohesion, that all of the personnel in a squad, platoon, or company are together, regardless of race or ethnic background, is vital to the elimination of racial tension. Commanders are made to realize that racial antagonisms or discrimination erode unit cohesion. They cannot hope for promotion if they do not work to prevent such destructive elements. Whether one is antiabortion or pro-choice, Democrat or Republican, a Protestant, Catholic, Jew, or Moslem is basically irrelevant to unit cohesion. But white suprematism or black separatism are obviously inimical to racial harmony and therefore fitting grounds for discharge. There is an obvious parallel in the world of athletics where the personal attitudes become subordinate to winning and a team effort is paramount. Not surprisingly, race relations in sports are better than other less-integrated sectors.

Efforts toward affirmative action and recognition of special situations for minorities occasion responses, "I see only Marine green, everyone is treated alike; there is only Navy blue, no other color," and variations on the theme. Under certain circumstances that is true, although during the segregated past marine green, navy blue, or army olive drab did not register the same if one's skin color was dark. In the course of a firefight, in carrying out a mission, the person of necessity loses identity. But an American in the service has his or her own individual genetic and environmental background —experiences, the family, the career path, and a host of other distinguishing elements. One of the curses of the interminable palaver about the performance of "the Negro soldier" is the tendency to classify every response and action as either typically black or typically white.

Genuine leadership from a noncom or petty officer, through a general or admiral requires cognizance of individual differences, ones based upon who the individual soldier, sailor, marine, or airman is. Until we achieve the impossible, a completely color-/ethnic-/gender-blind society, considerations must go beyond the uniform. Higher promotions in the enlisted ranks still require examinations but there is no mandate to add stripes because of a test score. There is room for a personal evaluation based upon performance. Prejudice and preference can insinuate themselves into the decision. That is perhaps truer in the commissioned ranks where promotions are entirely based upon performances. Evaluations by superiors play a critical role and the person writing up the subordinate can be influenced by bias, friendship, or his or her own skewed viewpoint. The boards that determine who moves up and who is passed over—witness the cases of John Lee, Jesse Brewer, Wesley Brown, Samuel Gravely, Colin Powell—rely on fitness reports and themselves are subject to the same perceptive influences.

In spite of this, the armed forces possess a great advantage in dealing with racial issues. The military, by the very structure of its units, emphasizes direction. The armed forces are not democratic institutions where major actions must be ratified by the rank and file through a vote. Indeed, the changes mandated by Zumwalt encountered resistance by some commanders who perceived any easing of the rules as a weakening of their power. Colin Powell notes, "The demands of the military and the coercive power to order behavior allowed us to be about ten years or so ahead of civilian society in dealing with these problems."

Those in uniform are forced into integrated work situations, to live and eat together. Unlike the civilian world, this is a twenty-four-hour-a-day condition, rather than just an eight-hour workday. A white in the service cannot move to the suburbs to avoid contact with African Americans. He or she risks status and career if hostility toward blacks is acted out through discrimination or verbal abuse. Like it or not, the members of the armed forces must learn to accept as equals those of another color or ethnic background. Wesley Brown's memories at Annapolis report a Southerner who found that close association with a black man forced him to change his attitude. In fact, historical experience suggests that familiarity rather than breeding contempt fosters understanding.

In a democratic society, the power to coerce is limited. Although laws may ban discrimination in the workplace, an employee unable to quell personal racial antagonism, unlike a serviceman, can change jobs. If you don't want your kids to associate with people of another race you can move or pick a different school. Although there is some self-segregation in the military—race members choosing to eat with one another or recreate with those of their own color—such choices are far more available to civilians.

The country at large might profit mightily if its people could realize the enormous price for their indulgence in racism. The costs lie in the deleterious effects racism inflicts upon the economy, the outlays for health, housing, education, and family support because of a hostile environment. We lack that valuable "unit cohesion" and the overall mission of the country is compromised. Colin Powell, in listing what he saw as major problems for the country, mentions among other things, "How do we end the ethnic fragmentation that is making us an increasingly hyphenated people?" The critics of affirmative action as carried out in the fashion of the military, and the self-righteously entrenched who smugly proclaim, "look how far we've come," ignore the obvious continuing existence of racism. The inequities due to this vice are clearly demonstrable in the low presence of minorities in the boardrooms, their lesser numbers in colleges and universities, their disproportionately high share of poverty, their excessive number of dysfunctional families.

While praising what has been achieved in the military, those who have been there, Emmett Tidd, Chick Rauch, Fred Black, know the job is never over. Retired for more than twenty years, Emmett Tidd says he remains in touch with today's navy through two sons on active duty—one an afloat chaplain and the other a destroyer commander—as well as other sources. "I conclude that compared to civilian life, the level of racial opportunity is much higher in the Navy. Physical violence resulting from racial tensions is virtually nonexistent. Gender and sexual issues are now more the areas of emotional tension than are the racial ones." Indeed, the Department of Defense Race Relations Institute at Patrick Air Force Base, which originally focused on African Americans, first widened its interests to cover other ethnic groups as well as certain categories of whites before shifting to emphasis upon alcohol and drug abuse and sexual harassment.

Chick Rauch notes, "The major thing I learned is that it takes a tremendous amount of organizational energy and capital to turn an institution around. I have worked at a very predominantly white university for fifteen years. Every year I have listened to a discussion of how we need more diversity (in particular for African Americans) at our university followed by the appointment of committees to look into what should be done. Each year the committees come up with the same thing, but no action is taken.

"By the time I retired from the Navy, I felt we had come a long way in correcting many of the obstacles faced by black members. Obviously, there were still personal differences and things you thought should be happening were not being done well, etc. But by and large I think a major change has occurred. The problem is that an organization like the Navy is constantly turning over, and large numbers continue to come into the Navy and positions of power who themselves have come from predominantly white Anglo-Saxon backgrounds and who are insensitive to the needs of those of a different ethnicity, race or culture. The question is how to keep the level of equality that you once had even though it was not perfect then. I do not think that most commanders have the patience and strength to periodically continue some of these programs that require a considerable amount of emotional and psychic as well as some financial capital. And if you do not keep at it, something is sure to fall back."

Fred Black echoes Rauch, "The supreme danger is that we become complacent and believe the war is won. Battles have been won but the war continues. Guards must remain in place and the military cannot let the situation slip back in any manner."

So long as there are men and women who believe and act on this premise, the fight for the right to fight and all that it entails promises victory.

Roll Call

George Allen. Military Policeman in Japan and Germany after World War II. After retirement in 1970, he was appointed special assistant to the governor of Massachusetts, responsible for minority and women's concerns. Later, when he learned that black veterans had problems obtaining benefits, he and several others established the Organization of African American Veterans. As an equal employment officer at Fort Huachuca in 1987 he recalls, "Someone painted a six-foot-high sign KKK on all sides of the two buildings that housed my staff. They placed stickers on the windows, DEATH TO RACE MIXERS. He is now a consultant on equal-employment matters in Sierra Vista, Arizona.

Joe Anderson. USMA, Class of 1965. Platoon and company CO in Vietnam. He retired as a major to pursue a civilian career and currently runs an automotive parts business in Detroit. "The automobile industry is well behind the military. Civilians can learn from it that if you're going to accomplish a mission, you need to have all resources aligned."

Ed Andrusko. Enlisted man, 1st Marine Division during World War II. After leaving the service, he moved to Denver to work in television, radio, electronics, and medical electronics.

De Witt Armstrong. USMA, Class of 1943. Command positions during World War II, Korea, and Vietnam. Upon retirement he settled in Alexandria, Virginia.

Vernon Baker. Medal of Honor winner with the 92d Division during World War II, and a career officer. After retirement he was a counselor for the Red Cross. He lives in St. Maries, Idaho.

Raymond Battreall. USMA, Class of 1949. Armor officer in Germany during the 1950s and advisor to South Vietnamese army for three and a half years. He retired as a colonel in Sierra Vista, Arizona.

Gary Bell. Sailor on the aircraft carrier USS *Cabot* in the South Pacific during World War II. Following separation from the navy he worked in broadcast radio. He lives in Anaheim, California.

Eli Bernheim. Paratrooper in the Philippines campaign during World War II and an officer with the 187th Airborne Regimental Combat Team in Korea. He lives in Jupiter, Florida.

Bradley Biggs. Paratrooper during World War II, company commander in Korea. After retirement he was an administrator in public works, a teacher, university official, as well as an author. He lives in North Palm Beach, Florida.

Fred Black. Served with the 82d Airborne in Vietnam. Following his combat tour, he attended graduate school and then taught political science at West Point. He retired to Chapel Hill, North Carolina.

Jesse Brewer III. Navy corpsman, Vietnam, dental officer U.S. Army. "Whatever happens in the general population one can expect to happen in the military. I don't think racial antagonism will ever disappear unless you can wipe the memories of this generation clean so they won't impart prejudices to their children." He practices dentistry in Tucson, Arizona.

Roscoe Brown. Pilot, 332d Fighter Group. "African Americans who had been in the military led the Civil Rights movement and those who stayed in service helped integrate it." Brown taught at the college level, became president of Bronx Community College, and developed the Center for Urban Education Policy. He resides in New York City.

Wesley Brown. USNA, Class of 1949. Upon retirement from the navy he went into practice as a civil engineer. His home is in Washington, D.C.

Ashley Bryan. Enlisted soldier, quartermaster unit in World War II. Honorably discharged, he became a teacher and artist. He lives on an island off the coast of Maine.

Charles Bussey. Pilot, 332d Fighter Group, company commander 77th Engineer Combat Company, Korea. "My Dad was a patriot who raised me to be one also. We differed slightly in that I took no slack from individuals or systems. I knew all about the 'master race.' All the stories you have heard about the South were true. I was not disappointed that changes were so few after the war. My experience was such that I knew improvements would be grudging and I was not disappointed." After he retired from the military Bussey established a construction business. He lives in Sun City, California.

Everett Copeland. Infantry soldier, Korea, career army officer. "I volunteered and was accepted to participate in the Atomic Bomb Tests, Desert Rock V. I made the entire series, ten bombs including the atomic cannon." He retired as a lieutenant colonel in 1967 and lives in Kansas City, Kansas.

John Costa. USMA, Class of 1949. Germany, Korea, and Vietnam. "We had been at the nadir in August–September 1973. Morale went up for a number of reasons. The influx of better quality soldiers and changes which streamlined procedures enabling company commanders to get rid of death weight undesirables, repeat offenders and addicts. Money was put into improving the living conditions of soldiers. I believe that the programs like race-relations seminars, drug treatment programs and new education programs were equally important." From 1977 to 1989, until he retired, Costa was a professor at West Point. He resides in Rhinebeck, New York.

Benjamin O. Davis Jr. USMA, Class of 1936. Pilot 99th Fighter Squadron and 332d Fighter Group, World War II, various air force assignments through the Vietnam War. On the cusp of retirement from the air force in 1972, he basked in the esteem of those who had previously ignored or mistreated him. The Washington, D.C., USMA, Class of 1936 alumni chapter unanimously honored him with the Benjamin F. Castle Award for Outstanding Service and Dedication. "I had no mixed feelings about accepting the award—to refuse it would have been ungracious. Through the years, several of my classmates had expressed regret about the way I had been treated at West Point and I held no grudges." Davis began a second career in security, first for the city of Cleveland and subsequently for the Federal Aviation Administration. He lives in Washington, D.C.

Frederic Davison. Platoon leader, 92d Division, World War II, Vietnam. He became the first of his race to command a division. His home is in Washington, D.C.

Michael Davison. USMA, Class of 1939. Cavalry squadron and company commander in Europe during World War II, command positions in Vietnam, commander of U.S. Army Europe. He lives in Arlington, Virginia.

William De Shields. Army officer, Vietnam. "The Race Relations Institute was superb in addressing racial issues, sexism, visibility of various ethnic groups. The mission of this school was later watered down under the guise that we no longer have such problems within the military. The real reason is that it was a burr in the saddle of many higher ranking officers who were unwilling to accept the fact that they may have had some racist or sexist hang-ups. We are paying a price for that miscalculation in our current military environment. The military because of its structure can do an excellent job of hiding or covering up problems." After retirement, De Shields founded the Black Military History Institute of America, Inc., to collect, provide, and exhibit materials pertinent to the military history of African Americans from the Revolutionary War to the current day. He lives in Arnold, Maryland.

Perry Fischer. Marine sergeant with a black ammunition company, World War II, army officer. "When I look back on my life, I see all the times when I could have and should have 'stood up' for my fellow men of color. I regret my silence every day." He retired as a major and lives in Turlock, California.

H. Minton Francis. USMA, Class of 1944. Artillery commander in Korea, member of the Army Concept Team in Vietnam. "I am a loyal son of West Point—it molded my character and instilled in me a determination to overcome all obstacles to my goals. But my reaction to the racism encountered in American society at large and reflected in microcosm at the Academy and in the Army was one of disgust and anger—never one of obeisance or accepting my 'place' among the majority of white men whom I considered my intellectual and cultural inferiors." Following his retirement, Francis worked for the first secretary of housing and urban development, the U.S. Post Office, the Department of Defense, Howard University, and as an unpaid adviser to the secretary of the army. He is president of the Black Revolutionary War Patriots Foundation, which is authorized to erect a memorial in Washington to the 5,000 African Americans who fought and supported the Revolution. He lives in Washington, D.C.

Milton Gish. Army officer, 93d Division, World War II. He makes his home in Shenandoah, Texas.

Samuel Gravely. Naval officer during World War II, Korea, and Vietnam, and the first black admiral. He resides in Haymarket, Virginia.

Harold Hayward. USMA, Class of 1944. World War II paratrooper, brigade commander, 101st Airborne Division, Vietnam; headquarters staff, U.S. Army Europe. He lives in Beaufort, South Carolina.

Frank Hodge. Noncom with the 92d Division, World War II. His hometown is Indianapolis, Indiana.

Edward Howard. USMA, Class 1949. With the 25th Division in Korea and CO and a signal battalion in Vietnam. "Structure and order in a military society assist in reducing problems of racial conflict. These features are not likely to prevail in the civilian world until such time as rational education, fearlessness and a sense of self-assurance become commonplace." He is a resident of Alexandria, Virginia.

Jehu Hunter. Communications officer, 92d Division, World War II. He worked as a scientist at the National Institutes of Health until retirement. His home is in Washington, D.C.

Joe Kornegay. Infantry sergeant, Korea. "When I returned to the United States I was ready to commit suicide and for many years lived very violently and recklessly. I have been in therapy for Post Traumatic Stress Disease, alcohol and drugs." Boarded out with an undesirable discharge, Kornegay, after thirty years of trying, petitioned successfully for a general discharge. He lives in Charlotte, North Carolina.

Tom LaMothe. Airman, 1980s. He is a minister on Long Island, New York.

John C. Lee. First black with a commission in the regular navy. He lives in Indianapolis.

Dick McDonald. Career marine officer, Vietnam, on the staff of chief of naval operations Admiral Zumwalt. "Ironically, Zumwalt's greatest, but less recognized heroism lay in his superb grasp of geopolitics. He was a major player in the SALT [Strategic Arms Limitation Talks] process and prevented Nixon, who was grasping at straws, from giving away the store in 1974. He finessed Diego Garcia from the British in a typically visionary move which has saved our bacon in the Middle East many times. I never see Zumwalt credited when there is a mention of the strategic value of that little island but he was the guy who did it, a CNO who always thought of the long haul." McDonald lives in Bartlesville, Oklahoma.

Spencer Moore. Officer with 92d Division, World War II. Haunted by his memories of combat in Italy, he could not concentrate upon college courses. He tried a number of jobs before a career with the Post Office. His home is in Magnolia, New Jersey.

Jeanne Murray. Career WAC officer. She lives in San Antonio, Texas.

William Murray. Career army officer. He lives in San Antonio, Texas.

Jim Pedowitz. Company commander, World War II. He lives on Long Island, New York.

Edgar Piggott. Soldier, 92d Division, World War II. His home is now Palm Coast, Florida.

Colin Powell. Career army officer, Vietnam, chairman of the Joint Chiefs of Staff. He lives in Alexandria, Virginia.

Robert Powell. Member of Provisional Infantry Platoon, World War II. He lives in Houston, Texas.

Chick Rauch. USNA, Class of 1948. Korea, Vietnam. After retirement from active duty, he worked in administration at a university and now lives in Orono, Maine.

John Rhoades. USMA, Class of 1935. World War II. He held jobs concerned with personnel in state government after retirement. He resides in San Antonio, Texas.

Percy Roberts. Supply officer, World War II, Korea. His home is in Three Rivers, Michigan.

Horace B. Robertson Jr. USNA, Class of 1945. "I think that after a slow start, the Navy has an admirable record in racial integration. Its progress may not have matched our hopes or expectations, but I think this is more the result of the initial reluctance to break from past tradition and the reputation the Navy had prior to 1948 among the black community. The affirmative steps taken by the Navy in recruiting, training and promotion of black and other minority personnel have made it a model of race relations in our society, second only to the Army and Air Force, which did not have quite the racist background of the Navy." After retirement he taught law at Duke University and now resides in Durham, North Carolina.

Burt Shepherd. Pilot, career Navy officer. "The lessons of race relations in the Navy are the same as in civilian life and in the Church. People are human. They want to be good. They want to follow the Golden Rule—most of them. They need guidance and leadership that is not bigoted and prejudicial. The church—like the Navy—seeks fairness and equality for all God's people. Sometimes we succeed. Sometimes we fail. But, God willing, when we fail, we recognize our failure and strive even harder in the future." He lives in Kingsville, Texas.

Harry Sheppard. Pilot, 332d Fighter Group, career air force officer. He lives in Arlington, Virginia.

Ed Simmons. Career marine officer, World War II, Korea, Vietnam. He lives in Alexandria, Virginia.

Michael Spiro. Career Marine officer, Korea, Vietnam, member of Admiral Zumwalt's staff. His home is in Bethesda, Maryland.

Clifford Stanley. A Career marine officer, he is on active duty in Washington, D.C.

John Suggs. Pilot, 332d Fighter Group, World War II, career air force officer. His home is in Washington, D.C.

William Thompson. Career navy officer, World War II, Korea, Vietnam. "Admiral Zumwalt's initiatives regarding race were an outstanding success. Equal opportunity exists today in the Navy, equal to any of the other services and exceeds many sectors of the U.S. social structure. It is the character and personality that Admiral Zumwalt brought to the job of CNO that made him different and outstanding. He was indefatigable and intelligent . . . his charisma and personality gave him the leverage to be one of the most influential CNOs in history. His *rap sessions* with young officers and enlisted personnel are legendary and were effective. The early 70s were bad years for the U.S. socially and certainly for the Navy. The younger people in the Navy trusted him and were confident that he would make the Navy a better place to service one's country. Older people did not want to accept change, nor admit that the Navy had to change and many of the older flag officers were jealous and kept shaking their heads in wonderment of, 'What's he doing with my Navy?'" He now lives in McLean, Virginia.

Emmett Tidd. Career navy officer, World War II, Korea, Vietnam. Member of Admiral Zumwalt's staff. From the military experience, the lessons for civilian sector: Recognize the value and need for education, sensitivity training, emphasis required by and example set from the top leadership down, communication of policies down to the lowest levels, unremitting followup of relevant personnel decisions to assure that they are enforced, and more education so that all minorities and genders can compete equally for the increasingly technical world in which they will live. Recognize the serious damage to mutual trust and confidence that can result from 'hot line' accusations made with an ulterior agenda and find a way of keeping such accusations confidential until confirmed to be either substantive or false— the solution to which the military is still seeking." He now lives in Arlington, Virginia.

Edwin Tifre. USMA, Class of 1985. He is on active duty as a helicopter pilot.

Harry Train D. II. USNA, Class of 1949. Since retirement, a board member of business and philanthropic organizations, He resides in Norfolk, Virginia.

Spann Watson. Pilot 332d Fighter Group, World War II, career air force officer. After retirement he served with the Federal Aviation Administration and lives on Long Island, New York.

Elliotte Williams. Career army officer. He lives in Fort Washington, Maryland.

Henry Williams. Soldier, 92d Division, World War II. His home is in Cleveland, Ohio.

Elmo R. Zumwalt, Jr. USNA, Class of 1943. World War II, Korea, Vietnam, chief of naval operations. He lives in Arlington, Virginia.

Bibliography

Allen, Robert L. *The Port Chicago Mutiny*. New York: Warner Books, 1989.

Appleman, Roy. *South to the Naktong, North to the Yalu*. Washington, D.C.: Center of Military History, U.S. Army, 1961.

———*Ridgway Duels for Korea*. College Station: Texas A & M University Press, 1990.

Barth, Chuck. *Buffalo Soldier History*. Tucson, Arizona: Blue Horse Productions, 1997.

Biggs, Bradley. *Triple Nickles*. Hamden, CT: Archon Press, 1986.

Blair, Clay. *The Forgotten War*. New York: Times Books, 1987.

Booth, Michael and Duncan Spencer. *Paratrooper: The Life of Gen. James M. Gavin*. New York: Simon & Schuster, 1994.

Boyne, Walter. *Beyond the Wild Blue*. New York: St. Martin's Press, 1997.

Bowers, William, William M. Hammond, George L. MacGarrigle, *Black Soldier, White Army*: Washington, D.C.: Center of Military History, U.S. Army, 1996.

Bussey, Charles M. *Firefight at Yechon*. McLean, Virginia: Brassey's (US),1991.

Carroll, John M. ed. *The Black Military Experience in the American West*. New York: Liveright Publishing Corp., 1971.

Cashin, Herschel V. *Under Fire with the Tenth Cavalry*. New York: Arno Press, 1969.

Dalfiume, Richard M. *Desegregation of the U.S. Armed Forces: Fighting on Two Fronts, 1939–1953*. Columbia: University of Missouri Press, 1969.

Davis, Benjamin O. Jr. *Benjamin O. Davis, Jr*. Washingon, D.C.: Smithsonian Institution Press, 1991.

Du Bois, W. E. B. *The Autobiography of W. E. B. Du Bois*. New York: International Publishers, 1968.

Fischel, Leslie Jr., and Benjamin Quarles,. *The Negro American*. New York: William Morrow and Company, Inc., 1967.

Fischer, Perry, and Brooks E.Gray, *Blacks and Whites Together Through Hell*. Turlock, California: Millsmont Publishing, 1993.

Fletcher, Marvin. *America's First Black General*. Lawrence: University Press of Kansas: 1989.

Flipper, Henry O. *Black Frontiersman*. Fort Worth: Texas Christian University Press, 1997.

Foner, Jack D. *Blacks and the Military in American History*. New York: Praeger, 1974.

Francis, Charles E. *The Tuskegee Airmen*. Boston: Bruce Humphries, Inc., 1955.

Freidel, Frank. *The Splendid Little War*. Boston: Little, Brown and Company, 1958.

Gatewood, Willard B. *Smoked Yankees*. Urbana: University of Illinois Press, 1971.

Gropman, Alan L. *The Air Force Integrates, 1945–1964*. Washington, D.C.: Office of Air Force History, 1978.

Hammond, William M. *The Military and the Media, 1968–1973*. Washington, D.C.: Center of Military History, U.S. Army, 1996.

Hickey, Donald R. *The War of 1812*. Urbana: University of Illinois Press, 1989.

Holway, John. *Red Tails, Black Wings*. Las Cruces, New Mexico: Yucca Tree Press, 1997.

Johnson, Jesse J. *Black Women in the Armed Forces 1942–1974*. Hampton, Virginia: Hampton Institute, 1974.

Kelly, Mary Pat. *Proudly We Served*. Annapolis: Naval Institute Press, 1995.

Lanning, M.L. *The African American Soldier from Crispus Attucks to Colin Powell*. New York: Birch Lane Press, 1997.

Leckie, William H. *The Buffalo Soldiers*. Norman: University of Oklahoma Press, 1967.

Lee, Ulysses. *The United States Army in World War II, Special Studies: The Employment of Negro Troops*. Washington, D.C.: Office of the Chief of Military History, 1966.

Lewis, David L. *W. E. B. Du Bois: Biography of a Race*. New York: Henry Holt and Company, 1993.

Lindenmeyer, Otto J. *Black and Brave*, New York: McGraw Hill, 1970.

Lord, Walter, *The Dawn's Early Light*. New York: W. W. Norton & Company, Inc., 1972.

McGregor, Morris. *The Integration of the Armed Services, 1940–1965*. Washington, D.C.: Center of Military History, U.S. Army, 1981.

MacGregor, Morris J., and Bernard C. Nalty, eds. *Blacks in the United States Armed Forces: Basic Documents*. 13 vols. Wilmington, Delaware: Scholarly Resources, 1977.

MacGuire, Phillip. *Taps for a Jim Crow Army: Letters from Black Soldiers in World War II*. Santa Barbara, California: ABC-Clio, 1983.

Means, Howard. *Colin Powell, Soldier/Statesman-Statesman/Soldier*. New York: Donald I. Fine, Inc., 1992.

Moore, George H. *Historical Notes on the Employment of Negroes in the American Army of the Revolution*. New York: Charles T. Evans, 1862.

Moser, Richard. *The New Winter Soldiers*. New Brunswick, New Jersey: Rutgers University Press, 1996.

Moskos, Charles, and John Sibley Butler. *All That We Can Be*. New York: Free Press, 1996.

Motley, Mary Penick. *The Invisible Soldier: The Experience of the Black Soldier, World War II*. Detroit: Wayne State University Press, 1975.

Nalty, Bernard D. *Strength for the Fight*. New York: Free Press, 1986.

————*The Right to Fight: African-American Marines in World War II.* Washington, D.C.: History and Museums Division, Headquarters, U.S. Marine Corp, 1995.

Phelps, J. Alfred, *Chappie: America's First Black Four Star General.* Novato, California: Presidio Press, 1991.

Powell, Colin. *My American Journey.* New York: Ballantine Books, 1996.

Quarles, Benjamin, *The Negro in the American Revolution.* Chapel Hill: University of North Carolina Press, 1961.

Schneider, Dorothy and Carl J. *Into the Breach: American Women Overseas in World War I.* New York: Viking, 1991.

Scott, Emmett. *History of the American Negro in the World War.* Chicago: Homewood Press, 1919.

Shaw, Henry I. Jr., and Ralph W. Donnelly. *Blacks in the Marine Corps.* Washington, D.C.: History and Museums Division, Headquarters, U.S. Marine Corps, 1975.

Smith, Graham. *When Jim Crow Met John Bull.* New York: St. Martin's Press, 1987.

Stillwell, Paul. *The Golden Thirteen.* Annapolis: Naval Institute Press, 1993.

Terry, Wallace. *Bloods: An Oral History of the Vietnam War by Black Veterans.* New York: Random House, 1984.

Vandiver, Frank Evers. *Black Jack: The Life of John J. Pershing.* College Station: Texas A & M University Press, 1977.

Wilson, Joseph T. *The Black Phalanx.* New York: Arno Press and the *New York Times,* 1968.

Wormser, Richard E. *The Yellowlegs.* New York: Doubleday & Company, 1966.

Zumwalt, Elmo R. Jr. *On Watch.* New York: Quadrangle, 1976.

Zumwalt, Elmo R. Jr., and Elmo R. Zumwalt III. *My Father, My Son.* New York: Macmillan Publishing Comapany, 1986.

Index

Jesse Brown